JIMMY SWAGGART
BIBLE
COMMENTARY

Hosea
Joel
Amos

JIMMY SWAGGART
BIBLE COMMENTARY

- Genesis (639 pages) (11-201)
- Exodus (639 pages) (11-202)
- Leviticus (435 pages) (11-203)
- Numbers
  Deuteronomy (493 pages) (11-204)
- Joshua
  Judges
  Ruth (329 pages) (11-205)
- I Samuel
  II Samuel (528 pages) (11-206)
- I Kings
  II Kings (560 pages) (11-207)
- I Chronicles
  II Chronicles (528 pages) (11-226)
- Ezra
  Nehemiah
  Esther (288 pages) (11-208)
- Job (320 pages) (11-225)
- Psalms (688 pages) (11-216)
- Proverbs (320 pages) (11-227)
- Ecclesiastes
  Song Of Solomon (11-228)
- Isaiah (688 pages) (11-220)
- Jeremiah
  Lamentations (688 pages) (11-070)
- Ezekiel (508 pages) (11-223)
- Daniel (403 pages) (11-224)
- Hosea
  Joel
  Amos (496 pages) (11-229)
- Obadiah
  Jonah
  Micah
  Nahum
  Habakkuk
  Zephaniah *(will be ready Spring 2013)* (11-230)
- Matthew (625 pages) (11-073)
- Mark (606 pages) (11-074)
- Luke (626 pages) (11-075)
- John (532 pages) (11-076)
- Acts (697 pages) (11-077)
- Romans (536 pages) (11-078)

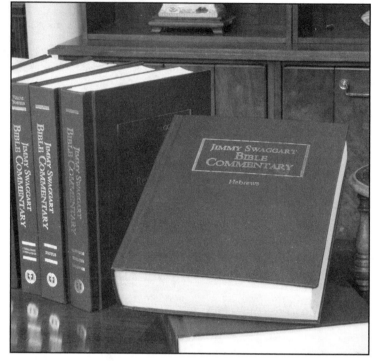

- I Corinthians (632 pages) (11-079)
- II Corinthians (589 pages) (11-080)
- Galatians (478 pages) (11-081)
- Ephesians (550 pages) (11-082)
- Philippians (476 pages) (11-083)
- Colossians (374 pages) (11-084)
- I Thessalonians
  II Thessalonians (498 pages) (11-085)
- I Timothy
  II Timothy
  Titus
  Philemon (687 pages) (11-086)
- Hebrews (831 pages) (11-087)
- James
  I Peter
  II Peter (730 pages) (11-088)
- I John
  II John
  III John
  Jude (377 pages) (11-089)
- Revelation (602 pages) (11-090)

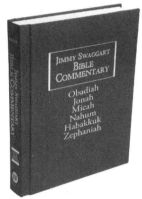

OBADIAH
JONAH
MICAH
NAHUM
HABAKKUK
ZEPHANIAH

For prices and information please call: 1-800-288-8350
Baton Rouge residents please call: (225) 768-7000
Website: www.jsm.org • E-mail: info@jsm.org

Jimmy Swaggart Bible Commentary

Hosea
Joel
Amos

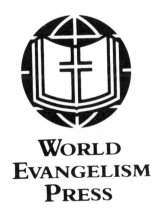

**WORLD
EVANGELISM
PRESS**

ISBN 978-1-934655-92-4
11-229 • COPYRIGHT © 2013 World Evangelism Press®
P.O. Box 262550 • Baton Rouge, Louisiana 70826-2550
Website: www.jsm.org • E-mail: info@jsm.org
(225) 768-8300
13 14 15 16 17 18 19 20 21 22 23 24 25 26 27 28 29 30 / RRD / 18 17 16 15 14 13 12 11 10 9 8 7 6 5 4 3 2 1

TABLE OF CONTENTS

THE
BOOK OF HOSEA

—■—

INTRODUCTION

It is October 29, 2009, as I begin work on the Commentary as it regards the first three of those referred to as the Minor Prophets. They are: Hosea, Joel, and Amos.

As is obvious, there are twelve Minor Prophets in number and in the Hebrew Bible, formed one Book, just as the Twelve Tribes of Israel formed one Nation.

Nine of these addresses or Prophecies were given before the captivity and three after it.

Even though some of the twelve Books are out of chronological order, in having them placed at the conclusion of the Old Testament, the Holy Spirit intended it for purpose. In fact, when one studies these Books, thereby, deriving twelve different messages, the entire focus of the Major Prophets take on a new and greater meaning. Even though these Prophets are referred to as *"Minor,"* to be sure, they are called such only because their Prophecies are shorter than the Prophecies of Isaiah, Jeremiah, and Ezekiel. However, they are no less important and no less inspired. In many ways, and as alluded to, the study of these Prophecies brings the entirety of the Old Testament into a greater harmony. It is as if the Holy Spirit designed His Own Chronology, which He no doubt did and, which, of course, serves its intended purpose.

FUTURISTIC EVENTS

Even though these Prophecies of old were directed toward Israel of that time, still, they sparkle, as well, with predictions of futuristic events. Almost without exception, the Holy

Spirit through each Prophet leaped from each gloomy present to a glorious future. Consequently, the Spiritual enrichment of the study of these men actually knows no limits, and failure to exercise one's privilege in this regard is failure indeed!

HOSEA

Hosea mainly addressed his Prophecy to the Ten Tribes shortly before their dispersion. His Book closes with a great Altar Call, to which the entirety of the Book could well be described.

JOEL

Joel ministered to Judah and while speaking of the present, wondrously leaped ahead to the future. As well, he is referred to by some as, *"the Holy Spirit Prophet of the Old Testament."* He was the one Peter quoted on the Day of Pentecost, because he was chosen by the Holy Spirit to outline as no other Prophet what the Pentecostal Way actually means.

AMOS

Amos is next and characterizes the Lord using one who did not call himself a *"Prophet, neither the son of a Prophet,"* but, nevertheless, was called such by God. This shepherd and fruit-gatherer would shake both Judah and Israel with his Spirit-inspired pronouncements. As well, he would speak to surrounding countries. His voice was like a thunder clap and carried similar power and was perhaps done so by the Lord because of his humble station in life.

The modern church, as well, can learn much from this *"herdman,"* and *"gatherer of sycamore fruit."*

OBADIAH

Obadiah follows and is the shortest Book in the Old Testament. His Prophecy concerns the Edomites who were the descendents of Esau, and who symbolized the Gentile powers through the centuries in their efforts to destroy Israel. It is the age-old struggle between the flesh and the Spirit, which, as well, characterizes every modern Believer.

JONAH

Jonah was the only Prophet sent to the Gentiles and was the only Prophet who tried to conceal his message. In effect, the entirety of the Book of Jonah is not only a history, the history of a man, but is actually Repentance in written form.

It is ironic, and yet beautiful, that the very port to which Jonah fled, Joppa, because he did not desire to take God's Message to the Gentiles of Nineveh, was the same port to which Cornelius sent his two servants and a soldier to *". . . call for one Simon, whose surname is Peter"* (Acts 10:5). Peter would take the Message of Salvation to the Gentiles from this very place.

How beautifully the Holy Spirit can bring small things such as this to pass even though separated by the centuries.

The Book of Jonah portrays the truth that at times, if not all times, it is more difficult to get the Messenger to take the message than it is for the poor sinner to receive it.

MICAH

Micah follows Jonah and ministered to both Judah and the Northern Kingdom of Israel as well as other nations.

Through this Prophet, the Holy Spirit repeats and confirms the Promise of Restoration made through Isaiah (Chpt. 2). There could be no change, for there was no reason for change, hence, the message is similar, for the moral facts were the same.

Micah's Message was strong because the times were desperate. In a short time, the Northern Kingdom would fall, and Judah, as well, would come to the trembling edge under Hezekiah before repenting and, thereby,

being saved with Judgment delayed.

Micah minced no words and, consequently, his words were like thunderbolts. No one had any trouble understanding what he was saying.

Even as I write these words, I sense the Presence of the Lord in that America and the world, for that matter, needs a Prophet or an Evangelist such as Micah.

However, even though his messages were strong and designed by the Holy Spirit thusly, still, he, as most, if not all the Prophets, never closed the door but always left it open by saying, *"Who is a God like unto You, Who pardons iniquity, and passes by the transgression of the remnant of His Heritage?"*

He then said, *"He retains not His Anger forever, because He delights in Mercy"* (Mic. 7:18).

MINOR PROPHETS?

Any and all of these called the *"Minor Prophets,"* as well as Isaiah, Jeremiah, and Ezekiel, could have readily fallen under the New Testament designations of *"Apostles, Prophets, Evangelists, Pastors, and Teachers,"* even though the Office of the Apostle had not yet been established (Eph. 4:11).

All of these individuals were definitely *"sent"* and had a special message, which characterizes the Office of the Apostle, yet, they were, as obvious, Prophets. As well, the thundering tones of the Ministry of the *"Evangelist"* rings in their messages. They served as a Clarion Call not only to Israel and Judah, but, as well, to the entirety of the world.

It is obvious that the *"pastoral heart"* resided in each of them, with their Ministries serving as a *"teaching"* vehicle to the Nation and to this present world also!

VARIETY OF BACKGROUND

One is amazed at the variety of backgrounds of these individuals, which spanned everything from Priest to day-laborer. And yet, God called them, used them, and made them the recipients of not only His Spoken Word, but, as well, His Written Word. In the annals of human history, no one could be honored more greatly.

Time and again, in attempting to write Commentary on these burning Words of the Lord as given to these Prophets, the Spirit of God would cover me, and the tears would freely flow. At times, it was as if I was there. I could see in my spirit their facial expressions, feel the palpitations of their heart, and even hear their thundering tones of Prophetic announcements. As well, I could feel the grief and disappointment, which characterized almost all of them, as their messages were rejected.

And yet, along with them, I soared to sublime heights as the Holy Spirit poured through their hearts and pointed through their lips to a brighter day that is coming—a day so glorious that it defies description.

In the Portals of Glory and in a coming day when all tears will be wiped away, I hope to enjoy a time of glorious reflection with those whom I have had the privilege of writing about. For you see, it is well nigh impossible to separate the message from the Messenger because the Messenger becomes a part of the message. In a sense, even though the message did not derive from them, being given by the Holy Spirit, still, its birth and its delivery became so much a part of these Prophets that it and them became indivisible. Consequently, Paul would write, *"And are built upon the Foundation of the Apostles and Prophets, Jesus Christ Himself being the Chief Corner Stone"* (Eph. 2:20).

APPLICABLE TO THE PRESENT

As is our custom, I have attempted in this Commentary to give whatever background information is available respecting these various Prophets and the times in which they lived. As well, we have attempted to place as many windows as possible in their pronouncements respecting their message as it applied to their day and age. Also, we have attempted to make it applicable to our modern circumstances, at least as the Holy Spirit helped us to do so.

As an Evangelist, I lay no claim to scholarship, which quickly becomes obvious as one attempts to digest our thoughts. And yet, I doubt that many, if any, of the Prophets of old were any different. Their

NOTES

Word was given by the Lord and was not the result of educational instruction, as valuable as that may have been. At the same time, our efforts are only thoughts and not, as theirs, Inspiration. And yet, I do boldly claim God's Help.

THE EVANGELIST

I am an Evangelist, which quickly comes through in my writings. As such, I have the tendency to see things in stark black or white with precious few variable shades in-between. As an Evangelist, I, as well, am a *"watchman"* (Ezek. 3:17). Consequently, there is a constant compulsion within my heart to graphically describe the Word of God, at least, to the best of my ability and as it applies to us, in terminology that is absolutely clear and simple. We must never forget, the Gospel of Jesus Christ is not an effort in diplomacy but is rather an ultimatum! It pulls no punches and is not meant to.

AN ULTIMATUM

As such, and at times, the description has a tendency to anger. However, if one is to notice, there is not much diplomacy that is used or tendered anywhere in the Bible. It, too, is a startling black or white. Even the Words of Christ, Who was the epitome of Love, were scathing and burning when dealing with the Pharisees (Mat. 23).

Our attention in all of our Commentaries is to first of all do our best to explain the Word of God and, secondly, to apply it to our personal and daily lives. If we have been, at least in some small measure, successful at doing this, then our efforts will have been worthwhile and your time spent in studying this Volume worthwhile as well!

SCHOLARSHIP

Even though, and as stated, I lay no claim to scholarship, still, I am indebted to a host of scholars from whom I have benefited, and greatly so. To attempt to name them would be difficult because of the goodly number and the passage of time. Especially in research, they have made my work a little easier, and, above that, hopefully, enabled me to elucidate my thoughts more perfectly.

THE MESSAGE OF THE CROSS

Actually, the work on both Volumes respecting all twelve of the Minor Prophets is a rewrite. The first Volume was written before the Revelation of the Cross was given to me in 1997. As a result, I feel like our work can be complete only as the present understanding of the Cross of Christ be given in our efforts. In fact, the Cross is of such moment that it is actually used by the Apostle Paul, and, no doubt, by countless others, as a synonym for the Gospel. As someone has well said, *"As one views the Cross of Christ, one thusly views God."* In other words, if one doesn't understand the Cross of Christ, then one's understanding of God of necessity is vastly confused. As well, one's degree of maturity is predicated solely on one's understanding of the Cross. All the Prophets of old, without exception, pointed to the One Who was to come, the very reason Israel was raised up from the loins of Abraham and the womb of Sarah. Whatever episode in their existence was taking place at the time, and whatever it may have represented, if it was righteous, was but another step toward the final objective, Who would be the Lord Jesus Christ. Unfortunately, as I'm afraid characterizes us all, at times, Israel took one or more steps backward instead of forward. But ultimately, the time came, the fulfillment of all the Prophecies, God becoming flesh, and for the purpose of going to the Cross, where there man would be totally and completely redeemed.

"Redeemed how I love to proclaim it!
"Redeemed by the Blood of the Lamb;
"Redeemed through His infinite Mercy,
"His Child, and forever, I am."

"Redeemed and so happy in Jesus,
"No language my rapture can tell;
"I know that the light of His Presence,
"With me does continually dwell."

"I think of blessed Redeemer,
"I think of Him all the day long;
"I sing, for I cannot be silent,
"His Love is the theme of my song."

"I know I shall see in His Beauty,
"The King in Whose Law I delight;

"Who lovingly guards my footsteps,
"And gives me songs in the night."

"Redeemed, redeemed,
"Redeemed by the Blood of the Lamb;
"Redeemed, redeemed,
"His Child, and forever, I am."

CHAPTER 1

(1) "THE WORD OF THE LORD THAT CAME UNTO HOSEA, THE SON OF BEERI, IN THE DAYS OF UZZIAH, JOTHAM, AHAZ, AND HEZEKIAH, KINGS OF JUDAH, AND IN THE DAYS OF JEROBOAM THE SON OF JOASH, KING OF ISRAEL."

1. The name *"Hosea"* means *"Salvation."* He was a contemporary of Isaiah.

2. His Ministry was to the northern kingdom of Israel.

3. He prophesied through the reigns of four kings of the southern kingdom of Judah, *"Uzziah, Jotham, Ahaz, and Hezekiah,"* and one king of the northern confederation of Israel, *"Jeroboam II."*

4. His Message was simple, *"Repent!"* It continued over a period of between 60 and 70 years and was one of, if not, the longest, on record.

5. His ministry began as a young man while *"Uzziah"* was on the Throne of Judah, and *"Jeroboam II"* was on the Throne of Israel. Uzziah and Jeroboam reigned contemporaneously for 26 years. Sometime during that period, Hosea commenced his Ministry. Uzziah survived Jeroboam some 26 years, giving Uzziah a reign of 52 years. Jotham and Ahaz in succession reigned16 years each.

6. During all of this time, Hosea continued his faithful Ministry, which lasted at least several years into the reign of Hezekiah. The destruction of Samaria (the northern kingdom of Israel) took place in the fourth year of Hezekiah, king of Judah.

7. The name *"Hosea"* means *"Salvation."* He is called *"Osee"* in Romans 9:25.

THE WORD OF THE LORD

The phrase, *"The Word of the LORD that*

came unto Hosea," places Hosea in the Prophetical Office. A Prophet is an individual inspired by God to instruct men for the present and inform them of the future, whether orally or by writing.

In effect, the Ministry of the God-called Prophet served, in a sense, as the Spiritual Leader of Judah and Israel. Tragically, the northern kingdom of Israel did not have one single godly king during its existence. While the southern kingdom of Judah had her share of kings who were wicked, she was blessed with a few who sincerely served the Lord, as did Hezekiah. So, the Ministry of the Prophet was very valuable, to say the least! In fact, the greater part of the Ministry of the Prophets was to serve as a Minister of Righteousness, in other words, to whip the Nation into shape, so to speak. Only a part of their Ministry was given over to foretelling the future. Actually, John the Baptist, whom Jesus proclaimed as the greatest Prophet born of a woman, said very little as it regarded the future, with basically all of his Ministry directed toward the Israel of his day. His greatness lay in the fact that he was the one to introduce Christ, and nothing could be higher than that. And yet Jesus said, *"Verily I say unto you, Among them who are born of women there has not risen a greater than John the Baptist: notwithstanding he who is least in the Kingdom of Heaven is greater than he"* (Mat. 11:11).

What did Jesus mean?

He wasn't meaning that Believers are greater in character than John the Baptist, but rather, the privileges that we have in Christ because of the Cross. John the Baptist was the last Prophet under the Old Covenant, with our Lord ushering in the New. All those who came before the Cross could only point to that which was to come but did not have the honor of enjoying its privileges. They were Saved, and they are all now with the Lord; however, in Christ, we presently have so much more!

THE CROSS OF CHRIST

The Scripture says, **"For the Law was given by Moses,** *but* **Grace and Truth came by Jesus Christ** (*proclaims Christ as the Representative Law-keeper for all humanity, i.e., to all who will believe; the Law*

manifested man [full of wickedness]; the Son manifested God [full of goodness])" **(Jn. 1:17).**

Paul said, **"But now** *(since the Cross)* **has He** *(the Lord Jesus)* **obtained a more excellent Ministry** *(the New Covenant in Jesus' Blood is superior and takes the place of the Old Covenant in animal blood),* **but how much also He is the Mediator of a Better Covenant** *(proclaims the fact that Christ officiates between God and man according to the arrangements of the New Covenant), which was established upon better Promises. (This presents the New Covenant, explicitly based on the cleansing and forgiveness of all sin, which the Old Covenant could not do.)"*

THE NEW COVENANT

"For if that First *Covenant* **had been faultless** *(proclaims the fact that the First Covenant was definitely not faultless; as stated, it was based on animal blood, which was vastly inferior to the Precious Blood of Christ),* **then should no place have been sought for the Second** *(proclaims the necessity of the New Covenant).*

"For finding fault with them *(the First Covenant was actually designed to glaringly portray the fault of the people, which it successfully did),* **He said** *(Jer. 31:31),* **Behold, the days come, says the Lord, when I will make a New Covenant with the House of Israel and with the house of Judah** *(that New Covenant was in Christ and what He did at the Cross; regrettably, Israel rejected Him)"* **(Heb. 8:6-8).**

BETTER

In fact, the New Covenant, which is all in Christ, is glaringly and beautifully described in the great Book of Hebrews as that which is *"better."* The Scripture says:

• Christ is *"better"* than Angels (Heb. 1:4).

• Christ brought us a *"better"* hope (Heb. 7:19).

• In Christ, we have a *"better"* Testament, i.e., *"Covenant"* (Heb. 7:22).

• Christ is the Mediator of a *"better"* Covenant, established upon *"better"* Promises (Heb. 8:6).

• Christ was a *"better"* Sacrifice (Heb. 9:23).

- In Heaven, every Believer has a *"better"* and an enduring substance (Heb. 10:34).
- In Christ, every Believer now has a *"better"* country, that is, an Heavenly (Heb. 11:16).
- In Christ, every Believer now has a *"better"* Resurrection (Heb. 11:35).
- In Christ, God has provided some *"better"* thing for us (Heb. 11:40).
- The Blood of Jesus has now provided *"better"* things than that of Abel (Heb. 12:24).

As stated, let us ever understand that while Christ is the Source of all things that we receive, of all things which are *"better,"* still, it is the Cross of Christ, which is the *"Means"* of these better things.

SALVATION

Inasmuch as Hosea's name means *"Salvation"* or *"Deliverer,"* it is very similar to Joshua, which means *"Saviour."* Joshua is different only as its prefix implies the Name of Jehovah as the Author of such Deliverance or Salvation. Actually, the name *"Jesus"* is the Greek derivative of the Hebrew, *"Joshua."* So, in Israel, during the time of Christ, our Lord was actually known as *"Joshua."*

Salvation has always had its foundation in Christ and what Christ would do at the Cross. From the dawn of time, actually, the first page of human history, the Lord gave a means to the First Family and those thereafter that they could have forgiveness of sins and communion with Him. It would be by means of the slain lamb, which would be a substitute until Christ would come. However, such was not a simple thing.

Concerning the world before the Flood, the Scripture says of mankind at that time, *"And God saw that the wickedness of man was great in the Earth, and that every imagination of the thoughts of his heart was only evil continually"* (Gen. 6:5).

All of this tells us that sin never remains static. It gets worse and worse until there is no redeeming factor in the individual whatsoever. In fact, the Lord would have to drown the world in water, with the exception of Noah and his family. For the Redeemer to come into the world, the Lord would have to raise up a people who would evidence

Faith in Him and, thereby, could be trained in the Ways of the Lord to make ready for the coming Saviour. The couple chosen approximately 400 years after the Flood was Abraham and Sarah. Through the loins of Abraham and the womb of Sarah, the Lord would miraculously bring forth a people who would serve Him, at least some of them would, and would prepare the way for the coming Redeemer. But still, it took nearly 2,000 years for the Saviour to be born, God becoming man, born of the Virgin Mary. So, this Salvation was not a simple thing, and is not a simple thing.

OUR LORD JESUS CHRIST AND THE CROSS

Our Lord came for many purposes and reasons, but the primary purpose was the Cross. He came to offer Himself as a Perfect Sacrifice, which would satisfy the demands of a thrice-Holy God. This was a debt that man could not pay. So, if it was to be paid, in other words, the human race be salvaged, God would have to become man, which is referred to as the Incarnation. He would then have to give Himself as a Perfect Sacrifice on the Cross, which He did, and which He did as our Representative Man, our Substitute. Simple Faith in Him and what He did for us at the Cross guarantees a perfect, pure, and spotless Righteousness, which is given immediately to such a one who believes. Actually, it is the Righteousness of God. It cannot be earned or merited; it is all by Faith, but it must be Faith in Christ (Rom. 5:1-2).

MERCY AND GRACE

Through the Ministry of Hosea, the Holy Spirit appealed diligently to the northern kingdom of Israel but to no avail! As Judah, some 133 years after the fall of Israel, would, likewise, fail to heed the Message of Jeremiah, Israel would not heed the Word of Hosea, even though faithfully delivered.

This long period of time shows the Mercy and Grace of God in attempting to bring His People, Israel, to their spiritual senses. Such is God's Manner! He will warn and even threaten, but if rebellion persists, whether in a nation or individual, His Righteousness demands Judgment. As well, as His Righteousness demands Judgment for disobedience, it demands blessing for proper obedience and a turning away from sin. But Israel would not obey!

If one is to notice in the First Verse, even though Hosea exercised his Prophetic function in Israel, the northern kingdom, and according to the Word of the Lord, the time during which he did so is reckoned by the reigns of the kings of Judah, with the single exception of Jeroboam II.

To be sure, the Holy Spirit did this for cause and reason.

While it is true that on the death of Jeroboam II, there was approximately 12 years during which a state of anarchy prevailed. At length, Zechariah (not the Prophet) succeeded to the throne in the northern kingdom, but he reigned only six months when he was murdered by Shallum. Shallum's reign only lasted a month, when he was put to death by Menahem.

However, even though anarchy prevailed, still, the reckonings were accounted by the reigns of the kings of Judah because Judah, although spiritually weak, was in God's Covenant, while the northern kingdom of Israel was out of Covenant. In other words, the Lord little recognized them, and only in a distant way.

The northern kingdom had forsaken the Temple and the Altar. In its place, they had set up idols. Therefore, they were not reckoned as in Covenant, and only *"Jeroboam II"* was mentioned. This was in order to signify the northern kingdom and the appeal to it to come back into Covenant.

THE NORTHERN KINGDOM OF ISRAEL

Some 200 years before Hosea, Ten Tribes had broken away, forming their own kingdom called Israel, Samaria, or Ephraim. This left only Judah and Benjamin to make up the southern kingdom, which was called *"Judah."* Possibly the Tribe of *"Simeon"* remained with Judah as their inheritance was within the inheritance of Judah (Josh. 19:1). And yet, there is some indication that the Tribe of Simeon, or at least some of them, migrated into the northern kingdom of Israel.

During this some 200 years, Israel had gone into deep apostasy and sin, forsaking the God of Abraham, Isaac, and Jacob, but was still greatly appealed to by the Lord. Such is evident in the great Ministries of Elijah and Elisha. Hosea would be the premier Prophet to Israel before her destruction; consequently, time was fastly running out, even though the Lord would appeal to them to repent even until the last.

(2) "THE BEGINNING OF THE WORD OF THE LORD BY HOSEA. AND THE LORD SAID TO HOSEA, GO, TAKE UNTO YOU A WIFE OF WHOREDOMS AND CHILDREN OF WHOREDOMS: FOR THE LAND HAS COMMITTED GREAT WHOREDOM, DEPARTING FROM THE LORD.

(3) "SO HE WENT AND TOOK GOMER THE DAUGHTER OF DIBLAIM; WHO CONCEIVED, AND BORE HIM A SON.

(4) "AND THE LORD SAID UNTO HIM, CALL HIS NAME JEZREEL; FOR YET A LITTLE WHILE, AND I WILL AVENGE THE BLOOD OF JEZREEL UPON THE HOUSE OF JEHU, AND WILL CAUSE TO CEASE THE KINGDOM OF THE HOUSE OF ISRAEL.

(5) "AND IT SHALL COME TO PASS AT THAT DAY, THAT I WILL BREAK THE BOW OF ISRAEL IN THE VALLEY OF JEZREEL."

1. (Vs. 2) *"Go, take unto you a wife of whoredoms and children of whoredoms,"* actually means *"children of idolatry."* The Nation of Israel, constituting the northern kingdom, is appealed to under the figure of an unfaithful wife because of its devotion to idols and forsaking of Jehovah.

2. (Vs. 3) There is some evidence that *"Gomer"* was the name of a harlot well-known at that particular time. If so, the shame heaped upon Hosea would have been multifold.

3. (Vs. 4) The name *"Jezreel"* means, *"God will scatter or sow."* This was Hosea's first son.

4. (Vs. 4) The phrase, *"And I will avenge the blood of Jezreel upon the house of Jehu,"* has reference to the commission given to Jehu by the Lord in carrying out of God's Judgment upon the house of Ahab. However, Jehu carried this commission too far, exacting greater Judgment than the Lord

intended. And then, above all, he went into the same sins for which the Lord had judged Ahab (II Ki. 10:31-36).

5. (Vs. 4) *"And will cause to cease the kingdom of the house of Israel,"* signals the beginning of the end for the northern kingdom of Israel, even though it would take some 70 years for it to be brought to a total consummation.

6. (Vs. 5) The sign of the coming fall of this kingdom was the breaking of the *"bow,"* because the northern kingdom of Israel was famous for its use of the bow.

THE BEGINNING OF
THE WORD OF THE LORD

When the Lord began to speak to Hosea, giving him a Message that he was to give to Israel, quite possibly he was but in his 20's. As stated, this Word began while Uzziah was reigning in Judah and Jeroboam II in Israel.

As to how the Lord spoke to Hosea, we aren't told. There is no indication that He spoke to the Prophet audibly, so this means that, more than likely, He spoke to him through His Spirit into his heart. However, the Lord most definitely can speak audibly if He so desires. There's nothing in Scripture that precludes such.

A WIFE AND CHILDREN
OF WHOREDOM

The phrase as given by the Lord to the Prophet, *"Go, take unto you a wife of whoredoms and children of whoredoms,"* would have been startling, to say the least. Actually the word *"whoredom"* is to be read *"idolatry."* The Nation is appealed to under the figure of an unfaithful wife because of its devotion to idols and forsaking of Jehovah, while, no doubt, immorality was also greatly involved.

The Prophet, who was a Spiritual son of Abraham and, perhaps, of the Children of Judah, was commanded to marry a wife belonging to the northern kingdom and to have children by her; hence, the symbolic language of this Verse. The verb *"begat"* may be supplied before the word *"children."*

The command for Hosea to take such a wife was not in Vision, as some such things had been given to Ezekiel, but is meant to be taken literally. By the phrase, *"a wife of whoredoms,"* we understand such to be a woman addicted to a life of immorality and would thus likely prove to be an unfaithful wife.

The short phrase, *"Children of whoredoms,"* referred to those, which of necessity, who would be born to such a union. In other words, there would be a terrible stigma attached to the children.

The word *"take"* clearly states that the Prophet must take a wife of the character indicated and beget children by her and not a wife of such character with children already born to her.

What must Hosea have felt when the Lord gave him these instructions, concerning the *"taking of a wife of whoredoms"*? Why would the Lord demand such a thing of His faithful Prophet? As a result, his life would be given over to pain and sorrow, for nothing is more sacred than the marriage bonds, symbolizing oneness and, therefore, unity.

Not only would it cause him tremendous grievance of heart and spirit but, no doubt, made him a target of scorn and ridicule. Therefore, the Prophet's love for God and his love for the lost Nation of Israel is overwhelmingly evident. What faithfulness and what godliness! What consecration and dedication!

And yet, Hosea, in many ways, is a Type of Christ Who came down to this sinful, wicked world and took unto Himself a wife (symbolically speaking) called the Church, who has proven so unfaithful so many times!

A MARRIAGE COVENANT

The Prophet's marriage to an unfaithful wife sets forth Jehovah's marriage to an unfaithful Nation, for this is what it is meant to imply. God often condescends—graciously condescends—to represent His Relation to His People as a marriage Covenant; consequently, unfaithfulness on our part is looked at as *"spiritual adultery."*

SPIRITUAL ADULTERY

Most Believers have probably never even heard the term *"spiritual adultery,"* and if they have, it has been linked, as here, to Old Testament experiences. But Paul graphically portrays this sin as a problem in the church, and does so, once again, by the means of the

NOTES

marriage bond.

He uses the example of a woman married to a man but, as well, goes and marries another man. Death or divorce is not mentioned, at least at this time. In the Eyes of God, this woman, whomever she may have been, now has two husbands. He said, *"So then if, while her husband lives, she be married to another man, she shall be called an adulteress"* (Rom. 7:3). He goes on to say, if the first husband of the woman had died, then she was free to marry someone else, but not so if her first husband was alive. Married to him, she, of course, was committing adultery by marrying someone else. But if he died, she was free then to marry someone else without breaking the Law.

Paul tells us that we as Believers are married to Christ. With the Cross, the great Apostle tells us, as well, that our first husband, the Law, died, and did so by Jesus going to the Cross and satisfying its just demands. Now we have one Husband Who is Christ, and we are to be faithful to Him in all things. He is to meet our every need and, in fact, is the only One Who can meet our every need.

However, if we place our faith in anything other than Christ and the Cross, we are being unfaithful to Christ and, in essence, committing the sin of *"spiritual adultery."*

THE MODERN CHURCH AND SPIRITUAL ADULTERY

As stated, Paul tells us that the Law was fulfilled in Christ totally and, in a sense, died with Him (Col. 2:14-15). At least, we are to look at it as though it is dead. In truth, the moral Law of God is still incumbent upon every Believer for the simple reason that moral laws cannot change. If it was wrong to steal 3,000 years ago, it's wrong to steal presently! Those moral Commandments are to be kept, as should be overly obvious! However, the question is, *"How do we keep them?"* We will address that momentarily.

Most of the modern church presently is living in a state of *"spiritual adultery."* How can we say such a thing?

If the Believer doesn't have his faith exclusively in Christ and the Cross as it regards our Sanctification, how we live for God on a daily basis, then this means the person has

his faith in something else. This means he's being unfaithful to Christ, which means he is living in a state of spiritual adultery. The problem is *"unfaithfulness to Christ."* That unfaithfulness comes about, as stated, by us placing our faith in something other than the Cross of Christ.

The Holy Spirit will not work in any capacity in our lives except by and through the parameters of the Finished Work of our Lord. He doesn't demand much of us, but He does demand that our Faith be exclusively in Christ and what Christ did for us at the Cross. In fact, our Lord must not be separated from the Cross. And, by that, we are not speaking of a wooden beam, as should be obvious, but rather what Jesus there did. He atoned for all sin at the Cross, thereby, defeating Satan and every power of darkness. Sin is the legal right that the Evil One has to hold man captive. With all sin atoned, which it was at the Cross, then that legal right is removed from the Evil One. That means he has no more right to hold anyone in bondage. And yet, we know and realize that most of the world lies in darkness, but it is because they will not take advantage of what Jesus has done for them.

But, we also know that most Christians are living in a state of spiritual bondage in one way or the other. Why?

It is because their Faith is not in Christ and the Cross, which greatly hinders the Holy Spirit. They are in a state of spiritual adultery. It is quite an analogy that Paul drew in those first four Verses of the Seventh Chapter of Romans.

IGNORANCE AND UNBELIEF

The truth is, most Christians have no knowledge whatsoever as it regards the Cross of Christ respecting Sanctification, in other words, how we live for God. They understand the Cross relative to Salvation but not at all relative to Sanctification.

But yet, whenever most Believers hear the Message of the Cross, which is what Paul gave to us, while some few accept, most, regrettably, don't! That is because of unbelief. So, we have a problem of ignorance, and we have a problem of unbelief. And please understand, *"spiritual adultery"* presently is just as bad as the idolatry of Old Testament times.

AND BEAR HIM A SON

Even though the Holy Spirit little describes it, still, the Prophet's Calling was, no doubt, greatly called into question. To purposely marry one of such reputation could only make the eyebrows of his contemporaries lift in a studied condemnation. One can well imagine the gossip that involved Hosea, which made the rounds, and was done so in an immoral manner! To think that such did not happen is wistful thinking, to say the least!

However, the evidence is that the Lord little bothered to explain His Purpose and Reason to the Prophet, and so the Prophet suffered the shame in silence. His only purpose was to obey God, not to win the plaudits of the crowd, *"so he went and took Gomer...."*

COMPLETION

The name *"Gomer"* means *"completion,"* as if stating that the Lord will fully execute on Israel the punishment of their transgressions that He may ultimately forgive them their iniquity.

Consequently, the meaning of Hosea's name, *"Salvation,"* and Gomer's, *"completion,"* produces that which God is attempting to do with the entirety of mankind. This alliance represents the relation into which Jehovah, with His Saving Power, had mercifully taken Israel and, not only Israel, but the whole of humanity.

Therefore, within this union, one is shown not only the wicked perfidiousness of the human heart but, likewise, God's Plan to change that heart. As we shall see, it is not done easily or quickly!

THE FIRST CHILD

The son mention in the phrase, *"Who conceived, and bore him a son,"* is the first of three children who will symbolically be used by the Lord, as well, to portray His Message to faithless Israel.

Hosea, faithful to his unfaithful wife, serves as an illustration of God Who is faithful to Israel even when they are unfaithful. And yet, as unfaithful and wayward as they have been, Israel will one day, once again,

become God's dearly loved Bride.

In Gomer's unfaithfulness, she would become enslaved to another man, actually, to many men, but would be bought back by Hosea. The action of his continuing love provides an object lesson for Israel, for in time, she will, as well, turn back to God. However, it will not be until the Second Coming, which, as is obvious, has not taken place even yet.

JEZREEL

The name *"Jezreel"* means, *"God will scatter or sow."* This was Hosea's first son.

The phrase, *"And I will avenge the blood of Jezreel upon the house of Jehu,"* has reference to the commission given to Jehu by the Lord in carrying out His Judgment upon the house of Ahab. However, Jehu carried this commission too far, exacting greater Judgment than the Lord intended, and then, above all, went into the same sins for which the Lord had judged Ahab (II Ki. 10:31-36).

While it was true that the slaughter of Ahab's sons, Jezebel and Joram, and that whole royal line, was in compliance with God's expressed Command, still, it seems that Jehu's zeal really was not for God, as he pretended, with a consequent diligence in obeying the Divine direction but, instead, was fueled by human passion and political advantage, which hurried him on. He exterminated the idolatry of Baal, but he did cleave to the calves of Jeroboam at Bethel and Dan because he, no doubt, felt it was expedient.

Consequently, what he did, therefore, the act itself, was right, for God commanded it and actually rewarded him by his family continuing to occupy the Throne of Israel to the fourth generation. However, his motive was wrong, for it was selfish ambition that prompted it and not a desire to obey the Lord.

MOTIVES

The lesson here taught is that God judges our motives even more so than He does our actions.

The Holy Spirit used the phrase, *"The blood of Jezreel,"* because this is where the slaughter commenced.

Let us say again that he did that which was right in this matter in the Eyes of Jehovah, at least, regarding his actions. However, since he did not observe to walk in the Law of Jehovah and did not turn aside from all the sins of Jeroboam, the son of Nebat, the blood that he shed was reckoned to him as innocent blood.

That is a powerful thought!

It means that, even though something is right, if done for the wrong motive, the Lord, consequently, attributes the same sin to the one carrying out His Will.

In other words, even though what is done is right, why, in effect, are we doing it? What is our motive?

If *"self"* enters the picture, as it did with Jehu and as it has with most, if not all of us, at one time or the other, then we become guilty of the same sin we are opposing.

The phrase, *"And will cause to cease the kingdom of the House of Israel,"* signals the beginning of the end for the State of Israel, even though it would take some 70 years for it to be brought to a total consummation.

The lesson taught in this Fourth Verse is powerful, to say the least! It should not go unnoticed.

THE VALLEY OF JEZREEL

"The Valley of Jezreel" is *"the Plain of Esdraelon."*

The phrase, *"And it shall come to pass at that day,"* describes an event that is far more than the downfall of a dynasty. It was the destruction of a kingdom. The close of Jehu's dynasty was once the preparation for and the commencement of the cessation of the kingdom of Israel.

The Valley that is here spoken of was where Israel, when judged by Deborah many years past, conquered the host of king Jabin. It was also where Gideon overthrew the Midianites. Saul, the first king of Israel, died here as well! Years later, king Josiah, one of the godliest kings to grace the Throne of Judah, would lose his life in this place while fighting the Egyptians.

The name of this Plain was derived from the city of Jezreel, situated near its eastern extremity on a spur of Mount Gilboa.

A PERSONAL EXPERIENCE

I have had two occasions to view this

particular Valley as it is presently. The first time, if I remember correctly, we shot some television footage there. Knowing of the great victory won by Deborah, the judge of Israel, I asked our guide who was with us if the little stream I was looking at was the same stream mentioned in the Bible. This stream had become a raging torrent during the battle with king Jabin. Some of the lines in the song says:

"They fought from Heaven; the stars in their courses fought against Sisera. The River of Kishon swept them away, that ancient River, the River Kishon. Oh my soul, you have trodden down strength" (Judg. 5:20-21).

According to Josephus, a great storm arose in the face of the Canaanites, which led to their utter defeat. This River is normally a very narrow stream; however, the storm evidently caused the River to flood, which played havoc with the chariots, etc.

As I looked at that little stream flowing in the midst of this beautiful Valley, all of a sudden, it was like I was transported back nearly 3,400 years ago. I could hear the din of battle, the neighing of the horses, the screams of the men, even as the Lord fought for Israel.

KING SAUL

As it regards this Valley, the second incident concerned our last trip to Israel. We were coming back from Tiberias on our way to Jerusalem. We were travelling immediately beside the Jordan River on the Israeli side.

At a certain juncture, the guide spoke up and said, *"Brother Swaggart, see that mountain to your right?"* which I did!

"That is Mount Gilboa where king Saul was killed by the Philistines."

Once again, it was almost like I could hear the roar of battle in which Saul and his son Jonathan died. It didn't have to be this way. He died because of his rebellion against the Lord. And, as far as we know, he died eternally lost!

But that's not so with Jonathan, who loved the Lord greatly and, in fact, is now with the Lord.

I WILL BREAK THE BOW

The phrase, *"That I will break the bow*

of Israel in the Valley of Jezreel," speaks of the chief weapon of Ephraim. The bow of Jonathan was known far and wide. The children of Ephraim were characterized as *"carrying bows."* And so, the chief weapon of the captain of the host of Israel was his bow. Therefore, the sign of the fall of this kingdom was the breaking of the *"bow."*

EPHRAIM

Ephraim was one of the Ten Tribes of the northern kingdom and was so strong that the entirety of the northern kingdom of Israel sometimes went by the name *"Ephraim."*

The Assyrians would be the instrument used by Jehovah to destroy Israel.

All of this, the child born to Hosea and Gomer, with him being named *"Jezreel,"* along with its corresponding Prophecy, was meant to serve as a warning to Israel that they must repent. However, the Actions of God were to no avail!

THE VOICE OF GOD

The Prophet was intended by the Lord to be the Voice of God; consequently, *"Hosea"* was God's Mouthpiece, delivering His Message. Actually, the status of the Office of the Prophet, at least in the northern kingdom of Israel, was the very highest Spiritual Authority.

The first person whom the Bible refers to as a Prophet was Abraham (Gen. 20:7), even though it alludes to *"Enoch"* serving in this capacity (Jude, Vs. 14). Enoch lived about 1,000 years before the Flood and, consequently, nearly 1,500 years before Abraham. However, it could probably be said that all Old Testament Prophecy received its form in the life and person of Moses, who constituted a standard of comparison for all future Prophets (Deut. 18:15-19; 34:10). Every feature, which characterized the true Prophet of the Lord, at least in the classical tradition of Old Testament Prophecy, was first found in Moses.

A MAN SENT FROM GOD

Moses received a specific and personal Call from God. The initiative in making a Prophet rests with God (Ex. 3:1-4; 17; Isa., Chpt. 6; Jer. 1:4-19; Ezek. 1:3; Hos. 1:2;

Jonah 1:1), and it is only the false prophet who dares to take the Office upon himself (Jer. 14:14; 23:21).

The primary object and effect of the Call was an introduction into God's Presence in order that the *"counsel"* of the Lord may be known (I Ki. 22:19; Jer. 23:22). Therefore, the God-appointed Prophet stood before men as a man sent from God.

The Prophet was the only one who could successfully interpret events as to their correct meaning, and again, this stemmed from Moses.

When Isaiah made his tremendous statements against idolatry, one of the most potent contentions was that Jehovah Alone is the Author of Prophecy and that the idols are, at best, wise after the event (Isa. 45:20-22). Isaiah's position stemmed directly from Moses and the Exodus.

Jehovah sent Moses into Egypt possessed of the clues necessary to interpret the great events, which were to follow. Therefore, history became Revelation because there was added to the historical happening a man prepared beforehand to say what it meant. Moses was not left to struggle for the meaning of events as or after they happened; he was forewarned of events and of their significance by the verbal Communications of God. So it was with all the God-called Prophets. Of the nations of antiquity, Israel alone had a true awareness of history. They owed it to the Prophets and, under the Lord of history, the Prophets owed it to Moses.

A MAN OF THE WORD OF GOD

Many of the Prophets of old were found confronting their kings and playing an active, statesman's part in national affairs. This, as well, was a function of the Prophet, which found its prototype in Moses who legislated for the Nation.

It is interesting that the first two kings of Israel, Saul and David, were also Prophets, but this union of offices did not continue and the Mosaic-theocratic rule was prolonged by the association of the anointed king and the anointed Prophet.

Regrettably, there was no anointed king in the northern kingdom of Israel. Therefore, the Nation was spoken to by Hosea, who occupied the high Spiritual Office, but, sadly, was given little regard by the leadership and the people of Israel.

The Prophet, as is obvious, was first a man of the Word of God. Even when he seemed to undertake other functions, such as the elaborate *"miming"* of Ezekiel, it was subordinated to the interests of bringing the Word of God to his fellowmen. Actually, the Prophet then and now was and is more a forthteller than a foreteller. In other words, he was a Preacher of Righteousness more so than a foreteller of futuristic events.

This Word was not, so to speak, a mere passive opinion, as though God were anxious simply that men should be aware of how He saw matters before they decided for themselves. It was, instead, the Prophet's conviction that the proclamation of God's Word would radically change the whole situation. For example, in Isaiah, Chapters 28-29, we are shown a picture of a people struggling for a satisfactory solution to a pressing problem of political expediency and, in the process, rejecting God's Word. Consequently, and at that particular time, the problem was no longer one of a political balance of power between Judah, Assyria, and Egypt, but one of Spiritual relationship between Judah, Assyria, and Egypt. Judah could accept the political alliance with these heathen powers or accept the Word of God. They could not accept both! Consequently, the Word became an active ingredient added to the situation, which became the criteria for a right direction, and was delivered by the Prophet.

THE PRACTICE OF FORETELLING

Even though God-called Prophets were first of all *"Preachers of Righteousness"* (I Pet. 2:5), the Prophets spoke to their situation primarily by means of warnings and encouragements concerning the future. Almost every Prophet first appears as a foreteller (Amos 1:2), which lends even greater credence to his forthtelling. There are four grounds of this practice of foretelling:

1. If people are to exercise due moral responsibility in the present, it is necessary that they should be aware of the future. This at once lifts the predictions out of the realm of mere prognostication and carnal curiosity.

2. Calls to Repentance (Isa. 30:6-9) and calls to practical holiness (Isa. 2:5) are equally based on a Word concerning the future. The vision of wrath to come is made the basis of a present seeking of the Mercy of God. The vision of bliss to come calls to a walking in the light now.

3. Prediction arises from the fact that the Prophets speak in the Name of the Holy Ruler of history. We have already mentioned that the Prophet's Call was primarily to a Knowledge of God. Out of this Knowledge sprang the awareness of what God would do as He guided history according to the unchangeable principles of His Holy Nature.

4. Prediction seems to belong to the very idea of the Prophetic Office. This is obvious in Deuteronomy 18:9. Israel, upon entering the Land of Canaan, is not only warned about the abominations of the Canaanite cults, such as infant sacrifice, but also about Canaanite religious practitioners, such as diviners. Certainly these individuals were involved with what we call *"fortunetelling"*; they offered to probe the future by one means or another. Actually, the world has always been full of these prognosticators.

THE ACCURACY OF THE FORECAST

For Israel, instead of being similar to the heathen nations which surrounded them, there was to be a Prophet whom the Lord would raise up from among their brethren. This Prophet, speaking in the Name of the Lord, was to be judged by the accuracy of his forecast—a clear proof that Israel expected Prophetic prediction, and that it belonged to the notion of Prophecy.

The Prophets came before their contemporaries as men with a word to say. The spoken Oracle is the form in which the Word of God is expressed. Each Prophet stamped the marks of his own personality and experience on this Word: for instance, the Oracles of Amos and Jeremiah are as unlike as are the personalities of the two Prophets. There is, therefore, a double awareness in the Books of the Prophets: on the one hand, these Words are the Words, which God gave to the Prophet. God took this man to be His

Mouthpiece; they are the Words of God.

On the other hand, these Words are the Words of a certain man, spoken at a certain time, under certain circumstances.

INSPIRATION

Even though the men were fallible and, therefore, imperfect, still, that which they spoke was perfect because it was inspired by the Holy Spirit. In other words, the Holy Spirit searched through their vocabulary to find the exact word He wanted each time. Then they were to write down that particular word and, in fact, all the words, into a sentence. That's the manner in which the Holy Spirit inspired the Prophets to speak and, as well, to make a copy of that which had been spoken (Mat. 4:4).

Consequently, one can search the Books of the Prophets without discovering any trace of suggestion that the Prophets thought the Word through them was in any way less than the Word of God.

Sometimes the Prophets of old couched their Oracles in the form of Parables or Allegories; however, the most dramatic presentation of their message was by means of the *"acted Oracle."*

AN EXAMPLE

An example is the meeting between king Joash and the dying Elisha (II Ki. 13:14). In Verse 17, the arrow of the Lord's Victory is shot against Syria. The Prophet has introduced the king into a sphere of symbolic action. He now inquires how far the king has Faith to embrace the Word of Promise: the king smites three times, and that is the extent to which the effective Word of God will achieve accomplishment and not return void.

Here we see very vividly the exact relation in which the symbol stood to the Word, and in which both stood to the course of events.

The Word embodied in the symbol is exceedingly effective; it cannot fail to come to pass; it will accomplish exactly what the symbol declared. Thus, Isaiah walked naked (wearing only his under tunic) and barefoot (Isa., Chpt. 20); Jeremiah smashed a potter's vessel in the place of potsherds (Jer., Chpt. 19); Ahijah tore his new coat into twelve pieces and gave Jeroboam ten (I Ki. 11:29); and,

NOTES

Ezekiel besieged a model city (Ezek. 4:1-3) and dug through the house wall (12:1).

As well, these are actions that originated not at all with the Prophet but, instead, with God, and which the Prophet carried out according to direction. In other words, the initiative rested solely with God.

Even though, the Messages from God and delivered by the Prophets were, in fact, most of the time, Messages of warning and Judgment, still, the true Prophet had a Message of peace at times.

However, when peace is the Message of God, it will always be in Exodus terms, meaning that peace can only come when Holiness is satisfied concerning sin.

THE MESSAGE

It should suffice to say that the mark of false prophets is, as well, their message. Most of the time, it is one of prosperity and shallow optimism or error concerning the Word of God. As well, it will, most of the time, be devoid of moral content, therefore, grieving the righteous and encouraging the wicked.

True Prophecy from a true Prophet will not direct itself to the ostensible queries but according to sinful hearts. For the Word of God, at least in this context, is always against sin.

However, it should be quickly added that Prophecy also involves itself, as given by the Prophet of God, *"to edification, and exhortation, and comfort"* (I Cor. 14:3).

PROPHECY AND PROPHETS

Prophecy and Prophets form the greatest line of continuity between the Old Testament and New Testament. This is evident from the Attitude of Christ and the Apostles to Old Testament Prophecy. The continuance of the phenomenon of Prophecy up to and after the Ministry of Christ, the Prophetic character of His Own Ministry, the placing of the Inspiration of New Testament Apostles and Prophets alongside that of Old Testament Prophets, and the general outpouring of the Holy Spirit—the Spirit of Prophecy—upon the Church, leads to a continuing acceptance of Prophets and Prophesying in New Testament Churches.

The Old Testament Prophetic line did not

end with Malachi, but rather with John the Baptist, as our Lord expressly declares (Mat. 11:13). Prophetic Utterances of John's father, Zechariah, and of Anna, Simeon, and Mary at the beginning of Luke's Gospel, all bear witness to the continuance of Prophetic Inspiration (Lk. 1:46-55, 67:79; 2:26-38).

Unfortunately, the customary division into two *"Testaments"* obscures this marvelous unity of God's Program of Revelation, but the line is continuous from Moses to John, even though there was a void of some 400 years between Malachi and John the Baptist. However, the Office of the Prophet under the New Covenant continues, as we shall see.

THE HOLY SPIRIT

Christ promised His Disciples that after His Ascension, He would send them His Holy Spirit Who would empower them to bear witness of Him in the world and would bear witness with them (Lk. 24:48-49; Jn. 14:26; 15:26-27; Acts 1:8). That this includes Prophetic Inspiration is clear from Matthew 10:19-20 and John 16:12-15.

The Apostles and those who preached the Gospel at the first did so in the Power of the same *"Holy Spirit sent from Heaven,"* Who inspired the predictions of the Old Testament Prophets as they looked forward to the coming Sufferings and Glory of Christ (I Pet. 1:10-12).

Hence, in Peter's message on the Day of Pentecost, he concludes that a major result of the infilling of the Holy Spirit is that *"they shall prophesy,"* which includes not only Prophetic Words but also Visions and Dreams (Acts 2:18).

Actually, every Christian is potentially, although not actually, a Prophet, thus, realizing Moses' wish expressed in Numbers 11:29. This is so because the Spirit given generally to the Church for its testimony to Jesus is the *"Spirit of Prophecy"* (I Cor. 14:31; Rev. 19:10). Consequently, Paul tells the Corinthian Christians, *"desire Spiritual Gifts, but rather that you may prophesy"* (I Cor. 14:1).

When Believers initially received the Power of the Holy Spirit, the commonest manifestations resulting at the time were speaking in other Tongues and prophesying (Acts 2:4, 17-18; 10:44-46; 19:6; I Cor. 1:5-7).

Jesus predicted that people would prophesy in His Name (Mat. 7:22; though attention should be paid to His Warning against reliance on this or any other work for one's Spiritual standing). So, Prophecy is repeatedly mentioned as one of the Gifts of the Holy Spirit with which Christ equips His Members to function as His Body in each place (Rom. 12:4-7; I Cor. 12:10-13; I Thess. 5:19-20; I Pet. 4:10-11).

THE SPIRITS OF THE PROPHETS ARE SUBJECT TO THE PROPHETS

The Scripture plainly tells us that in the New Testament Church, *"the spirits of the Prophets are subject to the Prophets"* (I Cor. 14:32). Therefore, Prophecy is not to be abused by people succumbing to any supposedly uncontrollable ecstatic frenzy. Neither is it to be exercised without the check of other members of the Body, notably the Elders and Prophets, weighing or discerning the accuracy and reliability of Utterances purporting to issue from the Holy Spirit (I Cor. 14:29-33).

No doubt, just such abuses are what led the Apostle to write to another young Church, *"Quench not the Spirit. Despise not Prophesyings. Prove all things; hold fast that which is good"* (I Thess. 5:19-21). A similar balance is shown by Paul concerning Tongues—I Corinthians 14:39-40.

Testing or weighing Prophetic Utterances is all the more necessary in view of the warnings of the New Testament and in the spirit of the Old Testament against false prophets and false prophecy, by which Satan seeks to lead the unwary astray (Mat. 7:15; 24:11, 24; II Pet. 2:1; I Jn. 4:1).

The testing of any Prophetic Utterance will be in accordance with our Lord's warning, *"Wherefore by their fruits you shall know them"* (Mat. 7:20). As well, the criteria will always conform to the teachings of Scripture.

PROPHETS AND PROPHESYING

However, it must be noted that there is a great difference in the *"Gift of Prophecy"* (I Cor. 12:10) and the *"Office of the Prophet"*

NOTES

(Eph. 4:11). All who have the New Testament Gift of Prophecy as one of the nine Gifts of the Spirit do not necessarily stand in the Office of the Prophet. These are two different Ministries altogether. While all those who stand in the Office of the Prophet definitely have the Gift of Prophecy, all who have the Gift of Prophecy don't stand in the Office of the Prophet. The Office of the Prophet is a much higher Calling than one who has the Gift of Prophecy although they are both from the Lord.

Probably the best known in Acts, as it regards the Office of the Prophet, is Agabus (Acts 11:28; 21:10-11), but others are also named (Acts 15:32), and the whole of the Book of Revelation is an extended Prophecy revealed to John the Beloved (Rev. 1:3; 10:11; 22:7, 10, 18-19).

All the evidence from the examples of Prophetic Ministry in the New Testament shows that it is entirely in harmony with Old Testament Prophecy in its character and form.

For instance, the Ministries of John the Baptist, Agabus, and John the Beloved, who wrote the Apocalypse, comprise the classic unity of prediction and proclamation, of foretelling (the future) and forthtelling (a Preacher of Righteousness). The same is true of Zechariah, Simeon, and others. Similarly, they combined prediction of wrath to come or trouble in store and of coming Grace (Lk. 3:7, 16; Jn. 1:29; Acts 11:28; Rev. 19:21).

THE MANNER OF PROPHECY

Equally, we find Prophecy and Revelation given by Visions and occasionally by Dreams, as well as by the Word of the Lord (Lk. 3:2; Rev. 1:10, 12; Acts 10:9-16; Mat. 1:20). Also, the use of parable and symbol, exactly as in the Old Testament, are well attested, including the acted Oracle (Acts 21:11).

It should be noted that Agabus' word was accepted by Paul as descriptively accurate but not personally directed (Acts 21:12-14).

ERROR

It is claimed by some that there can be no Prophecy or Prophets in the New Testament sense in the Church today or in any other post-apostolic age. There are those

NOTES

who claim that the term *"Prophesy"* simply means the preaching of the Gospel. However, that is untrue.

While evangelistic proclamation or a teaching ministry may on occasion approximate to Prophesy, they are not the same.

A PERSONAL EXPERIENCE

In 1985, if I remember the year correctly, Frances and I, along with others, had the privilege to go into what was then the Soviet Union to minster in several cities. We caught a train out of Moscow late in the afternoon and rode all night to the city of Minsk. I was to preach that morning in a Pentecostal Church and that night in a Baptist Church.

The Service in the Pentecostal Church was to prove to be extremely informative as it regarded the future.

The place was packed with not an available seat and, once again, if I remember correctly, not even standing room.

I was preaching through an interpreter, incidentally, who gave his heart to the Lord in the midst of that message; however, that's another story.

As I was preaching, I sensed an unusually heavy Anointing for a few minutes. And then the Lord began to speak through me with a Prophecy that contained information concerning the entirety of the great land of Russia and, actually, all 15 of its provinces. As stated, it was then under the heavy yoke of communism.

All of a sudden, I felt led to stop the Message I was preaching. And then, the Lord spoke through me with a Word of Prophecy, and I will quote it as best as I can remember. It said:

"The Gospel of Jesus Christ is going to be proclaimed in every city, town, and village in the Soviet Union."

When I said it, even though I knew it was the Lord, it startled me, as would be obvious. How in the world could that be? The heavy yoke of communism rested upon the entirety of the land, with most every means of presenting the Gospel facing a closed door. But yet, and as stated, I knew it was the Lord.

A STARTLING STATEMENT!

As Frances and I left the Service that day,

I mentioned to her the Prophecy that I had given. How in the world could it be? How could such a thing come to pass?

Well, of course, the Lord knew exactly what He was saying and what He was doing.

THE FAITH OF JIM WOOLSEY

Some three years had passed since that Service that Sunday morning in Minsk. The year was now 1988. Jim Woolsey, who had worked with us for years and had been instrumental in placing the telecast all over the world, which had resulted in a phenomenal harvest of souls, came into my office. He said to me, *"Brother Swaggart, I believe we can get on television in Latvia,"* which was one of the Soviet Provinces. I just looked at him for a few moments, wondering how in the world this could be done, considering the iron curtain of communism! I will be frank, I really didn't have the faith to believe for this situation. So, that means it was Jim Woolsey's Faith that brought all of this about.

A few weeks later, it happened exactly as Jim said; we went on television in the capital city of Latvia. The KGB tried to get the program taken off the station but to no avail. The response was so overwhelming as to defy description.

And then in 1989, Jim came back into my office saying, *"Brother Swaggart, I believe I can get the telecast on TV1 out of Moscow."* TV1 was the largest television Network in the world, with over 7,000 stations covering all 15 of the Soviet Republics.

I looked at Jim like he had lost his mind. Our telecast, translated into Russian, going all over the Soviet Union? How in the world could this be done?

Actually, Jim had been traveling to Moscow over and over again, meeting with the television people, always getting a little closer but never quite getting them to say *"yes."*

And then it happened. They quoted Jim a price, and we were to air the telecast, translated into Russian, over TV1, covering all 15 of the Soviet Republics.

The results were so phenomenal as to be staggering. We received over a million letters in the two-year period that the telecast was allowed to air. In fact, the entire nation of Russia, plus all of its provinces, were

touched with the Gospel. How we give the Lord the praise and the glory for bringing this to pass, which with man was impossible, but with God, all things are possible.

When the Lord spoke that Word that day in the Church in Minsk, while it was a part of the preaching, one might say, that did not mean that all the other preaching was Prophecy, for it wasn't. So, there is a difference in preaching and Prophecy, as ought to be obvious! While evangelistic proclamation, as stated, or a teaching ministry may on occasion approximate to Prophecy, they are not the same.

DENIAL OF THE GIFTS

Others have sometimes sought to identify the completion of the New Testament Canon of Scripture with the time when Prophecy would pass away. They use I Corinthians 13:8 as their Scriptural evidence. However, this does violence to the context, which clearly shows that these Gifts will pass away *"when the Perfect comes,"* which is defined as when we *"see face-to-face,"* or beyond this life and age altogether.

All should certainly agree that there is no new Revelation as it regards the Word of God, or, in other words, to add to Scripture. However, the Word of God leaves every impression that the Living God Who both speaks and acts (in contrast to dead idols) will definitely use the Gift of Prophecy and the Office of the Prophet to give particular local guidance to a Church, nation, or individual, or to warn or encourage by way of prediction as well as by reminders. This is in full accord with the written Word of God, by which all such utterances must be tested.

THE TRUTH

Certainly, the New Testament does not see it as the job of the Prophet to be a doctrinal innovator. However, it definitely does consider him to be one who delivers the Word the Spirit gives in line with the Truth, which was once for all delivered to the Saints (Jude, Vs. 3), and to challenge and encourage our Faith.

In the New Testament, the Prophets of both Testaments are always regarded as the pioneers of Faith, who stand in the front-line in every age and reap the full blast of the wind of persecution stirred up in the world by the Devil against the People of God. Ironically enough, much of that opposition will come from the church (Mat. 23:37; Lk. 11:47-50; Acts 7:52; I Thess. 2:15; Rev. 11:3-8; 16:6; 18:20, 24).

We must never forget, *"the Testimony of Jesus is the Spirit of Prophecy,"* and all His People are called to bear that Testimony faithfully in various ways by the Power of the Holy Spirit.

(6) "AND SHE CONCEIVED AGAIN, AND BORE A DAUGHTER. AND GOD SAID UNTO HIM, CALL HER NAME LO-RUHAMAH: FOR I WILL NO MORE HAVE MERCY UPON THE HOUSE OF ISRAEL; BUT I WILL UTTERLY TAKE THEM AWAY.

(7) "BUT I WILL HAVE MERCY UPON THE HOUSE OF JUDAH, AND WILL SAVE THEM BY THE LORD THEIR GOD, AND WILL NOT SAVE THEM BY BOW, NOR BY SWORD, NOR BY BATTLE, BY HORSES, NOR BY HORSEMEN."

1. (Vs. 6) *"Lo-ruhamah"* means *"not pitied."* Because of Israel going into total idolatry and refusing to repent, even though great Prophets were sent unto them, the northern kingdom would be destroyed as a nation, never to rise again, at least in that capacity.

2. (Vs. 7) About 200 years before the time of Hosea, Ten Tribes from the commonwealth of Israel, so to speak, had broken away and continued to refer to themselves as *"Israel."* The larger Tribe of Judah remained and referred to itself as *"Judah,"* with the Tribe of Benjamin throwing in their lot with Judah (II Chron. 10:12-19). Even though the Lord here pronounces Judgment upon the northern kingdom of Israel, He says here that the southern kingdom of Judah will be spared.

3. (Vs. 7) The Lord is referring here to the deliverance from Sennacherib in the days of Hezekiah, when in one night the Angel of the Lord smote 185,000 of the flower of the Assyrian host (II Ki., Chpt. 19; Isa. Chpt. 37). Still, its total fulfillment belongs to the future (II Thess., Chpt. 2).

NO MORE MERCY

As stated, *"Lo-ruhamah,"* means *"not*

pitied." One can compare this with Romans 9:25 and I Peter 2:10. Other references to Hosea in the New Testament are Matthew 2:15; 9:13; 12:7; and I Corinthians 15:55.

The phrase, *"For I will no more have Mercy upon the House of Israel; but I will utterly take them away,"* was fulfilled in totality.

However, God did have Mercy on the house of Judah, and they were restored. The reason for this is obvious and does not take away from the Mercy and Grace of God.

The northern kingdom of Israel, to which these Prophecies are addressed, had forsaken the Temple and sacrifices, therefore, they had forsaken the Word of God. They had substituted in their place idols of their own making; consequently, whenever the Word of God is forsaken, it is impossible for God to restore. At any time, if Israel had returned to the Word of God, Mercy, Grace, and Forgiveness would have been enjoined, ensuring their restoration. The same can be said for anyone.

However, if anyone refuses to abide by the Word of God, as Israel, there is nothing left but destruction. God cannot have *"Mercy"* upon those who will not meet His Terms.

THE WEAK AND DEFENSELESS CONDITION OF ISRAEL

The first birth symbolized the blood-guiltiness and idolatry of Israel and the consequent destruction.

Two other births follow to confirm the certainty of the coming calamity and to develop it further in order to show the prospect of deliverance to be hopeless because of Israel's failure to repent. If one is to notice, the first child was a boy, while the second is a *"daughter."* Such is not without purpose. Her name was Lo-Ruhamah.

The change of gender denotes the weak and defenseless condition of Israel after their bow was broken and their power crushed by the enemy. They were then ready to be led into captivity like a female, helpless and powerless, and exposed to all the insults of the conquerors.

After Gomer had borne a son, which was a proverbial reference to Jeroboam II, she now bears a daughter, who refers parabolically to Zechariah and to Shallum, both kings of

Israel, who were as weak as a female.

The phrase, *"For I will no more have Mercy upon the House of Israel,"* typifies the meaning of the name of the child, *"she-is-not-pitied,"* This emphasizes that inasmuch as Repentance was not forthcoming, the Mercy, which would have saved her from the miseries of captivity, is clean gone. To say the least, it is a solemn announcement!

THE FUTURE

The phrase, *"But I will have Mercy upon the house of Judah,"* definitely refers to Judah's present deliverance from Sennacherib in the days of Hezekiah when in one night the Angel of the Lord smote 185,000 of the flower of the Assyrian hosts (II Ki., Chpt. 19; Isa., Chpt. 37). However, its total fulfillment belongs even yet to the future (II Thess., Chpt. 2). Verse 7 also speaks of the Lord saving Israel from the hand of the Antichrist, which He will do at the Second Coming.

The phrase, *"And will save them by the LORD their God,"* is a peculiar form of expression. Instead of the pronoun, the proper name of Jehovah is employed. Instead of saying, *"I will save them by Myself,"* He says in a specially emphatic matter, *"I will save them by Jehovah."* At the same time, He adds the important adjunct of *"thy God,"* which reminds them of their relationship to Himself and virtue of which He interposes thus personally and powerfully on their behalf.

However, this in no way meant that the southern kingdom of Judah was without sin, for, in fact, Judah, even at this time, was spiritually deficient, and woefully so! Nevertheless, through the leadership of Hezekiah and the prophesying of Isaiah, and the fact that she still clung to the Temple and the sacrifices, Mercy would be shown as long as possible. However, in about 200 years Judah and Jerusalem would, as well, be destroyed, and because of sin. Still, Judah would be restored, whereas, the northern kingdom of Israel would never experience restoration.

(8) "NOW WHEN SHE HAD WEANED LO-RUHAMAH, SHE CONCEIVED, AND BORE A SON.

(9) "THEN SAID GOD, CALL HIS NAME LO-AMMI: FOR YOU ARE NOT MY PEOPLE, AND I WILL NOT BE YOUR GOD."

The exposition is:

1. (Vs. 8) Even though it would be about 70 years before the fall of Israel, still, the children are born to Hosea and Gomer in quick succession, proclaiming the finality of the Judgment of God.

2. (Vs. 8) As the three deportations would in later years be a warning to Judah, likewise, the births of these three children are warnings to Israel. However, whereas the deportations were some years apart, the births of these children were in quick succession, denoting the absence of any spiritual quality.

3. (Vs. 9) *"Lo-ammi"* means *"not My People."* As stated, the Prophet's children symbolized, step by step, Israel's fast coming calamity. There will be no reprieve because there will be no Repentance.

THE FINALITY OF THE JUDGMENT OF GOD

The weaning of the child could have taken from two to three years. However, it is merely a pause in the progress of the approaching calamity—pause indicative of the Divine loathness to execute the final sentence.

As well, the *"weaning"* may be referred to as the entire withdrawal of all Spiritual Nourishment and support, when promise and Prophecy, instruction and consolation, and symbol and sacrifice, would be totally abolished.

• The name *"Jezreel,"* the first child, means being scattered by God as a result of their sin. It represents the first blow that will soon be dealt to them by Divine providence, but from that, it was possible by Repentance to recover. Though dispersed, they were not beyond the reach of Divine compassion or beyond the Power of the Divine Arm to collect and bring them together again.

• The second child, *"Lo-ruhamah,"* meaning unpitied, imports another and a still heavier blow.

However, even though all pity from their Maker is gone, still, there is a glimmer of hope, even in this destitute name, that sometime in the distant future things may change, and their restoration be brought about.

• The name *"Lo-ammi,"* however, puts an end to hope, implying, as it does, a total rejection of an entire people on the part of the Almighty. The national Covenant is annulled. God has cast off His People, who are thus left hopeless and helpless, because of their sinful and ungrateful departure from the Source of all Mercy and the Fountain of all blessing.

By using the pronoun *"you,"* the Lord addresses this directly and personally. He says, *"You are not Mine, and I am no longer yours!"* Such is the literal rendering of this now sad but once tender expression.

WHY WOULD THE PEOPLE NOT REPENT?

The northern kingdom of Israel had had Prophet after Prophet sent to them, with now the great Prophet Hosea addressing them with a stronger Message than ever.

He is instructed by the Lord to marry a harlot, which is meant to symbolize Israel. The children born to this union were meant to signify the Lord's Dealings with Israel, which proclaimed their stiff-necked attitude of rebellion. Nothing He would say to them, nothing He could say to them, seemed to make any difference. They ignored the Prophets before Hosea, and now they ignore Hosea.

Let it be understood that God cannot condone sin in any fashion. Even though these were His People, still, after years, and even centuries, of dealing with them, but to no avail, there was no alternative left but Judgment. It would be the same as a wife being repeatedly unfaithful to her husband, which, after a while, would stretch to the breaking point the patience of even the most patient individual in the world. God is Merciful, Loving, Kind, Gracious, and Longsuffering; however, there comes a point to where the situation is worse, if allowed to continue, than the Judgment it takes to stop it.

(10) "YET THE NUMBER OF THE CHILDREN OF ISRAEL SHALL BE AS THE SAND OF THE SEA, WHICH CANNOT BE MEASURED NOR NUMBERED; AND IT SHALL COME TO PASS, THAT IN THE PLACE WHERE IT WAS SAID UNTO THEM, YOU ARE NOT MY PEOPLE, THERE IT SHALL BE SAID UNTO THEM, YOU ARE THE SONS OF THE LIVING GOD.

(11) "THEN SHALL THE CHILDREN OF JUDAH AND THE CHILDREN OF

ISRAEL BE GATHERED TOGETHER, AND APPOINT THEMSELVES ONE HEAD, AND THEY SHALL COME UP OUT OF THE LAND: FOR GREAT SHALL BE THE DAY OF JEZREEL."

The exegesis is:

1. (Vs. 10) There is no contradiction between Verses 9 and 10. Even though the northern kingdom of Israel was ultimately totally destroyed as a Nation and, in fact, will never, as such, rise again, still, *"the Children of Israel"* were not destroyed and, in truth, will be, in a future happy day, completely restored. Consequently, this Passage and Verse 11 have to do with the coming Kingdom Age.

2. (Vs. 11) The restoration under Zerubbabel did not satisfy the prediction of Verses 10 or 11, for it was very small and did not secure national independence. However, the future will satisfy the Prophecy, for then will God *"sow"* the Hebrew people unto Himself in Righteousness.

3. (Vs. 11) All of this will happen in the coming Kingdom Age, when, at the beginning of it, actually at the Second Coming of the Lord, Israel will then accept Christ.

THE FULFILLMENT OF PROPHECY

When the northern kingdom of Israel was taken captive by the Assyrians a little over 70 years from the time of Hosea, they would be scattered across the Assyrian Empire exactly as the name *"Jezreel"* suggests. There they remained for some 133 years until the fall of Judah.

Some of them intermarried, thereby, losing their Jewish identity; however, many did not, maintaining their nationality.

When Judah fell, some 133 years after the fall of the northern kingdom of Israel, they were assimilated, along with the other Jews, into the Babylonian Empire. Some 70 years after the fall of Judah, both groups, who had now become one, would be repatriated back to the Land of Israel, which was, in a sense, no longer divided.

SAMARITANS

Part of the former northern kingdom of Israel was populated by the Samaritans and was later called Samaria, with whom the Children of Israel would not have any dealings. This feeling was extremely prevalent in the time of Christ. However, the area known as Samaria did not include the entirety of the former area of the northern kingdom, in fact, excluding the area known as *"Galilee."*

Irrespective of the gathering that took place at the ending of the dispersion, still, that is not the gathering of the two Verses, 10 and 11. That gathering, which will take place at the beginning of the coming Kingdom Age, is yet to come!

The phrase from Verse 10, *"You are the sons of the Living God,"* has not yet been fulfilled. It will be fulfilled upon their acceptance of Christ immediately after the Second Coming.

Incidentally, the Samaritans were Gentiles sent into a part of the area of the northern kingdom of Israel by the king of Assyria. They were sent to replace the Jews who had been exported to Assyria. The Jews never recognized them as a part of Israel. But yet, Jesus ministered to them (Jn., Chpt. 4).

RIGHTEOUSNESS

The restoration under Zerubbabel, as stated, did not satisfy the prediction of Verses 10 or 11, for it was very small and did not secure national independence. However, the future will satisfy the Prophecy, for then will God *"sow"* the Hebrew people unto Himself in Righteousness.

The phrase, *"Gathered together,"* was, in fact, brought about after the 70 years dispersion of Judah; however, they never had *"one head"* as this Scripture predicts. This refers to one king over the entirety of the nation.

They never truly had a king after Jehoiachin, at least, *"appointed of themselves."* In fact, Herod was king during the time of Christ but was appointed by Rome and was not in the line of David.

The phrase, *"And they shall come up out of the land: for great shall be the day of Jezreel,"* refers to the terrible scattering of the people.

This reference extends even further than the defeat of the northern kingdom or even the defeat of Judah. In fact, it had reference to the terrible slaughter and scattering in A.D 70., when Titus destroyed Jerusalem, resulting in the Nation being destroyed and

the Jews being scattered all over the world.

Upon the second return of Christ, they will be gathered back to the Land of Israel from all over the world, even including the very last Jew, where they will rule and reign under Christ. This is the far-reaching meaning of the Eleventh Verse.

"O for a thousand tongues to sing,
"My great Redeemer's Praise,
"The Glories of my God and King,
"The Triumphs of His Grace."

"He breaks the power of cancelled sin,
"He sets the prisoner free;
"His Blood can make the foulest clean;
"His Blood availed for me."

CHAPTER 2

(1) "SAY YOU UNTO YOUR BRETHREN, AMMI; AND TO YOUR SISTERS, RUHAMAH.

(2) "PLEAD WITH YOUR MOTHER, PLEAD: FOR SHE IS NOT MY WIFE, NEITHER AM I HER HUSBAND: LET HER THEREFORE PUT AWAY HER WHOREDOMS OUT OF HER SIGHT, AND HER ADULTERIES FROM BETWEEN HER BREASTS;

(3) "LEST I STRIP HER NAKED, AND SET HER AS IN THE DAY THAT SHE WAS BORN, AND MAKE HER AS A WILDERNESS, AND SET HER LIKE A DRY LAND, AND SLAY HER WITH THIRST.

(4) "AND I WILL NOT HAVE MERCY UPON HER CHILDREN; FOR THEY BE THE CHILDREN OF WHOREDOMS.

(5) "FOR THEIR MOTHER HAS PLAYED THE HARLOT: SHE WHO CONCEIVED THEM HAS DONE SHAMEFULLY: FOR SHE SAID, I WILL GO AFTER MY LOVERS, WHO GIVE ME MY BREAD AND MY WATER, MY WOOL AND MY FLAX, MY OIL AND MY DRINK."

The exegesis is:

1. Verse 1 is addressed to a small company of true Believers, which was then ensconced in backslidden Israel, and which the Lord has in all ages, and which is here distinguished by the affectionate titles of

"My People" (Ammi) and "the engraced" (Ruhamah).

2. "Plead with your mother, plead," of Verse 2, speaks of the whole people of Israel taken together as a national unit. The "pleading" to Israel is to be done by those who still love and serve their Lord. In effect, they were to act as Evangelists.

3. (Vs. 2) "For she is not my wife, neither am I her husband," in its strict sense, refers to Gomer, who had left Hosea, even after bearing him three children, going back out into the world of sin and iniquity. As Gomer left Hosea for whoredoms, likewise, Israel had left God for whoredoms. So the marriage in both cases was dissolved.

4. The first phrase of Verse 3 refers to the fact that Gomer, rather than gaining prosperity, was instead reduced to abject poverty, as future Verses will portray.

5. (Vs. 4) The Nation of Israel as a whole with its body politic is spoken of as the parent. Its citizenry is spoken of as the "children." The children proved themselves to be no better than the mother who bore them. They were the worthless progeny of a worthless parent.

6. (Vs. 5) Likewise, Israel, of which Gomer was a symbol, ran after her "lovers," who were the Assyrians and the Egyptians. As a result, Israel worshipped the idols of these heathen nations, and also ascribed her blessings as not from Jehovah but from these idol gods.

THE SMALL REMNANT
WHO SERVED GOD

Some scholars feel that Verse 1 of this Second Chapter should have been the concluding Verse of the previous Chapter. However, I personally feel the King James translators were correct in placing the Chapter division where they did. The appeal of Verse 1 is this:

Verse 1, and the appeal it carries, is addressed to the small company of true Believers in the northern kingdom of Israel, who truly loved the Lord. Despite the fact that they were few in number, they were now to be given a tremendous responsibility. They were to plead with wayward Israel to come back to God. As stated, they were

distinguished by the affectionate titles of "My People," and "the engraced."

Believing the gracious Promises of the preceding Verses and energized by them, these followers of the Prophet Hosea are called to plead with the Nation and win it back to Jehovah. Thus, God invites His People into fellowship with Himself in His Love toward the guilty and sinful.

The Holy Spirit is giving an Altar Call and, actually, asking the small Remnant in the northern kingdom to take this Call to the balance of Israel.

In these Passages, one can easily see the Holy Spirit going to all lengths in order to bring Israel to her senses but, tragically, to no avail!

SCOFFERS

Considering that it would be some 70 years before the actual destruction took place, several years after the strong admonition by Hosea, no doubt, the scoffers abounded, desiring in sarcastic tones to know the date of this coming destruction. However, delay does not mean denial, only Mercy and Grace. But, sadly, it was Mercy and Grace that was heeded not at all.

Tragically, the attitude of the northern kingdom of Israel and, later, the southern kingdom of Judah is being repeated presently.

Peter said:

"Knowing this first, that there shall come in the last days scoffers, walking after their own lusts,

"And saying, Where is the Promise of His Coming? for since the fathers fell asleep, all things continue as they were from the beginning of the Creation" (II Pet. 3:3-4).

WHO ARE THESE SCOFFERS?

They are "enemies of the Cross." Paul said:

"Brethren, be followers together of me (be 'fellow-imitators'), and mark them who walk so as you have us for an example (observe intently).

"(For many walk [speaks of those attempting to live for God outside of the Victory and rudiments of the Cross of Christ], of whom I have told you often, and now tell you even weeping [this is a most serious matter], that they are the enemies of the Cross of Christ [*those who do not look exclusively to the Cross of Christ must be labeled 'enemies'*]**:**

"Whose end *is* destruction [*if the Cross is ignored, and continues to be ignored, the loss of the soul is the only ultimate conclusion*]**, whose God *is their* belly** [*refers to those who attempt to pervert the Gospel for their own personal gain*]**, and *whose* glory is** **in their shame** [*the material things they seek, God labels as 'shame'*]**, who mind earthly things.)** *(This means they have no interest in heavenly things, which signifies they are using the Lord for their own personal gain)*" **(Phil. 3:17-19).**

THE ALTAR CALL

The admonition of Verse 2, which the Lord gave to the Prophet Hosea to give to the small remnant in Israel, could be labeled as an *"Altar Call,"* so to speak. Two major things are said in Verse 2. They are:

1. Hosea, along with a small Remnant, was to *"plead"* with the people of Israel to get right with God.

2. They were to be faithful to the Word, showing Israel what they were facing unless there was Repentance. The persons addressed in this Second Verse are those individuals in Israel who had still retained their Spiritual Integrity, and who, not withstanding surrounding defection and abounding ungodliness, had continued steadfast in their loyalty and love to the Lord. They might be few in number, widely scattered, perhaps unknown to each other, and of comparatively little note; yet, they are here called on to raise their voices in solemn warning and earnest protest against the national defection and wickedness.

The phrase, *"Plead with your mother, plead,"* speaks of the whole people taken together as a national unit. The *"pleading"* is to be done by those who still love and serve their Lord. In effect, they were to act as Evangelists.

EVANGELISTS

At the present time, God-called Evangelists are scarcer than ever in the modern church. A Church that's on fire for God always has many Evangelists. The cooler it becomes,

Spiritually speaking, there are less and less Evangelists until, in some Christian denominations, there are precious few Evangelists at all, if any!

For instance, the major Pentecostal Denominations, which once were rife with Evangelists, have now, at least for the most part, been reduced to entertainers, singers, psychologists, and conductors of seminars, but, precious few Evangelists. Of all the signs of spiritual declension, this just might be the most telling of all.

Consequently, there are precious few to *"plead"* with the people to come back to God, which, for the most part, can only be done by God-called Evangelists.

The very word, *"plead,"* refers to a cry from a broken heart. More than all, it means to *"plead"* with tears.

DIVORCE

The phrase, *"For she is not my wife, neither am I her husband,"* in its strict sense, refers to Gomer, who had left Hosea, even after bearing him three children, to go back out into the world of sin and iniquity.

In effect, by the Lord making this statement, He is saying, *"Unless there is a change in Israel, unless there is Repentance, which alone can bring about change, the marriage will have to be dissolved."* In other words, the Lord could no longer claim Israel as His Wife, and He would not accept them claiming Him as their husband.

HOSEA

It is very difficult for us to understand what the Lord demanded of Hosea in asking him to marry such a woman. The Lord knew she would do what she did and how it would break the Prophet's heart. Actually, throughout history, few servants of the Lord have been asked for such a depth of consecration. But yet, it seems that the Prophet never questioned the Command of the Lord at all! He would faithfully obey, denoting a godliness that few in history have equaled.

As Gomer was here guilty of adultery, Israel was guilty of idolatry, which was Spiritual Adultery. The close and tender relationship into which God had graciously condescended to take Israel is rendered null and void, and that was through Israel's own fault. God threatens the renunciation of it unless perchance the pleading of the still faithful children might recall the erring mother to penitence and purity.

Consequently, and as a symbolic gesture, the children of the union of Gomer and Hosea, *"Jezreel, Lo-ruhamah, and Lo-ammi,"* are encouraged to plead with their *"mother"* to return to their father, and her husband, and to a life of godliness.

The phrase, *"Let her therefore put away her whoredoms out of her sight, and her adulteries from between her breasts,"* signifies the return of Gomer to her old pursuits of immorality. As stated, how this must have broken the hearts of Hosea and the children!

How old they were at this time is not stated; however, the implication is that they were old enough to *"plead with their mother."*

The expression is to be taken literally as the word, *"breast,"* in the parallel clause proves. Since the Holy Spirit compares her to a harlot, He attributes to her the ways of harlots.

THE JUDGMENT OF GOD

The phrase of Verse 3, *"Lest I strip her naked, and set her as in the day that she was born,"* refers to Gomer not gaining prosperity at all by her actions, but instead, being reduced to abject poverty, as future Verses will portray.

As well, this is meant to describe Israel. The removal of her garments would point to her degradation and disgrace. As Gomer, so Israel!

In other words, the Nation is threatened with depravation of all the blessings previously lavished upon them—property, prosperity, population, and privilege.

THE BLESSINGS OF GOD

Every Believer must understand the following: once the person is truly Born-Again, the Lord expects that individual to follow Him according to His Word. He then becomes the Source of all Blessings, all prosperity, and all freedom. In fact, He is the Source of everything that is good. If we love Him, obey Him, do our best to follow according to His Word, and continue to follow Him as we should, the Blessings will

continue to flow uninterrupted. Of course, this is with the understanding that Jesus Christ is the Source, and the Cross is the Means by which all of this is done and by which the Holy Spirit works. But, if the individual turns his or her back on God, in effect, ceasing to believe, or else placing his or her faith in something other than Christ and the Cross, then Judgment most definitely will come. While the Lord will do everything within His Power, short of forcing the individual to come back to the right way, if all fails, as stated, then Judgment will come. That is the pattern throughout the Word of God, and it is unvarying in its prediction.

Obedience to the Lord guarantees His Blessings. And we speak of Blessings of every nature, physically, domestically, economically, and above all, Spiritually.

WHAT DID JESUS SAY ABOUT THIS?

"And this know, that if the goodman of the house had known what hour the thief would come, he would have watched, and not have suffered his house to be broken through *(if one is truly watching for the Lord, then at the same time he will be watching as it respects Satan that the Evil One not destroy his 'house').*

"Be you therefore ready also: for the Son of Man comes at an hour when you think not *(regrettably, most of the modern church doesn't think the Rapture will take place; this means that it will definitely take place, and very soon!).*

THE FAITHFUL SERVANT

"Then Peter said unto Him, Lord, do you speak this Parable unto us, or even to all? *(Peter is thinking of an earthly kingdom about to begin, with the Twelve paramount in that kingdom; in fact, Jesus is speaking to all.)*

"And the Lord said, Who then is that faithful and wise steward *(some have claimed that the 'steward' refers to Ministers only; however, the very nature of the word pertains not to position, but to responsibility, which applies to all),* **whom *his* lord shall make ruler over His Household, to give *them their* portion of meat in due season?** *(It is the steward who is 'faithful and wise.')*

"Blessed *is* that servant *(stewards and servants are the same)*, **whom his Lord when He comes shall find so doing** *(being faithful in what the Lord has called us to do, proclaiming the fact that such are also wise)*.

"**Of a truth I say unto you, that He will make him ruler over all that He has** *(a ruler in the Kingdom of God, which is yet to come, is the reward which the 'faithful and wise' will seek, and not things of this world)*.

THE UNFAITHFUL SERVANT

"**But and if that servant say in his heart, My lord delays his coming** *(regrettably, most of the modern church falls into this category)*; **and shall begin to beat the menservants and maidens** *(to not properly love God is to not properly love our neighbor as ourselves)*, **and to eat and drink, and to be drunken** *(proclaims Believers who have ceased to believe and have, thereby, lost their way, which will ultimately conclude in the loss of their souls; as well, this completely refutes the unscriptural doctrine of Unconditional Eternal Security)*;

"**The lord of that servant will come in a day when he looks not for *Him*, and at an hour when he is not aware, and will cut him in sunder, and will appoint him his portion with the unbelievers** *(this clearly points to former Believers who have ceased to believe and will, thereby, die eternally lost [Heb. 6:4-6; 10:23-29])*" **(Lk. 12:39-46).**

I WILL NOT HAVE MERCY

Through the Prophet Hosea, the Lord said, *"And I will not have Mercy upon her children; for they be the children of whoredoms."*

The idea pertains to Israel of old, who perished in the wilderness, but yet, her children were spared. Now, however, the case is different and the punishment aggravated. The adulterous parent perishes, and the children of that parent perish also. The reason is that the children proved themselves no better than the mother who bore them. They were the worthless progeny of a worthless parent.

The Nation as a whole with its body politic is spoken of as the parent. Its citizenry is spoken of as the *"children."*

A PERSONAL ILLUSTRATION

Sometime back I was speaking with a lawyer who was Jewish. I had come to know the man quite well and considered him a friend.

In a particular conversation, he addressed me in this fashion, speaking of the Holocaust and all the Jews who had died in that inferno. *"Why would the Lord,"* he asked, *"judge us so cruelly? What happened between the Jews and Christ 2,000 years ago was not of our making. So,"* he continued, *"why would the Lord take such out on us now?"*

If I remember correctly, I said to him that the Lord is not the One Who engineered the Holocaust in World War II. I went on to relate to him how that some 2,000 years ago, the Jews purposely took themselves out from under the protective Hand of God and purposely placed themselves into the hand of Satan, who steals, kills, and destroys (Jn. 10:10). Concerning Christ, they purposely and with studied forethought stated, *". . . Let His Blood be on us, and on our children"* (Mat. 27:25). They then stated, *". . . We have no king but Caesar"* (Jn. 19:15).

As stated, they purposely took themselves out from under the protective Hand of the Lord, which placed them in the hand of Satan, so to speak. So, whatever happened to them in the future would not be the Lord's Doings but would be the result of their own choice.

The Jewish lawyer then said to me, *"But again I say to you that we had nothing whatsoever to do with that which happened some 2,000 years ago."*

I turned to him and answered, *"That is true; however, you do not have any more regard for Christ presently than they did those 2,000 years ago."* He had to admit that I was right.

WHY WOULD GOMER DO WHAT SHE DID?

The idea of Verse 5 is, Gomer would, once again, *"go after her lovers,"* and they would give her *"bread, water, wool, flax, oil, and drink."*

Why would she do this when her husband, Hosea, had, as well, given her these things?

The reason was Gomer did not really want

to live for God. Her heart was after her *"lovers"* instead of her husband; likewise, this is the cause of all Believers, as Israel, who cease to believe, thereby, turning from God.

Israel, of which Gomer was a symbol, ran after her *"lovers,"* who were the Assyrians and the Egyptians. As a result, Israel worshipped the idols of these heathen nations and, as well, ascribed her blessings as not from Jehovah but from these idol gods.

Little by little, the modern church follows suit! The way to life and happiness is no longer ascribed to the Word of God but, instead, to humanistic psychology.

THE MODERN CHURCH

Sadly, the modern church little sings anymore about the Blood, which cleanses from all sin, but, instead, *"fight songs,"* which subtly expresses the emphasis being changed from Christ to the so-called Believer! Even though it is in Pentecostal and Charismatic churches, still, it is just as humanistic as New Age philosophy. Whenever Christ and what He did at the Cross cease to be the center of all thought, ideas, action, and principle, man subtly takes His Place while all the time espousing His Cause. Therefore, this false way is easily believed, while all the time Christ and the Cross are quietly shoved aside. Consequently, Satan's work is done, with the people hardly being aware of what has happened.

(6) "THEREFORE, BEHOLD, I WILL HEDGE UP YOUR WAY WITH THORNS, AND MAKE A WALL, THAT SHE SHALL NOT FIND HER PATHS.

(7) "AND SHE SHALL FOLLOW AFTER HER LOVERS, BUT SHE SHALL NOT OVERTAKE THEM; AND SHE SHALL SEEK THEM, BUT SHALL NOT FIND THEM: THEN SHALL SHE SAY, I WILL GO AND RETURN TO MY FIRST HUSBAND; FOR THEN WAS IT BETTER WITH ME THAN NOW.

(8) "FOR SHE DID NOT KNOW THAT I GAVE HER CORN, AND WINE, AND OIL, AND MULTIPLIED HER SILVER AND GOLD, WHICH THEY PREPARED FOR BAAL.

(9) "THEREFORE WILL I RETURN, AND TAKE AWAY MY CORN IN THE TIME THEREOF, AND MY WINE IN THE SEASON THEREOF, AND WILL RECOVER MY

NOTES

WOOL AND MY FLAX GIVEN TO COVER HER NAKEDNESS.

(10) "AND NOW WILL I DISCOVER HER LEWDNESS IN THE SIGHT OF HER LOVERS, AND NONE SHALL DELIVER HER OUT OF MY HAND.

(11) "I WILL ALSO CAUSE ALL HER MIRTH TO CEASE, HER FEAST DAYS, HER NEW MOONS, AND HER SABBATHS, AND ALL HER SOLEMN FEASTS.

(12) "AND I WILL DESTROY HER VINES AND HER FIG TREES, WHEREOF SHE HAS SAID, THESE ARE MY REWARDS THAT MY LOVERS HAVE GIVEN ME: AND I WILL MAKE THEM A FOREST, AND THE BEASTS OF THE FIELD SHALL EAT THEM.

(13) "AND I WILL VISIT UPON HER THE DAYS OF BAALIM, WHEREIN SHE BURNED INCENSE TO THEM, AND SHE DECKED HERSELF WITH HER EARRINGS AND HER JEWELS, AND SHE WENT AFTER HER LOVERS, AND FORGOT ME, SAYS THE LORD."

The construction is:

1. (Vs. 6) Both Gomer and Israel had avowed their determination to pursue their evil course shamefully and sinfully, as if in despite and defiance of the Almighty. Consequently, the Lord affirms His Determination to thwart their course of sin and shame.

2. Partially so, regarding Israel, of which Gomer was a type, Verse 7 was fulfilled about 200 years later, with some of Israel returning with Judah from Babylonian captivity; however, it was only a partial fulfillment. The total fulfillment awaits the Second Coming of the Lord.

3. The phrase of Verse 8, *"For she did not know that I gave . . ."* portrays an unnecessary Spiritual ignorance. Israel forgot that the great Blessings she was showered with came from Jehovah. She claimed them as hers and as having been given to her by her idols. But God said that He gave them to her, that they were His, and that He would now take them back.

4. The action of Verse 9 is one of chastisement and, therefore, of love, for the Lord *"chastises those He loves"* (Heb.12:5-11).

5. As it states in Verse 10, Israel would find that none of her idols could deliver her from

the Assyrians, who would take her captive.

6. As Israel had said by her actions that she did not desire the things mentioned in Verse 11, which in truth were the cause of her blessings, the Lord in turn would remove her to where there would be no opportunity to partake of these Ordinances.

7. (Vs. 12) As Israel had forgotten Who truly was the Source of her prosperity, even attributing such to idols, the Lord would take away their prosperity. Then she would be made to see as to exactly Who had been her Benefactor. It definitely was not her idols.

8. The phrase of Verse 13, *"And I will visit upon her the days of Baalim,"* simply means, *"I will punish them for serving Baal."* The name of *"Baal"* came to be used generally as the designation of any idol or false god. Consequently, the *"days of Baal"* were the days consecrated to Baal, and on which the worship of the True God was transferred to that idol.

THE JUDGMENT OF GOD

Through the Ministry of the Prophet Hosea, the Lord would warn Israel of the Judgment that was coming, that is, if they did not repent. In fact, Hosea was just one of a long line of Prophets who had not ceased to warn Israel of such, but simply put, they would not hear. The Lord most definitely had no desire to bring Judgment upon these people, hence, He would warn them again and again. It must be remembered that even though Judgment may not come immediately, if sin persists, ultimately it will come. In fact, it would be several decades after Hosea before this Judgment would break upon Israel. However, when it did break, it destroyed the Nation in totality, bringing untold sorrow and sufferings. But yet, it was something that did not have to be!

The Lord said through Hosea, *"Behold, I will hedge up your way with thorns,"* which meant that He would make Israel's way very difficult. In other words, from then on, they would find the situation becoming more and more difficult with their Nation, which would impact every citizen in a negative way. The Lord affirms His Determination to thwart their course of sin and shame.

And then He said, *"And make a wall,*

that she shall not find her paths." This pertains to a double wall, the first one a hedge of thorns, which is sharp, prickly, and piercing, and the other a wall of stone that could not be climbed, leaped, or otherwise gotten over.

The idea is that Israel would not find help from other countries in her time of trouble. The Lord would see to that! Their help was in Him; however, they had forsaken Him for other gods.

The idea is that by their actions, they had turned the Lord, Who is Almighty and all powerful, against themselves; consequently, they had placed themselves in an untenable position.

AMERICA

As I dictate these notes, sadly and regrettably, they are so much parallel to what is happening in America presently. The Lord Alone is the Prosperity, the Strength, and the Power of this nation. However, many of the powers that be in this country have long since turned their backs upon God and actually disavowed Him. The American Civil Liberties Union (ACLU) has done and is doing everything within its power to erase the Name of God from anything that pertains to government. The present Administration under Barrack Obama has declared that America is not a Christian nation, completely disavowing the direction laid down by the Founding Fathers.

Of course, while everyone in this nation is not a Christian, with, in fact, only a few actually Born-Again, still, this nation was founded on the principles of the Word of God and can, therefore, be said to be *"Christian"* as it regards the dominant Faith.

Three sins were paramount in the empires of the past that finally fell. Those sins were:

1. Pedophilia;
2. Incest; and,
3. Homosexuality.

THE SIN OF HOMOSEXUALITY

While all sin is an abomination in the Eyes of God, most definitely some sins are worse than others. As it regards Israel, Jesus said of them, *"Therefore he who delivered Me unto you has the greater sin"* (Jn. 19:11).

The sin of homosexuality is at least one of the worst sins that can be committed. It is a gross insult to God as Creator by attempting to subvert the creation model of both man and woman. All sin is against God; however, this sin is the same as one brandishing his fist in the Face of God.

Homosexuality was the sin that caused the destruction of both Sodom and Gomorrah (Gen. 18:20; 19:4-5).

Moses wrote:

"If a man also lie with mankind, as he lies with a woman, both of them have committed an abomination: they shall surely be put to death; their blood shall be upon them" (Lev. 20:13). The Holy Spirit here through Moses speaks of homosexuality as *"an abomination."* The word *"abomination,"* in the Hebrew, is *"towebah,"* and means *"something disgusting, an abhorrence."*

He also stated:

"You shall not lie with mankind, as with womankind: it is abomination" (Lev. 18:22). Whatever man says, God says that homosexuality is an abomination. God help America to see the awfulness of so-called homosexual marriages.

Moses also wrote:

"There shall be no whore of the daughters of Israel, nor a sodomite of the sons of Israel *(whoredom in every capacity is banned, as well as homosexuality).*

"You shall not bring the hire of a whore, or the price of a dog *(the latter has nothing to do with the canine variety, but rather likens homosexuals to dogs),* **into the House of the LORD your God for any vow: for even both these are abomination unto the LORD your God** *(but yet, Rahab the harlot was allowed to come into the Family of God, and even to become an ancestress of Christ; she did so by Faith, which always overrides all law [Mat. 1:5]; none of this means that such people cannot be Saved, but only that Israel must oppose these sins greatly)"* (Deut. 23:17-18).

The Scripture also says:

"And he broke down the houses of the sodomites *(homosexuals),* **who were by the House of the LORD, where the women wove hangings for the grove** *(so we see here what God thinks of the terrible sin of* homosexuality; to be sure, the so-called same-sex marriages presently being engaged in certain parts of the United States indicate the nation's downward slide, which will ultimately guarantee Judgment)* **(II Ki. 23:7).**

"And there were also sodomites in the land: and they did according to all the abominations of the nations which the LORD cast out before the Children of Israel. *(Sodomites are homosexuals [Gen., Chpt. 17]. Here it refers to male prostitutes dedicated to idolatry involving this sin [II Ki. 23:7]. Such was forbidden by the Law of God [Deut. 23:17-18]. The Lord refers to this sin as an 'abomination.' A nation begins to lose its way when three sins become prominent, 'pedophilia, homosexuality, and incest')"* **(I Ki. 14:24).**

Paul said, **"For this cause God gave them up unto vile affections: for even their women did change the natural use into that which is against nature** *(in short speaks of Lesbianism):*

"And likewise also the men *(homosexuality),* **leaving the natural use of the woman** *(speaks of the sex act, which is performed between the man and his wife),* **burned in their lust one toward another** *(raging lust)*; **men with men working that which is unseemly** *(specifies its direction, which is total perversion),* **and receiving in themselves that recompence of their error which was meet** *(refers to the penalty attached to wrongdoing)"* **(Rom. 1:26-27).**

John the Beloved wrote, **"For without *are* dogs** *(homosexuals, the Jews referred to homosexuals as dogs),* **and sorcerers** *(witchcraft),* **and whoremongers** *(pertains to all types of immorality),* **and murderers** *(pertains not only to killing in cold blood but, as well, murdering one's reputation through gossip),* **and idolaters** *(pertains to placing anything above God or on a par with God; religion is the greatest idolatry of all),* **and whosoever loves and makes a lie** *(refers to anything that's untrue)"* **(Rev. 22:15).**

THE JUDGMENT OF HOMOSEXUALITY

Thirty percent of homosexual men between the ages of 17 and 29 attempt suicide. Sixty-seven percent try again if they fail the first time. Only 3.4 percent of heterosexual men attempt suicide.

The life expectancy of a heterosexual male is 75 years. The life expectancy of homosexuals is only 42 years. In fact, only two percent live past the age of 65.

A great part of the problem is guilt, and we speak of an inbred guilt that accompanies the sin of homosexuality. Of course, to try to place the blame elsewhere, many homosexuals claim that the guilt is in their hearts and lives because of we Preachers, who claim that the Bible says that homosexuality is a sin. So, if we would stop that, that would erase all guilt, they say!

Most definitely the Bible is the Word of God, and it does tell us what is right and what is wrong. The problem, however, is not with the Bible. The problem is with those who ignore the Word of God. No, if every Bible was taken off the face of the Earth, and no Preacher said one word about homosexuality, the guilt would remain.

ARE HOMOSEXUALS BORN THAT WAY?

No!

However, due to the fact of original sin, which began in the Garden of Eden with Adam and Eve, every single baby is born with a proclivity toward certain aberrations or perversions. This doesn't mean they are born a homosexual, a murderer, a thief, etc., but that there are tendencies toward certain proclivities, in some more than others. The word proclivity means, *"an inclination or predisposition toward something objectionable."*

The cure for that and, in fact, the only cure, which goes for any sin, is the Lord Jesus Christ and what He did for us at Calvary's Cross. Our Lord atoned for all sin at the Cross of Calvary, and that refers to every type of sin that one could think, past, present, and future, at least for all who will believe (Jn. 3:16). In fact, Christ and what He did at the Cross is the only answer for sin in any capacity. It's the answer for the homosexual, the liar, the thief, or even the good moral man or woman, at least as the world judges morality. The truth is, Jesus said, *". . . there is none good but One, that is, God . . ."* (Mat. 19:17).

Jesus wasn't saying in this statement that He wasn't good; in fact, He definitely was Good because He is God.

THE HOMOSEXUAL LOBBY

The homosexual lobby in this nation, which now has the ear of the president, wants to promote homosexuality in the schools, beginning down at the first grade. They even want to encourage little school children to experiment with this abomination. They want to make homosexual marriages acceptable all over this land. As well, they want to stop any Preacher in the country from referring to homosexuality as a sin, exactly as we are doing here. The so-called hate-crime bill that the president signed in October, 2009, is meant to address this very thing. While homosexuals should be treated with decency and respect, as all other human beings, still, their perversion is a sin. In fact, it is worse than sin; it is an abomination. As stated, all of this signals the fall of this nation as a world power. As Rome of old, while no outside power could destroy this country, it is rotting from within.

THE BLAME

The blame must be laid at the doorsteps of the church. As it regards morality and Spirituality, the church, as should be overly obvious, is supposed to be the guiding light. Sadly, it is anything but!

With the attack by the Muslims on the Twin Towers in New York City and the Pentagon in Washington, D.C., on September 11, 2001 (9/11), two well known preachers were being interviewed by the news media. They were asked the question as to why the Lord allowed this to happen, resulting in the deaths of over 3,000 people and the sorrow and heartache for untold thousands of families, plus costing this nation over a trillion dollars. And the expenses keep mounting!

Their answer was indicative to most. They stated it was because this nation has condoned abortion and homosexuality, etc. While those sins most definitely are abominable and are signs of the coming Judgment, even as stated, still, the acceptance of those sins is the result of what is first of all happening in the church. In other words, the blame for what happened on 9/11, and which, in one form or the other, continues unto this hour, must be laid at the doorstep of the church. The Scripture plainly says:

"For the time *is come* that Judgment must begin at the House of God *(Judgment always begins with Believers, and pertains to their Faith, whether in the Cross or otherwise; the Cross alone is spared Judgment, for there Jesus was judged in our place)*: and if *it* first *begin* at us, what shall the end *be* of them who obey not the Gospel of God? *(If God will judge His Own, how much more will He judge the unredeemed? The Cross alone stays the Judgment of God. Let that ever be understood.)*

"And if the Righteous scarcely be Saved *(can be Saved only by trusting Christ and the Cross and nothing else)*, where shall the ungodly and the sinner appear? *(If the great Sacrifice of Christ is rejected and spurned, where does that leave those who do such a thing? There is no hope for their Salvation)* (I Pet. 4:17-18).

WHY IS THE CHURCH TO BLAME?

The only thing standing between the world and the Judgment of God is the Cross of Christ. One could also say that the only thing standing between mankind and eternal Hell is the Cross of Christ. If, in fact, that is the case, and it most definitely is, then this means that the Message of the Cross must be the paramount theme of the Church.

Is it? It is anything but the paramount theme.

Paul said:

"For Christ sent me not to baptize *(presents to us a Cardinal Truth)*, but to preach the Gospel *(the manner in which one may be Saved from sin)*: not with wisdom of words *(intellectualism is not the Gospel)*, lest the Cross of Christ should be made of none effect. *(This tells us in no uncertain terms that the Cross of Christ must always be the emphasis of the Message)*" (I Cor. 1:17).

The Apostle also said:

"For the Preaching *(Word)* of the Cross is to them who perish foolishness *(Spiritual things cannot be discerned by unredeemed people, but that doesn't matter; the Cross must be preached just the same, even as we

shall see)*; but unto us who are Saved it is the Power of God. *(The Cross is the Power of God simply because it was there that the total sin debt was paid, giving the Holy Spirit, in Whom the Power resides, latitude to work mightily within our lives)*" (I Cor. 1:18).

Paul also said, "But we preach Christ Crucified *(this is the Foundation of the Word of God and, thereby, of Salvation)*, unto the Jews a stumblingblock *(the Cross was the stumblingblock)*, and unto the Greeks (Gentiles) foolishness *(both found it difficult to accept as God a dead Man hanging on a Cross, for such Christ was to them)*" (I Cor. 1:23).

And then the great Apostle said, "For I determined not to know anything among you *(with purpose and design, Paul did not resort to the knowledge or philosophy of the world regarding the preaching of the Gospel)*, save Jesus Christ, and Him Crucified *(that and that alone is the Message, which will save the sinner, set the captive free, and give the Believer perpetual victory)*" (I Cor. 2:2).

Actually, the very meaning of the New Covenant, which meaning was given to the Apostle Paul (Gal. 1:12), is the meaning of the Cross. One could turn it around and also state, *"The Cross is the meaning of the New Covenant."* While everything that Jesus did was of utmost significance, as should be obvious, still, it was at the Cross where all Atonement was made and satisfied. In other words, the Holiness and Righteousness of God were totally and completely satisfied in the Cross. The price was paid, and the price was the perfect physical body of our Lord and Saviour, Jesus Christ (Heb. 10:20; I Pet. 3:18; 4:1).

If the Church is to see men Saved, it must preach the Cross. If it is to see Believers live a victorious, overcoming life, victorious over the world, the flesh, and the Devil, it must preach the Cross. There is no other solution and no other answer, as there need be no other answer.

JUDGMENT DESIGNED TO BRING THE PERSON TO GOD

When I was about four years old, my Mother and Dad heard the Gospel for the first time. Actually, before my Dad was 25 years old, he had never even been in a church, seen a Bible, or heard a Gospel song. And yet, they tried to live, what one might call good, moral lives.

When they first heard the Gospel, with the Holy Spirit strongly dealing with them, my Dad rebelled against these pleadings. This was over a period of time and progressively grew stronger. Therefore, my Mother and Dad made plans to leave the area of Louisiana where they had been brought up and go to a distant state. The plans were grandiose, at least in their minds, however, the real purpose was to run away from God. They thought they could change locations, and He would not be there; however, they found Him to be there exactly as where they had left.

PNEUMONIA

After arriving at their intended destination, my baby brother, who was about four or five months old, came down with pneumonia. This was before modern antibiotics, etc., and was the cause of many deaths. The year was 1939.

My Dad went to a drugstore to get a prescription filled regarding this sickness. The druggist looked down at the doctor's name on the prescription and looked back at my Dad saying, *"You don't have a thing to worry about; this doctor has never lost a case of pneumonia."*

THE LORD SPEAKS

However, a few moments later, as the druggist attended to the filling of the prescription, the Lord spoke to my Dad. Even though he was unsaved, in a state of rebellion, and running from God, still, the Lord was dealing strongly with him. My Dad, having never been a Christian, understood nothing at all about Spiritual matters, but yet, he understood exactly what the Lord said to him.

"Your child will die!" said the Lord. It was short, cryptic, and straight to the point, leaving no room for misunderstanding.

About that time, the druggist walked out with the filled prescription in his hand and, looking at my Dad's ashen face, laid his hand

on Dad's arm, saying, *"As I said, you don't have anything to worry about; this doctor has never lost a case of pneumonia."*

However, my Dad knew better, and he knew that it was because of his rebellion.

A few hours later my baby brother died.

My Mother had also contracted pneumonia and was at that time in the hospital; therefore, she was not able to attend the funeral.

I'LL MEET YOU IN HEAVEN

Being only four years old, I was too young to understand all the things that were happening, but, still, some of it is imprinted indelibly upon my mind, and I will never forget it.

I remember walking with my Dad from the car to the graveside. I remember them opening the casket the last time, and me looking at the jet black curls that framed my baby brother's head. I remember my Dad so weak he could hardly stand, looking down into the casket, and I'll never forget what he said.

"I promise that I will meet you in Heaven!"

Those were his words, and a short time later, he and my Mother gave their hearts and lives to the Lord Jesus Christ.

Some may think the Lord cruel for doing such a thing! However, it was an act of Mercy rather than anger. Without such stern measures, it is possible that my parents would have never come to the Lord; consequently, our entire family came to know Christ.

Israel, as Gomer, would attempt to *"find her paths,"* but would not be able to because the Lord had set Himself against her.

I WILL RETURN TO
MY FIRST HUSBAND

Like the prodigal son and multitudes of others when in misery, she said, *"I will return to Jehovah, for then was it well with me."*

This Scripture was partially fulfilled about 200 years later when some of Israel returned with Judah from Babylonian captivity; however, it was only a partial fulfillment.

Its total fulfillment will be carried out in the latter half of the Great Tribulation yet to come. The phrase, *"And she shall follow after her lovers, but she shall not overtake them,"* will be starkly fulfilled at that time.

At the present, America stands behind Israel. Actually, at least as far as help is concerned, America is about her only friend. However, in the latter half of the time of *"Jacob's trouble"* (Jer. 37:7), America will not help her, and neither will any other nation. At that time, *"she shall seek them, but shall not find them."*

At her blackest period in her long history, she will then begin to call on Jehovah as she has never called on Him before. This long sojourn will climax in the Battle of Armageddon when she will come close to annihilation. She will then say, *"I will return to my first husband; for then it was better with me than now."* At that time, her *"First Husband"* will return, and she will find that it is the Christ she crucified!

SHE DID NOT KNOW

The Lord said through the Prophet, *"For she did not know that I gave her corn, and wine, and oil, and multiplied her silver and gold."* In other words, Israel forgot that the great Blessings with which she was showered came from Jehovah. She claimed them as hers and as having been given to her by her idols. But God said that He gave them to her, that they were His, and that He would take them back.

The phrase, *"For she did not know that I gave her . . ."* portrays an unnecessary spiritual ignorance.

WHY DID SHE NOT KNOW?

Upon the division of the Nation under Rehoboam some 200 years earlier, the northern kingdom forsook the Temple and the sacrifices and they substituted *"the calves"* instead (I Ki. 12:28). Consequently, they forgot the Ways of God.

The greatest sin of the church is to forsake the Ways of the Lord and replace those Ways with the ways of man.

CHRIST IS THE SOURCE, THE CROSS IS THE MEANS

The Cross of Christ is the Means of all Salvation, of all Believers being baptized with the Holy Spirit, the Means of all Blessings,

all prosperity, and all answer to prayer, in fact, every single thing that we receive from the Lord. But, as Israel of old, the modern church has forgotten the Cross of Christ.

Oh yes, the northern kingdom of Israel continued to offer sacrifices, even little lambs, exactly as were offered on the great Altar in front of the Temple in Jerusalem. As well, all of this was attended by so-called priests! But they were sacrifices to Baal and not to God.

The name *"Baal"* means, *"master or husband."* So, at the first, Israel, with Judah ultimately doing the same, thought of their sacrifice to Baal the same as to Jehovah. Both were referred to as *"husband."* They claimed they were sacrificing to Jehovah when in reality it was an idol.

First of all, they were not allowed to sacrifice anywhere except at the Temple in Jerusalem. Any place else was off limits. This specified that the Lord had one Means of Salvation, and that was the Cross of Christ. Not four, not two, only one.

As well, the Priests were to be of the Tribe of Levi, whereas the priests of Baal were whoever!

Also, they were to understand that the sacrifice itself could not save anyone. In other words, animal blood was insufficient to take away sins (Heb. 10:4). It was what the sacrifice represented, namely the coming Redeemer, Who would be the Lord Jesus Christ, Who would be the Saviour. The Sacrificial system, which was instituted on the first page of human history and continued unto Christ, a time frame of some 4,000 years, was meant to be representative of the One Who was to come, Who Alone could save the soul and set the captive free.

THE MODERN CHURCH AND THE CROSS

Simply put, the modern church is not preaching the Cross. While a few are preaching the Cross for Salvation, that number, tragically, is decreasing almost by the day. As it regards the Cross of Christ being preached for our Sanctification, this is almost not at all.

If the Cross is removed from Christianity, there is nothing left but a vapid, empty philosophy. It is the Cross alone, which provides the Means for all that the Lord gives to us. In other words, the Lord would not and, in fact, could not even look at us without the Cross of Jesus Christ. The Cross alone opened up the way for God to have personal fellowship with man. If the Cross is ignored, there is nothing left! And the Cross is by and large being ignored today.

I believe this is at least one of the reasons that the Lord has preserved Jimmy Swaggart Ministries. He has raised it up and preserved it, no doubt, for many reasons, but the greatest reason of all, in fact, that which is paramount, is the Revelation of the Cross that He has given to us. We now have a completed Message, and let me address that for a moment.

For the Message to be completely Biblical, to be what it is intended to be, the following must be the criteria:

1. Jesus Christ must be looked at as the Source of all things we receive from God (Jn. 1:1-3, 14, 29; 14:6).

2. The Cross, as repeatedly stated, is the Means by which all Blessings come to us from the Lord (Rom. 6:3-5; I Cor. 1:17-18, 21, 23; 2:2).

3. The Believer, at least to be used of the Lord as he or she should, must be baptized with the Holy Spirit with the evidence of speaking with other Tongues (Acts 2:4; 19:1-7).

That is the completed Message of the Word of God. To get New Testament results, New Testament Doctrine must be believed and possessed. Without it, very little, if anything, is going to be done for the Lord.

WILL TAKE AWAY THE CORN AND THE WINE

The Ninth Verse proclaims the fact that the Lord says that He's going to take away the prosperity of Israel. As well, He told them, decades ahead of time, that He was going to take away their freedom.

One might say that the action here is one of chastisement and, therefore, of love, for the Lord *"chastises those He loves"* (Heb. 12:5-11).

Perhaps it could be said that the worst thing of all is when God does not *"take away*

My Corn in the time thereof."

Sometime back, someone mentioned to me some individuals, who called themselves *"Christians,"* who never seemed to suffer any type of chastisement from the Lord although openly sinning.

"Why is this?" the person asked.

"Perhaps they are not sons, but bastards," was my answer (Heb. 12:8).

NOTHING CAN OVERCOME THE LORD

In the Tenth Verse, Israel is plainly told by the Lord through the Prophet that none of her idols could deliver her from the Assyrians. In fact, several things are said in Verse 10. They are:

1. Israel belonged to the Lord, Whom she would not serve. Her failure to serve Him and, in fact, turning to other gods, in no way lessened His Interest or Control.

2. The *"discovering of her lewdness in the sight of her lovers,"* refers to Him exposing her helplessness, which she was without Him, which brought shame, disgrace, and reproach.

3. The phrase, *"And none shall deliver her out of My Hand,"* means that the Lord would do with her as He desired, and no nation, irrespective of its power, could help her!

THE LORD WILL TAKE AWAY THAT WHICH BRINGS THE BLESSINGS

The Eleventh Verse proclaims particular times and days, as well as certain ceremonies, which were all designed by the Lord and, in fact, given in the Law of Moses, which were service to the Lord. Israel had forsaken all of these things when she made the golden calves nearly 200 years before. Therefore, the idea of the Verse is this.

As Israel had said by her actions that she did not desire these things, which, in effect, were the cause of her Blessings, the Lord in turn would remove her to where there would be no opportunity to partake of these Blessings.

While it was true that many from the northern kingdom came down to Judah in order to worship at the Temple and partake of these *"solemn feasts,"* still, the majority did not.

The idea expressed in the Eleventh Verse

is strong indeed! If the Believer does not want or desire the true worship of God, the Lord will see to it that the Believer is placed in a position to where these things are no longer forthcoming! Consequently, millions of modern Christians now find themselves in churches where the Word of God is no longer preached, and proper worship is no longer enjoined. Consequently, the joy that was once derived from these great benefits is now gone, fulfilling the phrase, "*I will also cause all her mirth to cease.*"

DESTRUCTION

As Israel had forgotten Who truly was the Source of her prosperity, even attributing it to idols, according to Verse 12, the Lord will take away that prosperity, hence, "*destroying her vines and her fig trees.*" Then she would be made to see what her idols (lovers) had actually given her, which was nothing!

ISRAEL WENT AFTER HER IDOLS AND FORGOT THE LORD

The phrase of Verse 13, "*And I will visit upon her the days of Baalim,*" simply means, "*I will punish them for serving Baal.*"

The name of "*Baal*" came to be used generally as the designation of any idol or false god. Consequently, the "*days of Baal*" were the days consecrated to Baal, and on which the worship of the True God was transferred to that idol.

The phrase, "*Wherein she burned incense to them,*" has to do with the true Offerings of the Lord. Just as the festivals of Jehovah were transferred to Baal, so His Service was turned into that of Baal. Thus, Israel prostituted herself and acted the part of a spiritual adulteress by her worship of idols.

THE TRUE WORSHIP OF GOD

In the true worship of God, at least under the old economy, every Meal Offering, which was presented by itself as a free-will offering, was accompanied with frankincense. This was done everyday, both morning and evening, actually, at the time of the morning and evening sacrifices, and was burnt in the Holy Place.

On the Great Day of Atonement, the High Priest carried a sensor of coals from

the Golden Altar into the Holiest of all and there burnt Incense before the Mercy Seat. This was done before he came in with blood to apply to the Mercy Seat, which was done for him and his house. The third time the Great High Priest came in on this Great Day of Atonement, blood was sprinkled on the Mercy Seat again, but this time it was for the whole of Israel. Thank the Lord it was referred to as a "*Mercy Seat*" and not a "*Judgment Seat.*" However, it must be understood that it was the blood that made it the Mercy Seat, which was typical of the Blood that our Lord would shed at Calvary's Cross. In effect, Jesus was the Great Day of Atonement as well as the Great High Priest, and it was His Blood, which was sprinkled on the ground, which proclaimed the veracity of the act.

The Children of Israel took this very Holy Offering, which typified the coming Redeemer and the Sacrifice of Himself on the Cross of Calvary, and transferred it to Baal.

The phrase, "*And she decked herself with her earrings and her jewels,*" refers to the lack of the "*Beauty of Holiness,*" with carnal ornaments serving as a substitute.

How much has the modern church followed suit!

Worship is conducted, but it is little worship to the Lord. Instead, it is orchestrated and, therefore, of the flesh and unacceptable to God.

Likewise, in the modern church, the true "*Beauty of Holiness*" is too often missing, with religious ceremony taking its place and, therefore, unacceptable as well!

The phrase, "*And she went after her lovers, and forgot Me, says the LORD,*" stipulates that one cannot have both. Jesus said, "*No man can serve two masters: for either he will hate the one, and love the other; or else he will hold to the one, and despise the other. You cannot serve God and mammon*" (Mat. 6:24).

The church, as well, has gone after "*her lovers*" in the form of humanistic psychology, with ". . . *philosophy and vain deceit, after the tradition of men, after the rudiments of the world, and not after Christ*" (Col. 2:8).

(14) "THEREFORE, BEHOLD, I WILL

ALLURE HER, AND BRING HER INTO THE WILDERNESS, AND SPEAK COMFORTABLY UNTO HER.

(15) "AND I WILL GIVE HER HER VINEYARDS FROM THENCE, AND THE VALLEY OF ACHOR FOR A DOOR OF HOPE: AND SHE SHALL SING THERE, AS IN THE DAYS OF HER YOUTH, AND AS IN THE DAY WHEN SHE CAME UP OUT OF THE LAND OF EGYPT.

(16) "AND IT SHALL BE AT THAT DAY, SAYS THE LORD, THAT YOU SHALL CALL ME ISHI; AND SHALL CALL ME NO MORE BAALI.

(17) "FOR I WILL TAKE AWAY THE NAMES OF BAALIM OUT OF HER MOUTH, AND THEY SHALL NO MORE BE REMEMBERED BY THEIR NAME.

(18) "AND IN THAT DAY WILL I MAKE A COVENANT FOR THEM WITH THE BEASTS OF THE FIELD, AND WITH THE FOWLS OF HEAVEN, AND WITH THE CREEPING THINGS OF THE GROUND: AND I WILL BREAK THE BOW AND THE SWORD AND THE BATTLE OUT OF THE EARTH, AND WILL MAKE THEM TO LIE DOWN SAFELY.

(19) "AND I WILL BETROTH YOU UNTO ME FOREVER; YES, I WILL BETROTH YOU UNTO ME IN RIGHTEOUSNESS, AND IN JUDGMENT, AND IN LOVINGKINDNESS, AND IN MERCIES.

(20) "I WILL EVEN BETROTH YOU UNTO ME IN FAITHFULNESS: AND YOU SHALL KNOW THE LORD.

(21) "AND IT SHALL COME TO PASS IN THAT DAY, I WILL HEAR, SAYS THE LORD, I WILL HEAR THE HEAVENS, AND THEY SHALL HEAR THE EARTH;

(22) "AND THE EARTH SHALL HEAR THE CORN, AND THE WINE, AND THE OIL; AND THEY SHALL HEAR JEZREEL.

(23) "AND I WILL SOW HER UNTO ME IN THE EARTH; AND I WILL HAVE MERCY UPON HER THAT HAD NOT OBTAINED MERCY; AND I WILL SAY TO THEM WHO WERE NOT MY PEOPLE, YOU ARE MY PEOPLE; AND THEY SHALL SAY, YOU ARE MY GOD."

The exegesis is:

1. (Vs. 14) The balance of the Verses of this Chapter predict the restoration of Israel under the Covenant of Grace as opposed to that of Law.

2. (Vs. 14) The Nation is pictured as a faithless and debauched wife betrothed as a spotless bride to Immanuel. This impossibility will be effected by the Miracle of the New Birth. The old impure Israel will die and a pure virgin will appear as the new Nation. As stated, this will take place at the beginning of the coming Kingdom Age.

3. The phrase of Verse 15, "And I will give her her vineyards from thence," signifies that the way to the "vineyards" is through the wilderness. Spiritual discipline precedes blessing and fits it for joy. Hence, the words "from thence."

4. The phrase also from Verse 15, "And the Valley of Achor for a door of hope," signals back to a vale of horror as described in Joshua 7:24, but which is to become for Israel "a door of hope."

5. (Vs. 15) The Truth is presented here by the Holy Spirit that where the Wrath of God justly fell, the Grace of God is to brightly shine. The valley of horror becomes the vale of hope. Such was Calvary—a place of horror to the Suffering Saviour under the Wrath of God, but a door of hope to the redeemed sinner under the Grace of God.

6. (Vs. 15) Thus, this "Valley of Achor" proclaims to the Believer who has suffered defeat that the very area of such defeat can become their area of victory.

7. The word "Ishi" of Verse 16 means "my Husband," while the word "Baali" means "my Lord." In other words, Israel will no more refer to Baal as her Lord but will rightly serve Jehovah.

8. (Vs. 17) The names of Baal shall become so abhorrent to blood-washed Israel that they shall pass away at once from their mouths and from their memories, nevermore to be mentioned and nevermore to be remembered.

9. The phrase of Verse 18, "And in that day will I make a Covenant for them," refers to the New Covenant, which Israel will accept immediately after the Second Coming. At that time, there will be no more war, which speaks to the universal safety of not only Israel, but of the entirety of the world.

10. The betrothal of Verse 19 between the

Lord and Israel will take place immediately after the Second Coming of Christ. Israel will then accept Him, not only as Saviour, but also as Messiah and Lord.

11. The phrase of Verse 20, *"You shall know the LORD,"* means that all evils come from not knowing Him (Isa. 1:3; Lk. 19:42, 44).

12. Verse 21 speaks of the *"Earth that shall be full of the Knowledge of the LORD, as the waters cover the sea"* (Isa. 11:9).

13. Whereas the name *"Jezreel,"* as used in Verse 22, pertained to Judgment when originally given, now it refers to the very opposite. Whereas the Lord scattered and sowed Israel in heathen lands, now He scatters and sows them in the Land of Israel proper, and in prosperity. In other words, the blessing of Israel will be the blessing of the entirety of the world, and the world will also realize that!

14. (Vs. 23) Israel was Lo-Ruhamah and Lo-Ammi, meaning *"no more Mercy"* and *"not My People."* Now, Israel will become *"Ruhamah,"* i.e., *"pitied one,"* and *"Ammi,"* i.e., *"My People."*

15. (Vs. 23) *"And I will say to them who were not My People, 'You are My People,'"* is quoted in Romans 9:25. It refers in that case to the Gentiles as an illustration of what may be true in their case as well as in Israel's.

THE RESTORATION OF ISRAEL

The phrase, *"Therefore, behold, I will allure her, and bring her into the wilderness, and speak comfortably unto her,"* refers to Revelation 12:6, when Israel will flee the Antichrist in the last three and one half years of the coming Great Tribulation.

The *"speaking comfortably unto her,"* refers to the beginning of the Salvation process, which will ultimately bring Israel back to God, and will do so at the Second Coming of Christ. The things He will then do are outlined in the following Verses.

Actually, the coming Great Tribulation, with all its attendant horror, is called, *"the time of Jacob's trouble"* (Jer. 30:7). While it will be a time of great trouble, still, it is designed to bring Israel to Repentance, which it shall! Therefore, if designed by the Lord, anything that happens to a Child of God is, actually, in the long run, for our benefit, no matter how seemingly destructive. Thus will it be to Israel!

A DOOR OF HOPE

This one phrase from Verse 15, *"And the Valley of Achor for a door of hope,"* tells every struggling Christian, especially those who have suffered defeat, that the very area of their defeat can become their area of victory. Such was Moses in that his temper caused him to be guilty of manslaughter, and that was at the beginning of his Ministry. However, the Holy Spirit made him instead *"the meekest man upon the face of the Earth"* (Num. 12:3).

The Apostle Paul was turned from an Apostle of hate to an Apostle of love (I Cor. 13:1).

Jacob of old was changed from a schemer to a *"Prince with God"* (Gen. 32:28).

Actually, such is the story of every single Bible great, as well as so many millions of others! Their *"Valley of Achor"* has been turned into a *"door of hope,"* which can only be brought about by Christ.

SANCTIFICATION

The glad tidings of Salvation is one thing; the struggle against the power that tries to keep the soul in bondage is quite another.

The modern church understands the Cross of Christ, at least after a fashion, as it refers to Salvation; however, it understands the Cross of Christ as it refers to Sanctification not at all. As a result, there is precious little victory in the hearts and lives of most modern Christians, and we are speaking of those who truly love the Lord.

Unfortunately, every Believer has to go through the Seventh Chapter of Romans, no exceptions. However, while that is inevitable, it is certainly not the Will of God for the Believer to stay in the Seventh Chapter of Romans. The tragedy is, most Christians never get out of the defeat of that Chapter but remain there all of their Christian lives.

Why?

They do not know God's Prescribed Order of Victory.

GOD'S PRESCRIBED ORDER OF VICTORY

When we speak of *"victory,"* we are speaking of Victory over the world, the flesh, and the Devil, to coin a phrase used by the Early Church Fathers.

That which the Lord has designed for the Believer is found all through the writings of the Apostle Paul because it was to Paul that the meaning of the New Covenant was given; however, the greater thrust is found in Romans, Chapters 6, 7, and 8.

As someone has well said, *"Romans 6 gives us the mechanics of the Holy Spirit, which tells us how He works. Romans 8 gives us the dynamics of the Holy Spirit, which tells us what He does for us after we understand how He does it."*

HOW DOES THE HOLY SPIRIT WORK?

It is the Cross of Christ that gives the Holy Spirit the liberty and the latitude to work within our lives (Rom. 8:2).

It is the Cross of Christ, which has given and does give the Holy Spirit the legal right to do all that He does. Before the Cross, the Holy Spirit was extremely limited as to what He could do. The reason being *"the blood of bulls and goats could not take away sins"* (Heb. 10:4). So, that meant that the sins remained. Before the Cross, this stopped the Holy Spirit from coming into the heart and life of Believers to abide permanently. While He did go into the hearts and lives of some to help them perform a certain task, still, when the task was completed, He left. There is no record in the Old Testament of the Holy Spirit helping at all as it regards the Sanctification process, i.e., how we live for God.

The Believer should understand that, through our own ability and strength, there is no way that we can effect within our lives that which must be done. The Holy Spirit Alone can do what needs to be done. As repeatedly stated, He Works exclusively within the parameters of the Finished Work of Christ. As stated, it is the Cross of Christ which gives the Holy Spirit latitude to function within our lives. This requires that our Faith ever be place in Christ and the Cross on a constant basis. That being done, the Holy Spirit will work mightily.

WARFARE

However, the Believer must understand that this great Plan of God does not mean

that once you understand what the Lord gave to us through Paul, this will end Satan's efforts against us. Not at all! In fact, Paul labeled the struggle that we're in as *"warfare"* (II Cor. 10:4). So, don't expect Satan to roll over or to strike his tent, so to speak, when you begin to understand what the Word of God says about all of this. Not at all! He is going to continue to hinder every way he can, but the difference is, by understanding what Christ has done for us at Calvary's Cross, the sin nature will no longer have dominion over us (Rom. 6:14). We're not talking about sinless perfection because the Bible does not teach such, but we are speaking of the fact that sin is to no longer have dominion over us. From the beginner stage, however, to the stage of perpetual Victory is not arrived at quickly or easily. And, please understand, there are no shortcuts.

VICTORY

The phrase, *"And she shall sing there, as in the days of her youth,"* refers to the *"joys of sins forgiven, and the bliss the blood-washed know."*

This has reference to Israel's deliverance from Egypt when they responded with songs of praise and thanksgiving as they sang the song of Moses by the Red Sea, while Miriam and the maidens of Israel in full chorus completed the harmony. Now, all these experiences of the past are to repeat themselves in the future history of Israel.

They were troubled in that Valley of Achor by the sin of Achan.

The punishment of the transgressor in that case and the putting away of sin in connection with penitence and prayer reopened, after defeat, the door of hope and restored the enjoyment of Divine help.

The discomfiture that so troubled the Host of Israel was immediately followed by the victory of Ai, which inspired them with the hope of soon possessing the entirety of the land.

So, with Israel, after the long dispersion among the nations for nearly 2,000 years, this dreary night of weeping will be followed by a bright and blessed morning. They will then accept Christ as their Saviour, and will rejoice, *"as in the day when she came up out of the land of Egypt."* It will happen at the Second Coming!

IDOLS

The further away from God that Israel (or Judah) strayed, the more she equated Jehovah with idols. When worshipping the idol, she, at least in her mind, was continuing to worship Jehovah and called the idol *"my Lord,"* referring to Jehovah. In their Spiritual declension, they demanded a god they could see, and which the idol amply served! As they bowed down to it, they continued to call it *"Lord"* exactly as they had referred to Jehovah.

So, in their minds, they had not ceased worship of God. They had only made it much more understandable and, consequently, much more desirable, at least to the carnal mind.

In effect, they *"changed the Truth of God into a lie, and worshipped and served the creature more than the Creator, Who is blessed forever. Amen"* (Rom. 1:25).

A MARRIAGE CONTRACT

When they did this, they broke their Covenant with the Lord, which He likened to a marriage contract. Now this Covenant will be restored, with them no longer serving idols thinking it is Jehovah, but will, in fact, serve the Lord in the *"Beauty of Holiness,"* and will then refer to Him as *"my Husband."*

Sadly and regrettably, the modern church follows suit, substituting ceremony in place of true Salvation. The Catholic church is virtually replete with this abomination, with the protestant church very little behind, if at all!

Many modern Christians are so divorced from the true Ways of God that they little understand what is being said when using the word *"ceremony."*

CEREMONY

The word refers to a formal act or series of acts prescribed by ritual, protocol, or convention, and performed with elaborate pomp. As such, man is lulled into a spiritual sleep, thinking that such an elaborate religious system (ceremony), along with one's participation, surely provides Salvation.

NOTES

However, if one knows his Bible at all, one knows and understands that such has absolutely no relationship to Salvation whatsoever. And yet, the majority of the church world, both protestant and Catholic, is glutted with this substitute for Salvation.

In effect, ceremony has absolutely nothing to do with one's Salvation, irrespective of the pomp and parade of its elaboration. The Scripture says, *"For by Grace are you Saved through Faith; and that not of yourselves: it is the Gift of God: not of works, lest any man should boast"* (Eph. 2:8-9).

In other words, the modern church too often bows down to an idol called ceremony and calls it *"Lord."* Irrespective of their denial, their trust is in the ceremony and not in Christ.

IDOLS ARE NO MORE

The actual meaning of Verse 17 is, *"You shall serve Me out of love and not out of fear; 'Ishi,' denoting marriage and youthful love; 'Baali,' denoting lordship and fear."*

As well, upon the return of Christ, all false religion and ceremony, along with man's false ways of Salvation, will pass into oblivion and will not be *"remembered"* anymore! Then it will be only Christ!

Sadly, most modern Christians, who claim to believe in Christ, actually believe in Christ plus! In other words, it is Christ plus Water Baptism, Christ plus speaking in Tongues, Christ plus the Lord's Supper, Christ plus church membership, Christ plus ad infinitum.

Such will not, and in truth, cannot be accepted by the Lord. Christ is Lord of all or not Lord at all! Actually, the Christ served and worshipped by most modern Christians is *"another Jesus"* entirely.

ANOTHER JESUS

Paul speaks to the Church at Corinth about *"another Jesus"* and *"another spirit,"* which presents *"another gospel"* (II Cor. 11:1-4).

If one separates Christ from the Cross in any manner, he is left with *"another Jesus,"* which refers to a Jesus of one's own making and not the Jesus of the Bible.

It is Satan's business to get the eyes of Believers off of Christ and what He did for us at the Cross and onto other things. The idea is, Satan enjoys man being very religious because he knows that such is the great deception and has caused much of the world to die eternally lost.

THE NEW COVENANT

The Covenant of which the Lord speaks in Verse 18 actually is the New Covenant, which covers the entirety of the New Testament. However, Israel, and it is Israel to whom the Lord is speaking, will not accept this New Covenant until the Second Coming. In essence, one might say that the Lord Jesus Christ is the New Covenant and to accept Him as one's Saviour and Lord is to accept the New Covenant, which untold millions have done from the Day of Pentecost until the present time. But, as stated, Israel will not accept Christ, i.e., *"the New Covenant,"* until the Second Coming.

THE KINGDOM AGE

At that time, which will begin the Kingdom Age, the entire complexion of everything will be changed. Satan will be locked away in the bottomless pit, along with all demon spirits and fallen Angels (Rev. 20:1-3). The difference that will make literally staggers the imagination.

And more importantly, much more importantly, the Lord Jesus Christ will set up His Kingdom, and do so personally. He will, in fact, be the President, so to speak, of the entirety of the world. Actually, He will be *"King of kings and Lord of lords"* (Rev. 19:11-16).

The entirety of the nature of creation will be changed. The time of tornadoes, hurricanes, earthquakes, famines, and droughts, will be forever ended (Rom. 8:19-22).

The very disposition of the animal kingdom, as well, will be changed. The great Prophet Isaiah said:

"The wolf also shall dwell with the lamb, and the leopard shall lie down with the kid; and the calf and the young lion and the fatling together; and a little child shall lead them. *(The character and nature of the Planet, including its occupants and even the animal creation, will revert to their posture as before the Fall.)*

"And the cow and the bear shall feed *(feed together)*; **their young ones shall lie down together: and the lion shall eat straw like the ox.** *(This Passage plainly tells us that the carnivorous nature of the animal kingdom will be totally and eternally changed.)*

"And the sucking child shall play on the hole of the asp, and the weaned child shall put his hand on the cockatrice' den. *(Even though some of the curse will remain on the serpent in the Millennium, in that he continues to writhe in the dust, still, the deadly part will be removed [Gen. 3:14])"* **(Isa. 11:6-8).**

THE EXTENT OF THE MESSIAH'S REIGN

Isaiah continues:

"They shall not hurt nor destroy in all My Holy Mountain: for the Earth shall be full of the Knowledge of the LORD, as the waters cover the sea. *(The 'Holy Mountain' refers to the Dwelling Place of Christ during the Kingdom Age, which will be Jerusalem. And from that vantage point shall go out the 'Knowledge of the LORD,' which will cover the entirety of the Earth.)*

"And in that day there shall be a root of Jesse, which shall stand for an ensign of the people; to it shall the Gentiles seek: and His Rest shall be glorious. *(The words, 'in that day,' as in most cases, refer to the Great Tribulation, the Battle of Armageddon, the Second Coming of the Lord, and the coming Kingdom Age.*

"The 'root of Jesse' refers to David and the Promise made by the Lord to David in II Sam., Chpt. 7. Hence, Christ is really the 'root of Jesse,' 'the Son of David')" **(Isa. 11:9-10).**

ISRAEL, GOD'S PEOPLE TO BE RESTORED

The great Prophet continues, regarding the restoration of Israel, which will take place, as stated, at the beginning of the Kingdom Age when they will then accept Christ. He said:

"And it shall come to pass in that day, that the Lord shall set His Hand again the second time to recover the remnant of His People, who shall be left, from Assyria, and from Egypt, and from Pathros, and from Cush, and from Elam, and from Shinar,

and from Hamath, and from the islands of the sea. *(Once again, 'in that day' refers to Christ reigning Personally in Jerusalem. The first gathering of the 'remnant,' as it refers to Israel, took place when Israel was gathered out of the Medo-Persian Empire and brought back to the Promised Land [Ezra 2]. In a sense, the second gathering began in 1948. It will be fulfilled in totality at the beginning of the Kingdom Age when Jews all over the world will recognize Christ as their Messiah and, thereby, desire to come to Israel and live near Him.)*

"And He shall set up an ensign for the nations, and shall assemble the outcasts of Israel, and gather together the dispersed of Judah from the four corners of the Earth. *(Here, Israel is called 'outcasts,' and they have been such ever since their rejection of Christ and the destruction of Jerusalem by Titus in A.D. 70.*

"The central theme of this Verse is Christ. Israel will now [during the Kingdom Age] recognize Him, and Him Alone, as their True Messiah. Jerusalem, the place of His Crucifixion, will now be the place of His Glory. The Jews will come to this Glory from 'the four corners of the Earth')" **(Isa. 11:11-12).**

THE BETROTHAL

In the Nineteenth Verse, the Lord said, *"And I will betroth you unto Me forever."* The word *"betroth,"* as here used, is a little different than in most of its meanings. Here, it refers not only to a pledge of marriage but that the marriage of old will now be renewed, with past offenses pardoned.

This betrothal will take place immediately after the Second Coming of Christ. Israel will then accept Him, not only as Saviour, but as Messiah.

Three times the words, *"I will betroth you,"* are used (Vss. 19-20), which confirms the engagement.

The betrothment, as listed in these two Verses, is:

• Will be perpetual (*"forever"*).
• Legal (*"in Righteousness"*).
• Well considered (*"in Judgment"*).
• Affectionate (*"in lovingkindness"*).
• Well endowed (*"in Mercies"*).
• Faithful (*"in Faithfulness"*).

Under this new contract (New Covenant), the divorced wife is to be taken back, with the marriage contract, which she had shamefully abrogated, now renewed, and, as stated, with past offenses pardoned. This certainly evidences extraordinary forbearances and affection. But that is not all.

A HIGHER RELATIONSHIP

A new and higher relationship is to be entered on. The Lord has so entirely forgiven and forgotten all the multiplied and aggravated transgressions of Israel against Him that the Jews are not to be received back as a repudiated wife, but to be henceforth regarded and treated as a chaste virgin, and in that capacity, betrothed unto the Lord.

Only the Lord could do such, so completely blotting out the past, that it is actually no longer a part of the present in any form or capacity. In essence, that is the part of the New Covenant referred to as *"Justification by Faith."* What the Lord will do with Israel in that coming glad day, He has already done so with every single Believer who has ever placed his Faith and Trust in Him.

JUSTIFICATION BY FAITH

Justification by Faith can be summed up in the following manner:

• All sins are forgiven.
• The sins are remembered no more against the individual as though the sin never existed.
• The forgiven individual is looked at by God as having never sinned, not even one time.
• The Perfection of Christ is given to the individual, who, in the Eyes of God, Whose Eyes Alone matter, is looked at as perfect.

As we have stated, the phrase, *"I will betroth you unto Me,"* is thrice repeated and each time with an additional element of Mercy. As well, this betrothal is not of temporary character and of short continuance, like the previous marriage contract, which the wife's guilt had rendered null and void. It is a betrothal, thrice repeated, because it will last forever.

FAITHFULNESS

The phrase from the Twentieth Verse,

"You shall know the LORD," means that all evils come from not knowing Him (Isa. 1:3; Lk. 19:42, 44).

The phrase, *"I will even betroth you unto Me in faithfulness,"* has a far greater meaning than appears on the surface.

The idea is this:

Notwithstanding Israel's failures, Jehovah's Faithfulness guarantees ultimate and lasting success. The special quality on Israel's side is true knowledge of God. It can probably be better explained this way.

Under the Old Covenant, the responsibility was on the keepers of the Law, which, sadly, could do nothing but fail.

Now, under the New Covenant, the responsibility is on Christ, Who can do nothing but succeed.

In other words, the Lord looks at Israel, rather will do so on that coming glad day, exactly as He looks at every Believer, which is through the Blood of Christ. All of their failures, as every Believer, are placed in Calvary's cleansing flow. Consequently, He will look at them in that coming Glad Day, as stated, as one perfect. In fact, Israel could have had such when Christ came the first time. Instead, they crucified Him and, therefore, destroyed their only Avenue of Life. Now, they accept Him!

THE HEAVENS AND THE EARTH

The Twenty-first Verse has reference to the fact that in the coming Kingdom Age, Earth, at least in a sense, will be made like unto Heaven. This speaks of the *"Earth that shall be full of the Knowledge of the LORD, as the waters cover the sea"* (Isa. 11:9).

The Earth and man have never been seen as God originally created them. All that has been seen is the cursed Earth and cursed man. Sadly and regrettably, even redeemed man continues to *"come short of the Glory of God"* (Rom. 3:23). It is because *"Earth"* is in a state of rebellion against *"Heaven."* However, *"in that day, I will hear, says the LORD,"* refers to prosperity, all spiritual, economical, physical, and domestical.

JEZREEL

The Twenty-second Verse says, *"And the Earth shall hear the corn, and the wine, and*

the oil; and they shall hear Jezreel."

Whereas the name, *"Jezreel,"* when originally given, pertained to Judgment, now, it refers to the very opposite.

Whereas the Lord scattered and sowed Israel in heathen lands, now, He scatters and sows them in the Land of Israel in prosperity.

In that coming Glad Day, one might say that Israel will cry to the corn, the wine, and the oil to supply her needs. They will cry to the Earth to fructify them. The Earth will cry to the heavens for the needed rain in order to produce the fruit. And, the heavens will cry to Jehovah to fill them with the required water. From Him there will be no further appeal, for He is the Great First Cause!

In response to this appeal, the Lord will fill the heavens with moisture, the heavens will discharge it upon the Earth, the Earth will produce, as the result, the corn, the wine, and the oil. Israel will have abundant provision, and, thus, Heaven and Earth will be bound together with the chain of love.

Then the great Promises of Christ, which we now know in part, we will then fully know (I Cor. 13:12).

MERCY

The phrase, *"And I will sow her unto Me in the Earth,"* pictures the name, *"Jezreel,"* being completely turned around to now speak of blessing. This pictures the sowing of Israel as a plant of His Own in the Earth, indicating their restoration.

Israel was *"Lo-Ruhamah"* and *"Lo-Ammi,"* meaning, *"no more Mercy,"* and, *"not My People."* Now, Israel will become *"Ruhamah,"* i.e., *"pitied one,"* and *"Ammi,"* i.e., *"My People."*

The phrase, *"And I will say to them who were not My People, You are My People,"* is quoted in Romans 9:25, and refers, in that case, to the Gentiles, as an illustration of what may be true in our case as well as in Israel's.

"There shall be showers of blessing,
"This is the promise of love;
"There shall be seasons refreshing,
"Sent from the Saviour above."

"There shall be showers of blessing,
"Precious reviving again;

*"Over the hills and the valleys,
"Sound of abundance of rain."*

*"There shall be showers of blessing,
"Send them upon us, O Lord!
"Grant to us now a refreshing;
"Come, and now honor Your Word."*

*"There shall be showers of blessing,
"Oh, that today they might fall,
"Now as to God we are confessing,
"Now as on Jesus we call!"*

*"There shall be showers of blessing,
"If we but trust and obey;
"There shall be seasons refreshing,
"If we let God have His Way."*

*"Showers of blessing,
"Showers of blessing we need,
"Mercy drops round us are falling,
"But for the showers we plead."*

CHAPTER 3

(1) "THEN SAID THE LORD UNTO ME, GO YET, LOVE A WOMAN BELOVED OF HER FRIEND, YET AN ADULTERESS, ACCORDING TO THE LOVE OF THE LORD TOWARD THE CHILDREN OF ISRAEL, WHO LOOK TO OTHER GODS, AND LOVE FLAGONS OF WINE.

(2) "SO I BOUGHT HER TO ME FOR FIFTEEN PIECES OF SILVER, AND FOR AN HOMER OF BARLEY, AND AN HALF HOMER OF BARLEY:

(3) "AND I SAID UNTO HER, YOU SHALL ABIDE FOR ME MANY DAYS; YOU SHALL NOT PLAY THE HARLOT, AND YOU SHALL NOT BE FOR ANOTHER MAN: SO WILL I ALSO BE FOR YOU.

(4) "FOR THE CHILDREN OF ISRAEL SHALL ABIDE MANY DAYS WITHOUT A KING, AND WITHOUT A PRINCE, AND WITHOUT A SACRIFICE, AND WITHOUT AN IMAGE, AND WITHOUT AN EPHOD, AND WITHOUT TERAPHIM:

(5) "AFTERWARD SHALL THE CHILDREN OF ISRAEL RETURN, AND SEEK THE LORD THEIR GOD, AND DAVID THEIR KING; AND SHALL FEAR THE LORD AND HIS GOODNESS IN THE

LATTER DAYS."

The construction is:

1. (Vs. 1) The phrase, *"Then said the LORD unto me,"* signals another step that is to be taken by the Prophet, this one perhaps even more severe than the first.

The short phrase, *"Go yet,"* means that the Lord is not through with His Object Lesson concerning Israel. That which will now be portrayed, even though painfully executed, will nevertheless portray the Love of God in a fashion that nothing else could.

2. The Command of the Lord to Hosea in Verse 1 is to *"love a woman beloved of her friend, yet an adulteress."* The idea of the entirety of this scenario is that Gomer, who was an adulteress, and which symbolized the idolatry of Israel, proved faithless to the Prophet and fell into degraded bondage. Nevertheless, Hosea was commanded still to love her, to redeem her from slavery, to remain faithful to her for a lengthened period, and then to fully restore.

3. (Vs. 1) The phrase, *"Beloved of her friend,"* is striking indeed! It means that Gomer was loved by Hosea, but she had forfeited by her misconduct the right to use the honorable words of *"wife"* and *"husband."* Therefore, the word *"friend"* instead would be used because she was *"yet an adulteress."*

4. As it regards Verse 2, the redemption price of a slave was 30 pieces of silver (Ex. 21:32) and so much barley. Fifteen pieces of silver and so little barley marked the worthlessness of this slave. No one can fully understand the pain and suffering evidenced in the words, *"So I bought her to me for fifteen pieces of silver."* Gomer was now used up, therefore, wanted and desired by no one!

5. (Vs. 2) One can only guess at the hurt that filled Hosea's heart as he stood before Gomer. She was, no doubt, dressed in rags and had been reduced by abuse to less than a slave. She must have reasoned, *"How could he love me after all this?"*

He could do so because about 800 years later One would hang on a Cross, Who had also been sold for 30 pieces of silver, the price of a slave. That One took her place of suffering that she might take His place of Glory.

And thus it is with us all!

6. The idea of Verse 3 is: Gomer had left

Hosea for *"many days"* and had now come back to him, even though in a deplorable condition; now she would be his wife again. This symbolizes Israel, who will come to Christ at the Second Coming. She will then call Him *"Ishi,"* i.e., *"my Husband"*; and she will never again *"play the harlot."*

7. (Vs. 4) Gomer leaving Hosea and going back into whoredoms typify Israel leaving the Lord, which has now lasted for nearly 2,000 years, i.e., *"many days."*

8. While Verse 4 is in the state of fulfillment, Verse 5 remains to be fulfilled. The words, *"His Goodness,"* should be translated *"His Gracious One,"* that is, the Messiah (Hos. 14:2; Eph. 1:6).

The phrase, *"Latter days,"* refers to the coming Kingdom Age.

HOSEA AND THE ADULTERESS

There is so much not said in this Chapter, and from that not said, the very silence itself speaks much.

According to the Word of the Lord, Hosea married Gomer, and the union produced three children. However, as this Chapter portrays, her heart was not with Hosea but, instead, with her old lovers. Therefore, she leaves the Prophet and her children, going back into her old sins. The pain this must have brought can only be spoken in the silence which suggests it!

AN OBJECT LESSON

That God was using this as an object lesson for Israel is plainly obvious now, but it is doubtful if anyone would have seen it in that light at that time. Undoubtedly, as the tongues wagged upon the marriage of Hosea to this woman, the tongues now wagged again in *"I told you so!"* The Prophet could only suffer all of this in silence. The pain he bore was, no doubt, looked at by his contemporaries as what he should have expected; consequently, *"What else could he expect!"* They did not know, and most did not even care, that everything he did was according to the Word of the Lord, and it was to be an object lesson for Israel, which would be spelled out in symbolic gesture. However, as Daniel said, *"Only the wise would understand!"* (Dan. 12:10).

NOTES

THE WORD OF THE LORD

The phrase, *"Then said the LORD unto me,"* signals another step that is to be taken by the Prophet, this one, maybe even more severe than the first.

Sometime before, Gomer had walked out on her family. As to exactly how long it had been, the Scripture is silent. At that stage, and for a period of time, the Prophet had no further direction from the Lord, therefore, he suffered in silence. Now the Lord will give him further direction.

Even though only two words, the phrase, *"Go yet,"* is pregnant with meaning.

It means that the Lord is not through with His Object Lesson concerning Israel, and that which will now be portrayed, even though painfully executed, will, nevertheless, portray the Love of God in a fashion that nothing else could.

SYMBOLIZING THE IDOLATRY OF ISRAEL

The Command by the Lord to Hosea is, *"love a woman beloved of her friend, yet an adulteress."*

The idea of the entirety of this scenario is that Gomer, who was an adulteress, and which symbolized the idolatry of Israel, proved faithless to the Prophet and fell into degraded bondage.

Hosea was commanded still to love her, to redeem her from slavery, to remain faithful to her for a lengthened period, and then to fully restore her.

This illustrated God's Action with Israel and is the teaching and argument of the Chapter.

FRIEND!

The word, *"love,"* is different than the word, *"take,"* as in Hosea 1:2. *"Take"* implies *"to take in marriage."* Now the Prophet, despite his wife's terrible conduct, was to renew his love for her, despite her guilt.

The phrase, *"Beloved of her friend,"* is striking indeed! It means that Gomer was loved by Hosea, but, by her misconduct, she had forfeited the right to use the honorable words of *"wife"* and *"husband."* Therefore, the word, *"friend,"* would be used instead because she was *"yet an adulteress."*

The phrase, *"According to the Love of the LORD toward the Children of Israel,"* in the action of Hosea was meant to illustrate the measure and fullness of the Divine Love to the guilty Nation. Therefore, the Lord had to place this love in Hosea's heart because the type of love he was to show to his wayward wife was to epitomize the Love of God. Such, at least within itself, is not a human commodity and can only be given by the Lord. It is what is referred to in the New Testament as *"agape,"* or the God kind of Love. Therefore, his love for her was genuine, sure, steadfast, unfailing, and involved far more than mere pity, even though it certainly would have included such!

TOTAL CARNALITY

The idea presented in the phrase, *"Who look to other gods, and love flagons of wine,"* speaks of the total carnality of Israel, which, as well, spoke of a total absence of Spirituality. They were not only in the world, they were of the world as well!

OTHER GODS

The words, *"other gods,"* and *"wine,"* characterize too much of the modern church also.

Even though the *"other gods"* have changed from the objects to which one bowed, still, the principle is the same respecting humanistic psychology, self-esteem, deceitful philosophies, etc. They are all *"gods!"*

The *"wine"* speaks of the heady enjoyment of this present world. It is obvious that the modern church is making plans to stay instead of leave. Its intention is to build a paradise on Earth instead of laying up *"treasure in Heaven."* As such, it is unscriptural and, thereby, ungodly!

THE PRICE OF A SLAVE

The redemption price of a slave in Old Testament times was 30 pieces of silver (Ex. 21:32) and so much barley. Fifteen pieces of silver and so little barley marked the worthlessness of this slave.

No one can fully understand the pain and suffering evidenced in the words, *"So I*

NOTES

bought her to me for fifteen pieces of silver," etc. Gomer was now used up, therefore, wanted and desired by no one!

One can only guess at the hurt that filled Hosea's heart as he stood before Gomer. She was, no doubt, dressed in rags and had been reduced by abuse to less than a slave.

As well, what must have gone through her mind and filled her heart when she saw the man who was buying her, her husband, Hosea? How could he want her now, she must have reasoned! How could he love her after all this?

THE CROSS

He could do so because about 800 years later, One would hang on a Cross, Who had, as well, been sold for 30 pieces of silver, the price of a slave. That One took her place of suffering that she might take His Place of Glory.

And thus it is with us all!

The picture here presented is one so altogether lovely that it defies description! It is beautiful even in the midst of its ugliness, and so is Salvation.

When the Lord purchases the sinner, there is nothing beautiful about the terrible ravages of darkness, which actually make slaves of men. And yet, the transaction is beautiful because it turns ugliness into beauty by changing the person by the Power of the Crucified Christ.

RESTORATION

Verse 3 proclaims the fact that Gomer had left Hosea for *"many days,"* and had now come back to him, even though in a deplorable condition, and would be his wife once again. She would not again *"play the harlot,"* or be *"for another man."* As well, the phrase, *"So will I also be for you,"* meant that he would forget the past, totally and completely, and would be to her as though she had never strayed at all. Such symbolizes Israel in every capacity, which it is meant to portray.

THE GREAT TRIBULATION

In the coming Great Tribulation and after some 2,000 years of being an *"outcast,"* Israel will be reduced exactly as Gomer. She will be on the edge of annihilation by the

Antichrist. No one wants her or desires her and, in fact, have written her off. She is desolate, forlorn, and used up.

And yet, at that very time, the Heavenly Hosea will come to her rescue, buying her back, so to speak. The price He pays will ever be a reminder to them of the price they paid—30 pieces of silver (Zech. 13:6).

Then Israel, as Gomer, *"shall abide for Me many days,"* actually, days without end. Never again will she *"play the harlot, nor worship idols,"* i.e., *"be for another man."*

As well, the Lord will forget all the past transgressions and will treat her as though she never strayed. Then, *"the Valley of Achor will be a door of hope."* Then, *"she shall sing there, as in the days of her youth, and as in the day when she came up out of the land of Egypt."*

As well, she will then call Him *"Ishi,"* i.e., *"my Husband."*

THE DESOLATION OF ISRAEL

Verse 4 says, *"For the Children of Israel shall abide many days without a king, and without a prince, and without a sacrifice, and without an image, and without an Ephod, and without teraphim."* This has been fulfilled and is being fulfilled to the letter.

There is some disagreement among scholars as to the exact disposition of Gomer when bought back by Hosea. There are two schools of thought on this subject. They are:

1. Some believe that after she was brought back, she and Hosea, at least for a long period of time, did not live together as husband and wife. But yet, and due to the agreement, she could not associate with another man either! Ultimately, they came together again as man and wife. This thinking is derived from the *"many days"* of both Verses 3 and 4.

2. Some think, which is the view that I hold, that after Gomer was purchased back, she immediately became the wife of Hosea. The leaving Hosea and staying gone for *"many days"* symbolizes the terrible dispersion of Israel in A.D. 70, which has lasted for nearly 2,000 years. In fact, it is continuing and shall continue through the coming Great Tribulation when, at the Second Coming, Christ will buy Israel back as Gomer was bought by Hosea.

BRITISH ISRAELISM

Verses 4 and 5 destroy the theory that the British nation constitutes the Ten lost Tribes of Israel, speaking of the northern kingdom.

This teaching claims that after the northern kingdom of Israel was defeated by the Assyrians, the Ten Tribes, which constituted that kingdom, were lost, at least as far as being joined together again with Judah and Benjamin. It is said that they ultimately wandered into the area now known as England. As a result (they say), the British, and later the American people, are the Ten lost Tribes of Israel. It is claimed that Britain is Ephraim and America is Manasseh.

They claim that the royal family of England constitutes the true legal heirs of the throne of David through Zedekiah's daughter, and that the throne of England is in reality the throne of David.

They also claim that the Coronation Stone, which reposed for some years under the chair in Westminster Abbey in London, where kings are crowned, is the same stone that Jacob used for a pillow (Gen. 28:18). By the way, this stone was returned to Scotland a few years back, from where it had been taken years ago.

As stated, Verses 4 and 5, plus many other Passages in the Word of God, completely refute this erroneous teaching.

THE NORTHERN KINGDOM OF ISRAEL

This Prophecy given by Hosea is addressed to the Ten Tribes. It predicted that they should remain for a long period of time (already some 2,800 years) without a government, a Priest, or a Levitical sacrifice, and yet, be free from idolatry. So it has been, so is it today, and so will it continue until they return to Jehovah their God and the Lord Jesus Christ, their King.

The phrase, *"For the Children of Israel shall abide many days without a king and without a prince,"* has been fulfilled to the letter. Since they were taken captive by the Assyrians approximately 800 years before Christ, they have not had a king or a prince. With the Tribes of Judah and Benjamin, which were taken captive by the Babylonians some 70 years later, they did return to Israel, at least some of them. At that time they renewed the Sacrificial system, which lasted until A.D. 70. Since that time, there has been no Nation of Israel until 1948.

ISRAEL NOW AS A NATION

Actually, at this time (2009), plans are being drawn to rebuild the Temple, with young men, supposedly from the Tribe of Levi, being trained in priestly duties in order to offer the sacrifices when the Temple is rebuilt. When this is done, and it most surely will be, this will fulfill Daniel 9:27.

The Dome of the Rock now sits in the exact spot where Solomon's Temple was and where the new Temple must be built. How can this be, considering, as stated, that the Dome of the Rock, the so-called third most holy place of Islam, occupies this place and position?

The Muslims claim that Muhammad went to Heaven on a winged horse from this particular spot. The truth is, there is no record that Muhammad was ever in Jerusalem, and for certain, he didn't go to Heaven when he died. At any rate, that is their legend, with many, if not all, Muslims believing this fabrication.

The Bible tells us that the Antichrist is going to formulate a peace treaty between Israel and the Muslim world, guaranteeing the safety and protection of Israel for some seven years. The moment it is signed, that will begin the coming Great Tribulation (Mat. 24:21).

We know that Israel will rebuild her Temple because the Prophet Daniel said so.

"And he (the Antichrist) **shall confirm the covenant with many for one week** (a week of years)**: and in the midst of the week** (three and a half years) **he shall cause the sacrifice and the Oblation to cease, and for the overspreading of abominations he shall make it desolate, even until the consummation, and that determined shall be poured upon the desolate"** (Dan. 9:27).

Concerning this, the notes from THE EXPOSITOR'S STUDY BIBLE say:

"'And he shall confirm,' refers to the Antichrist. The phrase, 'And in the midst of the week,' refers to three and a half years, at which time the Antichrist will show his

true colors and stop the sacrifices in the newly-built Temple. At that time, he will actually invade Israel, with her suffering her first military defeat since her formation as a Nation in 1948.

"'Even until the consummation,' means until the end of the seven-year Great Tribulation period. The phrase, 'And that determined shall be poured upon the desolate,' refers to all the Prophecies being fulfilled regarding the great suffering that Israel will go through the last three and a half years of the Great Tribulation [Mat. 24:21-22]."

HOW WILL THE ANTICHRIST BE ABLE TO PERSUADE THE MUSLIMS TO GIVE UP THE DOME OF THE ROCK SO THE JEWISH TEMPLE CAN BE REBUILT?

Some have suggested that this will not happen, meaning that the Temple will be built elsewhere. Some have said that possibly the Temple will be built beside the Muslim Dome of the Rock. Admittedly, there is enough room there to build several temples. Others have stated that possibly they will use the Great Synagogue in Jerusalem.

None of that seems plausible! The Word of God in the Old Testament is specific as it regards the site of the Temple. In fact, the location was chosen by the Lord Himself and not man at all (II Chron. 3:1). So, in all likelihood, the Temple will be built on the very site of the Dome of the Rock.

In fact, it is said that the Holy of Holies of Solomon's Temple resided over the direct spot where Abraham was to offer up Isaac as a sacrifice, and was stopped at the last minute by the Lord. Actually, the Scripture says, **"And He** (the Lord) **said, Take now your son, your only son Isaac, whom you love, and go into the land of Moriah; and offer him there for a Burnt Offering upon one of the mountains which I will tell you of"** (Gen. 22:2).

And now the Scripture says, **"Then Solomon began to build the House of the LORD at Jerusalem in Mount Moriah, where the LORD appeared unto David his father, in the place that David had prepared in the threshingfloor of Ornan the Jebusite"** (II Chron. 3:1). In fact, this is the first mention in this Scripture of Mount Moriah since Genesis 22:2; it is never mentioned after this.

Considering the emphasis placed upon the site, it is very doubtful that Israel would build the Temple anywhere else than this actual site.

Actually, the Dome of the Rock presently sits over the rock projection, where it is believed Isaac was placed when Abraham thought to sacrifice him in obedience to the Lord. As stated, the Lord stayed his hand at the last moment.

All of this was to show Abraham that Redemption had to be purchased by Sacrifice, which would be the Sacrifice of God's Son, even as Isaac was Abraham's son. Abraham and Isaac were used as Types.

So, the question still begs to be asked as to how the Antichrist will persuade the Muslims to give up their so-called third most holy site.

THE DECEPTION OF THE ANTICHRIST

Even though the Bible does not tell us how this will be done, the following perhaps may be close to that which will be carried out on that coming day.

The Antichrist could call together the leading clerics of Islam, proposing his plan for the supposed protection of Israel for seven years, etc. He will then relate to them that at the appropriate time, he will attack Israel, completely destroying her, with Islam then given the entirety of the Land of Israel. He will then say to them, *"You will have to give up the site of the Dome of the Rock for Israel to build their Temple."*

The Muslims will swallow long and hard over that demand! But considering that they're going to be given the entirety of the Land of Israel in a short period of time, they will agree.

Sure enough, three and a half years after the agreement has been signed with Israel, the Antichrist will attack Israel, showing his true colors, when she will suffer her first military defeat since becoming a Nation in 1948. In fact, the Antichrist would at that time completely annihilate her but for the fact that he will hear news out of the east and out of the north that shall trouble him greatly (Dan. 11:44). He will leave the destruction of Israel for the time being and

go to those parts of the world where great battles will, no doubt, be fought, with him coming out the victor.

However, not only will the Antichrist deceive Israel, for they will have thought at the beginning that he is their Messiah, but, as well, he will deceive the Muslims. Instead of him giving them the Land of Israel as he promises, if, in fact, that is what actually happens, he will outlaw every religion, including Islam.

The Battle of Armageddon will be the conflict where he proposes to completely destroy Israel and make himself the master of the world.

WHY IS HE SO DETERMINED TO DESTROY ISRAEL?

The tiny State of Israel as it now stands is only about the size of the State of New Jersey. Other than the Dead Sea, the Land of Israel has precious few resources. But yet, the Antichrist will be set on destroying this people at the expense of everything else.

Why?

Of course, Satan will fuel the mind of the man of sin with one specific purpose. If he can destroy Israel, this will cause the multitude of Promises in the Bible, concerning the restoration of Israel, to fall to the ground, so to speak. This will mean that the Word of God cannot be trusted. If he can do this, causing the Word of God to prove false, he will have won this age-old conflict and will be like the Most High (Isa. 14:13-14).

Many would ask the question, *"Doesn't Satan know what the Bible says about all of this?"*

Most definitely he does; however, the truth is, like the majority of mankind who follows him, he doesn't believe the Bible, and neither will the Antichrist.

During the Battle of Armageddon, Israel will cry to God, knowing that He is her only hope. She will then truly repent (Isa. 64:6-12). To be sure, the Lord will hear that prayer, which will precipitate the Second Coming, which will be the most cataclysmic thing the world has ever known in all of its history. Then the Antichrist, along with Satan, will meet their Waterloo, so to speak, with the Lord Jesus Christ completely restoring

Israel, but not before she repents. In fact, Israel at that time will accept the Lord Jesus Christ as Saviour, as Lord, and as Messiah (Zech. 13:6). Then all the Tribes of Israel will be restored to their rightful place and, in fact, Israel then will be the priestly Nation of the entirety of the world, serving and working under the Lord Jesus Christ, with David as their king.

TRUE WORSHIP AND FALSE WORSHIP

If the designations are to be noticed in Verse 4, one will find that it is not without design that the Holy Spirit intermingled the true Worship of God with false worship, and did so by including the *"sacrifice"* and *"Ephod"* with the *"image"* and *"teraphim."* Actually, this was Israel's problem all along! They worshipped God while, at the same time, worshipping idols. They often comingled the two. The meaning of the four is as follows:

THE SACRIFICE

This included the sacrifice of lawful animals to the Lord, as well as sacrifices to heathen idols, of which Israel, at times, did both.

THE IMAGE

This was probably the *"asherah,"* which consisted of a pillar or image of wood or metal, which was set up with the image of Baal. It was set upright erect in the ground like a totem pole. It was either a living tree with the top cut off and the trunk fashioned into a certain shape (Deut. 16:21), or a log fashioned into an idol and set erect in the ground (I Ki. 14:15; 16:33; Isa. 17:8).

It was originally worshipped as a symbol of the Tree of Life but later perverted to mean the origin of life and pictured as the male organ of procreation (Ezek. 16:17). It was a special object of God's Hatred; and it was at this idol that God revealed His Name as *"Jealous"* (Ex. 34:13-14).

THE EPHOD

From Exodus 28:6-14, we learn that this was a short cloak, covering shoulders and breast of the High Priest. It was wrought with colors and gold and formed of two halves connected by two shoulder-pieces.

On each half was an onyx stone engraved with the names of six of the Tribes. It was held together around the waist by a girdle of the same material. As stated, it was a part of the attire of the High Priest.

On the inside of the *"Ephod"* was a small pouch where the Urim and Thummim were kept, which was directly over the heart of the High Priest but hidden from view.

Exactly what the Urim and Thummim were, no one quite knows. Some think it was two small stones, with the word *"yes"* engraved on one, and the word *"no"* engraved on the other. This was the means, at least in some cases, of ascertaining the Will of God concerning present or future events. Consequently, the *"Ephod"* was also referred to as *"The Breastplate of Judgment."*

The word, *"Urim,"* means *"lights,"* while the word, *"Thummim,"* means *"perfections."*

THE TERAPHIM

This was a small image in human form, either graven in wood or stone; or graven in precious metal, such as gold. The first mention of them is in Genesis 31:19, and the name occurs 15 times in the Old Testament. They appear to have been of Syrian or Chaldean origin.

They were a household god and were supposed to bring good luck. They also were appealed to for direction, exactly as the *"Ephod"* worn by the High Priest. They were idols, pure and simple, and roundly condemned by the Lord.

MANY DAYS

The prediction was that Israel would be without either one for *"many days,"* the worship of the True God or the worship of idols. As stated, this has been fulfilled to the letter as Israel, even at the present time, little has any religion whatsoever, that is, if we would use such a term.

While it is true that there is a small but powerful contingent in modern Israel, who attempts to hold to ancient Judaism, still, it is mostly in name only, as such cannot be truly practiced without the Temple and its functions. Actually, one could probably say that the majority of modern Jews are either Atheistic or Agnostic.

THE RESTORATION OF ISRAEL

Of course, even though the restoration addressed began in 1948, it will not truly be brought together until the Second Coming when Israel accepts Christ as Saviour and Lord.

While Verse 4 is in the state of fulfillment, Verse 5 remains to be completely fulfilled. It says, *"Afterward shall the Children of Israel return, and seek the LORD their God, and David their king; and shall fear the LORD and His Goodness in the latter days."*

As stated, this will happen at the beginning of the Kingdom Age, with all the great Promises of God to these ancient people then to be literally fulfilled.

The words, *"His Goodness,"* from the Fifth Verse, should be translated, *"His Gracious One,"* that is, the Messiah (Hos. 14:2; Eph. 1:6).

The phrase from that Verse, *"latter days,"* refers to the coming Kingdom Age.

These terms *"many days,"* *"afterward,"* and *"the latter days,"* as found in this Chapter, define the periods of the dispersion and restoration of the Ten Tribes. As stated, they actually were never really lost.

THE DEFILEMENT

The conduct of Israel in defiling herself with idols, as symbolized by the action of Gomer, will appear more vile and debased if it be assumed, as some suggest, that in the excess of religious superstition, the unhappy woman left her husband and dedicated herself to the hideous life of a temple-woman, as we will see in the next Chapter.

From that bondage, as stated, Hosea redeemed her. It was a religious zeal, energized by Satan, which carried Israel, typified by Gomer, into idolatry.

This religious zeal, sad to say, is rampant in the modern church as well! Regrettably, the entirety of Catholicism is given over to idolatry because of this religious zeal. Sadly, the protestant world is little behind, if any at all!

However, as Gomer was redeemed, likewise, as Verse 5 declares, Israel will also be redeemed.

"I care not today what the morrow may bring,

"If shadow or sunshine or rain.
"The Lord I know rules over everything,
"And all of my worry is vain."

"Tho' tempests may blow and the storm clouds arise,
"Obscuring the brightness of life,
"I'm never alarmed at the overcast skies,
"The Master looks on at the strife."

"I know that He safely will carry me through,
"No matter what evils betide,
"Why should I then care, though the tempests may blow,
"If Jesus walks close to my side."

"Our Lord will return to this Earth some sweet day,
"Our troubles will then all be o'er,
"The Master so gently will lead us away,
"Beyond that blessed Heavenly Shore."

"Living by Faith, in Jesus Above,
"Trusting, confiding in His Great Love,
"From all harm safe, in His Sheltering Arm,
"Living by Faith, and I feel no alarm."

CHAPTER 4

(1) "HEAR THE WORD OF THE LORD, YOU CHILDREN OF ISRAEL: FOR THE LORD HAS A CONTROVERSY WITH THE INHABITANTS OF THE LAND, BECAUSE THERE IS NO TRUTH, NOR MERCY, NOR KNOWLEDGE OF GOD IN THE LAND.

(2) "BY SWEARING, AND LYING, AND KILLING, AND STEALING, AND COMMITTING ADULTERY, THEY BREAK OUT, AND BLOOD TOUCHES BLOOD."

The exegesis is:

1. (Vs. 1) All of this Chapter, except Verse 15, is addressed to the Ten Tribes; and yet, Grace calls them *"My People"* (Vss. 6, 8).

2. (Vs. 1) The phrase, *"For the LORD*

has a controversy with the inhabitants of the land," is a strong statement indeed! It refers to a judicial inquiry and cause.

3. The words, *"they break out,"* of Verse 2, speak of the terrible sins mentioned and present the illusion of water overflowing its banks and spreading in all directions. It means to *"break through the wall."*

THE WORD OF THE LORD

Chapters 1 through 3 were presented to Israel in Figure and Symbol in the persons of Hosea, Gomer, and their three children, *"Jezreel, Lo-Ruhamah, and Lo-Ammi."*

Beginning with Chapter 4, the symbolism having ended, the Message is now plainly and literally stated. In the First Verse of this Chapter, the Children of Israel are summoned to hear the charge preferred against them and the sentence pronounced.

The phrase, *"Hear the Word of the LORD, you Children of Israel,"* could well be addressed, not only to Israel of old, but to any and all presently. Nothing else but the Word of the Lord matters, as all else is fake and fabrication.

THE WORD OF THE LORD IN THE MODERN CHURCH

Satan is attacking the Word of God presently in the modern church, I believe, as never before. But yet, he is doing such in a different way possibly than ever. It is not a frontal attack, rather denying the Word, but an end run, so to speak. I am referring to the scores of translations of the Bible presently coming forth from the printing presses, which are really not translations at all, but rather paraphrases. At best, they can be referred to as religious books, but not at all as the Word of God. I speak of those such as the *"Message Bible,"* that at the time of this writing (November 2009) has sold over 2 million copies. It cannot, by any stretch of the imagination, be put in the category of the Word of God, and yet, scores of famous preachers are recommending it.

The other day Frances handed me an article advertising this religious book referred to as a Bible, and I was shocked to look at the names given who recommended it.

NOTES

WORD-FOR-WORD TRANSLATION

These paraphrases, i.e., *"religious books,"* are what is referred to as *"thought for thought"* translations. They hold no Scriptural validity. This means that if the Believer doesn't have a *"word-for-word"* translation, such as the King James Version, whatever it is he does have is not really a Bible, meaning it doesn't really contain the Word of God, but rather the word of man.

The Old Testament, as most understand, was written originally in Hebrew. The New Testament was written originally in Greek. In other words, when the Prophets of old wrote the Sacred Text as the Holy Spirit Moved upon them, they wrote it down in Hebrew, which was their natural language. The same goes for the Apostles of the New Testament, who wrote in Greek, which was the common language of their day.

A word-for-word translation means that the scholars, whether Hebrew or Greek, did everything within their power to bring the meaning of the Original Text over into English. They actually did it word by word. That is Scripturally proper simply because our Lord said, *". . . Man shall not live by bread alone, but by every Word that proceeds out of the Mouth of God"* (Mat. 4:4).

However, it must be understood that in the ancient Hebrew or Greek, there were no such words as *"thee,"* or *"thou,"* or *"hast,"* etc. Those words come out of Elizabethan English. In other words, when the King James scholars translated the Bible, those words were then a part of the English language. They are no longer. In fact, the King James has experienced some six revisions, with two of those revisions being major, and rightly so.

In our main Administration building at Jimmy Swaggart Ministries, we have a copy of a page from the very first printing of the King James Text. Written totally in Elizabethan English, it is very difficult to read. In fact, I doubt that most people could read it at all. So, the edits that took place with the King James were for valid reasons. In these edits they did not change the meaning of any Scripture or even any word, but rather used English that was more modern. It does no one any good to read something they can't understand. But yet, when one holds a King James Bible in his hands presently, he can be assured that he is holding in his hands the very Word of God.

THE WORD OF GOD, THE MOST IMPORTANT THING

As I've said many times, the Bible is the Word of God. As such, it is the only road map in existence for life and living. At the same time, it is the only blueprint for eternity. It is the single most important document on the face of the Earth.

That's the reason that every Believer should read the Bible completely through at least once a year. Also, the Believer should avail himself of every study aid that he can get to help him understand the Word of God a little better. That's one of the reasons that you as a Believer desperately need a copy of THE EXPOSITOR'S STUDY BIBLE, that is if you do not already have one.

If an individual is going to take a journey in his car, a journey that is quite lengthy, and if he doesn't have a road map, he is going to have difficulty. Or if he has a road map that is not accurate, such a journey will be freighted with peril. Tragically, as it regards the single most important thing of all, your soul, many Believers have an inaccurate road map.

A CHRONOLOGY OF BIBLE TRANSLATION

The following chronology includes events of major importance in the long and dramatic story of Bible translation. The list is necessarily selective and places special emphasis on the background of the English Bible, providing information basic to further study of a fascinating field.

• 1500 B.C. through 500 B.C.? – the Old Testament is put into writing.

• 250 B.C. through 100 B.C. – the Septuagint, a translation of the Old Testament in Greek, according to tradition, by 72 Hebrew scholars, was completed in Alexandria, Egypt. This Version contains 45 Books, the Alexandrian Canon, used by the Early Church, and continues to be the Old Testament Canon of the Latin and Greek Church.

• A.D. 52? through A.D. 100? – the New Testament is written, coming to us in Koine (common) Greek, the common language of the time, although some portions may have been first set down in Aramaic, the language spoken by Christ.

• A.D. 100? – formulation of Palestinian Canon of Hebrew Bible at Synod of Jamnia.

• A.D. 350 through A.D. 400 – first stabilization of New Testament Canon of 27 Books.

• About A.D. 400 – Jerome completes his final translation of the Bible, the Latin Vulgate, based on the Septuagint and translated from the Hebrew and other ancient versions.

• About A.D. 600 through A.D. 900 – the Masoretic Text in Hebrew was developed by the Masoretes, a school of Jewish textual critics. The Masoretic Text, used in the Jewish Bible, has been an important reference in preparing translations into other languages.

• A.D. 1382 – John Wycliffe completes his translation, the first complete Bible in English.

• A.D. 1456 – the Gutenberg Bible, a folio edition of the Latin Vulgate, is printed from movable type, an epochal event that inaugurated the era of printing.

• A.D. 1516 – Erasmus completes his translation in Greek.

• A.D. 1522 – Martin Luther translates the Bible into German.

• A.D. 1535 – William Tyndale issues his English translation, which powerfully influenced all of the English versions that followed.

• A.D. 1535 – Miles Coverdale issues his translation dedicated to King Henry VIII.

• A.D. 1537 – Coverdale's Bible becomes the first Bible to be printed in England.

• A.D. 1537 – Matthew's Bible is produced, based primarily on the Tyndale and Coverdale Bibles.

• A.D. 1539 – Coverdale issues the Great Bible, essentially a combination of his own earlier work and Tyndale's Bible. This work was authorized by King Henry VIII.

• A.D. 1560 – the Geneva Bible, produced by Coverdale, William Whittingham, John Knox, and others in Geneva after Mary became Queen. It is the first English Bible

NOTES

to divide the Chapters into Verses.

• A.D. 1582 through A.D. 1610 – Douay-Rheims (Catholic) Bible appears, a direct translation into English from the Vulgate by the Catholic College; the New Testament issued at Rheims, the Old Testament in 1609 and 1610 at Douay, France.

• A.D. 1611 – the great King James (or authorized) Version. Completed by the group of *"learned men,"* all renowned scholars, appointed by King James.

While there have been other translations from then until now, the King James is concluded by many scholars to be closer to the Original Text than any other effort. Down through the last several centuries it, by far, has been the most widely used and widely known.

THREE SUCCESSIVE STEPS IN PROPERLY UNDERSTANDING THE WORD OF GOD

They are:
1. Revelation;
2. Inspiration; and,
3. Illumination.

REVELATION

"But as it is written (Isa. 64:4), *Eye has not seen, nor ear heard, neither have entered into the heart of man, the things which God has prepared for them who love Him"* (I Cor. 2:9).

The first step in the transmission of Truth from the Heart of God to the heart of the Believer is *"Revelation,"* the Act of God the Holy Spirit uncovering the things in the Heart of God to the Bible writers, thus imparting the Truth of Scripture to them.

Paul explains that the Bible did not come by way of scientific investigation and human reason, because it could not come that way, but it came in another way, by Revelation. He further said, *"But God has revealed them unto us by His Spirit: for the Spirit searches all things, yes, the deep things of God"* (I Cor. 2:10).

The word *"revealed"* is the translation of a Greek word, which means *"to uncover, to lay open what has been veiled or covered up."*

The word *"us"* in I Corinthians 2:10 pertains to both the writers of Holy Scripture and, as well, to whom they were writing.

The Apostle continues by saying, *"For what man knows the things of a man, save the spirit of man which is in him? even so the things of God knows no man, but the Spirit of God"* (I Cor. 2:11).

Paul is actually saying in his explanation that while it may be possible for us as human beings to know and understand some things about our fellowman, even though that is very limited, we cannot know or understand God by that same means. What we are to know about God and His Word can only be revealed to us by the Holy Spirit. In fact, it can come no other way, even as the Holy Spirit here through Paul tells us. So, to attempt to understand God by natural means simply cannot be done. However, when we come to *"Illumination,"* the Holy Spirit will then inform us through the Word as to how the Lord actually does reveal Himself to us.

INSPIRATION

The Apostle Paul now says, *"Which things also we speak, not in the words which man's wisdom teaches, but which the Holy Spirit teaches; comparing Spiritual things with Spiritual"* (I Cor. 2:13).

Paul now tells us exactly how the Word of God was given by God to man, how it was received, and how it was written down.

The Apostle tells us that the Word of God is not words taught by human wisdom, but Words, which were given and written down by the writers who served as Instruments of the Lord. That is, the words, which the Bible writers used, were not dictated by their human reason or wisdom. In other words, none of the Bible writers embellished at all what God gave them to give to the world.

Paul plainly tells us that the way the Word of God was given was *"but in Words taught by the Spirit."* He says that the Words, which the Bible writers used, were taught them by the Holy Spirit.

It means that the Holy Spirit searched through the vocabulary of the writer and chose the correct Word that would give the content of meaning, which would give to the Believer the exact Truth God desires us to have. This, however, does not imply mechanical dictation or something different from the writer's own personality. The idea is, the Holy Spirit took the writers as He found them and used them infallibly.

That's the reason that every single Word of God is important, meaning, as we have related in this statement, that a word-for-word translation of the Bible is an absolute necessity. These books that claim to be Bibles, which give a thought for thought translation and are presently filling the land, are not Bibles at all but only religious books. These books will do no one any good whatsoever, but rather great harm.

When Paul used the phrase, *"Comparing Spiritual things with Spiritual,"* it tells us as to exactly how the Holy Spirit gave the Divine Text and how it was inspired. The word *"comparing"* means *"to judge,"* or better yet, *"to judge with."* It speaks of the action of judging something with something else.

In other words, somewhat like a computer that would search for the word, the Holy Spirit would search for the right Word in the writer's vocabulary to be used in every sentence. Thus, the Holy Spirit allowed the writers the free play of their personalities, vocabulary, and training while, at the same time, guiding them to make an infallible record of Truth that was infallibly revealed.

ILLUMINATION

We now come to this part, which is also very important, namely the Act of God, the Holy Spirit, enabling the Believer to understand the Truth, which was written down and given by *"Revelation"* and by *"Inspiration."* Paul says, *"But the natural man receives not the things of the Spirit of God: for they are foolishness unto him: neither can he know them, because they are Spiritually discerned"* (I Cor. 2:14).

The word *"natural,"* as the Holy Spirit used it through Paul, describes the unregenerate man at his best, meaning very educated. No matter how educated he might be, he simply cannot understand the Word of God by that means. So, the natural man here spoken of is the educated man at the height of his intellectual powers but devoid of the Spirit of God. Actually, the things of the Lord are but *"foolishness"* unto such a man. Paul says, *"But he who is Spiritual judges all things, yet he himself is judged of*

no man" (I Cor. 2:15).

The word *"judges"* is the translation of a Greek word rendered *"discerns."*

Continuing with our explanation of *"Illumination,"* we understand from the Word of God that it was to Paul that the Revelation, i.e., the meaning of the New Covenant, was given. In fact, the entirety of the New Covenant is wrapped up in the Cross of Christ (I Cor. 1:17-18, 23; 2:2). If we study Paul at all, we have to come to the conclusion that the Jew from Tarsus preached the Cross. Understanding this, we must come to the conclusion that unless one properly understands the Cross of Christ as it regards both Salvation and Sanctification, one cannot truly understand the Word of God as one should. Considering that the Cross of Christ is the Foundation of all that we know and understand as it regards the Plan of God, then we find that this is the key that unlocks the door (Rom. 6:3-5; 8:1-2, 11; Gal., Chpt. 5; 6:14; Eph. 2:13-18; Col. 2:14-15).

THE CROSS OF CHRIST

I think one could probably say, and without fear of Scriptural contradiction, that all error and all false doctrine stems from an improper understanding, an ignoring, or an outright denial of the Message of the Cross.

MATURITY AND THE CROSS OF CHRIST

Maturity in the Lord and in His Word is dependent solely on a proper understanding of the Cross of Christ. That's the reason that Paul further said:

"And I, brethren, when I came to you, came not with excellency of speech or of wisdom (means that he depended not on oratorical abilities, nor did he delve into philosophy, which was all the rage of that particular day)**, declaring unto you the Testimony of God** (which is Christ and Him Crucified)**.

"For I determined not to know anything among you (with purpose and design, Paul did not resort to the knowledge or philosophy of the world regarding the preaching of the Gospel)**, save Jesus Christ, and Him Crucified** (that and that alone is the Message, which will save the sinner, set the captive free, and give the Believer perpetual

Victory)" **(I Cor. 2:1-2).**

We must understand that the Lord strongly desires that we understand His Word. He hasn't made it hard or difficult; however, if we ignore His Way, which is the Way of the Cross, our understanding will be most unfruitful or even harmful!

"For the preaching (Message) *of the Cross is to them who perish foolishness; but unto us who are Saved it is the Power of God"* (I Cor. 1:18).

"Your Word is a Lamp unto my feet, and a Light unto my path" (Ps. 119:105).

The only *"Lamp"* in the world that produces *"true Spiritual Light"* is the Bible. It is the road map for life and the blueprint for eternity, and it is the only road map for life and the only blueprint for eternity.

TRUTH

The reason there was no *"Mercy,"* or *"Knowledge of God in the land of Israel"* was because there was no *"Truth."*

What is Truth?

That is the question that Pontius Pilate asked the Lord Jesus when the Master stood before him just before the Crucifixion (Jn. 18:38).

The way the question is posed by John, it seems that Pilate did not really want an answer from Christ. The question was asked in a way that said, *"No matter what You say, I don't think anyone knows what Truth actually is."*

In essence, Jesus told him what Truth was, which prompted Pilate asking the question. Our Lord said, **". . . You say that I am a King** (is the same as saying, 'Yes, it is so!')**. To this end was I born** (addresses the Incarnation, God becoming Man [Isa. 7:14])**, and for this cause came I into the world** (He is to be King in the hearts of all who believe Him)**, that I should bear witness unto the Truth** (carries in its statement the entirety of the embodiment of the Ways of God)**. Everyone who is of the Truth hears My Voice** (only those who sincerely desire Truth will know Christ, i.e., 'hear His Voice')**" (Jn. 18:37).**

WHAT IS TRUTH?

The answer to that question is one of the

most important in the world. Before we give the answer to the question, let's look at the manner in which *"truth"* is handled in the world.

There is what is known as objective truth and subjective truth.

Objective truth means that it doesn't change. It's the same now as it was 1,000 years ago or 5,000 years ago, for that matter. It is the same in every culture, every race, and every country. Irrespective, it doesn't change.

Subjective truth is the very opposite. It means that truth is subject to culture, race, etc., in other words, whatever someone wants it to be. For example, if a pregnancy is unwanted, the woman is to simply have an abortion. This means that *"truth"* is subject to the whims of whatever someone wants to make it.

A SYMPOSIUM!

I remember once watching a symposium over television where this very subject was being discussed. There were some very notable people in the discussion group, one of them actually being a sitting Supreme Court Justice, and I'm speaking of the Supreme Court of the United States.

During the course of the discussion, the host asked the question concerning a court case, *"Isn't it the responsibility of the court to find the truth of the matter?"*

The Supreme Court Justice jumped to his feet and stated, *"Oh there are two kinds of truth, one for the prosecution and one for the defendant."*

Such an answer would be ridiculous if it came from the most ignorant person in the world. However, the fact that it came from a Supreme Court Justice lets us know to a great extent what's wrong with this nation. What a ridiculous answer!

No, there aren't two kinds of Truth; there is only one kind of Truth.

THE DEFINITION OF TRUTH

• The Lord Jesus Christ is Truth: He said, *". . . I am the Way, the Truth, and the Life: no man comes unto the Father, but by Me"* (Jn. 14:6).

• *The* Word of God is Truth: Jesus said in His Prayer to the Father, *"Sanctify them through Your Truth: Your Word is Truth"* (Jn. 17:17).

• The Holy Spirit is Truth: John wrote and said, *". . . And it is the Spirit Who bears witness, because the Spirit is Truth"* (I Jn. 5:6).

Every law in the world that has a sense of fairness and equality about it has its origin in the Word of God. Every law, such as the right to abortion, etc., which is diametrically opposed to the Word of God, is that which mitigates against Truth. Such is the ruin of a person, a culture, a country, and even an entire empire.

MERCY

Truth and Mercy are both Divine Attributes and, as well, human virtues. It is in the latter sense that they are here employed.

Mercy always follows Truth, which is the Bible. The less adherence to the Word of God, the less Mercy. Consequently, one can easily look at the nations of the world, which repudiate the Word of God, and easily see the cruelty of man's inhumanity to man. In these countries and cultures, life is held cheap. Little regard is given to the old, infirm, or helpless, such as little children. Actually, Mercy is a by-product of Grace, which can only come from God.

Grace was a choice on the part of God. In other words, God purposely chose to use Grace in dealing with man. In fact, for Grace to be Grace, it has to be by choice. However, once Grace is chosen, there is no choice but that it be followed by Mercy. In other words, God, having chosen Grace, now has no choice but to grant Mercy. So, the more Truth there is, i.e., Word of God, the more Mercy is extended.

While Mercy does not ignore wrongdoing, as should be obvious, still, once the person properly repents before the Lord, Mercy is instantly granted. How wonderful it is to serve the Lord!

NO KNOWLEDGE OF GOD IN THE LAND

The more the Word of God is proclaimed, the more Knowledge of God is in the land. Regrettably and sadly, there is less Word of God being proclaimed in America at present than at any time, I think, since its founding

as a nation. The Word of the Lord is presently either ignored or twisted and perverted. In fact, in many churches the pastor doesn't really want the people to bring their Bibles to church. In effect, he wants them weaned away from the Bible in order to accept what he is presenting. I speak of the *"Purpose Driven Life Scheme"* and the *"Seeker Sensitive"* foolishness.

What is Seeker Sensitive?

It purports to find out what the people want and then gives such to them, whatever it might be. In other words, Seeker Sensitive churches, and there are some large ones, do not want the Word of God preached. They don't want to hear about Judgment, about sin, about Hell, about the Cross of Christ, etc.

Why?

Because such subject matter might offend people, and the Seeker Sensitive churches want to avoid such.

I heard the father of the Seeker Sensitive Movement state in an interview that they never mention sin, the Cross, the Blood, etc., in their sermons or singing. In other words, they never really mention the Bible. So, whatever is given to the people is not the Word of God.

I venture to say that not a single person in these churches is truly Saved. And if someone accidentally does get Saved, as if such could happen, he won't be able to stay in that atmosphere very long. You can't put a live chicken under a dead hen. If you do, you're going to have two dead chickens.

One can have the Knowledge of God only by understanding the Word of God. It cannot be obtained in any other manner or fashion. That's what grieves me about so-called Christian television.

People are told how to get rich when, in reality, it is only the preachers who get rich. Other preachers are motivators, and still others are social workers; however, precious few are actually preaching the Gospel. Thank God for the few who do, but that number is getting smaller almost by the day. In fact, most preachers presently are amateur psychologists. If they go to Bible College or Seminary, they will learn far more about psychology than they will about the Word of God. So, as one Methodist layman said to me:

"Brother Swaggart, the Methodist Church wasn't lost by its people carrying their Bibles to church, but rather by our Seminaries turning out preachers who no longer believe the Word of God."

It must be understood, when the Word of God is faithfully preached, it at times will bring *"joy unspeakable and full of glory"* to those who are privileged to know that great Word. But, on the other hand, at times it will also make a person feel like he's hanging over Hell on a rotten stick. Telling a cancer patient that all is well, when in reality he is dying, is not doing that person a favor. And that's exactly what preachers are doing in most churches presently. They are attempting to make the people feel really good about themselves, and, in most cases, they aren't doing their people a favor.

TWO MOUNTAINS

The Word of God is somewhat like two mountains in Old Testament history, which were located in Israel. They are *"Mount Gerizim"* and *"Mount Ebal."* Mount Gerizim was the *"Mount of Blessing,"* while Mount Ebal was the *"Mount of cursing."*

Consequently, we have some churches, actually many, which are altogether *"blessing churches,"* and some churches, which are altogether *"cursing churches."* Both are wrong!

The Word of God is a Blessing of unparalleled proportions for those who make every effort to obey its precepts, and do so by their Faith being in Christ and what Christ has done for us at the Cross. But, if the person does not obey and makes no effort to do such, the Word of God also, in essence, pronounces Judgment on those who disobey its concepts. So, for the Church to be what the Church ought to be, it must portray both, the Blessing and the Judgment.

Let not the reader think that because we're living in the Day of Grace that all Judgment is suspended. Not so! While the Lord is Merciful and Gracious and, in fact, is always Merciful and Gracious, still, if the individual will not humble himself before Him but insists upon flouting His Word, Judgment will ultimately come. It will come in the form of chastisement if the person is a Believer, but it will come in the form of

a curse if the person is an unbeliever, but come it shall!

As we have repeatedly stated, the only thing standing between man and eternal Hell is the Cross of Christ. God is unalterably opposed to sin in any form. It is the Cross alone that makes it possible for Him to deal with us on any level. He doesn't require much of us, but He most definitely does require that our Faith be in Christ and the Cross, and Christ and the Cross exclusively.

The Lord does not function by the means of merit or good works. If He did, we would be hopelessly lost. The reason being, our debt to God is so overwhelming that it's impossible for it to be rectified except through the Cross.

The more of the *"Knowledge of God"* that's in a person, the more of the *"Knowledge of God"* that's in the land, and the more Blessing there is.

SINS

"Swearing, lying, killing, stealing, adultery," which results in *"blood touching blood,"* is the result of a nation without God. Consequently, the similarity between Israel of old and modern America is chilling, to say the least! And if God judged Israel, who were His Chosen People, do we think that we are going to fair better?

(3) "THEREFORE SHALL THE LAND MOURN, AND EVERYONE WHO DWELLS THEREIN SHALL LANGUISH, WITH THE BEASTS OF THE FIELD, AND WITH THE FOWLS OF HEAVEN; YES, THE FISHES OF THE SEA ALSO SHALL BE TAKEN AWAY.

(4) "YET LET NO MAN STRIVE, NOR REPROVE ANOTHER: FOR YOUR PEOPLE ARE AS THEY WHO STRIVE WITH THE PRIEST.

(5) "THEREFORE SHALL YOU FALL IN THE DAY, AND THE PROPHET ALSO SHALL FALL WITH YOU IN THE NIGHT, AND I WILL DESTROY YOUR MOTHER.

(6) "MY PEOPLE ARE DESTROYED FOR LACK OF KNOWLEDGE: BECAUSE YOU HAVE REJECTED KNOWLEDGE, I WILL ALSO REJECT YOU, THAT YOU SHALL BE NO PRIEST TO ME: SEEING YOU HAVE FORGOTTEN THE LAW OF YOUR GOD, I

WILL ALSO FORGET YOUR CHILDREN.

(7) "AS THEY WERE INCREASED, SO THEY SINNED AGAINST ME: THEREFORE WILL I CHANGE THEIR GLORY INTO SHAME.

(8) "THEY EAT UP THE SIN OF MY PEOPLE, AND THEY SET THEIR HEART ON THEIR INIQUITY.

(9) "AND THERE SHALL BE, LIKE PEOPLE, LIKE PRIEST: AND I WILL PUNISH THEM FOR THEIR WAYS, AND REWARD THEM THEIR DOINGS.

(10) "FOR THEY SHALL EAT, AND NOT HAVE ENOUGH: THEY SHALL COMMIT WHOREDOM, AND SHALL NOT INCREASE: BECAUSE THEY HAVE LEFT OFF TO TAKE HEED TO THE LORD.

(11) "WHOREDOM AND WINE AND NEW WINE TAKE AWAY THE HEART."

The construction is:

1. (Vs. 3) *"Therefore shall the land mourn,"* is the result of the sins of Verse 2, for the evils detailed result from not knowing God.

2. (Vs. 3) The phrases concerning the *"beasts of the field,"* *"fowls of heaven,"* and *"fishes of the sea"* specify that all of Creation, animate and inanimate, suffer as a result of man's sin (Rom. 8:22).

3. Verse 4 refers back to the true position of the High Priest in Israel, whose word was law. Consequently, there was no point in striving with him. Consequently, it is also useless concerning the coming Judgment.

"Nor reprove another" refers to further admonishment as being hopeless!

4. The first part of Verse 5 has to do with both *"people"* and *"prophet,"* which actually refers to false prophets, and that all would fall alike, whether day or night. The destruction of the *"mother"* has to do with the entirety of the Nation. As a Nation, they would exist no more.

5. (Vs. 6) *"My People are destroyed for lack of Knowledge"* is the cause of all the problems in the church, and the world, for that matter! The *"Knowledge"* spoken of is the Bible. This *"lack of Knowledge"* was not ignorance, but rather a willful rejection of the Law of God. They didn't know, but it was because they didn't want to know!

6. The *"increase"* of Verse 7 speaks both numerically and economically. *"Therefore*

will I change their glory into shame" may also read, *"My glory have they changed into shame"*; that is, they substituted an idol for God.

7. The phrase of Verse 8, *"They eat up the sin of My People,"* actually meant that the Priests ate the Sin-Offering instead of offering it as a *"Burnt Offering,"* as they were supposed to do.

8. *"Like people, like Priest,"* they were one in guilt and, therefore, justly one in punishment. The word *"reward"* of Verse 9 is generally used in the positive sense, but here it is used in the negative!

9. The phrase of Verse 10, *"They shall commit whoredom, and shall not increase,"* means that because of *"whoredom,"* i.e., idolatry, the Lord will stop the numerical increase of the Nation. A large population was then desired because it represented strength. It was *"because they have left off to take heed to the LORD."*

10. (Vs. 11) Idol worship and its licentious rites destroy the understanding and make men insensible to their own good.

THE PEOPLE ARE DESTROYED FOR LACK OF KNOWLEDGE

As stated, the *"lack of Knowledge"* here addressed in Verse 6 pertains to the Bible. However, and also as stated, while it was true there was a lack of Knowledge of the Word of God in Israel at that time, it was a position they willfully desired to have. In other words, it was a willful rejection of the Word of God. They didn't know, but it was because they didn't want to know.

THE MESSAGE OF THE CROSS

It was to the Apostle Paul that the meaning of the New Covenant was given, which, in effect, is the meaning of the Cross (Gal. 1:1-12). Consequently, he gave to us this great Truth, which the Lord had given to him in his 14 Epistles. In fact, one might say that all of his teaching culminates in Chapters 6, 7, and 8 of the great Book of Romans. Chapters 1, 2, and 3 of that Book tell us of man's dilemma, which means that man is without God and, within himself, has no way to reach the Lord. But then, we are told in Chapters 4 and 5 how that God can justify an obviously guilty sinner, and do so by the means of the price paid at Calvary's Cross and the Faith of the sinner evidenced in that Finished Work (Rom. 5:1-2).

With the problem of Redemption now solved, i.e., *"Justification by Faith,"* Chapters 6, 7, and 8 of Romans proclaim to us how the Believer is to live for God. To be frank, if the Believer doesn't understand these three Chapters in Romans, while he can certainly be Saved, to be sure, his life and living is going to be far less than it should be. In other words, without understanding these Chapters, one does not know how to live for God.

BAPTIZED!

Due to the fact that the Holy Spirit through Paul used the word *"baptize"* in Romans 6:3-5, which pertains to the Cross, most Believers have a total misunderstanding of what this Chapter tells us. In fact, most Christians take the position that they have been baptized in water, so what is said in Chapter 6 is of little interest to them. That's the biggest mistake an individual ever made.

Paul said (both the Text and the notes from THE EXPOSITOR'S STUDY BIBLE):

"Know you not, that so many of us as were baptized into Jesus Christ *(plainly says that this Baptism is into Christ and not water [I Cor. 1:17; 12:13; Gal. 3:27; Eph. 4:5; Col. 2:11-13])* **were baptized into His Death?** *(When Christ died on the Cross, in the Mind of God, we died with Him; in other words, He became our Substitute, and our identification with Him in His Death gives us all the benefits for which He died; the idea is that He did it all for us!)"*

NEWNESS OF LIFE

"Therefore we are buried with Him by baptism into death *(not only did we die with Him, but we were buried with Him as well, which means that all the sin and transgression of the past were buried; when they put Him in the Tomb, they put all of our sins into that Tomb also):* **that like as Christ was raised up from the dead by the Glory of the Father, even so we also should walk in Newness of Life** *(we died with Him, we were buried with Him, and His Resurrection was*

our Resurrection to a 'Newness of Life')."

IN THE LIKENESS OF HIS DEATH

"For if we have been planted together *(with Christ)* **in the likeness of His Death** *(Paul proclaims the Cross as the instrument through which all Blessings come; consequently, the Cross must ever be the Object of our Faith, which gives the Holy Spirit latitude to work within our lives)*, **we shall be also** *in the likeness of His* **Resurrection** *(we can have the 'likeness of His Resurrection,' i.e., 'live this Resurrection Life,' only as long as we understand the 'likeness of His Death,' which refers to the Cross as the Means by which all of this is done)"* **(Rom. 6:3-5).**

But, as stated, most Believers mistake the two words, *"baptize"* and *"baptism,"* as referring to water. It doesn't!

One Believer wrote me the other day stating that Strong's Concordance states that these words, *"baptize"* and *"baptism,"* refer to water, to be *"dipped under."*

That is correct; however, Strong's also states that the word can be used either *"figuratively or literally."* Paul is using it here figuratively.

Listen to John the Baptist, for he used the words interchangeably as well. He said:

LITERALLY AND FIGURATIVELY

"I indeed baptize you with water unto Repentance (Used literally. Water Baptism is an outward act of an inward work already carried out)*: but He* (Christ) *Who comes after me is mightier than I, Whose Shoes I am not worthy to bear: He shall baptize you with the Holy Spirit, and with fire"* (Mat. 3:11).

As John used the word *"baptize"* in connection with the Holy Spirit, he used it figuratively, even as Paul did in Romans.

WHY DID THE HOLY SPIRIT CHOOSE THE WORD *"BAPTISM"*?

As John used the word, and even as Paul used it, it was used thusly by the Holy Spirit because it explains what is being done better than any other word. When a person comes to Christ, that individual, at least in the Mind of God, is literally placed *"in Christ."* We were and are *"in Christ"* in His Death,

His Burial, and His Resurrection. That's what Jesus was talking about when He said, **"At that day** *(after the Resurrection and the coming of the Holy Spirit on the Day of Pentecost)* **you shall know that I** *am* **in My Father** *(speaks of Deity; Jesus is God!)*, **and you in Me** *(has to do with our Salvation by Faith)*, **and I in you** *(enables us to live a victorious life [Gal. 2:20])*" **(Jn. 14:20).** In essence, through His Crucifixion, we are *"in Christ,"* and Christ is *"in us."* Actually, He is in us by virtue of the Holy Spirit (Mat. 3:11).

So, Paul was not speaking of water at all as he gave instructions regarding the Cross in Romans 6:3-5. But, as stated, most people think he is talking about Water Baptism, so they miss the entire scope of what the Holy Spirit is there telling us.

WILLFUL IGNORANCE

Even though most Believers miss what Paul is talking about in Romans, Chapter 6, still, the truth is, sad to say, most have little interest in what the Text actually means. In other words, they don't understand the Cross as it regards Sanctification, and the truth is, they simply have no desire to understand what it really means. To not know is one thing, while not desiring to know is something else altogether!

Our Lord is very patient, as should be well understood. However, when Light is given and then is rejected, not only does the person lose what he could have had, but, as well, what little Light he did have is removed from him. That's what happened to Israel, and I'm afraid that is what is happening to the modern church. In fact, the modern church has become almost pagan in many circles.

MY PEOPLE

Even though the phrase, *"My People,"* is collective, still, it comprehends all the individual members of the Nation. In other words, the Lord searches the heart of each individual person, ascertaining each one's Knowledge of Himself.

Let the reader not think that this was only with Israel of old! It is so with each and every person today and always!

The phrase used by the Apostle Paul, *"Let the Word of Christ dwell in you richly*

in all wisdom," has reference to a striking principle.

It really means that the Spirit of God can only deal with a Christian, regarding Leading, Guidance, Faith, and Holiness, according to the amount of Word residing in the Believer. Therefore, if a Believer knows very little of the Word of God, that means the Holy Spirit little works with that Believer because there is nothing there to work on. The Word of God is the Foundation on which all stands. If one is to notice, unbelievers are brought to Christ as the Word of God is delivered unto them in some form. There is no record, at least that I'm aware, of it being otherwise.

Considering that most of the modern church is Biblically illiterate, this means that most of the modern church is led little, or not at all, by the Spirit of God.

YOU HAVE FORGOTTEN THE LAW OF YOUR GOD

This speaks of a willful forgetfulness. Israel forgot it, and easily so, because it was no longer taught, studied, or even mentioned. If someone's name is never spoken, it gradually fades from memory. Therefore, they forgot *"the Law of God."* The word, *"your,"* is used because there was no God but Jehovah.

I WILL FORGET YOUR CHILDREN

The phrase, *"I will also forget your children,"* has reference to the time of the coming Judgment.

In effect, the Lord is saying that Judgment would not come in this generation but in the next, which it did! Consequently, the generation to which Hosea was speaking could have averted the tragedy that befell their *"children,"* but tragically, they saw no need to repent, and their children went to their doom.

NO BLESSING!

The idea of Verse 10 is that whatever the population of Israel would do would not satisfy. Someone has said that the soul of man is so big that only God can fill it. In fact, this is the basic problem of the human family.

Men eat, but it does not satisfy. They grow rich, but they do not have enough. They build new houses, but the ache and quest remain. It is as Christ said, *". . . for a man's life consists not in the abundance of the things which he possesses"* (Lk. 12:15).

The reason for all of this was, *"because they have left off to take heed to the LORD."*

IDOL WORSHIP

Hosea said, *"Whoredom and wine and new wine take away the heart."*

WHOREDOM AND WINE

It is obvious as to the sin of *"whoredom,"* but, seemingly, not so obvious, at least to the modern church, the sin of *"wine."* The Holy Spirit through the Prophet plainly says that the two *"take away the heart."* In other words, regarding sin, *"wine"* is put on the same low level as *"whoredom."*

Why is one frowned on and not the other by the modern church?

The answer is obvious! *"Whoredom"* is not socially acceptable, as it certainly should not be, while conversely, *"wine"* is! However, what is socially acceptable or not acceptable has no bearing with God and should have no bearing with the Church.

Considering the pain, suffering, and heartache caused by alcohol, how any Christian could condone such is a mystery. It certainly may be true that one glass of wine or one bottle of beer, if held to that, would be of little consequence. However, because of the 40 million alcoholics and problem drinkers in America, not counting the rest of the world, our attention should be drawn to the example set.

Considering the multiple millions who are not able to stop with one glass of wine, one bottle of beer, etc., any and all Christians, at least if they desire to do the Will of God, must act on the principle of total abstinence. Paul said, *"But take heed lest by any means this liberty of yours become a stumblingblock to them who are weak"* (I Cor. 8:9).

CULTURE

Many, especially on this issue, have attempted to fall behind the curtain of culture. However, every Christian must clearly understand that upon coming to Christ, our decayed culture must be thrown out the

NOTES

window, and the new culture of belonging to Christ must commence. The idea that it is acceptable for French Christians to drink wine or German Christians to drink beer simply because it's their culture has no Scriptural validity.

If that position is taken, then whatever is acceptable to the community is acceptable, be it gambling in Las Vegas or dealing in drugs in some of the South American cities, simply because a great part of that population is given over to that dealer of death.

No, the excuse of culture shows a woeful misunderstanding of the Word of God and little desire to do God's Will. If the Holy Spirit says that it *"takes away the heart,"* then it *"takes away the heart,"* and neither culture, nor anything else, can change that!

(12) "MY PEOPLE ASK COUNSEL AT THEIR STOCKS, AND THEIR STAFF DECLARES UNTO THEM: FOR THE SPIRIT OF WHOREDOMS HAS CAUSED THEM TO ERR, AND THEY HAVE GONE A WHORING FROM UNDER THEIR GOD.

(13) "THEY SACRIFICE UPON THE TOPS OF THE MOUNTAINS, AND BURN INCENSE UPON THE HILLS, UNDER OAKS AND POPLARS AND ELMS, BECAUSE THE SHADOW THEREOF IS GOOD: THEREFORE YOUR DAUGHTERS SHALL COMMIT WHOREDOM, AND YOUR SPOUSES SHALL COMMIT ADULTERY.

(14) "I WILL NOT PUNISH YOUR DAUGHTERS WHEN THEY COMMIT WHOREDOM, NOR YOUR SPOUSES WHEN THEY COMMIT ADULTERY: FOR THEMSELVES ARE SEPARATED WITH WHORES, AND THEY SACRIFICE WITH HARLOTS: THEREFORE THE PEOPLE WHO DO NOT UNDERSTAND SHALL FALL."

The pattern is:

1. The phrase of Verse 12, *"Their stocks,"* refers to wooden idols. *"Their staff"* refers to divination rods (Ezek. 21:21-22).

2. (Vs. 14) The tops of mountains, of hills, and of houses were chosen for the worship of idols because they were nearer to the sun, moon, and stars.

3. (Vs. 14) The wives and daughters were guilty of actual adultery because their husbands and fathers had volunteered them to temple prostitution. Consequently, the

Lord, impatient with the recital of such shameful licentiousness and indignant at such presumptuous sinning, closes abruptly with the declaration of the ruin of all such offenders with the words, *"the people who do not understand shall fall."*

4. (Vs. 14) In other words, anyone who would have no more spiritual sense than this, the worship of idols and all of its attendant evil, especially those who belong to God, can expect coming Judgment.

ISRAEL'S IDOLATRY: JUDGMENT

The phrase, *"their stocks,"* refers to wooden idols.

"Their staff" refers to divination rods (Ezek. 21:21-22).

The Assyrian monarchs are depicted on the monuments holding the rods in one hand. These rods were usually placed in a bag, and when one was drawn out, its markings directed the action or inaction in a proposed matter, or the decision to be made in either of two ways.

It should ever be understood that the spirit of idolatry causes one to err; the Spirit of God saves from error.

The Ten Tribes had gone from under the Protection and Authority of God, just as Gomer had from under the protection and authority of Hosea.

HUMANISTIC PSYCHOLOGY

The modern church's foray into humanistic psychology is actually no different than the consulting of wooden idols. How anyone, who claims to know their Bible, can succumb to such thinking has to be placed in the same category as the moderate drinking of the previous Verse.

The problems of man cannot be talked away or drugged away as psychology proposes! Such is far more acute than mere surface difficulties. They stem from the Fall of man and always constitute sin or an improper definition of Christ and His Power to save.

The northern kingdom of Israel had, sadly and regrettably, discontinued their seeking the Lord and had resorted to idols. So has the modern church! The actual direction may be somewhat different, but the principle is the

same. Either Christ holds all the answers, or else Christ doesn't hold all the answers! The excuse that most will not seek Christ and, therefore, must have another solution is facetious indeed because such thinking directly states that there is another solution other than Christ.

If such were true, then Christ could have saved Himself the terrible humiliation, pain, and suffering of coming down to this wicked, sinful world, and dying on Calvary.

No, there is no other answer than Christ for the ills, problems, and vicissitudes of life!

Likewise, it should be understood that the worship of Saints and images, or the appeal for help in that direction, is constituted by the Lord to be the same as *"asking counsel of wooden idols."* In God's Mind there is no difference.

THE CATHOLIC CHURCH

The Roman Catholic church teaches:

• The Saints function as mediators between the faithful and God.

• We should address prayers to the Saints and kneel before them to obtain their favor.

• The Saints are pleased to see their images venerated and adorned with costly treasures, and they will recompense the faithful who are generous in their worship.

• The images of the Blessed Virgin and the Lord Jesus Christ may be venerated under different names, they say! This actually gives rise to competition between different images of the same person.

• According to the Catholic position, which has no foundation whatsoever in Scripture, Saints are individuals of the New Testament (or later martyrs or notable persons of *"The Church"*) who have died and subsequently been declared to be Saints by the Pope.

It is difficult to understand how that Catholics are unaware of the direct contradiction between a belief in an Omnipotent God and the worship of Saints as advocates and intercessors.

A CONTRADICTION IN TERMS

In a conversation between an Evangelical and several Roman Catholics, the following inquiry was raised:

"Everyone accepts that the Saints are finite beings – not only on Earth but in Heaven as well. So, how can finite beings hear the prayers of men who are on the Earth? If one would stop to think about this, it would seem impossible for a finite being to hear the prayers of not just two or three people, but those of multiplied thousands who are all praying at the same time.

"The only way they could hear so many thousands of prayers and discern the heart attitudes of all of these people is if they were both omniscient and omnipresent. In other words, each Saint would have to be God in order to accomplish this."

When this question was put to the Roman Catholic representatives, they did not know how to reply. Finally, after a whispered conference, one of them offered:

"There is no difficulty. Even if Saints can't hear our prayers, God can, and He could reveal them to the Saints."

Dare we anticipate the resulting conclusion of this dialogue?

This would then mean that we would be approaching the Saints through God—instead of God through the Saints.

The idea becomes more absurd the further it is pursued.

The very thought of individuals speaking to frail and finite humans—whether in the field of psychology, as we have just mentioned, or whether expecting them to carry their ideas to God—is ludicrous. The Word of God states clearly that we can go directly to the Father, at any time, in the Name of the Lord Jesus Christ (Jn. 16:23).

THE CATHOLIC SYSTEM OF PATRON SAINTS

The Catholic system of patron Saints is nothing more or less than a continuation of ancient heathen beliefs in gods devoted to days, occupations, and the various needs of human life. Since the worship of Saints is really perpetuation of these false gods, Romanism is patently guilty of worshipping other gods, a practice that is condemned repeatedly in Scripture, as is obvious!

By the Tenth Century, some 25,000 Saints had been canonized by the Roman Catholic church. Of course, by that time, Rome had

hopelessly insinuated pagan religions into their brand of Christianity.

To make the apostasy less obvious, the leaders of the Roman Catholic church substituted Christian-sounding names that were similar to the original pagan names.

For example, the Goddess Victoria of the Basses-Alps was renamed St. Victoire. The pagan god Osiris was renamed St. Onuphrius. Apollo was renamed St. Apollinaris, and the heathen god Mars became St. Martine.

We are told that one of the best preserved of the ancient temples in Rome is the Pantheon, which was originally dedicated to *"Jove and all the gods."* It was reconsecrated, however, by Pope Boniface IV to the *"Mother of God and all the Saints."* An edifice formally consecrated to the Greek god Apollo now is displayed proudly as the Church of St. Apollinaris.

Where the ancient temple of Mars once stood, we now find the Church of St. Martine. Rome simply adopted the heathen gods into the so-called Christian church, renaming them as their worship continued uninterrupted.

Just as the pagans worshipped idols or statues of their gods, so does the Roman Catholic church utilize statues in their worship.

STATUES AND IMAGES

In many cases the same statue that was worshipped as a pagan god was rechristened with the name of a Christian Saint and worship continued. The statue of Jupiter, for example, was slightly changed and retitled *"Peter."*

Through the centuries, more and more statues have been crafted (and venerated) until today there are churches in Europe that contain as many as several thousand statues!

However, whether in a great cathedral, a small chapel, or on the dashboard of an automobile, these are still idols and are absolutely forbidden by the Word of God (Ex. 20:3-5).

It was not until the Fifth Century that pictures of Mary, Christ, and the Saints were made and used as objects of worship.

Scripture specifically condemns idol worship in countless places, as there is not a hint or a suggestion in the Word of God that the Early Church deviated from these age-old injunctions.

IRENAEUS

Irenaeus (about A.D. 130-202), a pupil of Polycarp (who sat at the feet of the Apostle John), said:

"As the Church has received liberally from the Lord, so let it minister liberally, and not ask to do anything through the invocation of Angels or through enchantments and other perverse rarities, but let prayers be addressed purely, clearly, and openly to the Lord, from Whom are all things, invoking the Name of our Lord Jesus Christ."

CLEMENT OF ALEXANDRIA

Clement of Alexandria, a Greek theologian (about A.D. 150-215), said:

"It is the height of foolishness to pray as though to gods to those who are no gods at all, for there is but one good God, to Him only do we and the Angels pray."

In another place he said:

"Every image or statue should be called an idol, for it is nothing but vile and profane material, and for this reason and to remove idolatry by the roots, God has forbidden the use of any image or likeness of anything in Heaven or in Earth, and has also forbidden the making of such images, and for this reason we Christians have none of these material representations."

ORIGEN

Origen, a Greek teacher and writer (about A.D. 185-254), said:

"The Angels are greatly interested in your Salvation. They have been given as helpers to the Son of God, but all prayers to God, whether they are supplications or thanksgiving, should be raised to Him through Christ, the High Priest, Who is above all Angels . . . men do not know the Angels, so it is unreasonable to address prayers to them instead of to Christ Who is known of men.

"And even were we to know the Angels, we should not be allowed to address our prayers to anyone except to God, the Lord of all Creation, Who is sufficient for all, and we come to Him through our Saviour, the Son of God."

The same writer said in another place:

"In the reproof of those who trust in the Saints, I would say, 'Cursed be the man who trusts in man' (Jer. 17:5), and 'It is better to trust in the LORD than to put confidence in man' (Ps. 118:8). If it is necessary for us to have confidence in anyone, let us leave all other and trust in the Lord."

CYPRIAN

Cyprian (martyred about A.D. 258), Bishop of Carthage (about 248-258), declared:

"Why bow down before images? Lift up your eyes and heart to Heaven; that is the place where you should seek God."

ATHANASIUS

Athanasius, a Bishop at Alexandria and the father of orthodoxy (about A.D. 300-373), said:

"It is written, 'God [is] my Rock; in Him will I trust; He is my Shield, and the Horn of my Salvation' (II Sam. 22:3) and, 'The LORD also will be a Refuge for the oppressed, a Refuge in times of trouble' (Ps. 9:9). And how many similar words do we find in the Sacred Scriptures? Should anyone reply that these are Prophecies that apply to the Son, which may be true, then let them admit that the Saints do not venture to call any created being their help and refuge."

Elsewhere he declared:

"The invocation of idols is a sin, and anything that is sinful at the beginning can never be good later."

AUGUSTINE

Augustine, Bishop of Hippo (about A.D. 354-430), said:

"Let not our religion be the worship of the dead, for if they lived a holy life, it is impossible to imagine that they desire such honors, rather they would wish that we should render our worship to Him through Whom we should be partakers with them of Salvation. Therefore, we should honor them by imitating them – not by worshipping them.

"The only Image of Christ that we should make for ourselves is to keep before us His Humility, Patience, and Kindness, and endeavor to make our lives like His in all things. Those who go in search of Jesus and the Apostles in mural paintings, or statues,

etc., far from conforming to Scripture, fall into error."

JEROME

Jerome (about A.D. 343-420), who translated the Old Testament directly into Latin from Hebrew (the Vulgate Bible), quoted a letter from Epiphanius in which he stated the following:

"In a part of the country that I visited I found a candle placed in the door of a Church over which was painted an Image of Christ, and another of a Saint. I was displeased that, in this defiance of Holy Scripture, the image of a man should be hung up in the Church of Christ, and I cut the candle down, advising the sacristan that it would be put to better use at the funeral of some poor person."

The use of images was condemned by all in the Early Church and even condemned as late as the Synod of Elvira (A.D. 305), the Council of Frankfort (A.D. 794), and the Council of Rouen (A.D. 1445). This latter assembly in its Seventh Canon condemned the practice of praying before images with names such as *"Our Lady of Piety," "Our Lady of Help,"* or *"Our Lady of Consolation."*

It said:

"Such practices tend to lead to superstition, as though there were more power in some than others."

DESIDERIUS ERASMUS

Desiderius Erasmus of Rotterdam (about 1466-1536), a Dutch scholar held in high esteem by the Roman Catholic church, was right when he said:

"No one who bows before an image or looks at it intentionally is free from some kind of superstition; and not only so, but if he only prays before an image."

WHAT DOES THE BIBLE SAY?

"You shall make you no idols nor graven image, neither rear you up a standing image, neither shall you set up any image of stone in your land, to bow down unto it: for I am the LORD your God" (Lev. 26:1).

". . . Be not deceived: neither fornicators, nor idolaters . . . shall inherit the Kingdom of God" (I Cor. 6:9-10).

"For there is One God, and One Mediator between God and men, the Man Christ Jesus" (I Tim. 2:5).

"Neither is there Salvation in any other: for there is none other name under Heaven given among men, whereby we must be Saved" (Acts 4:12).

WITH REGARD TO THE WORSHIP OF SAINTS . . .

"And as Peter was coming in, Cornelius met him, and fell down at his feet, and worshipped him. But Peter took him up, saying, Stand up; I myself also am a man" (Acts 10:25-26).

"And I John saw these things, and heard them. And when I had heard and seen, I fell down to worship before the feet of the Angel which showed me these things.

"Then said he unto me, See you do it not: for I am your fellowservant, and of your brethren the Prophets, and of them who keep the sayings of this Book: worship God" (Rev. 22:8-9).

A SAINT?

As well, there is no indication in the Word of God that a person becomes a Saint after he dies. In fact, it is not the Pope who makes someone a Saint, it is God. In Scripture, Saints are always living people—never the dead.

For example, when Paul wrote to the Ephesians, his letter was addressed *"to the Saints who are at Ephesus"* (Eph. 1:1).

Likewise, the Book of Philippians was written *"to all the Saints in Christ Jesus who are at Philippi"* (Phil. 1:1).

The early Christians in the Church at Rome were called *"Saints"* (Rom. 1:7; 16:15), as were the Christians who lived at Corinth (I Cor. 1:2; II Cor. 1:1).

Consequently, if a person wants a Saint to pray for him, he should find a Christian and ask him to join him in prayer, for all true Christians are Saints.

Anytime a person tries to contact people who have died, it is a form of spiritualism. The Bible repeatedly condemns any attempt to commune with the dead.

COMMUNING WITH THE DEAD

"There shall not be found among you . . . an enchanter (one who uses incantations),

or a witch, or a charmer, or a consulter with familiar spirits, or a wizard, or a necromancer (one who entreats the spirits of the dead). For all who do these things are an abomination unto the LORD . . ." (Deut. 18:10-12).

"And when they shall say unto you, Seek unto them who have familiar spirits, and unto wizards who peep, and that mutter: should not a people seek unto their God? for the living to the dead? . . . if they speak not according to this Word, it is because there is no light in them" (Isa. 8:19-20).

MIRACLES?

However, some would ask, *"But what about the miracles that have been performed by the intercession of the Saints?"*

These consist of statues that weep, form tears on faces, or produce (alleged) miracles. The Virgin of Lourdes is the most publicized.

Actually, there is absolutely nothing in the Word of God that even hints at such a thing. God has never healed or performed Miracles or done any kind of good works through inanimate objects except in the case of Paul's handkerchiefs and aprons, as described in Acts 19:12. And this one isolated case is not an example of worshipping or venerating an idol or image.

To use only one as an example, if a person were to visit Lourdes today, he would be appalled by the carnival atmosphere. This is, of course, totally foreign to the Word of God and the Work of God. There are no miracles at Lourdes, no healings or cures, or anything else of this nature, at least from God. There may be emotional reaction, but that is as far as it goes.

However, this should be said as well.

SATAN AND SICKNESS

Satan, who causes sicknesses by demon oppression (Acts 10:38; Lk. 13:11-16), can take off what he puts on without opposing himself or casting himself out. When he can damn a soul by getting a person to deny the essentials of the Bible that will save the soul, then it is to his advantage, at times, to deceive by taking away sickness.

Tragically, many people accept false religions, methods, or practices that promise

healing and other benefits. Satan cooperates with these religions, which he himself has founded to deceive men. He can even bring about a withdrawal of the sickness from people, as we have stated, without God being involved in the process. Such people will then think they are in the true religion. They reject Christ and see no need of being Saved from sin or of following the Saviour. Sadly and regrettably, they will be damned for doing so, Satan having won their souls.

DECEPTION

As any Bible student knows, one of the major works of Satan is the work of deception, and, in this vein, along with other efforts, he is leading much of the world astray.

Yes, Miracles and Healings, as given by the Lord, are real. As well, the Lord answers prayer; however, it, and without fail, will be the Biblical way.

Jesus said a long time ago:

"Come unto Me (Jesus Himself – not some Angel or dead Saint) . . . and I will give you rest.

"Take My Yoke upon you, and learn of Me (not some Angel or dead Saint) . . . and you shall find rest unto your souls" (Mat. 11:28-29).

PRAYER FOR THE SICK

Regarding prayer for the sick, the Lord uses living men and women to do such. He answers prayer when it is offered according to His Holy Word.

"Is any sick among you? let him call for the Elders of the Church; and let them pray over him, anointing him with oil in the Name of the Lord:

"And the prayer of Faith shall save the sick, and the Lord shall raise him up . . ." (James 5:14-15).

In conclusion, the worship or appealing to dead Saints and images has absolutely no foundation in the Word of God. It is an excursion into superstition and paganism, which will further unfold its web of deceit around the followers of Roman Catholicism or any other religion.

Jesus said:

". . . in that day you shall ask Me nothing. Verily, verily, I say unto you, Whatsoever

you shall ask the Father in My Name, He will give it you.

"Hitherto have you asked nothing in My Name: ask, and you shall receive, that your joy may be full.

"For the Father Himself loves you, because you have loved Me, and have believed that I came out from God" (Jn. 16:23-24, 27).

The reason for these sins of trusting in humanistic psychology or praying to dead Saints and images is *"the spirit of whoredoms,"* i.e., idolatry.

As stated, it is not merely an erroneous direction, but instead, is fostered and nurtured by demon spirits.

IDOLATRY

The tops of mountains, of hills, and of houses of Verse 13 were chosen for worship because they were nearer to the sun, moon, and stars.

The wives and daughters were guilty of actual adultery because their fathers and husbands were guilty of Spiritual Adultery. And it was reasonable that they should, therefore, not be further punished.

The unhappy women with whom these fathers and husbands dishonored themselves were the temple-women of ancient and modern idolatry. The violation of their bodies in honor of the god was a supreme act of worship to which they willingly dedicated themselves.

The phrase, *"I will not punish your daughters when they commit whoredom, nor your spouses,"* of Verse 14, actually means that God would not punish these women for their terrible iniquity any more than He punished their husbands or fathers for allowing such abominations.

The idea was that the fathers and husbands were involving themselves in idol worship and, thus, involving themselves with temple prostitutes. Therefore, all were equally guilty.

TEMPLE PROSTITUTES

These women (temple prostitutes) were females who devoted themselves to licentiousness in the service of Ashtaroth, the Sidonian Venus. Consequently, the lure of having beautiful women participate in these extremely immoral rituals guaranteed a

loyal following and a strong devotion.

The Lord stated the humiliating fact that instead of uniting with their wives in the worship of Jehovah, the fathers and husbands in Israel separated themselves and went aside with these female idolaters, sharing in their sinful sacrificial feasts. Moreover, He said that they even volunteered their own wives and daughters for the purpose of lewdness. Impatient of the recital of such shameful licentiousness and indignant of such presumptuous sinning, the Lord closes abruptly with the declaration of the ruin of all such offenders with the words, *"the people who do not understand shall fall."*

JUDGMENT

In other words, anyone, who has no more spiritual sense than this, especially those who belong to the Lord, can expect coming Judgment.

How is it possible for Israel of old, or even a modern Christian, to lose his or her way so badly?

The answers are many and varied; however, the basic reason is an improper relationship with our Lord.

Of course, Israel of old did not understand Christ as we understand Him presently. Still, all the Temple rituals, and we speak of the true Temple, were meant to point men to the coming Christ. So, the principle was the same!

RELATIONSHIP

As well, it must be understood that relationship with a religious denomination, of which millions are associated, is not, by any stretch of the imagination, a relationship with Christ. A relationship with the Lord is very personal and is meant, in every sense of the word, to be that way. As a result of such relationship, every aspect of the Christian life is purposely bent to His Will. The entire aspect is to please Him. And yet, He is not hard to please, for He said, *"For My Yoke is easy, and My Burden is light"* (Mat. 11:30).

HOW CAN ONE PLEASE THE LORD?

The Scripture says, **"By Faith Enoch was translated that he should not see death** *(refers to God transferring Enoch to Heaven* *in his physical body while he was yet alive)*; **and was not found, because God had translated him** *(refers to his translation being well-known at that time)*: **for before his translation he had this testimony, that he pleased God.** *(He pleased God because he placed his Faith exclusively in Christ and the Cross.)*

"But without Faith *(in Christ and the Cross; anytime Faith is mentioned, always and without exception, its root meaning is that its Object is Christ and the Cross; otherwise, it is faith God will not accept)* ***it is*** **impossible to please *Him*** *(faith in anything other than Christ and the Cross greatly displeases the Lord)*: **for he who comes to God must believe that He is** *(places Faith as the foundation and principle of the manner in which God deals with the human race)*, **and** ***that*** **He** *(God)* **is a rewarder of them who diligently seek Him** *(seek Him on the premise of Christ and Him Crucified)*" **(Heb. 11:5-6).**

Even though I think it was explained satisfactorily in the above notes, this is so important that I would ask that the reader indulge my repetition.

The only thing that pleases the Lord is for the Believer to exercise Faith in Christ and what Christ did at the Cross. That and that alone pleases the Lord!

Millions have Faith in Christ, or so they say, but they omit the Cross. As a result, they are following *"another Jesus"* (II Cor. 11:4).

WHAT IS ANOTHER JESUS?

Another Jesus is a failure to look at Jesus as the Word of God presents Him. In the Word, all the way from Genesis 1:1 through Revelation 22:21, Jesus is presented as the Saviour, and He is that by the Means of the Cross. Our Lord is many things, a Healer, a Provider, a Leader, a Teacher, and a Guide, in fact, everything and anything that one would desire that is righteous and holy. Still, until He is looked at as the Saviour, which can only be, as stated, by the Means of the Cross, then He is not understood correctly.

WHAT IS THE CROSS OF CHRIST?

The Cross of Christ is an act that was completed in time past, now nearly 2,000

years ago, but with continuing results, in fact, results which will never be discontinued. When we speak of the Cross, we aren't speaking of a wooden beam, but rather what Jesus there did.

WHAT HAPPENED AT THE CROSS?

On the proper explanation of that question, *"What happened at the Cross,"* rests the Redemption of the seeking soul. If what happened at the Cross is misunderstood, then everything about the Atonement is misunderstood, which can forfeit Salvation.

Let's look at what happened there.

THE PLAN OF REDEMPTION WAS FINISHED

The great Plan of Redemption, which was begun in the Mind of the Godhead from before the foundation of the world (I Pet. 1:18-20), and which was predicted by all the Prophets, was culminated and finished at the Cross of Calvary. What Jesus did at the Cross was the greatest act in human history, and, in fact, I think one could say, the greatest act in heavenly history. Everything pointed to this great Plan of God, which the Cross alone could carry out. So, it was at the Cross of Christ that the Plan of Redemption was totally and completely brought to a successful conclusion. It has resulted in untold millions being brought to a Saving Knowledge of Jesus Christ, both before the Cross and after the Cross. For those who died before the Cross but died believing, they were included in this glorious, great Redemption Plan.

THE PLAN WAS FINISHED AT THE CROSS

The Scripture plainly says concerning what Jesus did at Calvary, **"For in that He died, He died unto sin** *(the sin nature)* **once** *(actually means, 'He died unto the sin nature, once, for all')*: **but in that He lives** *(the Resurrection)*, **He lives unto God** *(refers to the fact that all life comes from God, and that we receive that life by virtue of the Cross and our Faith in that Finished Work)*" **(Rom. 6:10).**

The Scripture also says, **"And being made perfect** *(refers to being brought to* the goal fixed by God, which had to be if He was to be the Perfect Sacrifice), **He became the Author of Eternal Salvation** *(proclaims a perfect Salvation, because He was and is the Perfect Redeemer, because He was the Perfect Sacrifice)* **unto all them who obey Him** *(we obey Him by exhibiting Faith in the Cross, which then gives the Holy Spirit latitude to work; this Truth was given to Paul)*" **(Heb. 5:9).**

THE TORN VEIL

When Jesus died on the Cross, at the moment of His Death, God ripped the Veil that did hang in the Temple between the Holy Place and the Holy of Holies. No one was allowed in the Holy of Holies but the High Priest, and then only once a year when he applied blood to the Mercy Seat. However, there was no Ark of the Covenant or Mercy Seat in Herod's Temple. Nevertheless, the symbol of the Veil was still in place, which meant no entrance.

But when Jesus died, the price was forever paid, meaning that the demands of a thrice-Holy God were met, and were met forever. Due to what Christ did at the Cross, which was to atone for all sin, now anyone with a simple Faith in Christ and what He did at the Cross can *"come and take of the Water of Life freely"* (Rev. 22:17).

Concerning the torn Veil, the Scripture says, **"And, behold, the Veil of the Temple** *(that which hid the Holy of Holies; Josephus said it was sixty feet high from the ceiling to the floor [some say thirty feet], four inches thick, and was so strong that four yoke of oxen could not pull it apart)* **was rent in twain from the top to the bottom** *(meaning that God Alone could have done such a thing; it also signified that the price was paid completely on the Cross; signified by the rent Veil; regrettably, some say, the Cross – didn't finish the task with other things required; this Verse says differently)* . . ." **(Mat. 27:51).**

ALL SIN WAS ATONED

I think one could say without fear of contradiction that of all the things that were done at the Cross of Christ, all the victories won and all the accomplishments brought forth, the atoning for all sin was and is the

greatest accomplishment of all. When we say that He atoned for all sin, we mean all sin past, present, and future, at least for all who will believe (Jn. 3:16), Sin is the death knell of the human race. It is the destroyer of all that is good. All sin has death attached to it, meaning that it is the cause of everything decaying, being corrupted, being polluted, and finally falling into total chaos. Sin is the reason. As well, when one looks at the Cross with all of its attendant shame, misery, horror, pain, and suffering, all that it entails, one must say, *"my sin did that."*

We can only know how bad that sin is by understanding the price that had to be paid to address this monster. That price was God becoming man, and for the express purpose of offering Himself up as a Sacrifice, which payment was demanded. God cannot die, so in order for death to be brought about, because death was demanded, God would have to become man, which He did. Of all the things that Christ did, and all were of supreme significance, still, the chief end of His Mission, the purpose for all that was done, was the Cross. This we must never forget! To belittle the Cross, demean the Cross, register unbelief toward the Cross, and especially to deny the Cross, is to deny every single thing that God has done to redeem the human race. To know how bad that sin was and is, we need only to look at its remedy.

Concerning our Lord atoning for all sin, and again we emphasize, all had to be addressed, the Atonement had to be for all, not just part or some, but all. The Scripture says:

OUR HIGH PRIEST

"Wherefore He *(the Lord Jesus Christ)* **is able also to save them to the uttermost** *(proclaims the fact that Christ Alone has made the only true Atonement for sin; He did this at the Cross)* **who come unto God by Him** *(proclaims the only manner in which man can come to God)*, **seeing He ever lives to make intercession for them.** *(His very Presence by the Right Hand of the Father guarantees such, with nothing else having to be done [Heb. 1:3].)*

"For such an High Priest became us *(presents the fact that no one less exalted could have met the necessities of the* *human race)*, **Who is Holy**, **harmless, undefiled, separate from sinners** *(describes the Spotless, Pure, Perfect Character of the Son of God as our Great High Priest; as well, this tells us Christ did not become a sinner on the Cross, as some claim, but was rather the Sin-Offering)*, **and made higher than the Heavens** *(refers to the fact that He is seated at the Right Hand of the Father, which is the most exalted position in Heaven or Earth)***;"**

THE SIN-OFFERING

"Who needs not daily *(refers to the daily sacrifices offered by the Priests under the old Jewish economy)*, **as those High Priests, to offer up sacrifice, first for his own sins, and then for the people's** *(refers to the work of the Jewish High Priest on the Great Day of Atonement, which specified their unworthiness; Christ did not have to function accordingly)***: for this He did once, when He offered up Himself.** *(This refers to His Death on the Cross, which atoned for all sin – past, present, and future, making no further sacrifices necessary)***" (Heb. 7:25-27).**

Paul also said:

THROUGH THE ETERNAL SPIRIT

"How much more shall the Blood of Christ *(while the sacrifice of animals could cleanse from ceremonial defilement, only the Blood of Christ could cleanse from actual sin; so that throws out every proposed solution other than the Cross)*, **Who through the Eternal Spirit offered Himself without spot to God** *(in this phrase, we learn Christ did not die until the Holy Spirit told Him to die; in fact, no man took His Life from Him; He laid it down freely [Jn. 10:17-18]; as well, the fact that Jesus 'offered Himself without spot to God' shoots down the unscriptural doctrine that 'Jesus died Spiritually' on the Cross; had He died Spiritually, meaning He became a sinner on the Cross, He could not have offered Himself without spot to God, as should be obvious; God could only accept a Perfect Sacrifice; when He died on the Cross, He took upon Himself the sin penalty of the human race, which was physical death; inasmuch as His Offering of Himself was Perfect, God accepted it as payment in full*

for all sin – past, present, and future, at least for those who will believe [Jn. 3:16]), **purge your conscience from dead works to serve the Living God?** *('Dead works' are anything other than simple Faith in the Cross of Christ, i.e., 'the Blood of Christ')***" (Heb. 9:14).**

TO TAKE AWAY THE SIN OF THE WORLD

When introducing Christ, John the Baptist said, **". . . Behold the Lamb of God** *(proclaims Jesus as the Sacrifice for sin, in fact, the Sin-Offering, whom all the multiple millions of offered lambs had represented)*, **which takes away the sin of the world** *(animal blood could only cover sin, it could not take it away; but Jesus offering Himself as the Perfect Sacrifice took away the sin of the world; He not only cleansed acts of sin but, as well, addressed the root cause [Col. 2:14-15])***" (Jn. 1:29).**

Removing the sin debt, which characterized man from the dawn of human history, did all types of things:

• It made it possible for Justification by Faith to be an accomplished fact instead of a futuristic hope.

• With all sin removed because of one's Faith in Christ and what He did for us at the Cross, now the Holy Spirit could come into the heart and life of each and every Believer, which He did and does, there to abide permanently (Jn. 14:16-17).

• With the sin debt removed, which it was and is by what Jesus did at the Cross and our Faith in that Finished Work, such an individual can be labeled as perfect, and all because of Christ and His Atoning Work.

• With the sin debt removed, fellowship with God becomes more of a reality than a mere ceremony.

• With all sin atoned, the Believer can be granted a spotless, pure, perfect *"Righteousness of God,"* and instantly!

AT THE CROSS THE LAW OF GOD WAS SATISFIED IN EVERY RESPECT

The Law of God, and we speak of the moral Law, i.e., *"the Ten Commandments"* (Ex., Chpt. 20), presents God's Standard of Righteousness from which He cannot move. Unfortunately, due to the Fall, it was a Standard, as simple as it may have seemed to be, which man could not keep, no matter how hard he tried. In other words, not a single human being kept the Law of God, with one exception, and that Exception is Christ. In His earthly Life and Living, He kept the Law in every respect, not failing even one time in word, thought, or deed. The breaking of the Law was death, which meant separation from God, and actually, eternal separation. So, man was in a dilemma! There was no way within himself that he could extricate himself from this perilous situation. But Jesus did it for us and did it at the Cross. Concerning this, the Scripture says:

"And you, being dead in your sins and the uncircumcision of your flesh *(speaks of spiritual death, [i.e., 'separation from God'], which sin does!)*, has He quickened together with Him *(refers to being made Spiritually alive, which is done through being 'Born-Again')*, having forgiven you all trespasses *(the Cross made it possible for all manner of sins to be forgiven and taken away)*;

"Blotting out the handwriting of Ordinances that was against us *(pertains to the Law of Moses, which was God's Standard of Righteousness that man could not reach)*, which was contrary to us *(Law is against us simply because we are unable to keep its precepts no matter how hard we try)*, and took it out of the way *(refers to the penalty of the Law being removed)*, nailing it to His Cross *(the Law with its decrees was abolished in Christ's Death as if Crucified with Him)*" (Col. 2:13-14).

Paul also said:

A DISANNULLING OF
THE COMMANDMENT

"For there is verily a disannulling of the Commandment *(presents the end of the Law, which was all done by Christ, and was intended all the time)* going before for the weakness and unprofitableness thereof. *(This refers to the problems with the Old Law, and that it was of temporary character.)*

"For the Law *(Law of Moses)* made nothing perfect *(the Law was a mirror, which showed what man was, but had no power to change man)*, but the bringing in of a better hope *did (refers to Christ and what He did for us at the Cross)*; by the which we draw near

unto God. *(The Law of Moses could not open the door to the Holy of Holies for all of mankind, but the Cross did!)*" (Heb. 7:18-19).

And finally the Apostle said:

CHRIST IS THE END OF THE LAW

"For Christ is the end of the Law for Righteousness *(Christ fulfilled the totality of the Law)* to everyone who believes *(Faith in Christ guarantees the Righteousness, which the Law had but could not give)*" (Rom. 10:4).

While Jesus kept the Law perfectly in every respect in His Life and Living, still there remained the problem of the *"broken Law,"* which was incumbent upon every human being. To satisfy that terrible problem, a problem that man could not solve, Jesus went to the Cross, giving Himself as a Perfect Sacrifice, which satisfied the demands of a thrice-Holy God, and which totally addressed the broken Law. Simple Faith in Christ and what He did for us at the Cross satisfies the Law's demands upon us because Jesus has paid the price.

THE CROSS DEFEATED SATAN AND
ALL HIS MINIONS OF DARKNESS

Sin is that which gives the Evil One the legal right to hold man captive. With all sin removed, which it was at the Cross, Satan has lost his right to hold man captive. Concerning this, Paul said, "And having spoiled principalities and powers *(Satan and all of his henchmen were defeated at the Cross by Christ atoning for all sin; sin was the legal right Satan had to hold man in captivity; with all sin atoned, he has no more legal right to hold anyone in bondage)*, He *(Christ)* made a show of them openly *(what Jesus did at the Cross was in the face of the whole Universe)*, triumphing over them in it. *(The triumph is complete, and it was all done for us, meaning we can walk in power and perpetual Victory due to the Cross)*" (Col. 2:15).

WHY?

The question now begs to be asked, *"If Christ atoned for all sin at the Cross, which removed Satan's legal right to hold man in bondage, why is it that most of the world still is in bondage to Satan, even most of the church?"*

That is true!

However, it is true only in respect to the fact that men, whether unredeemed or redeemed, will not take advantage of what Christ has done for them. That being the case, as it mostly is, this gives Satan the legal right to continue, despite what Jesus did at the Cross.

The Work of the Cross is an effective Work only as long as human beings take advantage of what Jesus there did.

The world simply doesn't believe that what Jesus did at the Cross has any effectiveness to it. In fact, the Holy Spirit labeled the world as thinking of such as *"foolishness"* (I Cor. 1:23).

Christians do not have the benefit of what Jesus did at the Cross simply because of ignorance, unbelief, or a combination of both.

At the moment the sinner expresses Faith in Christ for Salvation, the bondage is broken.

It is the same with the Believer. But, unfortunately, most Believers try to live for God by means of the flesh, which causes untold problems.

Despite ignorance and unbelief, still, what Jesus did at the Cross defeated every single power of darkness for all time.

(15) "THOUGH YOU, ISRAEL, PLAY THE HARLOT, YET LET NOT JUDAH OFFEND; AND COME NOT YOU UNTO GILGAL, NEITHER GO YOU UP TO BETH-AVEN, NOR SWEAR, THE LORD LIVES.

(16) "FOR ISRAEL SLIDES BACK AS A BACKSLIDING HEIFER: NOW THE LORD WILL FEED THEM AS A LAMB IN A LARGE PLACE.

(17) "EPHRAIM IS JOINED TO IDOLS: LET HIM ALONE.

(18) "THEIR DRINK IS SOUR: THEY HAVE COMMITTED WHOREDOM CONTINUALLY: HER RULERS WITH SHAME DO LOVE, GIVE YOU.

(19) "THE WIND HAS BOUND HER UP IN HER WINGS, AND THEY SHALL BE ASHAMED BECAUSE OF THEIR SACRIFICES."

The pattern is:

1. The phrase from Verse 15, *"Though you, Israel, play the harlot, yet let not Judah*

offend," means that Israel had passed the point of no return. Judah is advised to not follow suit. *"Nor swear, The LORD lives,"* refers to idol worship, which associated God with idols.

2. Verse 16 could read, *"Israel is refractory as a refractory heifer,"* that is, one who throws the yoke off its neck.

3. (Vs. 16) *"Now the LORD will feed them as a lamb in a large place,"* means that He will scatter them in exile throughout the whole world of that day. They will resemble a lamb taken into a wilderness and left to range the wild and live at large, but without provision and without protection. Consequently, untended by the shepherd's watchful care, unguarded from ravening wolves or other beasts of prey, such a lamb is in a lost and perishing condition.

4. (Vs. 17) Ephraim, being the dominant Tribe, gave its name, along with Israel, to the northern kingdom. *"Joined to idols"* means that he is mated or united to his idols and will not get a divorce from them.

5. *"Let him alone,"* of Verse 17, refers to the Lord ceasing any and all effort to salvage the situation. Consequently, Jehovah says to the Prophet, *"Cease to reprove, for it is of no use."*

6. *"Committed whoredom continually,"* of Verse 18, shows that idolatry was the cause of their spiritual condition, which would result in their destruction.

7. (Vs. 18) *"Her rulers with shame do love, Give you,"* pertains to the leaders of the Nation, who were supposed to lead the people to Jehovah, but instead, led them toward idol worship, encouraging them in this direction, with the words, *"Give you,"* i.e., *"Give you devotion to idols!"*

8. *"The wind,"* of Verse 19, i.e., the spirit of idolatry (Vs. 12), carries its devotees into bondage, and the result of their sacrifices is that they are put to shame. As a result, the *"wind"* will become a strong storm of Divine Wrath, which will seize on Ephraim, wrapping her up with its wings, and will carry her away.

9. (Vs. 19) While the time would come that Israel would be *"ashamed because of these heathen sacrifices,"* still, it would be too late, for the Nation by then would have

been completely destroyed.

THE POINT OF NO RETURN

The terminology in these Verses is chilling, to say the least! Israel had gone so deep into idolatry, i.e., *"the worship of idols,"* that the Lord tells the Prophet Hosea that it is useless anymore in trying to reach them. All he can do is to send a warning message to Judah that they were not to follow suit. Regrettably and sadly, about 200 years later, Judah would follow suit and be effectively destroyed as a Nation.

ISRAEL COULD NOT DISTINGUISH JEHOVAH FROM IDOLS

The phrase of Verse 15, *"And come not you unto Gilgal,"* refers to the place where the school of the Prophets had been in the days of Elijah and Elisha. Incidentally, this was not the Gilgal between Jericho and the Jordan River, which was the encampment of Israel after they crossed over the Jordan and just before the capture of Jericho, but rather the Gilgal that was approximately 15 miles northwest of Jerusalem.

"Beth-aven" was actually *"Beth-el,"* where Jacob had had the Vision of the ladder and actually meant, *"House of God."* It was now a house of idols, for Jeroboam had set up the golden calf there. Satan had done his work well in taking that which had once been Holy and making it so very unholy.

The phrase, *"Nor swear, The LORD lives,"* refers to idol worshippers who associated God with idols. The association of idols with God is applauded by man even to this present day. This accusation by the Holy Spirit is serious indeed!

These people, who God had called *"My People"* in Verse 6, had, by now, become so spiritually disoriented that they did not know God from idols. I wonder today if it has changed any at all!

Many, if not most, modern Christians, do not know the false from the truth. They do not know the Anointing of the Holy Spirit from self-anointing. They do not know what is of God, and what is not of God because they do not know the Word of God. Consequently, like little children, they accept anything that shines or makes a noise.

BACKSLIDING ISRAEL

The phrase, *"Now the LORD will feed them as a lamb in a large place,"* means that He will scatter them in exile throughout the whole world of that day!

Carried into captivity, they may worship what they will and live as they like. In these circumstances, they will resemble a lamb taken away into a wilderness and left there to range the wild and live at large, but without provision and without protection. Consequently, untended by the shepherd's watchful care and unguarded from ravening wolves or other beasts of prey, such a lamb is in a lost and perishing condition. And thus was Israel!

LET HIM ALONE

The phrase, *"Let him alone,"* refers to the Lord ceasing any and all effort to salvage the situation. Consequently, Jehovah says to the Prophet, *"Cease to reprove him, for it is of no use."*

Left to his own recklessness, the northern kingdom of Israel is rushing toward ruin. Judah, the southern kingdom, is warned to stand aloof from the contagion, lest by interference he might get implicated in the sin and involved in the punishment.

To how many modern Christians has the Lord said the same, *"Let him alone!"*? Actually, how many entire religious denominations fall into the same category?

WHOREDOM CONTINUALLY

The phrase, *"Committed whoredom continually,"* shows that idolatry was the cause of their terrible spiritual condition, which would result in their destruction.

The phrase, *"Her rulers with shame do love, Give you,"* refers to the leaders of the Nation, who were leading the people to idol worship and not to God. The words *"Give you,"* encourage this direction of idolatry. They loved to give sacrifices to idols but had nothing but contempt for the sacrifices of Jehovah.

SHAME

Verse 19 teaches us that all sin, irrespective of who commits it, will ultimately bring shame. This is true whether in an individual, religious denomination, or the entirety of a nation.

"Righteousness exalts a nation: but sin is a reproach to any people" (Prov. 14:34).

"Alas! and did my Saviour bleed?
"And did my Sovereign die?
"Would He devote that Sacred Head,
"For such a worm as I?"

"Was it for crimes that I have done,
"He groaned upon the tree?
"Amazing pity! Grace unknown!
"And love beyond degree!"

"Well might the sun in darkness hide,
"And shut his glories in,
"When Christ, the mighty Maker, died,
"For man, the creature's sin."

"But drops of grief can ne'er repay,
"The debt of love I owe;
"Here, Lord, I give myself away,
"'Tis all that I can do."

CHAPTER 5

(1) "HEAR YOU THIS, O PRIESTS; AND HEARKEN, YOU HOUSE OF ISRAEL; AND GIVE YOU EAR, O HOUSE OF THE KING; FOR JUDGMENT IS TOWARD YOU, BECAUSE YOU HAVE BEEN A SNARE ON MIZPAH, AND A NET SPREAD UPON TABOR.

(2) "AND THE REVOLTERS ARE PROFOUND TO MAKE SLAUGHTER, THOUGH I HAVE BEEN A REBUKER OF THEM ALL.

(3) "I KNOW EPHRAIM, AND ISRAEL IS NOT HID FROM ME: FOR NOW, O EPHRAIM, YOU COMMIT WHOREDOM, AND ISRAEL IS DEFILED.

(4) "THEY WILL NOT FRAME THEIR DOINGS TO TURN UNTO THEIR GOD: FOR THE SPIRIT OF WHOREDOMS IS IN THE MIDST OF THEM, AND THEY HAVE NOT KNOWN THE LORD.

(5) "AND THE PRIDE OF ISRAEL DOES TESTIFY TO HIS FACE: THEREFORE SHALL ISRAEL AND EPHRAIM FALL IN THEIR INIQUITY; JUDAH ALSO SHALL FALL WITH THEM."

The pattern is:

NOTES

1. (Vs. 1) Neither the kings nor priests of the northern kingdom were legitimate, but they claimed to be kings and priests, and God met them on their own ground, and in Grace warned them of the Judgment about to fall upon them because of the idolatry established at Mizpah and Tabor.

2. (Vs. 1) Instead of being safeguards of the people, as they were supposed to be, these priests and kings of the northern kingdom had been a snare to them.

3. Verse 2 may be better translated, *"And the apostates are deeply resolved to slaughter victims in sacrifice, but I will be a rebuker of them all."* The idea of this Verse is that despite the *"rebukes"* of the Lord, which should have been a cause of warning, but which instead was ignored, they continued with this terrible sin of human sacrifice. God calls them *"revolters"*; to Him, they are *"revolting."*

4. (Vs. 3) *"Ephraim"* was the largest Tribe; consequently, the entirety of the northern kingdom went by that name. Similarly, Judah became the name of the southern kingdom because of it being the ruling Tribe.

"Ephraim," being the largest, led the other Tribes of the northern kingdom into idolatry and, hence, defiled the entirety of the Nation.

5. In these Prophecies, the term, *"to know the LORD,"* as used in Verse 4, means in Hebrew to know experientially rather than from a mere intellectual stance.

6. In Verse 4, the evil doings are traced to an *"evil spirit of whoredoms,"* i.e., of idolatries, which impels them blindly to not resist evil; and at the same time, it expels the Knowledge of God.

7. (Vs. 4) The phrase, *"And they have not known the LORD,"* means that this generation had not known Him at all. They were actually heathen at heart.

8. The phrase of Verse 5, *"And the pride of Israel does testify to His Face,"* means that this pride, as all pride, was in the very Face of God and, consequently, was an unending stench in His Nostrils. Now, Hosea mentions Judah, and in a negative sense.

JUDGMENT IS TOWARD YOU

The priests of the northern kingdom were

not in the Aaronic lineage and, therefore, were not recognized as true Priests of God. These were men chosen by men and, consequently, unacceptable. Only the Priests in the southern kingdom of Judah were recognized by God as legitimate, and this was because of their being in the Tribe of Levi. However, despite their lineage, even they would be rejected when they ceased following the Lord. This was evidenced in the destruction of the Temple and Jerusalem approximately 130 years after the fall of the northern kingdom, with the latter taking place some 70 years from the time of Hosea.

The phrase, *"O house of the king,"* was, as well, a king not recognized by the Lord because of not being in the lineage of David.

The Lord had told David and those who followed in his lineage that the sons of David would sit on the throne of Israel. Through this family, the family of David, the Messiah would ultimately come, which He did. In fact, Jesus was referred to as the *"Son of David."*

Unfortunately, after the death of Solomon, the kingdom was split, with some 10 of the Twelve Tribes forming a union, which they referred to as Israel, Samaria, or Ephraim. The remaining two Tribes, Benjamin and Judah, formed the southern kingdom, which continued with the Temple, the sacrifices, and the worship of Jehovah, at least after a fashion. So, for a king in Israel, using that name for both kingdoms, to be recognized by God, without fail, he had to be in the lineage of David. As stated, none in the northern kingdom were!

Concerning these *"false priests"* and *"false kings"* of the northern kingdom, the statement of the Lord was emphatic, *"for Judgment is toward you."* To be frank, that is a frightful place in which to be.

HOSEA THE PROPHET

Did this Word that came from the Lord to Hosea, a Word of Judgment, have any effect upon the leaders of Israel or its people?

Sadly and regrettably, no! Proverbially speaking, it went in one ear and out the other.

Why would they not hear and heed?

While we know Hosea to have been a Prophet Called of God, the people of Israel of his day simply did not believe such. They

didn't like what he had to say, and they didn't like the way he said it. To be sure, there was a bevy of false prophets in the land, who proclaimed smooth words, which the people of Israel and its leaders desired to hear.

THE MINISTRY OF THE PROPHET

The Ministry of the God-Called Prophet is basically twofold. It is as follows:

1. To foretell: we now speak of Prophecies regarding the future, which make up but a small percentage of the total Ministry of the Prophet.

2. To forthtell: this refers to the Prophet calling the people to Repentance exactly as Hosea was doing. While his great Prophecies were sprinkled with information about the future, mostly it pertained to the present. In other words, Hosea, as all true Prophets, was a Preacher of Righteousness.

True Prophets are seldom respected or appreciated. The reason is simple. The Message, which God desires them to deliver, is most of the time not in favor with the people. In other words, the people don't like what they are being told.

Concerning Israel, Jesus said shortly before His Crucifixion:

"O Jerusalem, Jerusalem (*presents Jesus standing in the Temple when He gave this sorrowing account*)**, you who kill the Prophets, and stone them who are sent unto you** (*presents the terrible animosity tendered toward these Messengers of God*)**, how often would I have gathered your children together, even as a hen gathers her chickens under *her* wings, and you would not!** (*Proclaims ever effort made by the Lord, and made 'often,' to bring Israel back to her senses.*)

"Behold, your house (*the Temple or Jerusalem, is no longer God's Habitation*) **is left unto you desolate** (*without God, which means they were at the mercy of Satan*)**.

"For I say unto you, You shall not see Me henceforth, till you shall say, Blessed *is* He Who comes in the Name of the Lord (*the Second Coming*)**" (Mat. 23:37-39).**

MURDER

It is believed that the Prophet Zechariah was the one Jesus spoke of in Matthew 23:35, who was murdered by the sons of Israel. If, in fact, that was the case, counting Christ, Israel murdered two of the last four Prophets sent to them.

Presently, America is filled with false prophets proclaiming all sorts of things, with none of it ever coming to pass, and with the people seemingly ignoring the false messages and hypocrisy. While there have always been false prophets and will continue to be false prophets, the truth is, there are precious few true Prophets, as there have always been precious few true Prophets. The true Prophet very seldom gains the plaudits of the people, but rather the very opposite. The people do not like to hear that *"Judgment is coming,"* but would rather hear words that are pleasing to the ears. As there was such a condition in Hosea's time, such is the condition presently as well!

A REBUKER OF THEM ALL

The word *"slaughter"* in Verse 2 has to do with the most horrible sin of human sacrifice. This is *"revolting"* in the Eyes of the Lord, as would be overly obvious.

To think that Israel would stoop so low that they would borrow from the surrounding heathen nations, thereby, instituting human sacrifice in their so-called worship is astounding to say the least! This is a sin that is so absolutely awful that it defies description. The following is the way that some of these sacrifices were carried out.

Virtually all of these human sacrifices were little children, involving ages of three or four and even younger. The idol being worshipped sat upright with protruding arms. A fire would be built in the belly of that thing, and the child would be tied to the arms, with the arms growing hotter and hotter until the child literally roasted to death.

Black robed priests would beat drums to drown out the screams of the child as it was dying. This was the Israel of God, and, regrettably, the southern kingdom of Judah would follow suit not too many years in the future.

ABORTION!

And yet, I ask the question, *"Is the hideous sin just mentioned any worse than*

modern abortions?"

I heard the testimony of a lady the other day who had previously worked for *"Planned Parenthood,"* which is anything but planned parenthood. When she saw a late term abortion and literally saw the baby on the scope fighting for its life, but to no avail, it so sickened her that she couldn't sleep. She then renounced her involvement in this gruesome crime, and a crime of murder it is.

She stated that the word *"baby"* is not allowed to be used in Planned Parenthood but only the word *"tissue,"* or something similar. However, I remind all and sundry, irrespective as to what man may call abortion, God calls it murder. To be sure, this nation is going to answer to God for this hideous crime.

First of all, at the moment of conception, in the Eyes of God, which had better be in our eyes, as well, that within the mother's womb is a child.

For long centuries no decent person, and certainly no respected Christian, has advocated killing an unborn baby. Like any other act of killing, it is murder. This is the law of civilized nations, or at least it was the law of civilized nations, and more importantly, it is the Law of God. But now, godless people are saying, *"Kill the baby. It will be good for the woman's mental health. She doesn't want the child."* She has become pregnant (much of the time) because of the sin of fornication and adultery. *"She doesn't want to feed, clothe, or rear the child."* She will then go to a doctor and pay him to kill the unwanted baby. And, somehow, greed will still the conscience.

ABORTION IS MURDER

All murder is wrong. In the Old Testament, even before the Law of God was incorporated, God said, *"Whoso sheds man's blood, by man shall his blood be shed: for in the Image of God made He man"* (Gen. 9:6). Under the Mosaic Law, God plainly commanded, *"He who smites a man, so that he die, shall be surely put to death"* (Ex. 21:12). The death penalty for cold-blooded murder is also clearly implied in the New Testament. Romans 13, Verses 1 through 7, states that the ruler of a nation is the minister of God, and he bears not the sword in vain. In the Book of Revelation, we are told that murderers are kept outside the heavenly Jerusalem (Rev. 21:8; 22:15).

To God, the killing of an unborn child is murder. The person guilty of that murder is subject to the same conviction and deserving of the same sentence (punishment) as the person who pulls the trigger of a gun used to kill another person.

Secondly, the unborn child is a human being—a person—and from the time of conception. Some have foolishly said that the unborn child is little more than a *"blob"* of flesh up to the sixth or seventh month. But, that is simply not true. The little unborn baby is not just a part of the woman's body. It is a separate life altogether. All of the child's particular traits have already been charted in its genes. The sex of the child, the color of the eyes and hair, the physical features, and the special talents and gifts are all determined at the time of conception. Both the mother and the father of the child have already, at this point, passed down to their baby every genetic characteristic they will contribute.

A LIVING SOUL

I believe the Bible also teaches that the fetus, from conception, is a person and, consequently, a living soul. David was inspired to say, *"Behold, I was shaped in iniquity; and in sin did my mother conceive me"* (Ps. 51:5). When David said, *"I was shaped,"* his honest inference was that from the very moment of conception, he was the person who would later be known as David, the great king of Israel.

Again, in Psalm 139, David was inspired to write, *"You have covered me in my mother's womb. I will praise You; for I am fearfully and wonderfully made."* From the moment of conception, and as the Holy Spirit gave the intent, David was, indeed, a person. It was David's body, his very substance, in the womb of his mother.

We have the same type of teaching concerning Jeremiah, where he said, *"Then the Word of the LORD came unto me, saying, Before I formed you in the belly I knew you; and before you came forth out of the*

womb I sanctified you, and I ordained you a Prophet unto the nations" (Jer. 1:4-5). God knew the Prophet Jeremiah before he was born. And if, by abortion, the fetus should have been murdered, it would have been Jeremiah who died. The mother would not have known his name, but God would have. And, the mother might not have known that this was to be a mighty Prophet of God, but God knew that, too.

I am saying that a fetus is a person, a living soul, from the time of conception.

A CHILD—BORN OR UNBORN

John the Baptist was filled with the Holy Spirit even from his mother's womb (Lk. 1:15). When Mary, the Mother of Jesus, came to greet Elisabeth, *"And it came to pass, that, when Elisabeth heard the salutation of Mary, the babe leaped in her womb"* (Lk. 1:41). The fetus of John the Baptist, in the womb of his mother, may not have understood clearly why he leaped at the sound of the voice of Mary (the Mother-to-be of the Saviour), but God knew.

It is interesting to note the words of Jesus in Mark 10:14, *". . . Suffer the little children to come unto Me, and forbid them not: for of such is the Kingdom of God."* He was speaking in reference to the infants brought to be blessed by Him. The term used for infants in the Greek is *"brephos;"* and *"Young's Analytical Concordance"* defines it as *"a child born or unborn."* Does that mean, then, that all the little ones who died before birth had an immortal soul (*"of such is the Kingdom of Heaven"*) and that they will meet us there? Well, that certainly seems to be what is implied in this Passage of Scripture.

PAIN AND GUILT

Thirdly, the pain of abortion is never quite erased from the mother's heart and mind. The psychic trauma and the sense of loss regarding personal mortality will persist throughout life. So, as a direct result of abortion, many times the woman will become troubled and consumed with guilt so that she develops significant psychiatric problems following. I believe it can be stated with certainty that abortion causes more deep-seated guilt, depression, and mental illness than it could ever cure. The woman will always wonder: what would the baby have looked like? Would it have had curly hair? What color would the hair have been? Would it have been a boy or a girl?

ONE SIN PLUS ONE SIN EQUALS TWO SINS

Fourthly, some have said that if the baby is illegitimate, then it should be aborted. Of course, the answer to that is you don't erase, correct, or even justify one sin by committing another. The only real answer to sin is Repentance and trusting the Saviour for forgiveness and for rearranging the soiled life. To compound sin upon sin is not the way to peace or mental health. Some say the end justifies the means: but, really, it never does.

Of course, some would ask the question, *"Would it not be proper to undergo an abortion in order to save the life or preserve the health of the mother?"* I suppose that in a few rare cases, probably not more than one in hundreds of thousands of cases, the doctor would have to choose between saving the life of the baby and saving the life of the mother. Actually, I've never known of such a case personally; of course, I'm confident they have existed. This so rarely happens, however, that it really is not worth the sake of argument.

IS ABORTION SCRIPTURALLY PERMISSIBLE REGARDING RAPE?

No!

We must understand that we are speaking of a human being in the womb of its mother even from the time of conception. It is not the child's fault, whatever the reason for conception. And even though rape is a horrible thing, as would be obvious, still, if a pregnancy should occur as a result of such, as it often has, killing the unborn baby is not going to make the situation right. In fact, the terrible trauma that the lady or the girl already is suffering will be increased by an abortion, not decreased.

My mind goes to Ethel Waters, who went on to be with the Lord not so long ago. She sang in many of the Billy Graham Crusades and blessed untold millions.

She came from a home of acute poverty, the eleventh of twelve children, if I remember correctly. I don't remember the circumstances of her birth, however, I do know that in today's moral climate, many would say that Ethel Waters, when conceived in her mother's womb, however it may have been brought about, should have been aborted. There were too many children in the family and considering that it was already poverty stricken, one more mouth to feed didn't help. But, thank the Lord, the little baby that would be named Ethel Waters was not aborted and grew up to bless millions of people. When we tamper with God's Creation Order, the results are catastrophic. No, while rape is a terrible thing for a woman to have to undergo, still, if pregnancy would be the result, such a child is to be loved and brought up in the fear of the Lord. If done so, that child can grow up and make an excellent contribution to society.

A MORAL QUESTION

The fact is, abortion is a sin. The killing of an unborn child is a terrible sin; actually, and, as stated, it is murder. It is a moral question. It is essentially the same thing as murdering the incompetent, the retarded, the handicapped, and the aged or senile.

If you're going to kill the unwanted, possibly there are many that are one-year olds, two-, five-, ten-, even fifty-year olds, who are unwanted. Why not just kill them, too? You see how horrendous this terrible crime becomes when carried to its ultimate conclusion. To slay the innocent because he cannot protest or swear out a warrant is a sin. The Scripture says, *". . . be sure your sin will find you out"* (Num. 32:23). There is a God Who cares for the weak, the unloved, and the unprotected. He will bring Judgment. Even though His Mills grind slowly, they will grind surely fine.

With the abortionists having gained the upper hand in this nation, where do we go from here? If you remember, Nazi Germany enacted a law permitting the elimination of *"useless"* members of society. Consequently, 18 million people were slaughtered (among them, 6 million Jews) because they represented a category that was considered useless.

We have the same pattern before us in America today in which a whole category of human beings—unborn babies, who cannot yet speak for themselves—are to be slaughtered at the whim of a mother or a doctor who decides that the mother is somehow unable or unwilling to have a baby.

Where do we go from here? What is the next class of humanity to be destroyed?

No, this is not of God. It is totally ungodly! It is a terrible case of man's inhumanity to man, and to make it worse, against the most helpless, the unborn baby. One day man will answer to God for the terrible stain upon this society, the terrible sin of abortion.

THE KNOWLEDGE OF GOD

The short phrase, *"I know Ephraim,"* given to us in the Third Verse, signals God knowing all the sins, such as the human sacrifices, that were committed by Ephraim and, hence, Israel, even though done in secret.

"Ephraim," being the largest of the Ten Tribes of the northern kingdom, led the other Tribes into idolatry and, thus, defiled the entirety of the Nation.

Men have ever attempted to hide their sins from God; however, they can only be truly hid in one place, and that's under the Blood of Christ. Otherwise, there is no hiding of anything from God.

As well, if the person, city, or nation refuses to avail themselves of the Precious Blood of Christ, sooner or later, their sin will find them out. Let no man think otherwise!

The short phrase, *"O Ephraim, you commit whoredoms, and Israel is defiled,"* is said, instead, with a sob by the Holy Spirit.

THE CLEANSING OF SIN

As we have just stated, the only thing that can cleanse sin to where there's not even a stain left is the Precious Blood of Christ. Peter said:

"Forasmuch as you know that you were not redeemed with corruptible things, as silver and gold . . . but with the Precious Blood of Christ, as of a Lamb without blemish and without spot" (I Pet. 1:18-19).

Sin carries with it the terrible attachment of death. *"The wages of sin is death"* (Rom. 6:23). Sin kills everything it touches.

NOTES

At this moment, it is killing untold thousands of marriages, untold thousands of lives, and untold thousands of ambitions and dreams that will never materialize simply because sin has brought death into those ambitions. And it is a death that keeps on dying. In other words, it can only be stopped by the Precious Blood of the Lord Jesus Christ, better known as the *"Born-Again experience"* (Jn. 3:3).

Tragically and sadly, churches are being filled today with people who have never really been Born-Again. They are religious but lost! In truth, unless the preacher preaches the Gospel, which is *"Jesus Christ and Him Crucified,"* there will be no Born-Again experiences. This means the guilt remains, and the terrible stain on the conscience remains because all that man does to address this situation can have no effect on it at all except the preaching of the True Gospel of Jesus Christ. If we fail to preach the Cross, people will not be Saved. If we fail to preach the Cross to Christians, Christians will not be victorious. That's why Paul said, *"We preach Christ Crucified"* (I Cor. 1:23).

TO KNOW THE LORD

The phrase, *"They will not . . ."* actually means that they *"cannot frame their doings to turn unto their God,"* at least within themselves. This is the power of darkness at its highest. Such shows the absolute helplessness of man to throw off, within himself, such a force. This is actually true of any bondage.

THE CROSS OF CHRIST

Sin, as we have stated, is a powerful force. It places individuals in a bondage from which they cannot extricate themselves. There is only one answer for this problem, and I mean only one. That is *"the Cross of the Lord Jesus Christ."*

A major part of the Victory of the Cross was for this very purpose, to break the stranglehold, the bondage of sin. The Scripture says, and I quote from THE EXPOSITOR'S STUDY BIBLE, Text and notes:

*"**And** having spoiled principalities and powers (Satan and all of his henchmen were defeated at the Cross by Christ Atoning for all sin; sin was the legal right Satan had to*

hold man in captivity; with all sin atoned, he has no more legal right to hold anyone in bondage), **He** *(Christ)* **made a show of them openly** *(what Jesus did at the Cross was in the face of the whole Universe),* **triumphing over them in it.** *(The triumph is complete and it was all done for us, meaning we can walk in power and perpetual Victory due to the Cross)"* **(Col. 2:15).**

WHY IS THE CROSS REJECTED IN THE MAJORITY OF THE CHURCH WORLD?

Most would not agree that they have rejected the Cross, but the truth is, most have. Let me explain.

A great part of the modern church definitely places their Faith and trust in the Cross of Christ as it regards Salvation, and rightly so. However, when it comes to Sanctification, in other words, how we presently live for God on a daily basis, they have no knowledge of that. And when that knowledge does come, most of the time, as stated, it is rejected simply because the Cross of Christ totally impacts all the religious devices of religious men. And what do we mean by that?

When we say that the Cross of Christ alone is the answer for the sin problem, we are speaking of Christians as well as the unsaved. This comes up against all the schemes, stratagems, and efforts by religious men to overcome this problem. They are not happy to be told that all of these stratagems are useless! Let me give you an example.

Sometime ago, Donnie was in an airport, waiting to catch a flight. He happened to look at the newsstand in the section where books were offered for sale. One was by a particular preacher. Actually, I'm not acquainted with the dear brother, and I do not mean at all to impugn his motivation. I'm sure he loves the Lord and is trying to help people. However, what he is suggesting will not help them whatsoever, at least to be the overcomer that they must be.

He was telling them that to overcome sin, they should fast twenty-one days, or some such number. Now, while fasting is most definitely Scriptural and will most definitely bless one, still, if fasting were the answer

to the sin problem, then Jesus died in vain. Paul plainly told us:

"*. . . If Righteousness come by the Law, then Christ is dead in vain*" **(Gal. 2:21).**

THE APOSTLE PAUL

In fact, Paul had this same problem in the Early Church. The Lord gave to him the meaning of the New Covenant, which is the meaning of the Cross of Christ (Gal. 1:1-12). This meant then the same as it does now, that the Cross of Christ is the answer, and the only answer.

Then Paul's problems were with the Judaizers. These were Jews from Judea who claimed that Christ was the Messiah and the Saviour, but, in order to be Saved, or at least to be a complete Believer, the Gentile men had to be circumcised. In answer to this, the great Apostle said:

"**. . . I Paul say unto you** *(presents the Apostle's authority regarding the Message he brings),* **that if you be circumcised, Christ shall profit you nothing.** *(If the Believer goes back into law, and law of any kind, what Christ did at the Cross on our behalf will profit us nothing. One cannot have it two ways.)*"

THE WHOLE LAW

"**For I testify again to every man who is circumcised** *(some of the Galatian Gentiles were being pressured by false teachers to embrace the Law of Moses, which meant they would have to forsake Christ and the Cross, for it's not possible to wed the two; as well, it's not possible to wed any law to Grace),* **that he is a debtor to do the whole Law** *(which, of course, is impossible; and besides, the Law contained no Salvation).*"

FALLEN FROM GRACE

"**Christ is become of no effect unto you** *(this is a chilling statement, and refers to anyone who makes anything other than Christ and the Cross the object of his faith),* **whosoever of you are justified by the Law** *(seek to be justified by the Law);* **you are fallen from Grace** *(fallen from the position of Grace, which means the Believer is trusting in something other than the Cross; it actually means, 'to apostatize')*" **(Gal. 5:2-4).**

BUT FASTING IS NOT LAW!

No, it isn't. However, anytime we place something in the position to where we are trusting in that something, whatever it might be, we turn it into law even though it's not a law within itself. This includes fasting. In fact, the biggest problem in the modern church is our turning that which is legitimate in its own right into a law.

When we do that, that's the same thing the Judaizers were doing in the Early Church, and that which caused the Work of God tremendous problems. Please understand the following.

The Faith of the Believer must be exclusively in Christ and the Cross, and we mean Christ and the Cross for everything. We must not try to manufacture another sacrifice. Let's say it in this manner:

Every single thing we receive from the Lord, and I mean every single thing, is given to us by the Means of what our Lord did at the Cross of Calvary. And, of course, I'm sure you understand that we aren't speaking of the wooden beam, but rather that which He there did.

SELF-RIGHTEOUSNESS

Anytime something other than the Cross of Christ is placed in the position of being the answer to man's dilemma, such will always, and without fail, produce self-righteousness in the heart and life of the Believer. And, to be sure, the modern church is eaten up with self-righteousness. I remind the reader that this is not a light thing. It was self-righteousness that nailed Christ to the Cross. The unredeemed have ever been trying to manufacture another god, while those who refer to themselves as Believers are trying to manufacture another sacrifice. God help us!

I have been in the Ministry over a half century. During that time, I have seen every type of scheme and stratagem that man can devise, proposing to be the solution, the answer to our dilemma. I watched Christians line up for hands to be laid on them for demons to be cast out of them, which was supposed to solve their problem. While most definitely demons are always

involved where there is sin, still, that was not the solution. Believers cannot be demon possessed. Oppressed, yes! Possessed, no! But yet, preachers were insisting that this was the solution. It wasn't! As stated, such only breeds self-righteousness. When these preachers are told that what they're doing is not Scriptural, just as the Judaizers, they are not too very happy. Self-righteousness never likes to be exposed! And to be sure, the Cross of Christ exposes this evil as nothing else!

THE STATE OF THE HEART

The actions of Israel at that time were an index of the state of the heart, and neither the thoughts of Israel nor their deeds, which indicated these thoughts, were in the direction of Repentance. In heart and life they were impenitent. Despite its evil results, they truly and sincerely wanted the sin in which they were mired, as do most!

The phrase of Verse 4, *"And they have not known the LORD,"* means that this generation had not known Him at all. They were actually heathen at heart.

THE PRIDE OF ISRAEL

The phrase from Verse 5, *"And the pride of Israel does testify to His Face,"* addresses their problem. It is pride!

At that time, Israel was prosperous and rich. As well, they attributed their prosperity to their own ability. They gave God no glory.

The phrase, *"And the pride of Israel does testify to His Face,"* means that this pride, as all pride, was in the very Face of God and, consequently, was an unending stench in His Nostrils.

The command is here given, *"Therefore shall Israel and Ephraim fall in their iniquity."* The Divine testimony saves or destroys as it is accepted or rejected.

Profuse profession of Repentance is only pride in the absence of contrition of heart and meets with no response from God.

The spirit of idolatry moves and energizes idolaters as the Spirit of God Moves and energizes Believers.

(6) "THEY SHALL GO WITH THEIR FLOCKS AND WITH THEIR HERDS TO SEEK THE LORD; BUT THEY SHALL NOT

FIND HIM; HE HAS WITHDRAWN HIM-
SELF FROM THEM.

(7) "THEY HAVE DEALT TREACHER-
OUSLY AGAINST THE LORD: FOR THEY
HAVE BEGOTTEN STRANGE CHILDREN:
NOW SHALL A MONTH DEVOUR THEM
WITH THEIR PORTIONS.

(8) "BLOW YOU THE CORNET IN GI-
BEAH, AND THE TRUMPET IN RAMAH:
CRY ALOUD AT BETH-AVEN, AFTER YOU,
O BENJAMIN.

(9) "EPHRAIM SHALL BE DESOLATE
IN THE DAY OF REBUKE: AMONG THE
TRIBES OF ISRAEL HAVE I MADE KNOWN
THAT WHICH SHALL SURELY BE.

(10) "THE PRINCES OF JUDAH WERE
LIKE THEM WHO REMOVE THE BOUND:
THEREFORE I WILL POUR OUT MY
WRATH UPON THEM LIKE WATER."

The pattern is:

1. The idea of Verse 6 is that in the not-
too-distant future, Israel would see the
calamity of Assyria coming upon them and
would then try to bargain with God, but
too late.

2. (Vs. 6) The *"flocks"* and *"herds"* speak
of sacrifice, but not with sincerity.

3. (Vs. 6) *"But they shall not find Him"*
refers to Ephraim seeking after the Lord in
all the wrong ways, as many do presently.

4. (Vs. 6) *"He has withdrawn Himself
from them"* proclaims such being done simply because the Lord had no other choice.
He could not tolerate a *"marriage of convenience,"* so to speak!

5. Verse 7 says, *"They have dealt treacherously against the LORD,"* and presents the
reason their sacrifices were not accepted.
"For they have begotten strange children"
refers to those who were not really serving
God, but rather bound to their idols.

The phrase, *"Now shall a month devour
them with their portions,"* probably refers to
Shallum reigning for only a month (II Ki.
15:13). The *"portions"* refer to idols (Deut.
32:9; Isa. 57:6).

6. The areas listed in Verse 8 seem to be
the line of march of the Assyrians coming
into the northern kingdom. Even though it
would be some 50 to 60 years into the future,
still, the Holy Spirit outlines it as if it has
already happened. The Tribe of *"Benjamin"*

NOTES

is mentioned because these areas were near
Israel's borders; consequently, they would
be affected by this excursion.

7. The first phrase of Verse 9 refers to
Ephraim's present prosperity but that which
shall surely end. *"Among the Tribes of Israel
have I made known that which shall surely
be"* proclaims the fact that the Lord was
constantly warning Israel before Judgment
came, so they were without excuse.

8. The *"Princes of Judah"* of Verse 10,
like those of Israel, removed *"the bound,"*
i.e., *"broke away from the Bible"* (Deut.
19:14; 27:17), just as the professing churches do today.

9. The pronoun *"them"* of Verse 10 actually refers to both Ephraim and Judah.
Ahaz, the king of Judah, set aside the Bible
and the Altar (II Ki. 16:10-18). To forsake
the Bible is to ultimately incur the Wrath of
God, whether then or now!

TOO LATE TO SEEK THE LORD?

Israel would see the calamity of Assyria
coming upon them and, therefore, would
offer sacrifices to God in hopes of escaping
the invader. However, to that moment, their
hearts really had not changed from idol worship. Therefore, the Holy Spirit says, *"But
they shall not find Him."* Meeting with constant rejection, He *"had withdrawn Himself
from them."*

The reason is given in the next Verse.

The Lord has never turned down sincere heartfelt Repentance, and He never
will (I Jn. 1:9)! However, He will never tolerate or involve Himself in a *"marriage of
convenience."*

Tragically, every Sunday morning, millions of individuals, calling themselves
"Christian," flock to churches, thinking by
their mere presence or the taking of the
Lord's Supper atones for the previous week
of sinning. They have no intention of having their lives changed. They full well plan
to continue their present course of action
and do so immediately upon leaving the
church. There is no Salvation in such, even
though millions participate each and every
week. God's Ways are not for sale or bargain. He does not *"cut deals"* or *"compromise His Word."*

STRANGE CHILDREN

The reason their sacrifices were not accepted, as per Verse 7, is because of their *"treachery."*

As the illegitimate children of a treacherous wife are *"strange"* to her husband, so are apostates *"strange"* to God.

Who were these *"strange children"*?

These *"strange children"* were supposed to be people of God. They had been recipients of the great Law of Moses, which was by far the fairest law on the face of the Earth. In fact, they were supposed to be a light to the darkness of the world. Actually, Israel had once been the only monotheistic people on the face of the Earth, meaning they worshipped one God, Jehovah. All the other nations of the world worshipped many gods, actually, demon spirits. So, Israel was to be a light in the darkness.

But tragically, Israel lost her way and, instead of light, became darkness. In essence, this is what Jesus was talking about when he said, **"But if your eye be evil, your whole body shall be full of darkness** *(if the spirit be evil, the entirety of the soul will be full of darkness)*. **If therefore the light that is in you be darkness** *(the light is not acted upon, but rather perverted)*, **how great *is* that darkness** *(the latter state is worse than if there had been no light at all)*" **(Mat. 6:23).**

The idea is, the darkness is worse where there has once been light.

Israel had come to the place that she was in worse spiritual condition even than the surrounding heathenistic nations. Therefore, they were *"strange children."*

Many years before, the Lord had given Moses a Message to give to the Children of Israel, which was shortly before they went into the Promised Land. The Message pulled no punches. It said:

THE LAW OF GOD

"If you will not observe to do all the words of this Law that are written in this Book, that you may fear this glorious and fearful name, THE LORD YOUR GOD *(this speaks of the entirety of the Book of the Law)*;

"Then the LORD will make your plagues wonderful, and the plagues of your seed, even great plagues, and of long continuance, and sore sicknesses, and of long continuance.

"Moreover He will bring upon you all the diseases of Egypt, which you were afraid of; and they shall cleave unto you.

"Also every sickness, and every plague, which is not written in the Book of this Law, them will the LORD bring upon you, until you be destroyed *(we learn from this, as should be obvious, that God controls all sickness and disease; He may use Satan as His Instrument to bring about such, but, still, it is the Lord Who is always in control)*."

DISOBEDIENCE

"And you shall be left few in number, whereas you were as the stars of heaven for multitude; because you would not obey the Voice of the LORD your God *(once again, disobedience of the Word of the Lord is the cause)*.

"And it shall come to pass, that as the LORD rejoiced over you to do you good, and to multiply you; so the LORD will rejoice over you to destroy you, and to bring you to naught; and you shall be plucked from off the land where you go to possess it *(the Lord rejoices in doing good for those who obey Him, and continues to rejoice over bringing evil on those who disobey Him; the idea is, the Lord rejoices in stamping out evil, even if such evil is found in His chosen People)*."

THE SCATTERING

"And the LORD shall scatter you among all people, from the one end of the Earth even unto the other; and there you shall serve other gods, which neither you nor your fathers have known, even wood and stone *(in other words, if they wouldn't serve God, then they would have to serve idols)*.

"And among these nations shall you find no ease, neither shall the sole of your foot have rest: but the LORD shall give you there a trembling heart, and failing of eyes, and sorrow of mind" (Deut. 28:58-65).

So, they had been warned, not once, but many times. And some 70 years from that time, the northern kingdom of Israel would be destroyed by the Assyrians exactly as the Lord said!

It was an adulterous generation. Israel's

infidelity to the Holy Covenant had as its result a graceless, godless race—children strange and superstitious in the spiritual sense.

PROSPERITY?

The phrase of Verse 9, *"Ephraim shall be desolate in the day of rebuke,"* refers to her present prosperity, but which shall surely end.

Some people consider prosperity a guarantee of the Blessings of God, which it certainly can be, but not necessarily so! Consequently, the modern church falls into this trap. It thinks that money, buildings, place and position in the community, worldly acclaim, or bigness equates with godliness. In the final analysis, those things have absolutely nothing to do with godliness.

Nearness to Christ, and nearness to Christ alone, which can only be brought about by an understanding of the Cross of Christ, equates to godliness.

Strangely enough, nearness to Christ is exampled by the Publican, who *". . . would not lift up so much as his eyes unto Heaven, but smote upon his breast, saying, God be merciful to me a sinner"* (Lk. 18:13).

Jesus said, *"I tell you, this man went down to his house justified rather than the other . . ."* (Lk. 18:14). The *"other"* was the Pharisee.

Israel is without excuse, even as the statement says, *"Among the Tribes of Israel have I made known that which shall surely be."* Therefore, they were without excuse!

REMOVING THE BOUND

The princes of Judah, like those of Israel, removed *"the bound,"* i.e., broke away from the Bible (Deut. 19:14; 27:17), just as many professing churches do presently.

The pronoun *"them"* of Verse 10 actually refers to both Ephraim and Judah. Ahaz set aside the Bible and the Altar (II Ki. 16:10-18).

Now, Judah, as Ephraim, is being warned even though Judgment on the southern kingdom would not come for nearly 200 years.

The literal meaning of *"removing the bound"* had to do with moving a landmark that separated properties. Such was looked at as a great sin. Even though it applied

literally to the nobles of Judah, as they oppressed the poor and helpless, even more so, the Holy Spirit is using the terminology to describe the spiritual boundaries drawn by the Word of God.

In effect, the leaders of Judah were substituting their word for God's Word. This sin that was rampant then is rampant now!

THE WRATH OF GOD

The word *"Wrath"* in Verse 10, as it applies to God, means *"to overflow."* It is thus the overflowing of Divine indignation, which will overwhelm these lawless leaders of a misguided and misgoverned people.

From the first page of human history, the only thing that has ever stood between mankind and eternal Hell is the Cross of Christ.

THE CROSS OF CHRIST

This is why the Sacrificial system was instituted at the very dawn of time, in fact, immediately after the Fall of Adam and Eve in the Garden of Eden. The only way that God could have any type of communion with our first parents was by and through the slain lamb, which would serve as a substitute until the Redeemer would come, the Lord Jesus Christ. The Sacrificial system was in vogue for some 4,000 years unto Christ. In fact, the Sacrificial system was at the very heart of the Mosaic Law. Actually, had it not been for this system, Israel would have been destroyed. The reason is simple; they could not keep the Law. So, their only recourse was the Sacrificial system, i.e., *"the Cross of Christ."*

Even in a bolder way at present, the Cross of Christ is so synonymous with Christianity that, in fact, the word *"Cross"* is actually used as a synonym for the Gospel. But, regrettably and sadly, most of the modern church is turning away from the Cross of Christ and resorting to other things. There could be nothing worse than that! Such a direction is the sure road to disaster!

And then, even with the part of the church who still believes in the Cross as it regards Salvation, knowledge concerning the Cross of Christ and Sanctification is, for all practical purposes, nonexistent. In its place, every scheme and stratagem that one can think is being offered up to the Christian public as a solution to victory over the world, the flesh, and the Devil. Please read the following very carefully.

SELF-RIGHTEOUSNESS

Any way or means proposing Salvation or victory outside of the Cross can only lead to self-righteousness. In fact, the only cure for self-righteousness is the Cross of Christ. Please note the following:

FOCUS: The Lord Jesus Christ (Jn. 14:6).

OBJECT OF FAITH: The Cross of Christ (Rom. 6:3-5; I Cor. 1:17-18, 23).

POWER SOURCE: The Holy Spirit (Rom. 8:1-2, 11).

RESULTS: Victory (Rom. 6:14).

Now, the above formula, in brief, is God's Prescribed Order of Victory. In fact, in essence, it is the meaning of the New Covenant.

Now let's look at the same formula but applied to the way it is commonly used.

Focus: Works.

Object of Faith: One's performance.

Power Source: Self.

Results: Defeat!

The first formula is God's Way, while the second formula is man's way.

You have a choice. What will you choose?

(11) "EPHRAIM IS OPPRESSED AND BROKEN IN JUDGMENT, BECAUSE HE WILLINGLY WALKED AFTER THE COMMANDMENT.

(12) "THEREFORE WILL I BE UNTO EPHRAIM AS A MOTH, AND TO THE HOUSE OF JUDAH AS ROTTENNESS.

(13) "WHEN EPHRAIM SAW HIS SICKNESS, AND JUDAH SAW HIS WOUND, THEN WENT EPHRAIM TO THE ASSYRIAN, AND SENT TO KING JAREB: YET COULD HE NOT HEAL YOU, NOR CURE YOU OF YOUR WOUND.

(14) "FOR I WILL BE UNTO EPHRAIM AS A LION, AND AS A YOUNG LION TO THE HOUSE OF JUDAH: I, EVEN I, WILL TEAR AND GO AWAY; I WILL TAKE AWAY, AND NONE SHALL RESCUE HIM.

(15) "I WILL GO AND RETURN TO MY PLACE, TILL THEY ACKNOWLEDGE THEIR OFFENCE, AND SEEK MY FACE: IN THEIR AFFLICTION THEY WILL SEEK

NOTES

ME EARLY."

The construction is:

1. (Vs. 11) Ephraim walked after the commandment of men rather than after the Commandment of the Lord.

2. We find from Verse 12, if the Ways of the Lord are followed, it means blessing; however, if the Ways of the Lord are rejected, it means Judgment.

3. (Vs. 13) The word *"Judah"* should be supplied before *"sent to king Jareb."* Jareb was king of Assyria and his name numerically spells *"666."*

4. Concerning Verse 13, Calvin says, *"Here God declares that whatever the Israelites might seek would be in vain. 'You think,' He says, 'that you can escape My Hand by these remedies; but your folly will at length betray itself, for he will avail you nothing; that is, King Jareb will not heal you.'"*

5. Verse 14 tells us that if no Repentance is forthcoming, which it was not, then the pressure would become fierce, as it did!

6. The phrase of Verse 15, *"I will go and return to My Place,"* refers to the Lord having carried out His Purpose and Design. He now withdraws His Presence and Spirit from the offending people.

7. (Vs. 15) The phrase, *"In their affliction they will seek Me early,"* refers to the fact of chastisement but does not guarantee Repentance. However, if Repentance is forthcoming, it will be because of *"affliction."*

THE COMMANDMENT OF MEN

As we said above, the phrase, *"Because he willingly walked after the commandment,"* should have been translated, *"because he willingly walked after the commandment of men."*

This is the great problem of the human race and, in fact, is the great problem of the church as well. It has before us the following:

- The Commandment of God and
- The commandment of men.

The pressure always is that the Commandment of God be ignored and, in its place, the commandment of men. In fact, this is even more of a problem with the church than it is with the world. The world doesn't know any better, and we speak of the unredeemed. So, they are going to automatically resort to the commandment of men. The church, however, is supposed to know better. But instead, religious men are ever seeking to replace the *"Commandment of God"* with the commandment of men. In regard to this, Jesus said:

VAIN WORSHIP

"Howbeit in vain *(means empty nothings, no profit)* do they worship Me, teaching *for* doctrines the commandments of men *(the State [Herod] put to death the Preacher of Righteousness [Mat. 14:10], and the church [the Scribes], corrupted the Word of Righteousness)*.

"For laying aside the Commandment of God, you hold the tradition of men, as the washing of pots and cups: and many other such like things you do *(said with sarcasm; they washed cups and pots but not their hearts; the ceremonial washing of their hands could not remove the guilt that stained them)*.

"And He said unto them, Full well you reject the Commandment of God, that you may keep your own tradition *(it was a studied and deliberate rejection)*" (Mk. 7:7-9).

So, this problem has been with us a long, long time!

THE FOUNDATION OF THE CROSS

Every Biblical doctrine, irrespective as to what it might be, must be built squarely on the Foundation of the Cross of Christ or else it will be spurious. This means that every false doctrine in the world today is because of a misunderstanding of the Cross of Christ, a misinterpretation of the Cross of Christ, an ignoring of the Cross, or an outright denial of the Cross.

We know this because the Cross of Christ was the very first Doctrine formulated in the mind of the Godhead, and done so even before the foundation of the world. Concerning this, Peter said:

THE PRECIOUS BLOOD OF CHRIST

"Forasmuch as you know that you were not redeemed with corruptible things, *as* silver and gold *(presents the fact that the most precious commodities [silver and gold] could not redeem fallen man)*, from your

vain conversation *(vain lifestyle)* received by tradition from your fathers *(speaks of original sin that is passed on from father to child at conception)*;

"But with the Precious Blood of Christ *(presents the payment, which proclaims the poured out Life of Christ on behalf of sinners)*, as of a Lamb without blemish and without spot *(speaks of the lambs offered as substitutes in the old Jewish economy; the Death of Christ was not an execution or assassination, but rather a Sacrifice; the Offering of Himself presented a Perfect Sacrifice, for He was Perfect in every respect [Ex. 12:5])*."

BEFORE THE FOUNDATION OF THE WORLD

"Who verily was foreordained before the foundation of the world *(refers to the fact that God, in His Omniscience, knew He would create man, man would fall, and man would be redeemed by Christ going to the Cross; this was all done before the Universe was created; this means the Cross of Christ is the Foundation Doctrine of all doctrine, referring to the fact that all doctrine must be built upon that Foundation, or else it is specious)*, but was manifest in these last times for you *(refers to the invisible God Who, in the Person of the Son, was made visible to human eyesight by assuming a human body and human limitations)*" (I Pet. 1:18-20).

THE HELPLESSNESS OF MAN

Bluntly and plainly, the Holy Spirit through the Prophet Hosea tells both Ephraim and Judah that man was not the solution to their problem. The Holy Spirit bluntly said, *". . . yet could he not heal you, nor cure you of your wound."* It is the same presently!

HUMANISTIC PSYCHOLOGY

Does psychotherapy hold the answer to man's problems?

In a word, no! Psychotherapy has no answers whatsoever concerning the problems that beset humanity.

Regrettably, almost all of today's church world has fallen for the lure of psychotherapy.

Psychotherapy (the psychological way) is rapidly replacing the Word of God (the Biblical Way). Additionally, the whole Christian ministry is being, to a great extent, subverted by this *"false religion"*—and a religion it is.

The phrase, *"professional help,"* has replaced much of the terminology that comes from a Biblical stance. The church world, which definitely includes the Pentecostal and Charismatic segments, is presently much more at home with psychological jargon than it is with the Word of God. Sadly, most of the sermons that are preached from most pulpits are more psychology than they are the Word of God. Most Christian books sold in Christian bookstores promote far more the *"religion of psychology"* than they do the Word of God. Many religious radio and television programs contain little, if any, Gospel at all. It is almost all psychology.

One Preacher told me, after he had taken a trip by car of more than a thousand miles, *"I listened to religious radio almost all the way. I heard many good things, but not much Gospel."*

That's the problem with our pulpits today. Many good things are said, but precious little of it is the Gospel: that is, *"Jesus Christ and Him Crucified."*

PSYCHOTHERAPY

Most of today's Bible Colleges and Seminaries afford at least some basic introduction to psychology for their would-be preachers of the Gospel. Thus, a foundation is laid for a subtle inflection away from the Bible and toward psychotherapy.

For the most part, the psychology courses offered to most of our future Preachers only touch on the rudiments of their association with the treatment of souls. However, the stage is set for a familiarity with (and affection for) things other than the Word of God.

I suspect that Preachers who earnestly desire to be of help to people are particularly vulnerable during these formative years. Lacking in experience and self-confidence, they are delighted to discover something that is boldly placarded as a certifiable tool in delivering such help. *"Christian psychology"*

supposedly offers an organized system for carrying out this weighted task, and formative minds are soon addicted to a method that seems to offer *"a whole new way."*

Bible Colleges and Seminaries of most denominations and fellowships now offer these courses, thereby, affording them a great legitimacy.

BIBLE KNOWLEDGE?

It is even suggested today that if a person has only Bible Knowledge, he is ill-equipped to handle the pressing needs of humanity. He must (along with a smattering of Bible training) be grounded in psychology to meet *"human needs."* This is implanted early, with the unspoken implication that the Bible in itself is insufficient to solve human problems.

It is constantly being suggested that ministers are ill-prepared and ill-equipped to meet the needs of modern man. If the preacher is to be truly effective and proficient in his role (it is said), he should be referring a large percentage of those who seek his help to *"professionals"* instead.

PROFESSIONALS?

"Professionals" and *"therapy"* used in this context mean, of course, psychologists and psychotherapy.

Psychotherapy has become widely accepted as *"scientific"*; therefore, it is assumed that it must be a useful tool. As a consequence, it has become accepted within most of the church world.

Most Pentecostal Bible Colleges and Seminaries now promote psychotherapy as a legitimate tool for meeting *"the human need."* As a result, most of our younger preachers are now convinced that psychotherapy is *"spiritually neutral."* Thus, it is considered a legitimate tool to be used with a clear conscience when trying to help humanity.

The old-fashioned, tried and true Word of Almighty God is given lesser place (if any place at all) when considering methods of solving man's problems.

WHAT IS PSYCHOTHERAPY?

The primary Greek word *"psycho"* is the root from which we derive the English terms *"psychology"* and *"psychologist."* Interestingly, the word *"psycho"* is utilized in the New Testament for *"soul."* Hence, a psychologist is a *"worker with souls."*

A specific distinction should be made, however. The secular psychotherapist considers himself a worker with *"minds,"* while the so-called *"Christian psychologist"* considers himself a worker with *"souls."*

Proponents of psychotherapy call it scientific and camouflage its discrepancies with scientific jargon and medical argot. However, the questions must be asked: *Is psychotherapy science or superstition? Is it fact or fabrication?*

These questions must be asked because we have come to venerate almost anything labeled as *"science."* If, indeed, psychology and psychotherapy are scientific, they should command our respect and should be used within every community. However, if they are not, we have valid grounds for questioning the propriety of intruding them into the preacher's methodology.

In Martin and Deidre Bobgan's book, *"The Psychological Way/The Spiritual Way,"* they state:

"In attempting to evaluate the status of psychology, the American Psychological Association appointed Sigmund Koch to plan and direct a study which was subsidized by the National Science Foundation. This study involved 80 imminent scholars in assessing the facts, theories, and methods of psychology. The results of this extensive endeavor were then published in a seven-volume series entitled 'Psychology: a Study of Science.'

"Koch then concludes,

"'I think it is by this time utterly and finally clear that psychology cannot be a coherent science.'

"He further declares that such activities as perception, motivation, social psychology, psychopathology, and creativity cannot be properly labeled 'science.'"

E. FULLER TORREY

E. Fuller Torrey, in *"The Death of Psychiatry,"* says:

"The medical model of human behavior, when carried to its logical conclusions

is both nonsensical and nonfunctional. It doesn't answer the questions which are asked of it, it doesn't provide good service, and it leads to extreme absurdities worthy of a Roman circus."

In a study (done some time ago) comparing modern day psychology with witchcraft, the results came out a dead heat. The only discernable difference was that the witch doctors charge less and kept their patients a shorter period of time.

"For My People have committed two evils; they have forsaken Me the Fountain of Living Waters, and hewed them out cisterns, broken cisterns, that can hold no water" (Jer. 2:13).

WILLIAM KIRK KILPATRICK

In his book, *"Psychological Seduction,"* William Kirk Kilpatrick had this to say:

"True Christianity does not mix well with psychology. When you try to mix them, you end up with a watered-down Christianity, instead of a Christianized psychology. But the process is subtle and is rarely noticed . . . it was not a frontal attack on Christianity . . . it was not a case of the wolf at the door: the wolf was already in the fold, dressed in sheep's clothing and from the way it was petted and fed by some of the shepherds, one would think it was the prize sheep."

JACOB NEEDLEMAN

Jacob Needleman, writing in *"Consciousness, Brain, States of Awareness, and Mysticism,"* says:

"Modern psychiatry arose out of the vision that man must change himself, and not depend on help on an imaginary God. Over a century ago, mainly through the insights of Freud, and through the energies of those he influenced, the human psyche was wrested from the faltering hands of organized religion and was situated in the world of nature as a subject of scientific study."

MARTIN GROSS

Martin Gross, in his book, *"The Psychological Society,"* says:

"When educated man lost faith in formal religion he required a substitute belief that would be as reputable in the last half of the

Twentieth Century as Christianity was in the first. Psychology and Psychiatry have now assumed that special role."[1]

THE ROOTS

Modern day psychotherapy has its roots in atheism, evolution, and humanism. Psychology pretends to have a cure for troubled souls. It is taught in atheistic universities, oftentimes by atheistic professors. And this same subject, with the same foundations and influences, is accepted today as an integral part of the Christian curriculum in most Bible Colleges and Seminaries.

There aren't too kinds of psychotherapy; there is only one. And as Paul Vitz says, *"It is deeply anti-Christian."*

Someone once said, *"America's problem is not ignorance; America's problem is that she accepts a lie."*

Psychotherapy is not scientific; it is not even an *"art"* as claimed. It is a lie, purely and simply, and has no basis in scientific or Biblical fact. When Bible Colleges offer it, they are offering a bold fabrication. When Seminaries teach it, they are teaching a lie. When would-be preachers immerse themselves in it, they immerse themselves in falsehood. When individuals accept a doctorate in this nefarious shamanism, they are receiving a certificate without scientific validity.

I say that preachers of the Gospel, attempting to meld psychotherapy with the Word of God, will help no one. They will deliver only confusion. There may be a temporary illusion of help, but that only leads people away from the true help that is available through the Word of God.

The two are as immiscible and as antagonistic as oil and water.

THE DIFFERENCES THAT CANNOT BE BRIDGED

• The Bible is the Word of God (Jn. 1:1). The *"bible"* for psychology is man's opinion, which changes almost on a daily basis.

• The Bible holds all answers relative to human behavior (II Pet. 1:3). Psychology claims to hold all answers relative to human behavior, and its supposed answers are totally contrary to the Word of God. So, both cannot be right.

• The Bible says man is an eternal soul (Jn. 3:16). Psychology has its roots in evolution.

• The Bible says man is a sinner (Rom. 3:23). Psychology says man is a victim.

• The Bible says the problem is man's evil heart (Jer. 17:9). Psychology says man's problem is his environment.

• The Bible says man is inherently evil (Jer. 17:9). Psychology says man is inherently good.

• The Bible treats the core of man's problem, which is an evil heart (Jer. 17:14). Psychology treats only man's symptoms.

• The Bible says that Jesus Christ is the answer (Mat. 11:28-30). Psychology says psychotherapy is the answer.

• The Bible says that we should deny self (Mat. 16:24). Psychology says we should love self.

• The Bible directs us to the Spirit of God (Zech. 4:6). Psychology directs us to the flesh.

• The Bible says the Cross of Christ is the answer (Rom. 6:3-5). Psychology says that the psychologist is the answer.

• The Bible directs us to Faith in God (Mk. 11:22). Psychology directs us to self-effort.

• The Bible directs us to Repentance (Acts 26:20). Psychology directs us to remorse.

• The Bible directs us to restoration (Gal. 6:1). Psychology directs us to rehabilitation.

• The Bible directs us to truth (Jn. 17:17). Psychology directs us to man's opinions.

• The Bible directs us to relationship with Christ (Jn. 3:16). Psychology directs us to idolatry.

• The Bible directs us to personal responsibility (Rev. 22:17). Psychology directs us to irresponsibility.

• The Bible directs us to free will (Rev. 22:17). Psychology directs us to determinism (causes other than oneself).

• The Bible deals with a *"cure of souls"* (Mat. 11:28-30). Psychology deals with a *"cure of minds."*

• The Bible says God's Truth is unchangeable (Ps. 119:89). Psychology says truth is determined by majority and culture.

• The Bible says it is sufficient (II Pet. 1:3).

Psychology says the Bible is insufficient.

• The Bible leads to love for God and man (Mat. 22:37-39). Psychology leads to love for self.

HUMANISM

Psychology is actually the religion of humanism. Humanism puts man in the center of all things; hence, psychology puts man in the center of all things. Conversely, the Bible puts Christ in the center as the only answer for man. Psychology (psychotherapy) and the Bible, therefore, are total opposites and cannot be reconciled.

THE TREE

If one goes back to the true roots of psychotherapy, one has to go back to the *"Tree of the Knowledge of Good and Evil."*

"But of the Tree of the Knowledge of Good and Evil, you shall not eat of it: for in the day that you eat thereof you shall surely die" (Gen. 2:17).

The *"evil"* part of this *"Tree of the Knowledge of Good and Evil"* is readily obvious to all of the world, even as it enslaves billions. However, the *"good"* part of the *"Tree of the Knowledge of Good and Evil"* is not so readily obvious. And, because it is *"good,"* at least to the natural mind, it is readily accepted. Yet, its enslavement is just as deadly, or even more so than the *"evil"* side of the Tree. The *"good"* part of this Tree comes under the heading of *"the pride of life"* and, as such, it camouflages its evil, which is even more insidious than its opposite (which is openly evil).

Psychotherapy comes from the *"good"* side of the *"Tree of the Knowledge of Good and Evil."* And just as the *"good side"* snared Eve (Gen. 3:6), so has this *"good side"* snared most of the billions who have lived since Eve. Psychotherapy is just one of the products of this *"good"* side of the *"Tree of the Knowledge of Good and Evil."*

CHRISTIAN PSYCHOLOGISTS?

The term *"Christian psychologists"* is a misleading term causing unsuspecting seekers of help to think that such individuals have a body of learning that is not available to secular psychologists—or to Preachers of the Gospel, for that matter.

There is no such thing as *"Christian psychology"* or *"Christian truck driving"* or *"Christian airplane piloting."*

There are psychologists who are Christians, and truck drivers who are Christians, and airplane pilots who are Christians. But there definitely is not any type of training for Christians who wish to be pilots other than the same type of training for non-Christians who wish to be pilots.

Likewise, there is no training or education that *"Christian psychologists"* receive that is any different from secular psychologists. The education that is given to a Christian who aspires to be a psychologist is the same education that is given to the individual who has no regard for Christianity whatsoever.

The term *"Christian psychologist"* subtly leads the seeker of help to believe that the practitioner has a body of knowledge that is not given in the Word of God. In other words, there is an implication that the Word of God does not hold the answer to the problems that beset modern man.

One so-called Christian Psychologist said:

"It is not a question of whether therapists rely upon the Holy Spirit or upon their counseling skills."

In other words, they are saying that it doesn't really matter where the help originates, whether it is from the Holy Spirit or from psychology. They then conclude that we *"must equip ourselves with the best tools available."*

A TOOL?

Is psychology a tool? When it was suggested that modern day psychology is not found in the Bible, one preacher stated that neither is the automobile, the airplane, or the computer. We do not, he reasoned, resist utilization of these tools in our lives, so why should we resist the tool of psychology (or any other self-help method or technique we might develop)?

My answer is, admittedly, the Bible has nothing to say about the automobile, computer, or a host of other crafts developed since it was written. The Bible does not claim to be a handbook on engineering, science, etc.

NOTES

Although, whatever it does say on these subjects is one hundred percent accurate. These extraneous subjects are not man's problems. A man can be an expert scientist, a qualified engineer, or a host of other things—and still be a moral and spiritual wreck. However, the Bible does claim to be a handbook on the *"human condition,"* and it does claim to hold all the answers in this particular human area.

THE WORD OF GOD

"According as His Divine Power has given unto us all things that pertain unto life and godliness, through the knowledge of Him Who has called us to Glory and Virtue:

"Whereby are given unto us exceeding great and Precious Promises: that by these you might be partakers of the Divine Nature, having escaped the corruption that is in the world through lust" (II Pet. 1:3-4).

Now, either the Bible did give us all things that pertain unto life or it didn't. If it didn't, it is a lie, and we then need to turn to other sources.

If there is such a thing as *"Christian psychology,"* I suppose then we could have *"Christian medicine"* or *"Christian physics."* Of course, such things don't exist in real-life terms.

Medicine is the same for the Christian as for the non-Christian. Chemistry is the same for the Christian as for the non-Christian. However, our Christian educators have taken an ungodly, atheistic, anti-Christian, unbiblical, worldly system and attempted to integrate it into Biblical counseling. And the church has bought it hook, line, and sinker.

IS THE PREACHER OF THE GOSPEL JESUS CHRIST QUALIFIED?

If the Preacher properly understands the Word of God, he not only is qualified but, in fact, is the only one in the world who is qualified to deal with the human problem.

The following, in very abbreviated from, is that which the Preacher of the Gospel must know and understand as it regards the human problem.

THE HOLY SPIRIT

The first thing the Preacher of the Gospel

NOTES

must know and understand, which actually applies to all Believers, is that the Holy Spirit Alone can make of us what we ought to be. Due to the Fall, man, even believing man, is incapable within himself of overcoming the powers of darkness. And the Believer must understand, what we are facing in the spirit world is beyond our capabilities. I speak of demon spirits, fallen Angels, and Satan himself. Paul said:

"For we wrestle not against flesh and blood (*our foes are not human; however, Satan constantly uses human beings to carry out his dirty work*)**, but against principalities** (*rulers or beings of the highest rank and order in Satan's kingdom*)**, against powers** (*the rank immediately below the 'Principalities'*)**, against the rulers of the darkness of this world** (*those who carry out the instructions of the 'Powers'*)**, against spiritual wickedness in high *places*.** (*This refers to demon spirits*)**"** (Eph. 6:12).

Considering what we are facing in the spirit world, and even with a modicum of understanding, it is easy to see that humanistic psychology holds no power against the spirit world of darkness. While all aberrations, perversions, and moral failings aren't caused by evil spirits, sooner or later, to be sure, evil spirits will become involved. These things respond only to the Power of God.

So, the Believer is to understand that the Holy Spirit, Who is God, Alone can overcome these things that are arrayed against us.

The following will relate to us as to how we can have the Holy Spirit to work mightily within our lives, making us what we ought to be.

THE LORD JESUS CHRIST

Every Believer must understand that our Lord is the Source of all things that we receive from God. Jesus plainly said:

". . . I am the Way, the Truth, and the Life (*proclaims in no uncertain terms exactly Who and What Jesus is*)**: no man comes unto the Father, but by Me** (*He declares positively that this idea of God as Father, this approach to God for every man, is through Him – through what He is and what He has done*)**"** (Jn. 14:6).

THE CROSS OF CHRIST

While the Lord Jesus Christ is the Source of all things that we receive from God, the Cross of Christ is the Means by which all of this is done. In fact, this is the story of the entirety of the Bible, *"Jesus Christ and Him Crucified"* (Jn. 1:1-3, 14, 29). When one properly understands the Cross of Christ, then one properly understands the Bible.

Paul told us in the first two Verses of the Sixth Chapter of Romans that sin is the problem. He then gave us the answer to that problem, which is the Cross of Christ. He said:

"Know you not, that so many of us as were baptized into Jesus Christ *(plainly says that this Baptism is into Christ and not water [I Cor. 1:17; 12:13; Gal. 3:27; Eph. 4:5; Col. 2:11-13])* **were baptized into His Death?** *(When Christ died on the Cross, in the Mind of God, we died with Him; in other words, He became our Substitute, and our identification with Him in His Death gives us all the benefits for which He died; the idea is that He did it all for us!)"*

NEWNESS OF LIFE

"Therefore we are buried with Him by baptism into death *(not only did we die with Him, but we were buried with Him as well, which means that all the sin and transgression of the past were buried; when they put Him in the Tomb, they put all of our sins into that Tomb as well)***: that like as Christ was raised up from the dead by the Glory of the Father, even so we also should walk in Newness of Life** *(we died with Him, we were buried with Him, and His Resurrection was our Resurrection to a 'Newness of Life')."*

THE LIKENESS OF HIS DEATH

"For if we have been planted together *(with Christ)* **in the likeness of His Death** *(Paul proclaims the Cross as the instrument through which all Blessings come; consequently, the Cross must ever be the Object of our Faith, which gives the Holy Spirit latitude to work within our lives)***, we shall be also** *in the likeness* **of** *His* **Resurrection** *(we can have the 'likeness of His Resurrection,' i.e., 'live this Resurrection Life,' only as long*

as we understand the 'likeness of His Death,' which refers to the Cross as the Means by which all of this is done)" **(Rom. 6:3-5).**

Once again, let us emphatically state that it is the Cross of Christ, which is the Means by which everything is given to us from the Lord.

THE CROSS OF CHRIST, THE OBJECT OF OUR FAITH

We must understand that the Cross of Christ is the Means of all things we receive from the Lord. In other words, it is the Cross that has made it all possible, and we speak of what Jesus there did. This means that the Cross of Christ must be, and without fail, the Object of our Faith, and the only Object of our Faith. Millions have Faith, but it's in the wrong object. Unequivocally, the Cross of Christ must be the Object of our Faith, and nothing else (I Cor. 1:17-18, 21, 23; 2:2; Gal., Chpt. 5; 6:14; Eph. 2:13-18; Col. 2:14-15).

Concerning the Cross, Jesus said:

". . . If any *man* **will come after Me** *(the criteria for Discipleship)***, let him deny himself** *(not asceticism as many think, but rather that one denies one's own willpower, self-will, strength, and ability, depending totally on Christ)***, and take up his cross** *(the benefits of the Cross, looking exclusively to what Jesus did there to meet our every need)* **daily** *(this is so important, our looking to the Cross; we must renew our Faith in what Christ has done for us, even on a daily basis, for Satan will ever try to move us away from the Cross as the Object of our Faith, which always spells disaster)***, and follow Me** *(Christ can be followed only by the Believer looking to the Cross, understanding what it accomplished, and by that means alone)"* **(Lk. 9:23).**

CANNOT BE MY DISCIPLE

Our Lord then said, **"And whosoever does not bear his Cross** *(this doesn't speak of suffering as most think, but rather ever making the Cross of Christ the Object of our Faith; we are Saved and we are victorious not by suffering, although that sometimes will happen, or any other similar things, but rather by our Faith, but always with* the Cross of Christ as the Object of that Faith), **and come after Me** (one can follow Christ only by Faith in what He has done for us at the Cross; He recognizes nothing else), **cannot be My Disciple** (the statement is emphatic! if it's not Faith in the Cross of Christ, then it's faith that God will not recognize, which means that such people are refused)" **(Lk. 14:27).**

HOW THE HOLY SPIRIT WORKS

Understanding that our Lord is the Source of all things good, that the Cross of Christ is the Means by which these things are given to us, and that the Cross of Christ must be the Object of our Faith, and that exclusively, then the Holy Spirit will begin to work mightily on our behalf.

The Holy Spirit works exclusively within the parameters, so to speak, of the Finished Work of Christ. In other words, it's the Cross of Christ that gives the Holy Spirit the legal means to do all that He does with us, for us, of us, by us, and in us.

Concerning the way and manner in which the Holy Spirit Works, the Apostle Paul said:

"**There is** **therefore now no condemnation** (guilt) **to them who are in Christ Jesus** (refers back to Rom. 6:3-5 and our being baptized into His Death, which speaks of the Crucifixion), **who walk not after the flesh** (depending on one's personal strength and ability or great religious efforts in order to overcome sin), **but after the Spirit** (the Holy Spirit works exclusively within the legal confines of the Finished Work of Christ; our Faith in that Finished Work, i.e., 'the Cross,' guarantees the help of the Holy Spirit, which guarantees victory)."

VICTORY IN JESUS

"**For the Law** (that which we are about to give is a Law of God, devised by the Godhead in eternity past [I Pet. 1:18-20]; this Law, in fact, is 'God's Prescribed Order of Victory') **of the Spirit** (Holy Spirit, i.e., 'the way the Spirit works') **of Life** (all life comes from Christ, but through the Holy Spirit [Jn. 16:13-14]) **in Christ Jesus** (anytime Paul uses this term or one of its derivatives, he is, without fail, referring to what

Christ did at the Cross, which makes this 'life' possible) **has made me free** (given me total victory) **from the Law of Sin and Death** (these are the two most powerful Laws in the Universe; the 'Law of the Spirit of Life in Christ Jesus' alone is stronger than the 'Law of Sin and Death'; this means that if the Believer attempts to live for God by any manner other than Faith in Christ and the Cross, he is doomed to failure)" **(Rom. 8:1-2).**

GOD'S PRESCRIBED ORDER OF VICTORY

What we have given you is God's Prescribed Order of Victory. That Prescribed Order is the Cross of Christ.

We must understand that Jesus defeated every enemy at the Cross (Col. 2:14-15). Our Faith anchored accordingly, as stated, gives the Holy Spirit latitude to Work within our lives and to make us what we ought to be, which He Alone can do!

EPHRAIM AND JUDAH

Due to the sin of both *"Ephraim"* and *"Judah,"* both kingdoms became conscious of their disease and decline. Ephraim felt its sickness or internal consumption, while Judah felt its wound or external corruption. They were both conscious of rottenness in their condition.

However, their diseased condition was spiritual rather than political, even though this was connected as cause and effect.

Instead of these nations applying to Jehovah for help, as the Lord intended, they applied to outside sources, namely Assyria or Egypt.

Their appeal was in vain, for no earthly power could avert the Divine Judgments.

One scholar translated Verse 13 accordingly:

"When Ephraim and Judah saw that the enemies were constantly invading and plundering them, they seek help from the king of Assyria; but turn not back to Me, nor seek help from Me, but from flesh and blood, which, however, cannot help them when it is not My Pleasure."

Calvin said, "Here God declares that whatever the Israelites might seek would be in vain. 'You think' He says, 'that you can escape My Hand by these remedies; but your folly will at length betray itself, for he will avail you nothing; that is, King Jareb will not heal you.'"[2]

ALMIGHTY GOD

The last sentence of Verse 14 should read, *"I will carry off, and none shall rescue."*

Verse 13 proclaims Israel's judgments as slow and silent but with a steady erosion that affected all parts of life and liberty. But now it will be public and obvious to the eyes of all, as well as decisive and powerful, as intimated by the comparison of a *"lion"* and a *"young lion."*

The lion was an apt example because, before removing the prey, he would tear it in pieces and then carry it away.

Likewise, the northern kingdom was first rent and broken by Shalmaneser, with the population finally carried into captivity. In like manner, about 130 years later, the southern kingdom experienced the same at the hands of Nebuchadnezzar.

One should well notice the manner of the Working of the Lord. First, the pressure was applied. It was not destructive, yet, it was debilitating. It was designed to bring Israel and, later, Judah to Repentance.

If no Repentance was forthcoming, which it wasn't, then the pressure would become fierce, as it did!

The phrase, *"I will take away, and none shall rescue him,"* renders mighty empires helpless in the Face of the Almighty. What God sets out to do, He does, with none able to stop or hinder. However, Israel and then Judah would try mightily to solicit the help of other nations, all to no avail!

"My soul in sad exile was out on life's
  sea,
"So burdened with sin and distress,
"Till I heard a Sweet Voice saying,
  'Make Me your choice,'
"And I entered the Haven of Rest."

"I yielded myself to His Tender
  Embrace,
"And, Faith taking hold of the Word,
"My fetters fell off, and I anchored my
  soul:
"The Haven of Rest is my Lord."

"The song of my soul, since the Lord
  made me whole,
"Has been the old story so blest,
"Of Jesus, Who'll save whosoever will,
"Have a home in the Haven of Rest."

"Oh, come to the Saviour, He patiently
  waits,
"To save by His Power Divine;
"Come, anchor your soul in the Haven
  of Rest,
"And say, 'My Beloved is mine.'"

CHAPTER 6

(1) "COME, AND LET US RETURN UNTO THE LORD: FOR HE HAS TORN, AND HE WILL HEAL US; HE HAS SMITTEN, AND HE WILL BIND US UP.

(2) "AFTER TWO DAYS WILL HE REVIVE US: IN THE THIRD DAY HE WILL RAISE US UP, AND WE SHALL LIVE IN HIS SIGHT.

(3) "THEN SHALL WE KNOW, IF WE FOLLOW ON TO KNOW THE LORD: HIS GOING FORTH IS PREPARED AS THE MORNING; AND HE SHALL COME UNTO US AS THE RAIN, AS THE LATTER AND FORMER RAIN UNTO THE EARTH."

The exposition is:

1. Verse 1 speaks of Israel in the last half of the Great Tribulation, under great persecution, finally turning back to the Lord. And how do we know that? We know it because Israel as a Nation has never come to the Lord in the fashion represented here, but which they will do immediately before and after the Second Coming (Zech. 13:1).

2. Verse 2 could very well apply prophetically to the period of Israel's subjection, affliction, and Restoration. Her subjection has lasted now nearly 2,000 years (two days), and her Millennial Reign will last for 1,000 years (the third day).

3. (Vs. 2) The word *"day"* normally refers to a 24-hour period of time. However, it can be, and often is, used figuratively for a specified or unspecified period of time.

4. (Vs. 2) *"In the third day He will raise us up"* refers to the Second Coming of

Christ when He will deliver Israel from the Antichrist.

5. The phrase, *"His going forth is prepared as the morning,"* from Verse 3, signals that His Second Coming is fixed as surely as the morning is eternally fixed to come at a certain time daily.

6. (Vs. 3) The *"latter and former rain"* actually refer to two outpourings of the Spirit, the *"former"* pertaining to the Early Church, with the *"latter"* pertaining to the present time, stretching into the Millennium (Acts 2:17-21). The *"latter"* is mentioned here before the *"former"* because Christ was rejected at His First Advent but will be accepted by Israel at the Second Advent.

REPENTANCE

Verse 1 pertains to a repentant Israel. This will be during the time of the Battle of Armageddon when it looks like all is lost and, in fact, Satan has won. The great Prophet Zechariah said, in essence, that the Antichrist has taken all of Israel, with even half of Jerusalem having fallen, and with the other half seemingly to fall at any moment. The Prophet said:

THE BATTLE OF ARMAGEDDON

"Behold, the Day of the LORD comes, and your spoil shall be divided in the midst of you. *('Behold, the Day of the LORD comes' presents this day as beginning with the Second Coming and lasting until the end of the Millennium. At that time, the end of the Millennium, the 'Day of God' begins and will continue through eternity [I Cor. 15:24-28; Eph. 1:10; II Pet. 3:10-13].*

"'And your spoil shall be divided in the midst of you' concerns the Antichrist coming against Israel [Ezek. 38:11-12].)"

HALF OF JERUSALEM HAS FALLEN

"For I will gather all nations against Jerusalem to battle; and the city shall be taken, and the houses rifled, and the women ravished; and half of the city shall go forth into captivity, and the residue of the people shall not be cut off from the city. *(The first phrase refers to the mobilization of the nations to Armageddon [Ezek., Chpts. 38-39; Joel, Chpt. 3; Rev. 16:13-16; 19:11-21].*

"'And the city shall be taken' actually means that the Antichrist will prepare to take Jerusalem, with actually half of it being taken. The phrase, 'And the houses rifled, and the women ravished,' expresses extreme cruelty practiced by the army of the Antichrist.

"'And half of the city shall go forth into captivity' means that half of Jerusalem will fall to the advances of the Antichrist, with the other half fighting furiously to save themselves, but with futility, other than the Coming of the Lord. Actually, the phrasing of the sentence structure portrays Israel fighting with a ferocity that knows no bounds, but yet, not able to stand against the powerful onslaught of the combined armies of the man of sin.

"'And the residue of the people shall not be cut off from the city' refers to the army of Israel already cut to pieces but determined to defend the city, even house to house, and, if necessary, to die to the last man)" **(Zech. 14:1-2).**

Then Israel will begin to cry to God in true Biblical Repentance. The great Prophet Isaiah told us basically the prayer that they will pray at that time.

THE PRAYER OF REPENTANCE

In that hour, Israel will cry:

"But we are all as an unclean thing, and all our righteousnesses are as filthy rags; and we all do fade as a leaf; and our iniquities, like the wind, have taken us away. *(Here Israel confesses the reason for their desperate condition. At long last, they own up as to exactly what it is, 'our iniquities.'*

"'But we are all as an unclean thing' is actually saying before God that they are spiritual lepers. They now recognize that their self-righteousness is no more than 'filthy rags,' which refers to the menstrual flux of a woman regarding her monthly period.

"It is very difficult for men, and especially religious men, to admit to such! Hence, not many religious men are Saved!)"

OUR INIQUITIES

"And there is none who calls upon Your Name, who stirs up himself to take hold of You: for You have hid Your Face from us,

and have consumed us, because of our iniquities. *(Once again, Israel admits that it is her 'iniquities' which have brought about the Judgment of God upon her. She has only herself to blame!)*"

THE POTTER AND THE CLAY

"But now, O LORD, You are our Father; we are the clay, and You our Potter; and we all are the Work of Your Hand. *(In this Passage is the gist of the great Salvation Message of Christianity. Only God can change the shape of the clay, thereby, molding the vessel into the shape and design that is desired, thereby, mending the flaws and weaknesses.)*"

WE BESEECH YOU

"Be not wroth very sore, O LORD, neither remember iniquity forever: behold, see, we beseech You, we are all Your People. *(The appeal here is for God to begin all over again, like the potter with the clay. The idea of the phrase, 'Be not wroth very sore,' refers to the fact that God had become very angry with His People. The reason for that anger was sin on the part of Israel. God cannot abide sin in the lives of His Own People any more than He can in the wicked.)*"

JERUSALEM IS A DESOLATION

"Your holy cities are a wilderness, Zion is a wilderness, Jerusalem a desolation. *(As we have stated, the entirety of this prayer of Repentance, which began in the Fifteenth Verse of the previous Chapter, will be prayed by Israel at the end of the Great Tribulation – at the Second Advent of Christ.)*"

OUR TEMPLE IS DESTROYED

"Our Holy and our beautiful House, where our fathers praised You, is burned up with fire: and all our pleasant things are laid waste. *(This speaks of the Temple that is yet to be built in Jerusalem. In fact, when the Antichrist turns on Israel, he will make their Temple his religious headquarters, committing every act of vileness that one could think.)*"

O LORD, WILL YOU HOLD YOUR PEACE?

"Will You refrain Yourself for these

things, O LORD? will You hold Your Peace, and afflict us very sore? *(Israel first repents of her terrible sins, pleading God's Mercy, Grace, and Love. They then bring to His Attention the terrible plight of the 'holy cities' and of 'Jerusalem.' Last of all, they proclaim to Him the destruction of the Temple.*

"They then ask, 'Will You refrain Yourself for these things, O LORD?'

"The answer is certain. He will not refrain Himself! He will not hold His Peace!)" (Isa. 64:6-12).

THE LORD WILL HEAR AND ANSWER THEIR PRAYER

Israel's prayer of Repentance will trigger the Second Coming, in fact, the most cataclysmic moment in human history. Actually, by television, there is a possibility that most of the entire world will observe the Lord Jesus Christ coming in the clouds of Glory, accompanied by a Host of Angels and every Born-Again Believer who has ever lived. In fact, the Scripture tells us exactly how He will come. It says:

"Then shall the LORD go forth, and fight against those nations, as when He fought in the day of battle. *('Then' is the key word!*

"1. 'Then': when Israel will begin to cry to God for deliverance, knowing that He is their only hope.

"2. 'Then': when half of Jerusalem has fallen, and it looks like the other half is about to fall.

"3. 'Then': when it looks like every Jew will be annihilated, with two-thirds already killed.

"4. 'Then': when it looks like the Promises of God made to the Patriarchs and Prophets of old will fall down.

"5. 'Then': when it looks like the Antichrist will win this conflict, which will make Satan the lord of the Earth

"'Then shall the LORD go forth' refers to the Second Coming, which will be the most cataclysmic event that the world has ever known. 'And fight against those nations' pertains to the nations under the banner of the Antichrist, which have set out to destroy Israel, and actually with annihilation in mind.

"'As when He fought in the day of battle'

probably refers to the time when the Lord led the Children of Israel out of Egypt by way of the Red Sea [Ex. 14:14; 15:3]. This was Israel's first battle when Jehovah Messiah 'went forth' and fought for them. Israel then passed through a valley between mountains of water; in this, their last battle, they will escape through a valley between mountains of rock, which the next Verse proclaims)" **(Zech. 14:3).**

When the Lord comes back, He will most definitely *"heal"* Israel. He will most definitely *"bind us up."*

THE CAUSE OF ISRAEL'S PLIGHT

The Prophet Hosea said, *"After two days will He revive us."* In effect, this speaks of the 2,000 years from the time of the Crucifixion of Christ to the time of the Second Coming. This does not mean 2,000 years to the day but, actually, in that vicinity, so to speak. Peter said, *"That one day is with the Lord as a thousand years, and a thousand years as one day"* (II Pet. 3:8).

If the calendar is correct going back to the time of Christ, counting the Day of Pentecost as the beginning of the Church Age, the Church is now (2009) 1976 years old. As stated, whether the numbers regarding the calendar are absolutely correct or not, we have no way of knowing. However, one thing we do know, whatever the correct number is, we are very close to the end of the Church Age. Please note the following:

At 2,000 and 1,000 year intervals, or rather near that number, something tremendously important has happened in the realm of the Work of God.

• From Adam and Eve to the time of Abraham was a time frame of approximately 2,000 years. This was a milestone in the progressive Work of God. At that time, the Lord gave the meaning of *"Justification by Faith"* to the great Patriarch.

• From the time of Abraham to the time of David was a period of approximately 1,000 years. This is so important simply because the Lord chose David to be in the direct lineage of the Lord Jesus Christ. Hence, our Lord was referred to at times as the *"Son of David."*

• From David to the time of Christ was another approximate 1,000 years. The First

Advent of Christ was of staggering significance in that Christ came to give Himself as a Sacrifice on the Cross so that fallen man could be Saved. The Cross of Christ is, without a doubt, the most remarkable happening in the annals of human history.

• From the time of Christ to this present hour has been, as stated, nearly 2,000 years. So, if the Lord holds true to form, and, to be sure, He most definitely will, we are nearing, as stated, the end of the Church Age. The end of this Age will see the rise of the man of sin, the Antichrist, the Great Tribulation, the Battle of Armageddon, and most important of all, the Second Coming of the Lord when Israel will then accept the Lord as Saviour, Messiah and Lord. Then He will truly *"revive Israel."*

THE KINGDOM AGE

The phrase, *"In the third day He will raise us up, and we shall live in His Sight,"* refers to the coming Kingdom Age, which will last for 1,000 years. Counting the 2,000 years from the time of Christ until the conclusion of the Kingdom Age is 3,000 years, i.e., *"three days."*

The word *"day"* normally refers to a 24-hour period of time; however, it can be, and often is, used figuratively for a specified or unspecified period of time.

In fact, during the 1,000-year Kingdom Age when Jesus will rule Personally from Jerusalem and, in fact, be the President of the entirety of the world and, as the Bible describes Him, *"King of kings and Lord of lords,"* then Israel will be the Priestly Nation of the world. This is described to us in the last nine Chapters of Ezekiel.

TO KNOW THE LORD

The Prophet Hosea said, *"Then shall we know, if we follow on to know the LORD,"* meaning to know Him experimentally and not merely in an intellectual sense. This pertains to the day that Israel will truly know the Lord, which is yet future.

The phrase, *"His going forth is prepared as the morning,"* signals that His Coming is fixed as to a certain time as surely as the morning is eternally fixed regarding the 24-hour day (Gen. 1:14-19; 8:22).

THE LATTER AND THE FORMER RAIN

The Prophet Joel mentioned this first. He said:

"**Be glad then, you children of Zion, and rejoice in the LORD your God: for He has given you the former rain moderately, and He will cause to come down for you the rain, the former rain, and the latter rain in the first month**" (Joel 2:23).

Concerning this Passage, the notes from THE EXPOSITOR'S STUDY BIBLE say:

"*The phrase, 'Be glad then, you children of Zion,' refers to Israel now restored as the premier Nation of the world, which is her rightful place. In other words, the world cannot be properly blessed until Israel is in her rightful place, which she will be not long after the Second Coming.*"

THE TWO RAINY SEASONS IN ISRAEL

"*The 'former rain' and the 'latter rain' refer to the two rainy seasons in Israel. The first, or 'former,' coming in October, promoted the germination and growth of the seed previously sown; the 'latter,' coming in April, matured the crops and got them ready for harvest. Spiritually speaking, the 'former rain' speaks of the outpouring of the Holy Spirit on the Early Church. The 'latter rain' speaks of the outpouring of the Spirit, which began at approximately the turn of the Twentieth Century and which will continue on through the Millennial Reign.*"

Actually, the Holy Spirit had the Prophet Hosea to invert the phrase *"former rain and latter rain,"* to read *"the latter and former rain."* The *"latter"* is mentioned by the Prophet Hosea before the *"former"* because Christ was rejected at His First Advent but will be accepted by Israel at the Second Advent.

The *"Latter Rain"* had to do with the harvest in Israel and is here meant to symbolize the Lord making a complete Harvest of Israel at His Second Coming (Zech. 10:1; 12:10-13:1; Rom. 11:25-29), which refers to a Harvest of souls.

James alluded to this *"early and latter rain,"* referring to the Harvest of souls before the *"Coming of the Lord."* He said:

"**Be patient therefore, Brethren, unto the Coming of the Lord.** (*This tells us the* cure and, in fact, the only cure for the injustices in the world. It is the Coming of the Lord.*) **Behold, the husbandman waits for the precious fruit of the earth, and has long patience for it, until he receive the early and latter rain.** (*The Holy Spirit, through James, tells us in a few words that the Coming of the Lord will take place shortly after the 'latter rain' commences, which, in fact, the world is now experiencing in the outpouring of the Holy Spirit, but only in a limited way. And yet, this means the Second Coming is very near, with the Rapture being even at the door*)" (James 5:7).

Consequently, the Church, at least those who truly love the Lord, can also expect a great Harvest of souls while, at the same time, expecting a great falling away (II Thess. 2:3; Acts 2:17; Mat. 24:14).

(4) "O EPHRAIM, WHAT SHALL I DO UNTO YOU? O JUDAH, WHAT SHALL I DO UNTO YOU? FOR YOUR GOODNESS IS AS A MORNING CLOUD, AND AS THE EARLY DEW IT GOES AWAY.

(5) "THEREFORE HAVE I HEWED THEM BY THE PROPHETS; I HAVE KILLED THEM BY THE WORDS OF MY MOUTH: AND YOUR JUDGMENTS ARE AS THE LIGHT THAT GOES FORTH.

(6) "FOR I DESIRE MERCY, AND NOT SACRIFICE; AND THE KNOWLEDGE OF GOD MORE THAN BURNT OFFERINGS.

(7) "BUT THEY LIKE MEN HAVE TRANSGRESSED THE COVENANT: THERE HAVE THEY DEALT TREACHEROUSLY AGAINST ME.

(8) "GILEAD IS A CITY OF THEM WHO WORK INIQUITY, AND IS POLLUTED WITH BLOOD.

(9) "AND AS TROOPS OF ROBBERS WAIT FOR A MAN, SO THE COMPANY OF PRIESTS MURDER IN THE WAY BY CONSENT: FOR THEY COMMIT LEWDNESS.

(10) "I HAVE SEEN AN HORRIBLE THING IN THE HOUSE OF ISRAEL: THERE IS THE WHOREDOM OF EPHRAIM, ISRAEL IS DEFILED.

(11) "ALSO, O JUDAH, HE HAS SET AN HARVEST FOR YOU, WHEN I RETURNED THE CAPTIVITY OF MY PEOPLE."

The pattern is:

1. The question of Verse 4, "*What shall I*

do unto you?" refers to the Lord using every possible method to turn both kingdoms around, but to no avail.

2. (Vs. 4) *"For your goodness is as a morning cloud, and as the early dew it goes away"* refers to a superficial religious effort, which had no substance and quickly dissipated (Mat. 13:5-6).

3. The phrase, *"Therefore have I hewed them by the Prophets,"* of Verse 5 is a figurative statement borrowed from the hewing of hard wood and shaping it so as to assume the required form. Despite the powerful statements by the *"Prophets,"* which were given by the Lord, Israel was unmoved.

4. (Vs. 5) *"I have killed them by the Words of My Mouth"* refers to an Anointing so powerful upon the *"Prophets"* that it was enough to make anyone listen, but still, to no avail!

5. (Vs. 5) The phrase, *"And your judgments are as the light that goes forth,"* proclaims that Faith can always take refuge in God, Whose *"Judgments"* are perfect!

6. Verse 6 was quoted in part by Christ (Mat. 9:13; 12:7). Israel tried to replace *"Mercy"* and *"the Knowledge of God"* with mere ritual.

7. The word *"men"* in Verse 7 in the Hebrew is *"Adam"* and should have been translated accordingly. *"The Covenant"* spoken of concerns the prohibition respecting the forbidden fruit. Adam's children, like their father, perpetually transgressed and dealt treacherously. Loss of fellowship with God and expulsion from Eden were the penal consequences that immediately followed upon Adam's transgression; likewise, the expulsion of Israel from the Promised Land.

8. (Vs. 8) The area of *"Gilead"* consists of the east side of the Jordan. In the New Testament, it is spoken of under the name of *"Perea."* Jeremiah would say, *"Is there no balm in Gilead . . .?"* (Jer. 8:22).

9. (Vs. 9) *"Gilead"* was also known as *"Ramoth Gilead."* It had been originally chosen by the Lord as a City of Refuge. Now it was a city of workers of iniquity, and the road to it was tracked with blood.

10. (Vs. 9) *"By consent"* should have been translated *"Shechem,"* for it also was a City of Refuge. Likewise, its priests, instead of

Saving men, *"murdered"* them by making them idolaters, for they taught them to commit lewdness, i.e., to practice idol worship.

11. The *"whoredom of Ephraim"* of Verse 10 was idol worship. God calls it *"an horrible thing."*

12. The idea of Verse 11 spans a length of time all the way to the coming Great Tribulation. That will be the *"harvest of wrath,"* which will come upon Judah at that time. *"When I returned the captivity of My People,"* refers to Israel ultimately making her way back to God, which will take place at the Second Coming.

WHAT SHALL I DO UNTO YOU?

The question proclaims the Lord using every possible method, portraying His Mercy and Compassion, but still unable to bring Israel or Judah to a place of Repentance.

Admittedly, Hezekiah, king of Judah, just a few years later, would do *"that which was right in the Sight of the LORD,"* but his son and successor, Manasseh, *"wrought much wickedness in the Sight of the LORD, to provoke Him to anger."* But strangely enough, Manasseh gave his heart to the Lord and served Him faithfully shortly before his death. The Scripture says concerning this:

"And when he was in affliction, he besought the LORD his God, and humbled himself greatly before the God of his fathers *(this is evidently why the Lord allowed Manasseh to rule as long as he did; as well, and as stated, it was the reason the Lord allowed him to be taken captive to Babylon; it had the desired effect upon the monarch; time and time again, the Lord chastises His Children in attempting to bring them to a place of Repentance),"*

THE LORD HEARD HIS SUPPLICATION

"And prayed unto Him: and He was entreated of him, and heard his supplication, and brought him again to Jerusalem into his kingdom. Then Manasseh knew that the LORD He was God *(there could be no more beautiful illustration of the Mercy and Grace of God than that which was extended to Manasseh; the great lesson learned here is that if the Lord would do that for this king, who had wrought more evil in Judah than* *any other king before him, He will do it for anyone else; there are only two requirements: to humble oneself, and to pray unto God)."*

REVIVAL UNDER MANASSEH

The Scripture continues to say, **"And he took away the strange gods, and the idol out of the House of the LORD, and all the altars that he had built in the mount of the House of the LORD, and in Jerusalem, and cast them out of the city."**

REPAIRING THE ALTAR

"And he repaired the Altar of the LORD *(the great Brazen Altar, on which the sacrifices were offered)*, **and sacrificed thereon Peace Offerings** *(the 'Peace Offerings' were generally offered after the Sin and Trespass Offerings, signifying that Peace with God had now been restored; this tells us that the Peace of God had now come to Manasseh)* **and Thank Offerings** *(to be sure, this king had much to be thankful for, hence, the 'Thank Offerings' and the emphasis on this by the Holy Spirit)*, **and commanded Judah to serve the LORD God of Israel"** (II Chron. 33:12-13, 15-16).

Conversely, there was not one single godly king that graced the throne of the northern kingdom of Israel.

Perhaps Christ had Verse 4 in mind when He said, *"Some seed fell upon stony places, where they had not much earth: and forthwith they sprung up, because they had no deepness of earth:*

"And when the sun was up, they were scorched; and because they had no root, they withered away" (Mat. 13:5-6).

THE JUDGMENT OF GOD

God's Judgments are referred to as *"the light that goes forth."*

If, in fact, Judgment is forthcoming, which will always be for lack of true Repentance, it is meant as corrective and, therefore, for the good of the individual. Paul said, *". . . nevertheless afterward it yields the peaceable Fruit of Righteousness unto them who are exercised thereby"* (Heb. 12:11).

THE ANOINTING OF THE HOLY SPIRIT

The descriptive terminology of Verse 5

pertains to a powerful Anointing of the Holy Spirit on the Prophets in order to turn Israel around, but to no avail.

There is no greater persuasive Power than the Word of God preached under the Anointing of the Spirit. If that is spurned and rejected, as it mostly is, there is nothing left but Judgment. To be sure, such Judgment can take many forms but is always corrective instead of punitive as it regards God's People.

The bondages of sin are so strong that nothing, not even education, talent, ability, or anything else can break that bondage except the Anointing of the Holy Spirit upon the Word of God. The Prophet Isaiah said, *"And it shall come to pass in that day, that his burden shall be taken away from off your shoulder, and his yoke from off your neck, and the yoke shall be destroyed because of the Anointing"* (Isa. 10:27).

Actually, it should be translated, *"because of the Anointed One,"* referring to Christ.

THE CROSS: ONE SACRIFICE FOR SIN

The first thing that Believers should understand is, the forces in the spirit world of darkness arrayed against us are more formidable than our ability to cope on a personal basis. That's why Paul said, **"For we wrestle not against flesh and blood** *(our foes are not human; however, Satan constantly uses human beings to carry out his dirty work)*, **but against principalities** *(rulers or beings of the highest rank and order in Satan's kingdom)*, **against powers** *(the rank immediately below the 'Principalities')*, **against the rulers of the darkness of this world** *(those who carry out the instructions of the 'Powers')*, **against spiritual wickedness in high** *places. (This refers to demon spirits)"* **(Eph. 6:12).**

THE INABILITY OF THE HUMAN BEING

Paul tells us why we are incapable within ourselves of overcoming these powers of darkness. He said:

"And if Christ *be* **in you** *(He is in you through the Power and Person of the Spirit [Gal. 2:20])*, **the body** *is* **dead because of sin** *(means that the physical body has been rendered helpless because of the Fall;*

consequently, the Believer trying to overcome by willpower presents a fruitless task); **but the Spirit *is* Life because of Righteousness** *(only the Holy Spirit can make us what we ought to be, which means we cannot do it ourselves; once again, He performs all that He does within the confines of the Finished Work of Christ)*" **(Rom. 8:10).**

THE CROSS OF CHRIST IS THE ONLY ANSWER

There is only one defense against the powers of darkness, and that is the Cross of Christ. Paul said:

"But this Man *(this Priest, Christ Jesus)*, **after He had offered One Sacrifice for sins forever** *(speaks of the Cross)*, **sat down on the Right Hand of God** *(refers to the great contrast with the Priests under the Levitical system, who never sat down because their work was never completed; the Work of Christ was a 'Finished Work' and needed no repetition)*" **(Heb. 10:12).**

OUR FAITH MUST REST EXCLUSIVELY IN THE CROSS OF CHRIST

Paul, knowing that Faith in Christ and what He did at the Cross is the only answer for sin, said:

"For I determined not to know anything among you *(with purpose and design, Paul did not resort to the knowledge or philosophy of the world regarding the preaching of the Gospel)*, **save Jesus Christ, and Him Crucified** *(that and that alone is the Message, which will save the sinner, set the captive free, and give the Believer perpetual victory)*" **(I Cor. 2:2).**

HOW THE HOLY SPIRIT WORKS

The Holy Spirit Works exclusively within the parameters of the Finished Work of Christ. In other words, it is the Cross of Christ that gave and gives the Holy Spirit the legal means to do all that He does. Before the Cross, due to the fact that the blood of bulls and goats could not take away sins (Heb. 10:4), the Holy Spirit was greatly limited as to what He could do for the Believer. But with all sin atoned, which it was at the Cross, the Holy Spirit comes into the heart

and life of the Believer at the moment of Conversion and there abides permanently (Jn. 14:16). He is there for many purposes and reasons but mostly to rid the Believer of all sin. This doesn't mean sinless perfection, for the Bible does not teach such, but it does mean that we are to come to the place that sin is to have no dominion over us (Rom. 6:14).

So, when we put our Faith exclusively in Christ and the Cross and don't allow it to be moved elsewhere (I Cor. 1:17-18, 23), the Holy Spirit will Work on our behalf, helping us to do what needs to be done. In fact, without the Holy Spirit, it cannot be done! As well, considering that the Holy Spirit demands that our Faith be exclusively in Christ and the Cross, we now begin to understand how important the Cross of Christ actually is.

WARFARE

Even with the help of the Holy Spirit, living this life as it ought to be lived is not a simple or easy thing to do. In fact, this is a *"war"* that will not end until we die, or the Trump sounds. So, there is nothing the Believer can do that will stop all temptation and attacks by the Evil One. Paul said several things about this. They are:

• He tells us that the Sanctification process, as outlined in I Thessalonians, Chapter 4, is an ongoing process. He couches his words in terms of the continuing struggle of the Believer.

• Whereas Believers are at least positioned to attain Sanctification, he indicates also that the Believer never quite attains this position. In other words, the school of the Cross has no graduating class (Rom. 6:2, 12).

• Paul himself admits that he has not personally attained to Sanctification in its fullness (II Cor. 9:27; Phil. 1:6; 2:12-18; 3:12-15).

• Complete Sanctification in Paul's eyes only occurs at the Return of Christ (I Thess. 3:13).

SIN IS NOT TO HAVE DOMINION

Even though the Bible does not teach sinless perfection because such is impossible in this particular state, still, the Bible most definitely does teach that *"sin is not to have dominion over us"* (Rom. 6:14).

The word *"dominion,"* as used here by Paul, means that a certain sin or sins dominate the person in some way. In other words, they are unable to stop committing this particular sin. This is the sin nature ruling the Believer in some way. In fact, if the Believer doesn't understand the Cross of Christ as it regards Sanctification, such a Believer is going to be ruled by the sin nature in some way no matter how hard he tries otherwise. So, due to the fact that the modern church has little or no understanding of the Cross of Christ as it refers to our Sanctification, this means that the sin nature is ruling most every modern Believer. And we're speaking of those who truly love the Lord!

WHAT IS THE SIN NATURE?

In essence, the sin nature is exactly what it says. It means that after the Fall, the nature of both Adam and Eve became one of sin, which passed down through original sin to everyone who would be born.

When we notice something that's done by someone that's a little different, the statement will often be made, *"That's his nature."* When Adam and Eve fell, they fell from a position of total God-consciousness down to the far, far lower level of total self-consciousness. Then, their every action and their every thought became one of sin. And that's exactly the way with every unredeemed person. If you will look back at your life before you came to Christ, you will have to admit that this was the case with you as well.

When the believing sinner comes to Christ, the Divine Nature now becomes a part of his life and living, his very being (II Pet. 1:4). In fact, the Believer has three natures. They are:

1. Human nature: Christ, as well, had a human nature.

2. Sin nature: as stated, due to Adam's Fall, every human being is born with a sin nature. Christ had no sin nature because He was Virgin Born.

3. Divine Nature: the Divine Nature comes into the Believer at Conversion.

When the believing sinner comes to Christ, the sin nature is made dormant. It is not removed, but it most definitely is made

ineffective. Paul said:

"Knowing this, that our old man is crucified with *Him (all that we were before Conversion)**, that the body of sin** (the sin nature) **might be destroyed** (made ineffective)**, that henceforth we should not serve sin** (the guilt of sin is removed at Conversion because the sin nature no longer rules within our hearts and lives)**" (Rom. 6:6).**

The Greek word translated *"destroyed"* actually should have been translated *"made ineffective."*

So, if the sin nature is made ineffective at Conversion, what causes it to be reactivated if, in fact, it is?

THE REACTIVATION OF
THE SIN NATURE

After the person comes to Christ, the mind is renewed immediately, with a hatred for sin becoming a part of the individual (Rom. 7:15). But, inevitably, and there has never been an exception, the Believer in some way will fail the Lord. Whenever this happens, the Believer is shocked. He reasons in his mind that he must take steps that this failure not reoccur. Instead of placing his Faith at that time exclusively in Christ and the Cross, he rather places it in something else. He will be more faithful to church! He'll give more money to the Work of the Lord! He will witness to more people about Christ, etc.!

Now, while all of these things are good and should be done by every Believer, that's not the way to overcome sin.

When such a course is taken, and it has been taken by every single Believer who has ever lived, this greatly hinders the Holy Spirit, Who works exclusively within the framework of the Finished Work of Christ. In other words, the Holy Spirit will not help us in such a situation. He'll do all that He can, but that's not the way to overcome sin, as necessary as those other things might be.

Now the sin nature has been reactivated and is once again beginning to rule the Believer in some way. It doesn't matter how hard the Believer labors to try to overcome the problem, unless he gets his Faith exclusively in Christ and the Cross, the failure will continue and get worse. That's why

Paul also said:

A RULING SIN NATURE

"Let not sin *(the sin nature)* **therefore reign** *(rule)* **in your mortal body** *(showing that the sin nature can once again rule in the heart and life of the Believer, if the Believer doesn't constantly look to Christ and the Cross; the 'mortal body' is neutral, which means it can be used for Righteousness or unrighteousness),* **that you should obey it in the lusts thereof** *(ungodly lusts are carried out through the mortal body, if Faith is not maintained in the Cross [I Cor. 1:17-18])"* **(Rom. 6:12).**

At this particular time the modern church knows precious little, if anything, about the Cross of Christ relative to Sanctification. Because of this, virtually all of modern Christians, even those who truly love the Lord, are being ruled in some way by the sin nature. Please understand this:

If the Believer doesn't understand God's Prescribed Order of Victory, which we have given to you in the last few pages, such a Believer is going to be ruled by the sin nature. To be sure, it makes for a miserable existence! That's why Paul said, *"Oh wretched man that I am . . ."* (Rom. 7:24).

THE MODERN CHURCH

This is a subject the modern church knows almost nothing about, and yet, it is one of the most important bodies of material found in the Word of God as it regards how we live for God.

As well, the Believer should understand that irrespective as to how much we may comprehend God's Prescribed Order of Victory, still, there is going to be a struggle, even as we have previously stated. Satan does not give up easily and, in fact, in a sense, never gives up. That's why Jesus told us that we had to *"take up the cross daily"* (Lk. 9:23). Inasmuch as He used the word *"daily,"* it carries the idea of us renewing our Faith each and every day simply because victories of yesterday, while absolutely necessary, will not suffice for today. There must be fresh victories each and every day.

The following is the manner in which people address the sin nature. I will be brief.

IGNORANCE

Regrettably, the far greater majority of the modern church simply doesn't know anything about a sin nature. They've never heard of it, never heard a sermon preached on the subject, and never read anything about such a problem. But yet, ignorance will not shield one from the evil effects of this ruling power.

DENIAL

There are many in the modern church who have some knowledge of the sin nature, but they deny that such exists in the Believer. They claim that while the person may have had a sin nature before Conversion, after they come to Christ, the sin nature, they say, is removed.

Now, that's strange when we consider that the Holy Spirit through Paul gave over the entirety of the Sixth Chapter of Romans to address this subject. We must remember that Paul is writing to Believers. If a sin nature did not exist, then the Holy Spirit was wasting His Time, and I can guarantee that the Holy Spirit never wastes time.

The word *"sin"* is mentioned 17 times in the Sixth Chapter of Romans. Fifteen of those times, Paul originally wrote it with what is referred to as the *"definite article"* in front of the word *"sin."* Actually, he stated, *"the sin."* He wasn't speaking of acts of sin, but rather the sin nature, or if one prefers, *"the evil nature."* You can look in your Greek lexicon, and you'll see what I'm saying is correct.

He only used the word *"sin"* one time as an act of sin, and that's in the Fifteenth Verse. While he didn't put the definite article before the word *"sin"* in the Fourteenth Verse, still, he used it as a noun instead of a verb, so it means the same thing—the sin nature.

LICENSE

What few people there are who have some inkling of knowledge regarding the sin nature, they use it as a license to sin. In other words, they state that inasmuch as they have a sin nature, they simply can't help but sin. So, due to the fact that Grace is greater than sin, they don't worry about it. This is the sure road to disaster.

The Apostle Paul answered this when he said:

"**What shall we say then?** *(This is meant to direct attention to Rom. 5:20.)* **Shall we continue in sin, that Grace may abound?** *(Just because Grace is greater than sin doesn't mean that the Believer has a license to sin.)*

"**God forbid** *(presents Paul's answer to the question, 'Away with the thought, let not such a thing occur').* **How shall we, who are dead to sin** *(dead to the sin nature),* **live any longer therein?** *(This portrays what the Believer is now in Christ)*" **(Rom. 6:1-2).**

STRUGGLE

Some Christians have the idea that one cannot really have victory over the sin nature; consequently, it's a struggle everyday to live for God. Strangely enough, some of the most consecrated Christians fall into this category.

While we do not deny that there is a struggle as it regards living for God, still, if we function God's Way, which is the Way of the Cross, the Scripture plainly says, ". . . *sin shall not have dominion over you . . .*" (Rom. 6:14).

The trouble is, many of these Christians make a religion out of their struggle. Because of this, self-righteousness is the result. In fact, if the person doesn't place his Faith exclusively in Christ and the Cross, self-righteousness is inevitably the result!

GRACE

Of all the things we've named, Grace is the only legitimate means by which Victory can be ours. Paul said:

"**For sin shall not have dominion over you** *(the sin nature will not have dominion over us if we as Believers continue to exercise Faith in the Cross of Christ; otherwise, the sin nature most definitely will have dominion over the Believer)*: **for you are not under the Law** *(means that if we try to live this life by any type of religious law, no matter how good that law might be in its own right, we will conclude by the sin nature having dominion over us)*, **but under Grace** *(the Grace of God flows to the Believer on an unending basis only as long as the Believer exercises Faith in Christ and what He did at the Cross; Grace is merely the Goodness of God exercised by and through the Holy Spirit, and given to undeserving Saints)*" **(Rom. 6:14).**

LAW AND GRACE

What did Paul mean by using the words *"Law"* and *"Grace"*?

If the Believer places himself under law, and that refers to anything other than the Cross of Christ, the Holy Spirit then becomes very much hindered as to the help He can give. So as there will be no misunderstanding, let me say it again.

When the Believer places his faith in anything except Christ and the Cross, he turns that direction into law, whether it's meant to be law or not. For instance, the Lord's Supper is definitely not law. However, when one places his faith in this Ordinance, thinking that by the participation it will bring victory over sin, he has just turned the Lord's Supper into law. The same could be said for fasting, etc. While these things certainly aren't wrong within themselves, they are not the answer for which we seek, which is Victory over the world, the flesh, and the Devil.

When the Believer places his or her Faith exclusively in Christ and the Cross, then the Holy Spirit, Who works exclusively within the parameters, so to speak, of the Finished Work of Christ, can then help the Believer. In other words, Grace is simply the *"Goodness of God"* extended to undeserving Saints, and proper Faith makes all of it possible.

The Lord has no more Grace now than He did 3,000 years ago.

THAT WHICH MAKES GRACE POSSIBLE

Before the Cross, the Holy Spirit could do very little with Believers simply because the blood of bulls and goats could not take away sins (Heb. 10:4). But since the Cross, with all sin atoned, the Holy Spirit has much greater latitude and liberty to Work on our behalf. Now the Grace of God, i.e., *"the Goodness of God,"* can be given to us unreservedly. When Believers place their faith in anything other than the Cross of Christ, it only serves to *"frustrate the Grace of God"* (Gal. 2:21). Frustrating the Grace of God means that its flow is impeded, which should be obvious.

MERCY AND KNOWLEDGE

The Lord said through the great Prophet, *"For I desire Mercy, and not sacrifice; and the Knowledge of God more than Burnt Offerings."*

The idea is, Israel had turned the sacrifices into a mere ritual. In other words, they had completely lost the meaning of what they represented, hence, the Lord saying that He desired Mercy and Knowledge more than the rituals. Consequently, the question begs to be asked, *"Can a Believer turn his Faith in Christ and the Cross into a mere ritual?"*

No!

It was easy to turn the sacrifices of old into a ritual simply because they were a physical thing. However, as it regards the Cross of Christ, one either has Faith in that Finished Work, or one doesn't.

IDOLATRY

The incessant denunciation of the popular religion as idolatry suggests that then, as now, the people fiercely denied that they were idolaters. They repeated the formula, *"Jehovah lives,"* i.e., claiming the images represented God, and they worshipped Him and not them. But God called it *"whoredom."* No wonder they were enraged.

The Priests failed to maintain moral relationships between the people and God; therefore, He, in His Grace, inspired the Prophet Hosea, as stated, to maintain those relationships.

The original Purpose of God was not a question of outward forms, as these *"sacrifices"* represented, but of Moral Relationship and Fellowship with Himself in and through Christ.

Sacrifices were constantly appointed, just as pictures are with children, to teach man his sinfulness and his need of an Atoning Saviour.

However, the Priests and the people turned the sacrifices into a religion within themselves and, consequently, made a salvation of these beautiful types, which they

were not and, in fact, could not be. As such, they forgot what they represented, namely the Coming Redeemer and, therefore, became salvation within themselves, at least in their minds.

As such, all who did not subscribe totally and completely to this false salvation, as represented in the sacrifices, were treated harshly.

Such is religion!

THE PROPHET HOSEA

The Prophet spoke to the hearts of the people and sought to bring them back to God. As such, the Book of Hosea is tremendously important because it furnishes a moral picture of a people whom God had judged and upon whom that Judgment was bound to fall. Here is found an affecting mixture on God's Part, of reproaches, of compassions, of appeals, and of reference to happier days, but all in vain! Consequently, the words of Christ in Mark 12:33, *"And to love Him with all the heart and with all the understanding, and with all the soul, and with all the strength, and to love his neighbor as himself, is more than all whole Burnt Offerings and Sacrifices,"* fulfill Verse 6.

The modern church, as well, has made a religion out of sacred things and, consequently, has made these things into salvation, which, in reality, does not exist.

As a result, millions join churches and constitute that as salvation. Other millions are baptized in water, thinking this act constitutes salvation. Actually, the list is quite endless.

Whenever religion (subscription to one's own works) becomes the salvation, no *"Mercy"* remains because all who do not immediately subscribe to the *"religion"* are automatically condemned. Such was Christ! He would not subscribe to the *"religion"* of that day and was summarily denounced and ultimately crucified.

Religion has no Mercy!

TRANSGRESS THE COVENANT

The Lord through the great Prophet said, *"But they like men have transgressed the Covenant: there have they dealt treacherously against Me."*

"The Covenant" spoken of concerns the prohibition respecting the forbidden fruit. Adam's children, like their father, perpetually transgressed and dealt treacherously.

Loss of Fellowship with God and expulsion from Eden were the penal consequences that immediately followed upon Adam's transgression.

Israel, like Adam, had been settled by God in Palestine, the glory of all lands. But, ungrateful for God's Great Bounty and Gracious Gift, they broke the Covenant of their God, the condition of which, as in the case of the Adamic Covenant, was obedience.

Thus the comparison projects the shadow of a coming event when Israel would lose the Land of Promise, which she did!

The world little understands that the real cause of all suffering, sickness, poverty, heartache, death, and destruction is Adam's transgression. In effect, Adam changed lords. Jehovah had been his Lord. Now, due to the Fall, Satan becomes his lord. Satan became, and is, the god of this present world (II Cor. 4:4). As such, he *"steals, kills, and destroys"* (Jn. 10:10).

GILEAD

The area in Hosea's day known as *"Gilead"* was on the east side of the Jordan. In New Testament times it is spoken of under the name of *"Perea."* Some years later, Jeremiah would say, *"Is there no balm in Gilead . . .?"* (Jer. 8:22).

When Jesus delivered the maniac of Gadara (Mk. 5:1-15), it was in this area. Therefore, Jesus' Ministry in this area answered Jeremiah's question. Jesus was the *"Balm"* and the *"Physician."* However, during the time of Hosea, it was an area of *"sin"* and *"murder."*

The words of Verse 8, *"polluted with blood,"* actually mean, *"foot-printed or foot-tracked from blood."*

It is said that the men of Gilead in general were fierce, wild mountaineers. And yet, they are represented as worse, much worse, in this Scripture. They were not only wicked but murderers as well!

THE SIN OF MURDER

As stated, *"Gilead"* had been originally

chosen by the Lord as a City of Refuge, but it had lost that meaning long before. Intentional murderers found a refuge there under the protection of its corrupt priests. Consequently, instead of Saving men, its priests *"murdered them"* by making them idolaters, for they taught them to commit lewdness, i.e., to practice idol worship.

It is interesting that the Holy Spirit through the Prophet uses the word, *"murder,"* regarding the activity of these priests. The Hebrew rendering implies that these priests committed spiritual murder instead of physical murder.

Could it be said today that every preacher who fails to preach the Word of God but, instead, preaches a gospel of his own making or the making of others commits spiritual murder?

I think the answer should be obvious and, sadly, applies to almost all!

The real sin of the church is not so much sins of passion, even though these sins are rampant and obviously destructive, but instead, the sin of pride. This sin, in one way or the other, fosters and nurtures all other sins.

It is the sin that caused the Fall of Adam and Eve in the Garden, and as the sin of the Fall, it continues to plague the human family and, especially, religious man.

THE WHOREDOM OF EPHRAIM

The Lord referred to the *"whoredom of Ephraim"* as *"an horrible thing."*

Let it be understood that anything anyone places ahead of the Lord becomes an idol. That's why John the Beloved said, *"Little children, keep yourselves from idols"* (I Jn. 5:21).

This statement as given by John does not refer to the heathen worship of idol gods but of the heretical substitutes for the Christian conception of God, or anything that pulls us away from Christ and the Cross.

I believe I can say without fear of contradiction that if the faith of the Believer is not exclusively in Christ and the Cross, in some way, he is worshipping an idol. It might be the religious denomination to which he belongs, his local church, the works that he performs supposedly for the Lord, etc. But, if it's not *"Christ Crucified,"* then it is an idol in the Eyes of God.

If a Believer selects a proposed way of victory other than the Cross of Christ, he is then embarking upon a course of *"spiritual adultery,"* i.e., *"whoredoms."* At least that's the way that the Lord looks at the situation.

God has a Way, and that Way is the Cross of Christ. To follow another way, as should be obvious, is that which constitutes acute unfaithfulness to the Lord. In fact, we as Believers are married to the Lord Jesus Christ (Rom. 7:4; II Cor. 11:1-4).

THE GREAT WHORE

Listen again to John the Beloved. He said:

"And there came one of the seven Angels which had the seven Vials, and talked with me (*probably is the seventh Angel; however, we actually have no way of truly knowing*), **saying unto me, Come hither; I will show unto you the judgment of the great whore who sits upon many waters** (*the 'great whore' refers to all the religions of the world that ever have been, which are devised by men as a substitute for 'Jesus Christ and Him Crucified'; God's Way is Christ and Him Crucified Alone; as well, the 'many waters' are a symbol for multitudes of people [Vs. 15]*)**:"**

SPIRITUAL FORNICATION

"With whom (*the great whore, i.e., all type of religions*) **the kings of the Earth** (*from the very beginning, most nations have been ruled by some type of religion*) **have committed fornication** (*all religions devised by men, and even the parts of Christianity that have been corrupted, are labeled by the Lord as 'spiritual fornication' [Rom. 7:1-4]*), **and the inhabitants of the Earth have been made drunk with the wine of her fornication** (*proclaims the addiction of religion; the doing of religion is the most powerful narcotic there is*)**" (Rev. 17:1-2).**

"To God be the glory Great Things He has done,

"So loved He the world that He gave us His Son,

"Who yielded His Life an Atonement for sin,

"And opened the Life Gate that all

may go in."

"O Perfect Redemption, the purchase of blood!

"To every Believer the Promise of God;

"The vilest offender who truly believes,

"That moment from Jesus a pardon receives."

"Great Things He has taught us, Great Things He has done,

"And great our rejoicing through Jesus the Son;

"But purer and higher and greater will be,

"Our wonder, our transport, when Jesus we see."

CHAPTER 7

(1) "WHEN I WOULD HAVE HEALED ISRAEL, THEN THE INIQUITY OF EPHRAIM WAS DISCOVERED, AND THE WICKEDNESS OF SAMARIA: FOR THEY COMMIT FALSEHOOD; AND THE THIEF COMES IN, AND THE TROOP OF ROBBERS SPOILS WITHOUT.

(2) "AND THEY CONSIDER NOT IN THEIR HEARTS THAT I REMEMBER ALL THEIR WICKEDNESS: NOW THEIR OWN DOINGS HAVE BESET THEM ABOUT; THEY ARE BEFORE MY FACE.

(3) "THEY MAKE THE KING GLAD WITH THEIR WICKEDNESS, AND THE PRINCES WITH THEIR LIES.

(4) "THEY ARE ALL ADULTERERS, AS AN OVEN HEATED BY THE BAKER, WHO CEASES FROM RAISING AFTER HE HAS KNEADED THE DOUGH, UNTIL IT BE LEAVENED.

(5) "IN THE DAY OF OUR KING THE PRINCES HAVE MADE HIM SICK WITH BOTTLES OF WINE; HE STRETCHED OUT HIS HAND WITH SCORNERS.

(6) "FOR THEY HAVE MADE READY THEIR HEART LIKE AN OVEN, WHILE THEY LIE IN WAIT: THEIR BAKER SLEEPS ALL THE NIGHT; IN THE MORNING IT BURNS AS A FLAMING FIRE.

(7) "THEY ARE ALL HOT AS AN OVEN, AND HAVE DEVOURED THEIR JUDGES; ALL THEIR KINGS ARE FALLEN: THERE IS NONE AMONG THEM WHO CALLS UNTO ME."

The exegesis is:

1. (Vs. 1) The first seven Verses of this Chapter declare the inherent evil of man's heart, and the remaining Verses the weakness, folly, and rebellion, which are its fruit.

2. (Vs. 1) The phrase, *"When I would have healed Israel,"* refers to the fact that the Lord not only wanted and desired to heal *"Israel,"* but eagerly searched for a way to do so! However, because of their great sin, there was no way to make this rotten apple whole.

3. The sense of Verse 1 is, *"When I wished to blot out the old sins of My People on account of ancient idolatry, Ephraim and Samaria discovered new idols."*

4. As Verse 2 records, evil conceived in the heart produces manifest fruits, which are seen by both God and man. *"And they consider not in their hearts that I remember all their wickedness,"* proclaims these people as placing God in a position of less than Deity. This is far more serious than meets the eye.

5. According to Verse 3, wicked kings and princes welcome religious teachers who assure them that there is no wrath to come or Lake of Fire. These lies make glad the hearers.

6. The phrase of Verse 4, *"They are all adulterers,"* speaks of idol worship, i.e., *"spiritual adultery."* This Verse, in essence, says, *"Sin, if left unchecked, will, as leaven, corrupt the whole."*

7. The idea of Verse 5 is: the corruption and spiritual rot permeated the whole of Israel from the throne to the hovel. All were leavened.

8. The idea of Verse 6 is that the heart of the people is compared to an oven, but with this difference: no baker was needed to sit up all night to keep up its temperature, for it was so inflamed with wickedness that it burned in the morning as a flaming fire. Thus, this Verse stands in relation to Verse 4.

9. The phrase of Verse 7, *"There is none among them who calls unto Me,"* means that amid the horrid scenes of blood and violence, of disorder and anarchy, there were

none of these kings who realized the calamities of the times or recognized the cause. Consequently, there was no one to discover the remedy and apply it to the True and only Source of relief, which was the Lord.

THE LORD WANTED TO HEAL

The phrase, *"When I would have healed Israel,"* refers possibly to the commencement of the reign of Jeroboam II (II Ki. 14:23-27).

In other words, the Lord not only wanted and desired to heal *"Israel"* but eagerly searched for a way to do so! However, because of their great sin, there was no way to make this rotten apple whole.

The *"iniquity of Ephraim"* was comparable to a thief, whose sin was inward and discovered.

The *"wickedness of Samaria"* was comparable to a public troop of robbers, and outward. Both practiced falsehood, but they professed a repentance which was not sincere.

The sense of Verse 1 is, *"When I wished to blot out the old sins of My People on account of ancient idolatry, Ephraim and Samaria discovered new idols."*

The old sins and ancient idolatry the Lord refers to was the making and worshipping of the golden calf in the wilderness, while the new idols were the calf-worship, which Jeroboam of the Tribe of Ephraim instituted, and the people of the capital, Samaria, adopted.

The idea is that in the entirety of the northern kingdom, there was no foundation whatsoever on which to build Righteousness. Consequently, and despite every effort of the Lord to *"heal,"* Israel went to her doom.

SIN

Sin is a horrible thing because it breeds more sin and blinds the spiritual eyes of the perpetrator. Deception becomes the hallmark, and more sin is sought and with eager participation.

This spiral to destruction can only be brought to a halt by sincere, heartfelt Repentance. However, the far greater majority of the time, the participants do not even see their need and, consequently, no repentance is forthcoming. It is too often, especially in modern times, the parable of Christ repeated again and again of *"certain which trusted in themselves that they were righteous, and despised others"* (Lk. 18:9).

AN IMPROPER KNOWLEDGE OF GOD

If we have an improper knowledge of Who God is, we will, as well, have an improper knowledge of what He does.

Too often in modern society, the Lord is cheapened as *"the Man upstairs."* Even the modern church has little fear of God. If they did, they would not dare do some of the things they do!

In effect, and upon proper Repentance, the Lord *"will be merciful to their unrighteousness, and their sins and their iniquities will I remember no more"* (Heb. 8:12).

However, if repentance is not forthcoming, God *"remembers all their wickedness."* Consequently, Judgment must follow.

THE ARK OF THE COVENANT

The phrase, *"They are before My Face,"* refers to their unconfessed sins, as it does all unconfessed sins.

This actually has reference to the Mercy Seat on the Ark of the Covenant in the Holy of Holies in the Temple.

The faces of the Cherubim, which were situated at either end of the Ark, perpetually looked down on the Mercy Seat. As well, the Lord, at least at that time, resided above the Mercy Seat.

In the Ark was a tablet containing the Ten Commandments. Every one of these Commandments, which were looked at by God continually, had been broken by man.

However, once a year, on the Great Day of Atonement, the Great High Priest would come into the Holy of Holies and offer up the blood of an innocent lamb upon the Mercy Seat.

When this was done, the gaze of the Cherubim and the Lord upon the broken Law was shielded by the shed blood, which had been applied.

This, as well, stemmed from the blood applied to the doorposts of the houses in Egypt of old, which occasioned the statement, *". . . when I see the blood I will pass over you . . ."* (Ex. 12:13).

NOTES

If our sins are not covered by the Blood of Christ, then *"they are before God's Face."*

Even though the Lord hungrily desired to wash and cleanse Israel from their sins, still, they would not allow Him to do so, as most of the world will not allow such presently!

FALSE PROPHETS

In England some time back, one of my associates, Jim Woolsey, was attempting to place our telecast on one of the British channels. Concerning that particular channel, the television executive laughed and said, *"Jesus Christ, if here in Person, could not get on this channel!"*

At that time, my associate witnessed an American preacher, Robert Schuller, interviewed on that same channel.

Schuller informed the viewers that there was no such thing as a literal Hell, and that Jesus Christ, if here in Person, would never call men *"sinners."*

It was the gospel of humanistic psychology called *"self-esteem."*

Paul said, *"In whom the god of this world has blinded the minds of them who believe not, lest the light of the Glorious Gospel of Christ, Who is the Image of God, should shine unto them"* (II Cor. 4:4).

LEAVEN

In bread-making, the leaven was probably a piece of dough retained from a former baking, which had fermented and turned acid. This was then either dissolved in water in the kneading-trough before the flour was added or was *"hid"* in the flour (Mat. 13:33), and kneaded along with it. The bread thus made was known as *"leavened."*

Leaven spoke of fermentation, which implied disintegration and corruption.

The Holy Spirit through the Prophet is using *"leaven"* as an example of sin. When the leaven was placed in the dough, it would do its work until the entirety of the loaf was leavened, for that is the nature of leaven. It is also the nature of sin.

This is what Paul was speaking of when he said, *". . . a little leaven leavens the whole lump"* (I Cor. 5:6).

Two things are said in the Fourth Verse:
1. Sin, as leaven, if left unchecked, will

corrupt the whole. It, as leaven, cannot be contained; therefore, the idea of self-improvement is facetious! Such cannot be until the sin (leaven) is rooted out, and such can only be done by Christ and our Faith in what He did for us at the Cross.

2. As the leaven fermented the entirety of the loaf of bread, likewise, it ferments the entirety of the person or nation. As stated, it cannot be checked or contained, at least not by man and all his efforts.

THE LEAVEN OF FALSE DOCTRINE

Concerning false doctrine typified by leaven, Paul said:

"**Your glorying *is* not good** (*these people had taken liberty into license*). **Do you not know that a little leaven leavens the whole lump?** (*Leaven is figurative of such that is miniscule in quantity but extremely pervasive in its penetrating force.*)

"**Purge out therefore the old leaven** (*spoken in Old Covenant terminology but with the same meaning carried over in the hearts and lives of New Testament Believers*), **that you may be a new lump** (*start acting like what you are, 'a new creation'*), **as you are unleavened** (*speaks of the position that one has in Christ; that is our 'standing'; it is the business of the Spirit to bring our 'state' up to our 'standing'*). **For even Christ our Passover is sacrificed for us** (*the Believer can have victory over all sin by placing his Faith exclusively in the Cross of Christ, which Sacrifice addressed all sin*):"

THE UNLEAVENED BREAD OF SINCERITY AND TRUTH

"**Therefore let us keep the feast** (*is meant to serve as a symbol of the Jewish Passover when all leaven was purged from the household*), **not with old leaven** (*old sins committed before Conversion*), **neither with the leaven of malice and wickedness** (*refers to the ways of the world from which the Child of God has been delivered*); **but with the unleavened *bread* of sincerity and truth** (*can only be attained by one's Faith being anchored solely in the Sacrifice of Christ*)" **(I Cor. 5:6-8).**

Any so-called Faith, which does not have as its Object the Cross of Christ, in some

way is leavened. That means that such a way is corrupt! God's Way is Christ and the Cross. He has no other way simply because no other way is needed!

WHY ISN'T THE CROSS READILY ACCEPTED?

It is because of self-righteousness!

Faith in Christ and the Cross exclusively gives no credit to man whatsoever, but rather all credit to God. Faith in anything other than Christ and the Cross gives credit to man and man alone! Such a direction will bring forth no positive results whatsoever. It only tends to breed self-righteousness. We must remember, it was self-righteousness that nailed Christ to the Cross.

Whatever religious man does outside of Faith in Christ and the Cross presents something that is devised by himself or other men. As such, it cannot be accepted by the Lord, not even a little bit. But religious man doesn't like to abandon that which he has devised. As a result, Abraham did not want to give up Ishmael. This young man was the fruit of the planning and scheming of both he and Sarah. So, he loved this work of the flesh, and a work of the flesh it was! We are still suffering the results of that direction even now. To understand that, all one has to do is to look at the religion of Islam, which came out of that wrong direction.

AS A FLAMING FIRE

The phrase, "*In the morning it burns as a flaming fire,*" serves as a symbol for sin and how it spreads. If one thinks that sin can be contained, then one should read this phrase over and over. It not only cannot be contained, but instead, it will be "*as a flaming fire,*" which means it consumes everything in its path.

CALLING UNTO THE LORD

The phrase, "*There is none among them who calls unto Me,*" means that amid the horrid scenes of blood and violence, and of disorder and anarchy, there were none of these kings who realized the calamities of the times or recognized the cause. Consequently, there was no one to discover the remedy and apply it to the true and only

Source of relief, which was and is the Lord.

All of this is very similar to our modern nation of America. The country goes headlong into sin and shame, and it is because the church, at least for the most part, no longer preaches the Gospel. It is fixated on place and position or money but definitely not the Lord and that which He desires.

(8) "EPHRAIM, HE HAS MIXED HIMSELF AMONG THE PEOPLE; EPHRAIM IS A CAKE NOT TURNED.

(9) "STRANGERS HAVE DEVOURED HIS STRENGTH, AND HE KNOWS IT NOT: YES, GRAY HAIRS ARE HERE AND THERE UPON HIM, YET HE KNOWS NOT.

(10) "AND THE PRIDE OF ISRAEL TESTIFIES TO HIS FACE: AND THEY DO NOT RETURN TO THE LORD THEIR GOD, NOR SEEK HIM FOR ALL THIS.

(11) "EPHRAIM ALSO IS LIKE A SILLY DOVE WITHOUT HEART: THEY CALL TO EGYPT, THEY GO TO ASSYRIA.

(12) "WHEN THEY SHALL GO, I WILL SPREAD MY NET UPON THEM; I WILL BRING THEM DOWN AS THE FOWLS OF THE HEAVEN; I WILL CHASTISE THEM, AS THEIR CONGREGATION HAS HEARD.

(13) "WOE UNTO THEM! FOR THEY HAVE FLED FROM ME: DESTRUCTION UNTO THEM! BECAUSE THEY HAVE TRANSGRESSED AGAINST ME: THOUGH I HAVE REDEEMED THEM, YET THEY HAVE SPOKEN LIES AGAINST ME.

(14) "AND THEY HAVE NOT CRIED UNTO ME WITH THEIR HEART, WHEN THEY HOWLED UPON THEIR BEDS: THEY ASSEMBLE THEMSELVES FOR CORN AND WINE, AND THEY REBEL AGAINST ME.

(15) "THOUGH I HAVE BOUND AND STRENGTHENED THEIR ARMS, YET DO THEY IMAGINE MISCHIEF AGAINST ME.

(16) "THEY RETURN, BUT NOT TO THE MOST HIGH: THEY ARE LIKE A DECEITFUL BOW: THEIR PRINCES SHALL FALL BY THE SWORD FOR THE RAGE OF THEIR TONGUE: THIS SHALL BE THEIR DERISION IN THE LAND OF EGYPT."

The pattern is:

1. (Vs. 8) *"Ephraim, he has mixed himself among the people,"* refers to them adopting the idolatries of the neighboring

NOTES

nations in addition to their own semi-idolatry of the calves.

2. (Vs. 8) The phrase, *"Ephraim is a cake not turned,"* has reference to the first phrase in that it is burned on one side and raw on the other. It has insinuation of being partly a Jew and partly a Gentile, at least in actions.

3. The *"gray hairs"* of Verse 9 signal the end of life and the approach of death. Yet, Israel *"knows it not."*

4. (Vs. 10) *"And they do not return to the LORD their God, nor seek Him for all this"* emphasizes their obstinate blindness and perverseness.

5. (Vs. 11) In effect, the Lord calls *"silly"* all those who refuse to seek Him, or else do so improperly.

6. As it regards Verse 12, the warnings in the Law and those given by the Prophets repeatedly declared that Judgments would fall upon the disobedient and rebellious (Lev. 26:14-39; Deut. 28:15-68; 32:15-35).

7. (Vs. 13) Spiritual declension is marked by the following:

• Turning away from the Lord;
• Transgressing against Him;
• Speaking lies respecting Him; and,
• Rebellion against Him.

8. (Vs. 14) *"They cried with a voice but not with the heart"* is the opposite of the soft sobbing of Repentance. It is more like the howling with pain of a hurt beast; in other words, a ritual, or an act, if you please!

9. According to Verse 15, the Lord helped Jeroboam II to win all his victories; yet his response and that of his subjects was to imagine mischief against that Gracious God. That is, they planned and kept on practicing idolatry (II Ki. 14:24).

10. *"They return, but not to the Most High"* of Verse 16 concerns them seeking help from other sources. *"They are like a deceitful bow"* refers to a bow that warps so that to shoot straight is impossible. In Egypt they trusted, and by Egypt they were ridiculed because of their fall.

A CAKE NOT TURNED

"Ephraim is a cake not turned" refers to this people having the disposition of a Jew on one side and a Gentile on the other.

Jehovah had raised up Israel as a people

unto Himself and had done so out of the loins of Abraham and the womb of Sarah. He had given them a special constitution, His Word. The object of this segregation was that Israel should be a peculiar people and a Holy Nation. Thus distinguished, they were to dwell alone. But, ungrateful for this high distinction and unmindful of their high destiny, they mingled with the nations, learned their heathenish ways, and worshipped their hateful idols.

Actually, they did worship the Lord, at least after a fashion, but served their own gods—they were neither true worshippers of Jehovah nor out-and-out followers of Baal.

In the modern church, the Christian is called to separation from the world. When he disobeys this call and mixes himself among the *"people"* and *"strangers,"* i.e., strangers to Grace and to God, he becomes worthless (Vs. 8), weak (Vs. 9), willful (Vs. 10), and wandering (Vs. 11).

At first, he is unconscious of his loss of power and spiritual decay, but when, like Samson, he becomes sensible of his weakness, he wanders off to *"Egypt"* or to *"Assyria,"* i.e., to man-made religions—anywhere except to God, in order to find recovery and enduement.

STRANGERS

The phrase of Verse 9, *"Strangers have devoured his strength,"* referred to the heathen nations surrounding Israel. Israel referred to all foreigners, whether near or far, as *"strangers."*

The foreign nations here mentioned were those with which Israel had entered into treaties or formed alliances in contravention of the constitution, which God had given them. These nations, moreover, devoured Israel's national resources by the imposition of taxes and hostile incursions.

The phrase of Verse 9, *"Yes, gray hairs are here and there upon him, yet he knows not,"* refers to this condition having existed even from the beginning. It was not a new sin but an old sin.

Spiritually speaking, *"found wanting"* was written on their walls, yet, they had no understanding of its meaning. Israel *"knew it not."*

NOTES

As Israel of old, major religious denominations fit the same category. They have lost their spiritual way, and *"yet they know it not."* This is the greatest danger of all!

It is bad enough to be in this spiritual condition, but to be thusly and not know it closes the door to any forthcoming help.

The modern church claims the Blessings of God because its buildings are big, its numbers are large, and its coffers are full of money. However, none of that has anything to do with the Moving and Operation of the Holy Spirit. In fact, the Presence of the Holy Spirit, constituting His Work and Operation, is the only True Sign of God's Favor and Blessing. Everything else is superficial; everything else is *"found wanting."*

PRIDE

The phrase, *"And the pride of Israel testifies to his face,"* refers to the haughtiness of Israel, which is characteristic of pride.

The word, *"testifies"* could be translated, *"humbled,"* as in *"humbled to his face."* This refers to humiliation at the hands of their enemies.

The phrase, *"And they do not return to the LORD their God, nor seek Him for all this,"* emphasizes their obstinate blindness and perverseness. They did not do so because, as stated in the previous Verse, they had reached the place that they did not even know how to turn to God. They did not seek Jehovah, but instead, made more treaties and alliances with foreign nations in hope of being lifted up out of their national impotence, but to no avail!

THE MODERN CHURCH

One must consider that the modern church, as well, has drifted so far away from the Lord, as a whole, that not only do they not turn to Him for help, but they, as Israel of old, don't even know how to do so.

Prayer was once the mainstay of the Church. It sought God, at least those who believed His Word. Now, and due to the psychological intrusion, the Lord is no longer sought for Leading, Help, or Guidance. As stated, they don't even know how to do so.

As well, great segments of the modern Charismatic churches actually do not even believe in seeking the Lord. To do so, at least to them, is an admittance of weakness and that something is wrong. They are taught that if something is wrong, an improper confession is the cause. Consequently, to correct the situation, they say, they are taught to confess properly.

As such, they do not even believe in seeking God, at least in the Biblical manner. Their seeking him mainly consists of confessing money, healing, etc., into existence.

In their teaching, the *"new creation man"* is always above the needs represented in these Passages.

THE CROSS OF CHRIST

As well, most in the modern Charismatic movement do not even believe in the Cross of Christ. They refer to it as *"past miseries"* or *"the greatest defeat in human history."* They claim that if the Preacher preaches the Cross, it will destroy the people.

That's very strange, especially when one considers that Paul said:

"Christ sent me not to baptize, but to preach the Gospel: not with the enticing words of man's wisdom, lest the Cross of Christ should be made of none effect" (I Cor. 1:17).

He then said, *"The preaching of the Cross is to them who perish foolishness; but to we who are Saved it is the Power of God"* (I Cor. 1:18).

And, *"We preach Christ Crucified, to the Jews a stumblingblock, and to the Greeks foolishness"* (I Cor. 1:23).

In other words, the great Apostle was saying that even though the Message of the Cross may be an offense to both the Jews and the Gentiles, still, that was the Message he preached, and the only Message he preached, simply because it was the only Message that would set the captive free.

So, you have your choice. You can believe the modern Charismatic group, or you can believe the Apostle Paul!

A SILLY DOVE

The Holy Spirit here uses the *"dove"* as an illustration because the dove has no bitterness, but neither is it very smart.

The *"dove"* is used as an example because in its search for food, it flies right into the

net of the bird-catcher without suspecting or observing it.

So Ephraim, when they went and asked help from Assyria or from Egypt, did not perceive that they went to their hurt.

Such typifies the majority of the modern church. They, as the *"dove,"* have drifted so far away from God that they no longer realize the terrible danger of false doctrines and fall into it as in a net. In other words, catching the hook of the *"greed message,"* they do not realize they are being led, instead, to destruction.

LIES AGAINST GOD

The phrase, *"Though I have redeemed them, yet they have spoken lies against Me,"* is not confined to their dealings with their fellowman, but instead, speaking lies against or concerning God.

The lies in question, no doubt, included His essential Deity or sole Divinity. As well, it probably pertained to His Power and Willingness either to protect or punish.

Or, it could well have been them drawing near to God with their lips without either true Faith or real affection in their hearts, which was probably the case.

In effect, and due to this, He says, *"I have withdrawn My Providential Oversight, and have hidden My Face from them, and, consequently, they shall be consumed."*

MODERN LIES

When the preacher stands before a television camera and tells the audience, whomever they might be, that if they will give so much money, at the end of the year all of their bills will be paid, etc., plainly and simply, they are lying. It's one thing to lie but something else altogether to make God a part of your lie. It would be better for these preachers to go down to a bank or a store, level a .38 revolver in the face of the clerk, and take the money, rather than lying about God.

It is certainly true that God will bless those who give to His Work; however, the giver should make certain it's truly the Work of God to which he is giving. If it is the Work of God, it is not going to lie, and above all, make God a part of the lie.

When a preacher, or anyone, for that

matter, says, *"The Lord told me . . ."* that is a very heavy statement. Only one thing can be said about it, and that is the person had better be certain that God has actually spoken to him in some way. Otherwise, he is telling a lie about God and, as well, making God a part of the lie. Such constitutes blasphemy!

A DECEITFUL BOW

The phrase, *"They return, but not to the Most High: they are like a deceitful bow,"* concerns Israel seeking help from other sources.

By now, the reader surely understands the significance and even insistence that the Believer seek the Lord instead of other remedies. And yet, this is the great sin of the modern church.

Men seek other men, i.e., humanistic psychology, religious denominations, soothsayers, fortune-tellers, psychics, or horoscopes, but they do not seek *"the Most High."*

As well, it should by now be obvious that the Lord places all other proposed solutions, everything other than the Cross of Christ, irrespective of it being religious or demonic, in the same category. This includes the Virgin Mary, along with dead Saints, Angels, etc. In other words, one will receive just as much help praying to a demon spirit as he will the Virgin Mary, and not meaning at all to take away from this dear lady in any capacity. It is in no way meant to place the blessed Mother of our Lord in association with spirits of darkness. All help comes from the Lord Alone, all made possible by the Cross and the Cross alone (I Cor. 1:17-18, 23; 2:2).

The phrase, *"They are like a deceitful bow,"* refers to a bow that warps so that to shoot straight is impossible.

The world regards with contempt and ridicules professing Christians who seek its support and fellowship. Consequently, the foray of the modern church into humanistic psychology has not drawn men to Christ but, instead, has belittled the God Whom we serve.

The idea of all of this is that all who trust in men will ultimately be ashamed, while all who trust in God will never be ashamed (Ps. 119:46).

"O blessed Life—the heart at rest,

"When all without tumultuous scenes,
"That trusts a higher Will, and deems,
"That higher Will, not mine, the best."

"O blessed Life, the mind that sees,
"Whatever change the years may bring,
"A Mercy still in everything,
"And shining through all mysteries."

"O blessed Life, the soul that soars,
"When sense of mortal sight is dimmed,
"Beyond the sense, beyond to Him,
"Whose Love unlocks the Heavenly Doors."

"O blessed Life, heart, mind, and soul,
"From self-born aims and wishes free,
"In all at one with Deity,
"And loyal to the Lord's Control."

"O Life, how blessed, how Divine,
"High Life, the earnest of a higher.
"Saviour, fulfill my deep desire,
"And let this blessed Life be mine."

CHAPTER 8

(1) "SET THE TRUMPET TO YOUR MOUTH. HE SHALL COME AS AN EAGLE AGAINST THE HOUSE OF THE LORD, BECAUSE THEY HAVE TRANSGRESSED MY COVENANT, AND TRESPASSED AGAINST MY LAW.

(2) "ISRAEL SHALL CRY UNTO ME, MY GOD, WE KNOW YOU.

(3) "ISRAEL HAS CAST OFF THE THING THAT IS GOOD: THE ENEMY SHALL PURSUE HIM.

(4) "THEY HAVE SET UP KINGS, BUT NOT BY ME: THEY HAVE MADE PRINCES, AND I KNEW IT NOT: OF THEIR SILVER AND THEIR GOLD HAVE THEY MADE THEM IDOLS, THAT THEY MAY BE CUT OFF.

(5) "YOUR CALF, O SAMARIA, HAS CAST YOU OFF; MY ANGER IS KINDLED AGAINST THEM: HOW LONG WILL IT BE ERE THEY ATTAIN TO INNOCENCY?

(6) "FOR FROM ISRAEL WAS IT ALSO: THE WORKMAN MADE IT; THEREFORE IT IS NOT GOD: BUT THE CALF OF SAMARIA SHALL BE BROKEN IN PIECES."

The construction is:

1. (Vs. 1) Menahem was king in Samaria at this time. He purchased the support of the Assyrians at a ruinous price for the state (II Ki. 15:19).

Uzziah was king in Jerusalem. He built fortified cities (II Chron. 26:9).

The one king trusted the Assyrians; the other, a *"defenced"* city. Neither sought help from God. Thus, there is no difference as to the *"flesh"* between an idolater and a nominal Christian.

2. (Vs. 1) *"He shall come as an eagle against the House of the LORD"* refers to the people of the northern kingdom of Israel and not the Temple. The pronoun *"he"* refers to the Assyrian monarch. The cause of this, as the last phrase implies, *"And trespassed against My Law,"* was disobedience to the Bible.

3. Referring to Verse 2, their profession of the Knowledge of God and of attachment to Him was false (Mat. 7:22; Jn. 8:54-55).

4. Addressing Verse 3, the *"good,"* which Israel rejected, is God, the One Good; Jehovah, the Greatest Good; the Law, which was good; and, also all the goodness that the Lord bestowed on those who keep His Covenant.

5. The short phrase, *"not by Me,"* given in Verse 4 means that these kings were not sanctioned by the Lord. As well, they took their prosperity, i.e., *"the silver and the gold,"* and made *"idols"* with it.

6. The actual meaning of Verse 5 is that idol worship had been the cause of their rejection. The question, *"How long will it be ere they attain to innocency?"* only shows their hypocrisy.

7. The phrase, *"For from Israel was it also,"* of Verse 6 refers to the people inventing the calf. It was broken in pieces by the Assyrians and thus was demonstrated its impotency to save. Regrettably, concerning most of that presently, which goes under the guise of Christianity, one also would have to say, *"The workman made it,"* meaning, *"therefore, it is not of God."*

SET THE TRUMPET TO YOUR MOUTH

The first phrase of Verse 1 should read, *"The trumpet to your mouth,"* leaving off

NOTES

the word *"set,"* because there was no time, inasmuch as the Assyrian invasion was imminent. This was the *"trumpet of war."*

The phrase, *"He shall come as an eagle against the House of the LORD,"* refers to the Assyrian monarch.

As an *"eagle,"* he would be swift and cruel.

As well, the *"House of the LORD"* refers to the people of Israel, as stated, and not the Temple at Jerusalem.

MY GOD, WE KNOW YOU

The profession of Israel of the Knowledge of God and of attachment to Him was false (Mat. 7:22; Jn. 8:54-55).

Their claim was based on them being originally chosen as the People of God. In fact, the southern kingdom of Judah and the northern kingdom called Israel were the only Nations in the world who had a true Knowledge of God. Actually, they were the only monotheistic people on Earth, meaning they worshipped one God, Jehovah. All the rest of the nations of the world were polytheistic, meaning they worshipped many gods, namely demon spirits. As such, Israel was to be the *"light"* opposing the darkness which reigned everywhere. However, due to going deeper and deeper into sin, their Knowledge of the Lord was now only ritualistic, superficial, and definitely not of the heart.

THE MODERN CHURCH

I fear that presently there are fewer people being truly Saved in the world than in any time since the Reformation. As well, there are fewer Believers baptized with the Holy Spirit with the evidence of speaking with other Tongues than at any time since the turn of the Twentieth Century, which occasioned the basic beginning of the Latter Rain. Churches are being filled with people who have never been Born-Again. They listen to preachers who tell them what they want to hear. Many of these preachers are little more than glorified social workers or amateur psychologists. Consequently, the modern church in too many circles is little more than a religious social center with the preacher little more than a motivator!

Even those who claim to be Spirit-filled all too often are *"walking after the flesh,"* rather than *"walking after the Spirit."* Considering that flesh appeals to flesh, they fall for almost anything that claims to be in the spirit realm. These preachers constantly prophesy, even giving dates to certain things, but with almost nothing ever coming to pass. But yet, precious few question the validity of such prophecies, instead, jumping hastily to the next fad.

HOW TO LIVE FOR GOD

The truth is, the modern church little knows how to live for God. And now we are speaking of those who truly know the Lord and truly love the Lord. As a result, it embraces one scheme after the other, the latest one as worthless as the one just abandoned.

JESUS SAID . . .

"Then if any man shall say unto you, Lo, here is Christ, or there; believe it not.

"For there shall arise false Christs, and false prophets, and shall show great signs and wonders; insomuch that, if it were possible, they shall deceive the very elect.

"Behold, I have told you before.

"Wherefore if they shall say unto you, Behold, he is in the desert; go not forth: behold, he is in the secret chambers; believe it not" (Mat. 24:23-26).

While in these Passages given on Olivet, Jesus admittedly was speaking of Israel and its sad state of affairs, which will commence shortly before the Battle of Armageddon, still, it most definitely can be applied, as well, to the present time.

THE CROSS OF CHRIST

Any so-called Move of God, which is really of the Lord, meaning it is truly Scriptural, will always, and without fail, be built squarely on the Message of the Cross.

When Paul left Athens, every evidence is that he was troubled in his spirit. And now the Lord had directed that he go to Corinth, the third most powerful city in the Roman Empire. As well, it was the most wicked! The twin great evils of Satan, vice and philosophy, were predominant in this city. These were shells, so to speak, that were hard to crack. The great Apostle, no doubt, wondered as he was coming from Athens

NOTES

to Corinth just how advancement could be made in this city. The Holy Spirit may have gently whispered to him at that time, *"Preach the Cross!"* And then the Holy Spirit may have said, *"If the Cross will work at Corinth, it will work anywhere."*

That's the reason the Great Apostle said the following:

JESUS CHRIST AND HIM CRUCIFIED

"And I, brethren, when I came to you, came not with excellency of speech or of wisdom *(means that he depended not on oratorical abilities, nor did he delve into philosophy, which was all the rage of that particular day)*, **declaring unto you the Testimony of God** *(which is Christ and Him Crucified)*.

"For I determined not to know anything among you *(with purpose and design, Paul did not resort to the knowledge or philosophy of the world regarding the preaching of the Gospel)*, **save Jesus Christ, and Him Crucified** *(that and that alone is the Message, which will save the sinner, set the captive free, and give the Believer perpetual victory)*.**"**

WEAKNESS AND TREMBLING

"And I was with you in *(personal)* **weakness** *(an expression of utter dependence on God)*, **and in fear** *(fear that he might not properly preach the Cross)*, **and in much trembling.** *(He realized the significance of what he was preaching and his inadequacy regarding his own person.)*

"And my speech and my preaching *was* **not with enticing words of man's wisdom** *(he knew that would not set anyone free; the modern church should take a lesson from this)*, **but in demonstration of the Spirit and of Power** *(which speaks of what the Holy Spirit can do in the hearts and lives of Believers if the Cross is properly preached)*:

"That your Faith should not stand in the wisdom of men *(speaks of any proposed way other than the Cross)*, **but in the Power of God** *(made possible only by the Cross)*.**"**

THE WISDOM OF GOD

"Howbeit we speak wisdom among them who are perfect *(only the spiritually mature* *can understand the Wisdom of God, which is the Cross)*: **yet not the wisdom of this world** *(the Wisdom of God pertaining to Salvation has absolutely no relationship whatsoever to the 'wisdom of this world')*, **nor of the princes of this world, that come to naught** *(the great sages and philosophers of the world contributed nothing to Paul, nor do they to us as well)*:

"But we speak the Wisdom of God in a mystery, *even* **the hidden** *wisdom (God's Wisdom leads sinful men to the great Sacrifice of history, the offering up of Jesus on the Cross of Calvary, which paid the terrible sin debt of man, at least for all who will believe)*, **which God ordained before the world unto our glory** *(in the Mind of God, Christ was offered up on the Cross even before the foundation of the world [I Pet. 1:18-20])*" **(I Cor. 2:1-7).**

THE CROSS OF CHRIST IS THE WISDOM OF GOD

To know and understand the Wisdom of God, i.e., the Cross, presents itself as the highest attainment of knowledge. That's the reason that Paul also said:

"Casting down imaginations *(philosophic strongholds; every effort man makes outside of the Cross of Christ)*, **and every high thing that exalts itself against the Knowledge of God** *(all the pride of the human heart)*, **and bringing into captivity every thought to the obedience of Christ** *(can be done only by the Believer looking exclusively to the Cross, where all Victory is found; the Holy Spirit will then perform the task)*" **(II Cor. 10:5).**

But instead, sadly, much of the modern church is seeking after the wisdom of the world instead of the *"Wisdom of God."* As a result, as it regards that which is positive, they get nothing. As it regards that which is negative, spiritual bondage is the end result. To abandon the Cross of Christ, which is the Wisdom of God, one, in effect, is abandoning God.

DO YOU WANT THE LORD?

The Lord through the Prophet said that *"Israel has cast off the thing that is good."* As a result, *"the enemy would pursue him."*

Living for the Lord, serving Him, and

working for Him is the most fulfilling, the most rewarding, and the most wonderful occupation in which one may engage himself. In fact, living for the Lord is so far ahead of anything the world has to offer that it is no contest. Now, that being the case, why is it that most of the world has no desire for Him whatsoever, and most of the church doesn't want or desire His Ways?

Deception is the reason!

Unredeemed men are deceived by the powers of darkness into believing the very opposite of that which is true. Regrettably and sadly, most of the church is also deceived into believing that which is incorrect.

Not wanting the Lord, He delivered Israel up into the hands of their pursuers. This tells us that the Lord has control of all things, as should be obvious!

USE IT OR LOSE IT

This lesson should not be lost upon modern Believers. If the church does not want the Bible, the Lord will see to it that the Bible is taken away. If the church does not want Righteousness, the Lord will take Righteousness away and see to it that the church has unrighteousness.

Thus is the Law of God, which, in effect, states that if a person wills Righteousness, God wills Righteousness to him. Conversely, if a person wills unrighteousness, the Lord wills unrighteousness to him.

The only thing that keeps Satan from the Believer is the Lord. If the Lord is rejected, the protection is removed, and *"the enemy shall pursue him."*

THE MESSAGE OF THE CROSS

Since the Lord was so gracious to give me the great Revelation of the Cross in 1997, little by little, more and more people are hearing this Word, and, thankfully, more and more people are believing this Word. But yet, the majority in the modern church has no desire for the Message of the Cross.

For those who accept it, they will find a place and position in Christ as they've never known previously. They will come to the place of understanding regarding the price that was paid at Calvary's Cross, and will learn that the Lord means for us to have all for which He paid such a price. In other words, they will know a *"joy unspeakable and full of glory"* as never before.

But for those who reject it, the increase in bondages of darkness is going to multiply. Such will have the tendency to turn some to the Cross, which is their only hope. But others, regrettably, will lose their way entirely. Regarding both sides, this will be in wholesale lots.

NOT BY ME

The phrase in Verse 4, *"Not by Me,"* means that these kings were not sanctioned by the Lord.

Likewise, the phrase, *"I knew it not,"* means *"I knew them not,"* i.e., *"I did not recognize them."*

This state of things began with Israel's revolt from the House of David and rebellion against the son of Solomon, their legitimate sovereign, and was repeated in subsequent usurpations.

However, in studying the account, we do know that God took a hand in seeing to the appointment of certain kings over Israel, such as Ahijah (I Ki. 11:37), and Jehu. Consequently, we must distinguish between the permission and approval of Jehovah. In His Government, He permits many things, which we know from His Nature He does not and, in fact, cannot approve.

IDOLS

The idea of the phrase, *"Of their silver and their gold have they made them idols,"* refers to Israel taking that which God had given them to use for God's Work but, instead, used it for idolatry.

The phrase, *"That they may be cut off,"* means that this *"gold and silver,"* which was used to fabricate idols, rather than bringing good, will instead bring destruction, i.e., *"cut off."*

THE MODERN CHURCH

Regrettably, as Israel of old substituted their choice for God's Choice, likewise, many modern religious denominations have, for the most part, set aside the pattern given by the Holy Spirit in the Early Church and have substituted their own.

NOTES

They have established man-made offices and attributed spiritual authority to them.

They have, if not in fact, definitely in principle, appointed little popes, consequently, abrogating the Headship of Christ as the Leader of the Church.

As a result, the same can be said of most modern religious denominations as Israel of old, *"they have set up kings, i.e., man-made offices, but not by Me."*

If one presently fully intends to follow the Word of God, one will find it very difficult, if not impossible, to associate with a religious denomination.

Many take the position that even though they are in the system, they do not approve of it, and, consequently, at least in their thinking, they are not guilty of its excesses. However, to be in something is to approve of it, whether one thinks so or not!

The compromising of convictions has always begun very quietly. Only a small part is trimmed from the whole, and the conclusion is that it will not be missed. However, after a period of time, we awaken to find that the entirety of the block of Spiritual and Scriptural Conviction has been whittled away until nothing remains.

THE ANGER OF GOD

The phrase, *"My Anger is kindled against them,"* shows how Jehovah is disgusted with their golden calf and hateful idolatry. The pronoun, *"them,"* proclaims the fact that even though the *"calf"* is mentioned, still, it is the stupid, sinful worshippers to whom the Lord points.

The question, *"How long will it be ere they attain to innocency?"* only shows their hypocrisy.

At the Prophet's Message, the people of the northern kingdom were claiming that they were totally unaware of their wrongdoing. In worshipping the *"calf,"* at least in their minds, they considered they were worshipping Jehovah.

Inasmuch as the Priests were not truly God-ordained, and they had long since forsaken the Temple with its sacrifices, which were truly of God, and inasmuch as they had been this way for nearly 200 years, they had no knowledge of the Word of God.

However, they were free to come at any time to Jerusalem to worship, which, in fact, many did! So, their reason was merely an excuse, which evoked this question.

GOD'S WRATH AGAINST SIN

C.H. Dodd regards *"the wrath of God"* not as *"the attitude of God to man, but an inevitable process of cause and effect in a moral universe. But a completely depersonalized concept is not adequate to cover Biblical teaching. The wrath of God is certainly no capricious passion, but it is the personal attitude of a personal God, the 'eternal recoil against the unholy on the part of the all-holy God.'"*[1] One side of God's Holiness is His Anger against sin; the other, and more fundamental aspect, is His Love and Mercy, to which the whole Bible bears witness. If we fail to recognize His Wrath, we shall not fully appreciate His Mercy.

WHY IS THE ANGER OF GOD SO PRONOUNCED AGAINST SIN?

Primarily it is because sin has death attached to it. Paul said:

"Know you not, that to whom you yield yourselves servants to obey, his servants you are to whom you obey (the Believer is either a slave to Christ, for that's what the word 'servant' means, or else a slave to sin, which he will be if he doesn't keep his Faith in Christ and the Cross); **whether of sin unto death** (once again allow us to state the fact that if the Believer attempts to live for God by any method other than Faith in the Finished Work of Christ, the Believer will fail, no matter how hard he otherwise tries), **or of obedience unto Righteousness?** (The Believer is required to obey the Word of the Lord. He cannot do that within his own strength, but only by understanding that he receives all things through what Christ did at the Cross and his continued Faith in that Finished Work, even on a daily basis. Then the Holy Spirit, Who Alone can make us what we ought to be, can accomplish His Work within our lives)" **(Rom. 6:16).**

THE WAGES OF SIN IS DEATH

The Apostle also said:

"For the wages of sin *is* death (speaks

of spiritual death, which is separation from God); **but the Gift of God *is* Eternal Life through Jesus Christ our Lord** (as stated, all of this, without exception, comes to us by the means of what Christ did at the Cross, which demands that the Cross ever be the Object of our Faith, thus giving the Holy Spirit latitude to work within our lives and bring forth His Fruit)" **(Rom. 6:23).**

DEATH BY SIN

Paul also said, **"Wherefore, as by one man sin entered into the world** (by Adam), **and death by sin** (both spiritual and physical death); **and so death passed upon all men** (for all were in Adam), **for that all have sinned** (all are born in sin because of Adam's transgression)" **(Rom. 5:12).**

Due to the fact of sin, death reigns over everything. Most marriages are dead or dying because of sin. The potential in untold millions of hearts and lives will never be realized because sin will kill such potential and does so repeatedly. Everything that sin touches ultimately dies. Considering that due to the Fall, sin is on everything, this means that everything is dying. Now we get an inkling of understanding as it regards why God unalterably hates sin. Sin is not a mere abstract negative condition, or is it a mere philosophical idea, but rather a spirit that *"steals, kills, and destroys"* (Jn. 10:10). Due to sin, man is dying, the Planet is dying, and all that is therein, and, at least, the heavens around the Earth. In fact, sin and death have existed from the first page of human history; therefore, man has never seen anything else but the dying and the decay.

THE NEW HEAVEN AND THE NEW EARTH

Concerning that coming time, the Scripture says:

"And I saw a New Heaven and a New Earth ('New' in the Greek is 'Kainos,' and means 'freshness with respect to age'; when it is finished, it will be new, as is obvious, but the idea is it will remain new and fresh forever and forever because there is no more sin): **for the first Heaven and the first Earth were passed away** (refers to the original Creation, which was marred by sin; 'passed away' in the Greek is 'parerchomai,' and means 'to pass from one condition to another'; it never means annihilation)**; and there was no more sea** *(refers to the giant oceans, such as the Pacific and the Atlantic; however, there will continue to be lakes, bodies of water, rivers, streams, etc.)***" (Rev. 21:1).**

Understanding the terrible destructive power of sin, God has to be unalterably opposed to sin in any form. Hence, the Word of God says:

THE REVELATION OF THE WRATH OF GOD

"For the Wrath of God *(God's Personal Emotion with regard to sin)* **is revealed from Heaven** *(this anger originates with God)* **against all ungodliness and unrighteousness of men** *(God must unalterably be opposed to sin)***, who hold the truth in unrighteousness** *(who refuse to recognize Who God is, and what God is)***" (Rom. 1:18).**

To understand how bad that sin really is, one has to look at Calvary. When we consider the price that was paid at Calvary's Cross for the Redemption of man, we then get an idea as to how bad that sin really is. There our Lord atoned for all sin, past, present, and future, at least for all who will believe (Jn. 3:16).

IT IS NOT GOD

The Holy Spirit through the Prophet said, *"For from Israel was it also: the workman made it; therefore it is not God."*

Anything that religious man does out of his own mind, no matter how righteous it may seem to be at the moment, purely and simply, *"is not God."* That means that if any Believer attempts to attain to Righteousness and Holiness by means other than the Cross of Christ, whatever it is he does, God cannot accept it. It doesn't matter how righteous it may seem to be or how Scriptural it might be in its own right. If it's not faith in Christ and the Cross, and that exclusively, then it means it's something that man has devised, which God cannot accept.

SCRIPTURAL?

Many Christians use things, which are Scriptural in their own right, such as Water

Baptism, the Lord's Supper, fasting, and confession of Scriptures, thinking by their use that they can attain to that which is desired. They cannot!

It is claimed by some, if problems of sin are faced, the Christian should just memorize and quote two or three Scriptures over and over, and this is going to bring victory. While the quoting of Scriptures is definitely right and will definitely bless the person, still, that will not help one overcome sin.

Others claim that the taking of the *"Lord's Supper"* will fall out to the same result. Again, the Lord's Supper is viable and Scriptural in its own right, but it will not give one victory over sin, and neither will it bring healing or prosperity, etc. The Cross of Christ alone will accomplish that task.

THE ALTAR OF INCENSE

If one were to go into the Holy Place in the Tabernacle, which was the first room, one would see to the right the Table of Shewbread, to the left the Golden Lampstand, and then immediately in front of the Veil was situated the *"Altar of Incense."*

While it was an Altar, sacrifices were not to be offered there. To do so would be a denial of the blood sacrifice at the Brazen Altar, which typified Calvary. While it was viable in its own right, as should be obvious, it was not meant to cleanse from sin, that being done at the Brazen Altar. That's what I mean by the use of that which is Scriptural in its own right but attempting to make it apply to the wrong purpose and reason. While obedience to the Word of God in any and every capacity will always bring blessing, we are not to use the Lord's Supper for that which Calvary is intended to be used, etc. Let's look closer at this Altar of Incense.

INTERCESSION

"And when Aaron lights the lamps at evening, he shall burn Incense upon it *(upon the Altar of Incense)***, a perpetual Incense before the LORD throughout your generations.** *(One or more coals of fire were to be taken from the Brazen Altar, which typified the Cross, and placed on the Altar of Incense, with Incense poured over the coals, which filled the Holy Place with a sweet* *fragrance, all typifying the Intercession of Christ on our behalf; however, it must be understood that the Intercession of Christ does not really pertain to Him doing anything in Heaven on our behalf, but that the fact of His Presence at the Throne of God guarantees that Intercession [Heb. 7:25-26]. If something other than His mere Presence was required, that would mean that the work which He did at the Cross was not a Finished Work. But it was a Finished Work and requires nothing else added [Jn. 19:30; Heb. 10:12-14].)"*

STRANGE INCENSE

"You shall offer no strange incense thereon *(the Incense poured on the burning coals had to be that which the Lord had designed and no other kind; anything else would be called 'strange incense' and would be unacceptable! As we will later study, the Incense was made of ingredients which pictured and portrayed Christ in His Atoning Work; that and that alone is what God will recognize)*, **nor burnt sacrifice** *(the Lord will recognize no sacrifice but that of the Cross, of which the Brazen Altar was a Type; the Altar of Incense was for worship and intercession only, all made possible by the Cross; 'works religion' typifies a sacrifice offered on the Altar of Incense, which God can never accept)*, **nor Meat Offering** *(concerning this, Pink says: 'This, in figure, tells us that our Great High Priest expects no blessings which His Blood has not purchased, and expects pardon from Divine Justice for no sins for which Faith has not been evidenced. And incidentally, the measure of the Blessings which are given is God's estimate of the life which He gave')*; **neither shall you pour Drink Offering thereon.** *(Anytime the Believer places his faith and trust in anything other than the Cross, he violates the Cross of Christ and wrongly uses the Altar of Incense, which, if continued, will bring on great chastisement from the Lord [Heb. 12:5-11])"* **(Ex. 30:8-9).**

Preachers who advocate anything as the vehicle of forgiveness for sins or Blessings from the Lord, other than the Cross, are, in effect, offering up strange incense. God can never accept such. Let it be forever understood:

GOD'S WAY

As we've already stated any number of times in this volume, let us do so again:

• Jesus Christ is the Source of all things that we receive from God. He said, *". . . If any man thirst, let him come unto Me, and drink"* (Jn. 7:37).

• However, the Cross of Christ is the Means by which these things are given to us. Salvation, healing, forgiveness, cleansing, blessings, and prosperity are all made possible by what Jesus did for us at the Cross (Rom. 6:1-14; I Cor. 1:17-18, 21, 23; 2:2; Gal., Chpt. 5; 6:14; Eph. 2:13-18; Col. 2:14-15).

• The Holy Spirit superintends all of this, and if our faith is in anything except Christ and the Cross, He will not allow entrance. The Scripture says:

"And that He *(Christ)* **might reconcile both** *(Jews and Gentiles)* **unto God in one body** *(the Church)* **by the Cross** *(it is by the Atonement only that men ever become reconciled to God)*, **having slain the enmity thereby** *(removed the barrier between God and sinful man)*:"*

ACCESS

"And came and preached peace to you who were afar off *(proclaims the Gospel going to the Gentiles)*, **and to them who were nigh.** *(This refers to the Jews. It is the same Message for both.)*

"For through Him *(through Christ)* **we both** *(Jews and Gentiles)* **have access by One Spirit unto the Father.** *(If the sinner comes by the Cross, the Holy Spirit opens the door, otherwise, it is barred [Jn. 10:1])"* **(Eph. 2:16-18).**

DO WE MAKE TOO MUCH OF THE CROSS?

It is impossible to make too much of the Cross. Was Paul making too much of the Cross when he said, *"But God forbid that I should glory* (boast), *save in the Cross of our Lord Jesus Christ, by Whom the world is crucified unto me, and I unto the world"* (Gal. 6:14)? Was he making too much of the Cross when he said to the Church at Corinth, *"For I determined not to know anything among you, save Jesus Christ, and Him Crucified"* (I Cor. 2:2)?

With purpose and design, Paul did not resort to the knowledge or philosophy of the world regarding the preaching of the Gospel. That and that alone, *"Jesus Christ and Him Crucified,"* is the Message which will save the sinner, set the captive free, and give the Believer perpetual Victory.

No, the sin of the modern church is making too little of the Cross of Christ.

(7) "FOR THEY HAVE SOWN THE WIND, AND THEY SHALL REAP THE WHIRLWIND: IT HAS NO STALK: THE BUD SHALL YIELD NO MEAL: IF SO BE IT YIELD, THE STRANGERS SHALL SWALLOW IT UP.

(8) "ISRAEL IS SWALLOWED UP: NOW SHALL THEY BE AMONG THE GENTILES AS A VESSEL WHEREIN IS NO PLEASURE."

The exegesis is:

1. (Vs. 7) The analogy drawn by the Holy Spirit is of a man attempting to sow seed in the face of a strong wind. Obviously, the seed will be blown away, with the harvest reaping only that which the *"whirlwind"* gives.

2. (Vs. 8) The Assyrians *"swallowed up"* the Ten Tribes, and they have been thrown aside as a despised vessel ever since.

3. What we sow, we reap!

SOWING AND REAPING

The Prophet is saying that they will weary themselves in vain in the service of idols, just the same as a man who sows to the wind, in which there is nothing substantial, shall only reap the wind.

As a result of the seed being whipped by the wind into unbroken land, the seed cannot germinate, and if it does, *"it has no stalk,"* and *"the bud shall yield no meal."*

THE NATION OF AMERICA HAS SOWED TO THE WIND

I'm afraid that this nation, as it regards the Obama Administration, has sowed to the wind and, consequently, will reap the whirlwind.

For some 20 years this man belonged to a church in Chicago whose pastor is a racist and, as well, a hater of America. During that

NOTES

20 years, the President was a close friend with this pastor and, accordingly, the Scripture says, *"Can two walk together, except they be agreed?"* (Amos 3:3). So, in truth, this means that this President is a racist and, as well, hates America, i.e., *"hates the Judeo-Christian concept on which this nation is founded."* As a result, we are about to reap the whirlwind.

The sadness of all this is, people elect to office that which they are! So that means this nation is in a sad shape. And it is in such a condition because the church has failed.

The Holy Spirit through Simon Peter said:

"For the time *is come* **that Judgment must begin at the House of God** *(Judgment always begins with Believers and pertains to their faith, whether in the Cross or otherwise; the Cross alone is spared Judgment, for there Jesus was judged in our place)***: and if** *it* first *begin* **at us, what shall the end** *be* **of them who obey not the Gospel of God?** *(If God will judge His Own, how much more will He judge the unredeemed? The Cross alone stays the Judgment of God. Let that ever be understood.)*

"And if the Righteous scarcely be Saved *(can be Saved only by trusting Christ and the Cross and nothing else)***, where shall the ungodly and the sinner appear?** *(If the great Sacrifice of Christ is rejected and spurned, where does that leave those who do such a thing? There is no hope for their Salvation)***"** (I Pet. 4:17-18).

PREACHING THE CROSS

Paul said:

"For after that in the Wisdom of God the world by wisdom knew not God *(man's puny wisdom, even the best he has to offer, cannot come to know God in any manner)***, it pleased God by the foolishness of preaching** *(preaching the Cross)* **to save them who believe.** *(Paul is not dealing with the art of preaching here but with what is preached)***"** (I Cor. 1:21).

He further said, **"But we preach Christ Crucified** *(this is the Foundation of the Word of God and, thereby, of Salvation)* **..."** (I Cor. 1:23).

In the Old Testament, the Lord said through Moses to the Children of Israel:

"For I will pass through the land of Egypt this night, and will smite all the firstborn in the land of Egypt, both man and beast; and against all the gods of Egypt I will execute judgment: I am the LORD. *(The words 'pass through' could be translated 'go through,' since the word used is entirely unconnected with the 'Passover.' According to Exodus 12:23, the Lord did not personally go through the land of Egypt that particular night, but rather that He used an Angel. The 'beasts' were included because animal worship was an important part of the religion of the Egyptians. So, the Lord directed His Judgment against every facet of Egyptian life and living.)"*

THE ANIMAL BLOOD WAS A TOKEN

"And the blood shall be to you for a token upon the houses where you are *(the blood applied to the doorposts meant that their Faith and trust were in the Pascal Lamb; the blood then applied was only a 'token,' meaning that it was then but a symbol of One Who was to come, Who would redeem mankind by the shedding of His Life's Blood)***:"**

WHEN I SEE THE BLOOD, I WILL PASS OVER YOU

The phrase, **"And when I see the blood, I will pass over you,** *(constitutes the great Doctrine of Redemption. This means that, without a doubt, this is one of the single most important statements or Scriptures in the entirety of the Word of God; the lamb had taken the fatal blow; and because it had taken the blow, those in the house would be spared; it was not a question of personal worthiness, self had nothing whatever to do in the matter; it was a matter of Faith; all under the cover of the blood were safe, just as all presently under the cover of the Blood are safe; this means that they were not merely in a savable state, but rather that they were 'Saved'; as well, they were not partly Saved and partly exposed to Judgment, they were wholly Saved, and because there is no such thing as partial Justification; the Lord didn't say, 'When I see you,' or, 'When I see your good works,' etc., but, 'When I see the blood'; this speaks of Christ and what He would do at the Cross*

in order that we might be Saved, which pertained to Him giving Himself in Sacrifice, which necessitated the shedding of His Precious Blood [I Pet. 1:18-19])."

THE PLAGUE

"And the plague shall not be upon you to destroy you, when I smite the land of Egypt. *(Salvation from the 'plague' of Judgment is afforded only by the shed Blood of the Lamb and Faith in that shed Blood)"* **(Ex. 12:12-13).**

The modern church is not preaching *"the Blood."* And considering that the Cross of Christ, i.e., *"the Blood shed at Calvary's Cross,"* is the only thing that stands between mankind and the Judgment of God, this means that our nation is in serious danger. Again I state, that which can save us is not being preached by the modern church, but something else entirely. God help us! Let us say it again:

"We have sown to the wind, and we are now about to reap the whirlwind."

ISRAEL IS SWALLOWED UP

The Assyrians *"swallowed up"* the Ten Tribes referred to as Israel, and ever since, they have been thrown aside as a despised vessel. They were intended to be the masters and teachers of the Gentiles, but their own sin brought them into centuries-long degradation.

Actually, that degradation continues still!

A modern Believer is sent into the world to bless it, but directly he ceases to live and fellowship with God, he becomes useless and despised.

The phrase, *"Now shall they be among the Gentiles,"* sadly came to pass and, even after these long centuries, still continues.

In 70 A.D., Jerusalem was so completely destroyed, with over one million Jews dying in that carnage, that they ceased to exist as a Nation.

From that time, their sojourn has been among the Gentiles, in Spain, Portugal, Romania, Poland, Russia, and Germany, as well as other parts of the world. Sooner or later, in each nation, they were expelled *"as a vessel wherein is no pleasure."*

THE WARSAW GHETTO

In 1984, Frances and I were in Warsaw, Poland. I asked to be taken to the site of the Warsaw Ghetto.

In September of 1939, Hitler began his quest for domination of the world. It began with Poland and signaled the beginning of World War II. Poland was overrun in a matter of days. Almost immediately, severe persecution against the extremely large Jewish community was instituted. It centered on the Warsaw Ghetto where most of the Jews were forced to live. They were basically blamed for any and all negative circumstances that took place in Warsaw in order to have an excuse for their extermination.

They refused to surrender and, in effect, held out for days but, ultimately, saw total defeat by the German High Command. Multiple thousands were killed, while thousands of others were marched off to slave camps. As stated, I asked to see this site.

It was a beautiful summer day when Frances and I were taken there, with the car being parked on a shaded street.

We got out of the car, and the guide, with a sweep of his hand, told us, *"This is the location of the Warsaw Ghetto."*

It was not large and was completely vacant!

He explained that the many buildings that once graced the site were destroyed in the conflict in 1940, and nothing had been built there since.

I stood there looking at the empty site, knowing that multiple thousands had laid down their lives in this place. It had been turned into a Hell, but now it was empty and silent.

However, let it be quickly known that God did not do this. In truth, He had done all that was Heavenly possible to bring Israel of old to her senses, but to no avail! Ultimately, He was forced to allow them to go their own way, as He will allow any and all to go the way they desire, if insisted upon! Their being a *"vessel wherein is no pleasure"* was of their own making.

Even their immediate suffering seemed to have little effect upon their spirituality. When Christ came, which was nearly 800

years later, they would crucify Him. Then the Lord lifted His Hand, allowing them their own direction, which saw their total destruction by the Roman Tenth Legion under Titus.

Only since 1948 have they had a home. And yet, their greatest test is still future.

However, not too long from now, they will no longer be *"a vessel wherein is no pleasure,"* but, instead, their negative circumstances will be changed.

And it will be by the One they crucified!

(9) "FOR THEY ARE GONE UP TO ASSYRIA, A WILD ASS ALONE BY HIMSELF: EPHRAIM HAS HIRED LOVERS.

(10) "YES, THOUGH THEY HAVE HIRED AMONG THE NATIONS, NOW WILL I GATHER THEM, AND THEY SHALL SORROW A LITTLE FOR THE BURDEN OF THE KING OF PRINCES.

(11) "BECAUSE EPHRAIM HAS MADE MANY ALTARS TO SIN, ALTARS SHALL BE UNTO HIM TO SIN.

(12) "I HAVE WRITTEN TO HIM THE GREAT THINGS OF MY LAW, BUT THEY WERE COUNTED AS A STRANGE THING.

(13) "THEY SACRIFICE FLESH FOR THE SACRIFICES OF MY OFFERINGS, AND EAT IT; BUT THE LORD ACCEPTS THEM NOT; NOW WILL HE REMEMBER THEIR INIQUITY, AND VISIT THEIR SINS: THEY SHALL RETURN TO EGYPT.

(14) "FOR ISRAEL HAS FORGOTTEN HIS MAKER, AND BUILT TEMPLES; AND JUDAH HAS MULTIPLIED FENCED CITIES: BUT I WILL SEND A FIRE UPON HIS CITIES, AND IT SHALL DEVOUR THE PALACES THEREOF."

The exegesis is:

1. (Vs. 9) *"For they are gone up to Assyria"* portrays Israel seeking help from the very ones who would destroy them.

2. (Vs. 9) *"A wild ass alone by himself"* portrays the nature of such an animal that stands alone by itself, even as stupid and stubborn as that animal is, which does so to secure its independence.

3. (Vs. 9) *"Ephraim has hired lovers,"* which portrays her as not even having as much sense as a stupid, wild ass. What an indictment!

4. (Vs. 10) Israel would find that Assyria

would demand great tribute, throwing a tremendous hardship on the people. Excavations at about the turn of the Twentieth Century at Nineveh show Menahem's name (king of Israel) as a vassal in the inscriptions.

5. The idea of Verse 11 is, to him who wills to sin, God wills further sin!

6. (Vs. 12) The *"strange thing"* was a matter with which they had no concern, speaking of the Bible. As then, so now! The Bible today is accounted as outside of and unconnected with personal, family, and political life.

7. The phrase of Verse 13, *"They shall return to Egypt,"* did not mean a literal return to Egypt, but that their captivity in Assyria would be, in its nature, as the Egyptian bondage.

8. The phrase of Verse 14, *"For Israel has forgotten his Maker, and built temples,"* refers to Israel building shrines to idol gods on high places. As well, the phrase, *"Judah has multiplied fenced cities,"* portrays her trusting in these *"fenced cities"* and not in Jehovah. The consequences would be disastrous!

HE WHO WILLS SIN, WILL BE WILLED BY GOD FURTHER SIN

The idea of Verse 9 is, *"lovers"* hire a loose woman, but Israel reversed what is usual. In other words, Israel is likened to a shameless harlot, who, instead of receiving money for her services, pays her lovers.

What an indictment!

If a person wills Righteousness, more Righteousness will be willed by God to them. The Scripture plainly says, **"Blessed *are* they who do hunger and thirst after Righteousness** *(God's Righteousness, imputed by Christ, upon Faith in His Finished Work)***: for they shall be filled** *(but first of all must be truly empty of all self-worth)***" (Mat. 5:6).** But the person who wills sin, in other words, desires sin, God will see to such that there is greater sin. The Eleventh Verse says, *"Because Ephraim has made many altars to sin, altars shall be unto him to sin."*

GREAT THINGS OF MY LAW

Verse 12 proclaims the fact that the Law of God was looked at by Israel *"as a strange thing."* Is that the case presently in America

as it regards the Bible?

The phrase, *"I have written to him the great things of My Law,"* proclaims the Writer as God and the pen, Moses. Moses did not originate the Law. This Verse, together with Luke 24:27 and many other Scriptures, declares that no inspired books were in existence prior to Moses.

The Athenians, whose city Paul found full of idols and altars, one of which was to an unknown God, had somewhat of an excuse, for they were not privileged with a Revelation of the Divine Will in a written Law. However, Israel had no such excuse. Actually, the Word of God was given through them and to them. In fact, they were the only people on the face of the Earth who had access to God's Word. But yet, to them, it was a *"strange thing."*

THE BIBLE

The Bible, as we have stated many times, is the only revealed Truth in the world today and, in fact, ever has been. As such, its preciousness knows no bounds; consequently, the learning of what it teaches should be a lifelong work. It should be revered, loved, studied, meditated upon, and taken as the rule of life in all matters that pertain to life. For it alone, and *"According as His Divine Power has given unto us all things that pertain unto life and godliness, through the knowledge of Him Who has called us to Glory and Virtue."*

And then it says, *"Whereby are given unto us exceeding great and Precious Promises: that by these you might be partakers of the Divine Nature, having escaped the corruption that is in the world through lust"* (II Pet. 1:3-4).

Where the Bible is a *"strange thing,"* be it a person, home, city, or nation, the results will be wreckage. The following pretty well applies the world over:

- No Bible, no freedom;
- A little Bible, a little freedom; and,
- Much Bible, much freedom!

A SIMPLE ILLUSTRATION

To show its power in a simple illustration: two men, who considered themselves atheists, were travelling many years ago in New

England. A violent winter storm quickly blew up, with them having no place of refuge for the night. In desperation, they stopped at a humble dwelling, asking shelter from the storm.

Only one man was there, a grizzled individual, of whom they were somewhat fearful.

He quickly invited them in and gave them his only bedroom in order that they may spend the night.

As stated, they were somewhat fearful, even though going ahead and retiring to bed. However, something happened that changed their minds completely, at least about this man.

Discussing his grizzled appearance and, as stated, fearful that he might attack them during the night, one of them arose from the bed and quietly walked to the door, which led to the only remaining room.

He gently opened it and peered inside without being seen; however, what he saw calmed all his fears.

He softly walked back to the bed, telling his companion that there was no need to worry.

He said, *"He is reading the Bible,"* hence, all fears were allayed.

No other book but the Bible has that type of Power.

I might quickly add that despite the efforts of Hollywood and television to denigrate the Bible, with all who believe in it painted as weirdos or worse, still, it is the only Book in the world, the teachings of which, as given through Christ, can change a person's life.

Actually, the Bible is the Story of Christ and His Redemption of humanity.

Wherever the Bible is *"strange,"* murder, rape, and robbery will be commonplace.

Where the Bible is loved, these abominations will cease.

ENSLAVEMENT

As previously stated, the phrase of Verse 13, *"They shall return to Egypt,"* was not speaking literally. It rather meant that their captivity in Assyria would be, in its nature, as Egyptian bondage.

Presently, if the Believer places his or her faith in anything except Christ and Him Crucified, ultimately bondage will be the

NOTES

result. The Cross of Christ is absolutely necessary for Salvation, as I would hope most Believers would agree. The Cross of Christ is absolutely necessary for our Sanctification as well. However, most modern Believers have little or no understanding at all as it regards the Cross of Christ and our Sanctification, in other words, how we live this life for the Lord.

DOMINION

Paul said:

"For sin shall not have dominion over you: for you are not under the Law, but under Grace" (Rom. 6:14).

The Greek word translated dominion is *"kurieuo,"* and means, *"to exercise lordship over."* In this case, it pertains to a sin that dominates an individual. In some way, it rules his life, and, as always, sin never remains static but gradually gets worse. Because of not understanding the Cross of Christ as it concerns Sanctification, multiple millions of Christians are being dominated by sin in some way. And please understand, I'm speaking here of those who truly love the Lord, and who truly want to please Him, but find themselves unable to do so.

HOW CAN A CHRISTIAN BE IN BONDAGE?

When an individual comes to Christ, in other words, is *"Born-Again,"* his entire world changes. The thing he once loved, which is sin, he now hates, and the things he once hated, such as the Word of God, he now loves. He has a renewed mind (Rom. 12:1-2). Such a person thinks, as all of us did, that he'll never sin again. However, very quickly he finds that in some way he has failed the Lord, in other words, he has sinned.

Such a position shocks the new Christian! How could he have done such a thing, he thinks within his own heart. Consequently, he sets about to build barriers to keep from committing that sin again, whatever it may have been. His Faith, he then finds, is in the barrier he has constructed, whatever it might be. He soon finds that it's not sufficient, and he fails again.

That's when the sin nature once again begins to come alive, so to speak. It was made dormant when the individual accepted Christ, meaning that it was no longer effective. But now, it is starting to exercise lordship over the individual. It might be to a small degree at first, but if one's faith continues in things other than the Cross, the dominion will increase even more and more until it totally dominates the individual. Millions of Christians are in this state and don't understand what is happening to them.

A LACK OF UNDERSTANDING

Paul gave us a chapter out of his own life in the Seventh Chapter of Romans. Reading this Chapter, we must understand that these things happened to Paul before he understood God's Prescribed Order of Life and Living. To be sure, when this great Revelation was given to him, which was the meaning of the New Covenant, the Apostle most definitely at that time knew how to live for God and how to walk in victory. While Paul did not teach sinless perfection, he most definitely did teach that sin was not to have dominion over us. That is the place, no more dominion, to where the Holy Spirit seeks to bring us.

During those several years that Paul lived in defeat, he said, **"For that which I do** (the failure) **I allow not** (should have been translated, 'I understand not'; these are not the words of an unsaved man, as some claim, but rather a Believer who is trying and failing)**: for what I would, that do I not** (refers to the obedience he wants to render to Christ, but rather fails; why? as Paul explained, the Believer is married to Christ but is being unfaithful to Christ by spiritually cohabiting with the Law, which frustrates the Grace of God; that means the Holy Spirit will not help such a person, which guarantees failure [Gal. 2:21])**; but what I hate, that do I** (refers to sin in his life, which he doesn't want to do and, in fact, hates, but finds himself unable to stop; unfortunately, due to the fact of not understanding the Cross as it refers to Sanctification, this is the plight of most modern Christians)**" (Rom. 7:15).**

Regarding the statement of the Apostle Paul, this Fifteenth Verse, which I've just quoted, is the very state in which most modern Christians find themselves. They don't understand what is happening to them. And

please remember, we are speaking now of Believers, who truly love the Lord and are trying to live a godly life, but find themselves unable to do so.

Such a Believer staggers from one supposed method to the other, all with no success. Most, not understanding God's Way, are confused, bewildered, and as Paul said, lacking in understanding.

PAUL'S EXPERIENCE

It must be understood, as all know, on the road to Damascus Paul had a personal experience with Christ, which was phenomenal to say the least. He actually saw the Lord and spoke with Him. As well, three days later, he was baptized with the Holy Spirit and immediately began to preach the Gospel (Acts 9:1-22). Even then, the Lord used him mightily, despite the fact that he did not know how to live for God.

Most Believers think that if someone has an experience, much less sees Christ, as did Paul, that surely he now knows how to live for God. But we find that these experiences, as wonderful and life-changing as they were, still were not the solution.

The thing that Paul thought that he should do when he came to Christ was to keep the Commandments. Now, in a sense, he was most definitely right about that; however, the question isn't that we keep the Commandments. The question is how they are to be kept! Concerning this very thing, the great Apostle said:

THE COMMANDMENT

"For I was alive without the Law once (Paul is referring to himself personally and his Conversion to Christ; the Law, he states, had nothing to do with that Conversion; neither did it have anything to do with his life in Christ)**: but when the Commandment came** (having just been Saved, and not understanding the Cross of Christ, he tried to live for God by keeping the Commandments through his own strength and power; in his defense, no one else at that time understood the Cross; in fact, the meaning of the Cross, which is actually the meaning of the New Covenant, would be given to Paul)**, sin revived** (the sin nature *will always, without exception, revive under such circumstances, which results in failure),* **and I died** *(he was not meaning that he physically died, as would be obvious, but that he died to the Commandment; in other words, he failed to obey no matter how hard he tried; let all Believers understand that if the Apostle Paul couldn't live for God in this manner, neither can you)"* **(Rom. 7:9).**

Many people simply quit and give up. In other words, they cease to even make an effort to live for God. In their minds, they reason that they don't want to be hypocrites, so they just quit.

While others do not quit, still, their entire life and living is that of confusion. Despite the fact that they are trying so hard, the failures increase instead of decrease.

The sin nature is ruling such a Believer simply because the Believer doesn't understand God's Prescribed Order of Life and Living.

GOD'S PRESCRIBED ORDER OF VICTORY

The Lord has one way, and only one way. In fact, that's all that is needed. It is very, very simple, and quite possibly because of its simplicity, it is unattractive.

Even though we have already given this simple formula in this Volume, please, because of the seriousness of the matter, allow the repetition.

FOCUS: The Lord Jesus Christ (Jn. 14:6).

OBJECT OF FAITH: The Cross of Christ (Rom. 6:3-5; I Cor. 1:17-18, 23; 2:2).

POWER SOURCE: The Holy Spirit (Rom. 8:1-2, 11).

RESULTS: Victory (Rom. 6:14).

Let's say it in another way, and even though this formula has already been given, as well, again we beg for privilege respecting the repetition.

• Jesus Christ is the Source of all things we receive from God (Jn. 7:37-39).

• The Cross of Christ is the only Means by which these things are given to us (Rom. 6:1-14; Col. 2:14-15).

• The Cross of Christ is to ever be the Object of our Faith, and the Cross of Christ alone (I Cor. 1:17-18, 23; 2:2; Gal. 6:14).

• All of this is superintended by the Holy Spirit (Eph. 2:13-18).

Getting back to the original thought, if the Believer doesn't function according to God's Prescribed Order, he *"shall return to Egypt,"* i.e., *"live in bondage."*

"What a wonderful change in my life has been wrought,
"Since Jesus came into my heart!
"I have light in my soul for which long I have sought,
"Since Jesus came into my heart!"

"I have ceased from my wandering and going astray,
"Since Jesus came into my heart!
"And my sins, which were many, are all washed away,
"Since Jesus came into my heart!"

"There's a light in the valley of death now for me,
"Since Jesus came into my heart!
"And the Gates of the City beyond I can see,
"Since Jesus came into my heart!"

"I shall go there to dwell in that City, I know,
"Since Jesus came into my heart!
"And I'm happy, so happy, as onward I go,
"Since Jesus came into my heart!"

"Since Jesus came into my heart,
"Since Jesus came into my heart,
"Floods of joy o'er my soul,
"Like the sea billows roll,
"Since Jesus came into my heart."

CHAPTER 9

(1) "REJOICE NOT, O ISRAEL, FOR JOY, AS OTHER PEOPLE: FOR YOU HAVE GONE A WHORING FROM YOUR GOD, YOU HAVE LOVED A REWARD UPON EVERY CORNFLOOR.

(2) "THE FLOOR AND THE WINEPRESS SHALL NOT FEED THEM, AND THE NEW WINE SHALL FAIL IN HER.

(3) "THEY SHALL NOT DWELL IN THE LORD'S LAND; BUT EPHRAIM SHALL RETURN TO EGYPT, AND THEY SHALL

EAT UNCLEAN THINGS IN ASSYRIA.

(4) "THEY SHALL NOT OFFER WINE OFFERINGS TO THE LORD, NEITHER SHALL THEY BE PLEASING UNTO HIM: THEIR SACRIFICES SHALL BE UNTO THEM AS THE BREAD OF MOURNERS; ALL WHO EAT THEREOF SHALL BE POLLUTED: FOR THEIR BREAD FOR THEIR SOUL SHALL NOT COME INTO THE HOUSE OF THE LORD.

(5) "WHAT WILL YOU DO IN THE SOLEMN DAY, AND IN THE DAY OF THE FEAST OF THE LORD?

(6) "FOR, LO, THEY ARE GONE BECAUSE OF DESTRUCTION: EGYPT SHALL GATHER THEM UP, MEMPHIS SHALL BURY THEM: THE PLEASANT PLACES FOR THEIR SILVER, NETTLES SHALL POSSESS THEM: THORNS SHALL BE IN THEIR TABERNACLES.

(7) "THE DAYS OF VISITATION ARE COME, THE DAYS OF RECOMPENCE ARE COME; ISRAEL SHALL KNOW IT: THE PROPHET IS A FOOL, THE SPIRITUAL MAN IS MAD, FOR THE MULTITUDE OF YOUR INIQUITY, AND THE GREAT HATRED."

The pattern is:

1. Evil Menahem, now king of the northern kingdom, had probably made a treaty with the Assyrians, which occasioned this *"joy"* of Verse 1. The Lord's admonishment, *"Rejoice not, O Israel, for joy, as other people,"* proclaims Him being extremely agitated at this act. *"As other people"* proclaims Israel attempting to be like the other nations, which the Lord pointedly tells them they are not! The phrase, *"For you have gone a whoring from your God,"* is what God calls this treaty!

2. (Vs. 1) *"You have loved a reward upon every cornfloor"* is a reference to them giving honor to their idol gods for the blessings of the harvest and for their treaty with Assyria. Loss of fellowship with God and loss of fruitfulness for God result from the association of idols with God. When the world, which is idolatry, is permitted to share the heart with Christ, fellowship and fruit cease (Jn. 15:1-11).

3. (Vs. 2) Treaties were made in order to secure the future. In essence, the Lord

is saying that instead of Israel making her future secure by making this treaty, she actually has guaranteed the insecurity of her future. To be sure, all such compromises, whether then or now, lead to the same conclusion. The bountiful harvest expected from their idols failed of realization.

4. The phrase of Verse 3, *"They shall not dwell in the LORD's land,"* is emphatic! In other words, this alliance, which they had made to secure the land of Israel, would now be the occasion of casting them out of the land. The effect of the Verse is that they should have made an alliance with the Lord instead.

5. (Vs. 3) *"But Ephraim shall return to Egypt"* did not refer to an actual sojourn into Egypt, but that, spiritually speaking, Israel had returned to the bondage of Egypt (II Pet. 2:22). *"And they shall eat unclean things in Assyria"* implies the coming captivity to Assyria (II Ki., Chpt. 17; Ezek. 4:13).

6. The worship addressed in Verse 4 in imitation of the Levitical model was observed but was disowned by God and declared by Him to be polluted.

7. The idea of Verse 5 is: the time would shortly come, which it did, that they, held captive in a strange land, would strongly desire to keep the *"Feasts of the LORD,"* but such would be impossible to do! Away in a distant foreign land, without Temple and without ritual, they would bewail the loss of their annual celebrations, their national festivals, and religious solemnities.

8. The answer to the question in Verse 5 is found in Verse 6. It means that religious festivals would be impossible because the land of Israel would be denuded of its inhabitants. This is evidenced in the phrase, *"For, lo, they are gone because of destruction."*

9. *"The days of visitation are come,"* addressed in Verse 7, refers to the Wrath of God. In this Verse, the Lord calls the false prophets *"fools."* As well, the Lord declares *"mad,"* i.e., spiritually insane, those who claim spirituality while at the same time worshipping idols.

REJOICING THAT ULTIMATELY WOULD BE TURNED TO WEEPING

Over and over again, the northern kingdom

of Israel was warned by several Prophets, in this case Hosea, of coming doom if they continued on this polluted path. The record is clear that they did not listen at all, but rather went even deeper into their alliances with foreign nations and, above all, went deeper into their idol worship.

For the present, their joy was deepened by a religious union of their church, so to speak, with the idol churches of the neighboring nations. It was their ruin! Furthermore, Satan has not ceased his activity in this arena. If possible, he has increased it.

Presently, there is a powerful push for unity in virtually all churches in America. Many, if not most, of the religious leaders of Protestantism, openly advocate union with Catholicism, if not, in fact, in principle. It is the same with the demonic religion of Islam. How in the world can Christians have any fellowship with Muslims?

All of this means that many of those in positions of leadership, as it regards the modern church, have no understanding whatsoever of the Word of God, much less the Moving and Operation of the Holy Spirit.

The Holy Spirit is intended to be the Power, Leading, Guidance, and Motivation of the Church; however, for the most part, He has been abandoned, ignored, or blatantly denied! As such, the far greater majority of the modern church is man-led, which means that God has no part in it. Such was Israel, and such is the modern church.

CAPTIVITY!

The idea of Verse 2, especially considering the following Verse, is that whatever the harvest was, they would not enjoy it due to the fact of being taken captive to Assyria. As a result, their treaty was of little consequence!

At the present time, spiritual captivity is the lot of the modern church. There is only one way of Victory in this Christian life, not ten ways, not even two, only one. That way is, *"Jesus Christ and Him Crucified"* (I Cor. 1:23).

The Believer must understand that the Cross of Christ is the Means by which we receive everything from the Lord. If the Believer places his faith in anything other than Christ and Him Crucified, irrespective as to what it is, spiritual captivity will be the

result! While the Cross of Christ is looked to and believed by many for Salvation, unfortunately, as it regards the Cross of Christ and Sanctification, the latter is a blank to most Believers. In other words, they have no knowledge of the Cross of Christ and Sanctification. This means that what Jesus there did plays little or no part in their everyday life and living for God. As a result, such Believers live a life of spiritual captivity and of spiritual bondage, in some manner. This includes virtually the entirety of the modern church, and we speak of those who truly love God. This means that they are being ruled by the sin nature in some way. It's not a very pleasant life or living. Please note the following:

• The only Way to God is through Jesus Christ (Jn. 14:6).

• The only Way to Jesus Christ is through the Cross (Lk. 9:23; 14:27).

• The only way to the Cross is a denial of self (Lk. 9:23; Rom. 8:1-2).

THEY SHALL NOT DWELL IN THE LORD'S LAND

Banishment from God's land and from God's Protecting Care was the necessary result of the action of Moral Law.

The geographical area known as Canaan was where Jehovah chose to dwell. It was evidenced by the visible Symbol of the Shechinah-glory. He had given the land of Canaan to His People; however, there were conditions attached to their occupation of the land. If the people did not keep the Commandments of the Lord, He had told them bluntly, ". . . you shall be plucked from off the land where you go to possess it" (Deut. 28:63).

He had also said, *"That the land spew not you out also, when you defile it, as it spewed out the nations that were before you"* (Lev. 18:28).

The land of Israel in Old Testament Times was a physical manifestation of the modern Believer's inheritance in Christ. As well, all should understand that as rebellion caused the Lord to dispossess them then, rebellion will cause the Lord to dispossess now.

Tragically, millions of modern Christians have been taught that if they are once in the land, so to speak, irrespective of what happens thereafter, they are forever in the land. The error of that teaching should, by now, be painfully obvious!

Israel's occupation of the Promised land was conditional, as the modern Believer's occupation of the Spiritual Inheritance of Salvation is conditional. What is that condition?

The condition of continued Salvation always has been and always is that the Believer maintains his Faith in Christ and what Christ has done for him at the Cross. That and that alone is the condition. If, however, the Believer ceases to believe in Christ and what Christ has done for us at the Cross, then such a person reverts to the position of unbeliever, as should be obvious. That being the case, that person is now in a lost condition (Jn. 3:16; Heb. 6:4-6; 10:26-29).

SACRIFICES?

The Sacrificial system, which was the core of the Law of Moses, was basically the only thing that kept Israel alive. However, the northern kingdom of Israel had long since abandoned the sacrifices of the Lord and the true worship of Him and, instead, set up *"golden calves"* (I Ki. 12:28). In fact, they had abandoned the entirety of the system of the Lord and substituted the worship of idols in its place. So, in effect, the Lord is saying that inasmuch as they did not desire His Way or His Sacrifices, which constituted true worship, they would summarily be placed in a land where such sacrifices would be impossible. And that's exactly what happened!

The situation hasn't changed from then until now. The only thing standing between mankind and eternal Hell is the Cross of Christ. But yet, the modern church has, for all practical purposes, abandoned the Cross of Christ, in a sense, exactly as Israel of old! To be frank, I wonder if God looks at the modern way, which has rejected the Cross, any different than He does the golden calves of Israel so long ago.

Christ is the Source of all things we receive from God, while the Cross is the Means by which those things are received. This demands that the Cross of Christ ever be the Object of our Faith. Only then will the Holy Spirit, Who functions entirely within the

NOTES

boundaries of the Finished Work of Christ, so to speak, work on our behalf.

EVERY BLESSING COMES THROUGH THE CROSS

Every single thing that mankind receives from the Lord comes by the Means of the Cross. In fact, it cannot come any other way. The Sacrificial system was instituted at the very dawn of time, in fact, on the first page of human history. We find that the Lord told the First Family, even though driven from the Garden in their fallen state, that by virtue of the slain lamb, which typified the coming Redeemer, they could have forgiveness of sins and communion with Him. However, it seems that they may have offered sacrifices for a short period of time and then discontinued them altogether. There is no record that Adam and Eve came back to the Lord. This must have been very grievous to the Heart of God, Who loved them dearly!

The Sacrificial system continued in small measure, evidently with a few obeying the Lord in this respect. We do know that Noah offered sacrifices after the Flood (Gen. 8:20-21). And then we find that Abraham offered sacrifices continually. In fact, he was referred to somewhat as *"the Altar Builder"* (Gen. 12:7-8; 13:4; 15:7-17; 22:9-14).

When the Law was given to Israel, the Sacrificial system, as stated, was at the very core of this Law, without which, Israel could not have survived. The truth is, Israel could not keep the Law of God, so the fall-back position, so to speak, was the Altar, which typified the Cross.

EVERYTHING COMES THROUGH THE CROSS

As we have repeatedly stated, the Cross of Christ is the Means by which we receive all things from God. Every single thing given to us, every answered prayer and every blessing, the Cross of Christ is the Means by which all of this is done. Without the Cross of Christ we could not approach the Lord in any fashion. The Cross alone opens that door!

Unfortunately, the modern church has all but abandoned the Cross of Christ. A great segment of it in the Charismatic world goes even further by denying its veracity. In those circles, it is referred to as *"past miseries"* and *"the greatest defeat in human history."* In fact, they claim that if the Preacher preaches the Cross, he is preaching death.

That's strange when we hear Paul saying:

"Christ sent me not to baptize, but to preach the Gospel: not with wisdom of words, lest the Cross of Christ be made of none effect" (I Cor. 1:17).

And then, *"The preaching of the Cross is to them who perish foolishness; but to we who are Saved it is the Power of God"* (I Cor. 1:18).

And then, *"I determined to know nothing among you save Jesus Christ, and Him Crucified"* (I Cor. 2:2).

So, we can take the word of these Christ rejecters, or we can take the word of the Apostle Paul. We cannot accept both!

DESTRUCTION

Verse 5 says, *"What will you do in the solemn day, and in the day of the Feast of the LORD?"*

The answer to the question in Verse 5 is found in Verse 6. It says, *"For, lo, they are gone because of destruction: Egypt shall gather them up, Memphis shall bury them: the pleasant places for their silver, nettles shall posses them: thorns shall be in their Tabernacles."*

It means that religious festivals would be impossible because the land would be denuded of its inhabitants. This is evidenced in the phrase, *"For, lo, they are gone because of destruction."*

The phrase, *"Egypt shall gather them up,"* refers to many who fled to Egypt upon the invasion by Assyria. They thought they would be safe there, but the Holy Spirit said, *"Memphis shall bury them."*

Memphis was the ancient capital of Lower Egypt; its location was on the western bank of the Nile and south of Old Cairo.

THE WRATH OF GOD

In that coming dread day, as recorded in Verse 7, Israel would know that her teachers, who professed to be prophets and, likewise, inspired, were, in fact, fools and liars.

As well, the fashionable preachers of today, who deny the fact of the coming Wrath

of God, and who promise peace and happiness to everyone, will be equally found liars in the coming Day of the Lord.

IDOLATRY

Israel provoked God with her idols, and this was the cause of their destruction and eventual captivity. Idolatry inflames the heart with hatred against God's Word and God's People.

Despite God's Word through Hosea, false prophets in Israel were continually predicting that this day of visitation would never come, and if it did come, it would be in the distant future, and there was nothing to worry about.

The true Prophet of God, Hosea, is saying the very opposite.

At the present, a large segment of the modern church, as well, is listening to false prophets who deny a coming Judgment. They are claiming that the world is getting better and better, with the Millennium soon to be ushered in. Actually, some are even foolishly claiming that we are already in the Millennium. Their churches are large and full of people, with their coffers full of money, because the *"prosperity message"* provides heady bait.

The false prophets love to prophesy false messages guaranteeing riches and plenty. The itching ears of spiritually depraved religious people love to hear such.

(8) "THE WATCHMAN OF EPHRAIM WAS WITH MY GOD: BUT THE PROPHET IS A SNARE OF A FOWLER IN ALL HIS WAYS, AND HATRED IN THE HOUSE OF HIS GOD.

(9) "THEY HAVE DEEPLY CORRUPTED THEMSELVES, AS IN THE DAYS OF GIBEAH: THEREFORE HE WILL REMEMBER THEIR INIQUITY, HE WILL VISIT THEIR SINS.

(10) "I FOUND ISRAEL LIKE GRAPES IN THE WILDERNESS; I SAW YOUR FATHERS AS THE FIRSTRIPE IN THE FIG TREE AT HER FIRST TIME: BUT THEY WENT TO BAAL-PEOR, AND SEPARATED THEMSELVES UNTO THAT SHAME; AND THEIR ABOMINATIONS WERE ACCORDING AS THEY LOVED."

The pattern is:

1. The phrase, *"The watchman of Ephraim was with my God,"* of Verse 8 refers to what Ephraim (Israel) had been but had now changed! In the days of Joshua, Israel was a true watchman in fellowship with Hosea's God, but she had now become a false prophet, a provocation in the house of her false god—and hence, a moral snare, with the result that she sank to the horrid depths of Gibeah in vileness, as recorded in Judges, Chapter 19.

2. This reference to the *"days of Gibeah"* in Verse 9 shows that at this time the Book of Judges was well known to all the people. The historical event here alluded to was the abominable and infamous treatment of the Levite's concubine by the men of Gibeah. This was the foulest blot on Israel's history during all the rule of the Judges.

3. (Vs. 10) Grapes in the wilderness and first-ripe figs are most refreshing and delicious to the traveler. Such was Israel to God at the first; but they went away from Him and served Baal-peor (Num., Chpt. 25; Deut., Chpt. 4) and consecrated themselves unto that shameful worship, prostitution being its highest religious action. Its moral result was that the worshippers became as abominable as the object of their worship.

THE WORSHIPPER BECOMES WHAT HE WORSHIPS

The heading, *"The Worshipper Becomes What He Worships,"* presents a startling statement, in fact, one that holds tremendous implications. Not only did this have reference to Israel of old, but it, as well, addresses the present.

The only true worship that God will recognize is that which is done by the means of Christ and the price that He paid at Calvary's Cross. In other words, God cannot accept anything that doesn't have Christ and the Cross as its foundation. Actually, He will not and, in fact, cannot hear and answer prayer that's not based strictly upon Christ and what Christ did for us at the Cross. It is the Cross alone, in effect, what Jesus there did, which gives us access to the very Throne of God. Otherwise, there is no access!

As it regards worship, every human being in this world worships at some altar. Almost all are altars fomented by Satan, with precious few that are truly of the Lord. Jesus, so long ago, addressed a Samaritan woman. Part of the conversation went according to the following:

YOU WORSHIP YOU KNOW NOT WHAT

"The woman said unto Him, Sir, I perceive that You are a Prophet *(had to do with the belief of the Samaritans and their interpretation of Whom the Messiah would be).*

"Our fathers worshipped in this mountain *(speaks of Mount Gerizim, which was about fifty miles north of Jerusalem; in a sense, they worshipped 'this mountain');* **and You say, that in Jerusalem is the place where men ought to worship** *(she admitted that Jesus fit the profile of the Great Prophet Who would come as Moses had predicted, but she was perplexed because He was a Jew and worshipped in Jerusalem, which the Samaritans believed were false).*

"Jesus said unto her, Woman, believe Me *(He is telling her to hear carefully what He is saying, and then to believe it),* **the hour comes, when you shall neither in this mountain, nor yet at Jerusalem, worship the Father** *(Calvary, which did away with the entire Jewish system, would introduce a new way of worship).*

"You worship you know not what *(He minced no words, telling her plainly that the Samaritan way of worship held no validity with God; regrettably, it is the same with most presently):* **we know what we worship: for Salvation is of the Jews** *(meaning that through the Jewish people came the Word of God and, as well, the Son of God, Who Alone brought Salvation, and did so by going to the Cross)."*

WORSHIPPING IN SPIRIT AND IN TRUTH

"But the hour comes, and now is, when the true worshippers shall worship the Father in spirit and in truth *(God is not looking for Holy worship; He is looking for Holy worshippers; as stated, Calvary would make possible an entirely different type of worship, which did not require ceremonies or rituals, etc.):* **for the Father seeks such to worship Him** *(means that by the word 'seeks' such are not easily found).*

"**God *is* a Spirit** (*simply means that 'God is a Spirit Being'*)**: and they who worship Him must worship *Him* in spirit and in truth** (*man worships the Lord through and by his personal spirit, which is moved upon by the Holy Spirit; otherwise, it is not worship which God will accept*)" **(Jn. 4:19-24).**

HOW DOES ONE WORSHIP IN SPIRIT AND IN TRUTH?

It means that we worship the Lord with our spirit. It might be said that man is a triune being. As such, he is and has:

• Man is a living soul. The Scripture says, **"And the LORD God formed man of the dust of the ground** (*proclaims the physical body made of clay*)**, and breathed into his nostrils the breath of life** (*the 'breath of life,' which comes from God, pertains to the soul and spirit of man; this was done with the first man, Adam, God breathing the soul and the spirit into man, and thereafter it comes automatically at conception*)**; and man became a living soul" (Gen. 2:7).** So, man, as stated, *"is a living soul."*

• He has a spirit, and with his spirit, he worships the Lord. He can, as well, worship Satan, or anything, for that matter; however, if one truly worships God, one must do so with one's spirit. This means that it's not done by ritual or ceremony, etc.

• The soul of man, as stated, addresses the physical body of man, while the spirit of man addresses God, which is the only way God can be addressed. The physical body addresses the world.

The soul of man is that which *"feels,"* while the spirit of man is that which *"knows."* This means that the soul of man is the seed of his passions and his feelings. The spirit of man is the seat of his intellect, his knowledge, his understanding, and his mind (I Cor. 2:11-12).

WHAT IS TRUTH?

Jesus said that we must worship God *"in spirit* (the spirit of man) *and in truth."*

The *"Truth"* of which He speaks has to do with the Plan of Redemption. This speaks of the way and the manner in which man is redeemed. It is from Christ and through the Cross. In other words, the Lord Jesus is

the Source of all things that we receive from God, while the Cross is the Means by which these things are received, all superintended by the Holy Spirit (Eph. 2:13-18). In short, the Truth of which He speaks is, *"Jesus Christ and Him Crucified"* (I Cor. 1:23).

If it is to be noticed, He said to the woman, *"But the hour comes, and now is, when the true worshippers shall worship the Father in spirit and in truth"* (Jn. 4:23).

He was speaking of the time when He would go to the Cross and there atone for all sin, past, present, and future, at least for all who will believe (Jn. 3:16). To be frank, before the Cross, most worship was carried on by means of ceremony and ritual. We speak of the Feast Days of the Jews, the Sacrificial system, and the rituals of the Priests, which, in fact, were a never-ending process. It was one ritual and ceremony after the other. However, when Jesus went to the Cross, He fulfilled all of that, which was a Type of His Atoning, Mediatorial, Intercessory Work. With the substance now a reality, i.e., *"the Cross,"* the Shadow is no longer needed. So, we come back to our original statement:

The only way that one can truly worship God is by understanding that all is made possible by the Lord Jesus Christ and what He did for us at the Cross. Now that Calvary is a fact, we worship the Lord strictly from our spirit, through no ritual or ceremony, because none is needed. And, as well, we must remember, we ultimately become what we worship.

If one worships money, he literally becomes greed and avarice. If one worships a religious denomination, such as Catholics worshipping the Catholic church, or any church, for that matter, that person becomes ritual and ceremony, which brings no joy, no happiness, and no peace of mind. Unfortunately, far too many Christians do not understand the Cross at all as it regards our worship, therefore, in those circles, there is very little true worship.

• Praise is what we do and
• Worship is what we are.

Israel worshipped idols, and so they became the abominations of which they worshipped. The Scripture says:

"But they went to Baal-peor, and separated themselves unto that shame; and their

abominations were according as they loved."

(11) "AS FOR EPHRAIM, THEIR GLO-RY SHALL FLY AWAY LIKE A BIRD, FROM THE BIRTH, AND FROM THE WOMB, AND FROM THE CONCEPTION.

(12) "THOUGH THEY BRING UP THEIR CHILDREN, YET WILL I BEREAVE THEM, THAT THERE SHALL NOT BE A MAN LEFT: YES, WOE ALSO TO THEM WHEN I DEPART FROM THEM!

(13) "EPHRAIM, AS I SAW TYRUS, IS PLANTED IN A PLEASANT PLACE: BUT EPHRAIM SHALL BRING FORTH HIS CHILDREN TO THE MURDERER.

(14) "GIVE THEM, O LORD: WHAT WILL YOU GIVE? GIVE THEM A MISCAR-RYING WOMB AND DRY BREASTS.

(15) "ALL THEIR WICKEDNESS IS IN GILGAL: FOR THERE I HATED THEM: FOR THE WICKEDNESS OF THEIR DO-INGS I WILL DRIVE THEM OUT OF MY HOUSE, I WILL LOVE THEM NO MORE: ALL THEIR PRINCES ARE REVOLTERS.

(16) "EPHRAIM IS SMITTEN, THEIR ROOT IS DRIED UP, THEY SHALL BEAR NO FRUIT: YES, THOUGH THEY BRING FORTH, YET WILL I KILL EVEN THE BE-LOVED FRUIT OF THEIR WOMB.

(17) "MY GOD WILL CAST THEM AWAY, BECAUSE THEY DID NOT HEAR-KEN UNTO HIM: AND THEY SHALL BE WANDERERS AMONG THE NATIONS."

The construction is:

1. Verse 11 predicts the complete destruc-tion of Ephraim and their dispersion among the nations.

2. The thrust of Verse 12 is that God would continue to deal with Israel, even in Judgment, attempting to bring them back to Himself. However, the day would come that upon continued rebellion, He would be forced to say to them, according to the name of Hosea's third child, *"Lo-ammi,"* i.e., *"not My People."*

3. As recorded in Verse 13, *"Tyre"* was also beautifully situated, as was Ephraim at the beginning; but now her fruitful birth-rate only provided victims for the murderer, i.e., Assyria.

4. The prayer of Verse 14 is a prayer of compassion. Of two evils, the Prophet chooses the lesser. Better to be childless

NOTES

than to provide children for the murderer.

5. Verse 15, in effect, says, *"In Gilgal"* they dethroned Immanuel (I Sam. 8:7; 11:14-15), and later they enthroned the golden calf under Jeroboam. Hence, the expression, *"All their wickedness,"* i.e., their chief guilt, was found there.

6. (Vs. 15) *"For the wickedness of their doings I will drive them out of My House"* portrays an outraged husband who has entered into divorce and has put his guilty wife outside the house. God is Love, and He must, of necessity, hate evil and judge it. His Righteousness demands no less!

7. (Vs. 15) *"I will love them no more"* does not mean that He doesn't love them now, but that if they continue on their pres-ent course, His Love and Protection will be withdrawn. The actual meaning is that love cannot be forever expressed to someone who will not return the love.

8. As it regards Verse 16, without the Love of God, *"Ephraim is smitten."* Even though they did not know it, their sustenance, bless-ing, glory, strength, and power existed totally in Jehovah. Without Him, *"their root is dried up, they shall bear no fruit."*

9. *"My God will cast them away,"* of Verse 17, refutes the unscriptural doctrine of Unconditional Eternal Security. History re-cords the fulfillment of the prediction, *"And they shall be wanderers among the nations."* In 1948, after nearly 2,000 years of *"wan-derings,"* Israel once again became a Nation, which again strains toward the fulfillment of Prophecy regarding their Restoration, which will take place at the Second Coming.

GOD CONTROLS ALL!

As we see from these Passages, the Lord has the final say on everything. If His Peo-ple follow Him, serve Him, and do their best to obey His Word, which can be done only by Faith expressed constantly in Christ and the Cross, the Lord will bless. If His People turn their backs on Him and ignore His Word, ex-actly as did Israel of old, the blessings and the protection will stop, with Satan then *"steal-ing, killing, and destroying"* (Jn. 10:10).

One should not and, in fact, cannot expect the Blessings of the Lord while, at the same time, purposely and knowingly violating the

Word of the Lord.

THE CROSS OF CHRIST

If the Believer doesn't understand the Cross of Christ relative to the Word of God, the Holy Spirit will be greatly hindered in the life of that Believer. This is true even in the lives of those who are sincerely trying to please the Lord and trying to obey His Word. It doesn't matter how sincere they might be. If they don't understand the Cross of Christ according to the Word of God, then the Believer is going in the wrong direction. The following should be noted:

• All true Wisdom comes through Christ and the Cross (I Cor. 1:18-31).

• All Spiritual Maturity comes from a knowledge of the Cross (I Cor. 2:2).

• All Blessings from the Lord are made possible by the Cross (I Cor. 1:17).

• All Victory over sin comes by the Means of the Cross of Christ (Rom. 6:13).

• All Deliverance comes by the Means of the Cross of Christ (I Cor. 1:18).

• All overcoming Victory comes by the Means of the Cross (Gal. 6:14).

• Anything and everything that one receives from the Lord comes from Christ as the Source and the Cross as the Means, all superintended by the Holy Spirit (Rom. 8:1-2, 11).

As we have said elsewhere in this Volume, the Lord could not even look at us, much less answer prayer and bless us, were it not for the Cross of Christ. What Jesus did at the Cross has made everything possible. That's the reason we continue to say that the Cross of Christ must ever be the Object of our Faith. That being the case, we then have our Faith anchored squarely in the Word of God. The story of the Bible is the Story of Christ and Him Crucified. This is typified by the untold millions of lambs that were offered up in sacrifice, all as a Type and Symbol of the One Who was to come, and Who did come and give Himself as a Perfect Sacrifice in order that we might be Saved.

THE HOLY SPIRIT AND
THE CROSS OF CHRIST

The Bible tells us that the Holy Spirit Works exclusively within the parameters, so to speak, of the Cross of Christ. What Jesus did in the Sacrificial Offering of Himself at Calvary gives the Holy Spirit the legal means to do all that He does. That's the reason that Paul wrote the following:

"For the Law (*that which we are about to give is a Law of God, devised by the Godhead in eternity past [I Pet. 1:18-20]; this Law, in fact, is 'God's Prescribed Order of Victory'*) **of the Spirit** (*Holy Spirit, i.e., 'the way the Spirit works'*) **of Life** (*all life comes from Christ but through the Holy Spirit [Jn. 16:13-14]*) **in Christ Jesus** (*any time Paul uses this term or one of its derivatives, he is, without fail, referring to what Christ did at the Cross, which makes this 'life' possible*) **has made me free** (*given me total victory*) **from the Law of Sin and Death** (*these are the two most powerful Laws in the Universe; the 'Law of the Spirit of Life in Christ Jesus' alone is stronger than the 'Law of Sin and Death'; this means that if the Believer attempts to live for God by any manner other than Faith in Christ and the Cross, he is doomed to failure*)**" (Rom. 8:2).**

THE MEANING OF THE CROSS

The very meaning of the Cross of Christ is the New Covenant, as the New Covenant is the Meaning of the Cross of Christ. In other words, the New Covenant is all wrapped up in the Cross, which has made everything possible. If one doesn't understand the Cross of Christ, then one doesn't understand the New Covenant.

When we speak of understanding the Cross of Christ, we are speaking not only of the Cross as it regards Salvation but, as well, as it regards Sanctification. In fact, Paul had far more to say about the Cross of Christ respecting Sanctification than he did Salvation. That should be obvious as to the reason.

The person doesn't have to know much about the Lord to be Saved; however, when it comes to living for God, that's another question altogether. In fact, over ninety-nine percent of the Bible, from Genesis 1:1 through Revelation 22:21, is given over to telling us how to live for God. If it were simple, I hardly think that the Holy Spirit would have devoted that much space to this all-important work. And yet, the modern

NOTES

Believers have at least a modicum of understanding as it respects the Cross of Christ relative to Salvation, but virtually none at all as it regards Sanctification. As a result, modern Christians, even those who truly love the Lord, little know how to live for God. That's the reason the modern church stumbles from one fad to the other, but all with little or no success.

As it regards Israel of old and Believers presently, the idea is that the Lord intended for His People to be *"The salt of the Earth: but if the salt have lost his savor, wherewith shall it be salted? it is thenceforth good for nothing, but to be cast out, and to be trodden under foot of men"* (Mat. 5:13).

"O Love, that will not let me go,
"I rest my weary soul in Thee,
"I give You back the life I owe,
"That in Your Ocean depths its flow,
"May richer, fuller be."

"O Light, that follows all my way,
"I yield my flickering torch to Thee;
"My heart restores its borrowed ray,
"That in Your Sunshine's Blaze its day,
"May brighter, fairer be."

"O Joy, that seeks me through pain,
"I cannot close my heart to Thee;
"I trace the rainbow through the rain,
"And feel the Promise is not vain,
"That morn shall tearless be."

"O Cross, that lifts up my head,
"I dare not ask to fly from Thee;
"I lay in dust life's glory dead,
"And from the ground there blossoms red,
"Life that shall endless be."

CHAPTER 10

(1) "ISRAEL IS AN EMPTY VINE, HE BRINGS FORTH FRUIT UNTO HIMSELF: ACCORDING TO THE MULTITUDE OF HIS FRUIT HE HAS INCREASED THE ALTARS; ACCORDING TO THE GOODNESS OF HIS LAND THEY HAVE MADE GOODLY IMAGES.

(2) "THEIR HEART IS DIVIDED; NOW

SHALL THEY BE FOUND FAULTY: HE SHALL BREAK DOWN THEIR ALTARS, HE SHALL SPOIL THEIR IMAGES.

(3) "FOR NOW THEY SHALL SAY, WE HAVE NO KING, BECAUSE WE FEARED NOT THE LORD; WHAT THEN SHOULD A KING DO TO US?

(4) "THEY HAVE SPOKEN WORDS, SWEARING FALSELY IN MAKING A COVENANT: THUS JUDGMENT SPRINGS UP AS HEMLOCK IN THE FURROWS OF THE FIELD.

(5) "THE INHABITANTS OF SAMARIA SHALL FEAR BECAUSE OF THE CALVES OF BETH-AVEN: FOR THE PEOPLE THEREOF SHALL MOURN OVER IT, AND THE PRIESTS THEREOF WHO REJOICED ON IT, FOR THE GLORY THEREOF, BECAUSE IT IS DEPARTED FROM IT.

(6) "IT SHALL BE ALSO CARRIED UNTO ASSYRIA FOR A PRESENT TO KING JAREB: EPHRAIM SHALL RECEIVE SHAME, AND ISRAEL SHALL BE ASHAMED OF HIS OWN COUNSEL.

(7) "AS FOR SAMARIA, HER KING IS CUT OFF AS THE FOAM UPON THE WATER.

(8) "THE HIGH PLACES ALSO OF AVEN, THE SIN OF ISRAEL, SHALL BE DESTROYED: THE THORN AND THE THISTLE SHALL COME UP ON THEIR ALTARS; AND THEY SHALL SAY TO THE MOUNTAINS, COVER US; AND TO THE HILLS, FALL ON US."

The pattern is:

1. *"Israel is an empty vine"* of Verse 1 meant that it was abundant in leaves but had no *"fruit."* And what little *"fruit"* that was brought forth was not unto God but *"unto himself."* The fruit that was brought forth was not used for the Lord but only to *"increase the altars,"* i.e., altars to idol gods.

2. The phrase of Verse 2, *"Their heart is divided,"* proclaims the fact that this was the source of their evil. Their heart was divided, so they halted between two opinions—between the worship of Jehovah and the worship of idolatry.

3. (Vs. 3) The natural heart, due to the Fall, is opposed to God. It sets up in self-will a king, declaring him to be a necessity, but, when God removes him in Wrath, they

at once say, *"We can do very well without him; what use is he?"*

4. (Vs. 3) In sin, all Israel had asked for a king, when the Lord was their King. In sin, Ephraim had made Jeroboam king. In sin, their subsequent kings were made without the Counsel and Advice of God. Now, at the close of all, they reflect how fruitless it all was.

5. (Vs. 4) Israel swore allegiance to the Assyrian monarch and, at the same time, made a treaty with the king of Egypt. Therefore, Divine Wrath would cover the whole land as the common weeds springing up in the furrow.

6. *"The calves of Beth-aven"* of Verse 5 refer to the Golden Calf of Beth-el. *"The people therefore shall mourn over it"* refers to the people of Israel now being called the people of the Calf as they once had been called the People of Jehovah. They had chosen the calf for their god. Now they mourn for their idol, which can neither help itself nor them.

7. *"King Jareb"* of Verse 6 is Shalmaneser. The phrase, *"It shall be also carried unto Assyria for a present,"* refers to the calf, the national god of Israel.

8. *"His own counsel"* of Verse 6 refers back approximately 175 years to the first king of the northern kingdom, Jeroboam, who set up the Golden Calf (I Ki. 12:28). He thought this was a very clever stroke of policy, which would keep the people of Israel from going down to Jerusalem to worship at the true Temple of the Lord. His *"counsel"* led to the destruction of Israel.

9. (Vs. 7) Such was the king of Samaria, sometimes called Israel and sometimes called Ephraim, because the position was not God-ordained, but was rather a position that was man-made.

10. *"The high places also of Aven,"* as portrayed in Verse 8, pertains to Beth-el. *"Aven"* means *"emptiness"* or *"vanity."* What was the House of God—Beth-el—became the house of vanity, the sin of Israel. Such is corrupt Christendom at the present.

This Verse speaks of the coming day when Israel will be destroyed, which it was by the Assyrians. Consequently, thorns and thistles grew up around these heathen altars.

ISRAEL'S IDOL ALTARS WILL CRUMBLE

It didn't happen overnight because the Lord was constantly trying to bring them to Repentance, but, ultimately, it was fulfilled in every capacity.

Despite the repeated warnings of the Lord and the abundant opportunities, Israel brought forth little to no fruit. What little fruit she did bring forth was used for idol worship and not the worship of the Lord.

An example of all of this is the fig tree that bore no fruit of the time of our Lord. It says, *". . . and when He came to it, He found nothing but leaves; for the time of figs was not yet.*

"And Jesus answered and said unto it, No man eat fruit of you hereafter forever . . ." (Mk. 11:13-14).

THEIR HEART IS DIVIDED

Perhaps in this short phrase, *"Their heart is divided,"* we find the cause of all spiritual problems. It's what Christ spoke of when He spoke of serving *"two masters."* He said, *"You cannot serve God and mammon"* (Mat. 6:24).

As well, this is what Jesus was referring to when He said, *"I know your works, that you are neither cold nor hot: I would you were cold or hot"* (Rev. 3:15).

About this *"divided heart,"* the Scripture says, *"now they shall be found faulty."*

Men love to subscribe to all types of standards, providing the measurement is theirs. However, God honors no standard but His Own!

Men ever strive to have credibility with other men but little with God; however, to have credibility with men and none with God results in the verdict, *"found faulty."* The truth of all of this is, the natural heart is opposed to God. That's the reason the heart has to be changed in the Born-Again experience before the person can know or understand God in any form.

TOTAL DEPRAVITY

The Scripture says:

"And you *has He quickened* (made alive), who were dead in trespasses and sins (*total depravity due to the Fall and original sin*);

"**Wherein in time past you walked according to the course of this world** (*refers to the fact that the unredeemed order their behavior and regulate their lives within this sphere of trespasses and sins*), **according to the prince of the power of the air** (*pertains to the fact that Satan heads up the system of this world*), **the spirit that now works in the children of disobedience** (*the spirit of Satan, which fills all unbelievers, thereby, working disobedience*):

"**Among whom** (*the children of disobedience*) **also we all had our conversation** (*manner of life*) **in times past in the lusts of our flesh** (*evil cravings*), **fulfilling the desires of the flesh and of the mind** (*the minds of the unredeemed are the laboratory of perverted thoughts, impressions, imaginations, etc.*); **and were by nature the children of wrath, even as others.** (*God's Wrath is unalterably opposed to sin, and the only solution is the Cross*)" (**Eph. 2:1-3**).

The phrase, "*Dead in trespasses and sins,*" means exactly what it says—dead. This means that such a person, spiritually speaking, is not bad sick or even terminal, but rather dead. When one is dead, and it speaks of dead toward God and the things of God, such a person cannot have any correct thoughts about God. This speaks of all unbelievers and for all time. Such a person cannot even have a desire to be Saved. If a desire is planted in such a heart, it is because someone is praying for that person, or they have come in contact with the Gospel in some way, giving the Holy Spirit latitude to Work in their hearts and lives. Otherwise, they are "*dead!*" And again we say, "*Dead is dead.*"

THE HOLY SPIRIT

A person cannot be Saved unless the Holy Spirit draws him, and such cannot happen unless the Word of God, from which the Holy Spirit Works, is somehow gotten to such an individual. That's the reason the preaching of the Gospel is so very, very important. In fact, without the preaching of the Gospel, people cannot be Saved.

Through our telecast we have seen hundreds of thousands, and I exaggerate not, brought to a Saving Knowledge of the Lord

Jesus Christ. We give the Lord all the praise and the glory!

Countless times I have read letters from individuals who had come to their homes in the wee hours of the morning greatly intoxicated. They would turn on the television set and hear me preach the Gospel. Most of the time, they thought their coming across the channel was an accident; however, it wasn't! The Spirit of God, through the Word of God, would begin to get a hold of their hearts and bring them under Conviction, with them then giving their hearts to Christ. Thank the Lord that when they passed our way, we were not telling jokes, but rather were preaching the Gospel. In fact, the chairman of our board (Jimmy Swaggart Ministries) was Saved in that exact manner.

THE CALVES OF BETH-AVEN

When men leave the Lord, they go to idols. To be sure, the idols take a different form presently than they did in Israel of old. Men will worship something, whether a "*calf,*" sports, money, etc. Some worship intellectualism or various philosophies. But perhaps the greatest idol of all is religion. What do we mean by that?

Millions think their churches will take them to Heaven. They think that because they are Catholic, Baptist, etc., this means something with God. It doesn't! Religion then becomes an idol! And to be sure, most in modern Christendom fall into the category of the idol of religion. Concerning the individuals who truly have a relationship with the Lord, that number, sad to say, is few. In fact, anything we look at other than God's Way, which is the Way of the Cross, can be constituted as an "*idol.*" That's the reason that "*religion*" is perhaps the greatest idol of all!

Israel of old looked to the mountains and hills crowned with their idols, unto which they lifted up their eyes for safety, in order to hide them from the Wrath of God.

Even though this was referring to the coming invasion by the Assyrians just a few years hence, still, it has a greater application pertaining to the Great Tribulation, which is yet to come (Lk. 23:30; Rev. 6:16; 9:6).

No direction without God can come to

a satisfactory conclusion. The end results, irrespective of the time frame involved, will ultimately lead to destruction.

(9) "O ISRAEL, YOU HAVE SINNED FROM THE DAYS OF GIBEAH: THERE THEY STOOD: THE BATTLE IN GIBEAH AGAINST THE CHILDREN OF INIQUITY DID NOT OVERTAKE THEM.

(10) "IT IS IN MY DESIRE THAT I SHOULD CHASTISE THEM; AND THE PEOPLE SHALL BE GATHERED AGAINST THEM, WHEN THEY SHALL BIND THEM-SELVES IN THEIR TWO FURROWS.

(11) "AND EPHRAIM IS AS AN HEIFER THAT IS TAUGHT, AND LOVES TO TREAD OUT THE CORN; BUT I PASSED OVER UPON HER FAIR NECK: I WILL MAKE EPHRAIM TO RIDE; JUDAH SHALL PLOW, AND JACOB SHALL BREAK HIS CLODS.

(12) "SOW TO YOURSELVES IN RIGH-TEOUSNESS, REAP IN MERCY; BREAK UP YOUR FALLOW GROUND: FOR IT IS TIME TO SEEK THE LORD, TILL HE COME AND RAIN RIGHTEOUSNESS UPON YOU."

The pattern is:

1. Regarding Verse 9, the Holy Spirit uses the incident at Gibeah, which took place nearly 500 years before, and pertained to the shameful outrage committed on the Levite's concubine by the men of Gibeah. In the battle that followed over this incident, the Tribe of Benjamin was all but exterminated, with only about 600 men left alive (Judg., Chpt. 19). Thus, the Holy Spirit is drawing a comparison in that the Ten Tribes will come close to extinction.

2. According to Verse 10, both Judah and Israel would be carried into captivity and made to toil like oxen, each in his own furrow. Judah would fall about 133 years after the fall of Israel. The phraseology of this Verse expresses God's Determination to punish sin and vindicate His Justice as the infinitely Holy One.

3. The sense of Verse 11 is that inasmuch as both kingdoms (Israel and Judah) were unwilling to bear the easy yoke of their Divine Ruler, they would, therefore, be sub-jected to the tyrant mastery of man. Sadly, these Prophecies, as given by Hosea to both the northern and southern kingdoms, would

NOTES

go unheeded.

4. Addressing Verse 12, in the midst of the dire warnings, Grace sends a message of Mercy, which, had it been accepted, would have saved them. However, it was not accepted.

The command, *"break up your fallow ground,"* denotes effort that must be ex-pended on the part of the individual. That effort is summed up in the invitation to *"seek the LORD"*!

A SOLEMN WARNING!

Over and over again through the Proph-ets, such as Hosea, the Lord warns the northern kingdom of Israel that unless there is sincere Repentance, Judgment will ultimately come. As an example, he used the shameful situation outlined in the Nineteenth Chapter of Judges, which ac-tually happened well over 500 years in the past. The Tribe of Benjamin was almost completely destroyed at that time. As well, untold thousands of the other Tribes were killed! Such an example should have put the fear of God into the hearts of the Israel-ites at the time of Hosea; however, there is little evidence, if any at all, that it had any effect on them whatsoever. In other words, it was sin as usual! Why did they refuse to heed the words of the Prophet?

UNBELIEF

The reason is simple. They simply did not believe what the Prophet said. No doubt, there were many false prophets at that time proclaiming the very opposite. To be sure, it was much easier to believe them than it was the words of Hosea. The false prophets were proclaiming peace and prosperity, and it was much easier to listen to them.

How so similar that is to modern times. The false prophets are in abundance. They are proclaiming peace and prosperity just as the false prophets did some 2,700 years ago. The situation has not changed one iota.

The false prophets presently are promis-ing silver and gold in abundance. It is what the *"itching ears"* desire to hear. A Preacher said to me the other day, *"The people want the Power of God."*

My answer to him was short and to the point. *"No,"* I said, *"While there is a small* remnant that definitely wants and desires the Spirit and Power of God, the far greater majority don't!" In fact, it has always been that way. While the numbers may vary, the general thrust has always been in the wrong direction.

I was a young Evangelist getting started back in the 1950's. At that time, there were many Preachers who were teaching Bible Prophecy. It was a subject of great interest to the Church of that day, as it should have been. While some Preachers presently continue to major in that all-important subject, the truth is, most of the modern church has no idea as to what the Rapture is. Neither do they believe in or understand the coming man of sin, i.e., "the Antichrist," who is going to make his debut for world dominion. The Bible is full of this information, and it is that which is going to happen very shortly. And yet, the church, which is supposed to understand these things, not only doesn't understand them but holds little interest in what the Bible actually says. In fact, the Bible itself is being slowly but surely pushed aside in favor of other things. The truth is, the modern church is almost Biblically illiterate! That is tragic but true!

Considering that the Word of God is the road map for life and living and, as well, the blueprint for eternity, it would seem that the Bible would take priority over everything else. It should, but it doesn't!

THE EXPOSITOR'S STUDY BIBLE

And yet, I am very pleased and happy at the favorable response we have had as it regards THE EXPOSITOR'S STUDY BIBLE. From the time it was published in 2005 unto this present time (2012), we have sold over 900,000 copies and are now pushing toward the 1,000,000 mark.

The Scripture does say, "So shall they fear the Name of the LORD from the west, and His Glory from the rising of the sun. When the enemy shall come in like a flood, the Spirit of the LORD shall lift up a standard against him" (Isa. 59:19). The notes regarding this Verse from THE EXPOSITOR'S say, "The 'Standard' is Christ! The 'Spirit of the LORD' anointed Christ to set the captive free [Lk. 4:18]. That 'Anointing,' which

NOTES

could have Saved Israel then, and has consequently Saved tens of millions since then, will now, and finally, save Israel.

"As our Lord attempted to proclaim the 'acceptable year of the LORD' at His First Advent and was refused, He will now declare the 'acceptable year of the LORD' at His Second Advent and be accepted."

As stated, the full thrust of this Verse pertains to the coming Battle of Armageddon when the Antichrist will be defeated by the Second Coming of the Lord. However, it can very well apply to the present time also. In fact, the great Prophet Daniel also said:

"And they who be wise shall shine as the brightness of the firmament; and they who turn many to Righteousness as the stars forever and ever" (Dan. 12:3).

DOES THE BIBLE TEACH A GREAT REVIVAL IMMEDIATELY BEFORE THE RAPTURE OF THE CHURCH?

Actually, it doesn't! It rather teaches the following, at least, as it regards that which we refer to as "Revival."

"Now the Spirit (Holy Spirit) speaks expressly (pointedly), that in the latter times (the times in which we now live, the last of the last days, which begin the fulfillment of Endtime Prophecies) some shall depart from the Faith (anytime Paul uses the term 'the Faith,' in short, he is referring to the Cross; so, we are told here that some will depart from the Cross as the means of Salvation and Victory), giving heed to seducing spirits (evil spirits, i.e., 'religious spirits,' making something seem like what it isn't), and doctrines of devils (should have been translated, 'doctrines of demons'; the 'seducing spirits' entice Believers away from the true Faith, causing them to believe 'doctrines inspired by demon spirits')" (I Tim. 4:1).

It also tells us, "This know also, that in the last days (the days in which we now live) perilous times shall come. (This speaks of difficult dangerous times, which Christians living just before the Rapture will encounter.)"

It then says, "Having a form of godliness (refers to all the trappings of Christianity but without the power), but denying the power thereof (the modern church, for all practical purposes, has denied the Cross; in doing this, they have denied that through which the Holy Spirit works, and in Whom the power resides [Rom. 8:1-2, 11; I Cor. 1:18]): **from such turn away.** *(No half measures are to be adopted here. The command is clear! It means to turn away from churches that deny or ignore the Cross)*" **(II Tim. 3:1, 5).**

WHAT DO WE MEAN BY THE TERM *"REVIVAL"*?

Actually, it refers to the Church returning exclusively to the Word of God. To be more precise, it refers to Believers coming back to the foot of the Cross, so to speak.

The Cross of Christ exposes self-righteousness as nothing else. It proclaims man's helplessness to extricate himself from the dilemma in which he finds himself. It pushes aside hypocrisy and elevates the Lord Jesus Christ to the center of all things. By contrast, anything and everything else elevates man, which, as should be obvious, is satanic.

While the Holy Spirit most definitely is now proclaiming to the Church world the theology of the Cross, one might say, still, there is little indication that the majority are accepting that which the Lord is doing. While some do and while some are, still, the vast majority don't and won't.

Why?

The answer should be obvious. Man loves his religion, with that word meaning such as has been developed by human beings. This means it is actually developed by Satan, which, of course, God can never accept. The Cross exposes this, obliterates this, and shows it up for what it is. Religious man doesn't like that at all! In fact, he loves his religion, even as he has always loved his religion. This is what Paul had to encounter upon the advent of the meaning of the New Covenant, the meaning of which the Lord gave directly to Paul. Actually, Biblical Christianity is not a religion, but rather a relationship with a man, the Man, Christ Jesus.

Religion consists of a series of *"dos and don'ts,"* in other words, rules and regulations, etc. Biblical Christianity has no rules or regulations of that nature. It operates strictly on the premise of Faith, and we speak of Faith in Christ and what Christ did for us at the Cross. That and that alone is the only means and the only way that an individual can have a relationship with God. True Christianity has no temples, no altars, at least the type that offers up sacrifice, etc., and no actual rules or regulations. Its central focus is Christ and what Christ did for us at the Cross. In fact, the entirety of the Bible is the Story of Jesus Christ and what He did for us at the Cross. So, when one understands the Cross of Christ, one, in essence, understands the Bible.

A HARVEST?

Even though I do not actually see that the Bible teaches a Revival in the last days, at least of any magnitude, I do believe, however, that it does teach a great Harvest of souls that will come to Christ immediately before the Rapture of the Church.

The great Prophet Joel said and was quoted by Simon Peter on the Day of Pentecost, *"And it shall come to pass in the last days, says God, I will pour out of My Spirit upon all flesh: and your sons and your daughters shall prophesy, and your young men shall see Visions, and your old men shall dream Dreams:*

"And on My Servants and on My Handmaidens I will pour out in those days of My Spirit; and they shall prophesy:

"And I will show wonders in Heaven above, and signs in the Earth beneath; blood, and fire, and vapor of smoke" (Acts 2:17-19).

Even though the *"days of My Spirit"* cover the entirety of the Church Age, even into the coming Great Tribulation, still, according to the Latter Rain Outpouring, which actually began at approximately the turn of the Twentieth Century, I believe this tells us the Lord will do great things at this time.

But perhaps one of the greatest Promises of all of a great Harvest of souls at this particular time and, actually, in the near future, is found in a Dream given to a heathen monarch, the Pharaoh who lived during the time of Joseph, which was approximately 3,700 years ago. The Dream given to Pharaoh was:

"And, behold, there came up out of the river seven well favored cattle and fat-fleshed; and they fed in a meadow.

"And, behold, seven other cattle came up after them out of the river, ill favored and

leanfleshed; and stood by the other cattle upon the brink of the river.

"And the ill favored and leanfleshed cattle did eat up the seven well favored and fat cattle. So Pharaoh awoke.

"And he slept and dreamed the second time: and, behold, seven ears of corn came up upon one stalk, rank and good.

"And, behold, seven thin ears and blasted with the east wind sprung up after them.

"And the seven thin ears devoured the seven rank and full ears. And Pharaoh awoke, and, behold, it was a Dream" (Gen. 41:2-7).

As we know, the magicians and prognosticators of Egypt at that time could not interpret the Dream for Pharaoh. Then the chief butler remembered Joseph, who was in prison, and how that Joseph had interpreted a Dream for him, who was also in prison, and how that he would be restored to his former place and position in the palace in three days. And so it was.

He related all of this to Pharaoh, insinuating that if the monarch would call for Joseph, perhaps he could interpret Pharaoh's Dream as well. That's exactly what happened.

THE INTERPRETATION

The following is what Joseph gave to Pharaoh as the Lord had given it to him. He said:

". . . The Dream of Pharaoh is one: God has showed Pharaoh what He is about to do. *(The Dream was doubled in order, as Joseph says in Verse 32, to denote its Divine certainty and, as well, to portray its immediate happening as well as its futuristic happening.)"*

He continues:

"The seven good cattle are seven years; and the seven good ears are seven years: the Dream is one.

"And the seven thin and ill favored cattle that came up after them are seven years; and the seven empty ears blasted with the east wind shall be seven years of famine. *(Discoveries many years ago at the First Cataract, and at El-Kab, record the fact of this seven years famine. The date is given as 1700 B.C. This date accords with accepted Bible chronology.)"*

He then said, **"Behold, there come seven years of great plenty throughout all the land of Egypt:**

"And there shall arise after them seven years of famine; and all the plenty shall be forgotten in the land of Egypt; and the famine shall consume the land;

"And the plenty shall not be known in the land by reason of that famine following; for it shall be very grievous.

"And for that the Dream was doubled unto Pharaoh twice; it is because the thing is established by God, and God will shortly bring it to pass" (Gen. 41:25-27, 29-32).

The following constitutes the notes from THE EXPOSITOR'S STUDY BIBLE as it regards this Dream and its meaning:

THE PRESENT AND THE FUTURE

"The interpretation, as given by Joseph, and which greatly concerned Pharaoh, was to take place in the immediate future. But due to the fact of the Dream being doubled, it has an Endtime meaning, as well, and which will be of far greater magnitude than that which would take place in Joseph's day. It is as follows:

"We know that this terrible famine, which would follow the seven years of plenty, would bring Joseph's brothers to him, ultimately, along with his father, Jacob. This represents Israel coming to Christ, for Joseph is a Type of Christ, which they shall do at the conclusion of the seven-year Great Tribulation Period. So, the seven years of famine point to the coming seven-year Great Tribulation Period prophesied by Daniel and foretold by our Lord (Dan. 9:27; Mat. 24:21)."

THE EAST WIND

"As well, the "east wind" mentioned in Verse 27 localizes the Great Tribulation Period that is coming, which will affect the entire Earth, but will have its beginning in the Middle East."

THE SEVEN YEARS OF PLENTY

"As it regards the seven years of plenty, which immediately preceded the seven years of famine, looking at it in the Prophetic sense, we can take the number "seven" in two different ways.

"The number 'seven,' which is God's Number of Perfection, could pertain to the Church and it being completed and then taken out of the world immediately before the seven years of Tribulation. Or, even as the seven years of famine correspond exactly to the coming seven years of Great Tribulation, the seven years of plenty could refer to a tremendous Harvest of souls immediately preceding the Rapture, which will be followed by the Great Tribulation. Quite possibly, both particulars will come into play. There will be a great Harvest of souls, fulfilling the Prophecy of Joel about the Lord pouring out His Spirit upon all flesh, which Peter infers will be in the last days in a greater way than ever, which will conclude the Church Age (Acts 2:16-21)."

However, if the seven years of famine refer to the coming seven years of Great Tribulation, which it most definitely does, then it follows to reason that the seven years of plenty, which portrays the greatest harvest that Egypt had ever known, will be fulfilled by a great Harvest of souls coming to Christ, happening immediately before the commencement of the Great Tribulation. And we must understand that a Harvest of souls is different than Revival.

THE MODERN CHURCH

In Chapters 9, 10, and 11 of Romans, the Holy Spirit through the Apostle Paul tells us that if the church ignores the Message of the Cross, it will be *"cut off"* exactly as was Israel of old. Paul said:

"You (the Church) **will say then, The branches were broken off, that I might be grafted in** (the Church must ever know and understand that it was and is second choice).

"Well; because of unbelief they (Israel) **were broken off** (unbelief respecting Christ and the Cross), **and you stand by Faith** (proclaims that the Church was brought in because of Faith and not merit, and stands in its present position by Faith and not merit). **Be not highminded, but fear** (the reason is given in the next Verse):

"For if God spared not the natural branches (Israel), ***take heed*** **lest He also spare not you** (again refers to the Church, as is obvious)."

CUT OFF

"Behold therefore the Goodness and Severity of God (don't mistake the Goodness of God for license)**: on them which fell, severity** (speaks of Judgment which came on Israel, God's Chosen People)**; but toward you, goodness, if you continue in *His* Goodness** (proclaims the condition; the continuing of that 'Goodness' pertains to continued Faith in Christ and the Cross)**: otherwise you also shall be cut off** (is the modern church on the edge of that even now? Revelation 3:15-22 tells us this is the case!)**" (Rom. 11:19-22).**

Actually, coming up to this present time (2010), I personally believe that the modern church has already apostatized and, in reality, has been *"cut off"* by God. Of course, I speak, as we might say, of the institutionalized church. There are millions of Believers, who truly love the Lord, all over the world. They make up the true Church and, in fact, will be used of the Lord greatly. But, as far as the institutionalized church is concerned, it is my personal feeling that it is no more. In other words, it is not recognized by God in any capacity.

THE LORD GAVE ME A WORD

On December 6, 2009, at about 3:30 a.m., I awakened from a deep sleep. I looked at the clock, so I remember the time.

Before going back to sleep, that is, if I did, I began to meditate on the message I was to deliver that Sunday morning at FAMILY WORSHIP CENTER. Actually, I was to preach on Joseph that day.

The Lord spoke to my heart that night, specifically bringing the Dream of Pharaoh to my mind, especially the seven years of harvest that would be greater than Egypt had ever known before. I believe he spoke the following to my heart:

"This Ministry (Jimmy Swaggart Ministries) is going to have a part in fulfilling that Dream given to Pharaoh some 3,700 years ago. That means that every person connected with this Ministry, and even in the most remote way, will have a part, irrespective as to where they might be in the world, in the greatest Harvest of souls the

world has ever known."

As I dictate these notes, we are gearing up for the new SONLIFE BROADCASTING NETWORK. It will operate 24 hours a day, 7 days a week. We believe that we have the message of the hour, which is *"Jesus Christ and Him Crucified."* In other words, as previously stated, I believe this is what the Holy Spirit is presently saying to the Churches. That being the case, whether the church accepts it or not, it must be delivered on a worldwide basis. This Network will help us to do exactly that.

BELIEVE!

The Lord that night also told me what I was to tell the people that they must do. It was simple and to the point, but yet, so very, very weighty.

The Lord told me to say to all the people who follow this Ministry that they must *"believe."* Now, what does that mean?

It means that they are to have Faith that there will be a great Harvest of souls. They are to believe that we will be a part of that Harvest. They are to believe that the Lord will open the doors wide for this Ministry to touch hundreds of millions. They are to believe that they are personally a part of this Move.

The greatest hindrance to the Child of God is unbelief. We need the very opposite of that. We need Faith! We need for people to believe!

If they will do that, the financial needs will be met, the doors will open, and a great Harvest of souls will be brought about for the Lord Jesus Christ.

I believe with all of my heart that this Dream given to Pharaoh so long, long ago includes a great Harvest of souls that will immediately precede the Great Tribulation. I also believe with all of my heart that this Ministry is going to be an integral part of that Harvest. And that includes all of you who are connected with this Ministry in any way.

What a privilege to be a part of something that far reaching! What a mighty God we serve!

THE VISION

I've had very few experiences in my living for God, which I considered to be a Vision,

NOTES

but the following is that which I definitely believe falls into that category. The year was 1985. It was Monday morning of July 1.

As was my custom in those days, I would drive my car to a railroad track, which is about a half mile from our house, park there for awhile and study the Word of God. I would then walk down the track, seeking the Lord. In those days, there were no houses or businesses along the track, so it afforded privacy. Now all of that has changed.

At any rate, that particular morning, I studied the Word for a little while and then got out of the car and proceeded to walk down the track, praying as I went.

I suppose I had not been seeking the Lord but for approximately ten minutes at the most when, all of a sudden, everything changed around me. As far as the eye could see in every direction, even stretching over the horizon, there was nothing but fields of cotton. In other words, the entire landscape was a sea of white.

While we preachers are accustomed to using wheat as a sign of the harvest, I wondered why the Lord showed me this vast field of cotton. But then, the Bible says in the Words of our Lord:

"Say not you, There are yet four months, then comes the harvest? behold, I say unto you, Lift up your eyes, look on the fields; for they are white already to harvest" (Jn. 4:35).

Our Lord also said:

". . . The harvest truly is great, but the labourers are few: pray you therefore the Lord of the harvest, that He would send forth labourers into His Harvest" (Lk. 10:2).

As Joseph, who was a Type of Christ, was the Lord of the harvest in Egypt in his day, likewise, our Lord Jesus Christ is the Lord of the Harvest as it refers to souls.

As I looked at the vast sweeping fields of cotton, with every stalk heavily laden, actually, with not a green leaf in sight, I saw three, if I remember correctly, mechanical pickers in the distance, trying to gather the harvest.

THE STORM

And then to my left, which was out of the east according to the way I was walking, I saw a storm gathering on the horizon. The clouds were the blackest I had ever seen in my life, with jagged forks of lightning playing through those clouds. I knew if the harvest was not gathered immediately, that storm was going to destroy it all. And then the Lord spoke to me. He said:

"I will delay the storm for a short period of time until the harvest can be gathered." He then said, *"I want you to put the telecast in every city in the world that will accept it, and whatever you do, don't fail Me."*

The Lord then related something else to me, which I do not feel at liberty to divulge.

In the years that followed, my heart was broken in a thousand pieces, so to speak, because I felt I had failed Him. Despite every effort that I made, there was nothing I could do. In fact, it seemed like the door was almost totally closed.

A WORD FROM THE LORD

And then in September, 2009, if I remember the month correctly, while in prayer, the Lord spoke greatly to my heart again. He said to me:

"For the last 20 years, Satan has tried to close the door to your Ministry in every capacity; however, I kept it open about ten percent." As I thought about it, that's exactly the approximate degree that the door was left open. And yet, He spoke to me that afternoon saying, *"I am now once again going to open that door wide."* He never said anything to me about the Vision given in 1985, but I firmly believe the two are connected. In other words, I believe that the Lord is going to help us fulfill that which He directed us to do in 1985. For years I had thought that the situation was hopeless, but with God, I am finding out, all things are possible! I believe that the SONLIFE BROADCASTING NETWORK, as well as the radio ministry, is going to play a major part in this effort. In fact, both are already carried all over the world by the Internet. Most every month, we get letters and e-mails from virtually every country in the world. But what we've seen in the last couple of years is really only a prelude to that which the Lord is going to do. That Harvest, I believe, is going to be gathered.

The Lord did not tell me how long He would delay the storm, but only that He

would delay it. At any rate, this is the time that we must accomplish the task. I solicit your prayers that the Gospel may have free course. I ask that you pray that we may stay in the center of God's Will, not veering to the right or to the left, but that we be exactly in the place and position in which He wants us. As stated, you are a part of this, an integral part!

SOW TO YOURSELVES IN RIGHTEOUSNESS, REAP IN MERCY

In the midst of the Lord's distraught Message through Hosea, the Prophet to Israel, He now gives a bright ray of sunshine.

In effect, this phrase as given by the Lord, *"Sow to yourselves in Righteousness, reap in Mercy,"* is a call to Repentance. And the sowing of such seed is that *"Righteousness"* may spring from it.

What is Righteousness?

In simple terms, Righteousness is merely that which is right. But the Standard is of God and not man. Anything that man produces, irrespective as to what it is, is labeled by the Lord as *"self-righteousness."* The idea is that we sow such seed as that *"Righteousness may spring from it."*

How do we do that?

We must place our Faith exclusively in Christ and the Cross, realizing this is the way the Holy Spirit Works (Rom. 8:2). If we are to receive the Righteousness of God, we are to realize that it comes from God and God Alone. This means that man cannot produce anything within himself or of himself that God can accept. And that goes for every Believer on the face of the Earth, even the godliest! So, our Faith must be exclusively in Christ and the Cross. This means that we know and understand that every single thing we receive from God, and I mean everything, comes to us from the Source, Who is the Lord Jesus Christ, but by the Means of the Cross, and only by the Means of the Cross.

When two imperatives, such as *"Righteousness"* and *"Mercy,"* are joined together, the latter indicates a Promise. In other words, *"Mercy"* is guaranteed to come upon such action.

The intimation is that Grace, i.e., *"Mercy,"*

surpasses Righteousness, or that God rewards men's actions, not according to merit, but according to Grace. Actually, that's the only way that God can reward anything.

As men sow, they reap. Accordingly, Israel is directed to sow according to Righteousness that their reaping or reward would be not in proportion to what they had sown, but in proportion to Mercy—Divine Mercy, and far above their highest deserts. They are promised a reward far above their poor doings, irrespective of their sad failings—a reward not of debt or of merit but of Grace.

The seed-time of Righteousness would be followed by a reaping-time proportionate to the boundless measure of the Divine Mercy.

In other words, as Divine Righteousness demands just Judgment upon sin unconfessed and unrepented of, likewise, the same Divine Righteousness demands Mercy and Grace upon proper Repentance and forsaking of sin.

As it was promised to Israel of old, likewise, it is promised to any and all!

In fact, the Promise is so great that it defies description.

THE PHARISEES

It is this that the Pharisees of Jesus' Day could not accept. The idea that a despised Publican could receive forgiveness, and above all, Justification, merely by saying, *"God be merciful to me a sinner,"* was a great offense to their self-righteousness, even as the Cross of Christ is always a great offense to self-righteousness (Lk. 18:9-14).

As well, the Righteousness promised and *"Mercy"* given are not after an extended probationary period, but instead, come immediately upon proper Repentance, as evidenced by the Publican. Jesus said, *"I tell you, this man went down to his house justified rather than the other . . ."* (Lk. 18:14).

JUSTIFICATION BY FAITH IS NEVER PROBATIONARY

In other words, the Lord never puts anyone on probation. When He forgives, it is done totally, instantly, and completely. As well, complete Restoration is made simply because there is no such thing as a partial Justification.

A self-righteous church cannot abide this because to do so, as the Pharisees of old, abrogates their man-made authority.

The modern church would have demanded that Israel of old, even upon proper Repentance, be placed in a secondary, probationary status, therefore, placing them in the position of a servant instead of a son.

Such thinking completely abrogates the Grace of God, substituting a man-made Salvation, which has no place or merit in the Eyes of God.

The modern church takes this position because its self-righteousness cannot abide an individual being unrighteous one minute and, because of the Mercy and Grace of God, being Righteous the next minute. Such is all of Faith and requires no works. Self-righteousness demands works and, therefore, the abiding by its unscriptural rules and regulations, which, in effect, denies the Grace of God. Such is an abomination in God's Eyes. Jesus said, *". . . You are they who justify yourselves before men; but God knows your hearts: for that which is highly esteemed among men is abomination in the Sight of God"* (Lk. 16:15).

It should be well understood that the world is slow to forgive, while the church forgives not at all!

BREAK UP YOUR FALLOW GROUND

Fallow ground is that which has not been cultivated in quite some time, resulting in it being hard and unyielding. The breaking up refers to a ploughman running his plough through the fallow field, breaking up the hard-packed soil, and clearing out the weeds and roots so that the ground may be pure and clean for the sowing of the seed in the spring.

Israel is here told that it is high time to begin this process, laying aside their stiff-necked, perverse ways, expelling from their hearts the noxious growth that had overspread it, resulting in a hardened heart.

Neither were they to relax their efforts till the blessed end was attained, with the guarantee that such efforts would not be in vain, but that the Lord would reign—bestow abundantly—upon them *"Righteousness."*

The Holy Spirit said through James,

"Draw near to God, and He will draw near to you. Cleanse your hands, you sinners; and purify your hearts, you double minded" (James 4:8). This can only be done by the means of our Faith being placed exclusively in Christ and the Cross. This will then give the Holy Spirit latitude to Work within our lives, thereby, making us acceptable unto God. We cannot do this ourselves, not in any capacity! We must make the effort, as is here obvious, but that is as far as we can go.

IT IS TIME TO SEEK THE LORD

The great Prophet Jeremiah said:

"For I know the thoughts that I think toward you, says the LORD, thoughts of peace, and not of evil, to give you an expected end. *(Upon obedience to the Lord, with a sincere attempt to follow His Ways and Word, His 'thoughts toward us' are always 'thoughts of peace, and not of evil.')*

"Then shall you call upon Me, and you shall go and pray unto Me, and I will hearken unto you. *(The Restoration under Cyrus fulfilled the Prophecy of Verses 10 through 14 of this Chapter in Jeremiah. That Restoration was an earnest of the yet greater one of the future.)*

"And you shall seek Me, and find Me, when you shall search for Me with all your heart. *(This glorious Promise is given to any and to all, and for all time!)*

"And I will be found of you, says the LORD: and I will turn away your captivity . . ." (Jer. 29:11-14).

So, these Passages from Jeremiah tell us unequivocally that whatever our situation, if we will earnestly seek the Lord in all Spiritual honesty and integrity, meaning that we are totally sincere, He has promised to hear and promised to answer. And, as well, that answer would be very, very positive!

Regrettably and sadly, the modern church little believes anymore in *"seeking the Lord."* It rather subscribes to the psychological way, which translates into *"seeking man."*

THE REIGNING OF RIGHTEOUSNESS

Therefore, the Promise is that such waiting, if persevered, will not end in disappointment. Not withstanding our great and manifold provocations, He will come and reign Righteousness in welcome, refreshing, and plenteous showers. This Righteousness will include the reward of Blessing and Salvation, both temporal and spiritual.

If men will only believe it, this Twelfth Verse in this Tenth Chapter of Hosea is one of the greatest found in the entirety of God's Word.

Consequently, I want all and sundry to know that I believe this of which the Lord has said, and I not only believe it but, as well, believe it is the only way to the fulfillment of the human heart. It is not one of several ways but the only way—God's Way.

Incidentally, the word, *"till,"* as found in the Twelfth Verse, speaks of true Repentance, which seeks till it finds, just as the True Shepherd seeks till He finds.

(13) "YOU HAVE PLOWED WICKEDNESS, YOU HAVE REAPED INIQUITY; YOU HAVE EATEN THE FRUIT OF LIES: BECAUSE YOU DID TRUST IN YOUR WAY, IN THE MULTITUDE OF YOUR MIGHTY MEN.

(14) "THEREFORE SHALL A TUMULT ARISE AMONG YOUR PEOPLE, AND ALL YOUR FORTRESSES SHALL BE SPOILED, AS SHALMAN SPOILED BETH-ARBEL IN THE DAY OF BATTLE: THE MOTHER WAS DASHED IN PIECES UPON HER CHILDREN.

(15) "SO SHALL BETH-EL DO UNTO YOU BECAUSE OF YOUR GREAT WICKEDNESS: IN A MORNING SHALL THE KING OF ISRAEL UTTERLY BE CUT OFF."

The pattern is:

1. (Vs. 13) Tragically, Israel did not *"sow Righteousness,"* but rather sowed wickedness; therefore, they reaped *"iniquity"* and *"lies."* Their inward trust was *"their way,"* i.e., their false religion, and their outward confidence was their standing army. Both these saviours would fail them and Samaria would perish at the hand of Shalmaneser.

2. The phrase from Verse 14, *"And all your fortresses shall be spoiled,"* refers to the invasion by Shalmaneser, king of Assyria, which would come in the near future. It is referred to in II Kings, Chapter 17.

3. (Vs. 14) *"As Shalman spoiled Beth-arbel in the day of battle"* pertains to one of

the previous invasions of Israel by Assyria. Actually, there were several invasions, of which the last saw their total captivity and destruction.

4. (Vs. 14) *"The mother was dashed in pieces upon her children"* portrays the ferocity of the former invasions, which should have been a warning of what would ultimately happen!

5. (Vs. 15) The phrase, *"So shall Beth-el do unto you because of your great wickedness"* refers to their idolatry and to where it had brought them, and that the cruelties to be suffered by them were not to be chargeable to God, but rather to themselves.

6. (Vs. 15) The *"king of Israel"* was Hoshea (II Ki., Chpt. 17). *"Cut off"* refers to the Nation literally ceasing to be.

THE PLOUGHING OF WICKEDNESS

The two fundamental errors, or rather evils, that led to Israel's ruin were apostasy from Jehovah and sinful self-confidence. Sunk in idolatry, they no longer looked to Jehovah as the source of their power and strength. They pursued their own ways, confident of the excellence of their own sagacity and foresight and, consequently, went to their doom.

The Scripture uses the phrase, *"Because you did trust in your way,"* meaning they placed their confidence in the wisdom of their own ways. By these means, whatever they were, they fancied themselves independent of God and sufficiently defended against their enemies. They leaned on the flesh of man and did not trust in God and, therefore, stumbled, as stumble they must!

As Israel of old, so the modern church! They trust in their own ways.

ISRAEL WILL BE DESTROYED

The phrase of Verse 15, *"In a morning shall the king of Israel utterly be cut off,"* refers to the destruction of the Nation. Their great wickedness was *"the Golden Calf."* The words, *"cut off,"* refer to the Nation literally ceasing to be, which is exactly what happened.

Thus, their main refuge, which was Beth-el and the Golden Calf, would come to an ignominious end, bringing along with

it the frustration of all their hopes and the conclusion of their mistaken and misplaced confidences.

"Grace! 'Tis a charming sound,
"Harmonious to the ear:
"Heaven with the echo shall resound,
"And all the Earth shall hear."

"'Twas Grace that wrote my name,
"In life's eternal Book:
"'Twas Grace that gave me to the Lamb,
"Who all my sorrows took."

"Grace taught my wandering feet,
"To tread the Heavenly Road;
"And new supplies each hour I meet,
"While pressing on to God."

"Grace taught my soul to pray,
"And made my eyes overflow;
"'Tis Grace has kept me to this day,
"And will not let me go."

"Grace all the works shall crown,
"Through everlasting day;
"It lays in Heaven the topmost Stone,
"And well deserves the praise."

"Oh, let that Grace inspire,
"My soul with strength Divine;
"May all my powers to You aspire,
"And all my days be Thine."

CHAPTER 11

(1) "WHEN ISRAEL WAS A CHILD, THEN I LOVED HIM, AND CALLED MY SON OUT OF EGYPT.

(2) "AS THEY CALLED THEM, SO THEY WENT FROM THEM: THEY SACRIFICED UNTO BAALIM, AND BURNED INCENSE TO GRAVEN IMAGES.

(3) "I TAUGHT EPHRAIM ALSO TO GO, TAKING THEM BY THEIR ARMS; BUT THEY KNEW NOT THAT I HEALED THEM.

(4) "I DREW THEM WITH CORDS OF A MAN, WITH BANDS OF LOVE: AND I WAS TO THEM AS THEY WHO TAKE OFF THE YOKE ON THEIR JAWS, AND I LAID MEAT UNTO THEM.

(5) "HE SHALL NOT RETURN

INTO THE LAND OF EGYPT, BUT THE ASSYRIAN SHALL BE HIS KING, BECAUSE THEY REFUSED TO RETURN.

(6) "AND THE SWORD SHALL ABIDE ON HIS CITIES, AND SHALL CONSUME HIS BRANCHES, AND DEVOUR THEM, BECAUSE OF THEIR OWN COUNSELS.

(7) "AND MY PEOPLE ARE BENT TO BACKSLIDING FROM ME: THOUGH THEY CALLED THEM TO THE MOST HIGH, NONE AT ALL WOULD EXALT HIM."

The pattern is:

1. Verse 1 was quoted concerning Christ in Matthew 2:15. It properly explains how Prophecy can have a double fulfillment.

2. First of all, Verse 1 pertains to Israel being delivered from Egyptian bondage. And then it also pertains to Christ, as a baby, being taken to Egypt by Joseph and Mary in order to escape the murderous intent of Herod. When King Herod died, which, evidently, was brought about shortly, an Angel then told Joseph in a dream that it would now be safe to leave Egypt and go back to Israel, which they did (Mat. 2:13-21).

3. *"As they called them,"* of Verse 2, refers to the Prophets calling Israel to Repentance. *"So they went from them"* pertains to Israel turning a deaf ear to those who were their truest friends and best advisers. They continued to offer sacrifices to Baal and *"burn incense to graven images."*

4. The first phrase of Verse 3 is a picture of God's Guiding and Guarding Care over His People, and that despite their waywardness.

5. (Vs. 3) The phrase, *"They knew not that I healed them,"* pertains to their going astray, suffering its consequences, and then being picked up by the Lord, Who handled them tenderly and gently, healing their hurts and misdirection. However, they did not apprehend or appreciate God's Gracious Design and Dealing with them. To use an old adage, they *"bit the hand that fed them."*

6. The idea of Verse 4 is that the Lord was abundantly good to Israel, and in every way, but they still had no desire for Him.

7. The phrase, *"He shall not return into the land of Egypt,"* of Verse 5, refers to Ephraim's expectation of help from the king of Egypt, as found in II Kings 17:4. However,

that help was not forthcoming because the Lord had decreed, *"But the Assyrian shall be his king."*

All of this happened because they refused to repent and *"return to the Lord."*

8. The phrase of Verse 6, *"Because of their own counsels,"* refers to their clever plan of playing off the king of Assyria against the king of Egypt. However, those *"counsels"* would lead to their destruction.

9. The first phrase of Verse 7 is extremely expressive, with almost every word having an emphasis of its own. With all their sinfulness and shortcomings, Israel was still the People of God—*"My People."* Moreover, the *"backsliding"* was not an occasional lapse but was their habit, their tendency.

10. (Vs. 7) *"Though they called them to the Most High"* refers to the Prophets calling Israel from their idols to Jehovah, but all to no avail. *"None at all will exalt Him"* refers to them refusing to abandon their idols and give allegiance to the *"Most High."*

THE TRUE ISRAEL

To preserve Israel's life, He sent him down into Egypt (Gen. 46:3), and to establish him in Canaan, He brought him up out of Egypt.

Satan obstructed these plans and seemed to have won a victory. But God retired into the True Israel, His Dearly Beloved Son. It was, therefore, necessary that He, as the True Israel, should seek safety in Egypt, be God's Son there and, as such, enter the Promised Land. In all of this, there was no defeat.

As Christ was the True Israel, and still is, likewise, Christ is the True Church (Col. 1:24).

IDOLATRY

Irrespective that Prophet after Prophet was sent to the northern kingdom of Israel, still, Israel turned a deaf ear to those who were their truest friends and best advisers. Despite the Word of the Lord given in thundering tones, still, *"they sacrificed unto Balaam, and burned incense to graven images."* This means they continued to offer sacrifices to these idols, even while the Prophets were calling them to Repentance.

As Israel of old, so the modern church!

NOTES

The analogy is almost, if not, identical. As most of Israel apostatized, likewise, most of the church apostatizes. Only a small Remnant in Israel truly followed the Lord, while only a small Remnant in the modern church truly follows the Lord.

As there were many false prophets then, with only a precious few godly Prophets, likewise, the false prophets abound today, with only a precious few godly Prophets to sound the Call. Likewise, as they stoned them then, they stone them now, if not by actual stones, then with verbal stones.

APOSTASY!

Some time back I saw over television the portrayal of a particular service conducted in a foreign country. The evangelist in question told a Catholic priest sitting on his platform how much he loved the Catholic church. Remember, this came out over television. A short time earlier I had seen that same evangelist with two Catholic Priests on his program, with him telling the world how wonderful and godly that Catholicism is. Ladies and Gentlemen, that is pretty close to blasphemy!

Anyone who embraces Catholic doctrine and continues in that way will die eternally lost. How many people in Catholic churches saw that program and were made to feel comfortable and secure in their false religion? Only God knows the answer to that, but the fact is, that popular evangelist was and is, simply put, preaching a lie! What did the Apostle Paul say about that?

"**But though we** (*Paul and his associates*), **or an Angel from Heaven, preach any other gospel unto you than that which we have preached unto you** (*Jesus Christ and Him Crucified*), **let him be accursed** (*eternally condemned; the Holy Spirit speaks this through Paul, making this very serious*).

"**As we said before, so say I now again** (*at some time past, he had said the same thing to them, making their defection even more serious*), **If any *man* preach any other gospel unto you** (*anything other than the Cross*) **than that you have received** (*which Saved your souls*), **let him be accursed** (*'eternally condemned,' which means the loss of the soul*)."

The great Apostle continues:

"**For do I now persuade men, or God?** (*In essence, Paul is saying, 'Do I preach man's doctrine, or God's?'*) **or do I seek to please men?** (*This is what false apostles do.*) **for if I yet pleased men, I should not be the Servant of Christ** (*one cannot please both men and God at the same time*)" (**Gal. 1:8-10**).

And yet, people, who conclude themselves to be Spirit-filled, keep pouring money into this obvious, blatant, false doctrine. And please understand, we are not here discussing the price of wheat but the eternal souls of men.

I TAUGHT EPHRAIM

Every single Believer is taught, one way or the other, by the Lord. And yet, the Lord will use many devices and many individuals. In fact, "*Apostles, Prophets, Evangelists, Pastors, and Teachers*" serve in this capacity, as well, at least those who are truly of the Lord. Unfortunately, those who are truly of the Lord are far, far less in number than those who have called themselves.

We have over 1,000 inmates a month from prisons all over this nation who write us, asking for an EXPOSITOR'S NEW TESTAMENT. We always fulfill that request at no charge. We also give thousands to our servicemen and women, as well, at no charge.

As someone has well said, "*When anyone gets an EXPOSITOR'S STUDY BIBLE, and in any form, they are getting not only the Word of God but, as well, instruction as to how to understand it, which accompanies almost every Scripture.*" In other words, they are getting a teacher along with the Text, which the Lord has intended all along, hence, the giving of these particular Ministries (Eph. 4:11). Paul said:

MINISTRY GIFTS

"**For the perfecting of the Saints** (*to 'equip for service'*), **for the work of the Ministry** (*to proclaim the Message of Redemption to the entirety of the world*), **for the edifying of the Body of Christ** (*for the spiritual building up of the Church*):

"**Till we all come in the unity of the Faith** (*to bring all Believers to a proper knowledge of Christ and the Cross*), **and of the**

knowledge of the Son of God *(which again refers to what He did for us at the Cross)*, **unto a perfect man** *(the Believer who functions in maturity)*, **unto the measure of the stature of the fulness of Christ** *(the 'measure' is the 'fullness of Christ,' which can only be attained by a proper Faith in the Cross).*"

EVERY WIND OF DOCTRINE

"**That we** *henceforth* **be no more children** *(presents the opposite of maturity, and speaks of those whose faith is in that other than the Cross)*, **tossed to and fro, and carried about with every wind of doctrine, by the sleight of men** *(Satan uses preachers)*, *and* **cunning craftiness** *(they make a way, other than the Cross, which seems to be right)*, **whereby they lie in wait to deceive** *(refers to a deliberate planning or system)*;

"**But speaking the Truth in Love** *(powerfully proclaiming the Truth of the Cross but always with Love)*, **may grow up into Him in all things** *(proper Spiritual Growth can take place only according to proper Faith in the Cross [I Cor. 1:21, 23; 2:2])*, **which is the Head,** *even* **Christ** *(Christ is the Head of the Church and is such by virtue of the Cross)*" **(Eph. 4:12-15).**

One of the great Works in the Ministry of the Holy Spirit is to teach us, in effect, to *"guide us into all Truth."* Concerning this very thing, Jesus said:

GUIDANCE INTO ALL TRUTH

"**Howbeit when He, the Spirit of Truth, is come** *(which He did on the Day of Pentecost)*, **He will guide you into all Truth** *(if our Faith is properly placed in Christ and the Cross, the Holy Spirit can then bring forth Truth to us; He doesn't guide us into some truth, but rather 'all Truth')*: **for He shall not speak of Himself** *(tells us not only what He does, but Whom He represents)*; **but whatsoever He shall hear,** *that* **shall He speak** *(doesn't refer to lack of knowledge, for the Holy Spirit is God, but rather He will proclaim the Work of Christ only)*: **and He will show you things to come** *(pertains to the New Covenant, which would shortly be given)*" **(Jn. 16:13).**

The idea is, the Lord wants us to know and understand the Word of God. He has

given us tremendously valuable aids to bring about this process. So, there is no excuse for the Believer not knowing and understanding the Word of God. But, unfortunately, like *"Ephraim"* of old, despite the availability of the knowledge that is needed, it is too often ignored! In other words, most in the modern church know more about Hollywood than they do the Holy Spirit, more about Babylon than they do the Bible!

DO YOU NOT KNOW . . .?

Out of the entirety of the Bible, Romans, Chapters 6, 7, and 8, proclaim to us as to how the Believer is to live a Victorious Life, in other words, victorious over the world, the flesh, and the Devil. One might say that everything in the Bible strains toward those three Chapters. Actually, in those three Chapters, the Holy Spirit through Paul uses the word *"know," "knowing,"* or *"known,"* some ten times. In other words, the Lord wants us to know (Rom. 6:3, 6, 9, 16; 7:1, 7, 18; 8:28). Every Christian ought to read the Bible through at least one time a year. To be sure, it will never get old because it is the Word of God. As we have said oftentimes, *"The Bible is the only revealed Truth in the world today and, in fact, ever has been."*

BANDS OF LOVE

The phrase, *"I drew them with cords of a man, with bands of love,"* actually means, *"I led them by strings."* This refers to one leading a little boy, who is just beginning to walk, that he may accustom himself to go little by little without trouble. This refers to Israel being led out of Egypt into the wilderness and being led from station to station.

The short phrase, *"Bands of love,"* is a remarkable statement in that it refers to the very opposite of that which is employed by men in taming or breaking wild and unmanageable animals.

In other words, the Lord did not force them into His Lifestyle, as one would drag a recalcitrant animal, but instead, as a man draws his fellowman without compelling him to go with resistance. It was done with gentleness, hence, *"bands of love."*

Such proclaims the Love and Grace of God in dealing with the human family. No wonder the Psalmist said, *"Unto You, O God, do we give thanks, unto You do we give thanks: for that Your Name is near Your Wondrous Works declare"* (Ps. 75:1).

THE YOKE OF THEIR JAWS

The phrase, *"And I was to them as they who take off the yoke on their jaws,"* refers to a man lifting the yoke of the ox that it may not press too heavily upon him or hinder him while eating.

The fact thus figuratively expressed is not the deliverance from the bondage of Egypt but the loving-kindness of Jehovah in making the Law easier to bear for Israel. In other words, He dealt kindly and graciously with them.

Some 800 years later, Jesus would refer to this by saying, *"For My Yoke is easy, and My Burden is light"* (Mat. 11:30).

ABUNDANT BLESSINGS

The phrase, *"And I laid meat unto them,"* refers to Him Blessing them abundantly. In other words, His Supply was bountiful.

He is actually saying that He did the very opposite with Israel as a man generally does with an ox by loosening the yoke, allowing him to get a mouthful of food occasionally. Instead, the Lord allowed Israel to feed abundantly.

So, Jehovah extended to Israel, notwithstanding their frequent acts of unfaithfulness, His Sparing Mercy and Tender Compassion, supplying them in abundant measure with all that they needed for the sustenance and even the very comforts of life.

Therefore, their turning aside to other gods, which, in effect, were no gods at all, was all the more inexcusable.

THEY SOUGHT DELIVERANCE FROM THE WRONG PLACE

The phrase, *"He shall not return into the Land of Egypt,"* refers to Ephraim's expectation of help from the king of Egypt, as found in II Kings 17:4. However, that help was not forthcoming because the Lord had decreed, *"But the Assyrian shall be his king."*

All of this happened because they refused to repent and turn to the Lord. If they had returned to God, foreign kings (literally,

"kings of the nation") would not have ruled over them, but they would have ruled over the nations as they had done in the days of David and Solomon when they did God's Will (Deut. 15:6).

All of these things, the pain, suffering, and ultimate bondage, were *"because they refused to return."*

THE CROSS AND THE MODERN CHURCH

Everything the Believer needs has been made possible by what Jesus did at the Cross. But yet, the modern church turns to humanistic psychology or else a humanitarian, social, material message. In the midst of all of this is an ethical message, which sounds good to the carnal ear. As someone has well said, *"The doing of religion is the most powerful narcotic there is."* One could put it in the following fashion:

• Much of what is being preached behind modern pulpits is psychology. In fact, untold thousands of preachers are preaching psychology and not even realizing it. This pertains to man's way of addressing problems, whatever those problems might be.

• The humanitarian, social gospel is that which involves the doing of good deeds and, thereby, proclaiming oneself as righteous.

• The money gospel (materialism) is that practiced by the majority of the Charismatic church world.

• The ethical gospel has to do with that which is morally right, which, again, sounds good to the carnal ear. Of course, the Child of God is most definitely to be moral. That's not the question! The question is, *"How do we attain this position of morality?"* To be sure, the ethical gospel that is presently being preached mostly stems from psychology. The reader must understand that there is only one way that Righteousness and Holiness can be developed in one's life. That is by our Faith being exclusively placed in Christ and what He did for us at the Cross, which gives the Holy Spirit the latitude to Work within our lives. It is the Holy Spirit Alone Who can bring about the change that all of us desperately need. Momentarily, I'm going to relate as to how, according to the Bible, the Holy Spirit Works within our lives.

THE TWO MAJOR HINDRANCES
TO THE GOSPEL

Those two hindrances are:
1. The wisdom of the world.
2. The legalism of religion.

The Biblical way and means of developing Righteousness and Holiness is strictly by the Means of the Cross of Christ and no other way. When man uses any other means, irrespective as to how good it may look on the surface, he is using the wisdom of the world, which God can never accept.

Paul said, *"That your Faith should not stand in the wisdom of men, but in the Power of God"* (I Cor. 2:5). But, sad to say, the *"wisdom of men"* is that which is mostly being promoted in the modern church. Let us say it again:

If it's not Faith in Christ and the Cross and Christ and the Cross exclusively, then it's the wisdom of men, no matter how right it may seem to be on the surface.

And then we have the *"legalism of religion."* Paul also said:

"I do not frustrate the Grace of God *(if we make anything other than the Cross of Christ the Object of our Faith, we frustrate the Grace of God, which means we stop its action, and the Holy Spirit will no longer help us)*: **for if Righteousness** *come* **by the Law** *(any type of religious law)*, **then Christ is dead in vain.** *(If I can successfully live for the Lord by any means other than Faith in Christ and the Cross, then the Death of Christ was a waste)*" **(Gal. 2:21).**

Legalism pertains to *"dos"* and *"don'ts"*! The idea of the Gospel of Jesus Christ is that Christ has already done at the Cross everything that needs to be done. For us to receive and be the beneficiary of that which He has done, we simply must register Faith in Him and His Finished Work. That being done, the Holy Spirit will then develop in our lives that which He Alone can develop. But, sad to say, the modern church is shot through with *"the wisdom of the world"* and the *"legalism of religion."*

HOW IS IT THAT VICTORY COMES BY
THE WAY OF THE CROSS OF CHRIST?

There is no magic charm and no manipulative power about the Cross, in fact, nothing

NOTES

that's beyond the pale of understanding regarding Believers. The Lord gave the meaning of all of this to the Apostle Paul, which he gave to us in his 14 Epistles. In other words, the Lord showed Paul the meaning of the New Covenant, which is the meaning of the Cross of Christ. Actually, the Cross is so much the Plan of Redemption that the Holy Spirit allowed Paul to use the word *"Cross"* as a synonym for the Gospel (I Cor. 1:17-18).

WHAT JESUS DID AT THE CROSS!

The Cross of Christ, as horrible as it was, was a designed purpose. Actually, it was designed by the Godhead from before the foundation of the world (I Pet. 1:18-20).

Jesus did two things at the Cross. They are:

1. He atoned for all sin, past, present, and future, at least for those who will believe (Jn. 3:16; I Jn. 1:7). He there satisfied every demand of the broken Law, of which all were guilty (Col. 2:14).

2. By atoning for all sin, the Lord removed Satan's right to hold man captive, at least for those who will believe. It is sin that gives Satan the legal right to hold man captive. With all sin removed in those who will believe, the Evil One now has no more right to hold anyone in bondage. If he does so, and, regrettably, he does in most cases, it is because that man will not believe and will not avail himself of that which our Lord has done at Calvary. Unfortunately, this goes for Christians also. Most of the modern church presently exhibits Faith in Christ as it regards their Salvation, but it's faith in themselves as it regards their Sanctification. God can never honor the latter. So, such a Christian remains captive to the sin nature, which causes all kinds of problems (Rom. 6:12-13).

Actually, the Work of Christ on the Cross is referred to as a *"Finished Work"* (Heb. 7:25-27; 8:6; 9:28; 10:9-12). That means nothing can be added because nothing needs to be added. It is a *"Finished Work."*

CHRIST, OUR SUBSTITUTE

We must know and understand that Jesus came to this world and did what He was to do as our substitute. In His Life and Living, He kept the Law perfectly in every respect, never sinning, not even one time, in word, thought, or deed. And, we must understand, He did this as the *"Last Adam,"* as the *"Second Man,"* meaning that He did it altogether for us. He was our Substitute. When we accept Him by Faith, which refers to Faith in Christ and what He did for us at the Cross and in His Resurrection, we are transferred from the position of lawbreaker to *"law-keeper."* But, we must remember, we are transferred to this position solely by virtue of Christ and what He did at the Cross on our behalf and our Faith in that Finished Work.

SUBSTITUTION, NOT IDENTIFICATION

While it is true that we identify with Christ in His Death, Burial, and Resurrection, and do so by Faith (Rom. 6:3-5), in no way does He identify with us as it regards our sin. In other words, He did not become a sinner on the Cross as some teach.

The only way it can be said that He identifies with us and our sin is by Him becoming a Sin-Offering, which, in fact, He most definitely did. This means that He took the penalty of our sin upon Himself by giving Himself in Perfect Sacrifice before God, which was accepted totally and completely by God.

The moment the believing sinner expresses Faith in Christ, in the Mind of God, the believing sinner is placed *"in Christ,"* as it refers to His Death on Calvary, *"in Christ,"* as it refers to His Burial, and *"in Christ,"* as it refers to His Resurrection. This is what Paul meant when he said the following:

COMPLETE IN HIM

"And you are complete in Him *(the satisfaction of every spiritual want is found in Christ, made possible by the Cross)***, which is the Head of all principality and power** *(His Headship extends not only over the Church, which voluntarily serves Him, but over all forces that are opposed to Him as well [Phil. 2:10-11])***:

"In Whom also you are circumcised with the Circumcision made without hands *(that which is brought about by the Cross [Rom. 6:3-5])***, in putting off the body of the sins of the flesh by the Circumcision of Christ** *(refers to the old carnal nature that is defeated by the Believer placing his Faith

totally in the Cross, which gives the Holy Spirit latitude to work)*:

"Buried with Him in Baptism *(does not refer to Water Baptism, but rather to the Believer baptized into the Death of Christ, which refers to the Crucifixion and Christ as our Substitute [Rom. 6:3-4])***, wherein also you are risen with *Him* through the Faith of the Operation of God, Who has raised Him from the dead.** *(This does not refer to our future physical Resurrection, but to that Spiritual Resurrection from a sinful state into Divine Life. We died with Him, we are buried with Him, and we rose with Him [Rom. 6:3-5], and herein lies the secret to all Spiritual Victory)***" (Col. 2:10-12).**

By all sin being totally and completely addressed at the Cross, meaning the price was paid, this took away Satan's right and privilege to hold men captive. If they are captive to him, it is because they do not avail themselves of that for which Christ has paid such a price.

THE SIN NATURE

The Cross of Christ, which we have dealt with first of all, is the only answer to the sin nature. Before we go to the Holy Spirit, Who Works entirely within the framework of the Finished Work of Christ, we must address the sin nature, which is the biggest problem for the Child of God.

After the Lord showed the Apostle Paul the manner and way of Salvation, which is Justification by Faith, found in Chapters 4 and 5 of Romans, He then showed Paul how to live for God. Paul shares this great Revelation with the Believer in the Sixth Chapter of Romans. It is sad, but the modern church simply does not know how to live for God, thereby, stumbling and staggering from one fad to the other, all to no avail. As stated, the Cross of Christ is the only answer.

In the Sixth Chapter of Romans, Paul mentions sin some 17 times. Fifteen of those times he uses what is now referred to as the *"definite article"* in front of the word sin, making it originally read, *"the sin."* This means that he is not speaking of acts of sin, but rather the root of sin, the sin principle, or the sin nature. Only in the Fifteenth Verse of the Sixth Chapter of Romans does Paul address himself to acts of sin. While the Fourteenth Verse does not have the definite article preceding the word sin, inasmuch as Paul used the word *"sin"* as a noun instead of a verb, we know that he is continuing to speak of the sin nature.

The moment the believing sinner comes to Christ, the sin nature is made dormant. In other words, one might say it is unplugged! So, before we go further, let's explain what the sin nature actually is.

A DEFINITION OF THE SIN NATURE

Before Adam and Eve fell, they were controlled completely by the Divine Nature. So, when they fell, they fell from a position of total God-consciousness down to the far, far lower level of total self-consciousness. Then their very nature became one of sin. In other words, their human nature was then controlled by the sin nature 24 hours a day, 7 days a week, one might say.

If you the reader will think back to your life before coming to Christ, you will have to admit that you, as well, were completely controlled in those days by the sin nature. This control was not partly so but totally and completely. When you came to Christ, the Divine Nature came into your heart and life, which, of course, is of God. Then the struggle commenced between the Divine Nature and the sin nature (II Pet. 1:4).

YOUR NEW LIFE IN CHRIST JESUS

When you were Born-Again, the things you once loved (sin), you now hate, and the things that you once hated (things of the Lord), you now love. In those days, in your mind you thought that you would never sin again. But then you found that sooner or later you failed the Lord. In fact, there has never been one who didn't.

When this happened, it shocked you, and you determined to take measures that it not happen again. That's when the problems began.

Not understanding anything about the sin nature or about the Cross of Christ relative to Sanctification, you placed your faith and confidence in something other than the Cross of Christ. In fact, that in which you

placed your faith was probably something good but was never meant by the Lord to function in the capacity in which you tried to make it function. Let me give you an example:

I heard a preacher say over television some time back that if the Believer would take the Lord's Supper once a day, or once a week, or whatever timeframe he said, the Believer would find prosperity, healing, victory over sin, etc.

Another one wrote, *"If one would fast 21 days, they would find total victory over every sinful problem in their life."*

Now, while the Lord's Supper and Fasting are definitely Scriptural, still, these things, or 101 other things we could name, were never meant by the Lord to be used in this manner. It's like trying to take a handsaw and make a hammer out of it. In fact, when the Believer does this, he has just committed Spiritual Adultery, even though he doesn't realize it.

SPIRITUAL ADULTERY

What is Spiritual Adultery?

When you as a believing sinner came to Christ, in effect, you married Christ. At least that's the way the Holy Spirit puts it (Rom. 7:1-4; II Cor. 11:1-4). This means that Christ is to meet your every need, whatever it might be, which He has done by the Means of the Cross. But when we look to other things for victory, we are being unfaithful to Christ, which Paul, in a sense, refers to as *"spiritual adultery."* As should be understood, the Holy Spirit doesn't work very well in such situations. While He won't leave us and will do all He can to help us, still, by us functioning in a state of Spiritual Adultery, we have greatly hindered the help that He can give. Unfortunately, due to the fact that virtually the entirety of the modern church little understands, if at all, the Cross of Christ relative to Sanctification, this means that most of the modern church is living in a state of Spiritual Adultery. This is the blueprint for tragedy. This means that the sin nature is going to rule the Believer in some way.

When the Believer places his or her faith in something other than Christ and the Cross, and due to the fact that we have greatly limited the Holy Spirit in what He can do for us, the sin nature is resurrected, one might say. Then, in some way, such a Believer will find himself controlled by the sin nature. Paul uses the word *"dominion"* (Rom. 6:14).

This creates confusion and consternation for the Child of God. He finds himself struggling with all his strength and might not to fail but finds that he fails anyway. This is what Paul was talking about when he said, *"For that which I do I allow not: for what I would, that do I not; but what I hate, that do I"* (Rom. 7:15).

Actually, the word *"allow"* should have been translated *"understand."* It would then read, and rightly so, *"For that which I do I understand not. . . ."* As we have stated, multiple millions of Christians are struggling and failing each day despite every effort they make otherwise, and they simply, as Paul, do not understand why.

Let it be understood that when Paul wrote the Seventh Chapter of Romans, he full well understood everything about the sin nature and how to have victory. But he's giving us a snapshot, one might say, out of his personal life before this great Revelation of the Cross was given to him. In fact, the best that one can chronologically put together, Paul probably lived in this state of spiritual failure for several years. But again we emphasize that when he wrote this, he very well understood God's Prescribed Order of Victory and was living accordingly. So, the question must be asked, *"If the great Paul, who had seen Christ on the road to Damascus, and had been baptized with the Holy Spirit three days later, and had immediately begun to preach the Gospel, could not successfully live for the Lord without understanding God's Order, no matter how hard he tried, how in the world do we think we can do so?"*

SIN

No true Christian wants to sin. In fact, every true Christian, and we speak of those who are truly Born-Again, hates sin in every form. While the flesh may want something that's not right, as a Born-Again Believer, we, in our spirit, definitely do not want that which is evil. As stated, and even as Paul

stated, we hate these things, whatever they might be. But yet, there are millions of Christians presently, who still are being dominated by the sin nature in some way, although hating sin with every fiber of their being. This means they are failing the Lord, actually sinning, despite all they can do otherwise.

IS SUCH A BELIEVER RESPONSIBLE?

Yes!

Every person who sins is responsible for that sin. However, we are not responsible in the way that most think.

Where we are responsible is that God has given us His Way in His Word, and it's our responsibility to find and understand that Way and walk therein. So, the failure is ours not so much in committing the act, although that is failure, but rather in failing to obey the Word of the Lord. In other words, and as stated, most modern Christians simply do not know how to live for God. Most Christians think that Paul is speaking of Water Baptism in the great Sixth Chapter of Romans and, thereby, dismiss the entirety of the teaching given therein because of a misunderstanding. That is tragic because the Sixth Chapter of Romans just might be the single most important Chapter in the entirety of the Word of God as it regards how to live for God. It is this Chapter that tells us how to have Victory over the sin nature.

We must understand that Paul is dealing here with Believers. The first two Verses in the Sixth Chapter of Romans tell us that sin is the problem.

Verses 3 through 5 tell us that the Cross of Christ is the solution to this problem and, in fact, the only solution. The balance of the Chapter deals with the sin nature and how it is to be overcome once we understand the meaning of the Cross as it regards our Sanctification.

CAN SATAN FORCE THE WILL OF A BELIEVER?

Yes, he can!

Once again, does that mean the person is not responsible?

No! When we sin, we are responsible, and for the reasons already given. Once again we go to the words of Paul.

He also said:

"For the good that I would I do not: but the evil which I would not, that I do" (Rom. 7:19).

This is not the statement of a man who is unsaved as some claim. In other words, some claim that Paul was speaking of himself before he came to the Lord on the road to Damascus. No! In the Fifteenth Verse of that Chapter Paul talked about hating sin. No unbeliever hates sin, in fact, he loves sin! So, the idea is, despite every effort that Paul made, he found that he could not successfully live for the Lord, no matter how hard he tried. This was before the Lord gave him the meaning of the New Covenant, which is the meaning of the Cross. Once again I ask the question, *"If the great Paul experienced this, and he most definitely did, where does that leave us?"* In other words, if you think you can successfully live for the Lord without understanding the Cross of Christ relative to Sanctification, then you should consider Paul. If he couldn't do it, how do you think you can?

Now, we must come to the conclusion that despite this problem, the great Apostle was Saved and baptized with the Holy Spirit, was actually preaching the Gospel, and, in fact, was being used by God greatly so! Many Christians don't understand this, but this is the case every day. Millions presently, who are struggling with the sin nature and failing the Lord despite all they can do otherwise, are being used by the Lord,. They are struggling because they do not understand God's Prescribed Order of Victory. And please understand, as well, if the Lord only used those who had the proper understanding of all of this, then He wouldn't use very many.

Yes, Satan can override the will of a Believer if he doesn't understand what Paul gave us in the Sixth Chapter of Romans. Satan can make that Believer do something he is struggling not to do. This happens every day by the millions of times all over the world. Regrettably, most don't understand it! The reason the church jumps from one fad to the other is because they don't understand God's Way. That Way is the Cross. Virtually all Believers have understanding of the Cross

of Christ as it refers to Salvation, with the words, *"Jesus died for me,"* being the greatest ever spoken. However, as it regards Sanctification respecting the Cross of Christ, in other words, how we live for God on a daily basis, the vast majority of Christians have absolutely no knowledge of this whatsoever. As a result, while they definitely are Saved, they live a life of spiritual defeat.

THE SEVENTH CHAPTER OF ROMANS

While every single Believer must go through the Seventh Chapter of Romans to a certain degree, in other words, live that Chapter, it most definitely is not God's Will that we stay there all the days of our lives. Tragically, that's what happens to most Christians. They never get out of the Seventh Chapter of Romans. Please read carefully the following:

What we must be in Christ, we cannot bring about by our own strength, ability, or personal efforts. In fact, the Holy Spirit through Paul refers to this as *"the flesh."*

WHAT IS THE FLESH?

The flesh, as Paul used the word, pertains to our human ingenuity, ability, strength, education, motivation, talents, etc. In other words, it's what we can do as human beings. There will be a struggle between the flesh and the spirit of man as long as we live, and we're speaking of the regenerated spirit of the Born-Again Believer. That's the reason that Jesus said that we must *"take up the Cross daily"* (Lk. 9:23). We must understand, religious flesh is just as hateful to God, if not more so, as regular flesh. Flesh is flesh, and Paul also stated, *"So then they who are in the flesh cannot please God"* (Rom. 8:8).

The following is going to be a very abbreviated diagram of the means and ways by which the modern church addresses the sin nature. It is as follows:

• IGNORANCE: the truth is, the vast majority of Christendom has no understanding whatsoever of the sin nature. Most Christians have never heard a sermon on this most important subject, never read a message about it, and have no understanding of it whatsoever. Even most preachers don't know what it is. In other words, as it regards the sin nature, the modern church is wrapped up in a blanket of ignorance.

• DENIAL: some few, who have a modicum of understanding regarding the sin nature, in other words, they do believe that such exists, claim that once a person comes to Christ, there is no more sin nature. My answer to that is simple: understanding that Paul is writing to Believers in Romans, Chapters 6, 7, and 8, why would the Holy Spirit take up so much time explaining something that doesn't exist? The truth is, we as Believers continue to have a sin nature. However, if we follow that given to us by the Apostle Paul as it was given to him by the Lord, the sin nature will prove no problem. Otherwise, it will be a severe problem!

• LICENSE: then there are some who have a modicum of understanding respecting the sin nature but erroneously think that because there is such a thing, they can't help but sin. This is where the *"sin a little bit every day"* has its roots. Paul answered that very succinctly by saying:

"What shall we say then? Shall we continue in sin, that Grace may abound? God forbid. How shall we, who are dead to sin, live any longer therein?" (Rom. 6:1-2).

• STRUGGLE: then there are some Christians who think that it is the lot of the Child of God to struggle with sin each and every day. Normally, these are what one would consider to be the best Christians. While there is a struggle, it is a struggle of our Faith and not with sin. We are to *"fight the good fight of Faith"* (I Tim. 6:12).

Jesus has already defeated sin at the Cross and did so by atoning for all sin, past, present, and future, at least for all who will believe (Jn. 3:16). So, we make a mistake when we try to fight with sin or struggle with sin. As stated, our struggle and our fight are with Faith and nothing else. We dare not try to do what we cannot do and which Jesus has already done.

The type of struggle that is engaged by most only tends to give birth to self-righteousness. In fact, anything we do, as it regards our Lord, other than Faith in Him and what He did for us at the Cross, will always and without exception lead to self-righteousness.

• GRACE: out of all these means and

NOTES

ways which have been named, *"Grace"* is the only one that is Scripturally valid. Grace is simply the Goodness of God given to undeserving Saints. We must understand that all Grace comes by the Means of the Cross. In other words, it is the Cross of Christ that makes it possible for the Lord to give us all of these good things. That is so because it was at the Cross where all sin was atoned. This made it possible for the Holy Spirit, Who is the Bearer of God's Grace (Eph. 2:13-18), to Work within our lives.

We are to place our Faith exclusively in Christ and what He did for us at the Cross. This then gives the Holy Spirit the latitude to take the good things of God, His Grace, and make them real to us. Then and only then can we be the overcomer we are meant to be. The Lord has all types of good things He desires to bestow upon us. It only takes one thing for those good things to be made real in our lives, and that is our Faith in Christ and His Cross. That's why Paul said:

"But God forbid that I should Glory *(boast),* **save in the Cross of our Lord Jesus Christ** *(what the opponents of Paul sought to escape at the price of insincerity is the Apostle's only basis of exultation),* **by Whom the world is crucified unto me, and I unto the world.** *(The only way we can overcome the world, and I mean the only way, is by placing our Faith exclusively in the Cross of Christ and keeping it there)"* **(Gal. 6:14).**

HOW THE HOLY SPIRIT WORKS

As we've already stated, the only way we can have Victory over the sin nature in every capacity and, as well, have the Fruit of the Spirit developed in our hearts and lives, and that Righteousness and Holiness may become a part of our demeanor and our very personality, is by the Person and Power of the Holy Spirit. These things, which we need and, in fact, must have from the Lord, we cannot bring about by our own ability, strength, education, motivation, or talent, in other words, the flesh. Such is impossible.

The Lord showed me in prayer two things we must consider:

1. The victory that we must have, we cannot bring about by our own strength and ability. It is impossible. It can only be done

by the Power of the Holy Spirit, which can be at our disposal according to our Faith in Christ and the Cross.

2. Even if we could develop these things in our lives, which we can't, the fallout would not be to our good but to our detriment. Such would only seek to develop self-righteousness in our lives, which the Lord can never condone. The very reason the Lord allows the sin nature to remain in our lives is for disciplinarial reasons. In other words, it is to serve as a discipline to us. The human spirit is such that if given half an opportunity, we will give the glory to ourselves instead of the Lord. Even when we're giving Glory to God, so oftentimes we try to claim that it's our Faith that gets it done. In other words, if you had the type of faith that I have, well then, you would never have a problem, etc. In reality, such thinking is really giving glory to ourselves and not to the Lord. So, the sin nature is ever present to warn us of our fallibility as well as our inability (Rom. 8:10).

THE CROSS AND THE HOLY SPIRIT

We are plainly told in Romans 8:2 as to how the Holy Spirit works within our lives. Having already given this Passage, I will not detail it again. To be brief, the Holy Spirit works entirely within the framework of the Finished Work of Christ, i.e., *"the Cross."* It only requires our Faith in Christ and the Cross for Him to do His Work.

The Holy Spirit is God. As such, He is All-Powerful, All-Knowing, and is ever-present everywhere. Consequently, He can do anything, as should be obvious.

Before the Cross, the Holy Spirit was very limited as to what He could do. The reason was the blood of bulls and goats could not take away the sins of Believers (Heb. 10:4), so this meant that the sin debt remained. That being the case, the Holy Spirit could only come into the hearts and lives of certain Believers to help them carry out particular tasks, such as the Prophets of Israel, etc. Even then, He had to remain for only a period of time, and then He would depart. There is no record in the Old Testament that the Holy Spirit helped at all with one's Sanctification, with His Work limited to the

task at hand, which concerned itself with a particular mission, etc.

In fact, that's the reason that when Believers died before the Cross, they were not taken to Heaven, but rather down into Paradise, which was in the heart of the Earth. In effect, they were captives of Satan even though He could not get them over into the burning side of the pit, that being separated from Paradise by a great gulf (Lk. 16:19-31). It was because the sin debt remained. With sin being the legal right that Satan had to hold man in bondage, they were still his captives although followers of the Lord.

But when Jesus paid the price at Calvary's Cross, thereby, atoning for all sin, this meant the sin debt was forever removed. Then our Lord could go down into Paradise, which He did after His Death on the Cross, and there liberate all of those righteous souls (Eph. 4:8-10). Now, when a Believer dies, in fact, ever since the Cross, the soul and the spirit of that Believer instantly goes to Heaven (Phil. 1:23). It is all because of what Jesus did at the Cross. That's the reason that Paul also said:

THE MEDIATOR

"But now (since the Cross) **has He** (the Lord Jesus) **obtained a more excellent Ministry** (the New Covenant in Jesus' Blood is superior and takes the place of the Old Covenant in animal blood), **but how much also He is the Mediator of a Better Covenant** (proclaims the fact that Christ officiates between God and man according to the arrangements of the New Covenant), **which was established upon better Promises.** (This presents the New Covenant, explicitly based on the cleansing and forgiveness of all sin, which the Old Covenant could not do.)

"For if that first *Covenant* had been faultless (proclaims the fact that the First Covenant was definitely not faultless; as stated, it was based on animal blood, which was vastly inferior to the Precious Blood of Christ), **then should no place have been sought for the Second** (proclaims the necessity of the New Covenant)" **(Heb. 8:6-7).**

So, the Victory of the Cross is not some magic talisman. It is a contrived Work carried out by the Lord from eternity past and culminates in the Cross of Christ. When the Believer places his Faith exclusively in Christ and the Cross, then the Holy Spirit, Who is God, can Work mightily within his heart and life. This is God's Prescribed Order of Victory. He does not have another because another is not needed.

ANGER OF THE EVIL ONE

And yet, do not think that because you understand God's Way Satan is going to fold his tent and leave. In fact, he will probably hit you harder than he ever has. In other words, the temptation will probably become more severe and the oppression with greater weight. All of this is to discourage you in order that you quit. He knows you're on the right track, so he'll do everything within his power to get you to shift your Faith from Christ and the Cross to something else. And, he doesn't too much care what the something else actually is just as long as it's not the Cross of Christ.

However, if you will not quit, if you will not stop, and if you will keep believing, there will come an hour that *"the sin nature will no longer have dominion over you"* (Rom. 6:14). But thereafter, even on a day-by-day basis (Lk. 9:23), we have to be vigilant respecting our Faith that it always be anchored in Christ and the Cross. In other words, Christ is to never be separated from the Cross or the Cross from Christ. Again, we aren't speaking of the wooden beam, but rather what Jesus there did. In fact, what He did at the Cross and the Means by which the Holy Spirit Works are of such consequence that, according to the Word of God, such are indivisible, meaning inseparable. Let's once again go to the Word. John the Beloved wrote:

THE LION AND THE LAMB

"And one of the Elders said unto me, Weep not (states that man's dilemma has been solved)**: behold, the Lion of the Tribe of Judah, the Root of David, has prevailed to open the Book, and to loose the Seven Seals thereof** (presents Jesus Christ).

"And I beheld, and, lo, in the midst of the Throne and of the four Beasts, and in the midst of the Elders, stood a Lamb as it had been slain (the Crucifixion of Christ is represented here by the word 'Lamb,' which refers to the fact that it was the Cross which redeemed mankind; the slain Lamb Alone has redeemed all things)**, having seven horns** (horns denote dominion, and 'seven' denotes total dominion; all of this was done for you and me, meaning that we can have total dominion over the powers of darkness, and in every capacity; so there is no excuse for a lack of victory) **and seven eyes** (denotes total, perfect, pure, and complete illumination of all things spiritual, which is again made possible for you and me by the Cross; if the Believer makes the Cross the Object of his Faith, he will never be drawn away by false doctrine)**, which are the Seven Spirits of God sent forth into all the Earth** (signifying that the Holy Spirit, in all His Perfection and Universality, functions entirely within the parameters of the Finished Work of Christ; in other words, it is required that we ever make the Cross the Object of our Faith, which gives the Holy Spirit latitude, and guarantees the 'dominion,' and the 'illumination' [Isa. 11:2; Rom. 8:2])**" (Rev. 5:5-6).

This is God's Prescribed Order of Victory. As previously stated, He has no other simply because no other is needed. When we function according to Christ and the Cross, we are functioning according to the Word of God. In fact, if we do not function according to Christ and the Cross, this means we aren't functioning according to the Word of God.

JESUS CHRIST AND HIM CRUCIFIED

All of this is why Paul said:

"For I determined not to know anything among you (with purpose and design, Paul did not resort to the knowledge or philosophy of the world regarding the preaching of the Gospel)**, save Jesus Christ, and Him Crucified** (that and that alone is the Message that will save the sinner, set the captive free, and give the Believer perpetual victory)**" (I Cor. 2:2).**

(8) "HOW SHALL I GIVE YOU UP, EPHRAIM? HOW SHALL I DELIVER YOU, ISRAEL? HOW SHALL I MAKE YOU AS ADMAH? HOW SHALL I SET YOU AS ZEBOIM? MY HEART IS TURNED WITHIN

ME, MY REPENTINGS ARE KINDLED TOGETHER.

(9) "I WILL NOT EXECUTE THE FIERCENESS OF MY ANGER, I WILL NOT RETURN TO DESTROY EPHRAIM: FOR I AM GOD, AND NOT MAN; THE HOLY ONE IN THE MIDST OF YOU: AND I WILL NOT ENTER INTO THE CITY."

The pattern is:

1. The agony of the love which pulsates in Verse 8 touches the heart. Admah and Zeboim were the companion cities of Sodom and Gomorrah and suffered like destruction (Gen. 14:2, 8). Ephraim had become so sinful that there was nothing left to do but destroy—hence, the Pleadings of God for the Nation to seek Him and do that which was right in His Sight.

2. (Vs. 8) The word *"repentings,"* as it refers to God, which it does in this case, implies no change of purpose on the side of God, but only a change of procedure consistent with His Purpose of Everlasting Love.

3. Verses 9 through 11 proclaim the Second Advent of Christ when the Lord will come from Heaven with all the Saints and will set up the Kingdom Age. *"I will not return to destroy Ephraim"* refers to the Lord's Second Coming, which will not be to destroy Ephraim, but instead to save Ephraim.

4. (Vs. 9) The phrase, *"For I am God, and not man,"* refers to Him being able to see the end from the beginning.

5. (Vs. 9) *"The Holy One in the midst of you"* pertains to Israel's stupidity in not accepting such a One, Who is able to Lead them, Guide them, and give them Protection from all their enemies. Even though He was *"in the midst"* of them and not in other nations, still, they would not serve Him, heed Him, or obey Him.

THE RUMINATIONS OF GOD CONCERNING ISRAEL

We find in this Eighth Verse statements made about God, which, in fact, are beyond our comprehension.

We know that God knows everything, past, present, and future. That being the case, how could it be said of Him, and it definitely was, that He was in the valley of decision as it regarded the northern kingdom of Israel?

Were they to be destroyed or spared?

As stated, Admah and Zeboim were the companion cities of Sodom and Gomorrah and suffered like destruction (Gen. 14:2, 8). Only Almighty Power could do such a thing. And, if He could do that, and He definitely did, at the same time, He could bless abundantly so and, in fact, desired to do so. But there are conditions to the Blessings of God.

We as Believers cannot repeatedly flout His Word with belligerence and arrogance and expect God to bless us. He doesn't require much of us, but He does require obedience.

The answer to the questions of Verse 8 is the Lord knew what He had to do simply because He knew the hearts of all the people of Israel, and what He knew was not good. It is love that makes these remarks. It is love that asks these questions. It is love that seeks to find a way that Israel not be destroyed but, at the same time, knowing there was no way.

Is the Lord at the present time ruminating over the United States of America? Have we drifted so far from Him, with the drift becoming even more pronounced, that there is nothing left but Judgment?

The question, *"How shall I give you up, Ephraim?"* refers to the Lord in a special way, actually grieving over the perilous condition of *"Ephraim."*

Does He do the same over modern Christians? If He did then, to be sure, He does now!

The question, *"How shall I deliver you, Israel?"* refers to every means being exhausted to cause Israel to see herself and, therefore, her perilous condition.

What more could the Lord do? He had sent the Prophets and had given them a powerful anointing to deliver His Word, but to no avail! Ephraim was so sinful that there was nothing left to do but destroy, hence, the Pleadings of God for the Nation to seek Him and do that which was right in His Sight.

THE RESTORATION OF ISRAEL

Verse 9 jumps thousands of years into the future, actually, from the time of the near destruction of Israel of old to the time of the Second Coming, which will redeem Israel.

The phrase, *"For I am God, and not man,"*

refers to Him being able to see the end from the beginning.

Even while He is speaking to Israel, pleading with them to repent, which they would not and, in fact, would suffer destruction, the Lord could look over 2,500 years into the future and predict what was going to take place. Only *"God"* and *"not man"* could do such a thing. However, in that Coming Glad Day of which He now speaks, the Lord will once again be in the *"midst of Israel."* However, this time, due to their perilous situation as a result of the Antichrist, they will not reject Him, but instead, wonderfully accept Him.

The phrase, *"And I will not enter into the city,"* as stated, refers to the Second Coming when He will definitely enter the city (Jerusalem), not to destroy it, but instead, to save it.

The next two Verses tell us what will happen:

(10) "THEY SHALL WALK AFTER THE LORD: HE SHALL ROAR LIKE A LION: WHEN HE SHALL ROAR, THEN THE CHILDREN SHALL TREMBLE FROM THE WEST.

(11) "THEY SHALL TREMBLE AS A BIRD OUT OF EGYPT, AND AS A DOVE OUT OF THE LAND OF ASSYRIA: AND I WILL PLACE THEM IN THEIR HOUSES, SAYS THE LORD."

The construction is:

1. The word *"west"* in Verse 10 is interesting! Of the approximate 12,000,000 Jews in the world, approximately 5,000,000 are in Israel proper, and approximately 5,000,000 are in the United States, which is *"west"* of Israel. These will gladly leave America in order to reside with Christ, Whom they will then recognize as their Messiah.

2. (Vs. 10) The word *"tremble"* is also interesting in that Israel, although delirious with joy because of their great Deliverance from the Antichrist, still, will realize that the One Who has Saved them is the One Whom they crucified so long ago—the Lord Jesus Christ.

3. The phrase from Verse 11, *"And I will place them in their houses, says the LORD,"* refers to all the Jews from all over the world being restored to the Land of Israel and

made safe and secure, i.e., *"in their houses."*

THEY SHALL WALK AFTER THE LORD

"Walk after the LORD," means to follow the Lord unabashedly. The amazing and beautiful thing about this is: the implication is that every single Jew on the face of the Earth at that time, and we're speaking of the Second Coming, will accept the Lord Jesus Christ to a man. They will accept Him as Lord, as Saviour, and their Messiah.

Israel will then be the priestly Nation of the world, with David as their king. Of course, all will be under the Lord Jesus Christ, Who will rule Personally from Jerusalem, and do so as King of kings and Lord of lords. In a sense, this means that He will be President of the entirety of the world. It will then be a one-world Ruler, a one-world government, and a one-world prosperity. In other words, there will not be a few with everything and most with nothing. In fact, I think one can say without fear of contradiction that in the coming Kingdom Age every single person in the world will be a millionaire, so to speak. There will be no poverty and no sickness anywhere in the world. Isaiah predicted saying, *"Of the increase of His Government and peace there shall be no end, upon the throne of David, and upon His Kingdom, to order it, and to establish it with judgment and with justice from henceforth even forever. The zeal of the LORD of Hosts will perform this"* (Isa. 9:7).

NO MORE WAR

The great Prophet also stated:

"And He shall judge among the nations, and shall rebuke many people: and they shall beat their swords into ploughshares, and their spears into pruninghooks: nation shall not lift up sword against nation, neither shall they learn war anymore" (Isa. 2:4).

THE DISPOSITION OF EVERYTHING WILL CHANGE

"The wolf also shall dwell with the lamb, and the leopard shall lie down with the kid; and the calf and the young lion and the fatling together; and a little child shall lead them. *(The character and nature of the Planet, including its occupants and even* *the animal creation, will revert to their posture as before the Fall.)*

"And the cow and the bear shall feed *(feed together)*; their young ones shall lie down together: and the lion shall eat straw like the ox. *(This Passage plainly tells us that the carnivorous nature of the animal kingdom will be totally and eternally changed.)*

"And the sucking child shall play on the hole of the asp, and the weaned child shall put his hand on the cockatrice' den. *(Even though some of the curse will remain on the serpent in the Millennium, in that he continues to writhe in the dust, still, the deadly part will be removed [Gen. 3:14])*" (Isa. 11:6-8).

ISRAEL WILL BE RESTORED

Isaiah continues:

"And it shall come to pass in that day, that the Lord will set His Hand again the second time to recover the remnant of His People, which shall be left, from Assyria, and from Egypt, and from Pathros, and from Cush, and from Elam, and from Shinar, and from Hamath, and from the islands of the sea. *(Once again, 'in that day,' refers to Christ reigning Personally in Jerusalem. The first gathering of the 'remnant,' as it refers to Israel, took place when Israel was gathered out of the Medo-Persian Empire and brought back to the Promised Land. In a sense, the second gathering began in 1948. It will be fulfilled in totality at the beginning of the Kingdom Age, when Jews all over the world will recognize Christ as their Messiah and, thereby, desire to come to Israel and live near Him.)*

"And He shall set up an ensign for the nations, and shall assemble the outcasts of Israel, and gather together the dispersed of Judah from the four corners of the Earth. *(Here, Israel is called 'outcasts,' and they have been such ever since their rejection of Christ and the destruction of Jerusalem by Titus in A.D. 70.*

"The central theme of Verse 12 is Christ. Israel will now [during the Kingdom Age] recognize Him, and Him Alone, as their True Messiah. Jerusalem, the place of His Crucifixion, will now be the place of His Glory. The Jews will come to this Glory from 'the four corners of the Earth')" (Isa. 11:11-12).

The Prophet then said:

"And many people shall go and say, Come you, and let us go up to the mountain of the LORD, to the House of the God of Jacob; and He will teach us of His Ways, and we will walk in His Paths: for out of Zion shall go forth the Law, and the Word of the LORD from Jerusalem. *(The 'Law,' as referred to here, has no reference to the Law of Moses, but rather to instruction, direction, and teaching. Again, this is the coming Kingdom Age when the Messiah, 'The Greater than Solomon,' will rule the world by Wisdom, Grace, and Love. He will do so through Israel)*" (Isa. 2:3).

(12) "EPHRAIM COMPASSES ME ABOUT WITH LIES, AND THE HOUSE OF ISRAEL WITH DECEIT: BUT JUDAH YET RULES WITH GOD, AND IS FAITHFUL WITH THE SAINTS."

The exegesis is:

1. The Prophecy of Verse 12 contrasts Ephraim and Jacob—the former, self-reliant and trusting the kings of Assyria and Egypt; the latter (Judah), weak, dependent, and trusting Jehovah, the God of his father Isaac.

2. (Vs. 12) So the lesson is here once more taught that God cannot give victories to the flesh, and that Jehovah's servant, Judah, is strong when he is weak (II Cor. 12:10).

3. It is amazing how the Holy Spirit changes the direction of the Prophecy from one sentence to another. In Verse 11, He is speaking of the Restoration of Israel, which is yet to take place but will do so at the Second Coming.

4. Without breaking stride, the Holy Spirit in Verse 12 brings the Prophecy back to the present time. Therefore, the two Scriptures are separated by at least some 2,500 years.

PROPHECIES

If it is to be noticed, with all the many judgments pronounced upon Israel by the Lord, time and time again, the Holy Spirit breaks through the tale of woe with tremendous Promises of Blessing, which will come in the coming Kingdom Age. Why does the Lord do this?

At least one of the reasons that it is done is because the Lord wanted and wants all to know and realize that He has given Promises to Abraham, Isaac, and Jacob as it regards the people of Israel and their blessing to the whole Earth. These Promises were true despite Israel's condition at that time, which necessitated the Judgment of God upon them. He wants everyone to know, and without reservation, that despite their situation at the time the Prophecies were given, those Promises and those Covenants will ultimately be realized, which they will be in the coming Kingdom Age.

"Earthly pleasures vainly call me;
"I would be like Jesus;
"Nothing worldly shall enthrall me;
"I would be like Jesus."

"He has broken every fetter,
"I would be like Jesus;
"That my soul may serve Him better,
"I would be like Jesus."

"All the way from Earth to Glory,
"I would be like Jesus;
"Telling o'er and o'er the story,
"I would be like Jesus."

"That in Heaven He may meet me,
"I would be like Jesus;
"That His words 'Well done' may greet me,
"I would be like Jesus."

CHAPTER 12

(1) "EPHRAIM FEEDS ON WIND, AND FOLLOWS AFTER THE EAST WIND: HE DAILY INCREASES LIES AND DESOLATION; AND THEY DO MAKE A COVENANT WITH THE ASSYRIANS, AND OIL IS CARRIED INTO EGYPT."

The pattern is:

1. The first phrase of this Verse refers to the treaties with the Assyrians and with the Egyptians.

2. *"Wind"* is employed figuratively to denote what is empty, vain, and of no real worth or practical benefit.

3. *"He daily increases lies and desolation"* refers to Israel's dependence on these foreign powers, which was based on *"lies,"*

and which resulted in *"desolation."*

4. The last phrase of the Verse refers to the abundance of olive oil in the land of Israel and the object of sending it to Egypt as a present to secure their interest and help against Assyria. They would be sadly disappointed!

DEPENDENCE ON THE WORLD INSTEAD OF GOD

When Israel went into idol worship, thereby, losing their relationship with God, they ceased dependence on Him and began a sojourn of cohabiting with the world. In other words, in Israel's case, they tried to make treaties with the Assyrians and the Egyptians. They would find that the Assyrians would little keep those treaties and, as well, Egypt would be of little help, in fact, no help at all.

As the modern church loses its way, we see it depending less and less on the Lord, if any at all, and resorting to the ways of the world, i.e., *"humanistic psychology,"* etc. As it regards life and living, purely and simply, and even bluntly, the world holds no answers whatsoever. The Lord Alone holds the answers to who we are and what He desires to make of us. And I might quickly add, the Holy Spirit Alone can develop Righteousness and Holiness within our hearts and lives. That particular state lies strictly in the domain of the Spirit of God. But yet, religious man continues to make every effort to bring about these qualities by his own ingenuity. He always fails, as fail he must! The Believer is to understand the following:

• Jesus Christ Alone is the Source of all things we receive from God the Father (Jn. 7, 9, 11, 15; 14:6).

• The Cross of Christ is the Means and, in fact, the only Means by which all of these things are given unto us (Rom. 6:3-5; I Cor. 1:17-18, 23; 2:2; Gal. 6:14).

• It is our Faith in Christ and what He did for us at the Cross alone which makes it possible for us to receive all of these good things (Lk. 9:23; 14:27; Rom. 6:3-5, 11).

• The Holy Spirit is the One, and the only One, Who superintends this great Plan of God. He is the One Who judges the legitimacy of our Faith or the lack thereof (Rom. 8:1-2, 11; Eph. 2:13-18; Rev. 5:5).

In brief, the simple formula given above expresses the great Plan of God for the human race. That's why Paul said, *"But we preach Christ Crucified . . ."* (I Cor. 1:23).

The entire Plan of Redemption and all of its concepts can be summed up in the statement made by Paul, *"Jesus Christ and Him Crucified."* Christ was God manifest in the flesh and was made so for the express purpose of going to the Cross (Jn. 1:1, 14, 29). When *"Jesus Christ and Him Crucified"* ceases to be the center of our circumference, that's when we lose our way.

(2) "THE LORD HAS ALSO A CONTROVERSY WITH JUDAH, AND WILL PUNISH JACOB ACCORDING TO HIS WAYS; ACCORDING TO HIS DOINGS WILL HE RECOMPENSE HIM.

(3) "HE TOOK HIS BROTHER BY THE HEEL IN THE WOMB, AND BY HIS STRENGTH HE HAD POWER WITH GOD:

(4) "YES, HE HAD POWER OVER THE ANGEL, AND PREVAILED: HE WEPT, AND MADE SUPPLICATION UNTO HIM: HE FOUND HIM IN BETH-EL, AND THERE HE SPOKE WITH US;

(5) "EVEN THE LORD GOD OF HOSTS; THE LORD IS HIS MEMORIAL."

The exegesis is:

1. While most of these Prophecies pertain to the northern kingdom of Israel, still, *"Judah,"* the southern kingdom, as addressed in Verse 2, was not without sin.

2. (Vs. 2) What was this controversy with Judah? It was little different than with Israel except, at least at that time, Judah had not abandoned themselves totally to sin and wickedness as their northern sister, Israel.

3. The phrase, *"He took his brother by the heel in the womb,"* of Verse 3, refers to Jacob's birth. It is recorded in Genesis 25:26. *"And by his strength he had power with God"* refers to his wrestling with the Angel (Gen. 32:24-32).

4. (Vs. 3) Prevention and humiliation are both Divine instruments. Jacob was prevented by the Lord from achieving what he desired through the flesh, and was humiliated by his weakness in the coming confrontation with his brother Esau, which drove

him to the Lord.

5. The phrase of Verse 4, *"Yes, he had power over the Angel, and prevailed,"* actually refers to Jacob wrestling with the Lord; for the Angel was God.

6. (Vs. 4) The short phrase, *"He wept,"* shows brokenness and humbling before the Lord, the place to which Jehovah had been seeking to bring him all along.

7. (Vs. 4) *"And made supplication unto Him"* refers to Jacob's statement, *"I will not let You go, except You bless me"* (Gen. 32:26).

8. (Vs. 4) The phrase, *"He found him in Beth-el, and there he spoke with us,"* refers to the fact that Beth-el, now a seat of idolatry (I Ki. 12:28-33), can be made into *"Beth-el,"* a *"House of God,"* that is, if Israel will only repent. As Jacob found God in Beth-el, likewise, Israel can find God in Beth-el but not in these idols!

9. (Vs. 5) The phrase, *"Even the LORD God of Hosts,"* is declared to be the hope of Israel as He was of Jacob. The Holy Spirit pleads with Israel that if they will allow the Lord to be their *"Memorial,"* as He was with Jacob, instead of foreign powers or idol gods, they too can reap the benefits given to Jacob.

JACOB

Now the Lord refers to Jacob of old from whom the thirteen sons came, which made up the Nation of Israel. Levi is counted as the priestly Tribe but yet given no inheritance of land, at least as the other Tribes.

This Prophecy contrasts Jacob and Ephraim—the latter, self-reliant and trusting the kings of Assyria and Egypt; the former, weak and dependent and trusting Jehovah, the God of his father Isaac. So, the lesson is here once more taught that God cannot give victories to the flesh, and that Jehovah's Servant is strong when he is weak (II Cor. 12:10).

In this scenario concerning Jacob, we find the key to all victory. It is:

• The Lord will punish Jacob according to his ways: the punishment is intended to bring the Patriarch to a place of Repentance.

• According to his doings will He recompense him: despite the fact that Jacob was chosen by God, nevertheless, what he sowed, he reaped. We must never forget that!

• He took his brother by the heel in the womb: this shows that he desired the blessing of the firstborn but in the beginning attempted to obtain it in the wrong way.

• By his strength he had power with God: his strength, strangely enough, was his weakness. Paul would say, *"When I am weak then I am strong"* (II Cor. 12:10).

• He had power over the Angel and prevailed: this spoke of Jacob's perseverance.

• He wept: this speaks of Repentance.

• He made supplication unto Him: *". . . I will not let You go, except You bless me"* (Gen. 32:26).

• He found him in Beth-el, and there he spoke with us: as Jacob found the Lord in Beth-el, likewise, Israel could find the Lord in Beth-el, but not in those idols!

Even though this admonition concerning Jacob was given to both Israel and Judah, still, it can most definitely apply to any hungry heart who will humble himself as did Jacob of old.

PREVENTION AND HUMILIATION

Prevention and humiliation are both Divine instruments. Jacob was prevented by the Lord from achieving what he desired through the flesh, and was humiliated by his weakness in the coming confrontation with his brother Esau, which drove him to the Lord.

Paul was saved from failing by prevention; Peter was permitted to fail in order to humiliate. There was no difference between them; they were both indwelt by a corrupt nature incapable of amendment.

THE LESSON FOR THE HUMAN HEART

This is one of the most bitter and humbling lessons for the human heart. It is painful but salutary for the Christian to have an experiential sense of the principle of evil which indwells him. But a greater Power also inhabits the temple of his body, and we speak of the Holy Spirit, and His Victorious Warfare is a profitable exercise for the heart (I Cor. 3:16).

If Jacob of old and the Apostle Paul of later years needed so humbling and painful an

experience of what the carnal nature is, it is evident that all Christians need it. It is plain that whatever weakens, belittles, and humiliates that proud and willful nature should be regarded by the Believer as most worthful.

It is humbling for the Christian to finally learn that his *"strength"* is his weakness, which demands that he depend totally upon the Lord, Who, in turn, gives us *"strength,"* which is of the Spirit, and far exceeds anything of the flesh.

WHAT IS THE FLESH?

Paul uses the term *"flesh"* in many ways and, in fact, throughout the entirety of the New Testament, it is used in many and varied ways. While we will not take the time to address ourselves to all of these ways, we will confine ourselves to the manner in which Paul used the word *"flesh"* as it regards our living for God.

The great Apostle said:

"So then they who are in the flesh cannot please God" (Rom. 8:8).

What did he mean by that statement and many others similar?

The Holy Spirit through the Apostle chose this word to define the capabilities or the lack thereof as it regards human beings. It speaks of our education, motivation, ability, strength, power, and talent, in other words, that which is indicative to a human being, meaning that which we can do by these means. In effect, the Lord is telling us that irrespective as to how strong the *"flesh"* may be, i.e., our ability and strength, etc., it is still inadequate for the task. In other words, we cannot make ourselves what we ought to be in the Lord by these means. Paul tells us why.

THE BODY IS DEAD BECAUSE OF SIN

He said, **"And if Christ *be* in you** (*He is in you through the Power and Person of the Spirit [Gal. 2:20]*)**, the body *is* dead because of sin** (*means that the physical body has been rendered helpless because of the Fall; consequently, the Believer trying to overcome by willpower presents a fruitless task*)**; but the Spirit *is* Life because of Righteousness** (*only the Holy Spirit can make us what we ought to be, which means* *we cannot do it ourselves; once again, He performs all that He does within the confines of the Finished Work of Christ)*.

"But if the Spirit *(Holy Spirit)* of Him *(from God)* Who raised up Jesus from the dead dwell in you *(and He definitely does)*, He Who raised up Christ from the dead shall also quicken your mortal bodies *(give us power in our mortal bodies that we might live a victorious life)* by His Spirit Who dwells in you *(we have the same Power in us, through the Spirit, that raised Christ from the dead and is available to us only on the premise of the Cross and our Faith in that Sacrifice)*" (Rom. 8:10-11).

In fact, this is the great struggle of the Child of God. We keep trying to do through the flesh, i.e., our own strength and ability, what the Holy Spirit Alone can do. One of the reasons is that we simply do not know how the Holy Spirit Works.

HOW THE HOLY SPIRIT WORKS

I've already dealt with this some paragraphs back and will not go through the entire scenario again. Suffice to say, the Holy Spirit Works exclusively within the parameters of the Finished Work of Christ, which demands that our Faith (and it's all by Faith) be placed exclusively in Christ and the Cross. This being done, the Holy Spirit will Work mightily on our behalf, which is God's Way and, in fact, His only Way.

(6) "THEREFORE TURN YOU TO YOUR GOD: KEEP MERCY AND JUDGMENT, AND WAIT ON YOUR GOD CONTINUALLY.

(7) "HE IS A MERCHANT, THE BALANCES OF DECEIT ARE IN HIS HAND: HE LOVES TO OPPRESS.

(8) "AND EPHRAIM SAID, YET I AM BECOME RICH, I HAVE FOUND ME OUT SUBSTANCE: IN ALL MY LABOURS THEY SHALL FIND NONE INIQUITY IN ME THAT WERE SIN."

The pattern is:

1. The argument of Verse 6 is: imitate Jacob, turn to Jehovah, live uprightly, and keep trusting the Lord.

2. (Vs. 7) The Hebrew word for *"merchant"* and *"Canaanite"* is the same word. With holy contempt, the Spirit of God here calls Ephraim a *"Canaanite."* Self-reliant

and clever, he defrauded (*"oppressed"*) and boastfully declared that *"they,"* i.e., the Prophets, should find nothing wrong in his business activities, for his commercial prosperity demonstrated his honest dealing. The idea of the Verse is that Jacob was once the *"deceiver"* and the *"oppressor"* but was changed by the Power of God. Israel can be changed, as well, if only they will turn to the Lord!

3. The short phrase of Verse 8, *"And Ephraim said,"* shows a haughtiness on Ephraim's part. The very phraseology speaks of pride, hardness, and dependence on self. Ephraim equated financial prosperity with the favor of God exactly as the modern church. They were to find to their dismay that they did not have the favor of God.

TURN TO THE LORD

The argument of Verse 6 is: imitate Jacob, turn to Jehovah, live uprightly, and keep trusting Him.

Saul lost the kingdom because he would not wait for God, though willing to wait on him.

The evidence of Repentance is found in Verse 6, which characterized Jacob and all who truly come to the Lord.

The evidence is twofold:

1. One aspect is manward, consisting of Mercy and Judgment.

2. The other is Godward, being a constant waiting upon God, but yet, given in a threefold manner.

Whenever the Holy Spirit spoke through the Prophet Hosea, *"Therefore turn you to your God,"* the literal rendering brings out the meaning more clearly. It is, *"And you, in* (or 'by') *your God you shall return."*

In the Hebrew, it can be translated either way, with the preposition *"in"* implying entire dependence on God or close and cordial fellowship with God. If we take it to mean *"by,"* it signifies the Power or Help of God.

Inasmuch as it can be rendered either way, most likely the Holy Spirit is referring to both ways, *"dependence on God"* and *"by the Power of God."*

The idea is that during all of Jacob's life, he had depended upon his own wits and abilities, hence, the scheming, etc. Now, he is told to place total dependence on the Lord and none upon himself.

As well, he cannot do this alone but must have the Power of God, which implies an experience in the Lord, which is graphically described in Genesis 32:24-32.

One is here reading the actual account of the victory won by Jacob of old, the manner in which he did it, and how the Lord brought it about. It is certainly meant to be an example to us.

SELF-ESTEEM

As well, this Sixth Verse teaches us that self-improvement, of which the world continually abounds, is a fruitless exercise. In other words, corrupt self cannot improve corrupt self. And yet, the apostate church majors in this illegitimate and fruitless spectacle as much or more than the world. Self-esteem is but one pitiful example!

The teaching of the modern church is that low-esteem is the cause of much of man's disorders. This is but one example of it veering away from the Bible and, consequently, the only truth which can really deal with these problems.

The teaching of self-esteem, be it low or high, is but another foray into humanistic psychology. Man's problem is not a low self-esteem, but instead, a corrupt, evil, wicked self, which can only be changed by the Miracle-working Power of God, here evidenced in the example of Jacob.

One of the finest explanations of evil, as it relates to the individual, that I have ever heard was given by a lawyer friend, who was writing to the President of the United States. Quoting from memory, I can only paraphrase:

EVIL

Beginning with Satan, evil is then characterized in his children. However, we make a mistake if we only judge the actions of the individual, which are but characteristic of the evil which dwells in the person.

I don't know if he fully understood what he said or not; however, he was dealing with the issue of evil, as it relates to self, and exactly as the Bible teaches it.

In other words, the thief is not a thief because he steals; he steals because he is a thief.

As such, it is impossible for man, at least

within himself, to improve self. Such can only be done by Christ, which necessitates a personal experience with the Lord, at least in some fashion, as Jacob of old. Jesus called it the *"Born-Again"* experience (Jn. 3:3).

THE STRUGGLE WITH THE FLESH

Even then, after the Born-Again experience, self is not easily brought under control, as it is actually a lifelong struggle. The Apostle Paul evidenced this in Romans, Chapters 7 and 8.

Chapter 7 portrays the struggle with the flesh, which always concludes in sin, with Chapter 8 portraying the ascendancy of the Spirit, which always gives Victory over the flesh and, thereby, over sin.

Nevertheless, the journey from Chapter 7 to Chapter 8 is sometimes, as with Jacob, long and hard. In fact, I think it possibly can always be said that it is *"long and hard."*

KEEP MERCY AND JUDGMENT

"Judgment and Mercy" characterize Repentance. They are, in effect, the Attributes of God. The Scripture says, *". . . I am the LORD Who exercises Loving-kindness, Judgment, and Righteousness, in the Earth: for in these things I delight, says the LORD"* (Jer. 9:24).

"Mercy" is an attribute of Grace. In other words, sometime in the distant past, God chose to deal with man from the premise of Grace. Therefore, Grace was a choice because Grace must be a choice, or else, it is not Grace. However, once the Lord chose Grace in His Dealings with the human family (and thank God he did), He had no choice but to grant *"Mercy"* because Mercy is a natural outflow of Grace.

JACOB AND THE MERCY OF GOD

The Holy Spirit is saying that Jacob was not given his new standing with the Lord as a result of his merit, but instead, as a result of the Mercy of God. In truth, Jacob had nothing good, could obtain nothing good, and deserved nothing good, but was given everything good!

Inasmuch as the Lord shows us abundant Mercy, we are, in turn, to exemplify the Mercy shown us by showing it to others.

If the Christian properly understands himself and God's Grace to him according to the Bible, he will then understand what he truly was, and now, what he truly is in Christ Jesus. In other words, the sinner doesn't know how lost he is, and the Christian doesn't rightly know how Saved he is!

He will, as well, understand that his newfound status is not at all according to his own strength or ability, but totally, a Gift of God. As such, he will have far more patience, love, and understanding for others.

So-called Christians, who are stern, unyielding, judgmental, and harsh, are really only portraying *"self"* and not Christ. In other words, what they are portraying is what they are. They have either never really experienced the Grace of God, or else, they have *"fallen from Grace"* and gone back under law (Gal. 5:4).

"Judgment" is, in effect, the Word of God. It alone is proper *"Judgment."* Therefore, the entirety of our living and existence should be guided totally and completely by the Word of God. It alone is *"Judgment."*

WAIT ON THE LORD CONTINUALLY

The phrase, *"And wait on your God continually,"* speaks of trusting in the Lord totally and giving oneself to a life of prayer and supplication. It is Faith that is placed exclusively in Christ and what He has done for us at the Cross, which provides the foundation of all that we are in the Lord.

To the carnal mind the statement just made would certainly not be appealing; however, the Spiritual Mind knows that this is the secret of all well-being, joy, happiness, fulfillment, and more abundant life. Sadly, in all the world of Christendom, only a tiny few take advantage of this admonition by the Holy Spirit. Consequently, only a tiny few have *"Righteousness to reign on them."*

Concerning Jacob, this latter phrase tells us that the scheming is over, with the Lord now drawing the blueprints.

If this one phrase was put into practice, all church politics would be ended. Men would *"wait on the Lord"* continually, desiring His Will and His Will alone; consequently, there would be no jockeying for position, place, and power. Self is hidden in Christ and desires

only that which characterizes Christ.

As such, it does not seek approval, commendation, applause, or earthly reward. It seeks only the Will of God.

CANAANITE

As stated, the Hebrew word for *"merchant"* and *"Canaanite"* is the same. With holy contempt, the Spirit of God here calls Ephraim a *"Canaanite."* Self-reliant and clever, the northern kingdom defrauded (*"oppressed"*) and boastfully declared that *"they,"* i.e., the Prophets, should find nothing wrong in their business activities, for their commercial prosperity demonstrated their honest dealing, or so they said!

They idea of Verse 7 is, Jacob was once the *"deceiver"* and *"the oppressor"* but was changed by the Power of God. Now his descendants are conducting themselves as Jacob, the schemer, before his great experience with the Lord. The idea is this:

God intended for Israel to be a *"light"* to a darkened world. He intended for them to exemplify Jehovah, thereby, pointing men to Christ, so to speak!

To help them do this, He gave them not only the Law, which was the only Revelation of God in the world, but, as well, prospered them greatly in the material sense. However, they forgot their true mission, which was of heavenly origin, and became worldly-minded, conducting themselves as their heathen neighbors and, in fact, pointing no one to the Lord.

The Message, as well, should not be lost on the modern church! The Apostle Paul grandly warned us by saying, *"No man who wars entangles himself with the affairs of this life; that he may please Him Who has called him to be a soldier"* (II Tim. 2:4).

Even though the modern Christian is in the world, he is definitely not to be of the world.

The Holy Spirit is endeavoring to impress upon Israel that the Lord can change them, as He changed Jacob of old, if they will only allow Him to do so.

PRIDE

The phrase, *"And Ephraim said,"* shows a haughtiness on Ephraim's part. The very phraseology speaks of pride, hardness, and dependence on self. It shows no humility, love, compassion, or devotion to God.

The phrase, *"Yet I am become rich, I have found me out substance,"* boasts of riches procured by fraud and violence, while all the time, maintaining, as previously stated, honesty. Such is hypocrisy!

The short phrase, *"I am become rich,"* is the exact opposite of *"wait on your God continually."*

The emphasis is that Ephraim did not wait on the Lord and did not acknowledge that the Lord gave the Nation strength to acquire wealth but, in effect, says, *"My own power and the strength of my hands have made for me this wealth."* Ephraim forgot that the Lord is the One Who blessed, and Who gave the Nation power to work, as it is written in the Law (Deut. 8:14).

This is what the Prophet means by the phrase, *"I am become rich."* He means to say, *"I have become rich from myself,"* i.e., by my own ingenuity.

In fact, at that time, Israel was in a state of great prosperity, which may have induced the self-confidence and forgetfulness of God, which prosperity, at times, has a tendency to do.

WHAT EPHRAIM SAID AND WHAT GOD SAID

Ephraim says, *"In all my labours they shall find no iniquity in me that is sin,"* while the Holy Spirit says, *"The balances of deceit are in his hand: he loves to oppress"* (Vs. 7).

Such characterizes almost all of humanity. Man is loath to admit that he is wrong and, consequently, a sinner.

In Ephraim's eyes, as the world, and even in most of the church, riches denote right. Therefore, the rich man must be right because he is rich; consequently, he ignores God's Laws and makes up his own. As a result, *"deceit"* and *"oppression"* are not sin in his eyes.

This Passage tells us many things, not the least being that riches are often gained by *"deceit"* and *"oppression."* In fact, the far greater majority of the riches of this world are gained accordingly.

Truly, blessed is the man whom the Lord has made rich and who, consequently, uses

NOTES

it for the glory of God. Regrettably, such are few and far between.

EPHRAIM AND THE MODERN CHURCH

The seven Messages that Jesus gave to the Seven Churches of Asia, in effect, pattern the entirety of the Church Age. They come all the way from the Early Church, typified by the Church of Ephesus, to the church of Laodicea, with the latter, sadly and regrettably, characterizing the modern church. As stated, we are now living in the time of the Laodicean church. What did the Lord say to the church at Laodicea?

THE CHURCH AT LAODICEA

Jesus said to this church and, thereby, to the modern church, **"And unto the Angel *(Pastor)* of the church of the Laodiceans write** *(this is the 'apostate church'; we do not know when it began, but we do know it has begun; it is the last church addressed by Christ, so that means the Rapture will take place very shortly)***; These things says the Amen, the faithful and true witness** *(by contrast to His Church, which is not faithful and true)*, **the beginning of the Creation of God** *(Jesus is the Creator of all things)***."**

LUKEWARM

"I know your works, that you are neither cold nor hot *(characterizes that which is prevalent at this present time)***: I would you were cold or hot** *(half measures won't do)***.**

"So then because you are lukewarm, and neither cold nor hot *(if a person is lukewarm toward something, it means he hasn't rejected it, but at the same time, he has by no means accepted it; in the Mind of God, a tepid response is equal to a negative response)***, I will spue you out of My Mouth.** *(There is no prospect of Repentance here on the part of this church, or Restoration. In fact, there is Divine rejection.)***"**

HAVE NEED OF NOTHING

"Because you say, I am rich, and increased with goods, and have need of nothing *(they equated the increase in material goods with Spiritual Blessings, which they were not)***; and know not that you are wretched, and miserable, and poor, and blind, and naked**

(the tragedy lay in the fact that while this church gloated over material wealth, she was unconscious of her spiritual poverty; again indicative of the modern church!)."

GOLD TRIED IN THE FIRE

"**I counsel you to buy of Me gold tried in the fire, that you may be rich** *(what they needed to 'buy' could not be purchased with money, but only with the precious Blood of Christ, which price has already been paid; but the modern church is not interested!)*; **and white raiment, that you may be clothed, and** *that* **the shame of your nakedness do not appear** *(refers to Righteousness which is exclusively of Christ, and is gained only by Faith in Christ and the Cross; this tells us that the Laodicean church is extremely self-righteous; not having the Righteousness of Christ, they are 'naked' to the Judgment of God)*; **and anoint your eyes with eyesalve, that you may see.** *(The modern church is also spiritually blind)*" **(Rev. 3:14-18).**

I'm certain the reader can see the similarity between Ephraim and the modern church, which is not a pleasant conclusion, to say the least.

(9) "AND I THAT AM THE LORD YOUR GOD FROM THE LAND OF EGYPT WILL YET MAKE YOU TO DWELL IN TABERNACLES, AS IN THE DAYS OF THE SOLEMN FEAST.

(10) "I HAVE ALSO SPOKEN BY THE PROPHETS, AND I HAVE MULTIPLIED VISIONS, AND USED SIMILITUDES, BY THE MINISTRY OF THE PROPHETS.

(11) "IS THERE INIQUITY IN GILEAD? SURELY THEY ARE VANITY: THEY SACRIFICE BULLOCKS IN GILGAL; YES, THEIR ALTARS ARE AS HEAPS IN THE FURROWS OF THE FIELDS.

(12) "AND JACOB FLED INTO THE COUNTRY OF SYRIA, AND ISRAEL SERVED FOR A WIFE, AND FOR A WIFE HE KEPT SHEEP.

(13) "AND BY A PROPHET THE LORD BROUGHT ISRAEL OUT OF EGYPT, AND BY A PROPHET WAS HE PRESERVED.

(14) "EPHRAIM PROVOKED HIM TO ANGER MOST BITTERLY: THEREFORE SHALL HE LEAVE HIS BLOOD UPON HIM, AND HIS REPROACH SHALL HIS

NOTES

LORD RETURN UNTO HIM."

The exegesis is:

1. The thrust of Verse 9 is yet future. As Hosea 11:9-11 spoke of the coming Kingdom Age, likewise, this Verse does also!

2. (Vs. 10) The three modes of Divine Communication referred to here are:

• *"Prediction."* This pertains to the word given by the Prophets. Of course, we are speaking of godly Prophets.

• *"Vision."* This speaks of Dreams and Visions given to particular individuals, but mostly the Prophets, as it regards present and futuristic events.

• *"Similitude."* This refers to illustrations, such as Hosea's marriage to Gomer and the birth of their three children, etc.

Thus, God left no means of admonishing them untried.

3. As it regards Verse 11, Gilead and Gilgal had become wholly idolatrous, and the idol altars were as numerous as the heaps of stones in the furrows of the field. In stony agricultural countries, such heaps are numberless.

4. The lowest form of servitude in the east of that time was that of a shepherd. Verse 12 is the fourth reference to Jacob and completes the argument that weakness wins victories.

• As an infant, his feeble hand won the birthright.

• As a penniless vagabond, he won the kingdom.

• As a slave, he won Rachel.

• And as a cripple, he won a title.

5. (Vs. 12) The Divine Jacob, i.e., Immanuel, is the Great Antitype; for, by weakness, He won the Birthright, the Throne, the Kingdom, and the Bride.

6. The Text in Verse 13 says, *"By a Prophet,"* i.e., Moses—not a soldier, but a Prophet. Nations are saved by Prophets such as Whitfield, Wesley, and Moody, and not by military generals.

7. (Vs. 14) Ephraim refused to listen to the Prophets and provoked Immanuel most bitterly. It is only love that can be thus provoked.

THE FEAST OF TABERNACLES

The phrase, *"To dwell in tabernacles,"*

refers to the *"Feast of Tabernacles,"* during which the people were to dwell some seven days in booths in commemoration of their having dwelt in booths in the wilderness after they had been delivered out of the land of Egypt. The Scripture plainly says that this will be revived in the coming Kingdom Age (Zech. 14:16-21). Actually, all nations will be gathered to Jerusalem year-by-year to worship the Lord and to keep this Feast.

How many other times during the Kingdom Age that representatives from all over the world will come to worship the Lord is not stated. However, there is no doubt that one may do so anytime he desires to visit Jerusalem where Christ will be reigning over earthly Israel and all the Gentile nations. There will be scheduled times, such as the new moons and Sabbaths, when this will be done (Isa. 66:18-24).

The idea of Verse 9 is, despite Israel's present condition (during the time of Hosea) and despite the fact that she would be totally destroyed because of her sin, still, in this Verse the Lord proclaims a coming Restoration. In fact, one might say and be Scripturally correct that the Restoration began in 1948 when Israel again became a Nation after some 1,900 years.

But the total fulfillment will not take place until the Second Coming of the Lord. Then, the Scripture intimates that every Jew in the entirety of the world will accept Christ as Lord, Saviour, and Messiah. They will also know and realize that this Jesus, Who they then accept, and Who will save them from the hand of the Antichrist, is the same One they crucified. That's the reason, even as the Prophet Zechariah mentioned, that there will be a great mourning in Israel at that time. Zechariah said, which was uttered some 2,500 years ago:

"And I will pour upon the House of David and upon the inhabitants of Jerusalem, the Spirit of Grace and of Supplications: and they shall look upon Me Whom they have pierced, and they shall mourn for Him, as one mourns for his only son, and shall be in bitterness for Him, as one who is in bitterness for his firstborn" (Zech. 12:10).

The notes from THE EXPOSITOR'S STUDY BIBLE regarding this Verse portray the following:

THE MESSIAH SPEAKS

"'And I will pour . . .' refers to the Lord pouring out fire upon Zion's adversaries, but the Holy Spirit upon her inhabitants (II Thess., Chpt. 1). If one is to notice, the Messiah Himself is speaking in the entirety of this Chapter as far as the word 'pierced'; then the Holy Spirit points to the moral effect produced by the Revelation.

"'Upon the House of David' proclaims the Promise originally given to David concerning his seed upon the throne of Israel (II Sam. 7:12-16)."

POURED OUT SPIRIT

The phrase from Zechariah, *"'I will pour upon them the Spirit of Grace,' concerns the Goodness of God and means they are no longer trusting in their law, but instead, the 'Grace of God,' which is found only in the Lord Jesus Christ. 'And I will pour upon them the Spirit of Supplications' speaks of Israel supplicating the Lord and the Lord supplicating the Father on their behalf. The word means 'to ask humbly and earnestly.'"*

WHO HE IS AND WHAT HE HAS DONE

"'And they shall look upon Me Whom they have pierced' identifies who and what they are and Who He is. 'And they shall mourn for Him, as one mourns for his only son' now proclaims the moral effect produced by this Revelation, as given by the Holy Spirit. They will then make their supplications to Him for Mercy and Forgiveness. 'And shall be in bitterness for Him' means 'a sense of intense shame.' It speaks of true Repentance."

THE FIRSTBORN

"The last phrase, 'As one who is in bitterness for his firstborn,' refers to the loss of an only son, the firstborn. In effect, they killed their own son, and the firstborn at that, which meant that the family line could not continue; it was, in fact, destroyed, at least as far as the Covenant was concerned; however, this 'Son,' or 'Firstborn,' rose from the dead. Even though they would not accept it then, they will accept it now—and

because He lives, they shall live also!"

MOURNING FOR WHAT THEY HAD DONE REGARDING THE CRUCIFIXION OF CHRIST

"In that day there shall be a great mourning in Jerusalem, as the mourning of Hadad-rimmon in the valley of Megiddon" (Zech. 12:11).

The notes from THE EXPOSITOR'S STUDY BIBLE continue:

"As Verse 10 proclaims, there is personal 'mourning,' with national 'mourning' in Verse 11, and domestic 'mourning' in Verses 12 through 14. Every man will feel himself guilty of piercing Immanuel, which is the way they should feel.

"The last phrase of the Eleventh Verse refers to King Josiah being killed in this place (II Chron. 35:22-25). His reign was the one gleam of light in the gloom that covered the Nation from Manasseh to the captivity. Consequently, there was great 'mourning' respecting his death." The Holy Spirit uses that as a type.

The entire Nation of Israel will mourn at the beginning of the Kingdom Age when they recognize that their Deliverer, the One Who has Saved them, is none other than the Lord Jesus Christ, the One Whom they crucified. In respect to that, the Prophet Zechariah continues:

EVERY FAMILY WILL MOURN

"And the land shall mourn, every family apart; the family of the House of David apart, and their wives apart; the family of the house of Nathan apart, and their wives apart;

"The family of the house of Levi apart, and their wives apart; the family of Shimei apart, and their wives apart *(the House of David and Nathan speaks of the princely line of Israel, while the family of Levi and Shimei speaks of the Priests. Consequently, these two Verses proclaim a personal and general Repentance on the part of both the civil and Spiritual leadership)*;

"All the families that remain, every family apart, and their wives apart. *('All the families that remain,' speaks now of the balance of Israel. Judah's Repentance and Conversion will not be motivated by fear of*

punishment but by the overwhelming sense of guilt affecting the heart, when they recognize that their Deliverer is Jesus Whom they crucified, and that all along, despite their hatred and their conduct, He kept on loving them)" **(Zech. 12:12-14).**

THE PROPHETS

The phrase as given by Hosea, *"I have also spoken by the Prophets,"* includes not only Hosea but, as well, Ahijah, Jonah, Shemaiah, Iddo, Azariah, Hananiah, Jehu, Elijah, Elisha, Micaiah, Joel, and Amos, to name some.

IS THERE INIQUITY IN GILEAD?

Gilead and Gilgal had become wholly idolatrous, and the idol altars were as numerous as the heaps of stones in the furrows of the fields. In a stony agricultural country such heaps are numberless.

Ephraim had claimed that *"they shall find no iniquity in me."*

Therefore, the Lord asked the question, *"Is there iniquity in Gilead?"* He raises the question in order to crush it with His Answer.

The statement, *"Surely they are vanity,"* proclaims that in Gilead there was nothing but iniquity.

It is strange but yet common. Men admit to no sin, while God says there is nothing but sin! Hence, Isaiah would say, and about that time, *". . . the whole head is sick, and the whole heart faint.*

"From the sole of the foot even unto the head there is no soundness in it; but wounds, and bruises, and putrefying sores: they have not been closed, neither bound up, neither mollified with ointment" (Isa. 1:5-6). The word, *"vanity,"* in Verse 11, actually refers to *"idols,"* which are often referred to in this manner. Incidentally, the word *"vanity"* means *"empty nothings."*

The phrase of Verse 11, *"They sacrifice bullocks in Gilgal,"* means that the inhabitants in the west were no better than the Gileadites on the east of Jordan. The whole kingdom, in fact, was overrun with idolatry.

ONLY CALVARY!

The sin of the people of Gilgal did not consist in the animals offered but in the unlawfulness of the place of sacrifice. There were only to be sacrifices offered to the Lord at the Temple in Jerusalem.

The phrase, *"Yes, their altars are as heaps in the furrows of the fields,"* denotes the number and prominence of these altars. In other words, they covered the country like a plough would make *"furrows in the fields."* And yet, they claim, *"They shall find no iniquity in me."*

When men leave the Word of God, they make up their own Bible, which is presently happening, and is filling the world with Christianized religion. In other words, it's a Christian philosophy, which, by its very nature, disallows Christ and what He did for us at the Cross, or else, it places Him in a secondary position.

The Word of the Lord was most strict as it regarded the sacrifices to be offered in Old Testament times.

• As stated, sacrifices could only be offered at the Tabernacle and then the Temple when it would be built. Sacrifices could not be offered any other place (Lev. 17:4). Concerning this, Mackintosh says:

"A man might say, can I not offer a Sacrifice in one place as well as another? The answer is, Life belongs to God, and His claim thereto must be recognized in the place where He has appointed – before the Tabernacle of the Lord. That was the only meeting-place between God and man. To offer elsewhere proved that the heart did not want God.

"The moral of this is plain. There is one place where God has appointed to meet the sinner, and that is the Cross – the antitype of the Brazen Altar. There and there alone has God's claims upon the life been duly recognized. To reject this meeting-place is to bring down judgment upon oneself – it is to trample underfoot the just claims of God, and to arrogate to one's self a right to life which all have forfeited."[1]

• As well, the lamb offered had to be perfect, i.e., without blemish (Deut. 17:1). The sacrifices were meant to be Types of Christ. As such, they had to be perfect; otherwise, they were an insult to God, as would be obvious.

• The Priests alone could officiate at the offering of the sacrifices. Priests were

Types of Christ. The moral is, Christ Alone could be the Sacrifice which God would accept. All the many sacrifices of the lambs that were offered up from the very dawn of time were mere substitutes until the reality would come, namely Christ (Lev. 7:28-38; Heb. 10:4; Jn. 1:29).

THE CROSS OF CHRIST, THE ONLY ANSWER

Understanding the meticulous regimen required under the Law of Moses regarding sacrifices and the way they were offered, etc., we should understand how important the Cross of Christ actually is. In fact, the Cross alone stands between man and the Wrath of God. God is unalterably opposed to sin, which should be obvious, because of its death-dealing effects. The Cross alone allows Him to deal with mankind with Grace and Mercy. If the Cross is abandoned, denied, or even ignored, as it is in most churches presently, there is nothing left that stands between God and man. And please believe me, that's a position in which no one desires to find himself.

As well, please understand that God is not mean, capricious, or overbearing. In fact, God is the very opposite; He is Love. But He knows, as no one else, the destructive power of sin. It cannot be tolerated, and He cannot be a part of its cause or effect. He can only deal with sin in that it be atoned, which it was at Calvary's Cross.

• It is the Cross of Christ alone that makes possible Salvation for lost humanity. I don't mean it's one of several means or ways; it is the only Way (Jn. 3:16; Rom. 5:1-2; Gal. 1:3-4).

• As well, the Believer's only avenue of Victory over the world, the flesh, and the Devil is by evidencing Faith in Christ and what Christ did at the Cross. That alone is God's Prescribed Order of Life and Living (Rom. 6:3-5; 8:1-2, 11; Gal., Chpt. 5; 6:14).

Understanding that, we certainly should realize how vastly significant the Atoning Work of Christ at the Cross actually is for both Salvation and Sanctification.

The two greatest hindrances to the Cross of Christ are the following:

1. The wisdom of the world (I Cor. 2:5-8).

2. The legalism of religion (Gal., Chpts. 1 and 5).

Regrettably, the modern church presently is up to its eyeballs in either the wisdom of the world or the legalism of religion. Either one produces self-righteousness, and only produces self-righteousness.

BY A PROPHET

The Text says, *"By a Prophet,"* which means it's not by the soldier, the educator, etc.

Had it not been for the Ministry of John and Charles Wesley, England probably would have gone the way of France as it regarded the revolution that took the lives of tens of thousands. Had it not been for Charles Finney, there's a good possibility that we would not have the America which we know today.

It should be understood that Prophets announce the Word of the Lord, which means they issue ultimatums. They do not function from the position of diplomacy.

At the head of God's Work in the Old Testament was the *"Prophet,"* and in the New it is the *"Apostle."* The tragedy in America and other so-called Christian countries is that there are precious few *"true Prophets"* and *"Apostles."* Tragically, in Old Testament times, many Prophets were stoned to death as the people rejected their Message. Today, it is the same, albeit with verbal stones, i.e., character assassination.

HOW ARE TRUE PROPHETS AND APOSTLES RECOGNIZED?

By their Message!

As well, if the Message is truly from God, it will always, and without exception, coincide with the Word of God.

And please understand, false prophets and false apostles are much of the time *"transformed into an angel of light"* (II Cor. 11:13-15). This means they look like the Lord, spiritually speaking, act like the Lord, speak like the Lord, etc., which means that if the Believer doesn't know the Word of God, such a Believer will be deceived (I Tim. 4:1).

That's the reason we keep saying, *"The Word of God is the only revealed Truth in the world today and, in fact, ever has been."* Considering how important the Word is, which means it is the only road map for life

NOTES

and living and the only blueprint for eternity, this means that we should do everything within our power to understand its content. Nothing is more important than that!

"Full Salvation! Full Salvation!
"Lo, the fountain opened wide,
"Streams through every land and nation,
"From the Saviour's Wounded Side.
"Full Salvation! Full Salvation!
"Streams an endless crimson tide,
"Streams an endless crimson tide."

"Oh, the glorious Revelation!
"See the cleansing current flow,
"Washing stains of condemnation,
"Whiter than the driven snow:
"Full Salvation! Full Salvation!
"Oh, the rapturous bliss to know,
"Oh, the rapturous bliss to know."

"Love's resistless current sweeping,
"All the regions deep within;
"Thought, and wish, and senses keeping,
"Now, and every instant, clean:
"Full Salvation! Full Salvation!
"From the guilt and power of sin,
"From the guilt and power of sin."

"Life immortal, Heaven descending,
"Lo! My heart the Spirit's Shrine:
"God and man in oneness blending,
"Oh, what fellowship is mine!
"Full Salvation! Full Salvation!
"Raised in Christ to life Divine!
"Raised in Christ to life Divine!"

"Care and doubting, gloom and sorrow,
"Fear and shame are mine no more;
"Faith knows naught of dark tomorrow,
"For my Saviour goes before:
"Full Salvation! Full Salvation!
"Full and free forevermore!
"Full and free forevermore!"

CHAPTER 13

(1) "WHEN EPHRAIM SPOKE TREMBLING, HE EXALTED HIMSELF IN

ISRAEL; BUT WHEN HE OFFENDED IN BAAL, HE DIED.

(2) "AND NOW THEY SIN MORE AND MORE, AND HAVE MADE THEM MOLTEN IMAGES OF THEIR SILVER, AND IDOLS ACCORDING TO THEIR OWN UNDERSTANDING, ALL OF IT THE WORK OF THE CRAFTSMEN: THEY SAY OF THEM, LET THE MEN WHO SACRIFICE KISS THE CALVES.

(3) "THEREFORE THEY SHALL BE AS THE MORNING CLOUD, AND AS THE EARLY DEW THAT PASSES AWAY, AS THE CHAFF THAT IS DRIVEN WITH THE WHIRLWIND OUT OF THE FLOOR, AND AS THE SMOKE OUT OF THE CHIMNEY.

(4) "YET I AM THE LORD YOUR GOD FROM THE LAND OF EGYPT, AND YOU SHALL KNOW NO GOD BUT ME: FOR THERE IS NO SAVIOUR BESIDE ME.

(5) "I DID KNOW YOU IN THE WILDERNESS, IN THE LAND OF GREAT DROUGHT.

(6) "ACCORDING TO THEIR PASTURE, SO WERE THEY FILLED; THEY WERE FILLED, AND THEIR HEART WAS EXALTED; THEREFORE HAVE THEY FORGOTTEN ME.

(7) "THEREFORE I WILL BE UNTO THEM AS A LION: AS A LEOPARD BY THE WAY WILL I OBSERVE THEM:

(8) "I WILL MEET THEM AS A BEAR THAT IS BEREAVED OF HER WHELPS, AND WILL REND THE CAUL OF THEIR HEART, AND THERE WILL I DEVOUR THEM LIKE A LION: THE WILD BEAST SHALL TEAR THEM."

The pattern is:

1. The thrust of Verse 1 speaks of Ephraim, who once walked with God, as in the days of Joshua, and spoke with authority to which the people trembled. He had a position of dignity and power. But he turned to idolatry and died spiritually as Adam did when he sinned.

2. (Vs. 1) The Christian has moral power and dignity so long as his heart is wholly governed by Christ and is free from idolatry, simply because any faith that's in anything other than Christ and the Cross constitutes idolatry.

3. The phrase of Verse 2, *"Their own*

NOTES

understanding," refers to a self-will worship (Col. 2:23), which is the principle of idolatry. And its ritual, as at the present day, necessitates the labor of many craftsmen, and I speak of anything in which faith is placed other than the Cross of Christ.

4. (Vs. 2) *"Let the men who sacrifice kiss the calves,"* was an expression of adoration. The kissing of images, statues, and so-called sacred pictures and icons is a prominent feature of modern idolatrous worship.

5. Israel is likened in the Third Verse to four figures: *"the morning cloud, the early dew, the chaff, and the smoke."* All express brevity and worthlessness.

6. (Vs. 4) Israel's greatest glory was that Jehovah was her God and Shepherd. The two titles, *"God"* and *"Saviour,"* present the Lord not only as Deity, but also as Deity Who will save.

7. (Vs. 4) The phrase, *"Yet I am the LORD your God from the land of Egypt,"* does not mean that He was not their God before this time, for actually He was, beginning with Abraham. But, never before had the evidence of His Power and Love to His People been so signal and conspicuous as the period of the Exodus and onward.

8. (Vs. 4) *"And you shall know no god but Me,"* should be studied carefully by modern Christians, as Israel of old! To worship Christ minus the Cross constitutes *"another Jesus"* (II Cor. 11:4), and is the bane of the modern church.

9. The phrase, *"I did know you,"* from Verse 5, refers to the Lord knowing them as a shepherd knows his sheep (Jn. 10:27). *"The wilderness, in the land of great drought,"* refers to the fact that there was absolutely no means of sustenance or livelihood in this howling waste except for Him. In fact, spiritually speaking, it is the same presently with this world. In Christ Alone, there is sustenance.

10. The phrase of Verse 6, *"According to their pasture, so were they filled,"* sadly refers to the fact that Israel did not know that it was the Lord Who was blessing them. *"They were filled, and their heart was exalted,"* means that in proportion as God prospered them, so did they forget Him. In Verse 2, they associated an idol with Him; in

this corresponding Verse, they forgot Him. Such is ever the moral action of the natural heart. It associates idols with God and then forgets Him; it degrades Him and then suppresses Him.

11. (Vs. 8) The four wild beasts of Verses 7 and 8 predict the military monarchies of Babylon (the lion), Persia (the bear), Greece (the leopard), and Rome (the wild beast). Forsaking the Lord, Israel was at the mercy of the Gentile powers.

THE OFFENSE

The phrase, *"When Ephraim spoke trembling, he exalted himself in Israel,"* corresponds to the statement of the Holy Spirit through Isaiah, *". . . but to this man will I look, even to him who is poor and of a contrite spirit, and trembles at My Word"* (Isa. 66:2).

The phrase, *"He exalted himself in Israel,"* does not mean a selfish exaltation sponsored by self-will, but, instead, that given by God because of the godly actions of Ephraim. Jesus said, *". . . for every one who exalts himself shall be abased; and he who humbles himself shall be exalted,"* as Ephraim, at least in the early days (Lk. 18:14).

The phrase, *"But when he offended in Baal, he died,"* refers to the sin and the result. *"For the wages of sin is death; but the Gift of God is Eternal Life through Jesus Christ our Lord"* (Rom. 6:23).

In this one Verse is found the secret to victory, i.e., *"humility,"* and, as well, in this Verse is found the road to destruction, i.e., *"sin."*

Verse 1, although given in very abbreviated Text by the Holy Spirit, still, carries the key to all life and, as well, the warning of all death. When a person, a people, or an entire nation humbles themselves before God, the Lord will see to it that such are exalted. But when they turn to idols, and that speaks of anything other than Christ and the Cross, the end result is always destruction. Let me quote it again:

". . . But to this man will I look, even to him who is poor and of a contrite spirit, and trembles at My Word."

THEIR OWN UNDERSTANDING

The Scripture says that all of the idol

worship of Verse 2 was according *"to their own understanding."* In other words, their minds had become so warped that they little understood the Ways of the Lord anymore.

The phrase, *"Their own understanding,"* of Verse 2, refers to will worship.

WHAT IS WILL WORSHIP?

Paul said, and I quote from THE EXPOSITOR'S STUDY BIBLE, **"Wherefore if you be dead with Christ** *(actually says, 'In view of the fact that you died with Christ')* **from the rudiments of the world** *(the way of the world)*, **why, as though living in the world, are you subject to Ordinances** *(refers to trusting something other than Christ and the Cross for Salvation and Victory)*,

"(Touch not; taste not; handle not *(there is no Salvation or victory in rules and regulations)*;

"Which all are to perish with the using;) *(This refers to the fact that they don't work because they are of human origin. Therefore, new ones are made that work no better than the old, which is the way of man.)* **after the commandments and doctrines of men?** *(This means it is not of God and must be avoided at all cost.)*

"Which things have indeed a show of wisdom in will worship *(refers to worship devised and prescribed by man, which characterizes most of the modern church)*, **and humility** *(false humility)*, **and neglecting of the body** *(speaks of the human body)*; **not in any honour to the satisfying of the flesh.** *(All ascetic observances, while they appeal to men as indications of superior wisdom and piety, have no value as remedies against sensual indulgence. That can be handled only at the Cross)"* **(Col. 2:20-23).**

CEREMONIES, RITUALS, ETC.

"Will worship" has to do with ceremonies, rituals, and religious schemes devised by men. In other words, and I think one can say without fear of contradiction, will worship involves the so-called worship of God under any guise other than Christ and the Cross.

Jesus said:

"But the hour comes, and now is, when the true worshippers shall worship the Father in spirit and in truth *(God is not*

looking for Holy worship; He is looking for Holy worshippers; as stated, Calvary would make possible an entirely different type of worship, which did not require ceremonies or rituals, etc.): **for the Father seeks such to worship Him** *(means that by the word 'seeks' such are not easily found).*

"God *is* a Spirit *(simply means that 'God is a Spirit Being'):* **and they who worship Him must worship *Him* in spirit and in truth** *(man worships the Lord through and by his personal spirit, which is moved upon by the Holy Spirit; otherwise, it is not worship which God will accept)"* **(Jn. 4:23-24).**

YOU WORSHIP YOU KNOW NOT WHAT

Every religion has its own mode and method of worship. For instance, the Hindu religion teaches that if one washes in the Ganges River, this will institute holiness, etc. Never mind that this river is little more than a sewage pit. In Thailand, I watched people bow down before the little jade god Buddha, bringing their offerings, which was their worship. In the demonic religion of Islam, they pray five times a day facing Mecca, etc. All of that is worship designed by man, which means it has nothing to do with the Lord.

All of that is understandable as being false; however, many aspects of Christianity have been given over to will worship. The Lord will only accept the following as it regards worship:

• We must know without reservation that everything we receive from God comes to us solely from Jesus Christ as the Source (Jn. 10:1, 7-11; 14:6).

• As well, we must know and understand that the Cross of Christ is the Means by which all of these things are given to us. In other words, they can come by no other way (Rom. 6:3-5; I Cor. 1:17-18, 23; 2:2).

• Understanding this, the Cross of Christ must be the Object of our Faith (Col. 2:14-15).

• The Holy Spirit oversees our Faith (Rom. 8:1-2, 11; Eph. 2:13-18).

The worship of the Lord is not bound up by ritual or ceremony but is done by Faith—and we speak of Faith in Christ and what He has done for us at the Cross.

Worship is what we are while praise is

what we do!

PLEASING GOD

As it regards Enoch, the Scripture says, **". . . for before his translation he had this testimony, that he pleased God.** *(He pleased God because he placed his Faith exclusively in Christ and the Cross.)*

"But without Faith *(in Christ and the Cross; anytime Faith is mentioned, always and without exception, its root meaning is that its Object is Christ and the Cross; otherwise, it is faith God will not accept)* **it is impossible to please *Him*** *(faith in anything other than Christ and the Cross greatly displeases the Lord):* **for he who comes to God must believe that He is** *(places Faith as the foundation and principle of the manner in which God deals with the human race),* **and *that* He** *(God)* **is a rewarder of them who diligently seek Him** *(seek Him on the premise of Christ and Him Crucified)"* **(Heb. 11:5-6).**

FOUR FIGURES

In Verse 3, Israel is likened to four figures, *"the morning cloud, the early dew, the chaff, and the smoke."* All express brevity and worthlessness.

At this time, the northern kingdom of Israel was prosperous, even what one might call rich; consequently, they thought of themselves as blessed, but God thought otherwise!

Despite their present prosperity and because of their great sin, they would soon pass away like a morning cloud, the early dew when the sun comes up, as chaff driven with a whirlwind, and smoke disappearing after coming from the chimney.

Regrettably, there are many modern Christians who loudly trumpet themselves as *"blessed"* when, in reality, their blessing is superficial and has little foundation, if any at all, in the Word of God. As such, when the storm appears, and sooner or later it will appear, the so-called blessing is soon gone because it is not anchored on the Rock of God's Word.

As well, many of these, who call themselves *"blessed,"* deny the possibility of any storm. However, the Lord says otherwise, *"And the rain descended, and the floods came, and the winds blew, and beat upon that house . . ."* (Mat. 7:25).

I AM THE LORD YOUR GOD

The Fourth Verse, *"Yet I am the LORD your God from the land of Egypt, and you shall know no God but Me: for there is no Saviour beside Me,"* presents Israel's greatest glory as that of Jehovah Who was her God and Shepherd. No god was associated with Him, or any saviour or shepherd, in the redemption out of Egypt and the preservation through the desert.

The use of the two titles, *"God"* and *"Saviour,"* presents the Lord not only as Deity but, as well, as Deity Who will save. In other words, He will go to any length, pursue any course, overcome any obstacle, or defeat any enemy in order to bring about the successful Salvation of His People. Actually, the lengths that God has gone to in order to save humanity are beyond the pale of human comprehension. Possibly the most oft quoted Passage in the Word of God proclaims this as no other, *"For God so loved the world, that He gave His Only Begotten Son, that whosoever believes in Him should not perish, but have Everlasting Life"* (Jn. 3:16).

The phrase, *"Yet I am the LORD your God from the land of Egypt,"* does not mean that He was not their God before this time, for actually He was, beginning with Abraham. However, never before had the evidence of His Power and Love to His People been so signal and conspicuous as at the period of the Exodus and onward.

NO GOD BUT ME

The phrase, *"And you shall know no god but Me,"* should be studied carefully by modern Christians, as Israel of old!

Presently, when one thinks of other gods, one thinks of the idols of ancient superstition, etc. However, anything that takes the place of Christ and the Cross becomes a *"god."* In its most simple translation, this means that every single person in the world, who does not serve Christ, has allowed and, in fact, is allowing another *"god"* to take His Place.

As well, every modern Believer in Christ, who allows someone or something else to share preeminence with Christ and the Cross, is making a *"god"* out of the person or thing.

Also, the modern Believer should carefully heed the words, *"For there is no Saviour beside Me."* Whatever the problems, difficulties, or vicissitudes of life, Christ and Christ Alone is the answer. Blatantly so, this means that neither modern psychology nor any other philosophy holds any answer for the Child of God, or for anyone else for that matter!

Bluntly, clearly, and plainly, the Lord tells us in very personal terms that He Alone is God and *"there is no Saviour beside Me."*

THE METHOD OF SALVATION AND SANCTIFICATION

The Cross of Christ did not begin some 2,000 years ago when Jesus died at Calvary. It actually began before the foundation of the world (I Pet. 1:18-20) but made its appearance at the very dawn of time, immediately after Adam and Eve were driven from the Garden. The Fourth Chapter of Genesis proclaims such. At that time, the Sacrificial system was instituted in order that fallen sinful man could have forgiveness of sins and communion with God. It would be by virtue of the slain lamb, which would serve as a substitute until the arrival of *"the Lamb of God Who would take away the sin of the world"* (Jn. 1:29). The Sacrificial system remained in vogue until the time of Christ, a period of approximately 4,000 years. The Sacrificial system was at the very heart of the Law of Moses. And, in fact, this is the only thing that kept Israel from the Judgment of God simply because they certainly didn't keep the Law.

And, please understand, when we speak of the Cross of Christ, we are not referring to a wooden beam, but rather to that which Jesus there did.

WHAT DID JESUS DO AT THE CROSS?

The Scripture says:

"Blotting out the handwriting of Ordinances that was against us, which was contrary to us, and took it out of the way, nailing it to His Cross.

"And having spoiled principalities and powers, He made a show of them openly,

triumphing over them in it" (Col. 2:14-15).

By the giving of Himself in Sacrifice, which, incidentally, was a Perfect Sacrifice, He satisfied the demands of the broken Law, of which every person was guilty. In doing such, He atoned for all sin, past, present, and future, at least for those who will believe (Jn. 3:16).

Sin was the legal hold that Satan had over man, allowing him to hold man captive. But with all sin atoned, Satan lost that legal right. So, if anyone is bound presently by sin, whether redeemed or unredeemed, it is because he will not avail himself of what Jesus Christ did at Calvary's Cross. In other words, he places his faith in something other than Christ and what He did for us at the Cross.

It is obvious at the unredeemed doing this, but not obvious as it regards Believers. But yet, not knowing *"God's Prescribed Order of Victory,"* which is Christ and the Cross, and Christ and the Cross alone, most Believers attempt to find victory in all the wrong ways. Let it be understood, and unequivocally so, there is no Salvation outside of Christ and the Cross, and there is no Sanctification outside of Christ and the Cross. Again we state, Christ is the Source while the Cross is the Means, which proclaims the fact that the Cross of Christ must ever be the Object of the Believer's Faith, and the only Object of the Believer's Faith.

Let us say it again in the Words of our Lord, *"For there is no saviour beside Me."*

THE SHEPHERD AND THE SHEEP

Verse 5 says, *"I did know you in the wilderness, in the land of great drought."*

The phrase, *"I did know you,"* refers to the Lord knowing Israel as a shepherd knows his sheep (Jn. 10:27).

The argument and the injunction of Verses 4 and 5 are that God manifested to Israel His Unity in Egypt and in the wilderness, and that, therefore, no god should be associated with Him.

The idea is also expressed that He acknowledged them when no one else would, and with great kindness and paternal care and kind providence, watched over them.

In effect, He is saying that inasmuch as

He did acknowledge them, and wonderfully so, in turn, they should gratefully acknowledge Him.

The phrase, *"The wilderness, in the land of great drought,"* refers to the fact that there was absolutely no means of sustenance or livelihood in this howling waste except for Him.

However, as it spoke of the *"wilderness"* of old, likewise, there is no spiritual sustenance in the entirety of this world and, in fact, never has been. As Christ was the only Sustenance for the Children of Israel in the wilderness of long ago, likewise, He is the only Sustenance presently and, in fact, ever has been. As it was a *"land of great drought"* then, it is a *"land of great drought"* now! Without Christ, a person is dead even while he lives (Eph. 2:5; Col. 2:13; I Tim. 5:6).

THE INEXHAUSTIBLE SUPPLY

Verse 6 says, *"According to their pasture, so were they filled; they were filled, and their heart was exalted; therefore have they forgotten Me."*

This Passage tells us that irrespective of the wilderness, irrespective of the difficulties, *"According to their pasture* (whatever their needs may have been), *so were they filled."* Such can Christ, and such is Christ! Only He can satisfy the thirst, hunger, and cravings of the human heart. If you drink of all else, you will thirst again. However, *"Whosoever drinks of the water that I shall give him shall never thirst; but the water that I shall give him shall be in him a well of water springing up into Everlasting Life"* (Jn. 4:14).

The phrase, *"They were filled, and their heart was exalted,"* means that in proportion as God prospered them, so did they forget Him. In Verse 2, they associated an idol with Him; in this corresponding Verse, they forgot Him. Such is ever the moral action of the natural heart. It associates idols with God and then forgets Him; it degrades Him and then suppresses Him.

Therefore, two consequences followed from God's Great Goodness to Israel:

1. The immediate consequence was pride of heart: this tells us that most that is gratifying to the flesh is hurtful to the soul.

2. *"Therefore have they forgotten Me"*: both these results were concurrent. They abandoned His Worship. They misused the Riches and Blessings of Jehovah by forgetting their Gracious Benefactor.

As then, so now! Many religious denominations graciously seek the Lord in the times of their humble beginnings; however, upon the advent of His Blessings, all too often, they forget Him.

THE LION, THE LEOPARD, THE BEAR, AND THE WILD BEAST

The four wild beasts of Verses 7 and 8, predict the military monarchies of Babylon (the lion), Persia (the bear), Greece (the leopard), and Rome (the wild beast).

If one is to notice the order, it is found that the leopard is designedly displaced. Why?

The empires as given in Daniel, and as history now records, were in the following order:

BABYLON

Babylon was the great persecutor of Israel during the time of Daniel, which would be approximately 200 years into the future, and was symbolized by a lion (Dan. 7:4). The phrases, *"I will be unto them as a lion,"* and *"and there will I devour them like a lion,"* refer to Nebuchadnezzar attacking and destroying Judah and Jerusalem along with the Temple. At this point, Judah went into captivity.

THE MEDO-PERSIAN EMPIRE

The Medo-Persian Empire followed Babylon and began also in the time of Daniel. It was symbolized by a bear (Dan. 7:5). The phrase, *"I will meet them as a bear that is bereaved of her whelps, and will rend the caul of their heart,"* refers to them remaining under subjection to this empire even when allowed to migrate back to the land of Israel. As a consequence, their heart was broken at being a vassal state for the first time in Judah's history.

THE GRECIAN EMPIRE

The Grecian Empire followed the Medo-Persian and was symbolized by a leopard (Dan. 7:6). The phrase, *"As a leopard by the way will I observe them,"* is interesting

NOTES

indeed! Actually, the Grecian Empire under Alexander the Great, although persecuting Israel, was not nearly as harsh as they could have been.

It is said that Alexander the Great, upon his siege of Jerusalem, was met outside the gate by the Great High Priest.

The night before, Alexander had a dream in which he saw a man come out of the gate at Jerusalem dressed in the most beautiful garments he had ever observed. Strangely enough, the High Priest had also had a dream the night before. In the dream, he was told to attire himself in his High Priestly garments and then go out the next morning, wearing these garments, and meet Alexander.

This he did! It is said that Alexander was so impressed by the beauty of the garments, and especially so since he had already seen them in a dream, that he ordered his army to stand down and for Jerusalem, accordingly, to be spared. Therefore he, as the Scripture said, *"observed them."* However, there is another meaning to this phrase, as we shall soon see.

THE ROMAN EMPIRE

The mighty Roman Empire followed the Grecian Empire and was symbolized by a wild beast (Dan. 7:7). The phrase, *"The wild beast shall tear them,"* was fulfilled when Titus, the Roman General, destroyed Jerusalem in A.D. 70, slaughtering over one million Jews in the process.

THE DISPLACED ORDER

However, in the order of empires, the leopard, as we have stated regarding Verse 7, is displaced. In Hosea's Prophecy, it follows the lion, whereas in Daniel's, it follows the bear.

The answer is found in the coming rule of the Antichrist. As the lion represented Babylon, we know from Revelation, Chapter 18, that Babylon will be rebuilt either literally or in spirit. It will actually serve as the first headquarters of the Antichrist where he will serve the first three and a half years of his reign (Isa. 14:4-6).

As well, when the man of sin begins to make his debut, he will do so aided and abetted by the same fallen Angel who helped

Alexander the Great but, of course, without him knowing such, even as Alexander did not know such. John said, *"And the beast which I saw was like unto a leopard,"* signifying the similarity with the old Grecian Empire. That similarity has to do, as stated, with the satanic prince of Grecia, who will come out of the abyss to help the Antichrist, even as he helped Alexander the Great (Rev. 17:8-11).

Therefore, as it concerns the last days, Babylon, as symbolized by the lion, and Greece, as symbolized by the leopard as is given in Verse 7, are linked together. Babylon will be rebuilt either literally or in spirit, and the Antichrist will have the spirit, as well, of the old Grecian Empire.

THE OBSERVANCE

Also, the phrase, *"As a leopard by the way will I observe them,"* has reference, as well, to the coming advent of the Antichrist when he will make a seven-year pact with Israel (Dan. 9:27). For three and a half years Israel will think the Antichrist is the Messiah. During this time, he will observe them, but not for good, rather for evil. He will be plotting all the time to destroy them, which he will attempt to do by actually invading them in the middle of the seven-year agreement.

Consequently, the seeming displacement by Hosea was actually no displacement at all but an explanation of the last days.

For more complete Commentary regarding Israel in the last days and the rise of the Antichrist, along with the advent of the coming Great Tribulation, we would strongly recommend our Commentaries on Ezekiel, Daniel, and Revelation.

(9) "O ISRAEL, YOU HAVE DESTROYED YOURSELF; BUT IN ME IS YOUR HELP.

(10) "I WILL BE YOUR KING: WHERE IS ANY OTHER WHO MAY SAVE YOU IN ALL YOUR CITIES? AND YOUR JUDGES OF WHOM YOU SAID, GIVE ME A KING AND PRINCES?

(11) "I GAVE YOU A KING IN MY ANGER, AND TOOK HIM AWAY IN MY WRATH.

(12) "THE INIQUITY OF EPHRAIM IS BOUND UP; HIS SIN IS HID.

(13) "THE SORROWS OF A TRAVAILING WOMAN SHALL COME UPON HIM: HE IS AN UNWISE SON; FOR HE SHOULD

NOTES

NOT STAY LONG IN THE PLACE OF THE BREAKING FORTH OF CHILDREN.

(14) "I WILL RANSOM THEM FROM THE POWER OF THE GRAVE; I WILL REDEEM THEM FROM DEATH: O DEATH, I WILL BE YOUR PLAGUES; O GRAVE, I WILL BE YOUR DESTRUCTION: REPENTANCE SHALL BE HID FROM MY EYES."

The exegesis is:

1. The argument of Verse 9 is: in turning away from her True Helper, Israel brought all her calamities upon herself.

2. (Vs. 10) In answer to the question, *"Where is your king?"* the reply to be supplied is, *"in prison,"* for it was there that Shalmaneser put Hoshea. As well, this Passage has reference to the coming Antichrist who, in effect, would be their king. Of all their sad choices of the past, this will be the saddest of all (Jn. 5:43).

3. The king given in anger according to Verse 11 was Jeroboam I, and the king taken away in wrath was Hoshea. Jeroboam was Ephraim's first king, and Hoshea was her last king. However, its future fulfillment concerns the Antichrist, whom the Lord, in *"His Anger,"* will allow Israel to have.

4. (Vs. 11) In the Battle of Armageddon, the Lord will *"take him away in My Wrath,"* referring to the Antichrist being destroyed by the Lord at the time of the Second Coming (Rev. 19:19-20).

5. The idea of Verse 12 is that the day of reckoning would certainly come for Ephraim because their sin was neither forgotten nor blotted out because they would not repent.

6. The Holy Spirit through the Prophet likens Verse 13 to a woman who cannot escape the anguish of childbirth—she is helpless. As well, a son who lingers where there is an abundance of men and a scarcity of work is foolish, for he does not look ahead and recognize the certain prospect of poverty.

The idea is: a prudent man foresees the evil, but the senseless sinner lives for the moment and takes no steps to escape approaching calamity.

7. *"I will ransom them from the power of the grave,"* from Verse 14, looks ahead to Israel's coming Redemption, which will take place at the beginning of the Kingdom Age. In effect, Mercy rejoices against Judgment,

and so Grace bursts out with a cry: *"Guilty, sinful, and foolish though they be, yet will I ransom them"* (I Cor. 15:55).

8. (Vs. 14) *"Repentance shall be hid from My Eyes"* has reference to that coming future day when Israel's *"Repentance"* will be *"hid,"* which means *"bound up"* and noted carefully by God, exactly as her sins had once been *"hid"* or *"bound up."* Now sins are replaced by Repentance. As a result, this *"Repentance"* causes the sins to be washed away and, therefore, *"hidden from God's Eyes."* It is called *"Justification by Faith."*

SELF DESTRUCTION

The phrase, *"O Israel, you have destroyed yourself,"* refers to Hosea's day, but more pointedly, refers to the coming day when Israel will accept the Antichrist as her Messiah. Paul dealt with this when he said, *"For when they shall say, Peace and safety; then sudden destruction comes upon them, as travail upon a woman with child; and they shall not escape"* (I Thess. 5:3).

Both Hosea's and Paul's statements refer to the seven-year treaty that Israel will make with the Antichrist (Dan. 9:27).

At this time, they will cry *"peace and safety."* No doubt, the entirety of the world will applaud them, and even more so, the Antichrist, with most every news agency in the world heralding the *"peace."*

Believing this man to be the Messiah, Israel will think that her time of glory, as in the days of David and Solomon, has now arrived. Nevertheless, she will soon find that this is not her time of Salvation, but instead, destruction. For the Antichrist will break his treaty with her and will invade her. He will desecrate the newly built Temple and would completely destroy her at this time were it not for certain things brought about by the Lord (Dan. 11:44). This will happen during the midst of the coming Great Tribulation.

THE LORD IS OUR ONLY HELP

The phrase, *"But in Me is your help,"* refers to the cause of the coming Great Tribulation, called the time of *"Jacob's trouble"* (Jer. 30:7).

In the last three and a half years of this coming terrible time, Israel, with great pain

and sorrow, will begin to come back to God. During the Battle of Armageddon, when pressed to the point of total destruction, she will cry out for her True Messiah to come, knowing, especially at this time, that this is her only hope (Zech. 13:10).

He, the Lord Jesus Christ, will then come back to this Earth, and Israel will find, and grandly so, that *"in Me is your help."*

As Israel, so every person!

REFUSING TO REPENT

Ephraim's iniquity, as addressed in Verse 12, was *"bound up"* by God and their sin *"reserved"* (hidden) by Him, meaning that it was not forgiven, and they, thereby, not cleansed (Deut. 32:34; Rom. 2:5).

To blot out the handwriting against the sinner (Col. 2:14) is the opposite action to binding up and reserving sin.

The idea of Verse 12 is that the day of reckoning would certainly come for Ephraim because their sin was neither forgotten nor blotted out, and because they would not repent.

As a miser puts his money in a bag and seals it to prevent it being lost, so the Almighty had, as it were, hoarded Ephraim's sin, putting it in a bag, so to speak, and tying the bag.

A parallel expression occurs in Job 14:17, *"My transgression is sealed up in a bag, and You sew up my iniquity."* Usually, when men put money into a bag, purse, or treasure-house, they count it, therefore, Ephraim's many sins were counted and laid up in the treasury of wrath.

Every sinner, in fact, is represented as treasuring up unto himself wrath against the day of wrath (Rom. 2:5).

Even though this Verse is very short, still, its implications are awful to behold. It should also be noted that as such was said of Ephraim of old, likewise, it is said of the majority of mankind, and for all time, because man will not repent before God. Consequently, Paul said, *"Blessed is the man to whom the Lord will not impute sin"* (Rom. 4:8).

THE ONLY PLACE FOR SIN IS THE CROSS OF CHRIST

To try to address sin in any manner other than by the Cross of Christ and our Faith in Christ and His Finished Work presents a wasted effort, to say the least! Concerning sin, the Scripture bluntly says:

"But this Man (this Priest, Christ Jesus)**, after He had offered One Sacrifice for sins forever** (speaks of the Cross)**, sat down on the Right Hand of God** (refers to the great contrast with the Priests under the Levitical system, who never sat down because their work was never completed; the Work of Christ was a 'Finished Work' and needed no repetition)**" (Heb. 10:12).**

Paul also stated:

"So Christ was once offered to bear the sins of many (the Cross was God's Answer to sin, and, in fact, the only answer)**; and unto them who look for Him shall He appear the second time without sin unto Salvation.** (This refers to the Second Coming. 'Without sin' refers to the fact that the Second Coming will not be to atone for sin, for that was already carried out at the Cross at His First Advent. The Second Coming will bring all the results of Salvation to this world, which refers to all that He did at the Cross. We now only have the 'Firstfruits' [Rom. 8:23])**" (Heb. 9:28).**

Unfortunately, the world tries to address sin by means of its own devising, which is guaranteed of failure. Sadder yet, the church seems to be adopting the ways of the world, which means they are ignoring the Cross of Christ!

THE RANSOM

Verse 14, somewhat like a meat cleaver, interrupts the sense of the whole Passage, as Scripture is oftentimes prone to do. In every essence, it is beautiful.

The phrase, *"I will ransom them from the power of the grave,"* looks ahead to Israel's coming Redemption, which will take place at the beginning of the Kingdom Age, which immediately follows the Second Coming of the Lord. In effect, Mercy rejoices against Judgment, and so Grace bursts out with a cry: *"Guilty, sinful, and foolish though they be, yet will I ransom them."*

In a sense, this glorious Verse is quoted in I Corinthians 15:55. Consequently, the phrase, *"O death, I will be your plagues; O grave, I will be your destruction,"* should have been translated, as in I Corinthians, *"O*

NOTES

death, where is your sting? O grave, where is your victory?" The Old Testament terms are Hebrew; the other terms, Greek—both express the same thing.

Not only does it have to do with the coming Resurrection of Life, as Paul applied it, but, as well, it speaks of Israel coming to the very brink of the grave in the Battle of Armageddon but Satan being denied that destruction because of the Coming of the Lord. At that time, the Lord will *"ransom them from the power of the grave, and redeem them from death."*

The phrase, *"Repentance shall be hid from My Eyes,"* has reference to that coming future day when Israel's *"Repentance"* will be noted carefully by God exactly as her sins had once been carefully noted. Now sins are replaced by Repentance. As a result, this *"Repentance,"* which will take place at the Second Coming, will cause their sins to be washed away and, therefore, *"hidden from God's Eyes."*

(15) "THOUGH HE BE FRUITFUL AMONG HIS BRETHREN, AN EAST WIND SHALL COME, THE WIND OF THE LORD SHALL COME UP FROM THE WILDERNESS, AND HIS SPRING SHALL BECOME DRY, AND HIS FOUNTAIN SHALL BE DRIED UP: HE SHALL SPOIL THE TREASURE OF ALL PLEASANT VESSELS.

(16) "SAMARIA SHALL BECOME DESOLATE; FOR SHE HAS REBELLED AGAINST HER GOD: THEY SHALL FALL BY THE SWORD: THEIR INFANTS SHALL BE DASHED IN PIECES, AND THEIR WOMEN WITH CHILD SHALL BE RIPPED UP."

The construction is:

1. (Vs. 15) As quickly as the Prophet switched from pronounced Judgment to coming Restoration regarding Israel, he as quickly switches back to Judgment.

2. *"An east wind shall come, the Wind of the LORD shall come up from the wilderness,"* of Verse 15, refers to the Assyrians. It was a wind, not coming by chance, but commissioned by Jehovah as a minister of vengeance to execute His Wrath. As a result, this *"flourishing tree of Ephraim"* will dry up.

3. (Vs. 15) *"He shall spoil the treasure of all pleasant vessels"* refers to Shalmaneser, the Assyrian monarch, as God's unwitting Instrument.

4. Verse 16 proclaims the Truth that the coming Judgment will not be tepid, but instead, flaming hot—in other words, *"awful"*!

JUDGMENT

The phrase, *"Though he be fruitful among his brethren,"* refers to the northern kingdom of Israel and the present prosperity.

The phrase, *"An east wind shall come, the Wind of the LORD shall come up from the wilderness,"* refers to the Assyrians. It was a wind, not coming by chance, but commissioned by Jehovah as a minister of vengeance to execute His Wrath.

"And his spring shall become dry, and his fountain shall be dried up" refers to this flourishing tree of Ephraim, planted near the living spring, to which it owed its vigor and prosperity, yet is doomed to wither in consequence of the drying up of the waters that nourished it.

Ephraim did not want the Lord, therefore, they rejected the Source of all their Blessings and, consequently, their *"spring"* and *"fountain"* dried up.

What an apt illustration!

SAMARIA

The phrase, *"Samaria shall become desolate,"* refers to the present prosperity being totally taken away, with its nationhood destroyed, and even its site and location presently obliterated.

Samaria was built by Omri as the capital of the northern kingdom. It was built near ancient Shechem (Jacob's well), which commanded the main trade routes through the Esdraelon Plain.

The hill on which the city was built commanded a view over the plain and was impregnable except by siege (II Ki. 6:24).

The city was some six years in building, with Ahab finishing the city and building a palace decorated or paneled with ivory (I Ki. 22:39).

In a temple for Baal of Sidon (Melquart), the deity whose worship Jezebel encouraged (I Ki. 18:22), Ahab set up a pillar near the altar, which Jehoram later removed (II Ki. 3:2). Other shrines and buildings used by the idolatrous priests must have been in use from this time until the reform undertaken

by Jehu (II Ki. 10:19).

A CENTER OF IDOLATRY

Samaria itself was long considered by the Prophets a center of idolatry (Isa. 8:4; 9:9; Jer. 23:13; Ezek. 23:4; Hos. 7:1; Mic. 1:6).

Benhadad II of Syria besieged Samaria, at first unsuccessfully (I Ki. 20:1-21), but later the Syrians reduced it to dire famine (II Ki. 6:25). It was relieved only by the panic and sudden withdrawal of the besiegers, which was discovered and reported by the lepers (II Ki., Chpt. 7).

Ahab was buried in the city, as were a number of Israelite kings who made it their residence (I Ki. 22:37; II Ki. 13:9, 13; 14:16).

Samaria was again besieged in the time of Elisha and miraculously delivered (II Ki. 6:8).

Later, Menahem preserved the city from attack by paying tribute to the Assyrian king, Tiglath-Pileser III (II Ki. 15:17-20). Pekah, however, drew the Assyrian army back again by his attack on Judah, then a vassal-ally of Assyria.

Later, the city was besieged by Shalmaneser V of Assyria in 725-722 B.C. II Kings records that he captured the city, agreeing with the Babylonian Chronicle, but, evidently, his death intervened before it was finally secured for Assyria.

The citizens of Samaria refused to pay the tax imposed on them, and in the following year (721 B.C.), Sargon II, the new king of Assyria, initiated a scheme of mass deportation for the whole area. According to his annals, Sargon carried off 27,270 captives, and the effect was to terminate the existence of the northern kingdom of Israel as a homogenous and independent state.

The Exiles were dispatched to places in Syria, Assyria, and Babylonia, and replaced by colonists from other disturbed parts of the Assyrian Empire (II Ki. 17:24).

ALEXANDER THE GREAT

During the time of Alexander the Great, Samaria was initially favorable to this monarch, who captured the city in 331 B.C. However, while Alexander was in Egypt, certain Samaritans murdered his prefect over Syria. On his return, Alexander destroyed Samaria, massacred the city's leaders in the cave to which they had fled, and resettled the area with Macedonians.

In 107 B.C., Samaria was besieged by John Hyrcanus, and the surrounding countryside was devastated. Finally, Herod, at least after a fashion, rebuilt the city and renamed it Augusta in honor of his emperor. It later became a Roman colony under Septimius Severus.

During the time of Christ, Samaritans were hated by the Jews, but Christ ministered to them, as is recorded in the Gospels (Lk. 17:11).

As well, Philip preached in Samaria, but perhaps the district rather than the city is intended, since the definite article in the Greek is absent in Acts 8:5.

REBELLION AGAINST GOD

Modern excavations of the site show the palace, which was probably built by Ahab, and was later adapted by Jeroboam II. It had a wide court in which lay a reservoir or pool, probably the one in which Ahab's blood-stained chariot was washed down (I Ki. 22:38). In an adjacent storeroom, more than 200 plaques or fragments of ivories were discovered. These show Phoenician and Pseudo-Egyptian styles and influences and may well have been inlays for furniture in Ahab's ivory house (II Ki. 22:39).

As stated, there is nothing left of the city presently. The phrase, *"For she has rebelled against her God,"* gives the reason!

In the phrase, *"Her God,"* love pulsates from the heart of the Heavenly Father. To sin against Righteousness is a great evil, but to sin against Love is the evil of all evils.

The terrible cruelties here spoken, *"They shall fall by the sword: their infants shall be dashed in pieces, and their women with child shall be ripped up,"* could not be charged to God, for her own misconduct caused them.

Just as a bird in its desire for the fruit flies into the net set in its sight (Prov. 1:17), so the sinner rushes into sin, not withstanding God's Earnest Warnings, and ruins himself, as well as his entire family.

Thus, Israel suffered the doom of Verse 16, though Divine Love tried to save them from it by foretelling it, but to no avail!

"I take Your Promise, Lord, in all its length,

NOTES

"And breadth and fullness, as my daily strength,
"Into life's future fearless I may gaze,
"For, Jesus, You are with me all the days."

"Days may be coming fraught with loss and change,
"New scenes surround my life and fancies strange;
"I thank You that no day can ever break,
"Saviour, when You will leave me or forsake."

"There may be days of darkness and distress,
"When sin has power to tempt, and care to press,
"Yet in the darkest day I will not fear,
"For, mid the shadows, You will still be near."

"Days there may be of joy, and deep delight,
"When Earth seems fairest, and her skies most bright,
"Then draw me closer to You, lest I rest,
"Elsewhere, my Saviour, than upon Your Breast."

"And all the other days that make my life,
"Marked by no special joy or grief or strife,
"Days filled with quiet duties, trivial care,
"Burdens too small for other hearts to share;"

"Spend these days with me, all shall be Thine,
"So shall the darkest hour with Glory shine.
"Then when these earthly years have passed away,
"Let me be with You in the Perfect Day."

CHAPTER 14

(1)　"O ISRAEL, RETURN UNTO THE

LORD YOUR GOD; FOR YOU HAVE FALLEN BY YOUR INIQUITY.

(2) "TAKE WITH YOU WORDS, AND TURN TO THE LORD: SAY UNTO HIM, TAKE AWAY ALL INIQUITY, AND RECEIVE US GRACIOUSLY: SO WILL WE RENDER THE CALVES OF OUR LIPS.

(3) "ASSHUR SHALL NOT SAVE US; WE WILL NOT RIDE UPON HORSES: NEITHER WILL WE SAY ANY MORE TO THE WORK OF OUR HANDS, YOU ARE OUR GODS: FOR IN YOU THE FATHERLESS FIND MERCY."

The pattern is:

1. (Vs. 1) This Chapter is the presentation of a glorious Altar Call. In fact, it also tells of Israel's Restoration in a coming Glad Day, but which could have taken place in Hosea's time or any time forward, if Israel had only repented. The Lord is always ready to receive all who come to Him. He will always do so gladly, kindly, and with open arms. He offers no condemnation, only acceptance.

2. As it regards Verse 2, Divine Love provides the fitting words for the truly repentant tongue. *"Take with you words,"* in essence, says, *"Not sacraments, not ceremonies, but 'words.'"*

3. (Vs. 2) *"Turn to the LORD,"* proclaims the fact that these *"words"* are not to be taken to men, but rather to the Lord.

The phrase, *"Say unto Him, Take away all iniquity,"* presents what these *"words"* ought to be.

4. (Vs. 2) *"And receive us graciously,"* refers to the fact that we are Saved by Grace through Faith, it is the Gift of God (Eph. 2:8-9). Grace is simply the Goodness of God extended to undeserving people. It is received, whether by the sinner or the Saint, by Faith evidenced in Christ and what He did for us at the Cross. In fact, the Cross is what makes the Grace of God (the Goodness of God) available to all.

5. (Vs. 2) *"So will we render the calves of our lips,"* refers to sacrifice and, in reality, the Sacrifice of the Cross. In essence, we are to thank the Lord for Saving us, and that it was made possible by and through the Cross.

6. Respecting Verse 3, *"Asshur shall not save us,"* pertains to the fact that man cannot

save man. The phrase, *"We will not ride upon horses,"* means that we will not trust in what man can do. *"For in You the fatherless find Mercy,"* refers to Israel as *"Lo-ruhamah"* (no more Mercy) and *"Lo-ammi"* (not My People). Despite these facts, the Lord says that if Israel (or anyone, for that matter) will truly turn to Him, He will receive and accept them (Eph. 2:13-18).

REPENTANCE

Israel's fall was caused by her own iniquity, but that did not set aside God's Faithfulness, and so Grace declared Him to be *"Jehovah your God."*

With some small exception, the previous Chapters of this Book abound with denunciations of punishment; however, this closing Chapter super abounds with Promises of pardon. It is the offer of God's Grace. Therefore, this Chapter will tell any and all exactly how to come to the Lord and even the words that should be said. As well, the Lord will abundantly proclaim what He will give in return. It is God's Great Offer of Salvation.

Some people erroneously think that people were Saved differently during Old Testament times than at the present. Such is not the case.

THE CROSS

The Plan of Salvation has always been the same, even from the very beginning. It has always been by Faith, and it has always been through Christ and what He did for us at the Cross. When Peter said, *"Neither is there Salvation in any other: for there is none other name under Heaven given among men, whereby we must be Saved,"* he was speaking not only of his day and the present, but for all time! (Acts 4:12).

Even though the Plan of Redemption was given through the sacrifices, still, *"it is not possible that the blood of bulls and of goats should take away sins"* (Heb. 10:4). Therefore, Salvation was in to Who and to what the sacrifices pointed, namely Christ and what He did at the Cross.

In Old Testament times, men were Saved by looking forward to Calvary, while men are now Saved by looking back to Calvary.

Calvary and the Resurrection have always been the focal point; therefore, men have always been Saved in exactly the same manner, as stated, *"By Faith in Christ."*

THE MEANS OF SALVATION

To fully explain Salvation, it must be looked at as Prophetic and historical. The Old Testament view of Salvation is effected through the Prophetic. In other words, the Prophets of old proclaimed One Who was to come, Who would redeem mankind (Gen. 12:3; 21:12; II Sam. 7:4-29; Isa., Chpt. 53). Man was told to place his Faith and trust in the coming Redeemer, Who at that time could be looked at as a Prophetic Christ. Now man is told to look backwards to a historic Christ, for the Work of Calvary is now a Finished Work.

As against Gnosticism, man is not Saved by wisdom, i.e., the wisdom of the world (I Cor. 1:18-31).

As against Judaism, man is not Saved by moral and religious merit (Eph. 2:8-10).

As against the Hellenistic mystery cults, man is not Saved by a technique of religious practice (Rev. 17:1-2).

As against Rome, Salvation is not to be equated with political order or works (I Cor. 1:17-18, 23; 2:2).

Man is Saved by God's Action in history in the Person of Jesus Christ and what He did at the Cross (Rom. 4:25; 5:10; II Cor. 4:10; Phil. 2:6; I Tim. 1:15; I Jn. 4:9-10, 14).

While the Conception, Birth, Life, and Ministry of Jesus are of tremendous significance, with, in fact, everything He did of vast significance, still the stress falls upon His Death and Resurrection, which alone saves man (I Cor. 15:5). In other words, we are Saved by the Blood of His Cross (Acts 20:28; Rom. 3:25; 5:9; Eph. 1:7; Col. 1:20; Heb. 9:12; 12:24; 13:12; I Jn. 1:7; Rev. 1:5; 5:9).

As this Message, Jesus Christ and Him Crucified, is proclaimed, and men hear and come to respond in Faith, God's Salvation is freely given to them (Rom. 10:8, 14; I Cor. 1:18-25; 15:11; I Thess. 1:4).

WHAT IS SALVATION?

Salvation is both moral and Spiritual. It

NOTES

relates to a Deliverance from sin and its consequences and, hence, from guilt (Rom. 5:1; Heb. 10:22). As well, it relates to a deliverance from the Law and its curse that was upon every man (Gal. 3:13; Col. 2:14). It delivers from the fear of death and, actually, from death altogether as it relates to separation from God, which is what death actually means (I Pet. 1:3-5; I Cor. 15:51-56). It delivers from Judgment, for all our sins were judged in Jesus Christ and what He did for us at the Cross, in giving of Himself as a Perfect Sacrifice, which was accepted fully by God as payment in full (Rom. 5:9; Heb. 9:28). It delivers from fear, for the Lord now guides our destiny in every capacity (Heb. 2:15; II Tim. 1:7, 9). His Death at Calvary delivers from bondage, at least if the Believer will place his Faith exclusively in Christ and what Christ did for us at the Cross, and maintain his Faith exclusively in that Finished Work (Rom. 6:1-14; 8:1-2, 11; Titus 2:11-3:6; Gal. 5:1).

Salvation gathers up all the contents of the Gospel, proclaiming Deliverance from sin and all its consequences, and, positively, the bestowal of all Spiritual and even material Blessings in Christ (Eph. 1:3). As well, and perhaps the most important result of Salvation, which delivers from sin, is the Gift of the Holy Spirit. Paul said, *"In Whom you also are built together for an habitation of God through the Spirit"* (Eph. 2:22). The Apostle also said:

"Know you not that you are the Temple of God, and that the Spirit of God dwells in you?" (I Cor. 3:16).

ETERNAL LIFE

As well, Salvation guarantees the life of Blessedness in the future age. This future perspective is crucial (Rom. 8:24; 13:11; I Cor. 5:5; Phil. 3:20; Heb. 1:14; 9:28; I Pet. 1:5, 9).

Actually, Salvation is eschatological. The theme of Christ in His earthly Ministry was the central category of the Kingdom of God, which is the manifestation of God's Sovereign Rule. In Revelation 12:20, Salvation and the Kingdom are virtually equated. Salvation in Christ is equivalent to Life under the Reign of God, or Eternal Life.

Some have said that Salvation is given

in three aspects, which is true, if properly understood.

THREE ASPECTS OF SALVATION

We have been Saved, we are Saved, and we are being Saved.

HISTORIC

First, historically, and as stated, Jesus died for us and thus accomplished our Salvation. Our initial belief in Him comes in conjunction with God's Application of Redemption to us by means of both Justification and Regeneration. In other words, Jesus died for me.

Thus, in both the historic and subjective senses, it is proper for the New Testament to speak of our having been Saved.

"According to His Mercy He Saved us," Paul writes (Titus 3:5), and he says to Timothy, *"God has Saved us and called us to a Holy life"* (II Tim. 1:9).

THE PRESENT

Second, it is also true that we are now Saved, not only have been, or only shall be, but presently are. Salvation has an impact on our present experience. Reconciled to God by virtue of the Cross, we are presently Saved because Jesus gave His Life as a ransom for sinners (Rom. 5:10). In other words, what He did in the past makes it possible for me to have Eternal Life in the present. This aspect of Salvation, which speaks of our Sanctification, is taught in Romans, Chapter 6. As it regards Believers, Paul taught us that sin is the problem (Rom. 6:1-2). He then taught us the solution for that problem, which is the Cross of Christ (Rom. 6:3-5). We were crucified with Him, we were buried with Him, and we were raised with Him in Newness of Life. Due to what was done at the Cross and our continued Faith in that Finished Work, we can overcome the sin nature.

WHAT IS THE SIN NATURE?

As stated elsewhere in this Volume, the sin nature pertains to the nature of the individual. In other words, when Adam and Eve fell in the Garden of Eden, their very nature, which was previously controlled by the Divine Nature, became controlled by sin, i.e.,

"the sin nature." In other words, their very nature became that of sin, unrighteousness, transgression, iniquity, etc.

WHY DOESN'T THE LORD REMOVE THE SIN NATURE AT CONVERSION?

While He doesn't remove it, He most definitely does make it ineffective (Rom. 6:6). To use a vernacular, it is *"unplugged,"* so to speak.

The Lord allows it to remain for disciplinary reasons. In other words, its presence disciplines us.

How does it discipline us?

THE DISCIPLINE OF THE SIN NATURE

The Believer, even the very best of us, is very quick to become prideful. While we disguise it with Scriptural quotations, nevertheless, the pride remains. The facts constitute the following:

What needs to be done, in fact, what must be done in the Believer's life, can only be done by the Holy Spirit. And that's where the rub comes in, so to speak. Now that we are Saved and baptized with the Holy Spirit, and even used of God, we tend to think that whatever it is that needs to be done in our lives, we can do it. In fact, one of the oft-quoted Scriptures in the Word of God is, *"I can do all things through Christ Who strengthens me"* (Phil. 4:13).

The truth is, most people quoting this Passage have no idea as to what it really means. In fact, it is the very opposite of what most Believers think.

It means that Paul can be either *"full or hungry, abound or suffer need"* (Phil. 4:12). He means that he can function either way if he has to. Let me say it again!

What needs to be done in our lives, and I speak of the development of Righteousness and Holiness, in other words, the Fruit of the Spirit, we cannot do ourselves. It's impossible!

Why?

Paul said, **"And if Christ *be* in you** *(He is in you through the Power and Person of the Spirit [Gal. 2:20]),* **the body *is* dead because of sin** *(means that the physical body has been rendered helpless because of the Fall; consequently, the Believer trying to* *overcome by willpower presents a fruitless task)*; **but the Spirit *is* Life because of Righteousness** *(only the Holy Spirit can make us what we ought to be, which means we cannot do it ourselves; once again, He performs all that He does within the confines of the Finished Work of Christ)*" **(Rom. 8:10).**

And now the great Apostle will tell us of the Working of the Holy Spirit within our lives. He said:

"But if the Spirit *(Holy Spirit)* **of Him** *(from God)* **Who raised up Jesus from the dead dwell in you** *(and He definitely does)*, **He Who raised up Christ from the dead shall also quicken your mortal bodies** *(give us power in our mortal bodies that we might live a victorious life)* **by His Spirit Who dwells in you** *(we have the same Power in us, through the Spirit, that raised Christ from the dead, and is available to us only on the premise of the Cross and our Faith in that Sacrifice)*" **(Rom. 8:11).**

Plainly, the Holy Spirit through the great Apostle tells us that the Holy Spirit Alone can help us to live this life as it should be lived. Now the Apostle addresses the problem that we will have if we try to live after the flesh, i.e., by our personal strength, ability, education, motivation, etc. In fact, the *"flesh"* is that which is indicative to a human being. In other words, it is what we can do as humans. The Holy Spirit through Paul is telling us that whatever it is we can do comes up woefully short. So, if we try to live for God by that means, sadly, as most do, we will fail, and fail every time. The Apostle continues:

THE FLESH

"Therefore, brethren *(means that Paul is addressing Believers)*, **we are debtors** *(refers to what we owe Jesus Christ for what He has done for us on the Cross)*, **not to the flesh** *(we do not owe anything to our own ability, meaning that such cannot save us or give us victory)*, **to live after the flesh** *('living after the flesh' pertains to our works, which God can never accept, and which can never bring us victory, but rather defeat)*."

TRYING TO LIVE AFTER THE FLESH

"For if we live after the flesh *(after our*

own strength and ability, which is outside of God's Prescribed Order), **you shall die** *(you will not be able to live a victorious, Christian life)*: **but if you through the Spirit** *(by the Power of the Holy Spirit)* **do mortify the deeds of the body** *(which the Holy Spirit Alone can do)*, **you shall live** *(shall walk in victory; but once again, even at the risk of being overly repetitive, we must never forget that the Spirit works totally and completely within the confines of the Cross of Christ; this means that we must ever make the Cross the Object of our Faith, giving Him latitude to work)*" **(Rom. 8:12-13).**

SELF-RIGHTEOUSNESS

If the Believer could, by his own Faith, or by whatever means, bring about victory within his life, the end result would not be what he would think. It would only tend to lead to self-righteousness, which is the Believer's biggest problem. We want to think that we can do it. As stated, we load our efforts up with Scriptures, but the truth is, it is *"self."* So, if we were able to accomplish the task, it would only generate pride, which would generate self-righteousness. In fact, every effort by Believers to live for God outside of the confines of the Cross of Christ leads to self-righteousness. It cannot do otherwise! That, in fact, is the bane of the Child of God and, in fact, the bane of the entirety of the church. We try to live this life outside of the means provided by the Lord, which is *"Jesus Christ and Him Crucified,"* which constitutes an impossibility. But, still we keep trying, even as we ever keep failing.

WHAT IS GOD'S WAY?

Even though the following formula has already been given in this Volume and will, no doubt, be given again because of its great significance, please read it carefully.

FOCUS: The Lord Jesus Christ (Jn. 1:1-2, 14, 29; 14:6).

OBJECT OF FAITH: The Cross of Christ (Rom. 6:3-5; I Cor. 1:17-18, 23; 2:2; Gal. 6:14).

POWER SOURCE: The Holy Spirit (Rom. 8:1-2, 11).

RESULTS: Victory (Rom. 6:14).

Now, what does all of this actually mean?

It means the following:

THE LORD JESUS CHRIST IS THE SOURCE OF ALL GOOD THINGS

If Jesus Christ were but a mere man, no matter how talented, how educated, or how charismatic, that would be one thing. However, if He is not only man but, as well, the Son of the Living God, in effect, God manifest in the flesh, then that's something else altogether. As it regards every other founder of the world's religions, their deaths were but a calamity. But with Jesus, not only was His Life that of Perfection, but His Death was as well. Due to the fact that He rose from the dead, and of that there is no doubt, what He accomplished in His Death is so overwhelming as to be mind-boggling. All of that puts Him into a category that nothing else or no one else could even remotely approach. Jesus Christ is God! Understanding that, and knowing that to be the Truth, puts a different complexion on the entirety of the proceedings.

THE CROSS IS THE MEANS BY WHICH HE HAS DONE ALL THINGS

Some of the detractors of the Cross are fond of asking the question, *"Was it Who He was, or what He did?"* In other words, they are insinuating that the Cross was no more than another incident along the way.

The truth is, it was both Who He was, because no one else could have done such a thing, and what He did, which speaks of the Cross. But let me remind the reader of the following:

Who He was actually never changed. In other words, Jesus Christ as God was unformed, unmade, and, in fact, always had been. But merely due to the fact that He was and is God, as absolutely demanded as that was, still that fact alone Saved no one. Now, read that line very closely. In other words, without the Cross, no one could have been Saved despite the fact that Jesus Christ was God.

Oh yes, the Lord could have Saved man without the Cross because He is God and can do anything. However, we must always understand that the Lord will never do anything contrary to His Nature of Pure Holiness and

Pure Righteousness. He has the Power to do anything, but He will never violate His Nature. So, in order for man to be Saved, God would have to become man, and we speak of the Incarnation (Jn. 1:1-3, 14, 29), which was absolutely necessary, that is, if man was to be Saved. So, while Jesus Christ is the Source of all of the good things that we receive, and I mean all, still, the Cross of Christ is the Means, and the only Means, by which these things can be done. This means that Believers must never separate Christ from the Cross. That's the reason that Paul stated, *"For I determined not to know anything among you, save Jesus Christ, and Him Crucified"* (I Cor. 2:2). And, of course, when we speak of the Cross, even as Paul spoke of the Cross, we aren't speaking of a wooden beam, but rather what Jesus there did.

WHAT DID JESUS DO AT THE CROSS?

In brief, He atoned for all sin, past, present, and future, at least for all who will believe (Jn. 3:16).

Sin is the commodity, so to speak, which gives Satan the legal right to hold man in bondage. That is his only claim on mankind—sin! When Jesus died on the Cross, thereby, offering Himself as a Sacrifice, and a Perfect Sacrifice at that, which God the Father accepted in totality, this took away Satan's right to hold man captive. Paul wrote:

"Blotting out the handwriting of Ordinances that was against us, which was contrary to us, and took it out of the way, nailing it to His Cross.

"And having spoiled principalities and powers, He made a show of them openly, triumphing over them in it" (Col. 2:14-15).

IF JESUS ATONED FOR ALL SIN AT THE CROSS, WHY IS IT THAT MOST OF THE WORLD IS STILL IN BONDAGE?

The bondage continues simply because man will not take advantage of that which Jesus did for us.

Our Lord predicted this when He said:

"And when He *(the Holy Spirit)* **is come, He will reprove** *(convict)* **the world of sin** *(the supreme sin of rejecting Christ)***, and of Righteousness** *(Jesus is Righteousness and declared so by the Resurrection)***, and of**

Judgment *(Satan was judged at Calvary, and all who follow him are likewise judged)*:

"**Of sin, because they believe not on Me** *(to reject Christ and the Cross is to reject Salvation)*" **(Jn. 16:8-9).**

The truth is, most of the world simply will not believe that Jesus Christ is God, and that He paid the price at Calvary's Cross for our Redemption. Therefore, they remain in bondage. Paul mentioned this when he said:

"**For after that in the Wisdom of God the world by wisdom knew not God** *(man's puny wisdom, even the best he has to offer, cannot come to know God in any manner)*, **it pleased God by the foolishness of preaching** *(preaching the Cross)* **to save them who believe.** *(Paul is not dealing with the art of preaching here, but with what is preached.)*

"**For the Jews require a sign** *(the sign of the Messiah taking the Throne and making Israel a great Nation once again)*, **and the Greeks seek after wisdom** *(they thought that such solved the human problem; however, if it did, why were they ever seeking after more wisdom?)*:

"**But we preach Christ Crucified** *(this is the Foundation of the Word of God and, thereby, of Salvation)*, **unto the Jews a stumblingblock** *(the Cross was the stumblingblock)*, **and unto the Greeks** *(Gentiles)* **foolishness** *(both found it difficult to accept as God a dead Man hanging on a Cross, for such Christ was to them)*" **(I Cor. 1:21-23).**

BUT WHY ARE MANY CHRISTIANS STILL IN BONDAGE IN SOME WAY?

That's a good question!

In short, the answer is the same for the Believer as it is for the unbeliever. It's a question of unbelief in both capacities.

You see, it's quite possible for an individual to fully trust Christ for Salvation but then trust themselves or something else for Sanctification, in other words, how we live this life. That's why Paul wrote the entirety of the Epistle to the Galatians. They had been gloriously Saved by trusting in Christ and what He did at the Cross, which is what Paul taught them. However, false teachers came in, telling them that if they wanted to be a complete Christian, they were also going to have to keep the Law of Moses. In

other words, all of the Gentile men who claimed Christ, at the same time, had to be circumcised. Paul answered that by saying:

"**Behold** *('mark my words!')*, **I Paul say unto you** *(presents the Apostle's authority regarding the Message he brings)*, **that if you be circumcised, Christ shall profit you nothing.** *(If the Believer goes back into law, and law of any kind, what Christ did at the Cross on our behalf will profit us nothing. One cannot have it two ways.)*

"**For I testify again to every man who is circumcised** *(some of the Galatian Gentiles were being pressured by false teachers to embrace the Law of Moses, which meant they would have to forsake Christ and the Cross, for it's not possible to wed the two; as well, it's not possible to wed any law to Grace)*, **that he is a debtor to do the whole Law** *(which, of course, is impossible; and besides, the Law contained no Salvation)*" **(Gal. 5:2-3).** And that in principle is the problem of the modern church as well. While it's not circumcision with the modern church, it is something else, in fact, anything else that one places as the means by which victory over sin is obtained.

Just this morning over television, I heard a preacher say that the taking of the Lord's Supper is the answer to all things. He went on to state that if one wanted to be physically well at all times, he should take the Lord's Supper continuously. And, if there is any sickness there, he should take it up to three times a day. By doing this, he went on to say, the person would guarantee health and long life.

Now, while the Lord's Supper most definitely is a viable Biblical Ordinance, still, when it's used in that fashion, we turn it into law. This means that if it's looked at in that fashion, *"Christ shall profit us nothing."*

In fact, the church continues to come up with one fad after the other. In other words, they place their faith in anything and everything except the right thing, which is Christ and Him Crucified. As a result, most Christians are in bondage in some way, which, in truth, makes life miserable.

Some would argue that the *"Lord's Supper"* is not law. Within itself, that is exactly right. However, when we try to use something in a wrong way, even as our dear brother was using the Lord's Supper, we are turning it into law, whether we realize it or not, which God can never honor. Please understand the following:

THE KEY TO THE LOCK

Every single thing that we receive from the Lord, and I mean everything, comes to us from Jesus Christ and by the Means of the Cross. The Cross of Christ is what makes Salvation possible, as well as the Baptism with the Holy Spirit, Divine Healing, the Fruit of the Spirit, the Gifts of the Spirit, all prosperity, answers to prayer, and Blessings of every type and nature, in other words, everything. All and without exception are made possible by what Jesus did at the Cross. We must understand that; we must believe that. If we don't believe it, thereby, putting something else up as the key and the answer, God will never accept it, whatever it is we are promoting. Paul also stated:

"I do not frustrate the Grace of God *(if we make anything other than the Cross of Christ the Object of our Faith, we frustrate the Grace of God, which means we stop its action, and the Holy Spirit will no longer help us)*: for if Righteousness *come* by the Law *(any type of religious law)*, then Christ is dead in vain. *(If I can successfully live for the Lord by any means other than Faith in Christ and the Cross, then the Death of Christ was a waste)*" (Gal. 2:21).

And that's exactly what all of these fads do. They frustrate the Grace of God. We must ever understand the following:

The Grace of God, which is the Goodness of God extended to undeserving Saints, is made possible totally and completely by the Lord Jesus Christ and what He did for us at the Cross. If we place our faith in anything other than Christ and the Cross, no matter how Scriptural the other *"thing"* might be in its own right, we will conclude by frustrating the Grace of God, which means we stop its flow, which means we are in trouble.

THE CROSS OF CHRIST MUST BE THE OBJECT OF OUR FAITH

I might quickly add, the Cross of Christ alone must be the Object of our Faith

(Rom. 6:1-14; I Cor. 1:17-18, 23; 2:2; Gal., Chpt. 5; 6:14; Eph. 2:13-18; Col. 2:14-15). Inasmuch as the Cross of Christ is the Means by which all of these great things come to us, this demands our Faith, and Faith that must not be divided. If we try to place our Faith in Christ and the Cross and something else, the Holy Spirit through James said that we are *"double minded."* He said:

"But let him ask in Faith *(some accuse James of denigrating Faith; however, he actually does the very opposite, making Faith a criteria for all things)*, nothing wavering *(nothing doubting)*. For he who wavers is like a wave of the sea driven with the wind and tossed. *(He who continuously veers from one course to another only reveals his own instability and lack of a sense of being under Divine control.)*

"For let not that man think that he shall receive anything of the Lord. *(This points to a particular type of individual, one who has a 'doubting heart.')*

"A double minded man *is* unstable in all his ways. *(One cannot place one's Faith in the Cross and something else at the same time. Such produces instability, a type of Faith that will never be honored by the Lord)*" (James 1:6-8).

Any time the Believer places his Faith in anything other than the Cross of Christ, in effect, such a Believer is committing the sin of *"spiritual adultery."*

WHAT IS SPIRITUAL ADULTERY?

In essence, we've already answered the question. Spiritual Adultery is the Believer placing his faith in anything other than Christ and the Cross. This means that such a Believer is being unfaithful to Christ, which greatly hinders the Holy Spirit in all that He can do for us. While the Spirit does not leave us, and thank God for that, still, the course of action taken by such a Christian, as it regards the placement of his faith in something other than the Cross of Christ, greatly hinders Him. This should be obvious! That's the reason that Paul said:

"For the Law of the Spirit of Life in Christ Jesus has made me free from the Law of Sin and Death" (Rom. 8:2).

In fact, most of modern Christendom is

living in a state of Spiritual Adultery because their faith is in something other than the Cross of Christ. I realize that I have just made a very strong statement, but I know it to be true. As I think it should be understood, this is the reason this Message, the Message of the Cross, is so very, very important. Actually, it is the meaning of the New Covenant. It is so much the meaning of the New Covenant that Paul actually used the word *"Cross"* as a synonym for the Gospel (I Cor. 1:17-18; Gal. 6:14).

HOW THE HOLY SPIRIT WORKS

The Holy Spirit works exclusively within the parameters, so to speak, of the Finished Work of Christ, i.e., the Cross. What Jesus did at the Cross is what gives the Holy Spirit the legal right to do all that He does, hence, Paul referring to this as a *"Law"* in Romans 8:2. In other words, the Holy Spirit will not work and will not function outside of the Cross of Christ. This demands that the Believer have his or her Faith exclusively in Christ and the Cross, and it be maintained exclusively in Christ and the Cross. In fact, this is the very heart of Christianity.

It was to the Apostle Paul that the meaning of all of this was given, and I speak of the meaning of the New Covenant, which is, in effect, the meaning of the Cross (Gal. 1:12). This is the way the Gospel works, and the only way that the Gospel works.

SATAN AND THE CROSS OF CHRIST

Satan, full well understanding this great Truth, will do everything within his power to destroy the Faith of the Believer. If he cannot do that, he will do everything he can to weaken it.

The truth is, Satan cannot deny the veracity of the Finished Work of Christ, i.e., *"the Cross."* This is a historic fact and is obvious to all; however, even though he is unable to deny the veracity of the Finished Work of Christ, he instead will seek to pervert it. He does such by having Christians place their faith in something else other than the Cross, and he doesn't too much care what the something else is. Paul also said:

"Now the Spirit (Holy Spirit) **speaks expressly** (pointedly)**, that in the latter times

(the times in which we now live, the last of the last days, which begin the fulfillment of Endtime Prophecies) **some shall depart from the Faith** (anytime Paul uses the term 'the Faith,' in short, he is referring to the Cross; so, we are told here that some will depart from the Cross as the means of Salvation and Victory)**, giving heed to seducing spirits** (evil spirits, i.e., 'religious spirits,' making something seem like what it isn't)**, and doctrines of devils** (should have been translated, 'doctrines of demons'; the 'seducing spirits' entice Believers away from the true Faith, causing them to believe 'doctrines inspired by demon spirits')**" (I Tim. 4:1).

HOW DO SEDUCING SPIRITS WORK?

The Holy Spirit through Paul tells us how. He said:

"For such *are* false apostles, deceitful workers (they have no rightful claim to the Apostolic Office; they are deceivers)**, transforming themselves into the Apostles of Christ.** (They have called themselves to this Office.)

"And no marvel (true Believers should not be surprised)**; for Satan himself is transformed into an Angel of light.** (This means he pretends to be that which he is not.)

"Therefore *it is* no great thing if his ministers (Satan's ministers) **also be transformed as the ministers of righteousness** (despite their claims, they were 'Satan's ministers' because they preached something other than the Cross)**; whose end shall be according to their works** (that 'end' is spiritual destruction)**" (II Cor. 11:13-15).

ENEMIES OF THE CROSS

The great Apostle also said, **"(For many walk** (speaks of those attempting to live for God outside of the Victory and rudiments of the Cross of Christ)**, of whom I have told you often, and now tell you even weeping** (this is a most serious matter)**, *that they are* the enemies of the Cross of Christ** (those who do not look exclusively to the Cross of Christ must be labeled 'enemies')**:

"Whose end *is* destruction (if the Cross is ignored, and continues to be ignored, the loss of the soul is the only ultimate conclusion)**, whose God *is their* belly** (refers to *those who attempt to pervert the Gospel for their own personal gain)*, **and whose glory is in their shame** *(the material things they seek, God labels as 'shame')*, **who mind earthly things.)** *(This means they have no interest in heavenly things, which signifies they are using the Lord for their own personal gain)*" **(Phil. 3:18-19).**

THE BELIEVER AND THE HOLY SPIRIT

Every Believer must understand that what we need to be in Christ, in fact, what we must be, cannot be done by our own ability, willpower, strength, talent, motivation, education, efforts, etc. While these things within themselves aren't wrong, they are woefully insufficient. What must be done in our lives can only be done by the Power of the Holy Spirit. In fact, it is the Cross of Christ alone, which has made it possible for the Holy Spirit to come into the heart and life of the Believer and abide forever, which He does immediately at Conversion. As stated, He is there for many reasons, but the greatest reason of all is to rid us of all sin.

No! This does not mean that the Believer can come to a place to where he is sinlessly perfect. The Bible does not teach sinless perfection. But it most definitely does teach, and that which we are attempting to give to you, that *"sin is not to have dominion over us"* (Rom. 6:14). Admittedly, this is not a condition in Christ to which we lay hold of quickly or easily.

WHAT IS THE DOMINION OF SIN?

Paul said:

"For sin shall not have dominion over you *(the sin nature will not have dominion over us if we as Believers continue to exercise Faith in the Cross of Christ; otherwise, the sin nature most definitely will have dominion over the Believer)*: **for you are not under the Law** *(means that if we try to live this life by any type of law, no matter how good that law might be in its own right, we will conclude by the sin nature having dominion over us)*, **but under Grace** *(the Grace of God flows to the Believer on an unending basis only as long as the Believer exercises Faith in Christ and what He did at the Cross; Grace is merely the Goodness*

of God exercised by and through the Holy Spirit, and given to undeserving Saints)" **(Rom. 6:14).**

The word *"dominion"* in the Greek is *"kurieuo"* and means, *"have dominion over, to lord it over, to exercise lordship over."*

This refers to a besetting sin, or possibly several sins, in the life of the Believer over which the Believer cannot obtain victory. The reason is, such a Believer is placing his faith in something other than the Cross of Christ. As a result, and as stated, the Holy Spirit, without Whom we cannot be what we ought to be, is woefully hindered in the help that He can give us. As stated, such a Believer is living in a state of Spiritual Adultery.

As a result, a certain sin or sins are going to lord it over the Believer, making life miserable, to say the least, with every intent to destroy that person. And please understand, this applies to preachers as well as to the laity. Considering that virtually the entirety of the modern church has its faith placed in something other than the Cross of Christ as it refers to life and living, this means that the sin nature is lording it over each Believer, making life miserable, and greatly hindering the growth process of such a Believer.

As we have already stated, the sin nature is unplugged, so to speak, when the believing sinner comes to Christ. However, when the Believer begins to place his or her faith in something other than Christ and the Cross, this denies the help of the Holy Spirit, which means that the sin nature is once again going to rule over the Child of God. Listen again to Paul:

"Let not sin *(the sin nature)* **therefore reign** *(rule)* **in your mortal body** *(showing that the sin nature can once again rule in the heart and life of the Believer, if the Believer doesn't constantly look to Christ and the Cross; the 'mortal body' is neutral, which means it can be used for Righteousness or unrighteousness)*, **that you should obey it in the lusts thereof** *(ungodly lusts are carried out through the mortal body, if Faith is not maintained in the Cross [I Cor. 1:17-18])*.

"Neither yield you your members *(of your mortal body)* **as instruments of unrighteousness unto sin** *(the sin nature)*: **but yield yourselves unto God** *(we are to yield* ourselves to Christ and the Cross; that alone guarantees victory over the sin nature)**, as those who are alive from the dead** (we have been raised with Christ in 'Newness of Life')**, and your members** as **instruments of Righteousness unto God** (this can be done only by virtue of the Cross and our Faith in that Finished Work, and Faith which continues in that Finished Work from day-to-day [Lk. 9:23-24])**" (Rom. 6:12-13).**

There is only one way to walk in Victory in this life, and that is for the Believer to place his or her Faith exclusively in Christ and the Cross, and maintain it exclusively in Christ and the Cross. That and that alone is *"God's Prescribed Order of Victory."* He has no other because no other is needed.

TAKE WITH YOU WORDS

The greater part of modern Christendom claims their Salvation from the premise of sacraments and ceremonies or the act of formally belonging to a particular church or denomination. Be it ever known, there is no Salvation in the church. In other words, fidelity to its functions and rituals cleanses no sin and saves no sinner. And yet, tragically so, the majority of *"Christians"* base their Salvation on this lie!

HUMANITARIANISM

And then, more than likely, the greatest seducer in the modern church presently is *"the gospel of humanitarianism."* This refers to doing good deeds of every sort, with the church becoming a big social center and the preacher no more than a motivator. None of this has anything to do with the Gospel, but people are deceived into believing that it does.

SELF-IMPROVEMENT

A short time ago, I read an article stating that whereas America's pastime once was baseball, now it is self-improvement. Admitting that all of us need improvement, the catch to all of that is, there is absolutely nothing that self can do to improve self. We may deceive ourselves for awhile in believing that whatever it is we are doing is going to bring about a great change. It isn't. How do I know that? Listen to the Word of God:

NOTES

"Can the Ethiopian change his skin, or the leopard his spots? then may you also do good, who are accustomed to do evil" (Jer. 13:23).

This Passage refutes any and all ideas that man can change himself. He cannot, yet, he keeps trying! So, the preacher who teaches self-improvement, using the wisdom of the world, always has a large audience simply because flesh appeals to flesh. While it is most definitely possible for an individual to change, it can only be done by the Power of the Holy Spirit as the Believer places his Faith and trust solely in the Lord Jesus Christ and what He did for us at the Cross. Even then, it's not easy!

We were told in the Second Verse, *"Take with you words."* What *"words"* are we to use?

Divine Love provides the fitting words for the truly repentant tongue.

TAKE AWAY ALL INIQUITY, AND RECEIVE US GRACIOUSLY

It is not possible, I think, for anything to be simpler. We are to say to the Lord, *"Take away all iniquity, and receive us graciously."* Basically, that is very little different than the words given by the Holy Spirit through John the Beloved some 800 years later. John said:

"If we confess our sins (pertains to acts of sin, whatever they might be, and refers to the Believer. The sinner is to believe [Jn. 3:16]; the Saint is to confess)**, He** (the Lord) **is faithful and just to forgive us** **our sins** (God will always be true to His Own Nature and Promises, keeping Faith with Himself and with man)**, and to cleanse us from all unrighteousness.** ('All,' not some. All sin was remitted, paid for, and put away on the basis of the satisfaction offered for the demands of God's Holy Law, which sinners broke, when the Lord Jesus died on the Cross)**" (I Jn. 1:9).**

In actuality, the Children of Israel were looked at by the Lord as Believers. Consequently, they were to confess their sins before the Lord, hence, the Lord saying, *"Take with you words, and turn to the LORD: say unto Him, Take away all iniquity, and receive us graciously."*

"Graciously" speaks of *"Grace!"* In effect,

the believing sinner is to ask the Lord to deal with him (deal with the sinner) with His (the Lord's) Goodness.

Sometime in eternity past, through omniscience, God knew He would make the world and, as well, would create man. He also knew that man would fall. So, it was determined by the Godhead that God would deal with man on the premise of Grace. It must be understood that Grace has to be a choice or else it's not Grace. However, once the premise of Grace was chosen by the Lord, then He had no choice but to extend Mercy. To obtain the Grace of God, i.e., *"the Goodness of God,"* all a person has to do is to confess his sins before Him and be of sincere heart. This means that such a one is determined to forsake sin with the guarantee then being given that God will deal with that one in the realm of Grace.

As well, it must be understood that all Grace comes by the means of the Cross. God had just as much Grace 3,000 years ago as He does now. But due to the fact that the blood of bulls and goats could not take away sins, meaning that the sin debt remained, this limited God as to what He could do as it regarded Grace being shown to individuals. But still, every single thing we see in the Old Testament, as it regards God doing great things for His People, is all because of Grace.

THE CROSS OF CHRIST

Inasmuch as the Cross is now a fact, which means that all sin was atoned, God can give unlimited Grace to anyone if they will meet His Conditions.

WHAT ARE THOSE CONDITIONS?

They are very simple!

The person is to simply ask the Lord to take away all iniquity, even as stated. As well, if a person is truly Born-Again, that person truly hates sin. This means that he doesn't want to commit sin of any nature. If and when it is committed, the heaviness, so to speak, is such that he cannot wait to go before the Lord that it be forgiven. But if the person will not confess his sin before the Lord, which is a private thing between the Lord and the individual, then such becomes grievous to the individual and even to the Lord.

NOTES

It is absolutely imperative for the Believer to seek forgiveness of any and all sin, and to do so instantly. As well, he must understand, even as we have taught the reader in these pages, how to overcome sin so that it not be committed over and over again. Despite the fact that the Lord will forgive again and again, actually, with no limitations, still, sin always has an extremely debilitating effect on the perpetrator. Death is always attached to sin (Rom. 6:23; 7:9; 8:2). This means that every time we sin, especially if the same sin is repeated over and over again, Righteousness and Holiness dies a little bit within us. While the Blood of Jesus Christ most definitely cleanses from all sin and its effects, repetitive sinning must never be looked at with a lackadaisical attitude. In such a case, Spiritual Growth is greatly hindered, if not stopped altogether. As well, sin always hardens the perpetrator. Paul said:

HARDENED THROUGH THE DECEITFULNESS OF SIN

"Take heed, Brethren (*proclaims Paul warning Believers by the examples of Israel's failures in the wilderness*)**, lest there be in any of you an evil heart of unbelief** (*the Greek order of words is, 'a heart evil with reference to unbelief'*)**, in departing from the Living God.** (*As stated, the problem is unbelief, and in modern terminology it refers to unbelief in Christ and the Cross.*)

"But exhort one another daily (*proclaims a constant frequency, which means the preacher should preach the Cross, and do so constantly*)**, while it is called today** (*it must be done today; in other words, start now talking and speaking about the Cross, which is the only answer [I Cor. 1:17; Gal. 6:14]*)**; lest any of you be hardened through the deceitfulness of sin.** (*This actually says, 'the deceitfulness of the sin,' which refers to a rejection of the Sacrifice of Christ*)**" (Heb. 3:12-13).** So, just because the Lord will forgive and will forgive an unlimited number of times, it doesn't mean at all that sin is to be looked at lightly. The person who does so is foolish indeed!

Sin is as dangerous to the Believer as a rattlesnake is when poised to strike. The only way to have victory over sin to where it is not habitually committed is for the Believer to place his Faith exclusively in Christ and what Christ did at the Cross, and do so on a continued basis. Jesus even spoke of *"taking up the Cross daily"* (Lk. 9:23).

TURN TO THE LORD

The *"words"* we are to take are not to be taken to men, but rather the Lord. The Catholic priest or the Protestant preacher cannot save. These *"words"* are to be taken directly by the seeker to the Lord. To be sure, He will never turn anyone away. Jesus said, *"All who the Father gives Me shall come to Me; and him who comes to Me I will in no wise cast out"* (Jn. 6:37).

CONFESSION

The Believers' confession of sin to the Lord, according to the Word of God, is one of the great Doctrines of the Bible and addresses itself to the great needs of every Believer, which means it is of extreme significance. As always, the Evil One has attempted to pervert this glorious privilege given to us in the Word of God. The following will give you some history as it regards this all-important subject.

THE CATHOLIC CONFESSIONAL

Inasmuch as the Catholic church little teaches confession to the Lord, but rather to the priest, the following thoughts are in order:

Catholic dogma states unequivocally that Jesus gave His Apostles the specific power to forgive or retain sins, and that this power has resided within the church (the Catholic church) from that day to this.

They claim that priests still have this power to forgive or retain sins, but for them to exercise this power, sins must be confessed to them verbally. The priest then imposes a penance to be performed and grants absolution (remission of the sin), with the understanding that the penance must be completed.

Until recently, the ritual for absolution included recitation of these precise words:

"May our Lord Jesus Christ absolve you, and by His Authority I absolve you from your sins, in the Name of the Father, and of the Son, and of the Holy Spirit."

NOTES

Further, the Church of Rome teaches that each Catholic must confess his sins to a priest at least once a year, preferably during Lent. This is known as *"the Easter duty,"* and is essential not only for Salvation, they say, but for membership and good standing in the Catholic church.

Annual confession is only a minimum standard for membership. Weekly (or even more frequent) confession is considered closer to the ideal.

ORIGINS OF THE CONFESSIONAL

This doctrine of Catholic Confession is neatly and logically presented within the Catechism and in official church histories. But its actual history as an accepted element within the Catholic structure is far less clear cut and rational. Even Catholic historians and theologians within the organized hierarchy are hard pressed to produce a convincing background for this practice of auricular (verbal) confession.

It is frustrating to attempt accurately to trace the story of its introduction, its spread, and its final imposition as a prerequisite to the forgiveness of sins. The story entails uncertainties, historical absurdities, hierarchical scheming, and theological revisionism, as Catholicism is prone to do.

So, if auricular confession was not established by Jesus Christ—or practiced by the Apostles—and it wasn't—where did Rome acquire this custom that was to become a basic building block of the Catholic faith? There can be little doubt that it came from the same source from which the Catholic church acquired a number of additional practices, which do not agree with Scripture. The following may throw some light on the subject.

THE UNSAVORY SOURCE IS
EARLY PAGAN RELIGIONS

Eusibias Salvarte, the Orientialist, refers to auricular confession as an integral part of Greek rites, which quite clearly demonstrates that they came from Babylonian origin. He says:

"All the Greeks, from Delphi to Thermopylae, were initiated in the mysteries of the Temple of Delphi. Their silence

in not revealing anything shows that they were enjoined to silence which was assured – not only by the penalties that were threatened should the mysteries be revealed – but also by the general confession required of the aspirants before being initiated. In this confession there was greater motive to fear the indiscreet Priest than the indiscretion of the initiate."

Dupius, in his work, Del Tous Le Sulte, says, *"There were certain Priests called Koes, whose task was to receive the confessions and judge the faults of the penitents."*

It is not unusual for Christian converts, coming from heathenism, to obstinately adhere to certain rituals and practices. Many found direct, personal confession to God unsatisfying, even though it was prescribed as such in the Holy Bible and confirmed by the most saintly men of the age. However, because of the inconvenience and embarrassment of public confession, private confession to a priest, it seems, was a logical and desirable compromise.

In the beginning, this amounted more to a confession to God with the priest participating by suggesting the penance, rather than an overt confession to the priest. At this point, the priest did not forgive the sin, he merely guided the meeting between the penitent and God.

EVOLUTION OF THE DOGMA OF CONFESSION

For many centuries confession was optional as a means of receiving counsel from a priest and of resolving the pangs of a person's conscience through the doing of some penance, which, of course, the priests would suggest, as it regarded the Catholic church. Many penitents continued in the traditional (and prescribed) manner of confessing their sins directly to God.

PUBLIC

We find in the history of the church that from the Second through the Fifth Centuries, confession of sins (after having first been made directly to God) was practiced from time to time before the whole congregation as a demonstration of public Repentance. Such public confessions could, of course,

have grave consequences, depending on the nature of the sins, and which method was not Biblical.

PENITENTIARY PRESBYTERS

To avoid this, confession before everyone, the first experiment in auricular confession was begun at Constantinople in A.D. 329 with the creation of *"penitentiary presbyters."* These were a special class of priests intended to hear confessions and to declare whether they were convenient (and prudent) to confess in public.

But in A.D. 390, the Office of Penitentiary Presbyters was abolished by Bishop Nestorius—due to a scandal involving one of the presbyters and a woman penitent.

In his pastoral letter abolishing the Office, Nestorius stated that in the future *"each person will be left in liberty to participate or not in the holy mystery of the communion, according to his conscience."*

Now, this begs a question!

If auricular confession had been practiced by all the Ministers of the Gospel since Apostolic times (as the Catholic church claims), why would there have been a need to create the penitentiary presbyters? Even more puzzling, did this mean Nestorius was abolishing the power of the priests to forgive sins, which Jesus had established among the Apostles, or so it was then claimed by some.

It was only very slowly, and as the priests gained influence, that it became more common to substitute confession to the priests for direct, personal confession to God.

However, even with all of this backward, forward, and lateral movement taking place, it would be 1,000 years before a priest would assume the responsibility of personally pardoning sins. Up until then, the penitent was dismissed after his confession with a simple and fitting phrase, *"May God forgive you and take away your sin."*

MODERN ABSOLUTION

The modern form of absolution, *"ego te absolve"* (*"I forgive you"*), considered to be essential to the Sacrament today, cannot be found in any authenticated document throughout the first twelve centuries of the Christian Era.

During this period, the absolution formula employed by the Roman Church was, *"Ablutio Criminum, Miscreatur Tui Omnipotens Deus, et dimittat tibi omnia pecatta tua"* (*"May God Omnipotent give you absolution and forgive you"*).

Thomas Aquinas, philosopher and scholar, who lived in the Thirteenth Century (about A.D. 1224-1274), inadvertently revealed the date of this important change from the traditional to the modern ritual. This respected writer and doctor of theology mentioned that a contemporary was complaining against the authoritarian form of absolution (where the priest takes the authority). In discussing this matter, he mentioned that it had been only 30 years since the professors had used the supplicatory (traditional, quoted above) form. So, we know that it was about A.D. 1200 that priests first assumed the authority to personally forgive sin.

OBLIGATORY

This important development was introduced, it seems, at the same time as the edict that made confession obligatory for all members of the church. This was at the Fourth Lateran Council, celebrated in A.D. 1215, where annual, auricular confession became mandatory for all persons who had reached the age of reason, on pain of mortal sin—which meant that eternal damnation was the penalty for ignoring this order.

In other words, irrespective as to what had happened during the year, the individual would still be consigned to eternal Hellfire—simply because he had not *"reported in"* to the priests during the year.

Claude Fleury, French ecclesiastical historian (A.D. 1640-1723), states:

"This is the first Canon I know of that commands general confession."

From this Fourth Lateran Council on, it has been the duty of every Roman Catholic to confess his sins to a priest to receive not only counsel but also absolution. This is, of course, contrary to the teaching and example of the New Testament.

PERILS OF THE CONFESSIONAL

The first thing that should be noted about the Roman Catholic confessional is that it is contrary to good morals.

How?

Because it encourages promiscuity in behavior by providing a simple and mechanical format for putting a person's sinful behavior behind him.

The thought that any transgression can be undone by observing a quick and simple ritual, thus, blotting out the pangs of conscience, makes future forays off the beaten path all that much more attractive. After repeated excursions into the realm of sin, with quick absolution each time, the practitioner soon becomes inured to the momentary tremors of conscience. *"Why not? I'll just go to confession tomorrow."*

Now, please understand. We are not minimizing the fact that the counsel and advice given by many Catholic priests can provide consolation and guidance to those coming for confession. But we maintain that this same ministry could be provided outside the confessional—in an environment relieved of the mechanical and dehumanizing aspects of a ritual and of the time pressures imposed by a waiting line of impatient parishioners.

They could further be provided without the incidental and baseless contention that the priests will *"broker"* God's Forgiveness.

Consequently, the remorseful Catholic could be directed to a personal audience with God for the dissolution of the sin element, and then the priest could offer ministry for the personal problems besetting the disturbed layman.

PRIESTLY DEFECTS

Every human priest, which, according to Scripture and under the New Covenant, does not even exist, has great (and human) defects in exercising the office of confessor:

• The priest does not know the Spiritual condition of the sinner, so he cannot be sure whether the person's repentance is genuine or not. Only God knows the secrets of the heart (Ps. 44:21).

• The priest knows even less of the thoughts of God. He can in no way ascertain whether God has, in fact, pardoned the supposed penitent, to whom he has almost obligated (by the very nature of the ritual) to provide his *"ego te absolbe."* Thus, his words may or may not conform to the truth—engendering the person receiving absolution a false sense of security.

• No mere mortal can forgive sin. Jesus said:

"Whose soever sins you remit, they are remitted unto them; and whose soever sins you retain, they are retained" (Jn. 20:23).

Of course, this is the very Scripture the Catholic church uses as authority for their priest's ability to forgive sins; however, the original Greek should be studied.

Here the words translated *"remitted"* and *"retained"* are in the perfect tense. This indicates an action already performed.

So, the Greek more accurately should be translated as, *"If you forgive the sins of any, they have already been forgiven. If you retain the sins of any, they have already been retained."*

The interpretation of the Catholic church reverses the order given in the original, saying instead (of the priest), *"You can forgive sins and then your decision will be approved in Heaven."*

But Scripture says, in essence, *"Your sins have already been forgiven in Heaven, through acceptance of your proclamation of forgiveness through the Blood of Jesus Christ."*

This means, in effect, that any Disciple (for Jesus addressed all present when He made this statement, not just the Apostles), can assure any sinner that his sins have been forgiven the moment he comes to Christ in repentant Faith. Likewise, the Disciple (and the Christian who trusts Jesus for Salvation) can assure any non-Believer that his sins are retained unless he trusts in Christ for his Salvation.

THE APOSTLES DID NOT HAVE THE POWER TO FORGIVE SINS

The remainder of the New Testament bears out the intent of this Passage. Furthermore, every major Doctrine within the Word of God appears more than once as self-confirmation. For example:

". . . that in the mouth of two or three witnesses every word may be established" (Mat. 18:16).

But there is no other statement in the Bible that even suggests that anyone can

forgive sin but God. There is no incident where a Disciple or Apostle forgives sins by his own authority.

Did the Apostle Peter give absolution to Cornelius (Acts, Chpt. 10)?

Did the Apostle Paul give absolution to the Philippian jailer (Acts, Chpt. 16)?

No! The Apostles preached Salvation to their hearers and led them to the opportunity to receive forgiveness through the Blood of Jesus Christ.

Only in this sense are there any recorded incidents of forgiveness through the actions of the Apostles. In no situation do we find the Apostles calling for a personal confession to them—followed by absolution. This would be in total opposition to the New Testament proclamation of forgiveness through Repentance and acceptance of the propitiatory Sacrifice of Christ at Calvary.

Peter confirmed this emphatically when he said, *"To Him give all the Prophets witness, that through His Name whosoever believes in Him shall receive remission of sins"* (Acts 10:43).

God has never given any person the authority to make a decision as to whether to forgive or retain another person's sins. Again, we must recall that the only Mediator between God and men is Christ Jesus.

"For there is one God, and one Mediator between God and men, the Man Christ Jesus" (I Tim. 2:5).

SOME TERRIBLE DANGERS

Not only does the confessional offer an easy way of becoming absolved of sin, which actually does not exist, but it also offers to the priest—an unmarried man—the most intimate thoughts of the opposite sex. He is the recipient of revelations of conjugal intimacies (proper or improper) and the most secret thoughts a wife may have regarding her husband. Every kind of sin is confessed to him, and it is no wonder that such revelations have produced such terrible scandals—and will go on doing so until the abandonment of this dangerous human institution.

How many priests (and preachers) have been started down the road to moral degradation by listening to confessions that open the door to their involvement? The confessional is a direct contradiction of the petition Jesus Himself said we should pray, *"Lead us not into temptation . . ."* (Mat. 6:13).

How many political figures, public servants, judges, and men of high and important positions are held in bondage because of intimate secrets revealed to their priests?

The most personal facts of every Catholic family and of every Catholic heart (which should be known only to God) are known by priests in their most intimate details. How many potential scandals within the Catholic church have been hushed up, and how many shameful situations concerning priests have been swept under the carpet by politicians and public servants—just because too many secrets are known to the priests?

Years ago, it was widely publicized that J. Edgar Hoover was politically untouchable because of his *"little black book,"* which contained intimate facts about all the political powers who might attempt to exert influence over him.

If such intimate knowledge could make an individual *"above the law,"* is it unreasonable to assume that similar knowledge could serve to make the Catholic church untouchable too?

One of the most powerful forms of bondage known to man can be the bondage of the confessional, where individuals can become the servants of priests because of revelations that become the property of the church through the confessional.

MODERN PSYCHOLOGY AND THE PROTESTANT CHURCH

Lest the reader think we are overly harsh regarding the Catholic confessional, let it be hurriedly said that as guilty as the Catholic church is regarding this unscriptural practice, likewise, the Protestant church follows suit in its confession to the psychologist.

It is true that the Protestant does not confess his sins to the psychologist in order to receive forgiveness for sins, and neither does the psychologist claim to forgive sin as the Catholic priest. Nevertheless, no help can be forthcoming by the engagement of such practices of confession to any human except in circumstances where an individual has been wronged.

To be sure, Protestant religious leadership is, for the most part, so taken up with psychological counseling that little credence is given anymore to Hosea's admonition to *"turn to the LORD."*

In fact, upon the advent of a problem respecting its ministers, such leadership demands a *"sign off"* by a psychologist before the individual can be accepted once again.

(How different is that than the Fourth Lateran Council of the Catholic church, which makes confession before a priest mandatory on pain of mortal sin?)

Consequently, the modern position of the Protestant church is fastly placing the role of the psychologist in somewhat the same role as the Catholic priest. Even though the former is secular, while the latter is religious, still, the end results are the same, the turning away from God and His Word to men.

Martin Gross, in his book, *"The Psychological Society,"* says:

"When educated man lost faith in formal religion, he required a substitute belief that would be as reputable in the last half of the 20th Century as Christianity was in the first. Psychology and Psychiatry have now assumed that special role."[1]

TRUE CONFESSION ACCORDING TO THE WORD OF GOD

"But you, when you pray, enter into your closet, and when you have shut your door, pray to your Father Who is in secret; and your Father Who sees in secret shall reward you openly" (Mat. 6:6).

In the Book of Acts and in all the Apostolic Letters, we do not find a single case where auricular confession takes place or is encouraged. Quite the contrary! One specific incident graphically illustrates the opposite: Simon the Sorcerer (Acts 8:9-24) offered the Apostles money if they would reveal to him the secret of receiving the Baptism with the Holy Spirit. Peter upbraided him for thinking that the Gift of God could be obtained for money and then told him:

". . . pray God, if perhaps the thought of your heart may be forgiven you" (Acts 8:22).

Note that Peter did not say, *"Confess your sin to me or to some other Apostle, and we will give you absolution."* He told him to pray to God for forgiveness.

It would seem that this one short Passage demonstrates convincingly that the Roman contention about priests forgiving sins is not harmonious with what the Word of God says about forgiveness.

ANOTHER KIND OF PARDON

In the New Testament we have an interesting example of a kind of pardon that has nothing to do with Divine Pardon for Salvation of the soul. Even here reconciliation was not bestowed by any one person but was granted by the group action of an entire community of Believers.

One of the members of the church at Corinth had fallen into sin and had refused to cease this action or to repent. The Christians of that church, meeting together in special session, had declared that the member was unworthy to partake of communion and had separated him from the fellowship of the church. The offending member then acknowledged his faults, and the Apostle Paul recommended charity toward him, saying:

"To whom you forgive any thing, I forgive also . . ." (II Cor. 2:10).

The words, "To whom you forgive any thing," clearly indicate that granting a pardon is not the exclusive office of any one person but is the responsibility of the entire assembly. Neither the Apostle nor any other Minister of the church at Corinth took on himself the individual authority to forgive. Even in this problem (involving fellowship rather than Salvation), the church as a whole had to make the decision and declare the repentant brother acceptable again to their Body (fellowship of Believers, or the church). In other words, getting back to the problem at hand, the man was on trial at the beginning, and now the church is on trial as it regards their forgiving him or not! Every evidence is that they did!

THE TEACHING OF THE EARLY CHURCH FATHERS

John Chrysostom, the great Preacher of the Fourth Century (aptly named "Golden Mouth"), wrote in one of his sermons:

"It is not necessary that anyone should

witness your confession. Recognize your iniquities and let God Alone, without anyone knowing, hear your confession. I exhort and entreat you to confess your sins to God. I do not tell you to reveal them to men, God Alone sees your confession.

"Confess your sins daily in your prayers . . . who can doubt to make us act this way? I do not urge you to go and confess your sins to a man who is a sinner like yourselves, who might despise you if you were to relate to him your faults. But confess them to God Who is able to forgive them."

Basil, the Bishop of Caesarea (A.D. 329-379), said:

"I do not make myself a spectacle before the world to confess with my mouth; I shut my eyes and make my confession in the privacy of my heart. Only before You, O my God, do I allow my sins to escape. You Alone are their witness."

Augustine, Bishop of Hippo (A.D. 354-430), and a great writer of apologetic and dogmatic works, declared:

"Why should I go to expose the wounds of my soul before men? It is the Holy Spirit Who remits sins; man is unable to do so for he stands in the same need or in the same position as he who comes to him for the remedy."

TRUE CONFESSION

So, without the confessional and absolution, how does the Christian find release from the sins that attack his conscience?

Every time the Christian realizes he has offended God, another person, or even himself (however unintentionally), he goes personally before God in private prayer, asking for pardon and for the strength to live a more genuine Christian life. We should all seek a life that honors the profession of Faith we made and make in our beloved Saviour (I Jn. 1:9).

In fact, it is the Cross of Christ that makes all of this possible. Jesus atoned for all of our sins at the Cross, whether past, present, or future, at least for all who will believe (Jn. 3:16).

As well, while the Bible does not teach sinless perfection, it most definitely does teach that sin is not to have dominion over us (Rom. 6:14). This place and position, where the sin nature no longer has dominion, is not reached easily or quickly. It can be reached only in one way, and that is by the Believer placing his or her Faith exclusively in Christ and what Christ has done for us at the Cross. This then gives the Holy Spirit, Who Works entirely within the parameters of the Finished Work of Christ, the latitude and liberty to Work within our lives, bringing about that which He Alone can bring about.

NO PRETENSIONS

In confession directly to God in the Name of Jesus, there is no possibility of *"shopping"* from one priest to another in the hope of finding one who has a philosophy of behavior similar to one's own. In true Christian confession—to God directly—there is no room for fraud, pretensions, or expectation of gullible acceptance of pleas of remorse—when we may not be feeling it. God, and God Alone, knows the heart.

I believe that the superior morality found in Protestant nations (which even non-fanatical Catholics will admit exists) is not so much a matter of culture or innate racial virtues as it is the question of the confessional. This is crucially important in defining the moral atmosphere of any nation where the majority of the population accepts Catholic Doctrine.

True Christian confession might, on the surface, appear to be easier than Roman Catholic confession. But it is actually more severe, much more severe, within the intimate realm of the Spirit—which is, after all, what really matters when we discuss Spiritual Growth and eternal Salvation, is it not?

"For You desire not sacrifice; else would I give it: You delight not in Burnt Offering.

"The Sacrifices of God are a broken spirit: a broken and a contrite heart . . ." (Ps. 51:16-17).

I think it should be obvious that the Catholic confessional is not Scriptural. We find that it has its origin in heathenistic, pagan rituals. We also note that the perils of the confessional are immorality among the priesthood, the creation of a false sense of security for the penitent, and the creation

NOTES

of a fertile field for promiscuous behavior.

It also places great numbers of individuals under bondage because the innermost secrets of the heart are bared to a priest. Such information can constitute a threat of moral extortion for such individuals.

We also find that true, Scripturally-founded confession must be made to God, and to God Alone. He Alone can forgive. He will forgive. Why, therefore, look elsewhere for false and confusing avenues to forgiveness?

NO FORGIVENESS

As well, there is every Scriptural evidence that all sins confessed to a priest, etc., with the hopes of forgiveness from God, in fact, are not forgiven by God. Therefore, multiplied millions of individuals are duped into believing that their sins are covered, washed, and cleansed by the Blood of Christ, when, in reality, they are not. Such is deception of the highest order!

Hosea cries, *"Turn to the LORD."* In doing so, one will find that He truly forgives.

TAKE AWAY ALL INIQUITY

"Say unto Him, Take away all iniquity": this is the same as the New Testament injunction by John the Beloved, *"If we confess our sins, He is faithful and just to forgive us our sins, and to cleanse us from all unrighteousness"* (I Jn. 1:9).

In the request, *"Take away all iniquity,"* is the admittance that sin has been committed. To be frank, if one will admit he is a sinner, which this demands, it is not too difficult to get him to seek forgiveness.

As well, the Lord will forgive not only some of the sins but *"all iniquity."* Satan is very adept at getting Christians to believe that God may possibly forgive some sins, but others, He will not! However, irrespective of the heinousness of the sin, the Lord, upon proper confession and Repentance, will abundantly forgive.

NO LIMITATIONS

Also, there is no limit to the number of times He will forgive. Men may forgive one time, or at the most, a few times. But then, at least for the most part, they will refuse to forgive anymore. However, God places no limitations on the times that He will forgive. He only demands that the person come to Him in humble contrition, admitting he is a sinner, and that the *"iniquity"* must be taken away (Mat. 18:21-22).

Many years later, John the Baptist would say, *"... Behold the Lamb of God, Who takes away the sin of the world"* (Jn. 1:29).

The words, *"take away,"* were used by Hosea by Faith, while John introduced the One Who would take the sins away.

JUSTIFICATION BY FAITH

Before the Death of Christ on the Cross, sins, in fact, were not taken away but only covered by the blood of bulls and goats. However, the writer of Hebrew says, *"It is not possible that the blood of bulls and goats should take away sins"* (Heb. 10:4).

Therefore, before the Death and Resurrection of Christ, these sins, ever how many they were, *"were only covered."*

Now, due to what Christ did at Calvary, all sins are *"taken away,"* upon proper Repentance. This means that they are washed clean by the Blood of Christ, and the sinner is looked at by God as though he never sinned. It is called, *"Justification by Faith"* (Rom. 5:1).

Therefore, considering that properly confessed sins are gone, Paul said, *"... forgetting those things which are behind, and reaching forth unto those things which are before.*

"I press toward the mark for the prize of the high calling of God in Christ Jesus" (Phil. 3:13-14).

THE GRACE OF GOD

"And receive us graciously": this refers to being Saved by Grace, as all have always been Saved (Eph. 2:8-9).

Some argue that Grace only came after the Death and Resurrection of Christ. However, Grace has always been the method through which the Lord has chosen to save men, and that both in the Old and New Testaments. Inasmuch as it was not possible for man to earn his Salvation, whether by works or merit, Grace was the only way that man could be Saved. Therefore, from Abel to the present, it has been Grace and Grace

NOTES

alone that has reconciled men unto God.

However, *"Grace"* is primarily a New Testament theme, inasmuch as it was only seen dimly in the Old Testament.

WHAT IS THE GRACE OF GOD?

It has been defined by many as *"unmerited favor,"* and, actually, that is correct; however, I prefer to say that Grace is the *"Goodness of God extended to undeserving people."*

The reason that the Grace of God could not be given as freely in Old Testament times as it is now in New Testament times is because, as stated, the blood of bulls and goats could not take away sins under the old economy of God (Heb. 10:4).

All of this means that while the sins of Old Testament Saints were covered, they were not taken away because animal blood was insufficient. It did serve as a stopgap measure until Christ would come, but only in that capacity. As a result, when Believers in Old Testament times died, they were not taken to Heaven, but rather down into Paradise, which was very close to Hell. Actually, only a gulf separated the burning side of Hell from Paradise (Lk. 16:19-31). In fact, all who were in Paradise were actually captives of Satan (Eph. 4:8). When Jesus died on the Cross, however, this meant that the great sin debt was paid, and paid for all, at least those who died believing, with Him going down into that place and delivering all of these souls. Now, since the Cross, when Believers die, they immediately go to be with the Lord in Heaven because all of their sins have been taken away. The sin debt was lifted, actually taken away, which was made possible by the Cross (Phil. 1:23).

Due to the sin debt being lifted by what Christ did at Calvary, now the door is open for Grace to be extended to any and every Believer upon proper Faith. However, we must understand, the Grace of God is made possible by what Christ did at the Cross, and the Cross exclusively. Therefore, it is required that our Faith be exclusively in Christ and the Cross, or else we will frustrate the Grace of God (Gal. 2:21).

OLD TESTAMENT FAITH

By Jesus' time, Old Testament Faith had

been seriously distorted by centuries of mis-interpretation. The religious Jew relied on his physical descent from Abraham and his knowledge of the Law. Relationship with God was considered an issue of ritual piety and obedience to the Letter of the Law.

The religious man had a claim on God, established by membership in the Covenant community and based on his own merits, or so he thought! The sense of helplessness that moved the Psalmist to call out to God, pleading only that the Lord show Mercy and stoop to meet his needs, was replaced in the religious life of the Pharisees by a smug sense of self-righteousness.

The Apostle Paul was thoroughly trained in this way of thinking and in rabbinical interpretation. But he was dramatically converted to Christ on the Damascus road and was driven to reexamine the beliefs of a lifetime.

THE APOSTLE PAUL

Paul's perspective on a person's relation-ship with God was transformed. As he was committed to missionary work, he was driv-en to the word *"Grace"* for a way to express the vital difference between human attempts to win God's Favor and the way in which personal relationship with God is actually established and developed. In fact, the Holy Spirit revealed all of this to Paul in totality. All that Paul gave us in his fourteen Epistles (and I believe he wrote Hebrews) was given to him by the Lord and the Lord exclusively. He was not influenced by anything else, as some have claimed!

THE EPISTLE OF PAUL
THE APOSTLE TO THE ROMANS

In Romans, Chapter 3, Paul quotes the Old Testament to show that all people are sinners. Law offered no way of Salvation, for Law stands as humanity's silent accuser, making us conscious of our sin (Rom. 3:19-20). So, in Jesus, God acted to reveal a Righteousness that has no relationship to Law. This is a Righteousness that comes from God through Faith in Jesus and is given to all who believe (Rom. 3:21-22). Because all have sinned, only God's spon-taneous and decisive Act in Christ—an act

of Grace—could purchase our Redemption (Rom. 3:23-26).

Then Paul, in Romans, Chapter 4, reviews sacred history. He shows that Abraham's relationship with God was not based on his works but on his Faith. Law and all human achievements are ruled out as avenues to a felicitous relationship with God. That can only come through Faith in God, Who has promised to do for us what we could not do for ourselves. This whole process—the Promise and the Faith—are rooted in Grace (Rom. 4:16).

Romans 5:15 through 5:21 again portrays Salvation as a gift that comes to us through Jesus and is an expression of God's Grace.

GRACE DOES NOT CONTRADICT OLD TESTAMENT REVELATION

Romans 11:1 through 11:6 argues that the concept of Grace in no way contradicts Old Testament Revelation, which was so badly misunderstood by Israel. God has always acted freely, and those who have found a per-sonal relationship with God have not found it by works but in Grace. The affirmations Grace makes about God and human beings stand in bold contrast to the normal human approach to relationship with the Lord. Grace holds that human beings are helpless, so locked in sin that their state can only be represented as death. Grace declares that God is Merciful and Loving, and that He is able to act to meet our deepest need. Grace teaches that God has acted in Jesus to bring us forgiveness and New Life through His Atoning Sacrifice at Calvary.

Because of motives rooted deeply within His Own Character, God has reached out in Jesus to save sinners.

For the religious people of Paul's day and for all people of every time, the Message of Grace is a powerful warning of our absolute need. And, it is an affirmation of the over-whelming Love of God that acts in Jesus to meet our need and provide forgiveness and Life.

This Grace affirmed in the New Testament is always mediated by Jesus. This Grace is a dynamic force that does more than affect our standing with God by crediting us with Righteousness.

Grace affects our experience as well.

ROMANS, CHAPTER SIX

In Romans 6, perhaps the greatest Chapter in the Word of God as it regards how the Believer is to live for God, Paul traces something of the transforming impact of Grace. Actually, Romans, Chapter 6, proclaims to us the meaning of the sin nature as it dwells in the Believer. The Holy Spirit through Paul tells us, as Believers, how to have victory over the sin nature and that it no more has dominion in our hearts and lives. Paul shows that when we are united with Jesus and what He did for us at the Cross, in other words, in His Death and Resurrection, we are removed from the realm of law, with its emphasis on works, and are established in the realm of Grace. Grace is marked always by God's Enabling Work within us to overcome our helplessness.

The first two Verses of Romans, Chapter 6, tell us that the problem is sin. Even though we are now Believers, Born-Again, Justified by Faith, still, the problem is sin. In Romans, Verses 3 through 5, the great Apostle gives us the solution to this dilemma. It is the Cross of Christ. He tells us how we are baptized into Christ, and he's not speaking of Water Baptism, but rather the Crucifixion of Christ, and how by Faith we are placed in Him, and that refers to His Death, His Burial, and His Resurrection. So, when Paul uses the phrase, *"in Christ,"* or one of its derivatives, such as *"in Him," "in Jesus,"* etc., which he does some 170 times in his fourteen Epistles, he is always, and without exception, speaking of the Death of Christ on the Cross and His Resurrection. When you accepted Christ as your Saviour, meaning when you were Born-Again, in the Mind of God, you were Spiritually placed in Christ in His Atoning Work at Calvary's Cross. You are to remain there all of your life, and this is the route to Victory.

GOD'S PRESCRIBED ORDER OF LIFE AND LIVING

• We are to understand that everything that man receives from God, whether Salvation or Sanctification, is made possible by the Cross of Christ. It begins and ends, so

to speak, at the Cross. Some may foolishly claim that they are little interested in the Cross but are very desirous of living the Resurrection Life. To be sure, the Resurrection Life is exactly what the Lord wants you to live, which refers to all Victory. However, that Resurrection Life cannot be achieved except that we understand the following:

Paul said, *"For if we have been planted together in the likeness of His Death, we shall be also in the likeness of His Resurrection"* (Rom. 6:5).

Resurrection Life refers to victory over the world, the flesh, and the Devil, which is the intention of the Lord, that for which He died. To have and enjoy Resurrection Life, we are to understand, and without reservation, that Resurrection Life is made possible by what Jesus did at the Cross. If we do not understand that we were planted together with Him, referring to the Cross, we are not going to have and enjoy Resurrection Life. It all comes by the Cross! (Rom. 6:14; I Cor. 1:17-18, 21, 23; 2:2; Gal., Chpt. 5; 6:14; Eph. 2:13-18; Col. 2:14-15).

THE RESURRECTION OF CHRIST

Some claim that the victory is in the Resurrection. That is not true!

In fact, despite what some say, there was never any doubt about the Resurrection of Christ. At the Cross, our Lord defeated every principality and power of darkness (Col. 2:14-15). So, when Jesus died and, thereby, went down into the heart of the Earth, where He remained for three days and three nights, He did not go down into that region as a defeated victim. He went down as a conqueror because the Victory had been won at the Cross. The Scripture tells us of only two things He did those three days and three nights. It says:

• First of all, the Scripture says, *"By which also He went and preached unto the spirits in prison"* (I Pet. 3:19). Incidentally, these *"spirits"* are fallen Angels, who had been locked up because of committing some terrible sin. More than likely, it was the sin of cohabiting with women, thereby, mongrelizing the human race to keep Jesus from coming into the world (Gen. 6:3-7). As well, the word translated *"preached"* in the Greek doesn't mean what it normally does, but rather that Jesus made an announcement to these fallen Angels. As to exactly what that announcement was, we aren't told. It probably had to do with the failure of their plan. He might have related to them that the price had been paid at Calvary's Cross for the Redemption of man, and that it would be an *"Everlasting Covenant,"* meaning that it would never need to be replaced. Whatever that announcement was, it was one of Victory.

• The second thing He did, and by far the most important, was to go into Paradise and deliver every single soul who had died in the Faith believing. In other words, their Salvation, deliverance from this place, and being brought out from under the dominion of Satan, were all dependent on the Cross of Calvary. The Cross was now a fact, meaning that all sin was atoned and Satan had no more claim on them. So, He led them out of this place. The Scripture says, *". . . He led captivity captive . . ."* (Eph. 4:8).

The term, *"He led captivity captive,"* is a strange statement. It means that they had been captives of Satan for all the time they were held there, but now, due to the Cross, meaning the sin debt was forever lifted, they all became our Lord's Captives. Now, when Believers pass away, they instantly go to be with the Lord Jesus Christ, and once again, all because of the Cross.

Some preachers claim that the Resurrection was in doubt. In other words, Jesus had to fight demons and devils, etc., in order to be resurrected. None of that is true! It's not found in the Bible because it didn't happen.

Before He went to the Cross, He made the following announcement several times to His Disciples:

". . . The Son of Man is delivered into the hands of men, and they shall kill Him; and after that He is killed, He shall rise the third day" (Mk. 9:31).

To be sure, had there been one sin left unatoned, and due to the fact that the Scripture says, *"The wages of sin is death,"* Jesus could not have risen from the dead. But with all sin atoned, death could not hold Him. So, there was no doubt about His Resurrection. The price was paid at Calvary's Cross, and Calvary's Cross alone. While, of course, the Resurrection is of immense significance, as should be overly obvious, never make the mistake that the Atonement was not finished until the Resurrection was a fact. The Atonement was totally and completely finished when Jesus uttered the words, *"It is finished"* (Jn. 19:30).

A PRACTICAL APPROACH

Romans, Chapter 6, shows us that Grace is not simply a basic orientation to relationship with God. It is also a practical approach to living the Christian life. This aspect of Grace helps us to understand the warning found in Galatians 5:4, that those *"who are trying to be justified by Law have been alienated from Christ; you* (they) *have fallen away from Grace."*

Any attempt by Believers to struggle toward a life of goodness by works of the law means a return to the futile way of religion. It involves reliance on ourselves and an abandonment of reliance on Christ, Who Alone can enable us to live righteous lives.

We cannot approach Christian experience from the old perspective, for Grace and religion are contradictory. We can only live by full commitment to the way of Grace and all that Grace involves.

The Biblical concept of Grace is much greater than is suggested in the common definition of *"unmerited favor."* *"Grace"* is a word that expresses a radical view of life and of relationship with God.

Grace teaches that God's Attitude toward us is one of acceptance and love. Knowing God's Heart, we can *"approach the Throne of Grace with confidence"* (Heb. 4:16) with every sin and need.

THE HUMAN CONDITION

Grace is a dramatic statement about the human condition. Each person is helpless, trapped in sin, and incapable of pleasing God or winning His Favor, except by Faith (Heb. 11:6).

Grace is a proclamation. It is the triumphant announcement that God in Christ has acted and has come to the aid of all who will trust Him for their Eternal Salvation.

Grace is a way of life. Relying totally on Jesus to Work within us, we experience

God's Own Unlimited Power, vitalizing us and enabling us to live truly good lives.

The Message of Grace, shadowed in the Old Testament and found in the New Testament, calls us to a completely different outlook on relationship with God and on Spiritual Achievement than is found in any religion of human invention.

Understanding the nature of Grace, we decisively reject any confidence in ourselves, and we trust ourselves totally to our Lord. He Alone is able not only to declare us truly Righteous men and women of God but, also, to make us so.

SACRIFICE

"So will we render the calves of our lips" refers to sacrifice and, in reality, refers to the offering a sacrifice of Praise to God as the fruit of our lips. Divine Love provides the fitting words for the truly repentant tongue (Heb. 13:15).

Along with the sacrifices of Thanksgiving, the Lord intended, as well, *"Praises of Thanksgiving."* Such is the fruit of the truly repentant heart, resulting in joy and thanksgiving. People who claim to know the Lord, with all its resultant work of Grace, and have no Praise of Thanksgiving, either are woefully failing the Lord or else have not truly repented and, thereby, do not truly know the Lord as their Redeemer.

Regrettably, this group makes up the far greater majority of the churches. In fact, in most churches, Praise to the Lord has never been offered.

These churches argue that Praise to the Lord is mere emotionalism and that their Salvation runs far deeper.

The truth is that most of these people do not really know the Lord, having embraced only a Christian philosophy and, consequently, have nothing for which to praise the Lord, at least, regarding Salvation.

Anyone who makes any pretense at studying the Word of God is stricken by the repetitive enjoiners to Praise the Lord, and to do so vocally and often! (Heb. 13:15; Ps. 145-150).

The truly redeemed soul will be a praising soul. There are several Hebrew words which express Praise: they are as follows:

NOTES

HALAL

This Hebrew word means *"to acclaim,"* *"to boast of,"* and *"to glory in."* It expresses deep satisfaction in exalting the wonderful acts and qualities of the One being praised.

The constant use of this verb in the plural shows that the joy found in recognizing God's Greatness is to be shared by the people who know and love Him. An example of such praise is seen in Psalm 65, which begins, *"Praise awaits You, O God, in Zion; to You our vows will be fulfilled. O You Who hears prayer, to You all men will come"* (Ps. 65:1-2).

YADAH

This Hebrew word means *"to Praise,"* *"to give thanks,"* and *"to confess."* This focuses on our acknowledgment of God's Works and Character, often in contrast with human failures.

Like all other Praise, this too is addressed to God Himself. It is significant that the Hebrews express thanks to God in Praise that included recounting God's Actions on their behalf.

Understanding that this word is essentially Praise in expression of acknowledgment of God's Goodness, we sense its power in Psalms 118:15-21, among other places.

ZAMAR

This Hebrew word means *"to sing Praise"* and *"to make music."* This word focuses on the use of instruments of music in praising God. It is found only in Bible poetry, usually in the Psalms. Again, this Praise focuses on Who God is and What He has done. Thus, David calls to Israel in Psalms 9:11, *"Sing praises to the LORD, enthroned in Zion; proclaim among the nations what He has done."*

Consequently, all the singing and music in our Church Services should follow suit.

SABAH

This Hebrew word means *"to Praise or commend."* This is Praise directed to the Lord, rich with adoration (Ps. 145:3-7).

Even though there are other Hebrew words which speak of Praise to God, these named sum up the Old Testament Revelation of Praise.

Inasmuch as the essential nature of Praise is established in the Old Testament, no New Testament Passage modifies its character. However, a variety of Greek words in the New Testament are used to express human awareness of and response to God's Greatness.

As all the words just given concerning Praise are from the Old Testament, and are, thereby, Hebrew words, let's look at the New Testament as it regards the Greek words used for Praise.

AINEO

The Object of this Praise is God Alone. It is found some nine times in the New Testament (Lk. 2:13, 20; 19:37; 24:53; Acts 2:47; 3:8-9; Rom. 15:11; Rev. 19:5).

EPAINEO

This Greek word means *"to commend"* and, thus, *"to Praise."*

Along with praising God for Himself, His Qualities and His Works, the word is also used in commending people. Excitingly, we learn that God will commend Believers for faithful service. This word is found six times in the New Testament (Lk. 16:8; Rom. 15:11; I Cor. 11:2, 17, 22). As well, its related noun, *"epainos,"* occurs 11 times in the New Testament.

EULOGEO

This Greek word means *"to bless"* or *"to speak well of."* This word and its cognates are found frequently in the New Testament (Mk. 14:61; Lk. 1:68; Rom. 1:25; 9:5; II Cor. 1:3; 11:31; Eph. 1:3; I Pet. 1:3).

EXOMOLOGEOMAI

This Greek word means *"to confess"* and is found 11 times in the New Testament. When such a confession is linked with sin or with public confession, it is translated *"Praise"* (Mat. 11:25; Lk. 10:21).

DOXAZO

This Greek word refers *"to giving glory to"* or *"to glorify."* This word or its cognates are found many times in the New Testament (Mat. 5:16; 9:8; 15:31; Acts 11:18; Rom. 15:7, 9, etc.).

HYMNEO

This Greek word means *"to sing a hymn"* or *"to sing praises."* It is found some four times in the New Testament (Mat. 26:30; Mk. 14:26; Acts 16:25; Heb. 2:12).

HYMNOS

This Greek word is referred to twice in the New Testament (Eph. 5:19; Col. 3:16).

PSALLO

This Greek word means *"to sing Psalms"* and is translated *"Praise"* in James 5:13. It is found three other times in the New Testament (Rom. 15:9; I Cor. 14:15; Eph. 5:19).

MEGALYNO

This Greek word means *"to magnify."* It is found some eight times in the New Testament (Lk. 1:46; Acts 10:46, etc.).

Praise in both the New Testament and the Old Testament is essentially the response of the Believer to God's Self-Revelation. God shows us His Attributes in His Mighty Works, in His Word, and especially in Jesus. The Believer recognizes the Hand of God and acknowledges the Person Whose reality he has come to know.

But Praise is more than acknowledgement. It is also an expression of delight. It is reveling in the God Who has shown Himself to us. It is expressing the love that wells up within us by speaking to Him.

As such, we can speak to God privately, with others in our homes, or assembled in congregations. When we speak to Him, we join with Believers through the ages who have expressed their love to the Lord by praising Him for His Great and Wonderful Acts and for His Great and Wonderful Self.

As well, Praise to the Lord is commanded from men as a duty and is obviously not meant to depend on mood, feeling, or circumstances. To *"rejoice before the Lord,"* is part of the ordered ritual of the common life of God's People (Deut. 12:7; 16:11-12).

NO DEPENDENCE ON MAN

The phrase from Verse 3, *"Asshur shall not save us,"* refers to Israel's great sin of trusting man and idols for Salvation. This Passage primarily speaks of Assyria but can mean man in general.

The phrase from the same Verse, *"We will not ride upon horses,"* refers to Egypt and trust in Egyptian cavalry (Deut. 17:16).

The phrase, *"For in You the fatherless find Mercy,"* refers to Israel as *"Lo-Ruhamah"* (no more Mercy) and *"Lo-Ammi"* (not My People).

Inasmuch as Hosea was appealing to Israel to repent collectively, therefore, her principal sin of trusting in others rather than Jehovah is here proclaimed. This was the practical side of Israel's Repentance. In other words, to do this would show forth the fruits of their Repentance.

Here was a renunciation of all hope of safety from the world-powers—both Assyria and Egypt.

While this renunciation of worldly power and carnal confidences is implied, as well, its opposite, unfaltering Faith in the protecting Power and Saving Strength of Jehovah is here heralded.

In effect, the Prophet Hosea is saying that if they would do such, to engage in heartfelt Repentance before God, they would have the consolation that the Father of the fatherless and the God of the orphan would have bowels of tenderest Mercy and Compassion.

As this cry was given by the Prophet to Israel of long ago, still the principal holds true even unto this hour.

TO REPENT OF THE GOOD

Regrettably, hundreds of millions in the ranks of Christendom are depending on Assyria and Egypt, i.e., ceremony, church membership, religious rituals, etc., to save them. Therefore, of these things, Repentance must be enjoined.

It is far easier to get religious man to repent of sins of the flesh than sins of pride, i.e., religious works. To repent of the *"bad"* is understood. To repent of the *"good"* is not understood at all! But that's exactly what it must be!

And yet, this is the need of the modern church, to repent of their dependence on the things of man, irrespective of how *"good"* it may seem. Regarding Salvation, one's trust must be solely in God.

When both John and Jesus came,

preaching Repentance, the primary thrust of their Message was that Israel repent of their *"goodness"* as well as their *"badness"* (Mat. 3:1-12).

WHAT DO WE MEAN BY REPENTING OF THE GOOD?

We are speaking of anything and everything that we think of as being good, believing that the doing will bring about favor with God. In fact, the thing might be good. To be sure, and sadder still, the modern church is filled with such. The truth is, the modern gospel is almost totally social and humanitarian. Anymore, man's lost condition is no longer mentioned. Sin, Hell, the Judgment, the Cross, and the shed Blood of Christ, are ignored altogether.

The reason?

Man is to be told how good he is, not how bad he is. So, in such an atmosphere, no one is Saved. To be sure, such a preacher is certainly not doing his adherents justice. In fact, he is the worst enemy they will ever encounter.

We as Believers must repent of these good things and of thinking that the doing of them, whatever they might be, brings about closeness with God. It doesn't! There is only one thing that pleases God, only one thing for which He looks, and only one thing on which He has fixed His Eye. That one thing is the Cross of Christ, and we speak of what Jesus there did, which is the atoning for all sin, which totally defeated the powers of darkness.

Sin is the legal right that Satan has to hold man captive. But with all sin atoned, which Jesus did at the Cross, Satan has no more legal right to hold anyone in bondage. If he is able to do so, it is because that mankind in some way gives him consent.

It is very hard for modern man to realize that all of his good works count for nothing in the Eyes of God—and I mean nothing!

SELF-IMPORTANCE

Religious people little mind engaging in all types of works, even at great expense and labor to themselves, because it ministers to their self-importance. As someone has well said, the *"doing"* of religion is the most powerful narcotic there is.

"Good works," within themselves, definitely aren't wrong. It's the dependence we place in these works, making us think that such pleases God, and declares us Righteous before God, etc. As we have stated, it doesn't! Listen carefully to what the Word of God says about this:

"By Faith Enoch was translated that he should not see death *(refers to God transferring Enoch to Heaven in his physical body while he was yet alive)***; and was not found, because God had translated him** *(refers to his translation being well-known at that time)***: for before his translation he had this testimony, that he pleased God.** *(He pleased God because he placed his Faith exclusively in Christ and the Cross.)*

"But without Faith *(in Christ and the Cross; anytime Faith is mentioned, always and without exception, its root meaning is that its Object is Christ and the Cross; otherwise, it is faith God will not accept)* **it is impossible to please** *Him (faith in anything other than Christ and the Cross greatly displeases the Lord)***: for he who comes to God must believe that He is** *(places Faith as the foundation and principle of the manner in which God deals with the human race)***, and** *that* **He** *(God)* **is a rewarder of them who diligently seek Him** *(seek Him on the premise of Christ and Him Crucified, which is our only access to God)***"** (Heb. 11:5-6).

PAUL

"For by Grace *(the Goodness of God)* **are you Saved through Faith** *(Faith in Christ, with the Cross ever as its Object)***; and that not of yourselves** *(none of this is of us, but all is of Him)***: it is the Gift of God** *(anytime the word 'Gift' is used, God is speaking of His Son and His Substitutionary Work on the Cross, which makes all of this possible)***:**

"Not of works *(man cannot merit Salvation, irrespective what he does)***, lest any man should boast** *(boast in his own ability and strength; we are allowed to boast only in the Cross [Gal. 6:14])***.**

"For we are His Workmanship *(if we are God's Workmanship, our Salvation cannot be of ourselves)***, created in Christ Jesus unto good works** *(speaks of the results of*

*Salvation and never the cause)***, which God has before ordained that we should walk in them.** *(The 'good works' the Apostle speaks of has to do with Faith in Christ and the Cross, which enables the Believer to live a Holy Life)***"** (Eph. 2:8-10).

ROMANS

The great Apostle then said:

"Therefore being justified by Faith *(this is the only way one can be justified; refers to Faith in Christ and what He did at the Cross)***, we have peace with God** *(justifying peace)* **through our Lord Jesus Christ** *(what He did at the Cross)***:**

"By Whom also we have access by Faith into this Grace *(we have access to the Goodness of God by Faith in Christ)* **wherein we stand** *(wherein alone we can stand)***, and rejoice in hope** *(a hope that is guaranteed)* **of the Glory of God** *(our Faith in Christ always brings Glory to God; anything else brings glory to self, which God can never accept)***"** (Rom. 5:1-2).

WHY DO WE SAY SO MUCH ABOUT THE CROSS?

The Believer must understand the following:

• Jesus Christ is the Source of all things we receive from God (Jn. 14:6).

• The Cross of Christ is the Means, and the only Means, by which all of these good things are given to us (I Cor. 1:17-18; 2:2; Gal. 6:14).

• Consequently, the Cross of Christ must always be the Object of our Faith (Eph. 2:13-18; Col. 2:14-15).

• Then the Holy Spirit, Who Works exclusively within the parameters of the Finished Work of Christ, can Work mightily on our behalf. It is the Cross of Christ that gives Him the legal right to do all that He does. That's the reason the Cross of Christ must ever be the Object of our Faith (Rom. 8:1-2, 11).

When one understands that every single thing we receive from God is given to us by the Means of the Cross of Christ, then one is beginning to understand the New Covenant, even as it was given to the Apostle Paul.

(4) "I WILL HEAL THEIR BACKSLIDING, I WILL LOVE THEM FREELY: FOR

MY ANGER IS TURNED AWAY FROM HIM.

(5) "I WILL BE AS THE DEW UNTO ISRAEL: HE SHALL GROW AS THE LILY, AND CAST FORTH HIS ROOTS AS LEBANON.

(6) "HIS BRANCHES SHALL SPREAD, AND HIS BEAUTY SHALL BE AS THE OLIVE TREE, AND HIS SMELL AS LEBANON.

(7) "THEY WHO DWELL UNDER HIS SHADOW SHALL RETURN; THEY SHALL REVIVE AS THE CORN, AND GROW AS THE VINE: THE SCENT THEREOF SHALL BE AS THE WINE OF LEBANON.

(8) "EPHRAIM SHALL SAY, WHAT HAVE I TO DO ANY MORE WITH IDOLS? I HAVE HEARD HIM, AND OBSERVED HIM: I AM LIKE A GREEN FIR TREE. FROM ME IS YOUR FRUIT FOUND.

(9) "WHO IS WISE, AND HE SHALL UNDERSTAND THESE THINGS? PRUDENT, AND HE SHALL KNOW THEM? FOR THE WAYS OF THE LORD ARE RIGHT, AND THE JUST SHALL WALK IN THEM: BUT THE TRANSGRESSORS SHALL FALL THEREIN."

The pattern is:

1. (Vs. 4) The Divine response of Verses 4 through 8 exhibits the moral result of true Conversion.

2. The *"dew"* of Verse 5 speaks of the Holy Spirit, the *"lily"* speaks of Righteousness, and the *"roots of Lebanon"* speak of one's place and position in Christ. All of this awaits the believing sinner!

3. The phrase of Verse 6, *"His branches shall spread,"* speaks of Spiritual Growth. *"And his beauty shall be as the olive tree"* speaks of *"fruit."* The phrase, *"And his smell as Lebanon,"* proclaims the fact that certain types of trees emit aromas which repel all insects and reptiles. Spiritually, it speaks of protection from the powers of darkness by Faith in Christ and His Cross (Rom. 6:3-5).

4. Verse 7 speaks of Israel restored and now reigning supreme in the coming Kingdom Age, which proclaims the fact that these ancient people will not be destroyed but will one day fulfill that which God has all along intended for them.

5. Verse 8 may be thus displayed:

Ephraim, *"What have I to do any more with idols?"*

Immanuel, *"I have heard him and observed him."*

Ephraim, *"I am like a green fir tree."*

Immanuel, *"Yes, but remember that from Me is your fruit found."*

The question concerning Ephraim, *"What have I to do any more with idols?"* is a full, final, and forever renunciation of idolatry.

6. Verse 9 forms the epilogue to the whole Prophecy. God's Way of Salvation is a stepping stone to the Believer but a stumbling stone to the unbeliever. Christ is a Rock of defense to the one but a Rock of offense to the other (I Cor. 1:23).

I WILL HEAL THEIR BACKSLIDING

The following great and glorious Blessings given by the Lord could have been had by Israel at the time of Hosea's Message, or any time previously. However, it was rejected, but yet, will be accepted in the coming Kingdom Age.

As well, these Divine Promises given to Israel of old apply to any and all who will respond accordingly. The following is what the Lord says He will do for those who meet His Conditions. They are as follows:

• *"I will heal their backsliding."*
• *"I will love them freely."*
• *"For My Anger is turned away from him."*

BACKSLIDING

The word *"backsliding"* refers to apostasy and idolatry.

In the New Testament, this refers to being *"turned away from the Truth, and being turned unto fables"* (II Tim. 4:4).

Many claim that inasmuch as the word *"backsliding"* or *"backslider"* does not appear in the New Testament, that such, under the New Covenant, is not possible. However, the word not being mentioned does not abrogate the principle thereof.

In the Old Testament, *"backsliding"* referred to disloyalty to the Covenant relationship and involved a refusal to live by the terms of that Covenant.

The same principle that held true for the Covenant of the Old Testament applies to the Covenant of the New Testament, commonly referred to as the *"New Covenant"* or the *"New Testament."*

In Paul's second Letter to the church at Corinth, at least of those we have a record, he admonished the Believers to *"not be unequally yoked together with unbelievers"* (II Cor. 6:14-18). Consequently, to do so would constitute an abrogation of the New Covenant and, in principle, could be classified as *"backsliding."*

As well, the Words of Christ to the church at Ephesus, *"Nevertheless I have somewhat against you, because you have left your first love"* (Rev. 2:4), definitely constitute *"backsliding."* Even though the word is not used, still, the principle is strongly implied. Consequently, too many churches are filled with backsliders, even though they do not think of themselves as such.

BACKSLIDING AND THE CROSS OF CHRIST

I think one can say without fear of contradiction that *"backsliding"* under the New Covenant, and it would have basically been the same under the Old Covenant, constitutes the Believer ceasing to believe. And what do we mean by that?

If the individual no longer believes that the Cross of Christ is the Means, and the only Means, by which the Lord gives all things to us, but rather transfers his faith to something else, this constitutes *"backsliding."*

Paul also said, *"Now the Spirit speaks expressly, that in the latter times some shall depart from the Faith, giving heed to seducing spirits, and doctrines of devils"* (I Tim. 4:1).

Any doctrine that pulls one away from the Cross of Christ can be labeled as none other than *"doctrines of demons."* Unfortunately, the land is presently full of such!

If it is to be noticed, every time there is true Revival, the Church finds itself at the foot of the Cross. In other words, for Revival to be brought about, the Holy Spirit must bring the Believer to the Cross. There is no other way! That being the case, it should tell us several things!

I WILL LOVE THEM FREELY

The love that is here freely promised can only be given upon the forgiveness spoken of,

which is tendered upon proper Repentance. The phrase means, *"Without a just cause."*

This means that such Love has its Source and Cause in God Alone, which, as well, speaks of the Cross. The Scripture still says, *"For God so loved the world that He gave . . ."* (Jn. 3:16). This Love is predicated totally upon God and none upon the recipient; consequently, this type of Love cannot respond to self-righteousness in any form. It is based solely upon the Grace of God and not the merit of man.

Whenever such true Repentance is engaged, the Lord promises favor as well as forgiveness so as to heal the moral malady under which one had long labored, and to remember the evil effects of one's apostasy and withhold the stripes He was going to inflict.

Going back to the Word, *"heal their backsliding,"* such means that the disease will be healed and its consequences averted.

Tragically, the majority of the modern church little practices God's Forgiveness and Love, even upon proper Biblical Repentance. Instead, it desires, in many cases, to demand and continue punishment. Such, in a sense, is a form of Catholic penance and, thereby, portrays a complete denial of the Grace of God or else, a misunderstanding of this most important principle of Biblical Christianity.

THE TURNING AWAY OF ANGER

Upon proper Repentance, the Lord has promised to turn His Anger away. This means that all punishment stops and all Judgment forestalled.

These phrases have to do with God's Righteousness in that, inasmuch as His Righteousness demands Judgment upon unconfessed and, thereby, unrepentant sin, likewise, the same Righteousness, upon proper Repentance, demands all Judgment to be stopped, with Blessing immediately taking its place.

Therefore, in these few words, the Holy Spirit through the great Prophet Hosea gives such grand Promises as to defy all description. As much as the scholar attempts to elucidate them, still, he falls so far short of that which is offered in these Passages.

The only thing that will cause God's Anger against an individual, or nation, is sin.

Proper Repentance turns that anger away.

As well, and by now, it should be concluded that God definitely does express *"anger."* However, it is no capricious thing, nor is it expressed in temper tantrums. God's Anger is always provoked. It is His Righteous Response to specific human failures and sin.

THE ANGER OF GOD

Knowing God's Moral Character, His People could avoid His Anger by being obedient to the Covenant in which He carefully defines right and wrong.

The Old Testament shows that the Lord is Angry when He is not trusted (Ex. 4:14), when His People complain against Him (Num. 11:1-33; 12:9), when He is disobeyed (Num. 32:10), and particularly when He is rejected in favor of idols (Ex. 32:7-12; Num. 25:3; Deut. 11:16-17).

God's Anger is a measured response to sin.

As well, God's Anger expresses itself in rebuke and discipline, so, consequently, it is positive rather than negative (Ps. 6:1; 38:1; 78:31-38).

However, the Bible does not present anger as an essential Characteristic of God. In fact, God's Wrath is set aside when God forgives (Ps. 85:2-3), and, as this Passage proclaims, even His Acts of Anger show restraint (Ps. 78:38). Compared to His Favor, which lasts a lifetime, God's Anger is momentary (Ps. 30:5). God intends only good to humanity, and when it is necessary to act in anger, the intention to do good is never lost.

RIGHTEOUS ANGER

The Bible's positive view of God's Anger brings us to the concept of righteous anger. God's Anger is righteous in several senses. It is provoked only by sin. It is expressed with only good in mind. And, strikingly, the Bible insists that God's Anger is never a controlling element in His Choices.

Conversely, it is impossible for human beings to exhibit righteous anger because in us anger tends to dominate and to control.

Exodus 34:6-7 describes God in this way:

"The LORD, the LORD God, the Compassionate and Gracious God, slow to anger, abounding in Love and Faithfulness,

maintaining Love to thousands, and forgiving wickedness, rebellion and sin. Yet He does not leave the guilty unpunished."

This significant statement places anger in a distinctive relationship with other qualities of the Lord. He is compassionate, gracious, loving, faithful, forgiving, and just. God's Anger never dominates to the extent that these other character traits no longer function. Consequently, God's Anger is always in harmony with His Compassion, Grace, Love, Faithfulness, Eagerness to forgive, and Commitment to do justice. Actually, some nine times in the Old Testament we are reminded that God is *"slow to anger"* (Ex. 34:6; Num. 14:18; Neh. 9:17; Ps. 86:15; 103:8; 145:8; Joel 2:13; Jonah 4:2; Nah. 1:3).

THE DIFFERENCES IN EMPHASIS REGARDING THE OLD AND NEW TESTAMENTS

Although the Old and New Testaments are consistent in viewpoint concerning anger, there are differences in emphasis. In the Old Testament, God's Anger is linked with violations of the Covenant relationship. Thus, the Jewish people are often the objects of His Wrath. But, in the New Testament, God's Wrath is focused on those who will not believe; however, in the final analysis, the end results are the same in both cases. *"Unbelief"* is basically the cause of all sin, whether under the Old or New Covenants.

It is argued by some that God's Anger, at least under the New Covenant, is directed only at those who refuse to respond to the Gospel.

They say that Believers are assured that *"since we have now been justified by His Blood, how much more shall we be Saved from God's Wrath through Him!"* (Rom. 5:9).

While this is certainly true in the final analysis, as God's Wrath against sin was directed at Christ's Self-Sacrifice at Calvary instead of the Believer, still, God's Attitude toward unrepentant sin does not change, irrespective of the Old Covenant or the New. David said, *". . . God is angry with the wicked everyday"* (Ps. 7:11). This actually means that He is angry not only with the *"wicked"* but with *"wickedness"* as well! Actually, God's Attitude toward sin does not change irrespective in whom sin abides.

Paul plainly spoke to *"followers of God"* (Eph. 5:1) and directed attention to various sins, and then said, *"Let no man deceive you with vain words: for because of these things comes the Wrath of God upon the children of disobedience"* (Eph. 5:1-6).

THE WRATH OF GOD

Paul did not say, as some claim, that such *"Wrath"* only came on unbelievers but not on Believers! Actually, he plainly states the opposite in that unconfessed and unrepented sin, irrespective in whom it dwells, will ultimately experience the Wrath of God.

So, to say that God's Anger against sin is exemplified in the Old Testament only is erroneous.

It is argued that the Lord only disciplines believing men and women, and that discipline is an expression of love, not of anger.

While it is certainly true that God definitely does discipline His Children (Heb. 12:6), still, according to Paul's writings, wrath will definitely come upon those who sin with impudence and refuse to repent.

It is true, as Paul says, that *"God has not appointed us to wrath . . ."* (I Thess. 5:9). Still, this Passage has no reference to unconfessed sin in one's life, but instead, to the coming Great Tribulation, as the entirety of this Chapter does through Verse 11 (I Thess. 5:1-11).

Paul spoke of Believers, who involve themselves in sin and refuse to repent, as *"children of disobedience."* As such, they can expect the *"Wrath of God"* (Eph. 5:6).

"I will be as the dew unto Israel":

• Redeemed Israel will be comparable to the *"lily"* for beauty.

• The *"cedar of Lebanon"* for strength.

• The *"olive"* for fruitfulness.

Her fragrance shall be as Lebanon itself; but all of this beauty, perfume, strength, and fruitfulness will be produced by the *"dew"* of Divine Grace, i.e., *"the Holy Spirit."*

In lands where there is little rain, the *"dew"* falling copiously fertilizes the earth, refreshes the languid plants, revives the face of nature, and makes all things grow. Thus, the *"dew"* becomes the source of fruitfulness. So God, by His Spirit's Grace, is the

Source of Israel's Spiritual Fruitfulness.

THE LILY

The phrase *"He shall grow as the lily,"* speaks of purity and beauty.

The *"lily"* is beautiful and, as well, extremely productive, inasmuch as a single root can produce some fifty bulbs. But still, its root is weak and, thereby, the next phrase.

"And cast forth his roots as Lebanon" implies that the *"lily"* will not have weak roots as normal, but will rather have *"roots"* as the great cedars of Lebanon. Regarding these trees, they strike their roots as far down into the depths as they lift their heads up into the air. Therefore, they cannot be shaken by storm, and their stability is here proclaimed.

All of this will Israel be upon coming to the Lord, which will take place in the coming Kingdom Age.

As well, and even at the risk of repetition, such can be any individual who places his trust wholly in the Lord.

THE SPREAD, THE BEAUTY, THE AROMA

The word *"spread"* speaks of both Spiritual Growth and material growth. In the coming Kingdom Age, and this pertains to that time, the boundaries of Israel will be what God promised Abraham some 4,000 years ago. He said:

"In the same day the LORD made a Covenant with Abram, saying, Unto your seed have I given this land, from the river of Egypt unto the great river, the river Euphrates" (Gen. 15:18). This will be fulfilled in the coming Kingdom Age. The territory will extend to the west to the Mediterranean Sea. On the south it will extend to the *"river of Egypt."* There has been disagreement among scholars as to exactly what the *"river of Egypt"* actually meant. I personally feel that it includes the entirety of the Sinai, extended to the Gulf of Suez. It will also include the Arabian Peninsula, which includes Saudi Arabia, Yemen, Southern Yemen, Oman, United Arab Emirates, Qatar, and Kuwait.

As it regards the Euphrates, this area includes about half of Iraq and almost all of Syria plus Lebanon. As stated, this will be realized in the coming Kingdom Age when Jesus rules supreme over the entirety of the world. The land area in question is almost half the size of the United States. Even though a great part of that area is now desert, Isaiah tells us that in the coming Kingdom Age, it will blossom as the rose (Isa. 35:1). So, the little word *"spread"* carries a phenomenal meaning. As we stated, the *"spread"* will begin Spiritually and then will spread to the material, etc.

Whenever and wherever the Gospel of Jesus Christ has sway, everything changes for the better, a thousand times over. Israel will then have accepted Jesus Christ as her Messiah, her Saviour, and her Lord, knowing that the One they crucified was indeed their Messiah.

THE GENTILE NATIONS AND ISRAEL

The phrase, *"His branches shall spread, and his beauty shall be as the olive tree,"* has to do with the Gentile nations that were always intended by God to dwell under Israel's beneficent shadow, and that they shall in the coming Kingdom Age. In fact, at that time, Israel will, once again, be the predominant Nation in the world. To be sure, her Power and glory will little pertain to great military preparation, if at all, but rather to her Messiah, the Lord Jesus Christ.

Israel, in that day, will be *"beautiful"* and is compared to an *"olive tree."* Her *"beauty"* will consist totally of the Righteousness of Christ, which now dwells in her. It is elsewhere called, *"the beauty of Holiness"* (Ps. 29:2).

The *"olive tree"* has been called the crown of the fruit trees of Israel. Its foliage makes it a vivid picture of the *"beauty of Holiness,"* or Spiritual Grace.

As well, its longevity, of which some are as much as 2,000 years old, here speaks of Israel's endurance, and because of the Promises of the Lord.

HIS SMELL AS LEBANON

The phrase, *"And his smell as Lebanon,"* refers to the giant cedars of Lebanon and the *"smell they produced,"* which made them pretty much insect and reptile free. In other words, noxious insects, such as mosquitoes,

gnats, etc., and, as well, poisonous snakes do not reside in the vicinity of this *"smell."*

Consequently, what is evil to these insects and reptiles is pleasant to all human habitation. Hence, the building of cedar closets in modern homes in order to keep out moths, termites, and other insects.

The Spiritual application is that the person properly in Christ is protected from the spirits of darkness. The aroma from the Lord repels these evil spirits.

UNDER HIS SHADOW

"They who dwell under His Shadow shall return," as well, speaks of the Gentile nations, even as Verse 6. These nations, which will include the balance of the world, will draw sustenance from Israel, who will then truly be the People of God. The nations of the world will then gladly run to her side because of her Glory, which is Christ.

This refers to what Israel was supposed to have been at the beginning, *"A light to lighten the Gentiles, and the glory of Your People Israel"* (Lk. 2:32). Tragically, they failed, and the world was thrown into that which is called *"the times of the Gentiles"* (Lk. 21:24). During this some 2,500 years, and even longer, which have already passed, the world has known little prosperity. It has rather known war, bloodshed, hate, privation, and want. Consequently, this Passage, plus many others, tells us that the nations of the world will never really know prosperity until Israel is fully restored, and the Promises of God made to the Patriarchs of old finally realized. When this glorious moment arrives, as surely it shall, the next phrases tell us what will then take place in the world.

THEY SHALL REVIVE AS THE CORN, AND GROW AS THE VINE

Paul alluded to the *"corn"* and the *"vine"* when he said, *"Now if the fall of them (Israel) be the riches of the world, and the diminishing of them the riches of the Gentiles; how much more their fulness?"* (Rom. 11:12).

Hosea is speaking of the nations of the world residing *"under his shadow,"* referring to Israel.

The word, *"revive,"* speaks of the seed being buried and upon the Advent of the *"dew"* spoken of in Verse 5, the blade springs forth as a healthy plant. It speaks of the Gentile nations and proclaims that they will *"grow as the vine,"* of which there is little limitation as to how long it will actually grow.

Such speaks of the prosperity of Gentile nations, as the Lord originally intended, because, at long last, Israel is in her place as the leader of the world, with the Gentile nations recognizing her as such because of the tremendous prosperity on all accounts enjoyed. As stated, the reason for Israel's prosperity, as well as the entirety of the world, is Christ.

The word, *"corn,"* actually refers to *"a corn of wheat,"* or barley, and not to corn as it's presently known in America and the other parts of the world. Corn, at least as we know it, was not grown in Europe, Asia, or the Middle East at that particular time, and was only introduced by the Indians in North America in the 1600's, when it was then introduced to Europe as well.

THE SCENT AS THE WINE OF LEBANON

This particular *"wine"* was actually used for medicinal purposes and is here intended; consequently, the meaning has to do with the healing of the nations inasmuch as Israel is now healed. So, because Israel's backslidings are *"healed,"* likewise, the result of that *"backsliding,"* i.e., the darkness of the nations, will likewise be healed.

IDOLATRY

The question concerning Ephraim, *"What have I to do anymore with idols?"* is a full, final, and forever denunciation of idolatry. The Words of the Lord, concerning His Answer to Ephraim's question, *"I have heard him, and observed him,"* refers to the Lord fixing His Eye on Israel in order to look after him, care for him, provide for him, and to protect and prosper him.

While it is true, regarding Israel's statement, *"I am like a green fir tree,"* still, though the fir tree is ever green, it is fruitless. As such, it must look to the Lord constantly in order to be fruitful. He will then prove, as we have stated, that He is the Source and can supply all that His People

shall or can ever need.

The *"fruit"* here *"found"* will be not only enough for Israel but, in truth, for the entirety of the world, for such is Christ!

The phrase, *"From Me is your fruit found,"* applies to Jesus as *"the True Vine, and My Father is the Husbandman"* (Jn. 15:1).

As such, He said, *"Abide in Me, and I in you. As the branch cannot bear fruit of itself, except it abide in the Vine; no more can you, except you abide in Me"* (Jn. 15:4).

WHO IS WISE?

The question, *"Who is wise?"* refers to those who know and follow the Bible and, therefore, the Lord. Otherwise, *"he shall not understand these things."*

The Holy Spirit through the Prophet emphatically, and even dogmatically, makes the statement, *"for the Ways of the LORD are right, and the just shall walk in them."*

What are the Ways of the Lord?

It is the Bible! Consequently, every Christian ought to make the Bible his life's work. If he does so, he will find that the Spirit of the Book, which is the Holy Spirit, will cause these Divine Promises, as well as warnings and admonitions, to increasingly live in the hearts and lives of all Believers.

In other words, it is not possible for one to be *"righteous"* or *"just"* outside of the teaching of the Bible and, as well, to know its Author.

TRANSGRESSORS AND TRANSGRESSIONS

The phrase, *"But the transgressors shall fall therein,"* simply speaks of unbelief. The Promises, at least in this Prophecy, are two-fold. They are as follows:

1. The Holy Spirit through the Prophet grandly proclaims the restoration of Israel, which is already in the making. But sadly, much of the church disbelieves these great Promises, claiming they have already been rejected by Israel in the Crucifixion of Christ.

While it is certainly true that they were rejected during Hosea's time, as well as thereafter, still, they will ultimately be realized.

The Holy Spirit calls those who will not believe this, *"transgressors,"* and, consequently, *"shall fall therein."*

2. These Great Promises could also be applied to any individual who dares to follow *"the Ways of the Lord."* Even though they apply to Israel as a Nation, still, in the Spiritual sense, they, as well, can apply to every Believer. To not believe this labels one a *"transgressor"* and will, sadly, ensure a *"fall."*

As Paul said, *". . . for I believe God, that it shall be even as it was told me"* (Acts 27:25).

"I'll tell to all that God is Love;
"For the world has never known,
"The great Compassion of His Heart,
"For the wayward and the lone."

"I'll tell of Mercy's boundless tide,
"Like the waters of the sea,
"That covers every sin of man;
"'Tis Salvation full and free."

"I'll tell of Grace that keeps the soul,
"Of abiding peace within,
"Of Faith that overcomes the world,
"With its tumult and its din."

"Eternal Glory is the goal,
"That awaits the sons of light;
"Eternal darkness, black as death,
"For the children of the night."

BIBLIOGRAPHY

CHAPTER 5
Martin & Deidre Bobgan, *The Spiritual Way,* Bethany House Publishers, 1981.
John Calvin, *Calvin's Bible Commentaries: Hosea,* Forgotten Books, 2007 (reprint), pg. 182.

CHAPTER 8
C.H. Dodd, *The Epistle of Paul to the Romans,* MNTC, 1932, pg. 50.

CHAPTER 12
C.H. Mackintosh, *Notes on the Pentateuch: Notes on Leviticus,* Neptune, New Jersey, Loizeaux Brothers, 1972, pgs. 388-389.

CHAPTER 14
Martin & Deidre Bobgan, *How to counsel from Scripture,* Chicago, Moody Press, 1985, pg. 12.

NOTES

REFERENCE BOOKS

Atlas Of The Bible — Rogerson
Expository Dictionary of Bible Words — L.O. Richards
Matthew Henry Commentary On The Holy Bible — Matthew Henry
New Bible Dictionary — Tyndale
Strong's Exhaustive Concordance Of The Bible
The Complete Word Study Dictionary
The Essential Writings — Josephus
The Interlinear Greek — English New Testament — George Ricker Berry
The International Standard Bible Encyclopedia
The Pulpit Commentary — H.D.M. Spence
The Student's Commentary On The Holy Scriptures — George Williams
The Zondervan Pictorial Encyclopedia Of The Bible
Vine's Expository Dictionary Of New Testament Words
Webster's New Collegiate Dictionary
Word Studies In The Greek New Testament, Volume I — Kenneth S. Wuest
Young's Literal Translation Of The Holy Bible

THE
BOOK OF JOEL

—■—

INTRODUCTION

The Book of Joel is referred to by Pentecostals as the Holy Spirit Book of the Old Testament, for it was in these Prophecies that Joel predicted the coming outpouring of the Holy Spirit. Even though other Prophets mentioned the Holy Spirit in this capacity, still, it was Joel who Peter quoted on the Day of Pentecost.

Therefore, that which multiple millions have enjoyed since the Day of Pentecost, the Mighty Baptism with the Holy Spirit, was foretold by this Prophet. What a privilege to study the times in which he lived as well as the events that occasioned this great Prophecy.

THE MINISTRY OF JOEL

Of course this, the Baptism with the Holy Spirit, is not the only Prophecy in Joel. He preached to guilty Judah, while Hosea preached to guilty Israel.

Even though the exact time of Joel's Ministry is not known, it is believed that he may have ministered approximately 80 years after Hosea.

Hosea's contemporaries were Jonah, Amos, Isaiah, Micah, and Nahum. Their ministries preceded the captivity of the Ten Tribes.

If our summation is correct concerning the time of Joel's Ministry, his contemporaries were Jeremiah, Habakkuk, Zephaniah, Daniel, Ezekiel, and probably Obadiah. Their ministries accompanied the overthrow of the throne of David and the captivity of the Two Tribes.

As well, and as alluded to, the Prophecy of Joel is undated, for it is general. It covers

NOTES

the period of the *"times of the Gentiles,"* that is, from Nebuchadnezzar to the Antichrist. Hence, the Prophecy speaks of the Temple and its Levitical worship but makes no mention of a king.

TIME

It is January 22, 2010, as I begin work on the Commentary respecting this great Book.

I am elated and thankful to the Lord for the positive response forthcoming as it regards the Commentaries. If there is good and that which is beneficial, we give the praise and glory to the Lord.

The study of the Word of God is the most profitable study in the world. The Bible is far and away the greatest help to mankind of anything that's ever been written simply because it is the Word of God. And, I might quickly add, irrespective of the claims, there is no other Word of God anywhere in the world. After reading behind some of the greatest Bible scholars of the recent past and surveying their exhaustive research, I realize that when one holds the King James Version of the Bible in one's hand, one can be absolutely certain that what he is holding is the Word of God.

UNDERSTANDING THE WORD OF GOD

Considering the value of the Word of God, one must make it a lifelong project as it regards the study of its contents. Nothing could ever be more profitable. Therefore, Books, such as this one held in your hands, which, hopefully, helps one to understand the Word of God a little better, are valuable assets and should be utilized!

REVELATION

In 1997, after some two prayer meetings a day for six years, the Lord opened up to me a greater understanding of the New Covenant as it was given to the Apostle Paul. It has revolutionized my life and Ministry. It is the Message of the Cross. I believe that this, the Message of the Cross, is what the Spirit is presently saying to the churches. Throughout this Volume, you will find us alluding to this great Truth.

As it regards the Holy Spirit, of which the Prophecy of Joel is famous, the great Truth that the Lord gave me, as it regards how the Holy Spirit Works, will be included in this Volume. Once you read it, you will see its simplicity. And yet, it is little known in the church world, if any at all, despite the fact that the Apostle Paul gave it to us nearly 2,000 years ago. If one doesn't know how the Holy Spirit Works within one's life, then one is going to miss so much for which Jesus paid such a price.

Please allow me to conclude this Introduction with an ultra brief account of what the Lord gave to the Apostle Paul, and which we will, no doubt, print again as the occasion arises.

• FOCUS: The Lord Jesus Christ (Jn. 1:1-2, 14, 29; 14:6).

• OBJECT OF FAITH: The Cross of Christ (Rom. 6:1-14; I Cor. 1:17-18, 23; 2:2; Gal. 6:14).

• POWER SOURCE: The Holy Spirit (Rom. 8:1-2, 11).

• RESULTS: Victory (Rom. 6:14; Gal. 2:20-21).

"Father, I know that all my life,
"Is portioned out for me,
"The changes that will surely come,
"I do not fear to see;
"I ask You for a present mind,
"Intent on pleasing Thee."

"I ask You for a thoughtful love,
"Through constant watching wise,
"To meet the glad with joyful smiles,
"And wipe the weeping eyes;
"A heart at leisure from itself,
"To soothe and sympathize."

"I would not have the restless will,

"That hurries to and fro.
"That seeks for some great thing to do,
"Or secret thing to know;
"I would be treated as a child,
"And guided where I go."

"Wherever in the world I am,
"In whatsoever state,
"I have a fellowship with hearts,
"To keep and cultivate;
"A work of lowly love to do,
"For Him on Whom I wait."

"I ask You for the daily strength,
"To none that ask denied;
"A mind to blend without outward life,
"While keeping at Your Side;
"Content to fill a little space,
"If You be glorified."

"In service which Your Love appoints,
"There are no bonds for me;
"My secret heart is taught the truth,
"That makes Your Children free:
"A life of self-renouncing love,
"Is one of liberty."

CHAPTER 1

(1) "THE WORD OF THE LORD THAT CAME TO JOEL THE SON OF PETHUEL.

(2) "HEAR THIS, YOU OLD MEN, AND GIVE EAR, ALL YOU INHABITANTS OF THE LAND. HAS THIS BEEN IN YOUR DAYS, OR EVEN IN THE DAYS OF YOUR FATHERS?

(3) "TELL YOU YOUR CHILDREN OF IT, AND LET YOUR CHILDREN TELL THEIR CHILDREN, AND THEIR CHILDREN ANOTHER GENERATION.

(4) "THAT WHICH THE PALMERWORM HAS LEFT HAS THE LOCUST EATEN; AND THAT WHICH THE LOCUST HAS LEFT HAS THE CANKERWORM EATEN; AND THAT WHICH THE CANKERWORM HAS LEFT HAS THE CATERPILLAR EATEN."

The exegesis is:

1. The phrase of Verse 1, *"The Word of the LORD,"* signifies that this Prophecy was not originated by Joel. God composed it and

gave it to him, as to all the Prophets of the Old Testament and Apostles of the New.

2. (Vs. 1) This Prophecy of Joel is undated, for it is general. It covers the period of the *"times of the Gentiles,"* that is, from Nebuchadnezzar to the Antichrist. Hence, it speaks of the Temple and its Levitical worship but makes no mention of a king.

3. (Vs. 1) The name *"Joel"* means *"Jehovah is God."*

Even though the exact time of Joel's Ministry is not known, it is believed that he ministered shortly before Jeremiah.

4. The idea of Verse 2 is that the Judgments to come would be so exceptional as to be without previous experience.

5. The manner in which the solemn announcement of Verse 3 is given, i.e., using the phraseology in the Second Verse, *"Hear this"* and *"give ear,"* is meant to impress upon the hearers the significance of the Message delivered. The coming Judgment is proclaimed, along with the sin that caused it, together with a plea for Repentance, and is meant to speak to every generation, etc.

6. (Vs. 4) At the time this Prophecy was given by God to Joel, quite possibly Judah was utterly devastated and ruined by a plague of locusts. This fact was used to illustrate the Divine Judgments that were about to be inflicted upon the land, which would have their climax in the dread *"Day of the LORD"* at the close of Judah's history. These Judgments, as previously stated, would be so exceptional as to be without previous experience, and all because of sin!

THE WORD OF THE LORD

The *"Word"* here addressed is that which we presently have and is referred to as *"The Book of Joel."*

There is nothing in the world more important than the Word of God. Every Believer should, with all diligence, make every effort to understand that which the Lord has given us. The Bible is the road map for life and living and the blueprint for eternity. I might quickly add, it is the only road map and the only blueprint; there is no other.

That's the reason that we strongly encourage Believers to secure for themselves a copy of THE EXPOSITOR'S STUDY BIBLE. We believe that it's the finest tool that could be placed into the hands of Believers to help them properly understand the Word of God. Anything that will do that, anything that will open up the Word more clearly, and anything that will shed more light on this all-important subject, proverbially speaking, is worth its weight in gold and much, much more!

The Lord began dealing with me back in the 1980's to develop a Study Bible. Looking back, I know that He did not intend for me to do it then, but, nevertheless, He planted the seed in my heart.

At first, I ignored what the Holy Spirit was saying to me because of a variety of reasons. I felt and, in fact, was totally inadequate for such a task. But, looking back, the Lord did not desire that which literary skill could give, but rather what He could give.

Feeling the push of this in my spirit, I began to look at the manner in which other Study Bibles were put together and really did not like anything I saw. That statement refers to the layout alone and not the material involved. In fact, there is some excellent material in other Study Bibles.

Looking back, I realize that the Lord did not desire that I develop this Bible until the Revelation of the Cross was given to me, which took place in 1997. I came to find out that without a proper knowledge of the Cross, one cannot properly understand the Word of God as one should.

THE LORD GAVE DIRECTION

If I remember the year correctly, it was 2004. I was working on one of the Commentaries. I began to dissect Scriptures, endeavoring to make them easier to understand, when the Spirit of the Lord spoke to my heart and said to me, *"This is the way that I want you to do this Bible."*

I had no doubt that the Lord had spoken to me. I also knew that my complaints had just been brushed aside.

• The Lord had told me to do this.

• The Lord had now shown me how to do it.

• And now the Lord would help me to do it.

NOTES

THE NEW TESTAMENT

We did the New Testament first. Despite what the Lord had said to me, not one time but many times, I was still somewhat skeptical.

How would it be received?

Would it really meet the need at hand of helping people to more properly understand the Word of God?

If I remember correctly, when I finished the New Testament, we printed 20,000 copies. Once again if I remember correctly, those 20,000 copies were gone in little more than a month.

I had immediately gone to work on the Old Testament, working almost day and night. As I would study the proofs, making corrections, etc., I could sense the Presence of the Lord. I related to Frances any number of times that I believed the Lord was going to use this Effort to help His People more properly understand the Word of God. So, when I say that the Lord told me to do this, showed me how to do it, and then helped me to do it, that's exactly what happened!

In 2005, the entirety of THE EXPOSITOR'S STUDY BIBLE was completed. To date (January, 2010), counting the New Testaments, which number about 100,000, we have sold some 600,000 copies. It has proven to be, and is proving to be, exactly as I felt the Lord told me it would be, a tool to help people understand the Word of God to a greater degree. And, as we have previously stated, anything that does that, give one a clearer picture of the Word, is valuable indeed!

A TREMENDOUS DEFENSE AGAINST APOSTASY

I personally believe that THE EXPOSITOR'S STUDY BIBLE, which is orthodox from Genesis through the Book of Revelation, is one of the greatest tools of defense against false doctrine in the world today.

At this particular time, Satan is, I believe, making his greatest attack against the Word of God; however, he is doing it in a different way, I think, than ever before. Instead of denying the Word of God as he generally does, he is seeking to pervert the Word of

NOTES

God, to shade its meaning, in fact, to rob it of its meaning. What do I mean by that?

I speak of so-called Bibles, such as the *"Message Bible,"* and scores similar, which, in reality, are not Bibles at all, but rather religious books. Please note the following:

A WORD FOR WORD TRANSLATION

If the Believer doesn't have a word for word translation of the Bible, such as the King James, then one really doesn't have a Bible. These books, which I've just mentioned, are thought for thought translations, even if they rise to that level. As such, the meaning of the Word of God has been robbed. The reason I say that Satan is making his greatest effort at this time is simply because these hybrid Bibles, if one could refer to them as Bibles, fall into that category.

WHAT IS A WORD FOR WORD TRANSLATION?

The statement means that the scholars, Hebrew for the Old Testament and Greek for the New, did their very best to give an exact word for word translation of that which was originally given in the Hebrew and the Greek. As most know, the Old Testament was originally written in Hebrew with the New Testament originally written in Greek. If that is not done, then one does not have a true picture of the Word of God.

LANGUAGES

Even though the King James translation is all that I use, still, it must be understood that while the Word of God itself is inspired, meaning it is error free, the translations are not inspired. While I believe the King James scholars did the very best they could to bring the Hebrew and Greek over into English without losing any of its meaning, still, translations are not inspired. Let me add another word about the King James!

It may come as a shock to most Christians, especially those who love the King James as I do, that Elizabethan English, such as *"thee,"* *"thou,"* and *"hast,"* etc., were not used by the Prophets of old or the Apostles of the New. Those are Old English words, which are no longer used even today in the English language. Some Christians erroneously think that when Jesus spoke, He used *"Elizabethan words,"* and, as well, when the Apostles wrote Matthew, Mark, Luke, and John, they wrote His Words in red. They didn't! That is silly. There wasn't even any red ink in those days.

The Words of Christ in red are no more than a marketing ploy that was used by individuals to help sell Bibles, which took place at about the turn of the Twentieth Century.

MANUSCRIPTS

As well, Manuscripts, as should be obvious, played the all-important part in Biblical translation. So, it must be said that there are no Original Manuscripts left of the Word of God because of the passing of time, etc. But yet, there are untold thousands of copies and fragments of Books of both the Old and the New Testaments that are presently available. Some of the New Testament copies of the Scriptures go back to a little under 200 years from the time the Original Manuscript was written. So, in doing translation work, the editors have to do their best to ascertain which Manuscript is the best because sometimes they may differ to a slight degree. Let me give you an example:

REVELATION 22:14

The Scripture listed in the heading is given in the King James Bible as, *"Blessed are they who do His Commandments, that they may have the right to the Tree of Life, and may enter in through the gates into the city"* (Rev. 22:14).

Now let's look at the notes from THE EXPOSITOR'S STUDY BIBLE as given with these phrases in this particular Scripture. I quote verbatim:

"Blessed *are* **they** (presents the seventh and last Beatitude in the Book of Revelation) **who do His Commandments** (should have been translated, 'who washed their robes in the Blood of the Lamb'; the Greek Text used for the King James Version of the Bible was the Textus Receptus; it is the Text that Erasmus, the famous Renaissance scholar, published in A.D. 1516; it was the first New Testament Greek Text ever published; since 1516, the world of scholarship and archeology has discovered thousands of earlier

Greek Texts; by comparing these thousands of Manuscripts, the scholars can easily ascertain the Original Text the Apostle wrote*), **that they may have the right to the Tree of Life** (proclaims the fact that this 'right' can be attained in only one way, 'by washing our robes in the Blood of the Lamb'*), **and may enter in through the gates into the city** (proclaims the Eternal abode of the Redeemed; we shall enter that city by means of His Grace, which is the Cross of Christ*)" **(Rev. 22:14).**

Now, as stated in the notes, the King James translators of nearly 500 years ago used the best copies, which were available at that time. But since then, copies have been found that are more true to the Original Manuscript as written by John the Beloved. Incidentally, there are some 24,000 copies of New Testament Books or fragments of Books, which have been discovered, some of them going back, as stated, to a little under 200 years after the Original was penned by the Apostles. As it regards the Old Testament, many copies of those Volumes exist, as well, such as the Dead Sea Scrolls, etc.

Scholarship states that if there are ten copies in existence of any Original, even though the Original may be lost, the veracity of the Manuscript in question is recognized. In fact, there are more copies of the Word of God in existence than any other literary effort. So, when you hold the King James Version in your hands, you can be doubly certain that you are holding the Word of God.

GIVE EAR

As it regards Verse 2, in that day and time, events of the past were handed down from generation to generation, even with the exact detail memorized as to the accuracy of the Account. This Prophecy is so important that Joel insists that its Message be handed down to the coming generations. The calamity predicted would be so great that such would be unknown in the memory of living men or unheard of in the days of their fathers. As such, it would be unparalleled in the past experience of their Nation.

The question, *"Has this been in your days, or even in the days of your fathers?"* in effect, asks that they recall every event and see if it will compare with this, which the Lord is giving him to give them.

Actually, this Prophecy given to Joel, which was some 600 years before Christ, not only pertained to that which would shortly come upon Judah, but it reaches on even to the time of the coming Antichrist. In fact, that is the reason for the terminology as given by the Holy Spirit. While it will affect the entirety of the world, the greater thrust of this Prophecy is toward Israel.

ISRAEL

At the present time as I dictate these notes (2010), the unredeemed world has absolutely no idea as to the significance of Israel as it regards world events, and especially that which is soon to come to pass in this world. We speak of the Great Tribulation. That particular time will be worse than anything the world has ever known before, even as it was said by our Lord (Mat. 24:21).

God made Promises to the Patriarchs of old as it regards Israel. To be sure, the Lord keeps His Promises.

In 1948, after being scattered all over the world for some 1,900 years, Israel once again became a Nation. That has never been done in history. We are speaking of people being scattered all over the world and then coming together to form a cohesive unit in the same area of land, which they originally occupied thousands of years ago. Israel becoming a Nation in 1948 concerns her preparation for what is going to take place in the future. In fact, the Great Tribulation that is coming upon this world in the near future, which will be some seven years in duration and, as stated, will be worse than anything the world has ever seen previously, will, no doubt, be for many reasons and purposes as tendered by the Lord. However, its greatest purpose is to bring Israel to God. It will succeed in bringing Israel to Repentance, which will take place at the Second Coming of the Lord.

Then Israel will do that for which she was originally intended by the Lord. During that coming time, the Kingdom Age, Israel will then be the leading Nation in the world under Christ. It will last for 1,000 years with the Lord Jesus Christ reigning supreme

over the entirety of the world, and doing so in Person. One might say that she will be the Priestly Nation, which characterization is given to us in the last nine Chapters of Ezekiel and the Fourteenth Chapter of Zechariah.

THE U.S.A., ISRAEL, AND THE MUSLIMS

Some 4,000 years ago, as it concerns Israel, which was not even then in existence, the Lord said through the great Patriarch Abraham: **"And I will make of you a great Nation** (the Nation which God made of Abraham has changed the world and exists even unto this hour; in fact, this Nation 'Israel' still has a great part to play, which will take place in the coming Kingdom Age), **and I will bless you, and make your name great** (according to Scripture, 'to bless' means 'to increase;' the builders of the Tower of Babel sought to 'make us a name,' whereas God took this man, who forsook all, and 'made his name great'); **and you shall be a blessing:** (Concerns itself with the greatest blessing of all. It is the glory of Abraham's Faith.

"God would give this man the meaning of Salvation, which is 'Justification by Faith,' which would come about through the Lord Jesus Christ and what Christ would do on the Cross. Concerning this, Jesus said of Abraham, 'Your father Abraham rejoiced to see My Day: and he saw it, and was glad' [Jn. 8:56].)"

THE BLESSING AND THE CURSE

"And I will bless them who bless you (to bless Israel, or any Believer, for that matter, guarantees the Blessings of God), **and curse him who curses you** (to curse Israel, or any Believer, guarantees that one will be cursed by God): **and in you shall all families of the Earth be blessed.** (It speaks of Israel, which sprang from the loins of Abraham and the womb of Sarah, giving the world the Word of God and, more particularly, bringing the Messiah into the world. Through Christ, every family in the world who desires blessing from God can have that Blessing, i.e., 'Justification by Faith')" **(Gen. 12:2-3).**

To be sure, the Lord meant exactly what He said.

Ever since Israel became a Nation, she has had the blessing of the United States. In effect, we have guaranteed her survival, despite the fact that over one billion Muslims are swearing her destruction. God has blessed us and blessed us greatly for our protection of this ancient people.

But under President Obama, who is, I believe, a sympathizer of the religion of Islam, our favor toward Israel is weakening. If it continues, that will be the greatest mistake this nation ever made.

If our nation stands firm behind Israel, guaranteeing her safety and protection, whatever problems come our way, to be sure, the Lord will see us through, otherwise, we are inviting destruction. When the Lord told Abraham, *"And I will bless them who bless you, and curse him who curses you,"* He meant exactly what He said.

The world of Islam hates Israel and America. Most all little Muslim boys and girls are taught to hate from the time they can comprehend anything. That hatred, as stated, is directed toward Israel and America. One of the other biggest mistakes that our nation can make, and is making, is to fail to see the intentions of the religion of Islam. To be sure, it is not a few fanatics who have hijacked that religion, but it is rather the religion of Islam, centered in the Koran, that turns Muslims into murderers. Let me be blunt, it is the religion of Islam that is the greatest threat to America and the world in general. Of all the religions of this world, the religion of Islam is inspired by Satan more so than any other false direction.

THE RESURGENCE OF ISLAM

This religion of Islam has had a resurgence in the last few years because it will be used mightily by Satan in these last days, with every effort to destroy Israel.

There are seven great events as it regards Bible Prophecy, with the first event soon to take place. These events are:

1. The Rapture of the Church (I Thess. 4:13-18; I Cor., Chpt. 15).

2. The Advent of the Antichrist (II Thess., Chpt. 2).

3. The coming seven years of Great Tribulation (Mat. 24:21; Rev., Chpts. 6, 18).

Incidentally, the moment the Antichrist signs the treaty, which will guarantee the safety and protection of Israel for some seven years, will begin the Great Tribulation (Dan. 9:27).

4. The Battle of Armageddon (Ezek., Chpts. 38-39; Zech., Chpts. 12-13; Rev. 19:15-21).

5. The Second Coming of the Lord (Zech. 13:6; 14:4; Rev. 19).

6. The Kingdom Age, which will last a thousand years (Isa., Chpt. 11; Rev., Chpt. 20).

7. The Perfect Age to come, which will be eternal (Rev., Chpts. 21-22).

THE GREAT DECEPTION OF THE ANTICHRIST

As we look at Israel presently, most of the modern world has little understanding of the situation, which is, no doubt, the greatest flash point on the face of the globe. Iran is working furiously, attempting to develop an atomic bomb, while all the time threatening Israel with total destruction, and doing so in an open, worldwide manner. Prime Minister Benjamin Netanyahu was asked the question a short time ago as to what Israel might do respecting Iran, that is, if the U.S.A. didn't step in first.

As I heard this question posed to the Prime Minister, he sat there for a few moments and said nothing. And then he finally stated, or words to this effect, *"The fate of Israel as a Nation is at stake, and we will do whatever we have to do to guarantee our survival."*

Much of the world thinks, or chooses to think, that if Israel would just give the West Bank, along with East Jerusalem, to the Muslims, this would satisfy the situation, and the contention would go away. What they don't realize, and, more than likely, they don't care, is that the Muslim intention is that they take the entirety of the land of Israel and slaughter every single Jew. Getting pieces of Israel, so to speak, is only a steppingstone to that ultimate goal.

I cannot even remotely see the Obama Administration doing anything to protect Israel since the President, I believe, is a Muslim sympathizer. So, that pretty much leaves Israel on her own. At any rate, this area, as stated, is the flash point of the world.

DANIEL

The great Prophet Daniel told us some 2,500 years ago of the rise of the man of sin, i.e., the Antichrist, who, for a short period of time, will solve this thorny problem. Who this man is, we do not now know. But we do know that his advent is very near. And yet, we believe, according to the Word of God, that the Antichrist will not be known as such until after the Rapture of the Church. Concerning this, the Apostle Paul said, and I quote directly from THE EXPOSITOR'S STUDY BIBLE:

"**Let no man deceive you by any means** (*in other words, don't listen to that which is Scripturally incorrect*)**: for** *that day shall not come*, **except there come a falling away first** (*should have been translated, 'for that day shall not come, except there come a departure first'; this speaks of the Rapture, which, in essence, says the Second Coming cannot take place until certain things happen*)**, and that man of sin be revealed, the son of perdition** (*this speaks of the Antichrist, who must come upon the world scene before the Second Coming*)**;**

"**Who opposes and exalts himself above all that is called God** (*pertains to his declaration of himself as Deity*)**, or that is worshipped** (*the Antichrist will put down all religions, at least in the area which he controls, making himself alone the object of worship*)**; so that he as God sits in the Temple of God** (*refers to the Jewish Temple, which will be rebuilt in Jerusalem; the Antichrist will take over the Temple, making it his religious headquarters*)**, showing himself that he is God.** (*This proclaims his announcement of Deity as it regards himself.*)

"**Don't you remember, that, when I was yet with you, I told you these things?** (*So, there was no excuse for the Thessalonians to be drawn away by false doctrine.*)

"**And now you know what withholds** (*speaks of the Church*) **that he might be revealed in his time.** (*This speaks of the Antichrist who will be revealed or made known after the Rapture of the Church.*)"

THE RAPTURE OF THE CHURCH

"**For the mystery of iniquity does already work** (*concerns false teaching by false teachers*)**: only he** (*the Church*) **who now lets** (*who now hinders evil*) **will let** (*will continue to hinder*)**, until he** (*the Church*) **be taken out of the way.** (*The pronoun 'he' confuses some people. In Verses 4 and 6, the pronoun 'he' refers to the Antichrist, while in Verse 7 'he' refers to the Church.*)

"**And then** (*after the Rapture of the Church*) **shall that Wicked** (*the Antichrist*) **be revealed** (*proving conclusively that the Rapture will take place before the Great Tribulation [Mat. 24:21]*)**, whom the Lord shall consume with the Spirit of His Mouth** (*should have been translated, 'the Breath of His Mouth' [Isa. 11:4]*)**, and shall destroy with the brightness of His Coming** (*both phrases refer to the Second Coming*)**.**"

THE ANTICHRIST

"*Even him* (*the Antichrist*)**, whose coming is after the working of Satan** (*means that Satan is the sponsor of the Antichrist*) **with all power and signs and lying wonders** (*proclaims the fact that the Antichrist's rise to power, at least in the beginning, will be very religious*)**,**

"**And with all deceivableness of unrighteousness in them who perish** (*refers to the fact that 'all lying powers and lying signs and lying wonders' will be used to deceive the world*)**; because they received not the love of the Truth, that they might be Saved** (*they rejected Christ and the Cross*)**.**

"**And for this cause** (*the rejection of Christ and the Cross*) **God shall send them strong delusion** (*if one doesn't want 'the Truth,' God will see to it one receives a 'delusion'*)**, that they should believe a lie** (*should have been translated, 'that they should believe the lie'; the Greek Text has the definite article 'the lie,' which refers to a specific lie; that 'lie' pertains to anything that leads a person away from the Cross*)**:**

"**That they all might be damned who believed not the Truth** (*who would not accept the Cross*)**, but had pleasure in unrighteousness.** (*The Greek has the definite article, which actually says, 'the unrighteousness,' specifying a particular unrighteousness; it is really referring to the results of rejection of the Cross of Christ*)" (**II Thess. 2:3-12**).

THE ADVENT OF THE MAN OF SIN

Not long after the Rapture of the Church, but could be as much as several years, the Antichrist will come on the scene. According to the great Prophet Daniel, there is some evidence that he will be a Syrian, Iraqi, or Iranian Jew. At any rate, Israel will accept him as their Messiah, so this tells us that he must be a Jew. They would not accept a Gentile.

He will be able to bring together the world of Islam, as it regards an agreement with Israel, guaranteeing her borders and her protection for a period of seven years. At the moment this treaty is signed, the seven years Great Tribulation will begin, even as foretold by our Lord (Mat.24:21). We must remember that while the Great Tribulation is, no doubt, for many reasons, the greatest purpose of all is to bring Israel to God. It does not pertain to the Church and, in fact, has nothing to do with the Church. That's the reason that the Church will be raptured away before the Advent of the man of sin and the Great Tribulation. The Scripture plainly tells us the following:

THE CHURCH WILL NOT GO THROUGH THE GREAT TRIBULATION

"For God has not appointed us to wrath (*has not appointed Believers to go through the Great Tribulation*), but to obtain Salvation by our Lord Jesus Christ (*again, pertains to the Rapture of the Church*),

"Who died for us, that, whether we wake or sleep, we should live together with Him (*again, the Rapture, all made possible by the Cross*)" (I Thess. 5:9-10).

Some claim that the Church must go through the Great Tribulation in order to be purified. Those who state such a thing do not understand the Cross of Christ. It was at the Cross where all sin was atoned and, thereby, where Believers, who place their Faith in the Finished Work of Christ, experience purification in its total sense. To claim that something else is needed presents an insult to the Finished Work of Christ at Calvary's Cross. No, "*. . . the Blood of Jesus Christ His Son cleanses us from all sin*" (I Jn. 1:7).

John the Beloved also said:

"My little children, these things write I unto you, that you sin not. (*This presents the fact that the Lord Saves us from sin, not in sin. This Passage tells us that, as Believers, we don't have to sin. Victory over sin is found exclusively in the Cross.*) And if any man sin, we have an Advocate with the Father, Jesus Christ the Righteous (*Jesus is now seated at the Right Hand of the Father, signifying that His Mission is complete, and His very Presence guarantees intercession [Heb. 7:25-26; 9:24; 10:12]*):

"And He is the propitiation (*satisfaction*) for our sins: and not for ours only, but also for *the sins* of the whole world. (*This pertains to the fact that the satisfaction is as wide as the sin. If men do not experience its benefit, the fault is not in its efficacy but in man himself*)" (I Jn. 2:1-2).

In this agreement formulated by the Antichrist, it will not only guarantee Israel's borders and protection but, as well, will give them the right to build their Temple, which the Prophet Daniel foretold would be done (Dan. 9:27).

WHERE WILL THE TEMPLE BE BUILT?

The Dome of the Rock, the supposed third most holy place in the world of Islam, Mecca being the first with Medina being the second, sits on the exact spot where Solomon's Temple was constructed some 3,000 years ago, and where Herod built the Temple, which was standing during the time of Christ.

If one would walk inside the Dome of the Rock, he would see a fence enclosing a rock outcrop. It is believed that Abraham placed Isaac on this rock in order to offer him up as a sacrifice as demanded by God, which was stopped at the last moment by the Lord. Abraham then saw a ram caught in the bush and offered him instead at the behest of the Lord (Gen. 22:12-14).

In addition, it is said, as stated, that this is the exact spot where Solomon built his Temple, even as directed by the Lord. Also, it is believed that the Holy of Holies in the Temple, wherein sat the Ark of the Covenant, was situated, as well, over the exact spot where Abraham was to offer Isaac.

Some have said that Israel will build her Temple immediately beside the Dome of the Rock or else will use the Great Synagogue in Jerusalem as such. There is no indication in the Bible of this.

In the first place, for the Temple to be that close to the Dome of the Rock would be sacrilege to the Muslims. As well, for the Dome of the Rock to be that close to the Temple would be sacrilege to the Jews. No, I personally feel that when Israel builds her Temple, which she will do, it will be in the exact spot where Solomon built his. I cannot see that they would accept any other place.

But the great question remains as to how in the world the Antichrist will get the Muslims to agree to the tearing down of their Dome of the Rock with a Jewish Temple to be built in its place.

The Muslims claim that Muhammad went to Heaven from this spot on a winged horse. Of course, that is ridiculous! In fact, there is no record that Muhammad was ever in Jerusalem. This claim by the Muslims is of fairly recent origin, considering that the religion itself is approximately 1,400 years old. But, what else is new! The entirety of the Muslim religion is a lie, actually instigated by Satan himself. Nevertheless, this Dome of the Rock is supposedly the third most holy place in the religion of Islam.

WITH ALL DECEIVABLENESS

As we quoted in one of the previous paragraphs, the Antichrist will not only be the master of deception, but he will incorporate all manner of *"deceivableness"* (II Thess. 2:10). Irrespective, how will it be possible for the Antichrist to convince the world of Islam to tear down the Dome of the Rock in order that the Jewish Temple be built?

The following is not given to us in the Word of God, but it could very well be the manner in which the Antichrist will be able to lure Israel into believing him. In fact, his effort will be to deceive the entirety of the world, and he will succeed grandly, at least, for a short period of time.

It is quite possible that the Antichrist will gather all the Muslim leaders together for a secret meeting. In this secret meeting, he will propose a seven-year peace treaty

between Israel and the Muslim world. Now, many treaties have already been made between Israel and the Palestinians, but they held no validity. However, this treaty is going to greatly appeal to Israel and, as well, to the entirety of the world, because it will allow Israel to build her Temple on the exact spot where Solomon's Temple sat. How in the world will he be able to get the Muslims to agree to tear down the Dome of the Rock for Israel to do this?

He could very well promise the Muslims that if they will go along with him, he will lure Israel in. Then, at an appropriate time, he will declare war on her and destroy her, with the entirety of the land of Israel now being given to the Muslims.

The truth is, the Antichrist will be deceiving the Muslims as well. He has no intention of allowing the religion of Islam to continue, and that goes the same for all religions. His desire is to set himself up as God, which he will do. Once again, the Scripture says, *"Who opposes and exalts himself above all that is called God, or that is worshipped; so that he as God sits in the Temple of God, showing himself that he is God"* (II Thess. 2:4).

However, he will not show his true colors until he has the power to do so.

The Muslim world, thinking they are going to acquire the entirety of the land of Israel, plus every Jew slaughtered, will go along with the so-called peace treaty formulated by the Antichrist.

When this happens, the whole world will applaud the man of sin. In fact, Israel will accept him as her Messiah, claiming to the world that this is the one, with much of the world then also believing that Jesus Christ was an imposter. This is what Jesus was speaking of when He said:

"I am come in My Father's Name, and you receive Me not (*proclaims the real reason they did not receive Him is because they did not know the Father, despite their claims*)**: if another shall come in his own name, him you will receive** (*actually speaks of the coming Antichrist, as well as all other false messiahs; shortly after the Rapture of the Church, Israel will receive a false messiah, claiming that he is the one for whom they* *have long looked; they will find, to their dismay, how wrong they are!)"* **(Jn. 5:43).**

While Israel is lured into this trap, the Muslim world will likewise be lured into the trap. As stated, the Antichrist is going to do away with every religion, irrespective as to what it is, showing himself, claiming that he is God. In fact, he will be worshipped as such by many in the world.

ISRAEL ATTACKED

At the midpoint of the Great Tribulation, the Antichrist will show his true colors, attacking Israel and defeating her, which will be her first military defeat since becoming a Nation in 1948. In fact, the Antichrist would destroy her then but for news he will hear from the north and the east, speaking of opposition to him. This will probably be the nations of Russia, China, etc. (Dan. 11:44). At any rate, he will have to leave off the destruction of Israel and go north and east to fight these great battles, which will take approximately three and a half years. He will win these great conflicts, with every intention of conquering the entirety of the world. But first, he must attend to the Jewish question. He is, in fact, inspired by Satan to do so as no other man has ever been helped by the Evil One. He will come close to succeeding, actually taking all of Israel in the Battle of Armageddon, with half of Jerusalem falling. But then, the most cataclysmic event the world has ever known will take place, and we speak of the Second Coming of the Lord.

In the Thirty-eighth and Thirty-ninth Chapters of the Book that bears his name, the great Prophet Ezekiel described what that is going to be like. But Israel is going to have to come to the place of near annihilation before they will finally call on the Lord, begging Him to intervene, which He most definitely will do. In fact, the great Prophet Isaiah recorded the very prayer they will pray at that time (Isa. 64:6-12).

So, the Prophecies of Joel have to do not only with Judah of his day but, as well, speak of the coming time of the man of sin when Israel will come close to being destroyed, but yet, will experience her greatest deliverance yet with the Second Coming of the Lord.

NOTES

TELL YOUR CHILDREN

The phrase, *"You tell your children of it,"* etc., is meant not only for this Prophecy but actually for the entirety of the Bible. It is the duty of parents to instill within their children several things concerning the Bible. They are as follows:

• The Bible is, in fact, the Word of God, and the only Word of God in the world. They must be taught that it is the only Revelation of Divine Truth.

• The children should be taught to study it diligently, constantly, making the learning of it the primary objective of their life's work. They should be taught to pray that the Lord will open up their understanding of it.

• Children should be taught that the Bible alone holds the moral concepts indigenous to mankind and for every generation. Consequently, they should be taught, and with all purpose, that their lives are to be guided by the Words of its Pages and that it alone sets the standard for living. Its Commandments, Precepts, Laws, Injunctions, and Instruction must, at all costs, be primary.

A PERSONAL EXPERIENCE

I personally started reading the Bible when I was eight years old. I would carry one with me everywhere I went, even to school. It was very small with exceedingly fine print; however, inasmuch as I was but a child, my eyes were very strong. During recess or the lunch hour, I would try to read one of these short Books of the Old Testament; therefore, I first read the Book of Joel when I was but eight years old.

I remember going to my Dad at times and asking him the meaning of certain Scriptures, especially regarding the Words of Christ. Sometimes he would know the answer, while, oftentimes, he would not.

If he did not know the answer, many times I would venture an answer myself, and he would remonstrate by saying he would ask our Pastor as to the meaning. Oftentimes, he would be amazed that the Pastor's answer was the same as mine.

PRAYER MEETINGS

From the time I was eight years old up to

10 or 11, I was in a prayer meeting almost every day of my life. They were conducted either at our Church, at my Grandmother's, or my Aunt's. Actually, I remember the exact time that World War II ended in August of 1945. I was in a prayer meeting at my Grandmother's with my Mother and Dad plus several others. If I remember correctly, it was a Saturday morning.

During those formative years, I even made an Altar out of a log in a small cope of woods at the back of our home. I would go out there two or three times a day, kneel down by this log, and begin to importune the Lord. Almost instantly I would be in the Spirit.

THE CALL OF GOD

The things that the Lord said and did in those formative years are almost beyond belief. For instance, when I was nine years old, I knew I would be an Evangelist. I also knew that my Ministry would be worldwide, covering many countries.

I remember in these prayer meetings, at least when they were conducted at my Grandmother's or my Aunt's, that each of us would first be seated. A box of Promise cards would then be passed to each one of us, with each taking one. As a child, this was always very special to me. When my turn came to read the Promise that I had drawn, I would read it with great rapture and joy, knowing that I held the very Word of God in my hands.

Invariably, my Grandmother would smile and encourage me in the Promise that I had received.

A PROMISE I DISTINCTLY REMEMBER

Of all the scores, even hundreds of times this was done, one particular time stands out greatly in my memory. At that particular prayer meeting, which was held at my Grandmother's, my Mother and Dad and baby sister were present, and possibly Aunt Irene. At any rate, Nannie (that's what I called my Grandmother) passed the box of Promise cards around, and I took mine.

When it came time for me to read mine, as all of us did, I read it out loud. As I read, I sensed greatly the Presence of God. The

NOTES

Promise said:

"Every place that the sole of your foot shall tread upon, that have I given unto you, as I said unto Moses" (Josh. 1:3).

I remember that when I read it aloud, my Grandmother commented by saying, *"Jimmy, that Promise is yours, if you will only believe it."* I have never forgotten that, and I hold it dear to my heart even unto this moment.

I firmly believe that every part of the Ministry, which the Lord has given to me, and I speak of television, radio, Family Worship Center, THE EXPOSITOR'S STUDY BIBLE, the Commentaries, the Books, and the Music, all, and without exception, have been used, is being used, and shall be used to touch the entirety of the world for the Lord Jesus Christ.

I WILL OPEN THE DOOR WIDE

Jumping up to November, if I remember the month correctly, of 2009, in prayer one afternoon, the Lord began to move upon me as it regards this Ministry. He said the following to me:

"The Evil One has tried to close the door to your Ministry, which I have given unto you, and I allowed him to do so, but keeping it open approximately 10%."

As the Lord spoke that to my heart, I instantly recognized the fact that that's exactly the approximate percentage that had remained from the times of the 1980's, when we touched much of the world for Christ. And then the Lord spoke this to me:

"Even though the Evil One tried to close the door, and do so completely, I would not allow it to happen, keeping it open a small amount, but I am about to open it wide."

When the Lord spoke that to me, I had absolutely no doubt that it was the Lord. As well, what He told me that He was going to do, He has already begun.

The Lord has called us to touch the entirety of the world, and that by the Grace of God we plan to do. We have already begun, and more beautiful yet, the Lord has already begun to open that door wide.

"I can see far down the mountain,
"Where I have wandered many years,

"Often hindered on my journey,
"By the ghosts of doubt and fears,
"Broken vows and disappointment,
"Thickly strewn along the way,
"But the Spirit has led unerring,
"To the land I hold today."

RAISED ON THE WORD OF GOD

I was raised on Abraham, Isaac, and Jacob. Peter, Paul, and Silas were my mainstays.

Yes, I was a boy like other boys, liking baseball, football, etc.; however, my walk with God, especially during those formative years, was the single most important thing in my life by far.

As a teenager, the struggles were severe with Satan attempting to destroy the Call of God in my life; however, even though the battle was hot, the Victory was sure!

The multiple tens of millions of people that the Lord has helped us to touch with this great and glorious Gospel of Jesus Christ, I owe to those formative years when the Bible and Prayer were the mainstay of my life and, in fact, continues to be. I realize that most would not understand a child having that type of interest in the Bible, and especially in prayer meetings; however, those who would think such have absolutely no conception as to Who God is. Actually, there is no way I can properly explain the glory and the joy of those times. The Spirit of God was so heavy upon me, almost constantly, producing a constant euphoria that words could not even begin to describe it.

MANIFESTATION

Many times, during those prayer meetings, I would begin to pray and go into a trance. When I would come back to consciousness a little later, I would think that only a few minutes of time had passed when, in reality, several hours had passed. It was, and is, truly, as Peter said, *"Joy unspeakable and full of glory!"*

ANOTHER GENERATION

The phrase, *"And their children another generation,"* refers to each generation making certain that the coming generation knows the Word of God. Presently, that is the only thing that will spare the child from

drugs, alcohol, immorality, etc. Any other defense against these evils is a mere façade, hence, the destruction of this generation.

It is so sad that this modern generation little knows the Word of God because the Bible, little by little, has been pushed from center stage to the periphery, if used at all. Humanistic psychology, with all of its varied tentacles and nuances, has taken its place. Actually, the entirety of the world has been so psychologized, even including the church, that religious terminology has even been changed from the Biblical concept to the psychological concept.

For instance, words like Victory, Deliverance, overcoming Power, Salvation, Born-Again, the Baptism with the Holy Spirit, etc., have gradually been changed, for the most part, to counseling, therapy, rehabilitation, self-esteem, treatment, psychological, etc.

As Isaac of old, the church desperately needs to redig the wells once dug by Abraham (Gen. 26:18).

Inasmuch as Joel's Prophecies were to cover a span of time, all the way from his day through the coming Antichrist, its Message must not be lost. Regrettably, for most of the world, it has been lost; however, this will not at all limit its fulfillment.

THE DESTRUCTIVE POWER OF SIN

The Fourth Verse presents an instance, not unusual in Prophetic teaching, of the Spirit of God using an event, such as this plague of locusts, to awaken the conscious of the people at the moment and, at the same time, to make use of it to picture a future event of much greater moment.

The development of the Judgment listed in Verse 4 actually exhibits four stages. These four stages are expressed in four Hebrew words here translated *"palmerworm," "locust," "cankerworm,"* and *"caterpillar."* This last stage is the most destructive of them all.

Possibly they prefigured the four military monarchies of Babylon, Persia, Greece, and Rome, which successfully devastated Judah as locusts had destroyed the land.

(Actually, all of these specifications are different species of locusts.)

(5) "AWAKE, YOU DRUNKARDS, AND WEEP: AND HOWL, ALL YOU

DRINKERS OF WINE, BECAUSE OF THE NEW WINE; FOR IT IS CUT OFF FROM YOUR MOUTH.

(6) "FOR A NATION IS COME UP UPON MY LAND, STRONG, AND WITHOUT NUMBER, WHOSE TEETH ARE THE TEETH OF A LION, AND HE HAS THE CHEEK TEETH OF A GREAT LION.

(7) "HE HAS LAID MY VINE WASTE, AND BARKED MY FIG TREE: HE HAS MADE IT CLEAN BARE, AND CAST IT AWAY; THE BRANCHES THEREOF ARE MADE WHITE."

The pattern is:

1. (Vs. 5) *"Awake, you drunkards, and weep"* has to do with the spiritual state of Judah. Instead of crying to God from a position of Spiritual Strength, they were, instead, faced with the problem of awakening the *"drunkards"* from their stupefaction. In other words, there was no spiritual base upon which to build.

2. (Vs. 5) *"Because of the new wine; for it is cut off from your mouth"* is meant to impress upon the *"drunkards"* that shortly the enemy was going to come into their country, with all vineyards being destroyed, with them either killed or taken captive. Consequently, there would be no more *"wine."*

3. (Vs. 6) *"For a nation is come up upon My Land,"* has a twofold meaning:

A. It refers to the soon-to-come Babylonian invasion of Judah. Actually, Babylon is symbolized by a *"lion"* (Dan. 7:4).

B. The phrase, *"And he has the cheek teeth of a great lion,"* refers to the coming Antichrist, who will come from Syria and Babylon (Ezek., Chpts. 38-39; Dan. 11:41-45; II Thess. 2:3-4; Rev. 13:2; 16:13-16; 19:11-21).

4. (Vs. 7) The destruction of the *"vine"* and *"fig tree"* denotes the devastation of the land of Judah, which would take place upon the advent of the Babylonian invasion.

AWAKE

The idea of Verse 5 is, so absolute would be the destruction of food in the coming invasion by the enemy that all classes would be plunged into a common misery.

The idea of the Verse is that Judah is in

the condition she is in, consequently, inviting the destruction predicted, because of sin. In other words, the Nation is drunk, literally and symbolically. They should have been teaching their children the Word of God, but, instead, they were teaching them how to drink alcohol.

It is the business of the Preacher of the Gospel to call the Church to account and, as well, the nation. But, if that is done, at least as it ought to be done, some people are going to have their feelings hurt. Others will grow very angry because the Gospel, if truly preached, will always illicit a response of anger or joy. It will seldom leave the individual neutral. However, the spiritual pabulum that is dished out presently to the church, and the nation as a whole, strikes no chord of Righteousness whatsoever because it is not designed to do such. Let it be understood that preachers can be religious leaders or they can be Prophets. They cannot be both! The former pleases men while the latter pleases God!

DRUNKARDS

While the word *"drunkards"* in Verse 5 has to do with the spiritual state of Judah, still, in the literal sense, it was true as well. Judah had become a Nation of drunkards.

The only position that a true Christian can take regarding alcoholic beverage is total abstinence. Any other position is an insult to the integrity of the Word of God.

The argument that moderate drinking should be acceptable in Christian circles is blown away by the word, *"drunkards,"* inasmuch as all of these began their dissipation with moderate drinking. Above all, as an example, the Christian must say a firm *"no"* to any and all imbibing, moderate or otherwise! Several things must be understood as it regards alcohol. They are:

• Every alcoholic began as a moderate drinker.

• It is a scientific fact that if it takes ten beers to make one drunk, then one beer makes one 1/10th drunk. In other words, impairment begins with the first drink.

• Of the automobile wrecks in this nation, which snuff out nearly 50,000 lives a year, plus the hundreds of thousands who are crippled for life, most are caused by drunk driving.

• Alcohol plays a part in over half of the crimes committed in this nation.

Considering all of that, if we as Believers are to have any type of positive Testimony, there must be a firm *"no"* to all alcoholic beverages.

GOD CALLS ISRAEL, *"MY LAND"*

As used by the Holy Spirit, the first phrase of Verse 6, which says, *"For a nation has come up upon My Land,"* signifies beyond the shadow of a doubt that Israel belongs to the Lord. It belonged to Him then, and it belongs to Him now! The passage of time does not alter that fact whatsoever.

Regrettably, most of the modern world does not agree with Israel's position regarding the boundaries of the State of Israel. Most of the world probably sides with the Palestinians, claiming that the land belongs to them. In fact, most of the world wouldn't care if Israel were completely destroyed and the name of that area changed to *"Palestine."* But, of course, the far greater majority of the world has absolutely no regard for Bible Prophecy and, in fact, registers gross unbelief toward the Word of God. Irrespective of the unbelief, everything that the Lord has said will happen as it regards Israel, or anything else, for that matter, is going to come to pass exactly as it is given in the Word of God. Concerning Israel and her present position in 2010, the great Prophet Isaiah said, and I quote directly from THE EXPOSITOR'S STUDY BIBLE:

ISAIAH

"And it shall come to pass in that day, that the Lord shall set His Hand again the second time to recover the remnant of His People, which shall be left, from Assyria, and from Egypt, and from Pathros, and from Cush, and from Elam, and from Shinar, and from Hamath, and from the islands of the sea" (Isa. 11:11).

Regarding this Verse, the notes from THE EXPOSITOR'S STUDY BIBLE read, *"Once again, 'in that day,' refers to Christ reigning Personally in Jerusalem. The first gathering of the 'remnant,' as it refers to Israel,*

NOTES

took place when Israel was gathered out of the Medo-Persian Empire some 2,500 years ago and brought back to the Promised Land. In a sense, the second gathering began in 1948, when Israel, after some 1,900 years, once again became a Nation. This second gathering will be fulfilled in totality at the beginning of the Kingdom Age, when Jews all over the world will recognize Christ as their Messiah and, thereby, desire to come to Israel and live near Him."

When we consider that this Verse in Isaiah pertains primarily to the gathering of the remnant, which has already begun, then it should make us realize how close we are to that which is referred to as the *"Endtime."* We are presently living in the very closing days, if not the closing hours, of the Church Age. We know that the final gathering of Israel will take place at the Second Coming, which will then totally fulfill this Passage in Isaiah. But when we consider that after a fashion, it has already begun, this should give us pause.

The Bible teaches seven great Prophetic events, which will take place in the near future and will, in fact, last forever. They are:

SEVEN PROPHETIC EVENTS OF THE LAST DAYS

1. THE RAPTURE OF THE CHURCH: The terms *"Rapture"* and *"Resurrection"* both refer to the same event. In I Thessalonians 4:13-18, Paul gives us the fact of the Rapture or, if preferred, the Resurrection. In I Corinthians, Chapter 15, he gives us the manner of this coming event, which could take place at any time (II Thess. 2:7-8).

2. THE ADVENT OF THE ANTICHRIST: The man of sin will be revealed not long after the Rapture of the Church (II Thess. 2:8).

3. THE GREAT TRIBULATION: At the moment the Antichrist signs the seven-year treaty of protection for Israel, guaranteeing her borders and protection, the Great Tribulation begins (Mat. 24:21; Dan. 9:27).

4. THE BATTLE OF ARMAGEDDON: (Rev. 16:16; Ezek., Chpts. 38-39; Zech., Chpts. 12-14).

5. THE SECOND COMING OF THE LORD: (Mat. 24:27-31; Rev., Chpt. 19; Zech. 14:1-7).

6. THE KINGDOM AGE: This time frame will last for 1,000 years (Rev. 20:47; Isa., Chpts. 2, 11).

7. THE PERFECT AGE: This Age will be eternal. God, in fact, will change His Headquarters from Heaven to Earth. The account is given in Revelation, Chapters 21-22.

ISRAEL, GOD'S PROPHETIC TIME CLOCK

If we want to know what time it is prophetically speaking, we need only look at Israel. Concerning this very thing, Jesus said:

"Now learn a Parable of the fig tree (the Bible presents three trees, the fig, the olive, and the vine, as representing the Nation of Israel, nationally, spiritually, and dispensationally); When his branch is yet tender, and puts forth leaves (is meant to serve as the illustration of Israel nationally), you know that summer is near (refers to Israel as the greatest Prophetic Sign of all, telling us that we are now living in the last of the last days):

"So likewise you (points to the modern church), when you shall see all these things (which we are now seeing as it regards Israel), know that it is near, even at the doors (the fulfillment of Endtime Prophecies)" (Mat. 24:32-33).

MY VINE AND MY FIG TREE

The Holy Spirit through Joel said, "He has laid My Vine waste, and barked My Fig Tree." To which we have just alluded, the Lord uses these two trees, "the vine and the fig," to illustrate Israel. As we have also stated, Verses 6 and 7 denote not only the coming desolation of the Babylonians upon Israel but, as well, the Antichrist, with the latter being yet future.

While the destruction of Israel by the Babylonians, which took place about 500 years before Christ, was terrible, to say the least, still, in the coming Great Tribulation, this period of time will be the most trying of all. In fact, the Antichrist will set out to completely annihilate Israel and would succeed were it not for the Second Coming of the Lord.

(8) "LAMENT LIKE A VIRGIN GIRDED WITH SACKCLOTH FOR THE HUSBAND OF HER YOUTH.

NOTES

(9) "THE MEAT OFFERING AND THE DRINK OFFERING IS CUT OFF FROM THE HOUSE OF THE LORD; THE PRIESTS, THE LORD'S MINISTERS, MOURN.

(10) "THE FIELD IS WASTED, THE LAND MOURNS; FOR THE CORN IS WASTED: THE NEW WINE IS DRIED UP, THE OIL LANGUISHES.

(11) "BE YOU ASHAMED, O YOU HUSBANDMEN; HOWL, O YOU VINEDRESSERS, FOR THE WHEAT AND FOR THE BARLEY; BECAUSE THE HARVEST OF THE FIELD IS PERISHED.

(12) "THE VINE IS DRIED UP, AND THE FIG TREE LANGUISHES; THE POMEGRANATE TREE, THE PALM TREE ALSO, AND THE APPLE TREE, EVEN ALL THE TREES OF THE FIELD, ARE WITHERED: BECAUSE JOY IS WITHERED AWAY FROM THE SONS OF MEN.

(13) "GIRD YOURSELVES, AND LAMENT, YOU PRIESTS: HOWL, YOU MINISTERS OF THE ALTAR: COME, LIE ALL NIGHT IN SACKCLOTH, YOU MINISTERS OF MY GOD: FOR THE MEAT OFFERING AND THE DRINK OFFERING IS WITHHELD FROM THE HOUSE OF YOUR GOD.

(14) "SANCTIFY YOU A FAST, CALL A SOLEMN ASSEMBLY, GATHER THE ELDERS AND ALL THE INHABITANTS OF THE LAND INTO THE HOUSE OF THE LORD YOUR GOD, AND CRY UNTO THE LORD."

The exegesis is:

1. The idea of Verse 8 concerns a young lady about to be married. But tragically, her sweetheart is killed before the wedding can take place. As she would "lament" for him, and rightly so, Judah is admonished to weep and cry for the destruction that is soon to come upon the land. Tragically, Judah would not heed!

2. (Vs. 8) It is believed, as stated, that Joel was prophesying to Judah a few years before Jeremiah.

3. The Ninth Verse proclaims the coming destruction of the Temple, which took place with the Babylonian invasion.

4. Verse 10 points to the devastation and desolation of the land upon the invasion of Nebuchadnezzar.

5. The idea of Verse 11 is "shame." There

was no excuse for Judah's plight. Sin was the cause of their ruin but could have been repented of at any time, thereby ensuring the commencement of the Blessings of God. But Judah would not repent!

6. Verse 12 shows a definite link of economic depression, which always follows spiritual depression. What are we presently seeing (2010) in the United States?

7. The idea of Verse 13 is: unless Repentance is enjoined, the sacrifices will be no more because the Temple will be no more. As well, the *"Priests"* were to take the lead if the Nation was to follow suit. Regrettably, the *"Priests"* did not take the lead.

8. As Verse 14 proclaims, step by step the Holy Spirit, through the Prophet Joel, tells Judah what she must do, which, if done, would avoid destruction. But sadly, it was all to no avail!

LAMENTATION

The Holy Spirit uses an apt illustration regarding the coming destruction of Judah, that is, if no Repentance was forthcoming. Over and over again the Lord would warn Judah through the Prophet Joel and other mighty Prophets, as well, such as Isaiah and Jeremiah, but it was all to no avail. They would not listen.

The illustration used by the Holy Spirit concerned a young lady who was engaged to be married to the love of her life, and then, tragically, he was killed. One can well imagine the heartache, the pain, and the suffering that would be caused by such a happening. Multiply that tens of thousands of times over, and you get an idea of the pain and suffering that is going to come upon Judah.

WHY WOULD THEY NOT REPENT?

Several reasons. They are:
• Unbelief: they simply did not believe what the Prophet said.
• They loved their sin, meaning they didn't want to give it up.
• The Nation at that time was relatively prosperous, so they reasoned that this was the Blessing of God and, as such, there was no need for Repentance.
• They felt the Message of the Prophet was too strict and too narrow, so it was

NOTES

much easier to believe the false prophets.

The idea of Verse 8 also falls into the category of the Lord telling Judah that she must now *"lament"* over her sins or else, in a coming day, she would tragically *"lament"* over her terrible loss.

If our calculations are correct concerning the time of Joel's Prophecies, Judah had from 25 to 40 years left before the horror of the Babylonian invasion. Quite possibly, at this present time (2010), Israel just might have a similar amount of time remaining, if that much, before the advent of the Antichrist!

A PATTERN FOR LIVING

Two things are said in Verse 9. They are as follows:

1. *"The Meat Offering and the Drink Offering is cut off from the House of the LORD"*: this refers to the Temple being destroyed and, therefore, the means of the sacrifices being brought to an end. Consequently, there was no way for Atonement to be made, which placed Judah and the entirety of the world, for that matter, in a perilous situation.

Judah was the only Nation on the face of the Earth who worshipped and served the True God and, therefore, had access to God Who made Heaven and Earth. Their worship was through the sacrifices, which were symbolic of the coming Redeemer. In fact, the Cross of Christ has always been the only way to God. Jesus Christ is the Source, and I speak of the Source of all things that we receive from God, and the Means by which these things are given to us and received is the Cross of Christ. The Lord does not have several means, only one, and that is the Cross. When Judah was destroyed by the Babylonians, which meant the Temple was also destroyed, which meant the sacrifices were no longer offered, the entirety of the world, at least in a sense, was cut off from God.

THE SITUATION IN
THE MODERN CHURCH

Considering that the Cross of Christ alone is, and has always been, the Means by which we reach the Lord, in fact, the only Means, where does that leave the modern church and the world? Except in a very limited way, the modern church is not preaching the Cross. The Seeker Sensitive program in the modern church looks to the Cross of Christ not at all. The Purpose Driven Life scheme follows suit. The Word of Faith doctrine, which, in reality, is no faith at all, at least, that which God will recognize, actually repudiates the Cross, referring to it as *"past miseries"* and *"the greatest defeat in human history."*

Considering the fact that virtually the entirety of the Charismatic church world has opted for the *"Word of Faith doctrine"* or the *"Purpose Driven Life scheme,"* and that many, if not most, Pentecostal churches and denominations have followed suit, this leaves only the denominational world, which, for all practical purposes, is cut through with modernism.

What few Churches are preaching the Cross, and thank the Lord for those, their messages almost altogether pertain to Salvation. The Churches preaching the Cross of Christ for both Salvation and Sanctification, which is what the Bible gives us, are few and far between. The upshot is, the Cross of Christ, which is the Wisdom of God, has been replaced by man's wisdom.

JUDAH

During the time of Joel, Judah was the only Nation on the face of the Earth who worshipped and served the True God and, therefore, had access to God Who made Heaven and Earth. In fact, this was the case from the time of Abraham to the time of Christ, a time frame of some 2,000 years. The other nations of the world worshipped idols, in other words, demon spirits; consequently, life was far better for all people in Judah than any other nation in the world. By and large, regarding most, if not all, nations other than Judah, the majority of the people were slaves, with only a few enjoying vast riches at the expense of all others. As a result, life was unbearable, at least for the far greater majority.

Judah, having the Law of the Lord, had a *"pattern for living"* (Ex. 25:8-9) as well as access to God. As such, He led and guided them, which no other nation enjoyed.

THE SACRIFICES

The sacrifices were so important because they provided a means for the atoning of sin. Even though the *"blood of bulls and goats could not take away sins,"* still, they served as a Symbol, pointing to the One Who could and, in fact, would, the Lord Jesus Christ.

With this *"cut off,"* there was no way the people could have their sins forgiven inasmuch as without the shedding of blood, there is no remission of sin (Heb. 9:22).

However, to the faithful Remnant, which was small indeed, the Lord would be to them as a *"little Sanctuary"* (Ezek. 11:16), even while in captivity. In other words, after the Temple was destroyed, their sins were forgiven by Faith. Tragically, only a few, at least in comparison to the whole, would have that type of Faith. This is the reason that the Lord urged the rebuilding of the Temple after the dispersion (Ezra 6:14).

THE LORD'S MINISTERS

2. The phrase of Verse 9, *"The Priests, the LORD's Ministers, mourn,"* speaks of the entirety of the Work of God being shattered. When the Temple would be destroyed, there would be no way for these *"Priests"* to be sustained, inasmuch as their livelihood was *"cut off."* Consequently, the entire Tribe of Levi was denied their occupation as *"Ministers of the LORD"* and, therefore, had no way to care for themselves.

This will happen, as well, when the Antichrist invades Israel at the midpoint of the coming Great Tribulation when the sacrifices in the newly-built Temple will be stopped, with that edifice then being taken over by the Antichrist (Dan. 9:27).

WASTED

The phrase of Verse 10, *"The field is wasted, the land mourns,"* portrays the devastation and, therefore, desolation of the land upon the invasion of Nebuchadnezzar.

All of this could have been avoided or could have been stopped, which speaks of a terror unequalled, if the people had only repented. However, they would not repent at least partially because *"the Priests"* spoken of in Verse 9 would not lead them to Repentance.

The two Verses, 9 and 10, are joined, signifying that the reason for the *"waste"* and *"mourning"* is because of the failure of spiritual leadership.

As then, so now! Consequently, the prosperity of the Nation in the economic sense was tied to the prosperity in the spiritual sense. To be sure, the economic prosperity continued unabated for a goodly number of years, even when there was no spiritual prosperity. However, ultimately, the lack of spiritual prosperity dragged down the economic prosperity, as well, as it always will!

THE PATTERN FOR DESTRUCTION

When a nation begins to lose its way, exactly as the U.S.A. is losing its way, the Spirituality dies first. In other words, the coming devastation can be laid at the doorstep of the Church.

If the preachers lose their way, the people will also lose their way. The people can little rise any higher, spiritually speaking, than the pulpit. The pulpit presently in America and the balance of the world, for that matter, is not in the best of spiritual health, to say the least. Of course, there are exceptions to the rule, and how we thank the Lord for that. I speak of the Preachers and people over this nation and elsewhere in the world, who truly hunger and thirst after Righteousness, who truly want the Ways of the Lord, who truly seek to abide exclusively by His Word, and who understand the Cross of Christ as it regards not only Salvation but, as well, our Sanctification.

What I'm about to give you, I placed in one of our Commentaries written approximately 14 years ago. Regrettably and sadly, it has come to pass exactly as stated. I said then, and I repeat now:

• Spiritual regression: according to the temperature, so to speak, of the Church, so will everything else in the nation follow suit. Regrettably, the temperature of the church presently (2010) is at, I personally believe, the lowest ebb it has known since the Reformation. The Word of God is adhered to presently in the modern church to a lesser degree than at any time, as stated, since the Reformation.

• Domestical regression: when the church

loses its way, the domestic or social condition of the nation plummets as well. Crime increases dramatically so, exactly as is presently happening. A great part of the leadership of the nation is advocating same-sex marriages, which is an abomination in the Eyes of God. Please note the following.

Every mighty empire of the past that rose and fell had three things that were pandemic in that empire. They were:

1. Homosexuality;
2. Pedophilia; and,
3. Incest.

Tragically, these three sins have become rampant in this nation at present. As well, abortion has become worse and worse, if such is possible. The Name of God is being ridiculed by court after court, instigated by the A.C.L.U. Let us say it again:

When the spiritual condition of the Church weakens, the domestic condition of the nation weakens as well.

• Economic regression: now for the first time in many decades, in fact, since the Great Depression of the 1930's, the economic picture in America is at an all time low. As I dictate these notes (February, 2010), unemployment stands near 11 percent, and if the truth be known, counting those who have given up looking for work, it probably stands at 15 percent or higher. The dollar as the world's currency would have been replaced months ago but for the fact that the other currencies of the world are in bad shape as well. In other words, when America catches a cold, so to speak, the rest of the world catches pneumonia.

Is it possible that the economic picture in this nation is not going to change until there is at least a modicum of Revival that sweeps the land?

THE ROLE OF AMERICA IN THE WORLD

The scepter of world leadership has been placed into the hands of the leadership of America by God Almighty. Let me explain Scripturally that of which I speak.

Some 2,500 years ago, the scepter of world power passed from the faltering hands of the kings of Judah and was placed into the hands of the Gentiles, first of all Nebuchadnezzar, and then with succeeding monarchs, where it has remained ever since. Concerning this, Jesus said:

"**And they** (*Israel*) **shall fall by the edge of the sword, and shall be led away captive into all nations** (*hundreds of thousands of Jews after the carnage of A.D. 70 were sold as slaves all over the world of that day; as well, the Jewish people as a whole were scattered all over the world, fulfilling exactly what Jesus said would happen*)**: and Jerusalem shall be trodden down of the Gentiles, until the times of the Gentiles be fulfilled" (Lk. 21:24).** Let's look at it a little closer.

Because of the spiritual declension of Judah, this scepter of world power was passed to the hands of the Babylonians. It was the intention of the Lord that Judah (Israel) would be the shining light to serve as a beacon for a world that was in darkness. Regrettably, Judah lost her way and instead of providing light, went into darkness herself.

Leadership passing from Judah to the Gentiles means that Israel would now be a subject Nation, subject to whatever power was in force at the time.

At a point in time, the Medes and the Persians defeated Babylon, by and large, becoming the ruler of the world of that day. Israel was then subject to the Medes and the Persians.

About 300 years before Christ, Alexander the Great came on the scene, with Greece becoming the dominant power, and the torch of leadership passing to them. After the death of Alexander the Great, at a point in time, world dominion passed to Rome where, in fact, it stayed for nearly 1,000 years.

At any rate, in A.D. 70, Israel was totally defeated by the Romans with Jerusalem totally destroyed, all because of insurrection on the part of Israel. Despite gargantuan losses, Israel, for the next few years, tried to bring herself back to nationhood and once again rose up against the Romans in A.D. 135. At that time, they were totally decimated and scattered all over the world, ceasing to be a Nation in any capacity whatsoever.

With Israel destroyed, world power, at least in that capacity, was of little consequence in the Eyes of God.

However, in 1948, as most know, Israel

NOTES

once again became a Nation. Even though they are not in full possession of the land and have no Temple, still, their being formed as a Nation at that time presents the beginning of fulfillment of Bible Prophecy, which will ultimately lead to the Second Coming.

Considering that, one might say that the turn of the Twentieth Century saw the scepter of power pass once again, this time to the United States, where it has remained unto this hour. To be sure, this became critical when Israel became a Nation. In fact, a great part of our prosperity and power in the world is tied to the tiny State of Israel. Of course, the powers that be do not agree to that whatsoever, irrespective, it happens to be the truth.

When the United States was given this responsibility by God, which, in effect, is a two-edged sword, He demanded two things of this nation.

THE TWO AREAS OF SPIRITUAL RESPONSIBILITY CONCERNING AMERICA

They are:

1. That the Church in America takes the Gospel to the world. Up unto the last few years, the Church in this nation has been very instrumental in touching the world with the Gospel of Jesus Christ. In fact, this Ministry (Jimmy Swaggart Ministries) has played and continues to play a strong part in this effort for the Cause of Christ. Through the telecast, we have translated every major language in the world, reaching untold millions of people for the Cause of Christ. We give the Lord all the praise and all the glory.

2. God requires of this nation that we serve as the Lord protector of Israel. In fact, the United States has been about the only friend that Israel has in the world. It has been our might and power that has kept the roaring lion at bay. It seems, however, that with this new Administration, our protection of Israel is weakening.

If we fail in these two particulars, it will destroy this nation. If we begin sending the True Gospel of Jesus Christ to the world by television, or by any other means at our disposal, and we strengthen our resolve respecting protection of Israel, somehow the Lord will bless us and pull us out of the present economic situation in which we find ourselves.

The following Word, even though given some 4,000 years ago, is still just as true today as it was then. The Lord put no time limit on it. He told Abraham:

"And I will bless them who bless you, and curse him who curses you: and in you shall all families of the Earth be blessed" (Gen. 12:3).

To be sure, the Lord said exactly what He meant and meant exactly what He said.

If we ignore this said by the Lord, we do so at our own peril!

Regrettably, this scepter of world power will pass to the Antichrist in the very near future. This will be after the Rapture of the Church, which will signal the beginning of the seven-year Great Tribulation (Dan. 9:27; Mat. 24:21). The Antichrist will be so deceptive that Israel will think that he is their Messiah and will accept him as such. After approximately three and a half years, he will show his true colors, attacking Israel, with her suffering her first military defeat since becoming a Nation once again. At that time, he would destroy her but because of negative news out of the north and the east, the Antichrist will be pulled away to fight other battles (Dan. 11:44). Some three and a half years later, at the very conclusion of the Great Tribulation, the Antichrist will come to Israel to settle the question once and for all. It will be the Battle of Armageddon. The man of sin will come upon Israel with quite possibly such a force as the world has never seen. In his mind, and energized by Satan, as the Evil One has energized no man, he will do what Haman, Herod, and Hitler could not do. He will totally annihilate Israel. To be sure, he most definitely would succeed were it not for the greatest event the world has ever known taking place at that time, and I speak of the Second Coming of the Lord. To be sure, when the Lord comes back that second time without sin unto Salvation, meaning He has already attended to sin at the Cross, He will now come to fight as He did in the days of old, with the Antichrist now learning just exactly Who Jesus Christ really is.

NOTES

THE SECOND COMING OF THE LORD

In fact, there will be millions of Angels accompanying our Lord at that time, along with every Saint of God who has ever lived, all with Glorified Bodies. As well, and according to the Thirty-eighth Chapter of Ezekiel, our Lord will use meteorites and hail by the millions as artillery, with some of the stones, no doubt, weighing well over 100 pounds. The Antichrist will be hit with power that he never knew existed. The Second Coming of the Lord will be the Salvation of Israel and the world, for that matter. It will be the greatest event in human history, with the exception of the price paid at Calvary's Cross by our Lord.

THE MEAT OFFERING AND THE DRINK OFFERING

The *"Meat Offering"* of Verse 9 was actually a Thanksgiving Offering. Of the five Levitical Offerings, it was the only one without blood. It must be understood that the word *"meat"* in those days stood for all types of food, whereas now, it speaks of flesh.

The *"Meat Offering"* was made of cereal, i.e., *"grain."* The grain was mixed with oil and frankincense. The Priests were to eat portions of it with the balance burnt on the Altar. As stated, it was meant to serve as a Thanksgiving Offering to the Lord for His many Blessings.

The *"Drink Offering"* was water and sometimes wine. It was poured out as an offering to the Lord, symbolizing several things. They are:

• It symbolized Christ pouring out Himself totally on the Cross of Calvary that mankind might be Saved.

• It typified the Believer pouring out himself before the Lord, in other words, giving the Lord our all.

• It typified the contrived weakness, which our Lord experienced at Calvary (II Cor. 13:4) and, as well, mankind's personal weakness as it regards the spirit world.

The idea of Verse 9 is that the Temple would be destroyed, making it impossible to offer up sacrifices anymore. In fact, Israel, for a span of time, would cease to be a Nation, taken over by the Babylonians.

The people came to the place that they

no longer revered the Offerings, all of which typified Christ. So, in essence, the Lord is saying that He will stop the sacrifices, which He did by allowing the Babylonians to destroy the Temple, the city, and, in fact, the entirety of Judah.

THE CROSS OF CHRIST

As the sacrifices of old were disdained by Israel and ultimately removed, likewise, the Cross in modern time is being either ignored or outright denied, as it is by the so-called Word of Faith people. I might quickly add, their faith is a faith that God does not recognize. Any faith, and read this carefully, that is not anchored squarely in Jesus Christ and Him Crucified cannot be said to be anchored in the Word of God and is, therefore, denied by the Lord. Merely having faith is not enough. The Object of our Faith must be correct, and that Object must be *"Jesus Christ and Him Crucified"* (I Cor. 1:23).

During the time of Judah, there were few Priests who continued to love the Lord. They saw the Temple destroyed and the sacrifices stopped. Concerning these Priests, the Scripture says, *"The Priests, the LORD's Ministers, mourn."*

JOY IS WITHERED AWAY
FROM THE SONS OF MEN

The great Prophet Joel is giving this Prophecy a little over 100 years before it would come to pass. The Lord warned Israel over and over again but, seemingly, to no avail. What the Prophet predicted here came to pass exactly as predicted, and sadly so!

If it is to be noticed, when the sacrifices would be stopped, everything else would be stopped as well. The Nation would lose its freedom, with hundreds of thousands slaughtered and many thousands of others taken captive into Babylon. God cannot abide sin in His Own any more than He can the world, in fact, not nearly as much as He can in the world.

CRY UNTO THE LORD

The Lord here plainly tells Israel, in effect, Judah, what they must do. He said to them:
• Dress in sackcloth, which typified humility.

• Call a fast.
• Call a solemn assembly for the purpose of seeking God, and do so at the House of the Lord.
• Cry unto the Lord.

The idea of Verse 13 and, in fact, all of these Passages, is that unless Repentance is enjoined, the sacrifices will be no more because the Temple will be no more. Ultimately, this did happen.

As well, the *"Priests"* were to take the lead if the Nation was to follow suit.

The phrase, *"Gird yourselves, and lament, you Priests,"* was meant to refer to sackcloth, which was the custom in that day for one who had sinned and was coming to the Lord, asking for Mercy.

The sackcloth was symbolic of one's guilt and the inability, at least within himself, to change the situation. It was a Sign to the Lord of humility on the part of the seeker.

Such is not followed under the New Covenant as there is no mention of this practice in the New Testament, except referring back to the Old Testament. Nevertheless, the principle is the same as the heart must take the same attitude of humility, with the demeanor accordingly!

It is not even necessarily meaning that these *"Priests"* were guilty of terrible sin, even though they may well have been. It is really referring to the intercession of these *"Ministers of the Altar"* on behalf of the entirety of the Nation. Night and day, they were to bewail their sins, as well as the sins of the people, with humble, penitent, and contrite hearts. They were to present an example to the people whose leaders they were and on whose behalf they ministered (I Cor. 9:13).

THE ALTAR

The *"Altar,"* speaking of the Brazen Altar where the sacrifices were offered, was referred to because such typified Calvary; therefore, the *"Ministry,"* as such, was as *"the Altar of God."* The Ministry was connected to the Altar wherein they ministered to Jehovah.

It is really no different presently in that the Preacher of the Gospel is the *"Minister of the Altar,"* i.e., Calvary. Hence, Paul would say, *"For I determined not to know anything among you, save Jesus Christ, and Him Crucified"* (I Cor. 2:2).

Consequently, any preacher who does not have Calvary as the central theme, the Foundation and principle of all he preaches and does, is not truly preaching the Gospel.

Even though the Old Covenant has been fulfilled by Christ and, consequently, passed away, still, that which it represented, namely Christ and Him Crucified, is ever-present and the central theme of the Gospel. In fact, the Cross of Christ is actually the meaning of the New Covenant, which means it is the Gospel. Paul said as much:

"Christ sent me not to baptize, but to preach the Gospel, not with enticing words of men's wisdom, lest the Cross of Christ be made of none effect" (I Cor. 1:17).

Presently, considering the condition of America, and the world, for that matter, the modern Ministry is, as well, enjoined by the Holy Spirit exactly as these Priests of old. However, the pleadings are presently little heard!

Instead, preachers are busily telling congregations how to get *"rich,"* how to be *"king's kids,"* and how to *"save"* the nation by humanitarian means.

God help us!

I wonder if anyone honestly believes that America is presently any better, Spiritually speaking, than Judah of old.

SANCTIFY A FAST

The word, *"sanctify,"* means, *"to set apart for sacred use."* In other words, the *"fast"* that is here called was abstinence from food in token of sorrow for sin. It was intended to be the external evidence of sorrow for sin.

These *"fasts"* were not long, mostly a single day. However, it was meant to symbolize the problem, the cause, and, therefore, the cure, which was total dependence on the Lord.

While fasting, as is obvious, is Scriptural and will greatly be a blessing to the Believer, still, one cannot fast oneself to victory over sin. The fasting then was, and the fasting now is, an admittance before God that whatever it is that is needed, we cannot within ourselves carry it out. As the fasting shows physical weakness, it is meant also to show our spiritual weakness.

Unfortunately, some have tried to claim that fasting will give one victory over sin. It won't! Jesus said, *"You shall know the Truth, and the Truth shall make you free"* (Jn. 8:32).

WHAT TRUTH IS JESUS SPEAKING OF?

He is speaking of the great Truth, which He would ultimately give through the Apostle Paul. It can be summed up in the following, although very abbreviated:

• Jesus Christ is the Source of all things that we receive from God (Jn. 1:1-2, 14, 29; 14:6).

• The Cross of Christ is the Means, and the only Means, by which all of these good things are given to us (Rom. 6:3-5; I Cor. 1:17-18, 23; 2:2; Gal., Chpt. 5; 6:14; Col. 2:14-15).

• The Cross of Christ must always be the Object of our Faith, for this is the only kind of Faith that God will recognize (Rom. 5:1-2; 6:11, 14; Eph. 2:13-18).

• The Holy Spirit is careful to superintend all of this, in other words, to ascertain if our Faith is correct, which refers to the Cross of Christ being its Object, and the Cross of Christ alone being its Object (Rom. 8:1-2, 11).

In an extremely abbreviated view, the *"Truth"* is *"Jesus Christ and Him Crucified"* (I Cor. 1:23).

In Old Testament Times, the Sacrificial system was the means by which sins were covered; unfortunately, animal blood was insufficient to take the sins away (Heb. 10:4). In other words, before the Cross of Calvary, men were Saved by looking forward to that coming event. Since the Cross, men are Saved by looking backward to that event. Salvation has always been the same, having never varied from the dawn of time unto the present, and, in fact, will never vary. It is Who He is, meaning that the Lord Jesus Christ is the Son of God, God manifest in the flesh, and What He did. That speaks of Calvary's Cross and the shedding of His Life's Blood, with the offering of Himself as a Sacrifice, which God accepted.

Let not the reader think we are minimizing fasting. We aren't! But we are putting it in its proper perspective.

WRONG DIRECTIONS OF
THE MODERN CHURCH

Let's establish the fact that sin is the problem. Whether it's the unredeemed or the redeemed, sin is the problem. As it regards unbelievers, Paul told us in Romans, Chapters 4 and 5, that the believing sinner is justified by Faith (Rom. 5:1-2). It is the Cross of Christ that makes it possible, and the Cross of Christ alone which makes it possible.

In Romans, Chapter 6, Paul deals with Believers, telling us how to live for God. In the first two Verses, he tells us that the problem is sin. He then gives the solution to that problem, which is the Cross of Christ. He said:

BAPTIZED INTO HIS DEATH

"**Know you not, that so many of us as were baptized into Jesus Christ** (*plainly says that this Baptism is into Christ and not water [I Cor. 1:17; 12:13; Gal. 3:27; Eph. 4:5; Col. 2:11-13]*) **were baptized into His Death?** (*When Christ died on the Cross, in the Mind of God, we died with Him; in other words, He became our Substitute, and our identification with Him in His Death gives us all the benefits for which He died; the idea is that He did it all for us!*)"

BURIED WITH HIM

"**Therefore we are buried with Him by baptism into death** (*not only did we die with Him, but we were buried with Him, as well, which means that all the sin and transgression of the past were buried; when they put Him in the Tomb, they put all of our sins into that Tomb as well*)."

RAISED IN NEWNESS OF LIFE

"**That like as Christ was raised up from the dead by the Glory of the Father, even so we also should walk in Newness of Life** (*we died with Him, we were buried with Him, and His Resurrection was our Resurrection to a 'Newness of Life'*)."

RESURRECTION LIFE BASED
ON SACRIFICIAL DEATH

"**For if we have been planted together**

(*with Christ*) **in the likeness of His Death** (*Paul proclaims the Cross as the instrument through which all Blessings come; consequently, the Cross must ever be the Object of our Faith, which gives the Holy Spirit latitude to work within our lives*), **we shall be also** *in the likeness of His* **Resurrection** (*we can have the 'likeness of His Resurrection,' i.e., 'live this Resurrection Life,' only as long as we understand the 'likeness of His Death,' which refers to the Cross as the Means by which all of this is done*)" **(Rom. 6:3-5).**

Unfortunately, the modern church faces sin in any one of several ways. The Word of Faith people, which, as stated, is no faith at all, at least that God will recognize, claim that the preacher is to never mention sin. If he mentions sin, they say, this will create a sin consciousness in the hearts of those who hear Him and will cause them to sin.

That seems strange when we realize that Paul mentioned sin some 17 times in the Sixth Chapter of Romans alone!

Then, other segments of the church, especially that of the Purpose Driven Life genre, claim that sin should not be mentioned because it might offend people.

And then, others try to deal with sin by coming up with every type of proposed scheme of which one could think. By the church coming up with all of these erroneous fads, it tells us that sin is the problem, irrespective as to what they say otherwise.

ONLY ONE ANSWER FOR SIN

That answer is the Cross of Christ and the Cross of Christ alone. Paul said:

"**So Christ was once offered to bear the sins of many** (*the Cross was God's Answer to sin, and, in fact, the only answer*); **and unto them who look for Him shall He appear the second time without sin unto Salvation.** (*This refers to the Second Coming. 'Without sin' refers to the fact that the Second Coming will not be to atone for sin, for that was already carried out at the Cross at His First Advent. The Second Coming will bring all the results of Salvation to this world, which refers to all that He did at the Cross. We now only have the 'Firstfruits' [Rom. 8:23]*)" **(Heb. 9:28).**

(15) "ALAS FOR THE DAY! FOR THE

DAY OF THE LORD IS AT HAND, AND AS A DESTRUCTION FROM THE ALMIGHTY SHALL IT COME.

(16) "IS NOT THE MEAT CUT OFF BEFORE OUR EYES, YES, JOY AND GLADNESS FROM THE HOUSE OF OUR GOD?

(17) "THE SEED IS ROTTEN UNDER THEIR CLODS, THE GARNERS ARE LAID DESOLATE, THE BARNS ARE BROKEN DOWN; FOR THE CORN IS WITHERED.

(18) "HOW DO THE BEASTS GROAN! THE HERDS OF CATTLE ARE PERPLEXED, BECAUSE THEY HAVE NO PASTURE; YES, THE FLOCKS OF SHEEP ARE MADE DESOLATE.

(19) "O LORD, TO YOU WILL I CRY: FOR THE FIRE HAS DEVOURED THE PASTURES OF THE WILDERNESS, AND THE FLAME HAS BURNED ALL THE TREES OF THE FIELD.

(20) "THE BEASTS OF THE FIELD CRY ALSO UNTO YOU: FOR THE RIVERS OF WATERS ARE DRIED UP, AND THE FIRE HAS DEVOURED THE PASTURES OF THE WILDERNESS."

The exegesis is:

1. (Vs. 15) This Prophecy leaps forward to the coming Great Tribulation, which has not even yet come to pass but will shortly (Rev. 6:17).

2. (Vs. 16) If it was true that locusts had already denuded the land, then the Prophecy concerned something already at least partially fulfilled, speaking of the time of Joel. However, it also refers to the coming Great Tribulation when Israel will experience suffering as never before (Mat. 24:21).

3. (Vs. 17) All that Joel here says took place in the Babylonian invasion, but the greater fulfillment concerns the coming Great Tribulation.

4. Regarding Verse 18, it is obvious from this Passage and many others in the Bible that animals suffer much because of the sins of man.

5. The words of Verse 19, "O LORD, to You will I cry," pertain to Faith, which hides herself in the very God Who executes the Judgment. Such is the reason for the Judgment, in that the people would realize their sin and cry to the Lord.

6. (Vs. 20) As all of this happened not too

NOTES

many years from Joel's day, even more so, and as stated, it will happen in the coming Great Tribulation, which coming time will be the worst trial that Israel will have ever endured (Mat. 24:21).

THE DAY OF THE LORD

The phrase, "The Day of the LORD," is used repeatedly in the Old Testament (Lam. 2:22; Isa. 2:12; 13:6, 9; Jer. 46:10; Ezek. 13:5; 30:3, etc.). The time frame pertained to in this phrase addresses several things. Some of them are:

• "The Day of the LORD," has to do with the Nation of Israel and not the Church. In fact, the Church was unknown to Old Testament Prophets. Peter stated that they searched the Prophecies, which the Lord gave them, trying to discover what would take place between the Cross and the Millennium. Paul telling us that Jew and Gentile would someday be one body, i.e., "the Church," was unknown until it was revealed to the Apostle (Eph. 3:4-7).

• The period designated by the term "Day of the LORD" is still future.

• The character of this time frame is one of Judgment upon Israel because of its sin. In fact, the great Prophet Jeremiah called it the time of "Jacob's trouble" (Jer. 30:7).

• It refers to the period of the Great Tribulation of some seven years predicted by the Old Testament Prophets. This account is given in Revelation, Chapters 6 through 19. It will be a time of unexampled trouble, which will take place after the Church is called out, and which Jesus also stated would come (Mat. 24:21).

• It also pictures the Second Coming of Christ, which will take place during the Battle of Armageddon. It does not refer to the First Advent of Christ but only to His Second Advent, which, of course, is the Second Coming.

While some of the references to the "Day of the LORD," as we are addressing here in Joel, had a fulfillment at that particular time, still, the complete fulfillment awaits a future day, namely the Great Tribulation.

The short phrase, "Alas for the day," as given by Joel, signifies that it will be the most terrible time the world has ever known.

Jesus said, *"For then shall be great tribulation, such as was not since the beginning of the world to this time, no, nor ever shall be"* (Mat. 24:21).

THE ALMIGHTY

As well, the phrase, *"And as a destruction from the Almighty shall it come,"* portrays the Lord being the Author of this Judgment. John said, *"For the great day of His Wrath is come; and who shall be able to stand?"* (Rev. 6:17).

"The Almighty" also means, *"the All-Bountiful."* The Hebrew root is *"shad,"* a woman's breast.

More than likely, the many breasted goddess of the Indian Pantheon was derived in a perverted fashion from the meaning *"Almighty."* As most heathen worship, it is actually a distorted view of the Scriptures.

The use of this Divine Title in this Passage augments its terror. Compare the term *"the Wrath of the Lamb"* (Rev. 6:16).

As is obvious, and as stated, the Holy Spirit in this Prophecy jumps from the present (Joel's time, or the near future from Joel's time), as evidenced in Verse 14, to the distant future, as evidenced in Verse 15, which has not even yet come to pass. In fact, such is done quite often in Bible Prophecy. Actually, there can even be a break of thousands of years in the middle of the sentence, as given by Christ in Luke 4:18-19.

THE MANNER OF PROPHECY

Jesus quoted the great Prophet Isaiah, taken from his Book in Chapter 61, Verses 1 and 2. He quoted it to the middle of the Second Verse, which states, *"To proclaim the acceptable year of the LORD."* He did not include the second part of the sentence, *"And the day of vengeance of our God; to comfort all who mourn."*

The reason He did not quote it is because the last half of the sentence, *"And the day of vengeance of our God,"* will not come about until the Great Tribulation, hence, called by Joel, *"The Day of the LORD."*

It would have been improper for Christ to have used the latter part of this Verse at that particular time because it was not ready for fulfillment. However, when the Holy Spirit

gave it to Isaiah, it was meant to include both the First and Second Advents of the Lord. When Jesus quoted it, it was meant to pertain only to His First Advent.

Therefore, when reading Prophecy, we have to read it, as here in Joel, and apply the proper part to the time at hand. Many Bible students do not understand this and, consequently, try to force the right Prophecy into the wrong time frame.

JUDGMENT

Verses 16 through 20 proclaim the coming Judgment by the Babylonians, which would take place probably between 100 and 150 years into the future. Actually, it is not certain as to the exact time frame of Joel's Ministry. And yet, the greater fulfillment of his statements concerns the coming Great Tribulation, which is yet future, and which will be the worst time this world will have ever known in all of its history. As we have stated, the Lord Himself will bring this Judgment upon the world, a world, we might quickly add, which has forgotten God days without number. Regarding the wars and, above all, the plagues that will be poured out upon the Planet by the Lord Himself, there is a possibility that at least half of the population of the world will die. As we've already stated, Chapters 6 through 19 of Revelation portray this coming time.

And yet, the world does not consider at all what we are taught in the Word of God about the near or the distant future. The incurable evil of the human heart has no time for God. In fact, if the truth be known, there is a greater animosity in America by much of the powers that be against the Lord Jesus Christ and the Word of God than it is any religion in the world, including Islam. And that despite the fact that the Muslims are directly responsible for thousands of Americans losing their lives and bringing our nation to the brink of bankruptcy. Our government officials do not seem to understand that it is the religion of Islam that is the cause of this terrorism. While all Muslims definitely aren't murderers, the far greater majority of Muslims, however, are in total sympathy with those who are murderers.

When September 11, 2001 (9/11), took

place in America, with the loss of nearly 4,000 lives, the Palestinians were seen jumping for joy until they were finally told by their leaders to cease and desist. They didn't want American television to see the rejoicing due to the fact that American taxpayers funnel tens of billions of dollars a year to the Palestinians for their sustenance. But, in truth, most of that money winds up in Swiss bank accounts.

We are supporting people who hate us and would destroy us down to the last man if they had the means to do so. Once again, it's not Uncle Sam, but rather Uncle Sap!

We are coming down to the very conclusion of the Church Age. In fact, we're living in the last of the last days concerning this period.

THE BOOK OF REVELATION

From the account given of the coming Great Tribulation in the Book of Revelation, it seems to me to leave no doubt as to who is controlling these Judgments. It is beyond question, the Lord. And it seems from the account given in the Book of Revelation that the world will know that it's the Lord Who is doing these things, and doing so because of man's constant rebellion. It is described as the Great Day of God's Wrath. But yet, the Scripture repeatedly states that despite the fact of the Judgments and despite the fact that men know that this is God, and I mean the God of the Bible, still, *"they repented not"* (Rev. 9:20, 21; 16:9; 16:11).

WILL THE HOLY SPIRIT BE TAKEN OUT OF THE WORLD AT THE TIME OF THE GREAT TRIBULATION?

No!

The Holy Spirit is God, which means that He is All-Powerful, All-Knowing, and, in fact, is everywhere at the same time. There will be millions Saved during the coming Great Tribulation, which the Scripture says, *"Which no man could number"* (Rev. 7:9-17). And to be sure, people cannot be Saved unless the Holy Spirit draws them (Jn. 6:44; 16:8-11).

Peter said, and I quote directly from THE EXPOSITOR'S STUDY BIBLE:

"And it shall come to pass in the last

NOTES

days, says God *(proclaims these 'last days' as beginning on the Day of Pentecost and continuing through the coming Great Tribulation)*, **I will pour out of My Spirit upon all flesh** *(speaks of all people everywhere and, therefore, not limited to some particular geographical location; as well, it is not limited respecting race, color, or creed)*: **and your sons and your daughters shall prophesy** *(includes both genders)*, **and your young men shall see Visions, and your old men shall dream Dreams** *(all given by the Holy Spirit; the Hebrew language insinuates, 'both your young men and old men shall see Visions, and both your old men and young men shall dream Dreams'; it applies to both genders as well)*:

"And on My Servants and on My Handmaidens I will pour out in those days of My Spirit *(is meant purposely to address two classes of people who had been given very little status in the past, slaves and women)*; **and they shall prophesy** *(pertains to one of the 'Gifts of the Spirit' [I Cor. 12:8-10])*:

"And I will show wonders in Heaven above, and signs in the Earth beneath; blood, and fire, and vapour of smoke *(pertains to the fact that these 'days of My Spirit' will cover the entirety of the Church Age, even into the coming Great Tribulation; that time limit has now been nearly 2,000 years).*"

SALVATION

"The sun shall be turned into darkness, and the moon into blood *(not meant to be literal, but rather that the moon will look blood red because of atmospheric conditions)*, **before that great and notable Day of the Lord come** *(the Second Coming)*:

"And it shall come to pass, *that* whosoever shall call on the Name of the Lord shall be Saved *(Joel 2:30-32; presents one of the most glorious statements ever made; it includes both Jews and Gentiles equally)*" **(Acts 2:17-21).**

It has been taught by some that the Holy Spirit at the Rapture of the Church will be taken out of the world. The Bible doesn't teach that.

While the Holy Spirit will definitely conclude His Work regarding the Church at that time, meaning that it has now been raptured away, still, He will continue to Move upon the hearts and lives of millions, persuading them to give their hearts to Christ. Many will, while many won't!

Every single thing done on this Earth by the Godhead, with the exception of Christ coming into this world and dying on the Cross, has been done by the Holy Spirit. In fact, the Holy Spirit superintended every single thing that Jesus did from His Conception to His Resurrection. So, the Bible in no way teaches that the Holy Spirit is going to be taken out of this world at the Great Tribulation.

"All is in Christ;
"God's Dear Son is Lord of all.
"Jesus Christ is Life's Perfection,
"Perfect Love and Perfect Life.
"Son of God, the True Reflection,
"Of the Father's Radiance bright.
"All the treasures of God's Riches,
"All the secrets of His Wisdom,
"All in Christ are hid away.
"Let His Name be praised today!"

"All is in Christ;
"God's Dear Son is Lord of all.
"Blessings are imparted to us,
"By the shameful Cross He bore.
"By His Suffering inglorious,
"We have peace forevermore.
"By the Cross we have forgiveness,
"Life eternal, endless Mercy,
"By God's Son is freely given,
"Everything in Earth and Heaven."

"All is in Christ;
"God's Dear Son is Lord of all.
"In me there is naught but weakness,
"I am worthless, full of sin,
"Stricken by its mortal sickness,
"Lacking light and hope within.
"Now in Christ I find abundant,
"Victory and strength and power.
"Saviour, come and live in me,
"Come and make me rich in Thee."

"All is in Christ;
"God's Dear Son is Lord of all.
"Saviour, pardon my transgressions,
"For my love is still so small;
"Though I gave all my possessions,
"This would profit scarce at all.

NOTES

"'Tis myself that You desire;
"So I give myself, Dear Master;
"No thing have You kept from me—
"Nor will I keep aught from Thee."

"All is in Christ;
"Your whole self present to Him.
"Vain your quest for lasting pleasure,
"Wealth, success, and worldly fame;
"Christ Alone must be your treasure,
"His Resource your only claim.
"Come, let Him disperse the famine,
"Of your arid, waste existence.
"Let God's Son, the Immortal King,
"Freely give you everything."

CHAPTER 2

(1) "BLOW YOU THE TRUMPET IN ZION, AND SOUND AN ALARM IN MY HOLY MOUNTAIN: LET ALL THE INHABITANTS OF THE LAND TREMBLE: FOR THE DAY OF THE LORD COMES, FOR IT IS NEAR AT HAND."

The pattern is:

1. The terms, *"Zion," "My Holy Mountain,"* and *"the land,"* define Israel and Jerusalem as the scene of these future events.

2. The phrase, *"Let all the inhabitants of the land tremble,"* refers to Israel, where the Battle of Armageddon will take place.

3. *"For the Day of the LORD comes, for it is near at hand,"* refers to the period in the future when the Messiah will interfere on behalf of His ancient People and deliver and restore them. This is the Second Coming! Its details are predicted in the Book of Revelation (Rev., Chpt. 19).

4. As well, modern Preachers must *"sound an alarm"* at the condition of the modern church, for these events of which Joel speaks are near at hand. This also means that the Rapture of the Church, which will precede these events, is very near (I Thess. 4:13-18; II Thess. 2:7-12).

BLOW THE TRUMPET IN ZION

The world little knows or understands the tremendous part that Israel will play in the near future as it regards world events.

"Why are these ancient people so very, very important?" many people might ask.

Some 4,000 years ago, from the loins of Abraham and the womb of Sarah, the Lord raised up these people, who we now refer to as *"Jews"* or *"Israelis."* At the time of Abraham, as far as we know, this family was the only people on the face of the Earth, with the exception of Melchizedek, who served Jehovah. It is thought that quite possible Melchizedek (Gen. 14:17-20) could actually have been Shem, the son of Noah. Shem was alive at that time and actually lived for about 60 more years. In fact, some think that Shem died when Abraham was about 150 years of age. The name Melchizedek means, *"King of Righteousness"* and *"King of Peace"* (Heb. 7:2).

Melchizedek, as a Priest, symbolized the coming Christ, Who is our Great High Priest (Heb.7:15-17). David prophesied, about 1,000 years after Abraham, *"The LORD has sworn, and will not repent, You* (Christ) *are a Priest forever after the order of Melchizedek"* (Ps. 110:4).

In fact, Melchizedek blessed Abraham, which means that the standing of Melchizedek as a Type of Christ was greater than that of Abraham.

At any rate, this was the limit of those who truly knew and served Jehovah, with every other nation in the world at that time worshipping demon spirits, etc.

So Israel was raised up by God for the purpose of the following:

• They were to give the world the Word of God, which they did. Every writer in the Bible was Jewish. Some think that maybe Luke was Gentile; however, I personally feel that Luke was Jewish as well.

• Israel was to serve as the womb of the Messiah, so to speak, which they did. Unfortunately, they did not recognize Him when He came and, therefore, crucified Him, but He rose from the dead after being in the heart of the Earth for some three days and nights. Israel still does not recognize Him, calling Him an imposter. However, at the Second Coming, they will realize that this One they crucified was actually their Messiah and now will fulfill that role upon Israel's Repentance.

• Israel, as well, was to evangelize the

world. In that, she failed but will accomplish the task in the coming Kingdom Age (Isa. 66:19).

At that time, Israel will be the Priestly Nation of the world and, in fact, the leading Nation. The Prophet Ezekiel gives the boundaries, in a sense, of their domain in that coming glad day. Israel at that time will incorporate not only that referred to presently as modern Israel but also Lebanon, Syria, all of Iraq up to the River Euphrates, as well as the Arabian Peninsula. Actually, Israel in that coming day will be nearly half as large as the United States.

But before that time comes, Israel will face its greatest trial, greater even than the Holocaust. In fact, the Prophet Zechariah said that two-thirds of the population of Israel will be slaughtered at that time, and done so by the Antichrist (Zech. 13:8-9). Were it not for the Second Coming of the Lord (Zech. 14:1-7), Israel would be destroyed. However, at that time, when all of Israel has fallen to the man of sin, with even one half of Jerusalem having fallen, as well, it will look like there is no hope (Zech. 14:1-2). But, according to the great Prophet Isaiah, Israel will repent at that time (Isa. 64:6-12). To be sure, the Lord will accept their Repentance and will answer by the most magnificent, glorious, stupendous, and miraculous event the world has ever known by far, and I speak of the Second Coming. Then the Antichrist will find out just exactly as to Who Jesus Christ really is. He won't like very much what he sees. In fact, the Second Coming will herald his demise, plus the end of Satan and all demon spirits, as well, at least for the most part (Rev. 19:15-21; 20:1-3).

All of it goes back, as previously stated, to the words given by the Lord to Abraham when He said to him, *"And I will bless them who bless you, and curse him who curses you: and in you shall all families of the Earth be blessed"* (Gen. 12:3).

But, as stated, before Israel comes to that glad day, she must see some dark times, in fact, the darkest ever!

SOUND AN ALARM IN MY HOLY MOUNTAIN

The great Prophecy of Joel, given approximately some 2,600 years ago, is, in effect, *"sounding that alarm."* But, regrettably, most of the world little heeds or even cares what the Lord gave to the great Prophet. In fact, Israel herself gives little heed to that given to us by Joel.

As it regards *"sounding the alarm,"* this should be the task of every modern Preacher as well! The world and the church should understand the following, and it's the Preacher of the Gospel who has been given the task of delivering the message. It is as follows:

• We are to sound the trumpet loud and clear that the great events of Bible Prophecy, such as the Rapture of the Church, the rise of the man of sin, and the onset of the Great Tribulation, are all very close.

• We are to proclaim the fact that the Rapture of the Church could happen at any moment.

• We are to *"sound the alarm"* that the things which are about to come upon this world are going to be more terrible than anything this Planet has ever seen previously. And, to be sure, that is saying something!

• As well, we are to warn every single person who doesn't know Christ that if he dies in that condition, he will die eternally lost, meaning he will be in Hell forever and forever.

• We are to *"sound the alarm"* that every Believer desperately needs the mighty Baptism with the Holy Spirit, especially, in these trying times.

• And, above all, we are to stress the fact, which means to *"sound the alarm,"* that every Believer must place his or her Faith exclusively in the Cross of Christ, understanding that Jesus Christ is the Source while the Cross is the Means by which all things are given to us. And, if the Message of the Cross is ignored, there remains no fallback position for the Child of God. It is either *"Jesus Christ and Him Crucified,"* or it is spiritual oblivion.

LET THE INHABITANTS OF THE LAND TREMBLE

This speaks of Judgment, and Judgment so terrible as to defy all description.

Why would the Lord allow such to come upon His ancient People? Admittedly, they have strayed and lost their way, but, still, God

NOTES

is a God of Mercy. So, why the Judgment?

Beginning with the Prophets of old, even with Moses thousands of years ago, the Lord began to warn Israel but all to no avail! Despite the Prophets and despite the warnings, still, Israel didn't even know her Messiah when He came and, in fact, crucified the very One Who had come to save them. Never mind that He rose from the dead on the third day. They still will not believe and have gone deeper and deeper into that quagmire of spiritual darkness. But yet, the Lord loves them and because of that Love, He must exact stringent measures in order to bring Israel to her senses. That is the reason for the coming Great Tribulation! That is the reason for the suffering these people will have to undergo! That is the reason, their Repentance, that all of these things are going to happen.

It would be much easier for the Lord to just turn elsewhere; however, it is love that will carry out this Judgment, and for the expressed purpose of bringing Israel to her senses.

Let the reader understand, if there is a chance for Repentance in any capacity in any Believer, and I speak of those who have seriously drifted and strayed, God will bring acute chastisement in order to bring the individual to his senses (Heb. 12:5-11). It is all done from a position of love.

Despite what a parent might say, one who will not correct his or her child simply does not love the child. If they love the child, they are going to correct them. This means to chastise it and to be as severe as they need to be in order to bring the child to its senses. The Lord will do no less with those who name His Name.

THE DAY OF THE LORD COMES

The phrase, *"The Day of the LORD,"* is mentioned five times in this Prophecy, plainly proving all of it is future (Joel 1:15; 2:1, 11, 31; 3:14).

The phrase, *"For the Day of the LORD comes,"* means that this coming terrible time, the time of the Great Tribulation, is most definitely going to come. Nothing can stop it. No action by the United States or any conglomerate of nations can stop it.

The Prophet has said it will come, and come it shall!

When the phrase, *"For it is near at hand,"* is used, it has reference to any number of things.

The Holy Spirit, in giving the Prophecy to Joel, leaps ahead to the time of the coming of the Judgment and says, *"For it is near at hand."* Concerning this, Jesus said, and perhaps referring to the same Verse:

THE PARABLE OF THE FIG TREE

"Now learn a Parable of the fig tree *(the Bible presents three trees, the fig, the olive, and the vine, as representing the Nation of Israel, nationally, spiritually, and dispensationally)*; **When his branch is yet tender, and puts forth leaves** *(is meant to serve as the illustration of Israel nationally)*, **you know that summer** *is* **near** *(refers to Israel as the greatest Prophetic Sign of all, telling us that we are now living in the last of the last day)*:

"So likewise you *(points to the modern church)*, **when you shall see all these things** *(which we are now seeing as it regards Israel)*, **know that it is near,** *even* **at the doors** *(the fulfillment of Endtime Prophecies)*.**"**

THIS GENERATION

"Verily I say unto you, This generation shall not pass *(the generation of Jews which will be alive at the beginning of the Great Tribulation; as well, it was a prediction by Christ that, irrespective of the problems that Israel would face, even from His Day, they would survive)*, **till all these things be fulfilled** *(there is no doubt, they will be fulfilled)*.

"Heaven and Earth shall pass away *(doesn't refer to annihilation, but rather a change from one condition or state to another)*, **but My Words shall not pass away** *(what the Word of God says, will be!)*.

"But of that day and hour knows no *man*, **no, not the Angels of Heaven, but My Father only" (Mat. 24:32-36).**

(2) "A DAY OF DARKNESS AND OF GLOOMINESS, A DAY OF CLOUDS AND OF THICK DARKNESS, AS THE MORNING SPREAD UPON THE MOUNTAINS: A GREAT PEOPLE AND A STRONG; THERE HAS NOT BEEN EVER THE LIKE,

NEITHER SHALL BE ANY MORE AFTER IT, EVEN TO THE YEARS OF MANY GENERATIONS.

(3) "A FIRE DEVOURS BEFORE THEM; AND BEHIND THEM A FLAME BURNS: THE LAND IS AS THE GARDEN OF EDEN BEFORE THEM, AND BEHIND THEM A DESOLATE WILDERNESS; YES, AND NOTHING SHALL ESCAPE THEM.

(4) "THE APPEARANCE OF THEM IS AS THE APPEARANCE OF HORSES; AND AS HORSEMEN, SO SHALL THEY RUN.

(5) "LIKE THE NOISE OF CHARIOTS ON THE TOPS OF MOUNTAINS SHALL THEY LEAP, LIKE THE NOISE OF A FLAME OF FIRE THAT DEVOURS THE STUBBLE, AS A STRONG PEOPLE SET IN BATTLE ARRAY.

(6) "BEFORE THEIR FACE THE PEOPLE SHALL BE MUCH PAINED: ALL FACES SHALL GATHER BLACKNESS.

(7) "THEY SHALL RUN LIKE MIGHTY MEN; THEY SHALL CLIMB THE WALL LIKE MEN OF WAR; AND THEY SHALL MARCH EVERYONE ON HIS WAYS, AND THEY SHALL NOT BREAK THEIR RANKS:

(8) "NEITHER SHALL ONE THRUST ANOTHER; THEY SHALL WALK EVERYONE IN HIS PATH: AND WHEN THEY FALL UPON THE SWORD, THEY SHALL NOT BE WOUNDED.

(9) "THEY SHALL RUN TO AND FRO IN THE CITY; THEY SHALL RUN UPON THE WALL, THEY SHALL CLIMB UP UPON THE HOUSES; THEY SHALL ENTER IN AT THE WINDOWS LIKE A THIEF.

(10) "THE EARTH SHALL QUAKE BEFORE THEM; THE HEAVENS SHALL TREMBLE: THE SUN AND THE MOON SHALL BE DARK, AND THE STARS SHALL WITHDRAW THEIR SHINING:

(11) "AND THE LORD SHALL UTTER HIS VOICE BEFORE HIS ARMY: FOR HIS CAMP IS VERY GREAT: FOR HE IS STRONG WHO EXECUTES HIS WORD: FOR THE DAY OF THE LORD IS GREAT AND VERY TERRIBLE; AND WHO CAN ABIDE IT?"

The synopsis is:

1. (Vs. 2) *"A day of darkness and of gloominess, a day of clouds and of thick darkness,"* refers to the beginning days of the

Battle of Armageddon, when the Antichrist *"shall ascend and come like a storm, and you* (he) *shall be like a cloud to cover the land"* (Ezek. 38:9).

2. (Vs. 2) *"Neither shall be any more after it, even to the years of many generations,"* describes the Coming of the Lord with His mighty Army, which the world has never seen before and will not see again until the end of the Millennium, when Satan and his Angels and demons will appear on Earth in an effort to once again take it over, at which time God will send His Army of Heaven against them for the second time (Isa. 24:22; Rev. 20:7-10).

This is what the *"many generations"* refer to, which concerns a timespan of about 1,000 years between the Second Coming and the end of the Millennium.

3. Verse 3 corresponds with Ezekiel 38:22, *"And great hailstones, fire, and brimstone,"* which refers to the Second Coming of the Lord, which will take place in the Battle of Armageddon (Zech. 14:3).

4. The pronoun *"them"* of Verse 4 pertains to all the Saints who will be with the Lord at the Second Coming, which corresponds with Revelation 19:14. All the Saints of God who have ever lived will then come back with the Lord and will be riding on *"white horses."* These, of course, will be spirit horses.

5. Verse 5 tells us that the Second Coming will not only be glorious, but its power will express itself in a manner the world has never known before. The phrase, *"As a strong people set in battle array,"* will be in answer to the boasts and taunts of the Antichrist, which will fill the world the last three and a half years of the Great Tribulation.

6. Referring to Verse 6, the Antichrist, seeing this tremendous power arrayed against him, *"shall be much pained."*

7. The initial thrust of Verse 7 is that the Second Coming of the Lord will not, at least in its initial stages, be for the blessing of the world, but instead for the destruction of evil. Hence, they are called *"men of war."* As well, *"they shall not break their ranks"* until this job of defeating the Antichrist and his armies is completed. And, completed it will be.

NOTES

8. The phrase of Verse 8, *"And when they fall upon the sword, they shall not be wounded,"* shows that the Glorified Saints, the Army of the Lord, will have Glorified Bodies, which are impervious to harm. In other words, they cannot be killed.

9. The idea of Verse 9 is that no place will be inaccessible to this Army of the Lord.

10. The sense of Verse 10 is that the coming of the Son of God will be so resplendent with Glory, with the very heavens lit up to such a degree that they will literally *"tremble."* Moreover, the *"sun,"* the *"moon,"* and the *"stars"* will be so outshone that it will seem as if they have no light. Jesus mentioned this (Mat. 24:27-30).

11. The phrase of Verse 11, *"And the LORD shall utter His Voice before His Army,"* speaks of all the happenings of Verses 2 through 11. *"For He is strong Who executes His Word,"* proclaims the Lord having the Power to back up His Word, and that all these predictions shall come to pass exactly as stated. All of this speaks of the Second Coming.

A DAY LIKE THERE HAS NEVER BEEN BEFORE

The Antichrist will have long since declared war on the Lord Jesus Christ. Of course, the question begs to be asked as to how he can do that.

He will do so by attacking God's Chosen People, the Nation of Israel, with every intention of completely annihilating them from the face of the Earth. As previously stated, what Haman, Herod, and Hitler could not do, the man of sin will set out above all to succeed.

WHY IS THE DESTRUCTION OF ISRAEL SO IMPORTANT TO HIM?

The idea is, if he can prove any Promise in the Bible to be untrue, in effect, he has won the conflict. If he can get even one Promise in the Bible to be proven untrue, this age-old conflict will be ended in his favor. And, the greatest Promise in the Bible concerns the restoration of Israel. Every Prophet of the Old Testament, along with Paul in the New Testament, mentioned that Restoration. If he can prove that untrue, as stated, he has won the conflict. He has said:

I WILL BE LIKE THE MOST HIGH

"How are you fallen from Heaven, O Lucifer, son of the morning! how are you cut down to the ground, which did weaken the nations! *(Isaiah's Prophecy now switches from the Antichrist to his unholy sponsor, Satan himself. 'Lucifer' is the name of Satan. Actually, he is an Angel, originally created by God, who served the Lord in Righteousness for an undetermined period of time.*

"When he fell, he led a revolution against God, with about one-third of the Angels, it seems, throwing in their lot with him [Rev. 12:4]. Therefore, all the pain, suffering, misery, heartache, death, and deception, which have ruled the nations from the very beginning, can be laid at the doorstep of this revolution headed up by Satan.)

"For you have said in your heart, I will ascend into Heaven, I will exalt my throne above the stars of God: I will sit also upon the mount of the congregation, in the sides of the north:

"I will ascend above the heights of the clouds; I will be like the Most High. *(In these two Verses, we see the foment of Satan's rebellion and revolution against God. It seems that Lucifer, while true to the Lord, was given dominion of the Earth, which was before Adam. After his fall, he worked deceitfully to get other angelic rulers to follow him in his war against God.)"*

THE FINAL END OF THE EVIL ONE

Concerning his boasts, the Lord says the following of him:

"Yet you shall be brought down to Hell, to the sides of the pit. *(This would be the lot of Satan and all who seek to be like God, but in a wrong way, in effect, by making themselves god)"* (Isa. 14:12-15).

So, the Antichrist will amass the greatest army possibly the world has ever seen as it comes down on Israel, referred to as the *"Battle of Armageddon."* Of course, it is Satan who puts all of these ideas in the heart of the man of sin. As stated, Satan will invest more in this man than he has ever invested in any man. In fact, this will be the fell swoop of Satan! All his eggs are in this basket, so to speak! And, for a short period

NOTES

of time, it will look like he is succeeding. In fact, he would succeed in this effort to completely annihilate Israel but for one thing, and that one thing is the greatest happening the world has ever known. It is the Second Coming of the Lord. That's what these Passages refer to.

THE BATTLE OF ARMAGEDDON

There is every reason to believe that hundreds, if not thousands, of television cameras will be at this momentous battle. The Antichrist will, no doubt, desire the entirety of the world to see his proposed great victory over Jerusalem, with the extermination of every Jew finally being brought to pass before the entirety of the world.

However, that which the world will see will be far different from that anticipated by the Antichrist. Instead, they will see the greatest Jew of all coming back in Power and great Glory, and with multiplied millions of Saints with Him, along with myriads of Angels. This, the television cameras and, no doubt, by satellite, will project into the homes of much of the world. Hence, the Holy Spirit in Verse 4, uses the word, *"The appearance of them."*

It will be a scene never before witnessed by human eyes. The grandeur, glory, and greatness of this moment will surpass anything ever known in human history. The very heavens will, no doubt, erupt in a cascade of joy as Jesus Christ, their Creator, comes back in order to set up a Kingdom for which so many millions have prayed, *"Thy Kingdom come, Thy Will be done. . . ."*

THE POWER OF THE SECOND COMING

Joel said, *"Like the noise of chariots on the tops of mountains shall they leap, like the noise of a flame of fire that devours the stubble, as a strong people set in battle array."*

This Verse tells us that the Coming of the Lord will not only be glorious, but its Power will express itself in a manner, which the world has never known before.

Everything seen previously, even though powerful, has been natural. This will be supernatural and, as such, will know no bounds.

During the outset of this Battle, when it seems as if Israel will be annihilated once and for all, and knowing that no one else will come to their aid, Israel will then begin to cry for the Messiah, the True Messiah. They will know at that time that He is their only Hope.

At that time, their prayer will be answered as it has never been answered. He will come, and, Oh, how He will come! He will be *"in battle array,"* and the world will see His Power expended against evil as never before. Israel, as well, will be saved!

No doubt, all of this will be going out all over the world through hundreds and, as stated, possibly even thousands of television cameras, taking the unfolding of the Second Coming into billions of homes all over the world. The Scripture says of this coming event:

"Behold, He comes with clouds *(the Second Coming of Christ is the chief theme of this Book; the word 'clouds' represents great numbers of Saints)***; and every eye shall see Him** *(refers to all who will be in the immediate vicinity of Jerusalem, and possibly even billions who may very well see Him by television)***, and they** *also* **who pierced Him** *(the Jews, and they will then know beyond the shadow of a doubt that Jesus is Messiah and Lord)***: and all kindreds of the Earth shall wail because of Him. Even so, Amen.** *(The 'wailing' will take place because of the Judgment Christ will bring upon the world for its sin and shame)"* **(Rev. 1:7).**

THE QUAKING OF THE EARTH

Verses 2 through 11 proclaim and give a descriptive account of the Armies of God at the Battle of Armageddon.

The phrase from Verse 2, *"A great people and a strong,"* and considering the corresponding Prophecies, denotes these people as supernatural.

The Scripture says, *"There has never been ever the like,"* and according to Verse 11, this is the Army of the Lord, which will appear at the Second Coming (Rev., Chpt. 19).

The phrase, *"Neither shall be any more after it, even to the years of many generations,"* describes the Coming of the Lord with His Mighty Army, which the world has never seen before and will not see again until the end of the Millennium. Then, Satan and his Angels and demons will appear on Earth

in an effort to once again take over. At that time, God will send this Army of Heaven against them for the second time (Isa. 24:22; Rev. 20:7-10).

This is what the *"many generations"* refers to, which concerns a timespan of about 1,000 years, between the Second Coming and the end of the Millennium.

Concerning the *"great people and a strong,"* this pertains to the Glorified Saints. It will include every Believer who has ever lived from the dawn of time through the conclusion of the Great Tribulation, which will be a time frame of some 6,000 or more years.

While the Glorified Body is flesh and bone, there is no evidence in the Word of God that it will contain blood. Presently, the life of the flesh is in the blood; however, as it regards the Glorified Body, the life force will be the Holy Spirit. In this particular body, which is the kind that Christ had after His Resurrection, there will be qualities which are totally foreign to us at present.

At that time, travel will be by the *"speed of thought."* In other words, when the person with the Glorified Body desires to be somewhere, all he will have to do is think it, and then he is there. As well, physical barriers, such as walls, etc., will prove no barrier at all for the Glorified Saint. While food will be eaten, it will not be necessary as it regards life and living, the life force then being, as stated, the Holy Spirit. All of this is derived from the conduct and actions of Christ after His Resurrection. As John the Beloved said, *". . . and it does not yet appear what we shall be: but we know that, when He shall appear, we shall be like Him; for we shall see Him as He is"* (I Jn. 3:2).

A DEVOURING FIRE

The phrase, *"A fire devours before them; and behind them a flame burns,"* corresponds with Ezekiel 38:22, *"And great hailstones, fire, and brimstone,"* which will actually be the artillery of the Lord in the Battle of Armageddon. The evidence is, the Lord will rain tens of thousands, if not hundreds of thousands, of hailstones. Some of these stones will, no doubt, weigh 100 pounds or more. Along with these hailstones will be meteorites, which, as would be obvious, will decimate the armies of the Antichrist, and do so in short order.

The great Prophet Zechariah said, *"Then shall the LORD go forth, and fight against those nations, as when He fought in the day of battle"* (Zech. 14:3).

FOLLOWING HIM ON WHITE HORSES

Joel said, *"The appearance of them is as the appearance of horses; and as horsemen, so shall they run."* This Verse corresponds with John's statement, *"And the armies which were in Heaven followed Him upon white horses, clothed in fine linen, white and clean"* (Rev. 19:14).

In other words, all the Saints of God who have ever lived will come back with the Lord, all, riding on *"white horses."* These, of course, will be spirit horses.

A STRONG PEOPLE SET IN BATTLE ARRAY

Verse 5 says, *"Like the noise of chariots on the tops of mountains shall they leap, like the noise of a flame of fire that devours the stubble, as a strong people set in battle array."*

This Verse tells us that the Coming of the Lord will not only be glorious, but its power will express itself in a manner in which the world has never known before.

Everything the world has is natural; however, all of this described in these Passages will be supernatural and, as such, will know no bounds.

The phrase, *"As a strong people set in battle array,"* will be the answer to the boasts and taunts of the Antichrist for the last three and a half years. Daniel said, *"And he shall speak great words against the Most High . . ."* (Dan. 7:25).

In fact, seeing these *"strong people"* set against him, these *"great words"* will stick in his throat.

LORD, WHY DO YOU WAIT?

Millions the world over have asked themselves the question as to why the Lord has not intervened in this world, thereby, bringing to a halt the pain, sickness, and suffering, along with man's inhumanity to man. That mystery will now be ended and that

NOTES

prayer answered. For the Lord will intervene in a way as the world has never known before.

The Eighth Verse is very interesting in that it says, *"Neither shall one thrust another; they shall walk everyone in his path: and when they fall upon the sword, they shall not be wounded."*

This refers to the fact that the Glorified Saints, as stated, the Army of the Lord, will have Glorified Bodies, which are impervious to harm. In other words, they cannot be wounded or killed. Therefore, the weaponry of the Antichrist, no matter how powerful, will be useless against them.

As it regards the Glorified Body, most Christians have a very dim understanding of what this will actually be. When will this take place?

At the time of the Rapture of the Church, or as some would prefer to use the term *"Resurrection,"* every Believer will be changed and given the Glorified Body. Concerning this, the Scripture beautifully states:

"Behold, I show you a mystery (a new Revelation given by the Holy Spirit to Paul concerning the Resurrection, i.e., Rapture)**; We shall not all sleep** (at the time of the Resurrection [Rapture], many Christians will be alive)**, but we shall all be changed** (both those who are dead and those who are alive)**."**

CHANGED IN A MOMENT

"In a moment, in the twinkling of an eye (proclaims how long it will take for this change to take place)**, at the last trump** (does not denote by the use of the word 'last' that there will be successive trumpet blasts, but rather denotes that this is the close of things, referring to the Church Age)**: for the trumpet shall sound** (it is the 'Trump of God' [I Thess. 4:16])**, and the dead shall be raised incorruptible** (the Sainted dead, with no sin nature)**, and we shall be changed** (put on the Glorified Body)**."**

INCORRUPTIBLE AND IMMORTAL

"For this corruptible (sin nature) **must put on incorruption** (a Glorified Body with no sin nature)**, and this mortal** (subject to death) **must put on immortality** (will never die).

"So when this corruptible *(sin nature)* shall have put on incorruption *(the Divine Nature in total control by the Holy Spirit)*, and this mortal *(subject to death)* shall have put on immortality *(will never die)*, then shall be brought to pass the saying that is written, Death is swallowed up in Victory *([Isa. 25:8], the full benefits of the Cross will then be ours, of which we now have only the Firstfruits [Rom. 8:23])*" **(I Cor. 15:51-54).**

THE HEAVENS SHALL TREMBLE

The sense of Verse 10 is that the coming of the Son of God will be so resplendent with Glory that it will light up the very heavens to such a degree that they will literally *"tremble."* As well, He will so outshine the *"sun," "moon,"* and *"stars"* that it will seem as if they have no light.

To imagine the brightness of the sun seeming as if it is not shining would demand a glory and brightness far beyond anything ever seen or known by the human eye.

With the Holy Spirit mentioning both *"sun"* and *"moon,"* it signifies that the entirety of the world will witness this phenomenon, at least in some regard.

In other words, even though it will be daylight in Israel at the time of the Coming of the Lord, on the other side of the world, it will be night. However, the implication is that His Coming will be so resplendent with Glory that it will actually cause the night on the other side of the world to seem as day. Zechariah said, *"But it shall be one day which shall be known to the LORD, not day, nor night: but it shall come to pass, that at evening time it shall be light"* (Zech. 14:7).

All of this signifies that the entirety of the world will know that something has happened because of the tremendous atmospheric changes.

To imagine such Glory is beyond comprehension! For nearly 2,000 years, most of the world has rejected and even cursed the Lord Jesus Christ. Then they will know that the One born of the Virgin Mary and raised in such humble circumstances was and is actually the Son of the Living God.

When one considers that the planetary bodies will, in effect, bow to Him, then how

NOTES

much more, *"That at the Name of Jesus every knee should bow, of things in Heaven, and things in Earth, and things under the Earth;*

"And that every tongue should confess that Jesus Christ is Lord, to the Glory of God the Father" (Phil. 2:10-11).

FOR THE DAY OF THE LORD IS GREAT AND VERY TERRIBLE; AND WHO CAN ABIDE IT?

The phrase taken from Verse 11, *"For He is strong Who executes His Word,"* proclaims Him having the Power to back up His Word, and that all of these predictions shall come to pass exactly as stated.

Therefore, whatever is read in these Prophecies and correctly interpreted, to be sure, shall come to pass exactly as predicted because it is the Word of the Lord.

The question, *"For the Day of the LORD is great and very terrible; and who can abide it?"* pertains to the Coming of the Lord.

Even though we have done our best to describe this momentous event, still, this *"Day of the LORD"* will be by far the most cataclysmic phenomenon the world has ever known! Even the Holy Spirit calls it *"great and very terrible."*

The question, *"And who can abide it?"* pertains to the evil of this world, and more particularly, the Antichrist. In effect, Satan's day is over and, to be sure, all opposition to the Lord will quickly be put down!

At that time Christ will set up His Kingdom, and He will do so with such Power and Glory that all opposition will immediately cease. As well, at that time, Satan, along with all the demon powers of darkness and fallen Angels, will be locked away in the *"bottomless pit,"* where he will be confined for a *"thousand years"* (Rev. 20:1-3).

(12) "THEREFORE ALSO NOW, SAYS THE LORD, TURN YOU EVEN TO ME WITH ALL YOUR HEART, AND WITH FASTING, AND WITH WEEPING, AND WITH MOURNING:

(13) "AND REND YOUR HEART, AND NOT YOUR GARMENTS, AND TURN UNTO THE LORD YOUR GOD: FOR HE IS GRACIOUS AND MERCIFUL, SLOW TO ANGER, AND OF GREAT KINDNESS, AND REPENTS HIM OF THE EVIL.

(14) "WHO KNOWS IF HE WILL RETURN AND REPENT, AND LEAVE A BLESSING BEHIND HIM; EVEN A MEAT OFFERING AND A DRINK OFFERING UNTO THE LORD YOUR GOD?

(15) "BLOW THE TRUMPET IN ZION, SANCTIFY A FAST, CALL A SOLEMN ASSEMBLY:

(16) "GATHER THE PEOPLE, SANCTIFY THE CONGREGATION, ASSEMBLE THE ELDERS, GATHER THE CHILDREN, AND THOSE WHO SUCK THE BREASTS: LET THE BRIDEGROOM GO FORTH OF HIS CHAMBER, AND THE BRIDE OUT OF HER CLOSET.

(17) "LET THE PRIESTS, THE MINISTERS OF THE LORD, WEEP BETWEEN THE PORCH AND THE ALTAR, AND LET THEM SAY, SPARE YOUR PEOPLE, O LORD, AND GIVE NOT YOUR HERITAGE TO REPROACH, THAT THE HEATHEN SHOULD RULE OVER THEM: WHEREFORE SHOULD THEY SAY AMONG THE PEOPLE, WHERE IS THEIR GOD?"

The structure is:

1. (Vs. 12) As Verses 2 through 11 spoke of the Second Coming, Verses 12 through 17 portray the call to Repentance for Israel, which will take place at the Second Coming and will guarantee her future Restoration. It also speaks to the Judah of Joel's day but more so to the Second Coming and what will then happen.

2. (Vs. 14) As the Righteousness of God demands Judgment upon unconfessed sin, likewise, the same Righteousness demands Blessing when sin is repented of and turned from.

3. In essence, Verse 15 speaks of the events in Israel immediately after the Second Coming. Even though Israel at that time will not be able to literally blow a trumpet, just the same, the image is sufficient. As well, even though none of this pertains to the Church, the example could also well apply!

4. (Vs. 17) The idea of this Repentance in that coming day pertains, in effect, to Israel's rejection of Christ and their crucifying Him. They will now learn that the One Whom they crucified is, in fact, their Messiah; hence, the religious leaders of Israel at that time

NOTES

will lead in this contrition before the Lord.

THE REPENTANCE OF ISRAEL

The chronology of this is perfect. When Jesus Christ comes back, as we've already stated, He will come with such Power and Glory as the world has never seen before in all of its history. Our Lord will make short work of the Antichrist, and of that one can be certain. In fact, five-sixths of the army of the Antichrist will be destroyed during the Battle of Armageddon, and all because of the Coming of the Lord.

Looking like Israel is going to be completely destroyed by the Antichrist, these beleaguered people will then begin to call on the Lord and cry to Him as never before. The Lord will hear that prayer and will answer it speedily and do so by the Second Coming. When Israel sees Him as He lands on the Mount of Olivet, at first, they will not know Who He actually is. In fact, they will ask Him, **"What are these wounds in Your Hands? Then He shall answer, Those with which I was wounded in the house of My Friends" (Zech. 13:6).**

The notes from THE EXPOSITOR'S STUDY BIBLE regarding this Passage give us the following:

THE TRUE PROPHET

"In these Passages, as it regards Zechariah [Zech. 13:3-5], false prophets are placed beside the True Prophet, the Lord Jesus Christ. They, before the Coming of the Lord, too oftentimes were rewarded, while He, as each True Prophet, was greatly opposed, even crucified. The false prophets thrust themselves forward and claimed reverence and position; He Himself, the greatest of the Prophets, did not claim to be a professional Prophet – that was not His Mission in coming to Earth – but became a Bond-servant and a Shepherd; made and appointed such in the Divine Purpose of Redemption. For man having sold himself into slavery, it was necessary that Christ should take that position in order to redeem him."

THE MOMENT OF RECOGNITION

*"'And one shall say unto Him,' refers to

the moment of recognition, as outlined in 12:10, where it says, 'And they shall look upon Me Whom they have pierced, and they shall mourn for Him.' This will be immediately after the Second Coming, with the Antichrist now defeated and Christ standing before Israel. They will then know, beyond the shadow of a doubt, that He is the Messiah; then will they ask, 'What are these wounds in Your Hands?' These wounds, which He will ever carry, will be an instant and constant reminder of Who He is and what was done to Him, which presents Him as the Sin-Bearer of the world. Even though He was the Redeemer of all mankind, still, this shows how He was treated by man, especially by His Own.

"'Then He shall answer,' will be an answer that will cause their terrible 'mourning' of 12:10-14. It will also be the cause of the 'Fountain opened to the House of David and to the inhabitants of Jerusalem for sin and for uncleanness' [13:1].

"'Those with which I was wounded in the house of My Friends,' proclaims His Crucifixion and those who did it to Him. The words, 'My Friends,' are said in irony."

REPENTANCE

Verses 12 through 17 portray the call to Repentance for Israel, which will guarantee her future restoration. This will happen immediately after the Second Coming of the Lord. Consequently, this Verse and following Passages are very similar to Verse 14 of the previous Chapter.

This will be demanded of Israel in that coming glad day. As well, it is demanded of all who would truly know the Lord and be delivered from sin and bondage. Unfortunately, the modern church and, actually, throughout the ages, has attempted to change God's Prescription for sin-cursed souls. Nevertheless, what was demanded then is demanded now!

The following is what the Holy Spirit through the Prophet tells us.

TURN TO THE LORD WITH ALL YOUR HEART

This speaks of Repentance and, as previously stated, that which will take place

NOTES

with Israel immediately after the Second Coming. It will be, again, as stated, when Israel comes to the quick realization that the One standing before them at that time is actually the One Whom they crucified. One can well imagine the feelings and thoughts of Israel at that time! And, then again, I think it would be impossible for anyone else to properly grasp what Israel will face at that time, which will precipitate Israel's Repentance.

We are told in this Passage that Repentance comes from the *"heart"* and is not subject to mere ceremony. Each and every year millions make a religious start, but it has no kinship whatsoever with these stipulations.

In fact, millions turn to churches, preachers, etc., but the admonition is *"even to Me."*

People have to be sorry for their sins before they will truly repent of their sins. When coming to God, millions attempt to justify themselves simply because most of the world, and even the church, actually trusts in a form of self-righteousness. They do not understand that God will not accept merit or good works but judges all alike as sinners and, therefore, corrupt.

It is not too difficult for some who have succumbed to sins of passion to admit this, but it is very difficult for the so-called good moral religious man to admit such. However, one must do so in order to be Saved, for these addressed here basically pertain to the religious elite of Israel.

Man thinks that if he belittles his sin and magnifies his Repentance, somehow this will justify him in God's Eyes. However, God demands that we magnify the sin (at least admit as to how wicked it is) and minimize the Repentance. On that basis, the Lord will abundantly pardon, even as Verse 13 describes.

REND YOUR HEART

The phrase, *"And rend your heart, and not your garments,"* expresses to us that even though there is great emotion involved at times respecting Repentance, still, such must come from the heart and not be mere outward manifestations, which avail nothing.

Among the Jews, to *"rend the garments"*

was a token of great grief and imparted that the individual who did so was overwhelmed with excessive sorrow.

However, it is possible to exhibit the external signs of grief without any such corresponding inward feeling of sorrow just as it is still possible for men to draw near to God with their lips while the heart is far from Him.

Evidently, many had gone through the motions of *"rending the garments"* when it was all outward show and evidenced no true spiritual renewal inwardly. Such is hypocrisy!

If true Repentance is brought about, truly coming from the heart and recognizing the terrible offense against God, then, *"He is Gracious and Merciful, slow to anger, and of great kindness."*

The phrase, *"And repents Him of the evil,"* simply means that, upon a true change of a man's heart, God wills a change then in His Own Direction. And yet, the word *"repent,"* as it is used of God, never refers to wrongdoing but always a change of direction only.

Neither does it mean that God literally changes His Mind, for His Plan always has been that if men will not repent, even after repeated warnings, Judgment will come. However, if they do repent, the Judgment that was coming will now be stopped or, at least, seriously curtailed. Actually, it presents no change in God but only a change in direction, which is according to His Word, and because of a change in the heart of the person involved in Repentance.

In other words, if a man repents, the Lord will forgive exactly as this Verse proclaims.

THE BLESSING

The phrase of Verse 14, *"And leave a Blessing behind Him,"* refers to the fact that the Blessing had been taken away because of sin on the part of Judah, but now that Repentance has been entered into, the Blessing can be restored.

The Passage concerning the *"Meat Offering"* and *"Drink Offering"* actually means that because of their Repentance, the Lord will now begin to bless His People. Consequently, they will now be able once again to offer sacrifices unto the Lord because of the

NOTES

bountiful harvest.

We have said it several times, but please allow us to repeat the gracious truth that as God's Righteousness demands Judgment upon unconfessed sin, likewise, that same Righteousness demands Blessing upon sin repented of and turned from.

BLOW THE TRUMPET IN ZION

The Holy Spirit through the Prophet Joel said, *"Blow the trumpet in Zion, sanctify a fast, call a solemn assembly."*

Dean Stanley, one of the scholars of over 100 years ago, drew this vivid picture of the circumstances and scene described by the Prophet in this Fifteenth Verse and following. It is as follows:

"The harsh blast of the consecrated ram's horn called an assembly for an extraordinary fast. Not a soul was to be absent.

"Like the fiery cross, it convened old and young, men and women, mothers with infants at their breast, the bridegroom and the bride on their bridal day. All were there stretched in front of the Altar.

"The Altar itself presented the dreariest of all sights – a hearth without its sacred fire, a table spread without its sacred feast.

"The Priestly caste, instead of gathering as usual upon its steps and its platform, were driven, as it were, to the further space; they turned their backs to the dead Altar, and lay prostrate gazing towards the invisible Presence within the Sanctuary.

"Instead of the hymns and music which, since the time of David, had entered into their prayers, there was nothing heard but the passionate sobs and the loud dissonant howls such as only an Eastern Hierarchy could utter.

"Instead of the mass of white mantels which they usually presented, they were wrapped in black goat's-hair sackcloth, twisted around them, not with the brilliant sashes of the Priestly attire, but with a rough girdle of the same texture, which they never unbound night or day.

"What they wore of their common dress was rent asunder or cast off. With bare breast they waved their black drapery towards the Temple, and shrieked aloud, 'Spare Your people, O Lord!'"[1]

THE SOUND OF THE HOLY SPIRIT IS ALSO ONE OF FASTING AND PRAYER

As the outpouring of the Holy Spirit was a *"sound of alarm"* in Verse 1, likewise, it is here also the sound of *"fasting and prayer."*

At least, it was when the Holy Spirit was primary and fundamental in our Churches. Now, sadly, too many churches have learned to function without Him. To be frank, *"fasting and prayer"* are a foreign language to most Christians, and yet, it is only by this method that souls are truly born into the Kingdom.

For souls to be Saved, they have to be *"Born-Again,"* snatched away from the powers of darkness. And Satan does not let go of his children easily!

Consequently, most modern church growth programs have, by and large, filled the churches with people who are unsaved. As well, most counseling programs have lulled people into a spiritual stupor, but, sadly, they remain undelivered. Our educational programs have psychologized the modern Body of Christ but have not taught them about Christ proper.

Actually, the modern church is filled with man-made programs of which the Holy Spirit has no part and, in fact, He is not wanted. Man, and especially religious man, does not like what he cannot control, and no man can control the Holy Spirit.

I maintain that it is not possible for a true Revival to be born, or even a Spiritual Work to be tendered in the heart and life of an individual, unless it is birthed by the Spirit of God.

The Holy Spirit is God and, as such, nothing is done on this Earth pertaining to God's Work but that it goes through Him, and through Him Alone. To be sure, He will not accept Cain's sacrifice even though so beautiful. And yet, that's about the only type of sacrifice presently being offered to Him.

BLOW THE TRUMPET

In Verse 1, the *"blowing of the Trumpet"* was directed at a sin-cursed world that had forgotten God days without number.

This *"blowing of this Trumpet"* is directed at a church, which has, as well, forgotten

God days without number.

FAITH

This present day is called the age or time of *"Faith,"* with thousands of churches actually referring to themselves as *"Faith churches"* or *"Word churches."* In fact, there has been more teaching on Faith in the last half century than possibly ever before; however, what these books seldom mention is the correct Object of Faith.

THE OBJECT OF FAITH MUST BE THE CROSS OF CHRIST

Men presently are taught to have Faith in the Word but seldom taught what the Word actually is.

The story of the Bible is the story of man's Redemption, with the theme of that Redemption being, *"Jesus Christ and Him Crucified"* (I Cor. 1:23).

John the Beloved tells us this in the First Chapter of his Gospel. He said:

"In the beginning *(does not infer that Christ as God had a beginning because as God, He had no beginning, but rather refers to the time of Creation [Gen. 1:1])* **was the Word** *(the Holy Spirit through John describes Jesus as 'the Eternal Logos'),* **and the Word was with God** *('was in relationship with God,' and expresses the idea of the Trinity),* **and the Word was God** *(meaning that He did not cease to be God during the Incarnation; He 'was' and 'is' God from eternity past to eternity future)"* **(Jn. 1:1).**

So, from this very first Verse in the Gospel according to John, we see that the *"Word"* is Christ, and Christ is the *"Word,"* i.e., *"the Living Word."*

This means, as well, that in some way, Christ is in every Book of the Bible, every Chapter in the Book, every Verse in every Chapter, etc. Therefore, to know the Word, we have to first of all know Christ. And now, John tells us in the same Chapter:

"And the Word was made flesh *(refers to the Incarnation, 'God becoming man'),* **and dwelt among us** *(refers to Jesus, although Perfect, not holding Himself aloft from all others, but rather lived as all men, even a peasant),* **(and we beheld His Glory, the Glory as of the Only Begotten of the Father,)**

(speaks of His Deity, although hidden from the eyes of the merely curious; while Christ laid aside the expression of His Deity, He never lost the possession of His Deity) **full of Grace and Truth** *(as 'flesh,' proclaimed His humanity, 'Grace and Truth' His Deity)"* **(Jn. 1:14).**

Now, this Word was made flesh and for a purpose. He did not do so to just merely come to this world. He did not do so to just merely take upon Himself flesh, which was a step down, so to speak, of unprecedented proportions. So, why did He become flesh, i.e., a human being?

John the Beloved gave us the answer to this question in the words of John the Baptist. The Text says:

"The next day *(refers to the day after John had been questioned by the emissaries from the Sanhedrin)* **John sees Jesus coming unto him** *(is, no doubt, after the Baptism of Jesus and the temptation in the wilderness)*, **and said, Behold the Lamb of God** *(proclaims Jesus as the Sacrifice for sin, in fact, the Sin-Offering, Whom all the multiple millions of offered lambs had represented)*, **which takes away the sin of the world** *(animal blood could only cover sin, it could not take it away; but Jesus offering Himself as the Perfect Sacrifice took away the sin of the world; He not only cleansed acts of sin but, as well, addressed the root cause [Col. 2:14-15])"* **(Jn. 1:29).**

IN THE LIKENESS OF SINFUL FLESH

Paul also addressed this very subject by saying, **"For what the Law could not do, in that it was weak through the flesh** *(those under Law had only their willpower, which is woefully insufficient; so despite how hard they tried, they were unable to keep the Law then, and the same inability persists presently; any person who tries to live for God by a system of laws is doomed to failure because the Holy Spirit will not function in that capacity)*, **God sending His Own Son** *(refers to man's helpless condition, unable to save himself and unable to keep even a simple Law and, therefore, in dire need of a Saviour)* **in the likeness of sinful flesh** *(this means that Christ was really human, conformed in appearance to flesh, which*

NOTES

is characterized by sin, but yet sinless), **and for sin** *(to atone for sin, to destroy its power, and to save and sanctify its victims)*, **condemned sin in the flesh** *(destroyed the power of sin by giving His Perfect Body as a Sacrifice for sin, which made it possible for sin to be defeated in our flesh; it was all through the Cross)"* **(Rom. 8:3).**

Jesus Christ came to this world for the express purpose of going to the Cross. In fact, this had been decided from before the foundation of the world (I Pet. 1:18-20). So, if our faith is not in Christ and what He did for us at the Cross, then it's not faith that God will recognize (Rom. 6:3-14; I Cor. 1:17-18, 23; 2:2; Gal., Chpt. 5; 6:14; Eph. 2:13-18; Col. 2:14-15).

THE NEW COVENANT

The *"New Covenant"* is the Lord Jesus Christ. The manner in which the benefits of the New Covenant come to us is by and through the Cross of Christ. In other words, our Lord is the Source while the Cross is the Means by which all of these things are given to us.

GATHER THE PEOPLE

Joel said:

"Gather the people, sanctify the congregation, assemble the Elders, gather the children, and those who suck the breasts: let the bridegroom go forth of his chamber, and the bride out of her closet."

While this was meant to be done in Joel's day, there is no record that such came about. The greater fulfillment concerns the coming Great Tribulation and the Battle of Armageddon with the efforts of the Antichrist to destroy Israel. All of that will be stopped by the Coming of the Lord. And, as stated, when Israel comes to the realization as to Who Christ really is, then these things proclaimed by Joel so long, long ago, will come to pass. At that time, Israel most definitely will repent. The great Prophet Zechariah said so (Zech. 12:10-14).

The manner in which this gathering is described portrays the acuteness of the times. The idea is severalfold:

• That the people know and understand how absolutely hideous sin is.

• That they realize how absolutely displeased the Lord is with their present condition.

• That the Spiritual Leadership takes the lead, but that they be followed by all in the Nation, and He means *"all."*

• That no excuse be allowed to hinder this gathering, even little children and weddings, which is meant to symbolize the normal affairs of life being set aside in favor of seeking God.

• That all would cry to God in a manner that portrayed no hypocrisy, but that it come truly from the heart, proclaiming that they realize their perilous situation.

Most of the modern church would probably not agree that the situation presently in America and in other nations of the world, as well, is just as acute as Judah of old. Nevertheless, it is that acute, or maybe worse!

THE MINISTERS OF THE LORD

The Ministry, i.e., *"Priests,"* were to take the lead in this contrition before the Lord as the Ministry must take the lead presently.

There is no nation, city, church, or person that could not be turned around if they would only truly follow this admonition as given by the Holy Spirit in this Seventeenth Verse plus other Verses as well. In these Passages, we find the blueprint for victory.

Every Revival, Renewal, Restoration, or Move of God that has ever taken place in history has basically followed these procedures. Regrettably, the modern church has attempted to institute other procedures! However, all such other efforts are works of men and will never be accepted by God.

Instead of Repentance and crying to God, the modern church refers its parishioners to the psychologists.

Then, there is another large group, which we have alluded to. They may not so much go the route of humanistic psychology, but rather *"confess their way to victory."* They claim that such procedures as outlined by Joel are strictly Old Testament theology and, consequently, have no place in the New Covenant for the *"new creation man."*

While it is certainly true that under the New Covenant there is no such thing as *"Priests," "Temples,"* or *"Altars,"* still, that

which all of this represented is very much applicable.

Spiritual declension cannot be *"confessed away"*! While a good confession is certainly important, still, the *"leaving of the first love,"* as Christ spoke concerning the church at Ephesus, cannot be handled by merely *"confessing"* the *"first love"* back into existence.

As well, we sadly deceive ourselves if we think the problems rife in the seven churches of Asia are not indicative of present problems.

Jesus called these individuals *"fallen"* and demanded that they *". . . repent, and do the first works; or else I will come unto you quickly, and will remove your candlestick out of his place, except you repent"* (Rev. 2:4-5).

Consequently, Repentance under the New Covenant, as plainly outlined by Christ, is the same as Repentance under the Old Covenant. Sin is the same whenever and wherever it is found, and the solution has always been the same, as well, namely Christ.

THE SEVEN CHURCHES OF ASIA

Incidentally, the seven churches of Asia were selected as examples by Christ and not man. As well, He spoke to each church individually, addressing first the Pastor and then even individual members. Also, the number *"seven"* was purposely chosen because this number denotes completion, fulfillment, universality, and totality. In other words, the number *"seven"* was meant to symbolize all churches and for all time.

WEEP BETWEEN THE PORCH AND THE ALTAR

The phrase, *"Weep between the porch and the Altar,"* pertains to the following:

The *"Altar"* proclaimed accomplished Redemption because it was a Type of Calvary.

The *"porch"* pertained to fellowship with God. This latter can only be enjoyed as the result of the former.

The *"porch"* was the entrance to the Temple. In the Temple proper were the *"Tables of Shewbread,"* which spoke of the partaking of Christ, along with the *"Golden Lampstands,"* which spoke of Christ as the Light of the world, and the *"Altar of*

Incense," which spoke of the Intercession of Christ, all on our behalf.

Even though the people could not actually go into this part of the Temple proper, still, the *"Priests"* were meant to be Types of Christ and, hence, mediators on the people's behalf.

When they passed the *"Altar,"* as stated, this spoke of Redemption in which Repentance must be anchored. In other words, everything must go through Calvary. God can recognize no other approach! It is always the Cross! The Cross! The Cross!

As well, the statement, *"Weep between the porch and the Altar,"* with the word *"porch"* being first, symbolizes that these were already Covenant people but had lost fellowship with God through sin.

Had he been speaking of the heathen who did not know God, the *"Altar"* would have been named first. However, these people, even as modern Christians, had already come by the *"Altar,"* i.e., *"Calvary,"* but because of sin, had lost fellowship with the Lord.

Actually, between the *"porch"* and the *"Altar"* were the *"Brazen Lavers,"* which the latter spoke of the Word of God. Hence, before fellowship with God could once again be enjoined, the water of the laver had to be applied to the hands and feet of the Priests. This symbolized the cleansing of the Word, and if properly abided by, would restore fellowship.

As well, the admonition, *"Spare Your People, O LORD,"* symbolizes that none of this was ceremony, but rather the very opposite!

RELIGIOUS CEREMONY

Millions engage in religious ceremony each and every day, which effects nothing with them spiritually because such cannot cleanse. Even though there was much ceremony in the Old Covenant, still, the Holy Spirit is properly proclaiming to all that this ceremony, as important as it was, could not effect Repentance. That must come from the heart.

Under the New Covenant, there is no more ceremony whatsoever because that to which the ceremony pointed, namely Christ, has been fulfilled with the Advent of Christ and, therefore, such is done away.

Paul said, *"Blotting out the handwriting of Ordinances that was against us, which was contrary to us, and took it out of the way, nailing it to His Cross"* (Col. 2:14).

THE GREAT INHERITANCE IN CHRIST

The phrase, *"And give not Your Heritage to reproach,"* speaks of the great inheritance in Christ given to God's People, whether the physical inheritance of old or the Spiritual Inheritance presently.

Under the Old Covenant, the land of Israel was carved out of the nations and given to God's People, who were meant to be a light to a darkened world.

As well, the modern church, even though not given any material substance, such as under the Old Covenant, still, is given a Spiritual Inheritance that is meant to portray the same light.

If, in fact, Joel's Ministry was contemporary with Jeremiah, then Judah was on the very edge of doom and would suffer a *"reproach"* as she had never suffered in all of her history.

If the time frame is correct, then the people were given every opportunity to repent, and with great Promises enjoined, as we shall soon see.

As well, the modern church is standing where Judah of old once stood. As only a small Remnant in Judah at that time was Saved, likewise, only a small Remnant in the modern church is ready to meet the Lord and, consequently, will do so in the Rapture. Otherwise, as Judah went to her doom, the modern church is being prepared right now for the advent of the Antichrist, who they will accept readily!

WHERE IS THEIR GOD?

The *"reproach"* spoken of was wrapped up in the question, *"Where is their God?"* It concerned the *"heathen"* ruling over them, which lends more credence to the time of Joel's Ministry corresponding with that of Jeremiah's.

The people are being plainly warned that if they do not repent, their Nation will fall, with the pagans mocking them, saying, *"Where is their God?"*

I wonder how much difference there is in

the present and the past.

The modern church equates God with money, buildings, education, and even politics. It seems to not realize that these things are secular and really have little to do with God.

Peter said, *"Silver and gold have I none; but such as I have give I thee: In the Name of Jesus Christ of Nazareth rise up and walk"* (Acts 3:6).

Sometime ago, someone in the modern church said, *"No longer do we have to say, 'Silver and gold have we none!'"*

The man to whom he spoke said, *"True, but no longer can we say, 'In the Name of Jesus Christ of Nazareth rise up and walk!'"*

Therefore, the question asked so long ago must be asked now, as well, *"Where is their God?"*

(18) "THEN WILL THE LORD BE JEALOUS FOR HIS LAND, AND PITY HIS PEOPLE.

(19) "YES, THE LORD WILL ANSWER AND SAY UNTO HIS PEOPLE, BEHOLD, I WILL SEND YOU CORN, AND WINE, AND OIL, AND YOU SHALL BE SATISFIED THEREWITH: AND I WILL NO MORE MAKE YOU A REPROACH AMONG THE HEATHEN."

The pattern is:

1. (Vs. 18) Upon Israel's Repentance, the phrase, *"Be jealous for His Land,"* proclaims the fact that as the Lord sought once to destroy it because of sin, now He will be quick to bless the land and all that is in it.

2. This will be at the beginning of the coming Kingdom Age when Israel will repent before the Lord and then be restored to their rightful place.

3. (Vs. 18) The phrase, *"And pity His People,"* means that the Lord will accept Israel's Repentance and restore them to their rightful place and position in the world.

4. (Vs. 19) Now, because Israel has properly repented before the Lord, the *"reproach"* is finally gone and prosperity now begins!

HIS LAND, HIS PEOPLE

The present political Administration in America (2010) should read again and again this line given in the Eighteenth Verse, *"Then will the LORD be jealous for His Land, and pity His People."* Then, the rest

of the world should read it, and above all, the Muslim world should read it.

It makes no difference that the Muslim world denies the God of the Bible and, in effect, denies the Bible itself. Irrespective of that, the land of Israel belongs to Jehovah, and these people, called in the Bible Israelites and presently referred to as Israelis, are *"His People."* To harm that which belongs to the Lord is the same thing as harming the Lord.

As we've already stated in this Volume, about the only friend in the world that Israel presently has is the United States. And, to be sure, the friendship of the present Administration is tepid at best! In fact, the only reason that America has stood behind Israel all of these years is because of the hundreds of thousands, if not millions, of Born-Again Believers in this nation.

A PERSONAL EXPERIENCE

If I remember correctly, the year was 1987. At any rate, I was invited to speak in Washington to a very distinguished group of Jews who had come in from all over America and even other parts of the world. The other speaker was the present Prime Minister of Israel, Benjamin Netanyahu. In fact, after the session was concluded, I had the opportunity to spend a short period of time with him.

Be that as it may, at a point in time after that meeting, I was informed that there was an automobile waiting for me to take me to another meeting. The meeting was to be with the Jewish liaison with Congress. I spent well over an hour with him.

In the course of our conversation, he made the statement that the Jewish community was somewhat nonplussed regarding the attitude of President Reagan toward Israel. The Ambassador said, *"Most Jews are liberal and vote democratic. This means we did not vote for President Reagan. But yet, he has been more gracious and kind to our Nation than any president before him."* The man sat there for a few moments then said, *"Why is that?"*

I had the opportunity then to tell this Ambassador that multiple millions of Christians in America stand behind Israel and, at the same time, are President Reagan's staunchest supporters.

I then went on to explain to him that his idea of Christianity was not exactly correct. All true Christians love Israel and, as well, they love the Jewish people. Christianity actually has its roots in Old Testament Judaism.

At one juncture I asked the Ambassador, *"Sir, do you ever sense the Presence of God?"* His answer was somewhat revealing.

"I don't know what you would call it," he said, *"but, at times, I will sit in synagogues and just cry, and I don't really know why I'm crying."*

THE REJECTION OF JESUS CHRIST

When Jesus came in His First Advent, Israel was already in sad shape, spiritually speaking. They had so perverted the Law of Moses till, anymore, it was no longer even a semblance of what had originally been. In fact, there was now no Righteousness to speak of in Israel, only self-righteousness. And it was this self-righteousness that murdered Christ.

This means that the Sacrificial system, which was a portrayal of Christ in symbolism and what He would do to redeem humanity, was now looked at and tendered as a mere ceremony. In other words, they had long since lost the meaning of this system. Considering that it is the Cross alone which makes the Righteousness of God possible, this is something we should look at more closely.

SELF-RIGHTEOUSNESS

As stated, it is the Cross alone and one's Faith in that Finished Work, which makes the Righteousness of God possible for the believing sinner. Understanding that the Cross alone makes all of this possible, and understanding that the Cross presently is little being preached, and understanding that the Church is proposing all types of self helps, then we should realize that the modern church is eaten up with self-righteousness. It cannot be any other way!

The Cross, as stated, if thought about at all in modern circles, basically is something that is taken for granted. Most don't know what it means, and the statement, *"Jesus died for me,"* is about the depth of

most understanding regarding the Cross. In fact, the modern church has basically no understanding at all as it respects the Cross of Christ and what was there accomplished, placing it more so in a sentimental mood than anything else.

To overcome sin, the modern church jumps from one fad to the other, all with no success. As Jeremiah said so long, long ago, *"They have healed also the hurt of the daughter of My People slightly, saying, Peace, peace; when there is no peace"* (Jer. 6:14). All of this means that if it's not the Cross of Christ, anything in which one places one's faith will result in self-righteousness, no matter how correct it might be in its own right. And please understand, self-righteousness is ugly, and to the core! As stated, that's what crucified Christ, and it is no less murderous presently than it was that sad day nearly 2,000 years ago.

This shows us, or, at least, it certainly should, just how important the Cross of Christ actually is. What Jesus there did was of such magnitude that eternity will not be able to proclaim the extent of the price that He paid and the Victory that He there won.

THE LORD WILL ANSWER

The Holy Spirit through the Prophet Joel said, *"Yes, the LORD will answer and say unto His People, Behold, I will send you corn, and wine, and oil, and you shall be satisfied therewith: and I will no more make you a reproach among the heathen."*

The word, *"Yes,"* signifies God's Response to proper Repentance. Paul said, *"For all the Promises of God in Him are yes, and in Him Amen, unto the Glory of God by us"* (II Cor. 1:20).

Therefore, and irrespective of what the problem has been or how heinous the sin, if anyone, even the most wicked of the wicked, will come God's Way, the Lord's Answer will always be *"Yes."* This means that every person can get up off the floor if they so desire. It means that every captive can go free! Therefore, there is no excuse for any.

The phrase, *"The LORD will answer and say unto His People,"* signifies that which most of the modern church no longer believes. The Holy Spirit through the Prophet says, *"God will answer!"* This Promise is very dear to me personally.

A PERSONAL EXAMPLE

When we began our daily prayer meetings in October of 1991, sadly and regrettably, almost every preacher I dealt with, in effect, said, *"God will not answer!"* It was not very encouraging, to say the least! And yet, it's more discouraging still to realize that the modern church has almost no Faith in God. They have faith in themselves, in their institutions, in their denominations, and in the psychologists, but almost none in God!

Therefore, we had almost no one to encourage us and were even being told that if we took our problem exclusively to the Lord, the churches would blacklist us. Nevertheless, I knew that if God did not do it, it could not be done. Consequently, I made up my mind that irrespective of what men said, I would trust God.

In fact, on that memorable day, I laid my Bible on the coffee table in front of me and Frances and others who were present, and stated, *"I don't know the answer to a victorious, overcoming, Christian life, where one has Victory over the world, the flesh, and the Devil, but I know the answer is found in the Word of God, and by the Grace of God, I'm going to find it."* That was the greatest thing I've ever done. While it didn't come quickly, and it didn't come easily, it did come! And what the Lord did was so far greater than I could ever have begun to imagine that it defies all explanation.

As it regards the struggle, and a struggle it is, Satan always takes full advantage of such. He joins in with his voice, as well as using well-meaning doubters, to constantly plant the seed, claiming that God will not answer.

We must always remember that what we're in is a *"fight."* However, it is a *"good fight,"* called, *"the good fight of Faith"* (I Tim. 6:12).

In fact, several months into our seeking the Lord, actually, in two prayer meetings each day, I experienced a particularly fierce struggle in my Faith. With Satan constantly saying how hopeless it was, along with doubting Christians preaching Satan's message, as well, it became very difficult to

NOTES

shake off the lies of the Evil One.

ENCOURAGEMENT FROM THE LORD

If I remember correctly, it was a Monday night. We had gathered for prayer meeting with about 35 or 40 present.

I stood up before this small prayer group and proceeded to read the Text that I had chosen for the 5 or 10 minute Bible Study before we went to prayer. It was II Chronicles 7:14.

I began to read, *"If My People, who are called by My Name, shall humble themselves, and pray, and seek My Face, and turn from their wicked ways; then will I hear from Heaven, and will forgive their sin, and will heal their land."*

As I read the Text that night, I in no way equated this Promise with my present struggle of Faith. However, all of a sudden, the Presence of the Lord came all over me.

The Holy Spirit, even while I was speaking to the people, gently whispered to me, saying, *"You have asked in your own heart if I will truly hear and answer."* Then He said, *"This is My Answer to you."*

He then quoted back to me His Own Words, *"Then will I hear from Heaven, and will forgive their sin, and will heal their land."*

As I was talking to the people, I began to weep, even though my statements to them little corresponded with what the Spirit of God was saying to me. It was like something warm flowed all over me, even from the top of my head to the souls of my feet. The Holy Spirit kept saying to me over and over again, *"I will hear, I will forgive, and I will heal."*

All that night, that phrase kept flowing like a stream through my heart and mind, *"I will hear, I will forgive, and I will heal."*

Even though there have been struggles between then and now, still, those phrases continue to flow through my heart. I can even sense the Presence of God as I relate these words into the Dictaphone.

As well, He did not say them to me only but to all who will dare to believe Him, *"I will hear, I will forgive, and I will heal."*

What a Promise!

BEHOLD, I WILL SEND YOU CORN

The phrase, *"Behold, I will send you corn,"*

actually refers to barley and wheat but, spiritually, has reference to the Word of God.

As I look back over my Christian experience, it is obvious that every single great Spiritual experience, coupled with a Promise from God, has always come through His Word. In other words, the Lord would take a Promise, exactly as I have just described regarding II Chronicles 7:14, and make it real to my heart and, as well, apply it to a particular problem we were presently facing. Paul said, *"Let the Word of Christ dwell in you richly in all wisdom . . ."* (Col. 3:16).

In other words, he is saying that the Lord can only move upon us according to the amount of Word that *"dwells in us."*

The reason that the Lord little speaks to most Christians is because there is almost no Word abiding in them. The more Word, the more He can lead and guide us.

BEHOLD, I WILL SEND YOU WINE

Of course, in the natural, this spoke of the vineyards of Judah once again producing a bountiful harvest; however, in the Spiritual, it speaks of *"joy."* Once Repentance is enjoined, we are brought back to the Word of God, i.e., the *"corn,"* then, great *"joy,"* i.e., *"wine,"* fills our hearts. This is *"joy unspeakable and full of Glory,"* as Peter said. The Word will always bring the joy!

BEHOLD, I WILL SEND YOU OIL

This spoke of an abundant olive crop, which produced the *"oil."* As well, in the Spiritual sense, it symbolizes the Holy Spirit.

And then He says, *"And you shall be satisfied therewith,"* meaning that the human heart cannot be satisfied with anything else.

Jesus said, *". . . a man's life consists not in the abundance of the things which he possesses"* (Lk. 12:15). Therefore, one's life consists alone of that which God gives, *"the corn, and wine, and oil."*

NO MORE A REPROACH

Actually, the true Church has always suffered reproach, as Paul said, *"We both labour and suffer reproach . . ."* (I Tim. 4:10).

As well, he said, *"Esteeming the reproach of Christ greater . . ."* (Heb. 11:26).

Therefore, this is not the type of

NOTES

"reproach" spoken of by the Holy Spirit in Verse 19.

As it regards Judah of old, the Lord is speaking of the *"reproach"* suffered by the People of God because they were overtaken by the heathen, with the heathen saying, *"Where is their God!"*

As well, the Lord, upon proper Repentance, which refers to a broken and contrite spirit, will always take away the reproach of sin. In fact, He Alone can do this, and if we meet His Conditions, the reproach will be lifted. He said through the great Prophet Isaiah:

". . . but to this man will I look, even to him who is poor and of a contrite spirit, and trembles at My Word" (Isa. 66:2).

(20) **"BUT I WILL REMOVE FAR OFF FROM YOU THE NORTHERN ARMY, AND WILL DRIVE HIM INTO A LAND BARREN AND DESOLATE, WITH HIS FACE TOWARD THE EAST SEA, AND HIS HINDER PART TOWARD THE UTMOST SEA, AND HIS STINK SHALL COME UP, AND HIS ILL SAVOUR SHALL COME UP, BECAUSE HE HAS DONE GREAT THINGS."**

The construction is:

1. The total fulfillment of this Prophecy speaks of the coming Antichrist, who will be defeated in the Battle of Armageddon (Ezek. 38:15).

2. The *"east sea"* is the Dead Sea and the *"utmost sea"* is probably the Mediterranean. Therefore, the defeat of the Antichrist will be total!

3. *"And his stink shall come up, and his ill savour shall come up,"* refers to the great number of the soldiers of the Antichrist being killed, as prophesied in Ezekiel 39:11-16.

4. *"Because he has done great things,"* refers to the Antichrist magnifying himself to do great things; for he will propose to attack and defeat Immanuel Himself (Rev. 19:19). The *"great things"* of the Antichrist will prove to be nothing, while the *"great things"* of the next Verse, as accomplished by the Lord, will be magnificent.

THE REMOVAL OF
THE NORTHERN ARMY

If Joel prophesied during the time of Jeremiah, this meant that the *"northern army,"* at least at that time, spoke of the coming Babylonian horde, which was actually from the east but entered Israel by the way of the north, hence, referred to as the *"northern army."*

In Verse 20, the Lord is especially speaking of the Antichrist and how he will be defeated, which, of course, has not happened even yet. However, if Judah had repented, and done so sincerely before the Lord, when the Babylonians came, they would have been totally and completely defeated, no matter how powerful and strong they may have been. Regrettably, Judah did not repent and was totally and completely destroyed by the Babylonian army.

But most definitely Israel will repent in the coming Great Tribulation in the Battle of Armageddon. She will then do what she did not do those many, many centuries before. In response, and to be sure, the Lord will do exactly what He said that He would do. He will *"remove far off from you the northern army."*

Ezekiel said, and with words similar to this given by the Prophet Joel, *"And you (Antichrist) shall come from your place out of the north parts, you, and many people with you, all of them riding upon horses, a great company, and a mighty army"* (Ezek. 38:15).

The Antichrist will, as well, originate in the east (rebuilt Babylon—Isaiah 14:4), but will actually come into Israel from the north, exactly as Nebuchadnezzar of old.

(21) "FEAR NOT, O LAND; BE GLAD AND REJOICE: FOR THE LORD WILL DO GREAT THINGS.

(22) "BE NOT AFRAID, YOU BEASTS OF THE FIELD: FOR THE PASTURES OF THE WILDERNESS DO SPRING, FOR THE TREE BEARS HER FRUIT, THE FIG TREE AND THE VINE DO YIELD THEIR STRENGTH.

(23) "BE GLAD THEN, YOU CHILDREN OF ZION, AND REJOICE IN THE LORD YOUR GOD: FOR HE HAS GIVEN YOU THE FORMER RAIN MODERATELY, AND HE WILL CAUSE TO COME DOWN FOR YOU THE RAIN, THE FORMER RAIN, AND THE LATTER RAIN IN THE FIRST MONTH.

(24) "AND THE FLOORS SHALL BE FULL OF WHEAT, AND THE VATS SHALL

OVERFLOW WITH WINE AND OIL.

(25) "AND I WILL RESTORE TO YOU THE YEARS THAT THE LOCUST HAS EATEN, THE CANKERWORM, AND THE CATERPILLAR, AND THE PALMERWORM, MY GREAT ARMY WHICH I SENT AMONG YOU.

(26) "AND YOU SHALL EAT IN PLENTY, AND BE SATISFIED, AND PRAISE THE NAME OF THE LORD YOUR GOD, WHO HAS DEALT WONDROUSLY WITH YOU: AND MY PEOPLE SHALL NEVER BE ASHAMED.

(27) "AND YOU SHALL KNOW THAT I AM IN THE MIDST OF ISRAEL, AND THAT I AM THE LORD YOUR GOD, AND NONE ELSE: AND MY PEOPLE SHALL NEVER BE ASHAMED."

The pattern is:

1. (Vs. 21) Basically, all the following pertains to what the Lord will do for Israel at the beginning of the Kingdom Age, which is immediately after His Return and Israel's Repentance.

2. Verse 22 portrays the coming Kingdom Age when the wild, carnivorous nature of the animal kingdom will be changed because the curse has been lifted.

3. (Vs. 22) *"For the pastures of the wilderness do spring,"* refers to the deserts blossoming as the rose (Isa. 35:1).

4. (Vs. 22) *"For the tree bears her fruit, the fig tree and the vine do yield their strength,"* refers, as stated, to the curse being lifted, with the land all over the world producing that which was originally intended. In other words, it will be a time of such plenty and prosperity as the world has never known.

5. The phrase, *"Be glad then, you children of Zion,"* of Verse 23, refers to Israel now restored as the premier Nation of the world, which is her rightful place. In other words, the world cannot be properly blessed until Israel is in her rightful place, which she will be not long after the Second Coming.

6. The *"former rain"* and the *"latter rain"* of Verse 23 refer to the two rainy seasons in Israel. The first, or *"former,"* coming in October, promoted the germination and growth of the seed previously sown. The *"latter,"* coming in April, matured the crops

and got them ready for harvest. Spiritually speaking, the *"former rain"* speaks of the outpouring of the Holy Spirit on the Early Church. The *"latter rain"* speaks of the outpouring of the Spirit, which began at approximately the turn of the Twentieth Century, and which will continue on through the Millennial Reign (James 5:7).

7. Verse 24 speaks of the harvest of prosperity, which will be gathered in the coming Kingdom Age. In fact, one might say that every person in the world of that day will be rich, and all because of Christ and what He did at the Cross.

8. The phrase of Verse 25, *"And I will restore to you the years,"* refers to that period of time which began with Nebuchadnezzar and which now has lasted for about 2,500 years. The mention of the *"locusts,"* etc., is meant to be symbolic of the years lost to the *"times of the Gentiles."*

9. (Vs. 25) *"My great army which I sent among you,"* speaks of the great empires that ruled Israel because of Israel's sin and refusal to repent.

10. According to Verse 26, Israel now will function as she should. As a result, they will *"eat in plenty, and be satisfied."* As well, never again will God's People *"be ashamed."*

11. Once again, in Verse 27, the Holy Spirit through the Prophet uses the phrase, *"And My People shall never be ashamed,"* and does so because Israel, in fact, has lived in *"shame"* for over 2,500 years.

THE LORD WILL DO GREAT THINGS

The grand Promises given here to Israel, which will take place in the future when they come to Christ, can be given to any and all, even at the present, who will dare to believe God. This is evidenced by Simon Peter quoting Verses 28 through 32 on the Day of Pentecost.

If the Holy Spirit allowed him to claim it then, and He definitely did, then He allows all to claim these great Promises presently, as well!

The modern church, and perhaps all of us, and perhaps for all time, has been very good at pointing to the past or the future, but never to the present. In other words,

NOTES

the implication is that one could have these great things if he had lived thousands of years ago or sometime in the distant future. However, the Bible student must ever learn that God is not necessarily a God of the distant past or the distant future but, instead, a *"now God."*

This He says, *". . . behold, now is the accepted time; behold, now is the Day of Salvation"* (II Cor. 6:2).

As well, He says, *"Wherefore (as the Holy Spirit says, Today if you will hear His Voice, harden not your hearts, as in the provocation, in the day of temptation in the wilderness)"* (Heb. 3:7-8).

He also said, *"Take heed, brethren, lest there be in any of you an evil heart of unbelief, in departing from the Living God"* (Heb. 3:12).

He then went on to say, *"So we see that they could not enter in because of unbelief"* (Heb. 3:19).

FAITH

Therefore, the modern church needs to take these great Promises, at least, where they can apply to us, and claim them as our very own, for God is no respecter of persons.

God can do *"great things"* for those who will believe Him and not allow *"fear"* to rule and reign.

When I was a child, my Grandmother taught me the Greatness of God. I will never forget one of her great sayings, which has helped me to touch this world for Christ. She said:

"Jimmy, God is a big God, so ask big!"

I have never forgotten that statement. As stated, it has helped me to believe the Lord for great and mighty things. I full well believe, also, that the greatest is yet to come! As I dictate these notes in February of 2010, I do so, anticipating a Move of God like we have never previously seen or known. To be sure, the Lord helped us touch the world in the 1980's for Christ, seeing literally tens of thousands brought to a Saving Knowledge of Jesus Christ. As well, multiple thousands were baptized with the Holy Spirit with the evidence of speaking with other Tongues as the Spirit of God gave the utterance. But I believe another Move is coming, a Move that will eclipse that of the past, for God never decreases but always increases.

Inasmuch as Israel will have repented in that coming glad day, they are enjoined to *"fear not, O land; be glad and rejoice."*

Upon Repentance, there need be no more *"fear"* of the enemy. He is forever defeated, therefore, *"be glad and rejoice."*

In fact, there is no *"joy"* or *"rejoicing"* like one who has experienced the *"joy of sins forgiven, and the bliss the blood-washed know."*

This is true *"joy"* and not some manufactured variety instituted by Pentecostal calisthenics or Charismatic orchestrated dancing.

The Scripture says that *"the LORD will do great things."* We must believe Him for that! We must expect Him to do great things! We must anticipate great things! And remember, as previously stated, He is not only a God of the *"past"* and will be a God of the *"future,"* He is, as well, a God of the *"now."*

THE BEASTS OF THE FIELD

The phrase of Verse 22, *"Be not afraid, you beasts of the field,"* portrays the coming Millennial Kingdom, when the curse will be lifted, and the animal kingdom, which now groans for deliverance, will then function as the Lord intended at the beginning. The great Prophet Isaiah said, *"The wolf also shall dwell with the lamb, and the leopard shall lie down with the kid; and the calf and the young lion and the fatling together; and a little child shall lead them"* (Isa. 11:6). The Prophet also said, *"And the cow and the bear shall feed; their young ones shall lie down together: and the lion shall eat straw like the ox.*

"And the sucking child shall play on the hole of the asp, and the weaned child shall put his hand on the cockatrice' den" (Isa. 11:7-8).

Reading these particular Passages in Isaiah, we are made to see that the entire complexion of the world will change in the coming Kingdom Age. There will be several major reasons, not the least being that our Lord will be here in Person. But the Scripture also says:

". . . for the Earth shall be full of the Knowledge of the LORD, as the waters cover

NOTES

the sea" (Isa. 11:9).

There is no way, even with the godliest, that any person can fully comprehend what life is going to be like in the coming Kingdom Age. The illustration given by the Holy Spirit as it regards the animal kingdom, within itself, is so far beyond our thinking as to defy description. In other words, the *"stealing, killing, and destroying,"* which characterizes Satan, will be no more. The entirety of the world will be pollution-free, crime-free, sickness-free, poverty-free, and hate-free, and death, for all practical purposes, will be banished. As well, the world will be storm-free, with earthquakes, hurricanes, tornadoes, famines, and droughts all a thing of the past. There will be so much food that the world will be hunger-free. All of this is because Jesus Christ reigns Personally from Jerusalem, and for the first time, the Earth will be full of the Knowledge of the Lord.

Plainly and clearly, the great Prophet Joel said the following:

• *"The pastures of the wilderness do spring:"* this means that every acre in the world will become fertile and productive.

• *"For the tree bears her fruit:"* all the crops will grow abundantly.

• *"The fig tree and the vine do yield their strength:"* there will be no bad crop years in the coming Kingdom Age. Every acre of land will yield its strength, which will, no doubt, be several times what it is presently.

THE FORMER RAIN AND THE LATTER RAIN

The phrase, *"Former rain and latter rain,"* have a physical meaning and, as well, a Spiritual meaning.

In the physical sense, during the Kingdom Age, the rains will come on time, ensuring the harvest and, as well, with implication that this *"rain"* will have a miraculous power about it, even beyond, far beyond, the normal. In other words, there will be something, it seems, in the raindrops, which will fertilize and energize the soil, thereby, producing crops beyond belief.

The phrase, *"Be glad then, you children of Zion,"* refers to Israel at long last being the premier Nation of the world, which the

Lord originally intended, but which Israel forfeited for so very, so long. Now, being in her rightful place, ensuring blessings upon this world as never before, a gladness and a joy fills the world simply because things are now being done according to the Will of God.

Presently, the Gentile nations do not understand Israel's rightful place and position because they do not understand the Bible or the Promises of God. They do not realize that Gentile powers hold sway, as stated, only because Israel, long ago, forfeited her position. Because of sin and rebellion against God, the Lord took the scepter of power out of the faltering hands of the kings of Judah and placed it in the hands of Nebuchadnezzar, with other powers following him. There it has remained ever since, with Jesus calling it, *"the times of the Gentiles"* (Lk. 21:24).

This *"times of the Gentiles"* have now lasted for approximately 2,500 years. However, during this time, even though Israel has been dissipated and scattered all over the world, still, her contributions to society are far beyond the normal.

In fact, many inventions, technological advancements, medical breakthroughs, etc., have been brought about by the Jewish community.

I remember speaking some years ago at a Jewish function where one of the other speakers referred to the Holocaust. He said:

"I wonder how many Jonas Salks and Albert Einsteins perished in the Holocaust?"

(Jonas Salk developed the polio vaccine, which has resulted in untold thousands of lives being saved, with almost all acquainted with the scientific achievements of Albert Einstein.)

He was right! Quite possibly, in that hell devised by Adolf Hitler, where 6,000,000 Jews died, there were those who, if they had lived, would have made a tremendous contribution to society.

THE WORLD OF ISLAM

What kind of contribution has the world of Islam made to society?

I think the answer is obvious. None!

It has contributed murder, starvation, ignorance, superstition, fear, and a little bit of Hell on Earth for its followers. Sadly and regrettably, they are locked in a world of superstitious, heathenistic, and satanic darkness.

The reason?

The answer to that is obvious! While the Jews most definitely have strayed from the Lord, still, they believe in God. The god of the Muslims is, in reality, a demon spirit.

The Muslim world hates the United States, referring to it as the *"great Satan,"* and Israel, which they refer to as the *"little Satan."* If they had the power to do so, they would blot these two Nations from the face of the Earth. And, to be sure, this problem is not caused by a few radicals in that religious world, but, in reality, the entirety of the Muslim world falls into that category. The only reason they do not destroy us is simply because they do not have the way. They have the will but not the way.

Our policy toward the religion of Islam is based on a lie.

That lie is that the religion of Islam is great and wonderful while only a few radicals have taken it over. The truth is, while every Muslim isn't a murderer, still, the vast majority of Muslims are in total sympathy with the murderers. We should understand that.

In thousands of Mosques across this nation, under the guise of freedom of speech and freedom of religion, they are plotting the destruction of this nation. And we are so stupid as to look the other way.

Freedom of worship is cherished by every sensible person in our nation. However, when that so-called freedom of worship is bent on destroying me, in other words, taking every freedom from us that we have and forcing this nation into servile slavery under the yoke of Islam, then the freedom ends. How long will it take for us to wake up? How long will it take for us to come to our senses?

As an aside, the hundreds of billions of dollars being used to build the super city of Dubai, for the most part, come from American taxpayers.

How?

We are so foolish, and even stupid, that we will not drill for oil in most areas of this nation when, in reality, we probably have greater reserves than any nation in the world, including Saudi Arabia. While it is true that a better form of energy will ultimately come along, until that time, we need to make use of the resources we presently have, which would save this nation trillions of dollars.

ANIMOSITY AGAINST THE LORD AND THE BIBLE

The statement I'm about to make is strong, but, regrettably, I believe it to be true.

There are powerful forces in the nation of America, who would do away with the Bible, in fact, any semblance of God, and who, as well, hate the Lord Jesus Christ. This group is pushing hard for same-sex marriages, for homosexuality to be predominant, in other words, any perversion! In fact, this powerful element in this nation would, if pushed, laud Islam while doing everything they can to destroy Biblical Christianity.

Why?

Of course, there are many reasons, but it all goes back to the very dawn of time. Immediately after the Fall, the Lord told Satan through the serpent, **"And I will put enmity** (animosity) **between you and the woman** (presents the Lord now actually speaking to Satan, who had used the serpent; in effect, the Lord is saying to Satan, 'You used the woman to bring down the human race, and I will use the woman as an instrument to bring the Redeemer into the world, Who will save the human race'), **and between your seed** (mankind which follows Satan) **and her Seed** (the Lord Jesus Christ); **it** (Christ) **shall bruise your head** (the Victory that Jesus won at the Cross [Col. 2:14-15]), **and you shall bruise His Heel** (the sufferings of the Cross)" **(Gen. 3:15).**

Pure and simple, this terrible animosity against the Lord Jesus Christ, against the Bible, and against those who truly follow Christ, is because the Lord is real, whereas all of these other claims are false.

At this present time, despite September 11, 2001 (9/11), where nearly 4,000 Americans lost their lives and cost this nation over one trillion dollars, still, there is probably far less animosity against the religion of Islam in

NOTES

this nation than Biblical Christianity. One noted Lesbian comedian made the statement the other day that she liked the religion of Islam much more than she did Christianity. In fact, she said she hated Christianity.

What the silly woman did not seem to know is if she lived in a Muslim country, being a Lesbian, they would kill her. They kill all homosexuals, at least those whom they know to be homosexuals.

The world of Islam, while beginning in the Seventh Century, has basically been asleep for all of these many, many years, being brought to the fore presently because of the role it will play regarding the coming Antichrist.

Will the Antichrist be Muslim?

No! In fact, while the Antichrist will, no doubt, feign being a Muslim, even though a Jew, the truth is, he will hate all religions, actually setting himself up as God. So, the man of sin will not only deceive Israel, and do so grandly, but will deceive the Muslim world also! Nevertheless, they will play their part in trying to destroy Israel at that time.

THE SPIRITUAL MEANING OF THE FORMER RAIN AND THE LATTER RAIN

James brought the phrase, *"The former rain and the latter rain,"* into the Spiritual sense, when he said, *". . . Behold, the husbandman waits for the precious fruit of the earth, and has long patience for it, until he receive the early and latter rain"* (Jam. 5:7).

Consequently, the natural phenomenon of the early and latter rains in Israel can, as well, symbolize the outpouring of the Holy Spirit in both the Early Church (former rain) and this Endtime outpouring (latter rain).

The *"former rain"* concerned the growth of the seed, which spoke of the outpouring of the Holy Spirit on the Early Church, ensuring its germination, growth, and development in the world.

As the *"latter rain"* had to do with the maturity of the crop immediately before the harvest, likewise, the latter day outpouring of the Holy Spirit has the same potential. The Church must be matured and the Harvest gathered. As it was then, concerning the natural harvest, so it is now, concerning the Spiritual Harvest.

A GREAT HARVEST

I believe the Lord has spoken to my heart that there is going to be a tremendous Harvest of souls in these last days. In fact, the stage is already being set for what I believe will be the greatest outpouring of the Holy Spirit the world has ever known. However, this outpouring will be somewhat different.

I doubt very seriously if this outpouring will morph into Revival. Revival is the church coming back to the Cross. I pray that will happen, but I really do not see such on the Spiritual Horizon.

I believe the outpouring refers to souls being Saved, which can now happen in a manner as never before. For instance, our telecast now goes all over the world. In fact, we have just begun a television network that is airing 24 hours a day, 7 days a week. We believe we have the Message for the world and the Church, and I speak of the Message of the Cross. We plan to cover the entirety of this nation and, in fact, are already airing in many major cities on Cable Systems, as stated, 24 hours a day, 7 days a week. We also plan to go up on Satellites to cover the entirety of the world. Untold thousands of people can be reached with a single Service, and if the Spirit of God Moves with the convicting Power of the Holy Spirit, tremendous numbers can be Saved.

The Lord has given me an Anointing of the Holy Spirit not only to reach the church but, as well, to reach the lost. I believe that we're going to see hundreds of thousands brought to a Saving Knowledge of Jesus Christ. I pray, as well, that God will use others to reach this world for Christ, and I believe that He will.

If the *"latter rain"* of old and the Blessings of God were indicative of a bountiful harvest then, for those who believe presently, there is going to be another bountiful Harvest, but this time, of souls.

WHAT I BELIEVE THE LORD SPOKE TO MY HEART

One early Sunday morning back in December of 2009, actually, at about 3:30 a.m., I awakened and began to meditate on the message I was to bring that Sunday morning at

Family Worship Center. The message pertained to Joseph, who was sold into Egypt by his brothers.

The Lord brought to my mind the Dream that He had given Pharaoh some 3,700 years ago. The Dream was in two parts. In the first part, the monarch dreamed that seven cattle came before him that were fat and sleek. In the second part, seven other cattle came forth that were lean and hungry and devoured the seven fat cattle. The Dream was doubled with seven stalks of grain appearing before Pharaoh, which were healthy and fat. Then seven stalks of grain came up, which were blasted and lean, and they consumed the seven fat stalks of grain.

The Lord gave to Joseph the interpretation of that Dream.

Taking the second part of the Dream first, the seven lean cattle and the seven lean stalks have to do with the coming Great Tribulation, which will last seven years. As that famine in Pharaoh's time brought Jacob and his family to Joseph, who was a Type of Christ, likewise, the coming Great Tribulation, which will also be seven years of duration, will bring Jacob to Jesus. However, it's the first part of the Dream to which I would call your attention.

THE HARVEST

That concerns seven fat cattle and seven fat stalks of grain. It represented the greatest harvest that Egypt had ever known. In fact, any number of granaries had to be built to take care of the surplus. Egypt, in fact, would feed the surrounding countries, which kept them from starvation during the coming seven years of famine.

At any rate, inasmuch as the seven years of famine represents the coming seven years of Great Tribulation, likewise, the seven years of fat cattle and healthy stalks of grain represent the greatest Harvest of souls, I believe, the world has ever known. And then I believe the Lord spoke the following to me:

THIS MINISTRY WILL HAVE A PART IN THIS COMING HARVEST

When I say, *"this Ministry,"* of course, I'm speaking of Jimmy Swaggart Ministries and all who are a part of this effort for the Cause of Christ. I'm speaking of all those in Family Worship Center. As well, I'm speaking of all those, irrespective as to where you might live in this world, who are blessed by this Ministry and, in essence, are a part of this Ministry. You are going to have a part in fulfilling this Dream given to this Egyptian monarch some 3,700 years ago. I believe firmly that's what the Lord spoke to my heart.

I want you to understand that! I want you to take it seriously!

THE LATTER RAIN OUTPOURING

After the Apostles went home to Glory, with John the Beloved being the last one to die, the Church, sadly and regrettably, began to apostatize after about two generations. It finally morphed into the Catholic system, which plunged the world into the Dark Ages until the Reformation. During those dark years, very few people were Saved and precious few baptized with the Holy Spirit. The reason was simple. The Catholic church literally locked up the Bible and basically quit preaching the Gospel altogether.

The Reformation changed that! The Lord greatly began to move as *"Justification by Faith"* once again began to be preached and understood. And then, at approximately the turn of the Twentieth Century, the Lord once again began to pour out His Spirit on searching, seeking hearts. Individuals were astounded as the Lord baptized them with the Holy Spirit with the evidence of speaking with other Tongues exactly as happened in the Early Church. It shook the entirety of the world.

As an aside, and if it is to be noticed, the nations of the world that embraced this Move of God or, at least, did not oppose it, with America leading the way, had blessings of unprecedented proportion poured out on them.

With the Holy Spirit, there is always an illumination of the Word of God and, in fact, of knowledge in every capacity. It doesn't mean that those who are baptized with the Spirit are suddenly catapulted into greater knowledge. That's not the idea! The idea is that ninety percent or more of all the

inventions in the world since the turn of the Twentieth Century have come out of America. I maintain that it's because of the outpouring of the Holy Spirit.

We are now coming to the very close of the Church Age. And, as stated, I believe the Holy Spirit is going to make one more great push before the Rapture.

Jesus said, *"And this Gospel of the Kingdom shall be preached in all the world for a witness unto all nations; and then shall the end come"* (Mat. 24:14).

So, as a result of this *"latter rain,"* the Harvest will be gathered, despite all that Satan can do. It is emphatically stated, *"He will cause to come down for you the rain."*

TO OVERFLOW WITH WINE AND OIL

The Holy Spirit through Joel said, *"And the floors shall be full of wheat, and the vats shall overflow with wine and oil."*

This, of course, speaks of the harvest of prosperity, which will be gathered in the coming Kingdom Age. Its meaning is literal, referring to an abundance of *"wheat, wine and oil."*

However, in the Spiritual Sense, the *"wheat"* speaks of the Harvest of souls, while the *"wine"* speaks of great joy, and the *"oil"* speaks of the Holy Spirit. The Holy Spirit emphatically states, *"the floors shall be full."*

When the Lord begins to work, the words *"full"* and *"overflow"* characterize His Actions.

The word *"wheat,"* as it is here used, actually denotes the pure grain separated from the husk or chaff and straw.

In other words, it is not wheat recently gathered but wheat having thoroughly been purged of all chaff and, therefore, clean (Mat. 3:11-12).

As well, the *"fats,"* as they were sometimes called, or *"vats,"* symbolize the end product of the vine and olive.

Therefore, the harvest is pictured as not only gathered but, as well, prepared for consumption.

THE RAPTURE

Likening this in the Spiritual Sense to the modern church, the Lord is not coming back after a church still covered with husks and chaff or grapes and olives unpressed. Instead, He is coming back for the finished product, as only the Holy Spirit can bring about. Therefore, this *"latter rain"* outpouring of the Holy Spirit, which I believe its conclusion is yet to come, will not only gather this tremendous Harvest but, as well, make ready the true Body of Christ, *"That He might present it to Himself a glorious Church, not having spot, or wrinkle, or any such thing; but that it should be Holy and without blemish"* (Eph. 5:27).

And yet, the Rapture of the Church could take place at any moment, without any of these things being totally fulfilled, because Jesus said, *"And when these things begin to come to pass, then look up, and lift up your heads; for your Redemption draws nigh"* (Lk. 21:28).

I think even the most casual observer, at least, in the Spiritual Sense, knows that the beginning of these things is already upon us.

RESTORATION

Joel also said, *"And I will restore to you the years that the locust has eaten, the cankerworm, and the caterpillar, and the palmerworm, My great Army which I sent among you."*

The mention of the *"locust"* and the *"cankerworm,"* etc., is meant to be but symbolic of the years lost to the *"times of the Gentiles."*

The phrase, *"And I will restore to you the years,"* refers to that period of time, which began with Nebuchadnezzar, when Judah and Jerusalem were overthrown, approximately 500 years before the birth of Christ. From that time until now, totaling about 2,500 years, Israel has wandered without much purpose in the world, having lost her place and position because of sin. However, in 1948, these things foretold by the Prophets began to come to pass, with Israel once again becoming a Nation.

Even though there are still some very dark days ahead for this Nation called *"Israel,"* and these people called *"Jews,"* in fact, the hardest ever, still, the *"Restoration"* will be brought about exactly as the Lord has promised.

The phrase, *"My great Army which I sent among you,"* refers to the plague of locusts,

NOTES

which came upon Israel because of rebellion against God. We must understand that the Lord controls the elements, the insects, etc. All of this means that He can send Blessing or the opposite. It is according to our obedience or the lack thereof. Also, the above phrase refers to the coming Antichrist and his army.

Don't think because we're living in the Day of Grace that the Lord doesn't personally deal with His People. It's different now in that He once dealt with the entirety of the Nation of Israel. Now, His Church is scattered all over the world. So, His Dealings now are with individuals and on an individual basis.

The modern Believer should do the following as it regards living for God.

THE BLESSINGS OF THE CROSS

As we've said repeatedly in this Volume and will continue to say such:

• Every Blessing comes from the Lord Jesus Christ. He Alone is the Source (Jn. 1:1, 14, 29; 14:6).

• The Cross of Christ and the Cross of Christ Alone is the Means by which all of these Blessings are given to us (Rom. 6:3-14; I Cor. 1:17-18, 23; 2:2).

• We must understand that the price paid at Calvary's Cross by our Lord guarantees every Blessing upon the Child of God, if we will only believe for such. In other words, every Blessing of which one can think comes by the Means of the Cross. They come no other way (Gal., Chpt. 5; 6:14; Eph. 2:13-18; Col. 2:14-15).

• Understanding that the Cross of Christ is the Means of every single thing we receive from God, including every Blessing, this means that the Cross of Christ and the Cross of Christ Alone must be the Object of our Faith (I Cor. 1:17-18, 23; 2:2).

• All of this said is overseen by the Holy Spirit and in every capacity. In fact, it is the Cross of Christ that has given the Holy Spirit the legal means to do all that He does for us (Rom. 8:1-2, 11).

If the Believer will place his Faith exclusively in Christ and the Cross and not allow it to be diverted to other things, and will earnestly seek the Lord regarding the things that are needed, whatever they might be, one can be assured that Christ will most definitely answer such a prayer. Considering the price paid by our Lord, don't you think that He wants us to have all for which He has paid this great price? I can assure you that He does! So, we have not because we ask not, and then too often, when we do ask, it's not from the right motive.

Every Believer can walk in purity and Righteousness, with the sin nature having no control over him whatsoever, if he will only place his Faith exclusively in Christ and the Cross. Also, every Believer can have material Blessings because the price was paid for that as well as everything else. There is nothing for which we can ask but that the Lord paid the price at Calvary's Cross. And, again, I will state the fact that the Lord desires, and does so strongly, that we take advantage of that for which He has given so much. He wants us to do that! He desires that we do that! And I personally think He is upset when we don't ask.

He said, *"For everyone who asks receives; and he who seeks finds; and to him who knocks it shall be opened"* (Lk. 11:10).

Please notice that He said *"everyone,"* and that includes you and it includes me! The secret is in the Cross. That's the reason that Paul said, *"Christ sent me not to baptize, but to preach the Gospel: not with wisdom of words, lest the Cross of Christ should be made of none effect"* (I Cor. 1:17).

All too often, we make the *"Cross of Christ of none effect"* by placing our faith elsewhere, which the Lord will never tolerate.

IS IT IN THE ATONEMENT?

That question in one form or the other has been asked, I suppose, from the time of the Cross. The answer can be ascertained once and for all.

Every single thing that the human being needs, whatever it might be, financially, materially, physically, domestically, mentally, and above all, Spiritually, was addressed at the Cross. Admittedly, we only have the firstfruits of that for which Jesus paid such a price, but one can be doubly certain that in the *"firstfruits"* our every need is met (Rom. 8:23).

OPPOSITION FROM THE POWERS OF DARKNESS

Now, once the Believer understands the Source of all life and living, which is the Cross of Christ, which gives the Holy Spirit latitude to Work within our lives, to be sure, Satan is not going to pull up stakes and leave. He's going to contest you with every iota of strength that he has. He'll try his best to discourage you, to frustrate you, to hinder you, and will work from inside the church to carry it out. Every effort that he makes is for but one purpose, and that is to destroy or, at least, seriously weaken our Faith. Now, please understand that. He wants you to divert your faith from the Cross of Christ to something else, and he doesn't too much care what the something else actually is. So, if you think that because your Faith is rightly placed, and you are truly believing God, everything is now going to be downhill with the wind at your back, think again. That's not the way it is, and that's not the way it's going to be. Concerning this very thing, Paul said:

"Fight the good fight of Faith (in essence, the only fight we are called upon to engage; every attack by Satan against the Believer, irrespective of its form, as stated, is to destroy or seriously weaken our Faith; he wants to push our Faith from the Cross to other things), **lay hold on Eternal Life** (we do such by understanding that all Life comes from Christ, and the means is the Cross), **whereunto you are also Called** (Called to follow Christ), **and have professed a good profession before many witnesses.** (This does refer to a particular occasion, but to the entirety of one's life for Christ)" **(I Tim. 6:12).**

Then Paul said:

"For though we walk in the flesh (refers to the fact that we do not yet have Glorified Bodies), **we do not war after the flesh** (after our own ability, but rather by the Power of the Spirit):

"(For the weapons of our warfare *are* not carnal (carnal weapons consist of those which are man-devised), **but mighty through God** (the Cross of Christ [I Cor. 1:18]) **to the pulling down of strongholds;)**

"Casting down imaginations *(philosophic strongholds; every effort man makes outside of the Cross of Christ)*, and every high thing that exalts itself against the Knowledge of God *(all the pride of the human heart)*, and bringing into captivity every thought to the obedience of Christ *(can be done only by the Believer looking exclusively to the Cross, where all Victory is found; the Holy Spirit will then perform the task)*" (II Cor. 10:3-5).

WARFARE

If it is to be noticed, Paul uses the words *"war"* and *"warfare,"* as it regards this present life that we're living for our Lord. In other words, it is war!

But one need not fear this warfare as long as his Faith is exclusively in Christ and His Cross. We must understand that every demon spirit, including Satan himself, and every fallen Angel were defeated at the Cross, and defeated in totality.

HOW DID JESUS DEFEAT SATAN AT THE CROSS?

Let's understand that this conflict was not physical. Anything in that nature, to be sure, Satan wants no part of, especially Christ. When the Lord tells the Evil One to jump, the only retort that Satan has is, *"How high?"* So, when we talk about our Lord defeating Satan and every power of darkness at the Cross, what happened there?

Sin is the legal means by which Satan holds men captive. As a result of sin, he has a legal right to do what he does regarding the stealing, killing, and destroying.

When Jesus died on the Cross, He gave Himself as a Perfect Sacrifice, which was accepted by God, and which atoned for all sin. This means that all sin is atoned by what Jesus did, past, present, and future, at least, for all who will believe (Jn. 3:16). That was what Jesus did at the Cross. Listen to Paul.

WHO GAVE HIMSELF A RANSOM FOR ALL

"For *there is* One God *(manifested in three Persons – God the Father, God the Son, and God the Holy Spirit)*, and One

Mediator between God and men, the Man Christ Jesus *(He can only be an adequate Mediator Who has sympathy with and an understanding of both parties, and is understandable by and clear to both; in other words, Jesus is both God and Man, i.e., 'Very God and Very Man')*;

"Who gave Himself a ransom for all *(refers to the fact that our Lord's Death was a spontaneous and voluntary Sacrifice on His Part; the word 'ransom' refers to the price He paid, owed by man to God, which was His Precious Blood [I Pet. 1:18-20])*, to be testified in due time. *(This refers to the planning of this great Work, which took place 'before the foundation of the World,' unto the 'due time' of its manifestation, which refers to when Christ was crucified)*" (I Tim. 2:5-6).

When Jesus atoned for all sin, this took away Satan's legal right to hold man captive. But in order for man to escape this bondage, he must first accept Christ as his Saviour, making Him the Lord of his life. And then, he must place his Faith exclusively in Christ and what Christ has done for us at the Cross. He must maintain his Faith in Christ and the Cross, not allowing it to be moved any place else. This will then give the Holy Spirit the liberty to Work in the heart and life of such a person, developing His Fruit and, above all, giving him Victory over the world, the flesh, and the Devil, which the Holy Spirit Alone can do.

HOW THE HOLY SPIRIT WORKS

The Holy Spirit Works exclusively within the parameters, so to speak, of the Finished Work of Christ (Rom. 8:1-2, 11). He will not work outside of those capacities simply because the Cross of Christ is what gives Him the legal Means to do all that He does for us.

Understanding that the Holy Spirit Works exclusively within the parameters of the Cross, this means that the Faith of the Believer must, without fail, be placed in the Cross of Christ, and maintained in the Cross of Christ.

In fact, the strongest admonition possible is placed upon this Doctrine, and we continue to speak of the Holy Spirit and how

He Works. Listen again to Paul:

THE LAW OF THE SPIRIT OF LIFE IN CHRIST JESUS

"For the Law *(that which we are about to give is a Law of God, devised by the Godhead in eternity past [I Pet. 1:18-20]; this Law, in fact, is 'God's Prescribed Order of Victory')* **of the Spirit** *(Holy Spirit, i.e., 'the way the Spirit works')* **of Life** *(all life comes from Christ but through the Holy Spirit [Jn. 16:13-14])* **in Christ Jesus** *(anytime Paul uses this term or one of its derivatives, he is, without fail, referring to what Christ did at the Cross, which makes this 'life' possible)* **has made me free** *(given me total victory)* **from the Law of Sin and Death** *(these are the two most powerful Laws in the Universe; the 'Law of the Spirit of Life in Christ Jesus' alone is stronger than the 'Law of Sin and Death'; this means that if the Believer attempts to live for God by any manner other than Faith in Christ and the Cross, he is doomed to failure)*" **(Rom. 8:2).**

I haven't bothered to count them, but I have read that Paul uses the term, *"in Christ Jesus,"* or one of its derivatives, such as, *"in Him," "in Whom," "in the Lord,"* etc., some 170 times in his 14 Epistles.

This means that this *"Law"* is the single most important thing for the Believer to learn. When Paul uses these terms, always and without fail, he is speaking of the Cross and what Jesus there did. The Cross and our Faith in that Finished Work on a continuing basis is what gives the Holy Spirit liberty to work within our lives. Never forget, He Alone can make us what we ought to be. He Alone can develop His Fruit in our hearts and lives. He Alone can give us Victory, and He does so by and through what our Lord did at the Cross.

That's the reason that Jesus said the following:

DENY YOURSELF

". . . If any *man* **will come after Me** *(the criteria for Discipleship)*, **let him deny himself** *(not asceticism as many think, but rather that one denies one's own will-power, self-will, strength, and ability, depending*

totally on Christ), **and take up his cross** *(the benefits of the Cross, looking exclusively to what Jesus did there to meet our every need)* **daily** *(this is so important, our looking to the Cross; that we must renew our Faith in what Christ has done for us, even on a daily basis, for Satan will ever try to move us away from the Cross as the Object of our Faith, which always spells disaster)*, **and follow Me** *(Christ can be followed only by the Believer looking to the Cross, understanding what it accomplished, and by that means alone)*" **(Lk. 9:23).**

And then Jesus said:

CANNOT BE MY DISCIPLE

"And whosoever does not bear his Cross *(this doesn't speak of suffering as most think, but rather ever making the Cross of Christ the Object of our Faith; we are Saved and we are victorious not by suffering, although that sometimes will happen, or any other similar things, but rather by our Faith, but always with the Cross of Christ as the Object of that Faith)*, **and come after Me** *(one can follow Christ only by Faith in what He has done for us at the Cross; He recognizes nothing else)*, **cannot be My Disciple** *(this statement is emphatic!; if it's not Faith in the Cross of Christ, then it's faith that God will not recognize, which means that such people are refused)*" **(Lk. 14:27).**

EAT IN PLENTY

Joel said, *"And you shall eat in plenty, and be satisfied, and praise the Name of the LORD your God, Who has dealt wondrously with you: and My People shall never be ashamed."*

The Lord is a *"Blessing God."* That means He wants to bless His Children. He wants to give us good things. He desires that we have *"plenty"* as it regards whatever it is that is needed.

We should believe that, understand that, act upon that, and look at God in exactly that posture. While at times He has to correct and has to chastise, that's not what He desires to do, although it is necessary at times. He wants to bless, and that we must realize, recognize, understand, act upon, and believe with all of our hearts.

To have those Blessings in an abundant supply, we only have to walk obediently according to His Word. He doesn't ask much of us. Jesus plainly said:

"**Come unto Me** (*is meant by Jesus to reveal Himself as the Giver of Salvation and, in fact, every good thing*), **all** *you* **who labor and are heavy laden** (*trying to earn Salvation by works*), **and I will give you rest** (*this 'rest' can only be found by placing one's Faith in Christ and what He has done for us at the Cross [Gal. 5:1-6]*).

"**Take My Yoke upon you** (*the 'yoke' of the 'Cross' [Lk. 9:23]*), **and learn of Me** (*learn of His Sacrifice [Rom. 6:3-5]*); **for I am meek and lowly in heart** (*the only thing that our Lord Personally said of Himself*): **and you shall find rest unto your souls** (*the soul can find rest only in the Cross*).

"**For My yoke** *is* **easy, and My burden is light** (*what He requires of us is very little, just to have Faith in Him and His Sacrificial Atoning Work*)" **(Mat. 11:28-30).**

ISRAEL AND THE CHURCH

As is obvious, all of these Passages refer to the coming Kingdom Age when Israel will have repented graciously before the Lord and, thereby, been restored to their rightful place and position in the world. But yet, any Promise made to Israel of old, in a sense, can be ours, as well, and I refer to the Church.

Some claim that the Lord gave many things to Israel that He will not give to the Church. I don't believe that!

Anything He promised Israel of old, be it material, economical, domestical, and, above all, Spiritual, He will do for modern Believers as well.

Paul said, "**But now** (*since the Cross*) **has He** (*the Lord Jesus*) **obtained a more excellent Ministry** (*the New Covenant in Jesus' Blood is superior and takes the place of the Old Covenant in animal blood*), **but how much also He is the Mediator of a Better Covenant** (*proclaims the fact that Christ officiates between God and man according to the arrangements of the New Covenant*), **which was established upon Better Promises.** (*This presents the New Covenant, explicitly based on the cleansing and forgiveness of*

all sin, which the Old Covenant could not do)" **(Heb. 8:6).**

As stated, some claim that while the Lord blessed Israel materially and economically, He will not do that for the Church. Not so! Let me say it again:

Anything He gave to Israel, He will do for us and more under this *"Better Covenant."* In fact, as it regards the New Covenant, probably one could say that the crowning word is *"better."*

• Christ is Better than the Angels (Heb. 1:4).

• The New Covenant contains a Better Hope (Heb. 7:19).

• Jesus is the Mediator of a Better Covenant (Heb. 8:6).

• The New Covenant is established upon Better Promises (Heb. 8:6).

• Our Lord offered a Better Sacrifice (Heb. 9:23).

• God has provided a Better thing for us (Heb. 11:40).

• Jesus speaks Better things than that of Abel (Heb. 12:24).

If the New Covenant is *"Better"* than the Old Covenant, and it most definitely is, then we should expect the Lord at least to do for us what He promised to do for Israel of old. And to be absolutely sure, He will do much, much more under this New Covenant!

WHAT THE LORD PROMISED ISRAEL OF OLD

"The LORD shall command the Blessing upon you" (Deut. 28:8).

• *"And the LORD shall make you plentiful in goods"* (Deut. 28:11).

• *"The LORD shall open unto you His good Treasure"* (Deut. 28:12).

• *"And the LORD shall make you the head, and not the tail"* (Deut. 28:13).

THE CONDITION LAID DOWN BY THE LORD

To receive these great Blessings, there was a condition, and it is as follows:

"And it shall come to pass, if you shall hearken diligently unto the Voice of the LORD your God, to observe and to do all His Commandments which I command you this day, that the LORD your God will set

you on high above all nations of the Earth" (Deut. 28:1).

Now, as we read that carefully, we very quickly come to the realization that none of us has kept all of His Commandments. And that is the condition! So, where does that leave us?

As it regards Israel, they were between the proverbial rock and the hard place. While the Promises, grand and glorious as they were, were given, still, none could claim perfect obedience. But, it is different with us presently.

The Last Adam, the Second Man, the Lord Jesus Christ, our Representative Man, our Lord, our Saviour, the One Who is the New Covenant, has, in fact, kept all the Commandments and has done so perfectly, not breaking even one in word, thought, or deed, and He did it for us.

When we place our Faith exclusively in Him and what He did for us at the Cross, then His Perfection becomes our perfection. His Obedience becomes our obedience! It only requires one thing on our part, and that is Faith in Him and in His Sacrificial, Atoning Work, which He carried out on our behalf at Calvary's Cross.

So, if my Faith is properly in Christ and what He did for me at the Cross, and I maintain that proper place and position, when the Lord looks at me, He doesn't really see me, but rather He sees Christ.

Whereas Israel could not claim these great Promises simply because they had failed to obey as they should have, as is overly obvious, we can claim them in totality all because of the Lord Jesus Christ and His Atoning Work at Calvary's Cross. Never forget it, the Lord Jesus Christ is the New Covenant. He is the Source of all things we receive from God, while the Cross is the Means by which these things are received. It only requires that the Cross of Christ ever be the Object of our Faith, and then the Holy Spirit, Who watches over all things, will guarantee that for us for which Christ has paid such a price.

Yes, He will give us every single thing that He gave Israel of old and much, much more!

(28) "AND IT SHALL COME TO PASS AFTERWARD, THAT I WILL POUR OUT

NOTES

MY SPIRIT UPON ALL FLESH; AND YOUR SONS AND YOUR DAUGHTERS SHALL PROPHESY, YOUR OLD MEN SHALL DREAM DREAMS, YOUR YOUNG MEN SHALL SEE VISIONS:

(29) "AND ALSO UPON THE SERVANTS AND UPON THE HANDMAIDS IN THOSE DAYS WILL I POUR OUT MY SPIRIT."

The exegesis is:

1. (Vs. 28) The word *"afterward"* refers to the occurrences predicted in Verses 30 through 32.

2. (Vs. 28) This Promise of the Spirit is placed out of chronological order in order to couple it with the material Blessings of Verses 21 through 27 and to provide for Acts, Chapter 2. In fact, the phrase, *"And it shall come to pass afterward, that I will pour out My Spirit upon all flesh,"* even though beginning on the Day of Pentecost, still, will not be totally fulfilled until the coming Kingdom Age.

3. (Vs. 28) *"And your sons and your daughters shall prophesy,"* refers to the Gifts of the Spirit, which accompanied the outpouring of the Holy Spirit during the time of the Early Church, and which continues unto this hour (I Cor. 12:7-11). However, as stated, this will have a complete fulfillment in the coming Kingdom Age. As well, the outpouring of the Spirit is for all—old and young, men and women.

4. (Vs. 29) *"In those days,"* actually refers to the coming Kingdom Age. Still, according to what was said by the Apostle Peter, that which happened on the Day of Pentecost was the beginning of the *"pouring out of My Spirit,"* which continues unto this day and, as stated, will be fully realized in the coming Kingdom Age.

ALL FLESH

All ranks will participate in the visitation, as proven by the words, *"That I will pour out My Spirit upon all flesh."* Pentecost was an earnest of it. The Apostle Peter did not say, *"Now is fulfilled that which was spoken by the Prophet Joel,"* but he said, *"This is that which was spoken by the Prophet...."* Its nature and characteristics are presently identical with what will happen in the coming Kingdom Age. This means that untold millions at that time will be baptized with the Holy Spirit with the evidence of speaking with other Tongues exactly as they were on the Day of Pentecost and have continued unto this hour.

Even though the phrase, *"And it shall come to pass afterward, that I will pour out My Spirit upon all flesh,"* will not be totally fulfilled until the coming Kingdom Age, still, as stated, the Day of Pentecost and forward have seen an earnest or down payment, so to speak, of that which will one day fill the entirety of the Earth.

And yet, if the *"earnest"* has been this wonderful, filling multiplied millions with the Spirit of God and energizing the Church, how much grander will it actually be when the Knowledge of the Lord covers the Earth as the waters cover the sea!

THE GIFTS OF THE SPIRIT

The phrase, *"And your sons and your daughters shall prophesy,"* refers to the Gifts of the Spirit (I Cor. 12:7-11).

No, this did not pass away with the Early Church, neither will it pass away at this present time but, instead, will continue until it totally engulfs the Earth in the coming Kingdom Age. Therefore, those who claim that such has passed away have no Scriptural validity whatsoever for their claims. No, it not only has not passed away but will actually increase. In reality, *"prophesying"* is very much of kindred spirit to the infilling of the Holy Spirit.

When Paul laid hands on the Believers at Ephesus, the Scripture says, *"The Holy Spirit came on them; and they spoke with Tongues, and prophesied"* (Acts 19:6).

Therefore, the Gift of Prophecy oftentimes accompanies the infilling of the Holy Spirit.

Incidentally, *"Prophecy,"* as here indicated, is not preaching, as many teach, even though it definitely can be exercised and, in fact, often is, during the preaching of the Word, especially when there is a heavy Anointing of the Holy Spirit.

The Gift of Prophecy, which is one of the nine Gifts of the Spirit (I Cor. 12:8-10), *". . . speaks unto men to Edification, and Exhortation, and Comfort"* (I Cor. 14:3). However, these three specifications of

NOTES

"Edification, Exhortation, and Comfort," can, in fact, involve themselves in either *"foretelling"* or *"forth-telling."*

(*"Foretelling"* speaks of futuristic events, while *"forth-telling"* speaks of present events, instructions, and specifications.)

PROPHETS AND THE GIFT OF PROPHECY

However, all people who prophesy, or, in other words, have this Gift of the Spirit, are not necessarily Prophets. In other words, they do not necessarily stand in the Office of the Prophet. In fact, few do! The Office of the Prophet comes under one of the fivefold Ministry headings of, *"Apostles, Prophets, Evangelists, Pastors, and Teachers"* (Eph. 4:11).

As well, *"sons and daughters,"* i.e., men and women, are put on an equal footing with neither one preferred over the other in respect to the outpouring of the Holy Spirit and being used by God.

Therefore, this destroys the idea that only men can be called to preach the Gospel because women are plainly inferred here as well.

YOUNG MEN AND OLD MEN

The phrase, *"Your old men shall dream Dreams, your young men shall see Visions,"* in the original Hebrew actually says, *"your old men and young men shall dream Dreams and see Visions."*

Therefore, as gender is not shown partiality, neither is age.

In a crusade we conducted in about 1985 in Anchorage, Alaska, among the many who were baptized with the Holy Spirit in the Holy Spirit rally on Sunday afternoon was a dear elderly gentleman, 101 years old. His wife also received, being either 99 or 100, if I remember correctly.

I'll never forget looking into his face as it was wreathed in a smile after he had partaken of this glorious experience, and he said to me:

"Brother Swaggart, my wife and I drove several hundred miles to be in this crusade. I know I don't have long left to live, but in the last few months, I have been so hungry for the Holy Spirit. I determined somehow to get to this meeting and prayed that God

would give me the strength to do so. That He did, and He also baptized me with the Holy Spirit with the evidence of speaking with other Tongues. Now, I can go home and die happy!"

Actually, we have seen tens of thousands of people gloriously and wondrously baptized with the Holy Spirit with the evidence of speaking with other Tongues as the Spirit of God gave the utterance, which is according to the Word of God (Acts 2:4).

THE LORD TOLD ME WHAT TO DO

In 1968, the Lord impressed upon both Frances and me that I should go on radio with a daily program. To be frank, I was very leery of doing such because, even though I had been on radio any number of times in meetings across the country, I had little or no knowledge as it regarded sustaining a program on a daily basis. As well, I did not really consider myself to be a Bible teacher, which was absolutely needed for radio, but rather a preaching Evangelist. Nevertheless, the Lord kept leaning on us to go in this direction.

If I remember the date correctly, our first program aired on January 1, 1969. It was 15 minutes in length, Monday through Friday.

I first went on three stations, Houston, Texas; Beckley, West Virginia; and, Atlanta, Georgia. I'm certain that my efforts were very meager, and, thereby, I had very little to offer the people as it regarded the teaching of the Word of God. Very soon, after about three months, we were out of money simply because of getting almost no response.

I reasoned in my spirit that whatever I was doing wasn't right, so I might as well go off the air. I didn't feel right about it, but the bills had to be paid. Our response was next to nothing, and so I seemed to have had no other choice.

I wrote the managers of the three stations, telling them that we were cancelling and gave them two weeks' notice according to our contracts. As far as I was concerned, this effort was over.

But the managers of these three radio stations didn't see it that way. Without my knowledge, all three of them went on the air at the scheduled time of our broadcast,

telling the people that we were cancelling the program. Without collaborating with each other, and, in fact, they didn't even know each other, they told the people that this program should remain because it was needed.

At any rate, I was in Louisville, Kentucky, in a meeting. Frances had stayed home with Donnie inasmuch as he was now in high school.

She called me with the most astounding news that I think I had ever heard.

She told me how she had heard the doorbell ring that morning and had gone to the door. When she opened it, the mailman was standing there, and a whole sack of mail was at his feet. He calmly looked at her and said, *"This is for you."*

There were 900 letters in that mail sack, with people telling us they did not want the program to be cancelled. The managers of these three stations had told the people that if they wanted the program to continue coming to them, they should write us and tell us. They did, and in a way none of us even remotely thought could happen.

NATIONWIDE

In a few months' time, we were on some 600 stations daily with the largest audience of a daily radio program, to my knowledge, in the nation. The Lord blessed it abundantly.

THE HOLY SPIRIT

At a given point in time, about 1970, the Lord began to deal with my heart about teaching on the Holy Spirit. I argued with the Lord, informing Him that I was not a teacher, but rather a Preacher. How brash we are through ignorance!

At any rate, in prayer one afternoon, the Lord spoke to my heart and said, *"I will show you how to teach."* I realize that's a short statement, but as short as it may be, it covers a wide territory. How in the world could the Lord show me how to teach His Word in a short period of time?

But, of course, He knew exactly what He was doing. In a few minutes' time, He taught me how to address a particular subject, how to take it apart, and how to present it to the people. It was just that easy and just that simple.

I began to teach on the Holy Spirit and continued for some two years on that one subject. In fact, I actually received mail in Baton Rouge addressed to *"Mr. Pentecost,"* and it would be delivered to us.

This was the time of the great outpouring of the Holy Spirit on Baptists, Methodists, Catholics, Presbyterians, Lutherans, etc. I firmly believe that our little short radio program, called *"The Campmeeting Hour,"* only 15 minutes in length each day, Monday through Friday, played a great part in this great outpouring. At any rate, what little part we were privileged to play, we give the Lord all the praise and all the glory.

BELIEVERS TO RECEIVE THE HOLY SPIRIT

We had just begun conducting crusades all over the nation when the Lord moved greatly upon me in prayer one particular morning. He stated that we should set aside one Service in our crusades in which we were to preach on the Holy Spirit and pray for Believers to be filled with the Spirit. In that prayer session that morning, the Lord told me, *"If you obey Me, I will bless your efforts, and, in fact, I will fill as many as a thousand people in a single Service."*

That was astounding to me because I remembered praying with countless people through the years. Seeing eight or ten people filled in a Revival was a big thing. But a thousand in a single Service? That was miraculous! At any rate, the Lord spoke that to my heart and I found that He would be true to His Word.

THE FIRST SERVICE

I set out to obey the Lord, and my next meeting was in Canton, Ohio. Actually, it was to be conducted in a church in which the Lord moved greatly, giving us many souls. The crowds were enormous, actually packing the building to capacity each night.

As the meeting convened, I began to announce that on Sunday afternoon, we would be having a special Service in one of the auditoriums in town, which we had rented, especially to pray for Believers to be baptized with the Holy Spirit. Considering that I was teaching on the subject every day over

our radio program, when Sunday afternoon arrived, again, if I remember correctly, the building was packed, with hundreds there wanting to be filled with the Spirit.

When the message concluded, and I called Believers forward who wanted to be baptized with the Holy Spirit, I was astounded that hundreds responded. The truth was, I did not have any idea as to how to deal with hundreds of people seeking the Holy Spirit. As stated, all through the years I had been accustomed to praying with people and stay with them until they were filled; however, this could not be done with hundreds of people. Please believe me, that afternoon, I tried. After just a little bit, I had no voice left, and I was physically exhausted. The truth is, only a few out of the hundreds who came were actually baptized with the Holy Spirit.

When the Service ended, I was totally dejected. I remember going back to the motel room where I was staying, throwing myself across the bed, and informing the Lord that I would never do that again. But, of course, the Lord knew a lot of things that I did not know.

THE REVELATION FROM THE LORD

Our next crusade some weeks later was in Toledo, Ohio. It was being conducted in an auditorium there in the city. At any rate, the Full Gospel Businessmen were having a meeting on Saturday morning and invited me to speak. They informed me that they wanted me to speak on the Holy Spirit, if I felt so led, etc.

That Saturday morning, I arose long before daylight. I went before the Lord in prayer, asking Him what I was to do.

That morning the Lord showed me exactly how I was to pray for hundreds of people to be filled with the Spirit, and to be filled instantly. He told me what to say to them as I gave them a few moments of instructions. He told me, as well, to have Spirit-filled people come stand behind the folk who wanted to be filled and to lay their hands on them when I told them to do so.

I knew beyond the shadow of a doubt that the Lord had spoken to my heart. I knew He had given me information that would see untold thousands baptized with the Holy Spirit. I could hardly wait for that Service to begin that morning.

The meeting was conducted in a large banquet hall in the Holiday Inn. It was full!

I preached on the Holy Spirit and then set out to do exactly what the Lord told me to do. I asked how many there wanted to be baptized with the Holy Spirit. Scores raised their hands.

I had them come forward, and it was so many that the line literally went all the way across the building to the back wall. I then told them to look at me as I gave them some short instructions. I did my best to tell them exactly what the Lord had told me to say.

To be brief, I told them that the only requirement to be baptized with the Holy Spirit was to be Born-Again. I then related to them that the Lord sincerely wanted them to be filled.

I went on to say that when we began to pray for them, and the people laid hands on them, they would sense a language that they had never known or heard beginning to be formed in their spirit. That was the Lord giving the utterance. I told them that the Holy Spirit would not force them to speak in Tongues. He would give the utterance, but they would have to do the speaking. And the moment they heard in their spirit these words, which were not English or any other language they had learned at their mother's knee, they were to speak those words out and to keep speaking them. I emphasized the fact that the Spirit of God would give the utterance but would not force them to speak. They had to do that themselves. The Bible didn't say that the Holy Spirit spoke in Tongues, but rather that the people did.

At the beginning of my instructions, I told them that every recipient of the Holy Spirit, with no exception, speaks with other Tongues when they are baptized with the Holy Spirit.

I gave those instructions that morning to the scores of people standing there, and I could hardly wait to see what happened.

I then prayed and after concluding my petition to the Lord for His Spirit to fall on these people, I told the workers standing behind them to lay their hands on their heads and, as well, do so speaking with Tongues themselves.

And, then it happened!

THE LORD HONORED HIS WORD

As this was done, all of a sudden, the Spirit of God fell in that building. If I remember correctly, every single person who came was baptized with the Holy Spirit. It must have been at least 50 to 75, or maybe even 100, who were instantly filled.

I remember a little Nazarene grandmother. Every time I would be in that part of Ohio in meetings, she would always attend. She wanted the Holy Spirit, but up to now, had not been filled. But that morning she was filled.

The Lord knocked her flat on her back on the floor, and she came up speaking with other Tongues as the Spirit of God gave the utterance. When I saw her a little later, her face literally beamed. She said, *"Brother Swaggart, you have said that it is wonderful, but it's greater than you have said."*

From that meeting forward, in every crusade, we would set aside a special Service to pray for people to be filled with the Spirit. It was usually Sunday afternoon, the closing Service of the crusade. The crowds began to grow, with thousands coming, actually filling the largest auditoriums and coliseums in the nation. I suddenly got it into my mind that possibly I should preach something else other than the Holy Spirit in these Sunday afternoon Services. I did not consult with the Lord and was to find out that whenever we do this, we always get into trouble.

At any rate, in the particular crusade at that time, Sunday afternoon came, and I began to try to prepare for the message. Nothing would come! I prayed and sought the Lord, but there was nothing. I got up some little message, but in my heart I knew it wasn't right. However, I did not know what else to do.

When Frances and I arrived at the coliseum, I found that every seat was packed. Thousands were present. I walked on the platform, and Thomas Sloane was leading the Praise and Worship, which was our usual procedure.

I was standing by the piano, waiting for him to introduce me, when all of a sudden, the Lord spoke to my heart. To be sure, I knew it was the Lord. There was no mistake about it.

He said to me, *"I did not tell you to change this Service. I told you to preach on the Holy Spirit and to call Believers forward to be filled with the Spirit at the end of the Service."* And then He said, *"Are you going to obey Me or not?"*

I stood there by the piano literally trembling, with tears rolling down my face. I said, *"Lord, if You'll continue to give me breath, the moment I take this Service, I will do exactly what You've called me to do."*

After the music, I announced my subject, which the Lord had given me in the last few minutes, *"There is a River!"* And then I did exactly what the Lord told me to do, I preached that Message on the Holy Spirit, and the Glory fell in the place.

When the message was concluded, I called for people to come forward who wanted to be baptized with the Holy Spirit. Hundreds responded, and hundreds were filled!

MADISON SQUARE GARDEN, NEW YORK CITY

If my memory serves me correctly, Madison Square Garden seats some 21,000 people. Our crusade there had begun on Friday night. This was our third or fourth time in this huge coliseum, always with phenomenal meetings. This meeting was to be no exception, and, in fact, Sunday afternoon was to prove to be a milestone, meaning that the Lord was faithful to His Promise as He always is.

The building was packed that Sunday afternoon. After I preached, I once again asked for a show of hands from those who knew they were Saved and wanted to be filled with the Holy Spirit but had not yet received. It was like a forest of hands that was raised.

I then asked them to come forward. They began to come and kept coming. They filled up the front and then filled up the aisles all the way back to the furthest reach of that gigantic coliseum.

There were so many who had come forward that there was little room for workers to stand behind each one as we normally did. But we did the best we could, and people crowded in as much as possible.

After I gave instructions and prayed and then asked the workers to lay hands on them, there was a powerful outpouring of the Spirit in that gigantic coliseum. I knew the Lord had done a wonderful thing; however, I really did not think very much about how many were filled.

After the crusade, we had to catch a plane that night for London, England. After flying all night long and getting an hour or two of sleep, if that, we arrived in London. London is normally about six hours ahead of New York. So, it was in the afternoon when we arrived.

After Frances and I got situated in the room, I told her that I was going to walk over to the park and pray awhile. The hotel was immediately beside Hyde Park.

In prayer that afternoon, all of a sudden, the Lord very freshly brought back to mind that great Service of the day before. The Lord then spoke to my heart saying, *"How many do you think were baptized with the Holy Spirit yesterday afternoon?"* It suddenly dawned on me the Promise the Lord had made me years before. He had said to me, *"If you obey Me, I will baptize at least a thousand people in a single Service with the Holy Spirit."*

As these thoughts came to my mind, the Lord spoke again and said, *"There were over 1,000 people baptized with the Holy Spirit yesterday afternoon exactly as I told you would happen."*

I'll never forget where I was at that moment. I stopped, with tears rolling down my face, thanking the Lord not only for what was done but for His Word being so meticulously kept.

We aired many of these Services over worldwide television. This also created a hunger in the hearts and lives of untold hundreds of thousands to be baptized with the Holy Spirit. Currently, everywhere that Donnie, Gabriel, and all the other Ministers of our organization go, they set aside a Service to pray for people to be filled with the Spirit. The Lord never fails to open the windows of Heaven. In fact, as our Ministry before them, they are seeing many, many Believers baptized with the Holy Spirit. The Vision continues!

I WILL POUR OUT MY SPIRIT

Joel said, *"And also upon the servants and upon the handmaids in those days will I pour out My Spirit."*

Even though the words, *"In those days,"* actually refer to the coming Kingdom Age, still, according to what was said by the Apostle Peter, that which happened on the Day of Pentecost was the beginning of the *"pouring out of My Spirit."* It continues unto this day and will be fully realized in the coming Kingdom Age.

Actually, the Lord intended for Israel to have this, beginning with the Day of Pentecost. However, Israel refused it, even as most of the world and most of the church refuses it presently.

Nevertheless, even though the religious leadership of Israel refused it, still, some few did not refuse it and were actually the recipients of this great Promise. As such, they became the nucleus of the Early Church. By the Power of the Holy Spirit, they evangelized a great part of the civilized world of that day.

As stated, it was poured out then and has continued to be poured out on hungry hearts and lives ever since.

Nevertheless, Israel, although rejecting the Holy Spirit on the Day of Pentecost, will, in fact, widely accept it in a coming glad day. Then, the whole of Israel, as well as a great percentage of all the Gentiles (*"all flesh"*), will be baptized with the Holy Spirit with the evidence of speaking with other Tongues.

In view of Joel's Prophecies regarding the Holy Spirit, perhaps further comments would be in order.

THE BAPTISM WITH THE HOLY SPIRIT

Salvation is God's greatest Gift to the world while the Holy Spirit is God's greatest Gift to His Children, the Church. The Baptism with the Holy Spirit might properly be called the *"Baptism of Power."* As such, it is an invaluable asset to the Christian committed to seeking the furtherance of God's Plan for the world.

WE BELIEVE . . .

• We believe that the Believer most

NOTES

definitely does receive the Holy Spirit at Conversion; however, this, in fact, is not the Baptism with the Holy Spirit that was poured out on the Day of Pentecost.

• There is a vast difference in being born of the Spirit and being baptized with the Spirit (Jn. 3:3-8).

• We believe the Baptism with the Holy Spirit is a distinct Work of Grace separate and apart from Salvation (Acts 2:4).

• We believe the only requirement to be baptized with the Holy Spirit is to be *"Born-Again"* (Acts 19:1-7).

• We believe that the Baptism with the Holy Spirit is for all Believers, irrespective as to whom they might be (Acts 2:17).

• We believe that speaking with other Tongues is the initial, physical evidence that one has been baptized with the Spirit (Acts 2:4, 44-46; 19:6).

• We believe the Baptism with the Holy Spirit, among other things, is given to the Believer for Power (Acts 1:8).

• We believe that unless one has been baptized with the Holy Spirit with the evidence of speaking with other Tongues, there is actually going to be very little done for the Lord (Acts 1:4-5).

• We believe that *"Tongues"* constitute a language spoken somewhere in the world but not known by the speaker (Acts 2:6-11).

• We believe that speaking with other Tongues is of great benefit to the Believer (Acts 2:11, 17; I Cor. 14:2, 4).

• We believe there is nothing in the Word of God that even remotely indicates that this great Gift from God ceased after the time of the Early Church but that it continues unto this hour and, in fact, will continue even in the Great Tribulation and into the Kingdom Age (Acts 2:17-21).

• We believe that as it was necessary for Jesus to be filled with the Spirit before commencing His Ministry, it is most definitely necessary for us as well (Mat. 3:16-17).

• We believe the Baptism with the Holy Spirit is so necessary for the Believer that Jesus instructed His Followers to be filled with the Spirit before they undertook anything for Him (Acts 1:4-5).

• We believe that Gifts of the Spirit are not possible in one's life until that individual has first been baptized with the Holy Spirit (I Cor. 12:4-11).

PROPHECY

The Baptism with the Holy Spirit was promised through Prophecy by John the Baptist, and Jesus would be the Baptizer. He said:

"**I indeed baptize you with water unto Repentance** *(Water Baptism was an outward act of an inward work already carried out)*: **but He** *(Christ)* **Who comes after me is mightier than I, Whose Shoes I am not worthy to bear: He shall baptize you with the Holy Spirit, and** *with* **fire** *(to burn out the sinful dross [Acts 2:2-4])*:

"**Whose fan** *is* **in His Hand** *(the ancient method for winnowing grain)*, **and He will thoroughly purge His Floor** *('purging it, that it may bring forth more fruit' [Jn. 15:2])*, **and gather His Wheat into the garner** *(the end product as developed by the Spirit)*; **but He will burn up the chaff with unquenchable fire** *(the wheat is symbolic of the Work of the Spirit, while the chaff is symbolic of the work of the flesh)*" **(Mat. 3:11-12).**

THREE PARTICULARS RESPECTING THE HOLY SPIRIT AND THE CHURCH

There are three things we should note, which I believe to be of immense significance as it regards the Work of God and speaking of that which pertains to the Baptism with the Holy Spirit.

JESUS NEEDED THE HOLY SPIRIT . . .

Our Lord was filled with the Spirit before He began his public Ministry. The Scripture says of this event:

"**And Jesus, when He was baptized** *(this was the beginning of His earthly Ministry)*, **went up straightway** *(immediately)* **out of the water** *(refers to Baptism by immersion and not by sprinkling)*: **and, lo, the Heavens were opened unto Him** *(the only One, the Lord Jesus Christ, to Whom the Heavens would be opened)*, **and he saw the Spirit of God** *(Holy Spirit)* **descending like a dove, and lighting upon Him** *(John saw a visible form that reminded him of a dove)*:

"**And lo a Voice from Heaven, saying** *(the Voice of God the Father)*, **This is My Beloved Son, in Whom I am well pleased** *(the Trinity appears here: the Father speaks, the Spirit descends, and the Son prays [Lk. 3:21])*" **(Mat. 3:16-17).**

Our Lord was born without a sin nature, which means He was born without original sin, hence, the Virgin Birth. He was and is the Son of the Living God, God manifest in the flesh. Now the question must be asked, *"If our Lord, altogether perfect, needed the Holy Spirit to carry out His Ministry, where does that leave us?"* I think the answer to that is overly obvious. If He needed the Holy Spirit, we most definitely need the Holy Spirit. In fact, our Lord set the Standard for Ministry, a Standard, incidentally, that we must follow. That Standard is the Holy Spirit helping us, anointing us, and empowering us, without which, precious little, if anything, is going to truly be done for the Lord.

THE LAST WORD OF OUR LORD BEFORE HIS ASCENSION

Concerning His last Message to His Disciples, the Scripture says:

"**And, being assembled together with** *them (speaks of the time He ascended back to the Father; this was probably the time of the 'above 500' [I Cor. 15:6])*, **Commanded them** *(not a suggestion)* **that they should not depart from Jerusalem** *(the site of the Temple where the Holy Spirit would descend)*, **but wait for the Promise of the Father** *(spoke of the Holy Spirit which had been promised by the Father [Lk. 24:49; Joel, Chpt. 2])*, **which, said** *He*, **you have heard of Me** *(you have also heard Me say these things [Jn. 7:37-39; 14:12-17, 26; 15:26; 16:7-15])*.

"**For John truly baptized with water** *(merely symbolized the very best Baptism Believers could receive before the Day of Pentecost)*; **but you shall be baptized with the Holy Spirit not many days hence** *(spoke of the coming Day of Pentecost, although Jesus did not use that term at that time)*."

THE KINGDOM

"**When they therefore were come together, they asked of Him, saying** *(seemingly presents the last meeting before the Ascension)*, **Lord, will You at this time restore** again the Kingdom to Israel? *(He would later answer this question through the Apostle Paul [II Thess., Chpt. 2].)*

"And He said unto them, It is not for you to know the times or the seasons, which the Father has put in His Own Power *(the Master is saying that it is not the business of the followers of Christ to know this information, but rather to 'occupy till I come' [Lk. 19:13]).*

POWER

"But you shall receive power *(Miracle-working Power)*, after that the Holy Spirit is come upon you *(specifically states that this 'Power' is inherent in the Holy Spirit, and solely in His Domain)*: and you shall be witnesses *(doesn't mean witnessing to souls, but rather to one giving one's all in every capacity for Christ, even to the laying down of one's life)* unto Me *(without the Baptism with the Holy Spirit, one cannot really know Jesus as one should)* both in Jerusalem, and in all Judaea, and in Samaria, and unto the uttermost part of the Earth *(proclaims the Work of God as being worldwide)*.

THE ASCENSION

"And when He had spoken these things *(refers to His last Instructions to His Followers)*, while they beheld, He was taken up *(refers to Him ascending before their very eyes)*; and a cloud received Him out of their sight *(represents the Shekinah Glory of God, which enveloped Christ as He ascended)*" **(Acts 1:4-9).**

The last word or the last message that anyone gives to individuals, whatever the occasion, should be understood as to be extremely important or, at least, intended to be so. And one can surely conclude that the last Message of our Lord to His Disciples, actually, to all His Followers, even including up to this very moment, was and is of extreme significance. In fact, it is so important that it would be impossible for anyone to gauge the significance of this particular time.

This would be the last word that He would give to them. The great Plan of Redemption was now complete. Calvary was a fact! Now, the job of world Evangelism would commence, in essence, the building of the

Church. So, He would give His Followers His final Instructions, which we have to assume were the single most important words they could ever hear.

He could have spoken on Prophecy. In fact, His Disciples attempted to get Him to deal with that subject by asking if the Kingdom would now be restored to Israel. He brushed it aside by telling them, in essence, that that was not the important thing at the time.

His last Message to them and to us was that they must wait for the Promise of the Father. He was speaking of the mighty Baptism with the Holy Spirit, which would take place a few days from then. In essence, He told them, *"Don't go try to testify for Me, don't go try to hold Services in My Name, in fact, don't do anything for Me, don't engage in My Work whatsoever until you first are baptized with the Holy Spirit."* That's how important it was.

He would use the last minutes of His Ministry on this Earth to give them these instructions. As we stated, He could have addressed anything, but He addressed this, their need and the absolute essentiality of them being baptized with the Holy Spirit.

That should tell us something. In fact, it speaks volumes! This was the Last Word, their receiving the Baptism with the Holy Spirit, before His Ascension. We must not allow the significance of this to be lost on us.

A COMMAND

The third thing to which I will call your attention is the manner in which He gave this Last Word. He Commanded them to obey His Instructions as it regarded their being baptized with the Holy Spirit. The Scriptures says:

"And, being assembled together with them, Commanded them that they should not depart from Jerusalem, but wait for the Promise of the Father, which, said He, you have heard of Me.

"For John truly baptized with water; but you shall be baptized with the Holy Spirit not many days hence" (Acts 1:4-5).

As we have noted, as it regarded them being baptized with the Holy Spirit, He *"Commanded them"* to obey His Instructions.

The word *"commanded"* in the Greek is *"taraggello,"* and means *"something that's most definitely not casually said, but rather a charge that is given."* In effect, it's the same as a military charge given by a commanding officer, in this case, the greatest Commander of all, the Lord Jesus Christ.

Now, the question, no doubt, can be asked, *"Is that Command for us today?"*

Most definitely, it is! That Command was meant not only for His Disciples, not only for His Followers of that time, but for every single follower who has ever existed from then until now and, in fact, will continue throughout the coming Kingdom Age. So, we have three particulars in this that we should carefully remember. They are:

1. Jesus needed the Holy Spirit for His Ministry, and so do we!

2. Considering the last Message that He gave to His Disciples and Followers, we learn how important that it is for all Believers to be baptized with the Holy Spirit.

3. In fact, when addressing this subject, He did more than merely suggest their need for the Baptism with the Holy Spirit. He *"Commanded"* them to be filled with the Spirit before beginning Ministry. That's how important this great subject of the Baptism with the Holy Spirit actually is.

WHO IS THE HOLY SPIRIT?

The Holy Spirit is a distinct and separate Member of the Divine Trinity. He works in association and in complete harmony with the Father and the Son. Actually, the Father, the Son, and the Holy Spirit are One in essence.

The word *"essence"* refers to the properties or attributes by means of which something can be placed in its proper class or identified as being what it is, meaning that it is of the same nature.

However, although the Godhead is One in essence, the Holy Spirit should not be confused with either the Father or the Son. I John 5:7 tells us, *"There are Three Who bear record in Heaven, the Father, the Word, and the Holy Spirit...."* (The *"Word"* is the same as Christ—John 1:1.)

Our Lord Jesus Christ Himself said (Mat. 28:19), *"... Preach to all nations, baptizing them in the Name of the Father, and of the Son, and of the Holy Spirit."*

The Holy Spirit is God, just as the Father is God, and just as the Son is God. There are, however, differences between the Father, the Son, and the Holy Spirit. The Three are not carbon copies. They have individual characteristics, which set Their Roles apart, even though Their Purposes and Their Aims are inseparable.

It might be said that the Father is the Owner of all Creation, while the Son is the Builder of all Creation, with the Holy Spirit being the Worker Who actually carries out the task.

DOES ONE RECEIVE THE HOLY SPIRIT AT CONVERSION?

There is controversy as to whether one receives the Holy Spirit at the moment of Conversion. Actually, the only proper answer to this question is *"Yes."* However, receiving the Holy Spirit at Conversion is not the same as being baptized with the Holy Spirit. These are two different things.

The responsibilities of the Holy Spirit are many and varied. One of the most important of these responsibilities is that of Regeneration. Paul states, *"... no man can say that Jesus is the Lord, but by the Holy Spirit"* (I Cor. 12:3). This demonstrates without question that the Holy Spirit plays a unique role in bringing a sinner to Conviction, Repentance, and Salvation.

As well, the activities of the Holy Spirit are many. He is a Comforter, a Leader, a Helper, a Communicator, and a Guide. He is the Director of all God's Activities on Earth today and, in fact, ever has been. So, when the sinner comes to the moment of Salvation, certainly he has received the Holy Spirit within the context of having been influenced and even occupied by Him. However, to assume that this Work of the Holy Spirit is the same as the Baptism with the Holy Spirit is erroneous.

Even though every Believer is definitely Saved, still, every Believer has not been baptized with the Holy Spirit even though every Believer can if he or she so desires. There is a vast difference in being *"born of the Spirit"* and being *"baptized with the Spirit."*

SERVICE FOR GOD

At Salvation, life is imparted to someone who has heretofore been spiritually dead. In the Baptism with the Holy Spirit, power is imparted to the Christian who was previously weak and ineffectual. He is henceforth fitted for service to God. Therefore, according to Scripture, it is clearly the mandate of the Lord that every Christian should be baptized with the Holy Spirit (Acts 1:4).

Salvation and the Baptism with the Spirit are two separate and distinct experiences. They are different as to time and nature. A person, as we have stated, may experience Salvation without experiencing the Baptism with the Holy Spirit. He cannot, however, experience the Baptism with the Holy Spirit without first experiencing Salvation. The Baptism with the Holy Spirit must, therefore, be preceded by Regeneration (Salvation), and only then can the Holy Spirit actually begin to function within his life as He so desires. Jesus said, *"Even the Spirit of Truth; Whom the world cannot receive, because it sees Him not, neither knows Him: but you know Him; for He dwells with you, and shall be in you"* (Jn. 14:17).

It is this indwelling of the Holy Spirit that endows us with power and enables us to be of greater service to God (Acts 1:8).

THE WORD OF GOD

Does the Word of God support the contention that the Baptism with the Holy Spirit and Salvation are not simultaneous? Let's see what it says:

In Luke 10:20, Jesus said to the Disciples upon their return from spreading the Gospel, *". . . rejoice, because your names are written in Heaven."* What can we assume from this?

We can assume that these men were Saved. If their names were written in Heaven (in the Lamb's Book of Life), they were unquestionably Saved. But they didn't receive the Baptism with the Holy Spirit until the Day of Pentecost, sometime later!

And then there was Paul (Saul of Tarsus). Acts, Chapter 9 tells of the dramatic, glorious, and sudden Conversion of Paul as he traveled from Jerusalem toward Damascus.

When Jesus appeared to Paul at that time, Paul there gave his heart to the Lord and was instantly Converted. But it was some three days later before the Lord sent Ananias to Paul for the laying on of hands for healing and for the Baptism with the Holy Spirit! The Scriptures says in the words of Ananias, *". . . the Lord, even Jesus, Who appeared unto you in the way as you came, has sent me, that you might receive your sight, and be filled with the Holy Spirit"* (Acts 9:17).

As stated, this plainly and clearly tells us that Paul wasn't baptized with the Holy Spirit when he was Saved, but rather some three days later.

EPHESUS

Acts 19:1 through 6 tells us of Paul's experience at Ephesus. He found there some twelve men, and upon speaking with them, found that even though they were Saved, they had not yet been baptized with the Holy Spirit. He said to them:

"Have you received the Holy Spirit since you believed?"

In the Greek, this is literally, *"Having believed, did you receive?"* We know these men were already Saved because every time the word *"Disciples"* is used in the Book of Acts, it refers to individuals who have accepted Christ. Paul could tell that these individuals, although Saved, had not yet been baptized with the Holy Spirit.

Upon Paul asking the men the question as to whether they had been baptized with the Holy Spirit, they said **". . . And they said unto him, We have not so much as heard whether there be any Holy Spirit** (*this doesn't mean that they didn't know of the existence of the Holy Spirit, but that they were not aware that the Age of the Spirit had come, and that Believers could literally be baptized with Him; at Salvation, the Holy Spirit baptizes believing sinners into Christ; at the Spirit Baptism, Jesus baptizes Believers into the Holy Spirit [Mat. 3:11])"* **(Acts 19:2).**

It is almost as if the Lord anticipated the future debate over whether the Holy Spirit Baptism comes simultaneously with Salvation. He would include the phrase as given by Paul, *"Have you received the Holy Spirit since you believed?"* to prove that these men were Believers, who had not been baptized with the Holy Spirit at the time of Salvation. This should have laid the question to rest before it has even begun.

Some, though, see what they want in Scripture despite all the evidence to the contrary. Was the Lord foreseeing this when He said in Mark 8:18, *"Having eyes, see you not?"*

THE BELIEVERS IN SAMARIA

Acts, Chapter 8, records Phillip going to Samaria where he preached Christ unto these people. During the course of this meeting, many were delivered and many were healed. Upon seeing all these Miracles, the people were convicted and accepted Christ as their Saviour.

The Scripture says the following concerning this momentous event:

THE HOLY SPIRIT

"Now when the Apostles which were at Jerusalem heard that Samaria had received the Word of God *(many had been Saved)*, **they sent unto them Peter and John** *(for a reason which we will see)*:

"Who, when they were come down, prayed for them, that they might receive the Holy Spirit *(this was their purpose for coming, and this is how important it is for Believers to be baptized with the Spirit)*:

"(For as yet He *(the Holy Spirit)* **was fallen upon none of them** *(evidently Philip had strongly preached Salvation, but had not preached the Baptism with the Holy Spirit)*: **only they were baptized in the Name of the Lord Jesus.)** *(This is meant to infer that they had been baptized in water but not the Baptism with the Spirit.)*

"Then laid they *their* hands on them *(presents one of the ways Believers can be baptized with the Spirit, but this is not necessary in order to be filled [Acts 2:4; 10:44-48])*, **and they received the Holy Spirit** *(doesn't give any more information, but we know from Verse 21 that they also spoke with Tongues)*" **(Acts 8:14-17).**

In these Passages, we are told the following:

• The Salvation experience does not automatically include the Baptism with the Holy Spirit, with the latter being received after Conversion, whether moments later, years later, etc.

• As well, Water Baptism, as important as that is, is not the Baptism with the Holy Spirit.

We see from this, and unequivocally so, that the Baptism with the Holy Spirit is an experience separate and apart from Salvation. In fact, the Believer must ask for this experience. Concerning this, Jesus said, *"How much more shall your Heavenly Father give the Holy Spirit to them who ask Him?"* (Lk. 11:11-13). The facts are, no unbeliever is going to ask the Lord to baptize him with the Holy Spirit, which should be obvious. Only people who have truly been Born-Again will want and desire such a thing.

We must understand that the Baptism with the Holy Spirit is not something imposed unknowingly or unwillingly upon anyone at the moment he becomes a Christian. But yet, unless it is preached to the people, for Faith comes by hearing, and hearing by the Word of God, there will be little or no desire for this experience (Rom. 10:17).

DOES EVERY RECIPIENT SPEAK WITH OTHER TONGUES?

We teach and preach, according to the Word of God, that every recipient of the Baptism with the Spirit speaks with other Tongues, and there are no exceptions. In other words, if one doesn't speak with other Tongues, while one may be greatly blessed, that particular individual has not yet been baptized with the Holy Spirit. While speaking with other Tongues is not the only evidence that one has been filled, it most definitely is the initial, physical evidence that one has been baptized with the Spirit. Again, this is according to the Word of God. Some think that if they have some type of experience from the Lord, whatever it might be, this constitutes the Baptism with the Spirit. That experience may be perfectly Scriptural and viable and a great Blessing; however, if the individual doesn't speak with other Tongues, then he has not been baptized with the Holy Spirit.

LET'S LOOK AT THE APOSTLE PAUL

I think it would be agreed by all that Paul had one of the most tremendous experiences on the road to Damascus that anyone could ever have as it regards the Lord. He plainly said that he saw the Lord at that time, using the words, **"And last of all He was seen of me also** (and this was after the Ascension of Christ), **as of one born out of due time"** (I Cor. 15:8).

As well, he not only saw the Lord but actually held a conversation with Him (Acts 9:4-6). In fact, he was wondrously and gloriously Saved when he said to the Lord, *"What will You have me to do?"* (Acts 9:6). The light that surrounded Christ was of such magnitude that it blinded this future Apostle (Acts 9:3).

So, if one wants to speak of experiences, I think it would be very difficult to improve upon that which Paul had. But yet, despite seeing Christ, speaking with Christ, and actually being Born-Again at that time, still, he wasn't baptized with the Holy Spirit. That took place some three days later when Ananias, having been instructed by the Lord, went to where Paul was staying and prayed for him that *"he might receive his sight, and be filled with the Holy Spirit"* (Acts 9:17). Therefore, we must not mistake experiences from the Lord, as wonderful as they might be, as being baptized with the Holy Spirit, as some have! I might quickly add, if one is baptized with the Holy Spirit automatically at Conversion, what was Ananias doing praying for Paul to be baptized with the Spirit three days after his Conversion? As well, if, in fact, it all happens at Conversion, what in the world were Peter and John doing going to Samaria some days after Philip had preached the great meeting there in order to pray for these Believers to be baptized with the Holy Spirit? No, the Scripture is clear that the Baptism with the Holy Spirit is an experience separate, distinct, and apart from Salvation. As well, one might quickly add the following:

NOT FOR SALVATION

As we have repeatedly stated, Salvation is an experience separate and apart from being baptized with the Spirit. In fact, one must be Saved before one can be filled with the Spirit (Jn. 14:17).

A person can be Saved in a church, in his home, on a street corner, or anywhere. It is not the place, it is the action. The person who believes in his heart and confesses with his mouth is Saved (Rom. 10:9-10). And once he is Saved, he can't be more Saved by speaking in Tongues. But yet, *"Tongues"* are extremely valuable in our Christian experience, which we will momentarily address.

IF ONE IS SAVED, WHY DOES HE NEED THE BAPTISM WITH THE SPIRIT?

Once again, we must go to the Word of God. Salvation is one thing; however, the Baptism with the Holy Spirit is quite another. Salvation gets us ready for Heaven, while the Baptism with the Holy Spirit gets us ready for this world and our work for God.

During our Lord's Ministry here on Earth, the Disciples had Him as a Personal Advisor, Comforter, Leader, and Manager, one might say. Today, we don't have Him on hand Personally to fill these essential roles. And this is why He said, before He left, that He would send another Comforter.

He knew His Personal Time on Earth would be short; that He would Personally oversee only the beginning of the great Salvation story still going on; and that those committed to sharing the responsibility for bringing the unsaved millions to Salvation would need direction beyond their human capabilities. Basically, this is the inestimable value of the infilling of the Holy Spirit.

As well, every Christian, active or passive, is going to be forced to confront the powers of darkness described by the Apostle Paul in Ephesians 6:12. Satan has his army of demons committed to interfering with and even destroying Christian lives.

The mighty power of the indwelling Holy Spirit, Who functions exclusively within the parameters of the Finished Work of Christ, which demands that our Faith at all times be in Christ and the Cross, is the only thing which can augment our feeble powers to the point where we can live the lives we should live, overthrowing the powers of darkness, and, thereby, become the type of Christians

NOTES

we ought to be.

As well, the Holy Spirit ever draws us nearer to Christ and, in truth, glorifies Christ within us (Jn. 16:14).

CONCERNING THE HOLY SPIRIT, JESUS SAID . . .

"Howbeit when He, the Spirit of Truth, is come (*which He did on the Day of Pentecost*)**, He will guide you into all Truth** (*if our Faith is properly placed in Christ and the Cross, the Holy Spirit can then bring forth Truth to us; He doesn't guide into some truth, but rather 'all Truth'*)**: for He shall not speak of Himself** (*tells us not only What He does, but Whom He represents*)**; but whatsoever He shall hear,** *that* **shall He speak** (*doesn't refer to lack of knowledge, for the Holy Spirit is God, but rather He will proclaim the Work of Christ only*)**: and He will show you things to come** (*pertains to the New Covenant, which would shortly be given*)**."**

TO GLORIFY CHRIST

"He shall glorify Me (*will portray Christ and what Christ did at the Cross for dying humanity*)**: for He will receive of Mine** (*the benefits of the Cross*)**, and shall show** *it* **unto you** (*which He did, when He gave these great Truths to the Apostle Paul [Rom., Chpts. 6-8, etc.]*)**.**

"All things that the Father has are Mine (*has always been the case; however, due to the Cross, all these things can now be given to the Believer as well*)**: therefore said I, that He shall take of Mine, and shall show** *it* **unto you** (*the foundation of all the Holy Spirit reveals to the Church is what Christ did at the Cross [Rom. 6:3-14; 8:1-2, 11; I Cor. 1:17-18, 21, 23; 2:2; Gal., Chpt. 5, etc.]*)**" (Jn. 16:13-15).**

HOW THE HOLY SPIRIT WORKS

Understanding the Baptism with the Holy Spirit, it is absolutely imperative that the Believer also understand and realize how the Holy Spirit Works within our hearts and lives, carrying out the revealed Will of God. Unfortunately, most Christians take the Holy Spirit for granted. Regarding the denominational world, the Holy Spirit is

mentioned once in awhile, but that's about it. As it regards Pentecostals and Charismatics, most knowledge in those circles begins and ends with speaking in Tongues and the Gifts of the Spirit. But we must realize, almost all of Paul's teaching, and it was to him that this information was given, centers up on how the Holy Spirit Works within our lives on a daily basis.

It is the Cross of Christ that has given the Holy Spirit the latitude and liberty to Work within our hearts and lives. In fact, before the Cross, the Holy Spirit could only come into a few hearts and lives, such as the Prophets, etc., to enable them to carry out the mission assigned for them, but that was the extent of His Working with them. Although great and mighty Miracles were done, still, there's almost nothing in the Old Testament that refers to the Holy Spirit involving Himself in Believers at that time, regarding the Sanctification process, in other words, how we live for God on a daily basis.

Why?

It was because the blood of bulls and goats could not take away sins (Heb. 10:4). This means that the sin debt remained even in the godliest. Consequently, whenever Believers in Old Testament times passed away, they did not go to Heaven, but rather down into Paradise, and were actually held captive by Satan. While he could not hurt them, still, due to the sin debt remaining, and due to the fact that sin is what gives Satan his legal right to hold men captive, they were still captives of the Evil One despite their trust in the Lord. In fact, they were incarcerated in this place called Paradise to await the coming Crucifixion of our Lord when all sin would be totally and completely atoned.

When the price was paid at Calvary, Jesus went down into this place, during the three days and nights of His Death, and liberated all of these particular souls. The Scripture says concerning this, **"Wherefore He said** (*Ps. 68:18*)**, when He ascended up on high** (*the Ascension*)**, He led captivity captive" (Eph. 4:8).**

The Scripture then said, "*. . . what is it but that He also descended first into the lower parts of the earth?*" (Eph. 4:9).

Now, when a Believer dies, and we speak

of the entire time frame from the Cross unto the present, and which will extend through the Great Tribulation, instantly such person goes to be with the Lord Jesus Christ (Phil. 1:23). All of this was made possible exclusively by the Cross of Christ.

Due to the fact of the sin debt being lifted because of the Cross, the Holy Spirit can now come into the heart and life of the Believer, which He does at Conversion, and can work mightily in the heart and life of such a person, providing that individual places his or her Faith exclusively in Christ and the Cross.

THE OBJECT OF ONE'S FAITH

In the last 50 years, I suppose, more books have been written on Faith than all the other time of the Church put together. But almost all of these books pertain to faith as Faith and not in what the Object of Faith ought to be. The truth is, every human being in this world has faith. But the facts are, as it regards the unredeemed, their faith is in things other than the Lord. It's in themselves, their money, politicians, other individuals, etc. As it regards Believers, regrettably and sadly, most Believers have Christ, but not the Cross, as the Object of their Faith. And, such a faith is faith that God will not recognize.

If one wants the help of the Holy Spirit on a continuing basis, which helps us to overcome sin in every capacity, which is the greatest task of the Spirit, the Cross of Christ must be the Object of one's Faith, and the Cross of Christ alone! That being done, the Holy Spirit will grandly help us!

Unfortunately, while most Christians, and we speak of those who are truly Born-Again, understand the Cross after a fashion as it regards Salvation, they do not understand the Cross of Christ at all as it regards Sanctification, in other words, how we live for God on a daily basis. As we've already stated in this Volume, almost all of Paul's instructions concern how we live for God with very little information given as to how to be Saved. And, of course, we certainly should know the reason.

Unsaved people don't read the Bible. Consequently, the Word of God, while it does

definitely give us instructions regarding the Salvation of the soul, still, almost altogether is given over to telling us how to live for God.

That's why Paul said to the church at Corinth, **"And I, brethren, when I came to you, came not with excellency of speech or of wisdom** (means that he depended not on oratorical abilities, nor did he delve into philosophy, which was all the rage of that particular day), **declaring unto you the Testimony of God** (which is Christ and Him Crucified).

"For I determined not to know anything among you (with purpose and design, Paul did not resort to the knowledge or philosophy of the world regarding the preaching of the Gospel), **save Jesus Christ, and Him Crucified** (that and that alone is the Message, which will save the sinner, set the captive free, and give the Believer perpetual victory)**" (I Cor. 2:1-2).**

Once again, we must ever understand that the Holy Spirit Works exclusively within the parameters of the Finished Work of Christ. This gives Him the legal means to do all that He does, which demands that our Faith be exclusively in Christ and the Cross. That's the way the Holy Spirit Works.

THE SCRIPTURAL EVIDENCE FOR TONGUES

Acts 2:4 says, *"And they were all filled with the Holy Spirit, and began to speak with other Tongues, as the Spirit gave them utterance."*

This is very clear and uncomplicated. It says plainly, *"And they . . . began to speak with other Tongues."*

Acts, Chapter 8, records the incident of the Samaritans being baptized with the Holy Spirit (Acts 8:14-17).

It doesn't plainly say they spoke with Tongues when they were filled, but it does tell us that *"when Simon the Sorcerer saw that through laying on of the Apostles' hands the Holy Spirit was given,* (that) *he offered them money, saying, Give me also this power, that on whomsoever I lay hands, he may receive the Holy Spirit."*

Peter's answer was instant. He said, *"Your money perish with you, because you have thought that the Gift of God may be purchased with money. You have neither part nor lot in this matter"* (Acts 8:18-21).

In the Greek, the word *"matter"* as here translated in the King James, is *"Logos,"* and means *"a word or speech."* So, it should have been translated, *"You have neither part nor lot in this utterance."* Peter is referring to these Believers speaking with other Tongues.

Acts, Chapter 9, records Paul being Saved and baptized with the Holy Spirit, with the latter taking place some three days after his Conversion.

It gives us no information whatsoever as to what happened, simply that Ananias said, *"Brother Saul, the Lord, even Jesus, Who appeared unto you in the way as you came, has sent me, that you might receive your sight, and be filled with the Holy Spirit"* (Acts 9:17).

That's all the information we are given, which tells us nothing at all about what happened.

But yet, later, Paul said in his Epistle to the Corinthians (I Cor. 14:18), *"I thank my God, I speak with Tongues more than you all."* Some have tried to make this into Paul's linguistic ability to speak several languages. It is true that Paul could speak both Hebrew and Greek; however, the entirety of this Fourteenth Chapter of I Corinthians has to do with *"Tongues"* and *"Prophecy."* No, Paul is talking about speaking with other Tongues and makes the claim that he utilized this Gift constantly. Obviously, he spoke in Tongues as a result of his Baptism with the Spirit, or he wouldn't have mentioned it here.

Acts, Chapter 10, proclaims the Salvation of Cornelius and his household as well as their Baptism with the Spirit. The Scripture says:

"And they of the Circumcision which believed were astonished, as many as came with Peter, because that on the Gentiles also was poured out the Gift of the Holy Spirit.

"For they heard them speak with Tongues, and magnify God" (Acts 10:45-46).

We have already mentioned the incident of Paul laying hands on the twelve at Ephesus and their being baptized with the

Holy Spirit. Plainly, the Scripture says, *"And when Paul had laid his hands upon them, the Holy Spirit came on them; and they spoke with Tongues, and prophesied"* (Acts 19:6).

There are five incidents of Believers being baptized with the Holy Spirit during the time of the Early Church, with the last account, the Disciples at Ephesus, being about 25 years after the Day of Pentecost. In three of those accounts, it plainly says they spoke with Tongues. In the other two, it strongly implies such.

CONTROVERSY!

Why is it that there is such controversy about this phenomenal experience given by the Lord? About half of the Protestant world accepts the Biblical account of the Baptism with the Holy Spirit and speaking with other Tongues, with the other half registering unbelief. In fact, nearly 800 years before Christ, the great Prophet Isaiah prophesied that this would happen. He said:

"For with stammering lips and another tongue will He speak to this people.

"To whom He said, This is the rest wherewith you may cause the weary to rest; and this is the refreshing: yet they would not hear" (Isa. 28:11-12).

Why?

The problem is unbelief! In fact, Paul, in his teaching given in the Fourteenth Chapter of I Corinthians, quoted the statement as given by Isaiah (I Cor. 14:21).

At the turn of the Twentieth Century, the great latter rain outpouring began, which has seen over a half billion people since that time baptized with the Holy Spirit with the evidence of speaking with other Tongues. At the beginning, it was referred to as a mere *"fad,"* which would quickly pass. It was, as well, passed off as being accepted only by the uneducated, etc. Nevertheless, despite the opposition of much of the church world, the Lord Moved mightily, not only Saving untold numbers of people but, as well, baptizing untold thousands with the mighty Baptism with the Holy Spirit. Today, it can hardly be looked at as a mere fad, when about half of the Protestant Church population believes, as stated, the Biblical account of the Baptism with the Spirit with the evidence of speaking with other Tongues. As it regards world missions, and I speak of taking the Gospel to the world, almost all that has been accomplished in this realm has been by individuals baptized with the Holy Spirit with the evidence of speaking with other Tongues. I maintain, while there may be much religious machinery operating among those who disavow the Baptism with the Holy Spirit, the truth is, in those circles, almost nothing is truly done for the Lord.

I'll admit that we who claim the mighty Baptism with the Holy Spirit with the evidence of speaking with other Tongues are poor examples. But still, with these poor examples, our Lord has touched this world with the Gospel. I know that of which I speak because this Ministry (Jimmy Swaggart Ministries) has been very much involved in world Evangelism.

As to the *"why"* of rejection, the things of God have never been popular with the world and neither are they popular with religion. We have defined religion as that, which is devised solely by man as a way to reach God or to better oneself in some way. As is obvious, the Lord is not in it.

People like to associate themselves with that which is popular. To be sure, the Baptism with the Holy Spirit with the evidence of speaking with other Tongues is not popular. In fact, nothing truly of God is popular, but the more of the Lord it is, the less popular it is.

Sad to say, it is my belief that most people in denominational churches simply have never been Born-Again. Some few have, most haven't! Sadder still, it's getting to be that way in many Pentecostal churches, etc. This happens when the ways of man are inserted in place of the Ways of God.

As a Believer, I have no personal preference as to what the Bible teaches. I just want to know what it teaches and then accept it and receive it for my own benefit and then to do my best to give it to others. That's the reason that I encourage our people at Family Worship Center, and all those who listen to us over the SONLIFE BROADCASTING NETWORK, be it radio or television, to check out what we teach and

NOTES

preach according to the Word of God. To be sure, all of us are going to be judged by the Word and nothing else!

WHAT ARE TONGUES?

"Tongues" are not incoherent babble, chatter, or gibberish. Tongues, as it regards the Baptism with the Holy Spirit, are a language known somewhere in the world but not by the speaker. The Bible plainly tells us this. Concerning this very thing, the Scripture says:

"And there were dwelling at Jerusalem Jews, devout men, out of every nation under Heaven (*Jews were then scattered all over the Roman World, with thousands coming in from every nation to keep the Feast*)**.**

"Now when this was noised abroad (*multitudes who were in the Temple heard and saw the proceedings and, as well, began to tell others*)**, the multitude came together** (*what was happening attracted a multitude*)**, and was confounded, because that every man heard them speak in his own language** (*means that these onlooking Jews heard these people speaking in many different languages, in fact, languages of the nations of their residence, wherever that might have been, proving that this was not gibberish or babble as some claim*)**."**

AMAZED

"And they were all amazed and marveled (*mostly centered upon this speaking with other Tongues*)**, saying one to another, Behold, are not all these which speak Galilaeans?** (*This means that the Galilaean accent was peculiar and well-known [Mk. 14:70; Lk. 22:59].*)

"And how hear we every man in our own tongue, wherein we were born? (*This proves once again that this was not babble, mere chatter, or gibberish, but rather a language known somewhere in the world but not by the speaker.*)**"**

MANY DIFFERENT NATIONALITIES

"Parthians, and Medes, and Elamites, and the dwellers in Mesopotamia, and in Judaea, and Cappadocia, in Pontus, and Asia,

"Phrygia, and Pamphylia, in Egypt, and in the parts of Libya about Cyrene, and

strangers of Rome, Jews and proselytes,

"Cretes and Arabians, we do hear them speak in our tongues the wonderful Works of God (this tells us what speaking in Tongues actually is, a recitation of the 'Wonderful Works of God').

"And they were all amazed, and were in doubt (should have been translated, 'and were perplexed;' they had no rational answer to their perplexity), saying one to another, What does this mean? (This was asking more in wonder than demanding an answer.)

"Others mocking said (they scoffed; whether by gesture or word, they jeered at the Testimony of this given by the Holy Spirit), These men are full of new wine (was actually an accusation that they were drunk, i.e., 'intoxicated'; some were amazed and some 'mocked,' which continues to be done even unto this hour).

PETER

"But Peter, standing up with the Eleven, lifted up his voice, and said unto them (Peter will now preach the inaugural Message of the Church on that Day of Pentecost), You men of Judaea, and all you who dwell at Jerusalem, be this known unto you, and hearken to my words (the Message was probably delivered on Solomon's Porch, a part of the Court of the Gentiles; it was where debates and such like were commonly conducted):

"For these are not drunken, as you suppose (in effect, says they are drunk but not in the common manner), seeing it is but the third hour of the day (9 a.m.).

"But this is that which was spoken by the Prophet Joel (please notice that Peter did not say, 'This fulfills that spoken by the Prophet Joel,' but rather, 'This is that . . .' meaning that it will continue)."

I WILL POUR OUT OF MY SPIRIT UPON ALL FLESH

"And it shall come to pass in the last days, say God (proclaims these 'last days' as beginning on the Day of Pentecost and continuing through the coming Great Tribulation), I will pour out of My Spirit upon all flesh (speaks of all people everywhere and,

therefore, not limited to some particular geographical location; as well, it is not limited respecting race, color, or creed): and your sons and your daughters shall prophesy (includes both genders), and your young men shall see Visions, and your old men shall dream Dreams (all given by the Holy Spirit; the Hebrew language insinuates, 'both your young men and old men shall see Visions, and both your old men and young men shall dream Dreams'; it applies to both genders as well):

"And on My Servants and on My Handmaidens I will pour out in those days of My Spirit (is meant purposely to address two classes of people who had been given very little status in the past, slaves and women); and they shall prophesy (pertains to one of the 'Gifts of the Spirit' [I Cor. 12:8-10])" (Acts 2:5-18).

As stated, Tongues are a language known somewhere in the world but not by the speaker and is amply proven by Scripture.

WHAT VALUE IS SPEAKING WITH OTHER TONGUES?

Many detractors have asked the question, as it regards worshipping the Lord with other Tongues, "What good is it?" or "What good does it do one?"

Well, in answer to that question, let's see what the Bible says about this matter.

• The Word of God tells us that the Baptism with the Holy Spirit with the evidence of speaking with other Tongues is from Heaven (Acts 2:2-4). I should think that anything that's from Heaven, meaning the abode of God, should be of tremendous worthwhile.

• It is the Holy Spirit Who gives the utterance respecting the individual speaking in Tongues (Acts 2:4). Once again, I think it should be obvious that whatever it is the Holy Spirit does is of tremendous worth.

• The Scripture tells us that when Tongues are spoken, as the Spirit of God Moves on a person, it is the "Wonderful Works of God" being related (Acts 2:11). That is of immense significance.

• Speaking with other Tongues is the fulfillment of Bible Prophecy (Acts 2:16-18; Isa. 28:11-12).

• Speaking with other Tongues magnifies God (Acts 10:46). Anything that does that is of great comport.

• Speaking in Tongues *"speaks not unto men, but unto God"* (I Cor. 14:2). I certainly should think that one could well see the worth in that.

• Speaking in Tongues edifies the Believer, which all of us constantly need (I Cor. 14:4).

• *"Tongues are for a sign, not to them who believe, but to them who believe not"* (I Cor. 14:22). What kind of sign?

Even though they do not understand it, it is a sign to the world, especially in this latter rain outpouring, that we are nearing the end of things as they now are.

• Tongues are God's Way *"wherewith you may cause the weary to rest"* (Isa. 28:12). We live in pressing times. Speaking with other Tongues provides a *"rest"* for a person's emotions, their spirit, and, as well, for their physical bodies.

• Speaking with other Tongues is not only a *"rest,"* but, as well, it is a *"refreshing"* (Isa. 28:12). While speaking with other Tongues brings about a *"rest"* from the tiredness of the journey of life, as well, speaking with other Tongues brings about a *"refreshing,"* which rejuvenates the person.

I can hardly see how anyone could read the Scriptural evidence we have given regarding the value of speaking with other Tongues and not understand its extensive worth. As someone has said, while those who oppose this may have an argument, those who embrace it have an experience. And, it is an experience sanctioned and proclaimed by the Word of God!

SOME ERRONEOUS CONTENTIONS

The worst thing a person can do is to read into the Sacred Text that which is not there or, conversely, to refuse to see what is plainly obvious. Unfortunately, as it regards the Baptism with the Holy Spirit with the evidence of speaking with other Tongues, this problem magnifies itself.

The following will deal with some of these examples.

DO ALL SPEAK WITH TONGUES?

Some have deduced from this question, as asked by the Apostle Paul, that while some may speak in Tongues, all do not, meaning that one can be baptized with the Spirit without Tongues, etc. Let's see what the Word of God says:

"Have all the Gifts of Healing? *(The answer is obviously, 'no.')* **do all speak with Tongues?** *(Paul is not addressing himself here to the initial Baptism with the Spirit, which is always and without exception accompanied by speaking with other Tongues, but rather is addressing the Gift of Tongues, which is one of the nine Gifts of the Spirit, which all do not have, although baptized with the Spirit.)* **do all Interpret?** *(Again, the answer is 'no,' but some do!)*" **(I Cor. 12:30).**

Paul is speaking here of the *"Gifts of the Spirit"* (I Cor. 12:8-10). As stated, he is not addressing speaking with other Tongues as the initial physical evidence that one has been baptized with the Holy Spirit, but only as it regards various Gifts.

He says, *"And God has set some in the Church, first Apostles, secondarily Prophets,"* etc. If it is noticed, he said *"some,"* meaning that all aren't Apostles, and all aren't Prophets, etc.

As well, he goes on to say that some are called to be teachers, and some are called to be workers of Miracles, while others are called to pray for healing. In the body of all of this, he asked the question, *"Do all speak with Tongues?"* meaning when Tongues are used in a public service and intended to be interpreted. It has absolutely nothing to do with the initial, physical evidence of being baptized with the Spirit, and neither is it speaking of one's prayer language as we worship the Lord everyday (at least, I do) by speaking with other Tongues.

So, to try to use this question as asked by Paul as a claim that while some may speak in Tongues, all don't, holds no Scriptural validity.

WHETHER THERE BE TONGUES, THEY SHALL CEASE

Others are fond of using I Corinthians 13:8-10, *"Whether there be Tongues, they shall cease,"* as an example of proving their contention that Tongues are not for today. However, this is another example of taking a few words out of context and building a doctrine on them, in other words, not *"rightly dividing the Word of Truth"* (II Tim. 2:15).

In order to put this statement in proper perspective, one must read all of I Corinthians 13:8-10 to get the full meaning of what Paul was saying. He was not saying, as some claim, Tongues would cease when the last Apostle died. This is what he did say:

"Charity never fails: whether there be Prophecies, they shall fail; whether there be Tongues, they shall cease; whether there be Knowledge, it shall vanish away."

Paul went on to say, *"For we know in part, and we prophesy in part. But when that which is Perfect is come, then that which is in part shall be done away"* (I Cor. 13:8-10).

Paul is comparing Spiritual Gifts with love, i.e., *"charity."* Where *"love"* never fails (Agape Love), Prophecies, at times, fail because they were not truly given by the Holy Spirit. As well, *"Tongues cease,"* because of unbelief. Also, our *"knowledge,"* Scriptural or otherwise, at times, *"vanishes away,"* i.e., imperfect light on the subject.

Consequently, he said that we only have part knowledge, and, as well, at times, Prophecies come from the flesh and are not valid.

In all of this, Paul is not criticizing *"Prophecy, Tongues, or Knowledge,"* but, he is stating that even the most mature of us, in this state, are imperfect.

He then went on to say, *"But when that which is Perfect is come, then that which is in part shall be done away"* (I Cor. 13:10).

The word, *"Perfect,"* in this case, speaks of Christ. In other words, upon the First Resurrection of Life, when corruption will put on incorruption, and mortality will put on immortality, then every Believer will put on the Glorified Body and will come back with Christ at the Second Coming to rule and reign on this Earth, which will then be done in perfection.

As well, the word, *"Perfect,"* does not refer to the Bible, as some claim, stating that when the Canon of Scripture was completed in about 100 A.D., then all Gifts of the Spirit ceased, etc.

Full well knowing the frailties of the human family and the imperfection of all

Christians, through whom the Gifts of the Spirit must work, the Holy Spirit through Paul is cautioning the Corinthian Believers, as well as all of us, that we should understand the Gifts in that context. We must always remember that even though, at times, we may fail (because of our imperfection and not their imperfection), still, *"love never fails."* Consequently, love must be the foundation on which all things work in the Body of Christ. Therefore, he would say, *"Though I speak with the tongues of men and of Angels, and have not charity* (love), *I am become as sounding brass, or a tinkling cymbal"* (I Cor. 13:1).

Again I state, the Apostle is not repudiating Tongues, Prophecy, Knowledge, etc., but instead, placing *"love"* as the foundation principle of all Christian experience and endeavor.

I HAD RATHER SPEAK FIVE WORDS WITH MY UNDERSTANDING . . . THAN TEN THOUSAND WORDS IN AN UNKNOWN TONGUE

This is a favorite Scripture for those who are antagonistic to the concept of speaking in Tongues and is taken from I Corinthians 14:19.

However, once again, the choosing of a few words out of context, and assigning meaning not apparent when viewing the entirety of the Text, can only lead to an erroneous conclusion. A careful reading of the whole Scripture (the Fourteenth Chapter of I Corinthians—not just 14:19), puts an entirely different impression on what Paul is saying.

Obviously, the church at Corinth had become unbalanced in their worship Services, concentrating unduly on the matter of speaking in Tongues during the Service. Paul spends the whole Fourteenth Chapter teaching the proper place of Tongues, etc., in a Church Service.

Obviously, if someone were opposed to speaking in Tongues, he would hardly devote the amount of teaching encompassed in the Fourteenth Chapter to its proper utilization. If he had been opposed to Tongues, all he had to do was say, *"Do not speak in Tongues."*

But does he say this? Hardly! He says, *"I*

would that you all spoke with Tongues." As well, *"I thank my God, I speak with Tongues more than you all."*

Finally, in discussing the Fourteenth Chapter of I Corinthians, one would have to ask those opposed to Tongues why they stress the Nineteenth Verse but completely ignore the Thirty-ninth. It would seem that the seeker of truth would want to receive the truth concerning the Word of God in relation to any subject under question. And what does the Word of God say in the Thirty-ninth Verse?

It says, *"Forbid not to speak in Tongues."*

YET SHOW I UNTO YOU A MORE EXCELLENT WAY

The heading containing the Text is found in I Corinthians 12:31, and some contend that this statement by Paul indicates a Scriptural position where love is an alternative to speaking in Tongues. They say Paul was suggesting that *"a more excellent way"* would preclude the need to speak in Tongues.

No, and as we have already stated, Paul was not saying that, but instead, that everything must be put in its proper perspective, with love as the ultimate foundation and the expression of everything Jesus taught.

He is plainly saying that everything that is done for the Lord, no matter how spectacular or charismatic, still, love must be the undergirding foundation of all we do. In other words, if we had all the Gifts of the Spirit and did not have love, we still would not have anything.

Actually, in I Corinthians 12:28, he ranks the Gifts according to their importance. This is what he said:

"And God has set some in the Church, first Apostles, secondarily Prophets, thirdly Teachers, after that Miracles, then Gifts of Healings, Helps, Governments, Diversities of Tongues."

He then goes on to ask, *"Are all Apostles? are all Prophets?"* etc., which obviously they are not!

In Verse 31, he says, *"But covet earnestly the best Gifts: and yet show I unto you a more excellent way."*

He then proceeds to give the great dissertation on love, which supersedes all, but

does not exclude any (I Cor., Chpt. 13).

THE LEAST OF ALL THE GIFTS?

Some say, since Paul placed Tongues last in his index of Gifts (I Cor. 12:28), it might well be eliminated from the Gifts to be sought after and utilized.

What a hornet's nest of satanic confusion would be opened if we were to accept this proposal.

Do we start with the Ten Commandments and eliminate the Tenth because it is listed last? Then, with the Tenth removed, do we strike out the Ninth, etc.?

Obviously, any list has to contain something first and something last. It should not imply, however, that items on the list become optional to a greater or lesser degree depending on their position. Nothing from God is insignificant. No statement from God is to be considered *"optional"* by man.

The Lord through Paul did list the correct order of Offices and Gifts to the Church, in I Corinthians 12:28 through 30, beginning with *"Apostles,"* which He placed *"first."* However, that in no way meant that *"Prophets"* or *"Teachers"* were not needed. Such thinking would be silly, to say the least!

God set up a complete roster of Spiritual Gifts. He intended all the Gifts to be operational in anybody. Without all the Gifts, a body (the Church) becomes less effective than it would be with all Gifts.

Any man who decides to take over God's Authority and starts picking and choosing from among those God-given Gifts is assuming an authority that is not Scriptural. The mere fact that placement on a list might be above or below something else is small authority to remove anything instituted by God.

I think the argument that *"Tongues"* is the least of all Gifts is a dangerous argument, and one belittling God's Ability to decide if something is of value to man and the Church is very dangerous. In reality, whatever Gift is needed at the moment, at least, at that particular time, is the most important.

FOR US TODAY?

The question, ultimately, is this, *"Is the mighty Baptism with the Holy Spirit with the evidence of speaking with other Tongues for every Believer today?"*

Unequivocally and, above all, Scripturally, I know it is.

And more than that, I believe it is a *"must"* for every Christian. It isn't something to be placed on the *"optional"* shelf where the Christian shopper can browse and debate whether or not it would be *"desirable."* Please remember, in the last address given to His Disciples, our Lord *"Commanded them"* to first be filled with the Spirit before work for Him would commence (Acts 1:4-5). And to be sure, that *"Command,"* which, incidentally, is not a suggestion, is just as binding on us presently as it was then. Make no mistake about it, the Holy Spirit Himself set the pattern for the Church as given to us in the Book of Acts and the Epistles. It was a Church where people were Saved by trusting Christ and what He did for us at the Cross and, as well, were baptized with the Holy Spirit with the evidence of speaking with other Tongues, with Healings and Miracles and the great Works of God manifested in their midst. The Holy Spirit, I firmly believe, desires and even demands no less of us today!

Without the Baptism with the Holy Spirit, the Christian will never be what he could be within God's Plan for his life. John the Baptist said, *"He shall baptize you with the Holy Spirit and with fire!"* (Lk. 3:16). Anyone who has seen a lukewarm Christian transformed by the Power of the Holy Spirit knows what John was talking about.

In effect, the Holy Spirit Baptism is the most important tool a Christian can ever have. That's the reason that Jesus commanded that it be received by Believers.

As we close this Chapter on Verse 29, which, to say the least, has been quite lengthy, what better way to close than by quoting this Verse once again, as Peter also quoted it:

"And on My Servants and on My Handmaidens I will pour out in those days of My Spirit" (Acts 2:18).

One can believe that God did not mean what He said, or else one can believe He meant exactly what He said.

Unequivocally, and without a doubt, I believe He meant exactly what He said!

(30) "AND I WILL SHOW WONDERS

IN THE HEAVENS AND IN THE EARTH, BLOOD, AND FIRE, AND PILLARS OF SMOKE.

(31) "THE SUN SHALL BE TURNED INTO DARKNESS, AND THE MOON INTO BLOOD, BEFORE THE GREAT AND TERRIBLE DAY OF THE LORD COME.

(32) "AND IT SHALL COME TO PASS, THAT WHOSOEVER SHALL CALL ON THE NAME OF THE LORD SHALL BE DELIVERED: FOR IN MOUNT ZION AND IN JERUSALEM SHALL BE DELIVERANCE, AS THE LORD HAS SAID, AND IN THE REMNANT WHOM THE LORD SHALL CALL."

The exegesis is:

1. Verse 30 pertains to the Great Tribulation, which will immediately precede the Second Coming.

2. The prediction of Verse 31 is fulfilled in Revelation 6:12 under the *"sixth seal."*

3. (Vs. 32) The entirety of these Passages proclaim three great outpourings of the Holy Spirit. They are:

• On the Day of Pentecost, which continues unto this hour (Acts 2:1-28, 31).

• During the future Great Tribulation (Acts 2:16-21).

• During the Millennium (Isa. 32:15; 44:3; Ezek. 36:26-27; 39:29; Zech. 12:10).

THE GREAT TRIBULATION

Verses 30 and 31 pertain to the coming time, in fact, which is just ahead, which Jesus referred to as the worst time the world has ever known before and will never know again (Mat. 24:21).

This coming time, which will last for seven years, will usher in some astounding things. And one should know, when our Lord says it will be worse than any time the world has ever known, one can be certain that it will be such as the world has never seen before. Some of the things that will happen during that time are as follows:

• As stated, it will be seven years of Great Tribulation such as the world has never known before. It will not merely be *"tribulation,"* as bad as that would be, but rather, and in the words of our Lord, *"Great Tribulation."*

• This seven-year period, called the

NOTES

"Great Tribulation," will experience the Wrath of God poured out on this Earth as never before. This *"wrath"* will be because of the great evil perpetrated by the man of sin, i.e., the Antichrist. In other words, the world will know evil at that time as never before (Rev. 6:17).

• Israel at that time will accept the Antichrist as their Messiah, who, of course, is a false Messiah, but who will solve the Muslim problem regarding the borders of Israel, at least for a period of time (Jn. 5:43).

• It is possible that during this seven-year period, half of the population of Planet Earth will die (Rev. 14:15-20).

• At the very outset of the Great Tribulation, the Antichrist will make his debut. He will set out to take over the entirety of the world and, in fact, would succeed but for the Second Coming of the Lord Jesus Christ (Rev. 6:1-2).

• Ironically enough, the Great Tribulation Period will begin with what looks like peace but will quickly graduate to war, with the Antichrist setting out to conquer the world (Rev. 6:3-4).

• This seven-year period will see climate changes and happenings with planetary bodies, which will affect the Earth as never before (Rev. 6:12-16).

• Some three and a half years into the Great Tribulation, the Antichrist will show his true colors, attacking Israel, and would destroy her at that time were it not for pressing business elsewhere (Dan. 11:44).

• Despite the terrible activity of the powers of darkness, still, there will be millions who will come to Christ during the seven years of Great Tribulation, and yet, most, the overwhelming majority, will not repent (Rev. 7:9-15; 9:21).

• During the Great Tribulation, there will be three types of Judgments rendered by God. They will be referred to as the *"Seal Judgments,"* the *"Trumpet Judgments,"* and the *"Vial Judgments."* They will each be seven in duration. Also, there will be three *"Woes."* These three Woes will be interspersed among the other Judgments.

• The Great Tribulation will conclude with the Battle of Armageddon, which, no doubt, will be the most horrific conflict ever fought (Rev. 16:16).

• The Battle of Armageddon will conclude with the most cataclysmic event the world has ever known, the Second Coming of the Lord Jesus Christ (Rev., Chpt. 19).

THE SALVATION OF THE LORD

The phrase, *"For in Mount Zion and in Jerusalem shall be deliverance,"* speaks of the Jews being Saved as a Nation during this time, which will immediately follow the Second Coming (Isa. 66:7-8; Zech. 12:10-13:1; Rom. 11:25-29).

The phrase, *"And in the Remnant whom the LORD shall call,"* refers to the Jews left alive after the Battle of Armageddon, in which the Prophet Zechariah said that two-thirds will be killed (Zech. 13:8).

As well, and as we have previously stated, many Gentiles will be killed during the seven-year Great Tribulation, whether in war or by the Judgments of God. It is possible that fifty percent or more, as it regards the population of the Planet, will suffer annihilation at that time!

Going back to Verse 1 of this Chapter, the Trumpet announcing the Wrath of God is the same Trumpet that announces the Grace of God in Verse 15. The Gospel tells of the Lake of Fire and of the Redeeming Blood. A Gospel that omits either of these is a false Gospel.

Linking together the *"sound from Heaven"* of Acts 2:2 with this Second Chapter of Joel, one finds the Work of the Holy Spirit outlined. It is, at least in part, as follows:

• The *"Sound of Pentecost"* is the *"sound of alarm"* (2:1). As previously stated, every time an individual is baptized with the Holy Spirit with the evidence of speaking with other Tongues, it is the *"sound of alarm"* to a world that has forgotten God days without number. In other words, time is almost up, for this is the *"latter rain"* outpouring, which will immediately precede the Great Tribulation soon to come upon this world.

• The *"Sound of Pentecost"* is the sound of fasting and prayer (2:15).

• The *"Sound of Pentecost"* is also the sound of gladness and rejoicing, for the Lord will do great things (2:21).

- The *"Sound of Pentecost"* is the sound of the outpouring of the Holy Spirit all over the world, *"all flesh"* (2:28-29).
- The *"Sound of Pentecost"* is the sound of Signs and Wonders in the heavens and in the Earth (2:30).
- The *"Sound of Pentecost"* is the sound of the Coming of the Lord (2:32).

"In the crimson of the morning,
"In the whiteness of the noon!
"In the amber glory of the day's retreat.
"In the midnight robed in darkness,
"Or the gleaming of the moon,
"I listen for the coming of His Feet."

"I have heard His weary Footsteps,
"On the sands of Galilee,
"On the Temple's marble pavement,
"On the streets filled with suffering,
"Faltering up the slopes of Calvary,
"I hear the sound of the coming of His Feet."

"Down the minster aisles of splendor,
"From between the Cherubim,
"Mid the wandering throng with motion strong and fleet,
"Sounds His Victor's Tread approaching,
"With the singing far and dim,
"Sounds the music of the coming of His Feet."

"He is coming says the Spirit,
"With His Everlasting Peace,
"With His Righteousness immortal and complete.
"He is coming says the Spirit,
"And His Coming brings release,
"I listen for the coming of His Feet."

—◼—

CHAPTER 3

(1) "FOR BEHOLD, IN THOSE DAYS, AND IN THAT TIME, WHEN I SHALL BRING AGAIN THE CAPTIVITY OF JUDAH AND JERUSALEM."

The synopsis is:

1. This Chapter follows the preceding one without a break.

2. The Spirit describes:

- The future Deliverance of Israel.
- The Judgment of the nations that oppressed her.
- The ascension of Immanuel upon the Throne of Jehovah at Jerusalem.
- His Vindication of His ancient People.
- The destruction of the army of the Antichrist.
- The moral glory of Jerusalem.
- The appointment of Jerusalem as a center of blessing to the Earth.
- The future amazing fertility of the land of Israel.

3. The phrase, *"When I shall bring again the captivity of Judah and Jerusalem,"* is a Hebrew idiom for Restoration.

IN THOSE DAYS AND IN THAT TIME

The phrase, *"For behold, in those days, and in that time,"* concerns cataclysmic happenings, which will take place in the very near future. The study of eschatology pertains to futuristic events according to the Word of God. In fact, the Bible is the only Book in the world that deals with futuristic events. About one third of the Bible is Prophecy, with nearly half already fulfilled, about one third is teaching, and about one third is history. Futuristic events, which the Bible teaches are coming upon this world in the very near future, are as follows:

- The Rapture (Resurrection) of the Church (I Thess. 4:13-18).
- The Advent of the Antichrist (Dan. 8:23-25).
- The Great Tribulation, which will last for seven years (Dan. 9:27; Rev., Chpts. 6-18).
- The Battle of Armageddon (Zech. 14:1-3; Rev. 16:16).
- The Second Coming of the Lord (Zech. 14:4; Rev. 19:11-21).
- The Kingdom Age, which will last for 1,000 years, with the Lord Jesus Christ reigning Personally from Jerusalem as King of the entirety of the world (Rev. 20:4-6; Isa. 2:1-4; 11:1-9; 35:1-10).
- The Perfect Age to come, which will be eternity without end. Actually, the Lord will transfer His Headquarters, so to speak, from Heaven to Earth. As well, the entire topography of Planet Earth will be totally and completely changed (Rev., Chpts. 21-22).

HOW DO WE KNOW THESE PREDICTIONS WILL COME TO PASS?

We know simply because every prediction of the past, with some of those predictions being given many centuries before the fact, came to pass exactly as described. A perfect case in point is the Birth, Life, Death, and Resurrection of the Lord Jesus Christ. Those Prophecies are as follows:

• At the very dawn of time, in fact, immediately after the Fall, God predicted to Satan through the serpent the coming of the Redeemer. He said:

"And I will put enmity (animosity) **between you and the woman** (presents the Lord now actually speaking to Satan, who had used the serpent; in effect, the Lord is saying to Satan, 'You used the woman to bring down the human race, and I will use the woman as an instrument to bring the Redeemer into the world, Who will save the human race'), **and between your seed** (mankind which follows Satan) **and her Seed** (the Lord Jesus Christ); **it** (Christ) **shall bruise your head** (the Victory that Jesus won at the Cross [Col. 2:14-15]), **and you shall bruise His Heel** (the sufferings of the Cross)" **(Gen. 3:15).**

As is obvious, this Prophecy was fulfilled when some 4,000 years later the Lord Jesus Christ was born for the purpose of going to the Cross where He would redeem humanity.

• The prediction made by the Lord to Abraham as it regarded the *"Everlasting Covenant."* He said:

"And God said, Sarah your wife shall bear you a son indeed; and you shall call his name Isaac (the name Isaac means 'laughter'): **and I will establish My Covenant with him for an Everlasting Covenant, and with his seed after him.** (The Covenant is to be established with Isaac and not Ishmael. This completely shoots down the contention of the Muslims that Ishmael was the chosen one, unless you don't believe the Bible. Through Isaac the Lord Jesus Christ, the Saviour of mankind, would ultimately come)" **(Gen. 17:19).**

• Jacob, Abraham's grandson, predicted on his dying bed that the Messiah would

come from the Tribe of Judah. He said:

"The sceptre shall not depart from Judah (the 'Sceptre' is defined as 'a staff of office and authority,' which pertains to Christ), **nor a Lawgiver from between His Feet** (refers to the fact that Judah was meant to be a guardian of the Law, which they were; the Temple was in Jerusalem, which was a part of the Tribe of Judah, and which had to do with the Law), **until Shiloh come** (when Jesus came, typified by the name 'Shiloh,' Who, in fact, was, and is, the True Lawgiver, He fulfilled the Law in totality by His Life and His Death, thereby, satisfying all of its just demands); **and unto Him shall the gathering of the people be** (the only way to God the Father is through Christ the Son; the only way to Christ the Son is through the Cross; the only way to the Cross is through an abnegation of self [Lk. 9:23-24])" **(Gen. 49:10).**

As is obvious, Jesus came from the Tribe of Judah.

THE VIRGIN BIRTH

Isaiah prophesied nearly 800 years before Christ, saying, *"Therefore the Lord Himself shall give you a sign; Behold, a virgin shall conceive, and bear a Son, and shall call His Name Immanuel"* (Isa. 7:14).

Without a doubt, this Prophecy is one of the greatest, if not the greatest, in the Bible.

In Hebrew, the word *"virgin"* is *"haalmah,"* which means *"the virgin—the only one that ever was or ever will be a mother in this way."* The *"Son"* Who would be born would be the *"Son of God."* The word *"Immanuel"* means *"God with us."* Such was fulfilled in Christ.

This Prophecy was given by God as a rebuttal to the efforts of Satan working through the kings of Syria and Israel to unseat Ahaz. In other words, their efforts to make void the Promise of God given to David would come to naught.

As is obvious, Jesus was born of the Virgin Mary, fulfilling this Prophecy in totality.

BETH-LEHEM

The Prophet Micah prophesied about 700 years before Christ that Jesus would be born in Beth-lehem. He said:

"But you, Beth-lehem Ephratah, though you be little among the thousands of Judah, yet out of you shall He come forth unto Me Who is to be Ruler in Israel; Whose goings forth have been from of old, from everlasting" (Mic. 5:2).

"But you, Beth-lehem Ephratah," speaks of the birthplace of Christ. *"Though you be little among the thousands of Judah,"* signifies a small place, though the birthplace of David, as well! *"Yet out of you shall He come forth unto Me Who is to be Ruler in Israel,"* speaks of Christ coming from the Tribe of Judah. This was prophesied, as well, by Jacob long before (Gen. 49:10).

"Whose goings forth have been from of old, from everlasting," is meant to portray to any and all that this is not just any person, but rather, as Isaiah prophesied, *"Immanuel, God with us"* (Isa. 7:14).

THIRTY PIECES OF SILVER

Nearly 500 years before Christ, the Prophet Zechariah prophesied that Christ would be sold for thirty pieces of silver. He said:

"And I said unto them, If you think good, give Me My Price; and if not, forbear. So they weighed for My Price thirty pieces of silver" (Zech. 11:12).

The first phrase of Verse 12 refers to the Lord speaking, even though He uses the Prophet as His Instrument. The Lord is speaking in the Person of the Great Shepherd. He asked His Hire of the flock because the flock represents men.

"And if not, forbear," means, *"I leave it to you to decide."* The phrase, *"So they weighed for My Price thirty pieces of silver,"* proclaims what Israel thought of their Messiah and His Care through all the many centuries. They valued Him at thirty shekels, the price of an injured slave (Ex. 21:32).

It is amazing that the Pharisees, who claimed to be such sticklers for the Law, would read these words, especially, after the act had been performed, and still not relate it to themselves. Such is the marvel of unbelief!

THE ANOINTING OF JESUS

The Prophet Isaiah also prophesied as to the manner of the Ministry of our Lord. In

fact, Jesus quoted Isaiah in His Message at Nazareth. Isaiah said:

"The Spirit of the Lord GOD is upon Me; because the LORD has anointed Me to preach good tidings unto the meek; He has sent Me to bind up the brokenhearted, to proclaim liberty to the captives, and the opening of the prison to them who are bound" (Isa. 61:1).

The first nine Verses of Chapter 61 of Isaiah present the Messiah and His People. Actually, the Speaker in Verse 1 is the Messiah Himself as He proclaims His First and Second Comings. That the Speaker is the Messiah is proved by Jesus, as stated, quoting Isaiah (Lk. 4:16-21).

The *"Anointing"* of Jesus was the Sanctification of His Human Nature by the Holy Spirit, which commenced in the womb of the Blessed Virgin (Lk. 1:35), and continued as He grew to manhood (Lk. 2:40, 52). This was openly manifested at His Baptism and never ceased till He took His Glorified Body and Soul to Heaven.

That which the Father anointed Him to do addressed itself to every aspect of life and living. In truth, Christ Alone can address these problems, which means that humanistic psychology holds no answers.

TORTURE

The Prophet Isaiah also predicted that Jesus would be beaten, which took place immediately before His Crucifixion, and, as well, have the beard pulled from His Face. He said:

"I gave My Back to the smiters, and My Cheeks to them who plucked off the hair; I hid not My Face from shame and spitting" (Isa. 50:6).

This Verse addresses itself to the hours before the Crucifixion. Matthew 26:67 and 27:26 fulfill this Passage.

That our Lord, of such Power as is described in Verse 3, could contain Himself, when His Own People would treat Him thusly, is beyond comprehension! Their response to His Love was their hate. They whipped Him, pulled His Beard from His Face, and spit on Him.

Their doing it was no surprise. By His Omniscience, He knew before He came what the results would be. And yet, He came anyway!

THE CRUCIFIXION OF CHRIST

The Prophet Isaiah also predicted the Crucifixion of our Lord, even though the word *"crucify"* or *"Crucifixion"* is not used. Isaiah gave us this information in the Fifty-third Chapter of his Book.

All of these Prophecies concerning Christ, plus others we have not named, were fulfilled to the letter. And, of course, there were scores of Prophecies given concerning Israel, with many already fulfilled and many others yet to be fulfilled. So, whatever the Lord has said in His Word that He will do, one can feel assured that that is exactly as to what will happen. In other words, every single Prophecy given will be fulfilled to the letter. Concerning this very thing, Jesus Himself said:

"For verily I say unto you (*proclaims the ultimate authority!*)**, Till Heaven and Earth pass** (*means to be changed or pass from one condition to another, which will take place in the coming Perfect Age [Rev., Chpts. 21-22]*)**, one jot** (*smallest letter in the Hebrew alphabet*) **or one tittle** (*a minute ornamental finish to ancient Hebrew letters*) **shall in no wise pass from the Law, till all be fulfilled"** (Mat. 5:18).

WILL BRING AGAIN THE CAPTIVITY OF JUDAH AND JERUSALEM

As we previously stated, the phrase, *"When I shall bring again the captivity of Judah and Jerusalem,"* is a Hebrew idiom for restoring everything that has been lost.

The Lord is the Source of all Blessings, and I mean all Blessings! If mankind attempts to obey Him, God being Good, and Good beyond our comprehension, will bestow all manner of good things upon those who love Him and try to obey His Word. The truth is, none of us obey His Word as we should, which should be overly obvious. However, there is One Who came as our Substitute, and I speak of the Lord Jesus Christ, Who, in fact, kept the Law perfectly. He did it all on our behalf and, as well, satisfied the demands of the broken Law by giving Himself as a Perfect Sacrifice on Calvary's Cross. He

NOTES

shed His Life's Blood, giving Himself totally and, once again, did it all for us. So, our Faith in Him and what He did for us at the Cross guarantees us His Perfection. In other words, our Faith is that which the Lord requires. However, it must be understood that the Cross of Christ must be the Object of that Faith, or else, it is faith that God will not recognize. So, the way to have all the good things of God, all of His Blessings, all of His Largess, and all the mighty and wonderful things which He can do and, in fact, desires to do, is to render obedience to Him. We do this by placing our Faith where it should be placed, and maintaining our Faith where it should be maintained, which, again we state, is always the Cross of Christ (Rom. 6:1-14; 8:1-2, 11; I Cor. 1:17-18, 23; 2:2; Gal., Chpt. 5; 6:14; Eph. 2:13-18; Col. 2:14-15).

A NEW START

In effect, in the coming Kingdom Age, Israel will finally be what the Lord wants them to be and intended for them to be. But, of course, it will be after their Repentance, and we might quickly add, Repentance to the last man (Zech. 12:11-14). There should be, as well, a tremendous lesson in this for all of us, and I speak of the present time.

If the modern Believer doesn't have his faith exclusively in Christ and the Cross, while he can still be Saved, still be a Christian, etc., the truth is, he cannot live a victorious, overcoming, Christian life. And we speak of Victory over the world, the flesh, and the Devil. In fact, the *"more abundant life"* promised by our Lord, which, in effect, every true Believer has, can only be enjoyed when one places one's Faith exclusively in Christ and the Cross. Every Believer has more abundant life, but only a few are enjoying more abundant life.

I've been on both sides of this proverbial fence, and I know that of which I speak. The side of *"law"* is not that in which the Believer wants to engage himself, and yet, this is where most modern Believers are, and we speak of those who truly love the Lord. This means the Holy Spirit can little help them, at least, as much as He desires. While He will do all that He can, still, we greatly hinder Him when we misplace our faith.

Please understand, the Faith of the Child of God, as previously stated, and which we will keep stating, must, without exception, be in Christ and the Cross.

• Jesus Christ is the Source of all things we receive from God.

• The Cross of Christ is the Means by which we are given everything from the Lord.

• Understanding that, the Cross of Christ must ever be the Object of our Faith in order for us to receive all of these things, which the Lord desires to give us.

• The Holy Spirit superintends all of this. In fact, if we try to come to the Lord by any means other than Faith in Christ and the Cross, the Holy Spirit will bar the door, so to speak. Paul said:

"For through Him (through Christ) **we both** (Jews and Gentiles) **have access by One Spirit unto the Father.** (If the sinner comes by the Cross, the Holy Spirit opens the door, otherwise, it is barred)" **(Eph. 2:18).**

Jesus also said:

THE DOOR

"Verily, verily, I say unto you, He who enters not by the door into the sheepfold (proclaims to us that there is a 'door,' and, in fact, only one 'door!'), **but climbs up some other way, the same is a thief and a robber** (using a 'way' other than Christ; He Alone is the Door).

"But he who enters in by the Door (Way) **is the Shepherd of the sheep** (Jesus Alone is the True Shepherd)" **(Jn. 10:1-2).**

A BLOOD-SPLATTERED DOOR

To learn what that Door really is, and how that Door really is, we must go back to the deliverance of the Children of Israel from Egyptian bondage.

The Lord told Moses to tell every family in Israel that they were to take a lamb without blemish, one for each household, and keep it four days, inspecting it minutely. It must be a lamb, as stated, *"without blemish"* (Ex. 12:5). And then, if they found the lamb to be perfect, for it had to be this way simply because it was a Type of Christ, they were then to kill it and *"take of the blood, and strike it on the two side posts and on the upper door post of the houses"* (Ex. 12:7).

The Lord then said, **"And the blood shall be to you for a token upon the houses where you are** (the blood applied to the door posts meant that their Faith and trust were in the Pascal Lamb; the blood then applied was only a 'token,' meaning that it was then but a symbol of One Who was to come, Who would redeem mankind by the shedding of His Life's Blood): **and when I see the blood, I will pass over you** (this is, without a doubt, one of the single most important Scriptures in the entirety of the Word of God; the lamb had taken the fatal blow; because it had taken the blow, those in the house would be spared; it was not a question of personal worthiness, self had nothing whatever to do in the matter; it was a matter of Faith; all under the cover of the blood were safe, just as all presently under the cover of the Blood are safe; this means that they were not merely in a savable state, but rather that they were 'Saved'; as well, they were not partly Saved and partly exposed to Judgment, they were wholly Saved, and because there is no such thing as partial Justification; the Lord didn't say, 'When I see you,' or, 'When I see your good works,' etc., but, 'When I see the blood'; this speaks of Christ and what He would do at the Cross in order that we might be Saved, which pertained to Him giving Himself in Sacrifice, which necessitated the shedding of His Precious Blood [I Pet. 1:18-19]), **and the plague shall not be upon you to destroy you, when I smite the land of Egypt.** (Salvation from the 'plague' of Judgment is afforded only by the shed Blood of the Lamb and Faith in that shed Blood)" **(Ex. 12:13).**

IN THOSE DAYS

Basically, as we have stated, Israel must ultimately come the same way every Born-Again Believer has come, and that is by expressing Faith in the Lord Jesus Christ and do so with a broken and contrite spirit. This will take place *"in those days,"* referring to the Battle of Armageddon, when it will look like, at long last, Satan has won the day, with Israel totally and completely destroyed, even annihilated. However, and to be sure, the Lord *"in those days"* will hear the supplication of Israel as she desperately calls upon

His Name, in effect, asking for their True Messiah to come. They were woefully deceived by the false Messiah, the Antichrist, and have suffered terribly for that wrong direction, even as sin hurts all who participate in its web of deceit. But now, at long last, their priorities are correct, their petition is right, and their thinking is Biblical. To be sure, the Lord will answer that prayer. Jesus will come back with such Power as the world has never known before.

When He came the first time, they beat Him, laughed at Him, ridiculed Him, spit on Him, and finally crucified Him. However, when He comes the second time, it will not be as a Lamb, but rather as a Man of War, actually the King of kings and the Lord of lords, and with such Power as the world has never seen, witnessed, or experienced. In short order, the Antichrist is going to find out just exactly Who Jesus Christ really is. For him and his armies, it won't be a pretty picture. In fact, the great Prophet Ezekiel said that five-sixths of his armies would be totally and completely destroyed, and in just a few hours time (Ezek. 39:1-5).

(2) "I WILL ALSO GATHER ALL NATIONS, AND WILL BRING THEM DOWN INTO THE VALLEY OF JEHOSHAPHAT, AND WILL PLEAD WITH THEM THERE FOR MY PEOPLE AND FOR MY HERITAGE ISRAEL, WHOM THEY HAVE SCATTERED AMONG THE NATIONS, AND PARTED MY LAND.

(3) "AND THEY HAVE CAST LOTS FOR MY PEOPLE; AND HAVE GIVEN A BOY FOR AN HARLOT, AND SOLD A GIRL FOR WINE, THAT THEY MIGHT DRINK.

(4) "YES, AND WHAT HAVE YOU TO DO WITH ME, O TYRE, AND ZIDON, AND ALL THE COASTS OF PALESTINE? WILL YOU RENDER ME A RECOMPENCE? AND IF YOU RECOMPENSE ME, SWIFTLY AND SPEEDILY WILL I RETURN YOUR RECOMPENCE UPON YOUR OWN HEAD;

(5) "BECAUSE YOU HAVE TAKEN MY SILVER AND MY GOLD, AND HAVE CARRIED INTO YOUR TEMPLES MY GOODLY PLEASANT THINGS:

(6) "THE CHILDREN ALSO OF JUDAH AND THE CHILDREN OF JERUSALEM HAVE YOU SOLD UNTO THE GRECIANS,

NOTES

THAT YOU MIGHT REMOVE THEM FAR FROM THEIR BORDER.

(7) "BEHOLD, I WILL RAISE THEM OUT OF THE PLACE WHITHER YOU HAVE SOLD THEM, AND WILL RETURN YOUR RECOMPENCE UPON YOUR OWN HEAD:

(8) "AND I WILL SELL YOUR SONS AND YOUR DAUGHTERS INTO THE HAND OF THE CHILDREN OF JUDAH, AND THEY SHALL SELL THEM TO THE SABEANS, TO A PEOPLE FAR OFF: FOR THE LORD HAS SPOKEN IT."

The pattern is:

1. The phrase of Verse 2, "I will also gather all nations," refers to soldiers from many nations of the world aiding and abetting the Antichrist in his efforts to destroy Israel. Whatever the plans of these people, it will be the Lord Who is doing the gathering.

2. (Vs. 2) The phrase, "And will bring them down into the Valley of Jehoshaphat," pertains to the Valley of Megiddo. The name "Jehoshaphat" means "Jehovah has judged."

3. (Vs. 2) The words, "And will plead with them there for My People and for My Heritage Israel," refers to the Second Coming of the Lord when He will fight as He once fought in the day of battle (Zech. 14:1-3).

4. The idea of Verse 3 speaks for all time. Even though the statements pointedly concern the coming Antichrist and, consequently, the Battle of Armageddon, still, the Holy Spirit is referring to all ages and times. In other words, He is saying that such treatment of Israel is over.

5. (Vs. 4) Even though the Jews are presently far away from God, still, the Promise the Lord made to Abraham ever holds true. He said, "And I will bless them who bless you, and curse him who curses you" (Gen. 12:3).

6. The idea of Verse 5 is, when people or nations touch Israel in a negative way, they touch God. That goes, as well, for any Believer and for all time.

7. The "Grecians" of Verse 6 have reference to the Antichrist, who will come from the Syrian division of the old Grecian Empire.

8. The words, "sold them," of Verse 7, do not necessarily refer to selling them as slaves, at least in this case, but actually refers to the dire straits to which they have been forced as a result of the actions of the Antichrist.

"Out of the place," no doubt, pertains to Petra, where Israel will be forced to flee in the Great Tribulation when the Antichrist declares war on her (Rev., Chpt. 12). The last phrase says that the Antichrist is now going to be called to account.

9. The phrase, "And I will sell your sons and your daughters into the hand of the children of Judah," of Verse 8, refers to the defeat of the Antichrist in the Battle of Armageddon, when all Gentile powers will then come under the domain of Israel, including the Arabs, symbolized by the "Sabeans."

THE BATTLE OF ARMAGEDDON

This great battle, which will come at the conclusion of the seven-year Great Tribulation, will be fought in the "Valley of Jehoshaphat," at times referred to as the Valley of Megiddo. This valley is located about 35 miles southwest of the Sea of Galilee. It is in the area once occupied by the Tribe of Manasseh.

When Israel took this area in 1948, once again becoming a Nation even after some 1,900 years, the Valley of Jehoshaphat was a swamp. They shortly drained the area, until today, it is, no doubt, the most fertile area in the entirety of Israel, with crops growing there 12 months out of the year. This will be where the Antichrist, under the tutelage of Satan, makes his debut. It's an area excellent for tank warfare, actually, the only area in Israel so situated.

THE DOINGS OF THE LORD

If it is to be noticed, the first part of Verse 2 states that the Lord will actually be the Instigator Himself of the act of bringing the Antichrist and his army against Israel. In other words, He will allow the Antichrist freedom of activity in the gathering of the nations at that particular time. The Lord will do so in order to prove His Mighty Power. This is, as stated, the Battle of Armageddon (Zech. 14:1-3; Rev. 16:13-16; 19:19).

In fact, the very word, "Armageddon," means, "Mount of Megiddo," which is on the south side of the Valley of Megiddo or, as it is sometimes also referred to, "Esdraelon."

Megiddo was the capital of a portion of

NOTES

Canaan that was given to Joshua (Josh. 12:21; 17:11; Judg. 1:27). It is at the entrance to a pass across the Carmel mountain range on the main highway between Asia and Africa, and is the key position between the River Euphrates and the River Nile.

It has been the battleground of many people throughout the ages. Thothmes III, the founder of the old Egyptian Empire, said, "Megiddo is worth a thousand cities."

Sometime ago on a trip to Israel, I stood on a hill northwest of the town of Nazareth where Jesus was brought up. With my back to the city and the expanse spread out before me, the Valley of Jehoshaphat lay immediately in front of me. It is sometimes called, as stated, "the Valley of Megiddo," "the Valley of Jezreel," or "the Valley of Esdraelon."

In the distance from where I stood was Mt. Gilboa, where Saul and Jonathan were killed. To the left of that and further in the distance was Mt. Carmel, situated nearby the Mediterranean, where Elijah called fire down from Heaven.

This valley, at least, where I stood, must be about eight to ten miles wide, and possibly, some 30 miles long.

And yet, the Battle of Armageddon will cover almost, if not the entirety, of the land of Israel, with Jerusalem as its main objective. However, this "Valley of Jehoshaphat" is perfect, as stated, for great tank battles as well as the movement of large armies.

MY PEOPLE

It is beautifully interesting that in Verse 2 the Holy Spirit refers to these outcasts as "My People." This portrays the truth that, even though they disowned Him, He never disowned them. Such is Grace!

This does not mean that Christ-rejecters were Saved, for, in truth, they were eternally lost. However, the short phrase, "My People," refers to what the Lord will do in bringing them to Himself once again, as this proclaims!

MY LAND

The phrase, "Whom they have scattered among the nations, and parted My Land," is interesting indeed!

The pronoun, "they," refers to the

Romans, who scattered them all over the world of that day after the terrible defeat of A.D. 70.

It, as well, refers to all the nations, which took part in persecuting Israel during the intervening some 2,000 years.

In fact, even though Israel has been a Nation proper since 1948, still, there are more Jews outside of Israel than in Israel. There are approximately five million Jews in Israel proper with approximately 15 million in other countries of the world, with the majority of that number now being in America.

The phrase, *"And parted My Land,"* is, as well, interesting indeed. From this statement and any number of others in the Bible, as it regards the land of Israel, all and sundry should know and understand that the land of Israel is totally different than any other geography on the face of the Earth. While all the Earth, in essence, belongs to the Lord simply because He created it, still, there is a special significance to the land of Israel itself, indigenous to that particular area, which cannot be said about any other part of the world. So, that means that every nation of the world should understand that when they make decisions regarding the land of Israel, they are dealing with that which directly belongs to God, with the guarantee that He is going to do with it as He so desires.

It must be ascertained that He has reserved that area for the Jews and the Jews alone! Some 4,000 years ago, He said to Abraham, *"Get thee out of your country, and from your kindred, and from your father's house, unto a land that I will show you"* (Gen. 12:1).

According to the Word of God, and unequivocally so, that land is the land of Canaan. The Lord said to Moses:

"Get thee up into this mountain Abarim, unto Mount Nebo, which is in the land of Moab, that is over against Jericho; and behold the land of Canaan, which I give unto the Children of Israel for a possession" (Deut. 32:49).

This means that it doesn't belong to the Palestinians or anyone else, for that matter. God has given it to Israel.

NOTES

Incidentally, there is really no such thing as Palestinians. These people that refer to themselves as such are actually Jordanians, Syrians, Egyptians, etc.

Since 1948, the combined Arab nations have attacked Israel several times with every intent of completely destroying her. Had that happened, there would be no Israel today, and if they were allowed to have their way, there would be no Jews in that part of the world left alive. But Israel won every conflict, even against overwhelming odds. Still, they allowed the *"Palestinians"* to remain in the land. Again we state, had the situation been reversed, one can be dead certain that the Muslims in no way would have allowed Israel to remain.

America has been greatly blessed by God simply because of our standing with Israel these decades. Tragically, we are about the only friend that Israel presently has, and I speak of the entirety of the world. However, under the Obama Administration, that friendship is weakening greatly because this President, in my opinion, is a Muslim sympathizer, etc. Of all the mistakes we have made as a nation, to pull away from Israel will be the worst mistake of all. To be sure, the Lord still means what He said when He told Abraham, *"And I will bless them who bless you, and curse him who curses you . . ."* (Gen. 12:3). One can be certain that God says what He means and means what He says!

THE PARTING OF THE LAND

The phrase, *"And parted My Land,"* goes all the way back to the division of Judah from Israel proper. Ten Tribes went their way, forming the northern confederacy, calling themselves either *"Israel,"* *"Samaria,"* or *"Ephraim."*

The Two Tribes of Judah and Benjamin formed the southern confederacy called *"Judah."* Jerusalem, along with the Temple, was in the southern division. After the terrible destruction of A.D. 70 by the Romans, the land of Israel continued to be occupied by Jews, with an insurgence over the centuries of Turks and Arabs.

Today the land continues to be parted, with the Gaza Strip being administered, at least, after a fashion, by the Palestinians, with Jericho, the West Bank, and East Jerusalem being contested. To be sure, all of this will cease when Jesus comes back, with Him utilizing the entirety of the land of Israel, even according to the ancient Prophecies. In other words, Israel will then be solely for the Jews and not for the Arabs or anyone else!

The manner the Holy Spirit uses designations in Verse 2 is interesting. He said:

• *"My People"*: this speaks of the Jews, the sons of Jacob, and their ancestors, even unto today.

• *"My Heritage Israel"*: this speaks of the Promises made to the Patriarchs, kings, and Prophets. Israel's *"Heritage"* was threefold:

1. Give the world the Word of God.
2. Bring the Messiah into the world.
3. Evangelize the world.

They succeeded in the first two and failed in the last, but which they will now fulfill.

• *"My Land"*: this pertains to the geographical boundaries of Israel originally promised to Abraham, which said, *"... Unto your seed have I given this land, from the river of Egypt unto the great river, the river Euphrates"* (Gen. 15:18).

This geographical boundary borders the Mediterranean on the west, the Suez Canal on the south, with the Euphrates River on the north and the east. This includes modern Syria along with the Arabian Peninsula, even with about half of modern Iraq. Only a fraction of this area was ever fully occupied, and that was under the reigns of David and Solomon; however, in the coming Kingdom Age, all promised will be realized and utilized.

MY PEOPLE

The Holy Spirit through the Prophet Joel said, *"And they have cast lots for My People; and have given a boy for an harlot, and sold a girl for wine, that they might drink."*

The idea of this Verse speaks for all time. Even though the statements pointedly concerned the coming Antichrist and his treatment of Jews, still, the Holy Spirit is referring to all ages and times. In other words, He is saying that such treatment is over.

Actually, such treatment had been

predicted ages before, that is, if Israel forsook the Lord, which, tragically, they did (Lev. 26:33; Deut. 28:36).

Josephus, the Jewish historian who was born A.D. 38, spoke of such happenings, which took place with the fall of Jerusalem in A.D. 70. Concerning one particular lot of Jews held captive, he said:

"Ninety-seven thousand prisoners were disposed of as follows: those under 17 years of age were publicly sold; some exiled to work in Egyptian mines; others reserved to fight with wild beasts in the amphitheatre. Also, in the time of Hadrian four Jewish captives were sold for a measure of barley."

The Prophet Joel, however, looks forward in Prophetic Vision to the day of final Judgment when God will, in just retribution, pour out the vials of His Wrath on all the oppressors of His People. Not only is it *"My Land,"* but, also, it is *"My People!"*

WHAT HAVE YOU TO DO WITH ME?

Verse 4 says, *"Yes, and what have you to do with Me, O Tyre, and Zidon, and all the coasts of Palestine? will you render Me a recompense? and if you recompense Me, swiftly and speedily will I return your recompense upon your own head."*

The mention of Tyre, Sidon, Philistia, and Greece supports the view that this Prophecy covers the whole period of the times of the Gentiles.

The phrase, *"And all the coasts of Palestine,"* refers to Philistia, which included the famous cities of Tyre and Sidon. Actually, the names *"Palestine"* and *"Palestinians"* are derived from the name *"Philistines,"* which comes from *"Philistia."* To be sure, there are no more Philistines left, actually ceasing to be a nation or a people many, many centuries ago.

The question, *"Will you render Me a recompense?"* rather means, *"What have you to do with Me?"*

The question, *"And if you recompense Me, swiftly and speedily will I return your recompense upon your own head?"* in effect, says, *"What will you do to stop Me?"*

The Lord is speaking to the whole of Gentile nations, with a view in mind that spans thousands of years, even beginning with Egypt, but more pointedly referring to the coming Antichrist.

These Passages portray God's Anger at the way His People, the Jews, have been treated down through the many centuries. Of course, the same could be said for His People, the Church, as well!

Soon the Gentile nations of the world will join together with the Antichrist in what is referred to as *"Armageddon,"* with a determination to completely annihilate these people called the Jews. As such, God's Anger comes up in His Face.

It must be remembered, *"To touch that which belongs to God is to touch God!"*

These Passages, and other similar Passages, are the very reason that America's present handling of the situation in Israel is so very, very important.

Even though these people, the Jews, are presently far away from God, still, the Promise the Lord made to Abraham nearly 4,000 years ago ever holds true. Let me say it again, He said:

"And I will bless them who bless you, and curse him who curses you . . ." (Gen. 12:3).

MY SILVER AND MY GOLD

The Holy Spirit through the Prophet Joel also said, *"Because you have taken My Silver and My Gold, and have carried into your temples My goodly pleasant Things."*

It was *"My Land,"* and then *"My People,"* and now it is *"My Silver and Gold."*

All of this means that *"the silver and gold"* taken from Israel by invading armies through the many centuries past, He likens as *"My Silver and My Gold."* Therefore, that which belongs to His, in fact, belongs to Him. We must never forget that!

As well, if such deeds are not repented of, which they seldom are, neither does He forget these infractions and will ultimately visit it once again upon the heads of the perpetrators exactly as stated in the previous Verse.

The phrase, *"And have carried into your temples My goodly pleasant Things,"* refers basically to the Vessels of the Temple, which were taken by Nebuchadnezzar to Babylon and placed in the temple of the god Bel (II Chron. 36:18).

SOLD UNTO THE GRECIANS

The Sixth Verse says, *"The children also of Judah and the children of Jerusalem have you sold unto the Grecians, that you might remove them far from their border."*

This Passage has a double fulfillment:

• It possibly has reference to the event narrated in II Chronicles 21:16-17, where it is written, *"The LORD stirred up against Jehoram the spirit of the Philistines. . . .*

"And they came up into Judah, and broke into it, and carried away all the substance that was found in the king's house, and his sons also, and his wives."

It is said that the Phoenicians sold some of these slaves to the Ionian Greeks of Asia Minor in order to prevent the possibility of their return to their own land.

• As well, and more so, the *"Grecians"* also has reference to the Antichrist, who will come from the Syrian division of the old Grecian Empire.

He will make a Covenant with Israel, guaranteeing her borders and her protection for some seven years. At midway point of this seven-year Covenant, he will actually declare war upon these people. At that time, he will transfer his headquarters from rebuilt Babylon to Jerusalem and will, no doubt, maltreat the Jews severely who were not quick enough to escape him (Dan. 9:27).

HOW WILL THE ANTICHRIST CONVINCE THE MUSLIMS TO GO ALONG WITH A COVENANT GUARANTEEING THE PROTECTION OF ISRAEL FOR SEVEN YEARS?

We know from the Biblical account that the Antichrist will make a seven-year Covenant with Israel, guaranteeing her borders and her protection, and, as well, that he will break that Covenant at the midpoint of the time frame (Dan. 9:27). That Covenant will not only include Israel's borders and protection but, as well, will give her the right to rebuild her Temple, and, no doubt, on the exact spot where Solomon's Temple originally was built. Considering that the Muslim Dome of the Rock sits on the exact spot of the Temple site, with the Dome of the Rock being the so-called third most holy site of the Muslims, and meaning it will have to be torn down, how will the Antichrist convince the Muslims to go along with this Covenant?

THE PRESENT EFFORTS TO BRING PEACE TO THE MIDDLE EAST

The brightest minds in America have not been able to solve this thorny problem that, in fact, is the flash point of the world. The president of Iran (2010) has sworn the destruction of Israel. As well, the Iranian scientists are working feverishly, trying to develop an atomic bomb.

On the other hand, the Muslim world is demanding for the Palestinians, not only the West Bank but, as well, East Jerusalem, as their capital. Prime Minister Benjamin Netanyahu has firmly said *"no"* to the idea of East Jerusalem being the capital of the Palestinians, and rightly so! As we have stated, this land is God's Land, and He has given it to the Jews while still retaining ownership. But, of course, the Muslim world does not believe the Bible is the Word of God, doesn't believe in Jehovah, and doesn't believe in the Lord Jesus Christ.

Before President Bush left office, he vowed that he would have a peace treaty between Israel and the Palestinians. He didn't! Basically, President Clinton said the same thing, but without success. And now (2010), the most dangerous thing for the U.S.A. is that President Obama is, in my opinion, a Muslim sympathizer. He is very little attempting to work out a fair solution but, in reality, is issuing statements that, if complied with, will cause Israel serious problems.

THE ANTICHRIST

But yet, when the Antichrist comes on the scene, he will be able to accomplish, and by the powers of Satan, we might quickly add, what the brightest minds in America have not been able to accomplish. He will work out a seven-year Treaty, which will guarantee Israel's borders as well as her safety and protection. In this Covenant, he will also solve what seems to be an impossible situation, which concerns the rebuilding of Israel's Temple. The term *"rebuilding"* is used advisedly because they haven't had a

Temple in this particular place, or anywhere else, for that matter, in nearly 2,000 years.

So, how will he be able to convince the Muslims that the Dome of the Rock be torn down with the Jewish Temple being put in its place?

Some claim that the Dome of the Rock will not be torn down, but rather that Israel will build her Temple elsewhere on the Temple Mount. Others have even suggested that she might possibly use the Great Synagogue in Jerusalem.

All of this is highly doubtful for the simple reason that the Bible is very specific as to where this Temple must be. I cannot see that Israel would tolerate the Dome of the Rock, which they consider to be blasphemy, and rightly so, being adjacent to their Temple. Likewise, I cannot see the Muslims allowing the Jewish Temple, which they consider to be blasphemy, to be situated near their so-called third most holy place in Islam! Also, I cannot picture Israel trying to use their largest synagogue in the city for this purpose. Every evidence is, I think, that the Temple will be built on the exact spot where Solomon's Temple was built, which was the first Temple, and where Herod's Temple was also built, the one in which Jesus ministered.

Even though this information is not given to us in the Bible, we do know several things about the Antichrist and about the Muslims as well. There is no truth in either one.

DECEPTION

The Antichrist could very well have a meeting with the leading Muslim clerics and relate to them his plan, which will be very hard for them to swallow, but the prize they think they are going to gain will be well worth it.

To get them to agree to his plan, which means that they will tear down the Dome of the Rock, with the Jewish Temple taking its place, he could make them this promise. At a point in time, that is, when he is strong enough, he will attack Israel without warning, with the land of Israel in its totality then being given to the Muslims. However, what they don't realize is, the Antichrist will be setting them up as well. He has no intention of giving place to any religion, planning at a given point to declare himself as *"god."* So, he will most definitely turn on the Muslims even as he turns on the other religions of the world. But, of course, he will hate Judaism and Christianity to a far greater degree than any other religion. Nevertheless, he will tolerate no other form of worship, at least, in the countries which he controls.

GREECE?

Why did the Holy Spirit include the word *"Grecians,"* i.e., *"Greece,"* in this Sixth Verse?

As previously stated, even though this Passage could definitely have had something to do with the Phoenicians selling some of the Israelites as slaves to the Greeks of Asia Minor (II Chron. 21:16-17), the greater weight of the meaning has more to do with the coming Antichrist than anything else.

Daniel said that the *"little horn,"* or the Antichrist, will come out of the Syrian division, as stated, of the Grecian Empire (Dan. 8:5-12). The Syrian division included modern Lebanon, Syria, Iraq, Iran, Afghanistan, and even part of Pakistan. So, that means the Antichrist could come from any one of these countries; however, more than likely, he will come from the Syrian division because he is referred to as the *"king of the north."* With the exception of Syria, all of these countries listed are east of Israel. Irrespective, the countries listed presently constitute the flash point of the world, meaning they are the most dangerous.

FALLEN ANGEL

Daniel told us, as it regards one of his Visions, that the *"Prince of Grecia"* would play a major part as it regards aiding and abetting the Antichrist. But please understand, this *"Prince of Grecia"* is not a human being, but rather a fallen Angel. This is the Angel that greatly aided and abetted Alexander the Great in his many conquests. Of course, Alexander had no knowledge whatsoever of this prince of darkness who was helping him, nevertheless, this was actually the secret of his great conquests (Dan. 10:20). When Alexander died at 32 years of age, this fallen Angel was incarcerated in a place in the heart of the Earth referred to as

"the bottomless pit." He will be released out of this pit upon the advent of the Antichrist in order to help the man of sin. As well, the Antichrist will not know that he is being aided by a powerful fallen Angel, but will rather take all the credit to himself, even as did Alexander the Great (Rev. 17:8-14). Of course, the overriding ambition of the Antichrist will be to totally and completely destroy Israel, which he will attempt to do in the Battle of Armageddon. He will not succeed because of the Second Coming of the Lord.

THE ARABS

Verse 8 says, *"And I will sell your sons and your daughters into the hand of the children of Judah, and they shall sell them to the Sabeans, to a people far off: for the LORD has spoken it."*

As previously stated, Verse 8 refers to the defeat of the Antichrist in the Battle of Armageddon when all Gentile powers will then come under the domain of Israel.

Of course, such seems to be totally impossible at the present time, considering the smallness of Israel and the might and power of mighty nations such as America, etc. However, upon the Second Coming of the Lord, the entire complexion of the world will change drastically! The Lord Jesus Christ will Personally reign supreme from Jerusalem, and with a might, majesty, and power such as the world has never known.

He is the One Who will elevate Israel to her rightful place, thereby, fulfilling the Prophecies made to the Patriarchs and Prophets of long ago. Consequently, the phrase, *"To sell into the hand,"* means to deliver over into the power of the children of Judah, which shall be done at that particular time, which is the coming Kingdom Age.

The phrase, *"And they shall sell them to the Sabeans, to a people far off,"* refers to *"Sheba"* in Arabia.

Consequently, this has to do with the age-old conflicts of the Arabs and Jews, going all the way back to Abraham, Isaac, and Ishmael. That conflict rages today hotter than ever!

The phrase simply means that the seed was Isaac, a work of the Spirit, and not

Ishmael, a work of the flesh.

As a result of this conflict, which has raged for thousands of years, the religion of Islam made its debut in A.D. 622.

Tragically, most Americans have little knowledge as to what the religion of Islam actually is. And please believe me, this is ignorance that can lead to extremely adverse circumstances. The Muslim world hates Israel and the United States. Their hatred for Israel goes all the way back to Abraham as it regards his two sons, Isaac and Ishmael, which we will deal with more directly. Their hatred of the United States is twofold. It pertains to our protection of Israel, but most of all, because of the Lord Jesus Christ, Whom they see as the great competitor of Muhammad. We will look at this religion from its Spiritual aspects according to the Word of God, and from its practical aspects as it regards its present ambitions.

WHAT IS THE RELATIONSHIP OF ISLAM TO THE BIBLE?

In truth, none!

While the Muslims have misquoted the Bible, falsely interpreted the Bible, misapplied the Bible, and even changed the Bible, the truth is, Islam has absolutely no part in the Word of God. While the Koran contains illustrations from the Bible, generally, those illustrations are twisted and perverted. In fact, while many religions have borrowed somewhat from the Bible, the Bible, the oldest Book in the world, has not borrowed from anything.

The Muslims claim that Ishmael is the promised seed and not Isaac.

The Bible portrays Ishmael as a work of the flesh and that he, along with his mother Hagar, were driven out of the household of Abraham.

The Scriptures say, and I quote from THE EXPOSITOR'S STUDY BIBLE:

"And the LORD visited Sarah as He had said, and the LORD did unto Sarah as He had spoken (despite all of Satan's hindrances, Isaac, the progenitor and Type of the Messiah, is born).

"For Sarah conceived, and bore Abraham a son in his old age, at the set time of which God had spoken to him. (Referring back

to the past Chapter, if it be objected that this whole occurrence is incredible because no heathen prince would desire to marry a woman upwards of 90 years of age, or to conceive such a passion for her that to secure her he would murder her husband – the very fate which Abraham feared for himself – it may be replied that God must have miraculously renewed her youth, so that she became sufficiently youthful in appearance to suitably be desirable. Three times in these first two Verses, the clause points to the supernatural character of Isaac's birth.)

"And Abraham called the name of his son that was born unto him, whom Sarah bore to him, Isaac. (The name means 'laughter.' It speaks of blessing, increase, healing, life, and well-being [Jn. 10:10]. As Isaac was a Type of Christ, it would not be wrong to say that one of the names of Christ is 'laughter.')"

ISAAC

"And Abraham circumcised his son Isaac being eight days old, as God had commanded him (this was a sign of the Covenant that God would ultimately send a Redeemer into this world).

"And Abraham was an hundred years old, when his son Isaac was born unto him (this Verse is placed in the Text so that all may know that Isaac's birth was indeed miraculous).

"And Sarah said, God has made me to laugh, so that all who hear will laugh with me. (The mention of Sarah's name some five times thus far in this Chapter is done for purpose and reason; the Holy Spirit is impressing the fact that Sarah was in truth the very mother of this miraculous child. Sarah had once laughed in unbelief; she now laughs in Faith, a laughter, incidentally, expressing joy, which will never end. It all pointed to Christ. Because of Christ, untold millions have laughed for joy.)

"And she said, Who would have said unto Abraham, that Sarah should have given children suck? for I have born him a son in his old age (this is a poem, and could very well have been a song, and probably was).

"And the child grew, and was weaned

(the custom in those days was to nurse children for two to three years before they were weaned; however, there is some indication that Isaac was approximately five years old when he was weaned): **and Abraham made a great feast the same day that Isaac was weaned** *(at this time, the boy was turned over to his father for training, at which time his education began).*"

ISHMAEL

"**And Sarah saw the son of Hagar** *(Ishmael)* **the Egyptian, which she had born unto Abraham, mocking.** *(The effect of the birth of Isaac, a work of the Spirit, was to make manifest the character of Ishmael, a work of the flesh. The end result of the 'mocking' was that Ishmael actually desired to murder Isaac [Gal. 4:29]. Ishmael was probably eighteen to twenty years old at this time, and Isaac was probably about five years old.)*

"**Wherefore she said unto Abraham, Cast out this bondwoman and her son:** *(Isaac and Ishmael symbolize the new and the old natures in the Believer. Hagar and Sarah typify the two Covenants of works and Grace, of bondage and liberty [Gal., Chpt. 4]. The birth of the new nature demands the expulsion of the old. It is impossible to improve the old nature. How foolish, therefore, appears the doctrine of moral evolution!)* **for the son of this bondwoman shall not be heir with my son, even with Isaac.** *(Allowed to remain, Ishmael would murder Isaac; allowed to remain, the flesh will murder the Spirit. The Divine way of holiness is to 'put off the old man,' just as Abraham 'put off' Ishmael. Man's way of holiness is to improve the 'old man,' that is, to improve Ishmael. The effort is both foolish and hopeless.)*

"**And the thing was very grievous in Abraham's sight because of his son.** *(It is always a struggle to cast out this element of bondage, that is, salvation by works, of which this is a type. For legalism is dear to the heart. Ishmael was the fruit, and, to Abraham, the fair fruit of his own energy and planning, which God can never accept.)*"

HEARKEN TO SARAH

"**And God said unto Abraham, Let it not**

be grievous in your sight because of the lad, and because of your bondwoman; in all that Sarah has said unto you, hearken unto her voice; for in Isaac shall your seed be called. *(It is labor lost to seek to make a crooked thing straight. Hence, all efforts after the improvement of nature are utterly futile, so far as God is concerned. The 'flesh' must go, which typifies the personal ability, strength, and efforts of the Believer. The Faith of the Believer must be entirely in Christ and what Christ has done at the Cross. Then, and then alone, can the Holy Spirit have latitude to work in our lives, bringing forth perpetual victory [Rom. 6:14]. It must ever be understood, 'in Isaac [in Christ] shall your seed be called.')*

"**And also of the son of the bondwoman will I make a nation, because he is your seed** *(out of this 'work of the flesh' ultimately came the religion of Islam, which claims that Ishmael is the promised seed, and not Isaac)*" **(Gen. 21:1-13).**

GOD'S PROMISE CONCERNING ISHMAEL

Some years before, Hagar, the bondwoman, and her son, Ishmael, were cast out of the home of Abraham. Actually, just before Isaac was born, the Lord said unto Abraham:

"**As for Sarai your wife, you shall not call her name Sarai** *('my princess,' referring to the fact that she was Abraham's princess alone)*, **but Sarah shall her name be** *(simply means 'princess;' the idea is, whereas she was formerly Abraham's princess only, she will now be recognized as a princess generally and, in fact, in a sense, could be referred to as the 'mother of the Church').*

"**And I will bless her, and give you a son also of her** *(this is the first time in all of God's Dealings with Abraham that He had mentioned the fact that the promised son would be of Sarah)*: **yes, I will bless her, and she shall be a mother of nations; kings of people shall be of her** *(her 'blessing' spoke of increase, which includes even the Church and, in a sense, the Lord Jesus Christ).*

"**Then Abraham fell upon his face, and laughed, and said in his heart, Shall a child be born unto me who is an hundred years old** *(Abraham's laughter was that of joy [Jn. 8:56])*? **and shall Sarah, who is ninety**

years old, bear? *(Paul said of him: 'He considered not the deadness of Sarah's womb' [Rom. 4:19].)*

"And Abraham said unto God, O that Ishmael might live before You! *(Abraham asked the Lord that Ishmael might have some place and not be completely left out.)*

"And God said, Sarah your wife shall bear you a son indeed; and you shall call his name Isaac *(the name Isaac, as stated, means 'laughter')*: **and I will establish My Covenant with him for an Everlasting Covenant, and with his seed after him.** *(The Covenant is to be established with Isaac and not Ishmael. This completely shoots down the contention of the Muslims that Ishmael was the chosen one, unless you don't believe the Bible. Through Isaac the Lord Jesus Christ, the Saviour of mankind, would ultimately come.)*

"And as for Ishmael, I have heard you: Behold, I have blessed him, and will make him fruitful, and will multiply him exceedingly *(the Lord would bless Ishmael, but not as it regards the Covenant)*; **twelve princes shall he beget, and I will make him a great nation** *(the blessing here pronounced was not because of Ishmael but because of Abraham, and Abraham alone)*.

"But My Covenant will I establish with Isaac, who Sarah shall bear unto you at this set time in the next year *(so now they knew when the child would be born)*.

"And He *(the Lord)* **left off talking with him, and God went up from Abraham** *(Communion with the Lord is the most profitable exercise there is)*" **(Gen. 17:15-22).**

THE WORD OF GOD

This, which we have given, concerns the statement given by the Lord as it regards Isaac and Ishmael. Even though we have dealt with it in a Spiritual sense, it can be likened to the flesh and the Spirit, even as Paul addressed it in Galatians 4:21 through 31. But yet, the information given is meant to proclaim what the Word of God says as it regards both Isaac and Ishmael, which completely refutes the claims of Islam. As stated, they claim that the Lord chose Ishmael instead, and not Isaac. This all came from the supposed revelation given to

Muhammad in approximately the year 622.

Actually, the Lord foretold, even before the birth of Ishmael, as to what type of man he would be. He said:

"And he will be a wild man; his hand will be against every man, and every man's hand against him; and he shall dwell in the presence of all his brethren. *(These predictions describe the Arab people perfectly. They cannot get along with anyone in the world; they cannot even get along among themselves. The descendants of Ishmael dwell in the presence of all his brethren [Israel], but do not subdue them and, in fact, never will subdue them!)*" **(Gen. 16:12).**

THE LAST DAYS

There are some who claim that the Muslims will play a great part in the activity of the last days and, no doubt, will. By the term *"last days,"* we're speaking of the beginning of the Great Tribulation. The Scripture says concerning this:

"And he (the Antichrist) *shall confirm the covenant with many for one week* (a week of years – seven years) *. . ."* (Dan. 9:27).

In effect, the Antichrist will make his debut on the world scene by brokering a peace treaty between Israel, the Palestinians, and the Arabs, and, no doubt, other nations of the world, as well, and, undoubtedly, including the U.S.A. The Antichrist will receive instant recognition for his ability to do this, so much so, in fact, that Israel will acclaim him as their long awaited Messiah. This is what Jesus was talking about when He said concerning this very thing:

"I am come in My Father's Name, and you receive Me not: if another shall come in his own name, him you will receive" (Jn. 5:43).

As would be obvious, the Muslim Middle East will be tremendously involved in this. In fact, the situation, as it regards Israel and the balance of the Middle East, grows more difficult with each passing day. Iran is claiming publicly that Israel should be wiped off the face of the Earth; so, anyone who can solve this problem will be heralded as a superman. The Antichrist will solve it, at least, for a short time. The moment this seven-year treaty is signed will signal the beginning of the Great Tribulation referred to by Christ and the Prophets (Mat. 24:21).

As to how the Antichrist will be able to bring Israel and the Muslims to the negotiating table and, thereby, accomplish something that the brightest minds in America have not been able to accomplish, we have addressed some pages back. It would be well worth the time of the reader to peruse it carefully. It possibly will answer many questions.

During the first three and one half years of that time, referred to, as well, as Daniel's Seventieth Week, Israel will fare very well, it seems, even though the Judgment of God will begin to be poured out. But then, they will be rudely awakened and, in fact, will now face their most horrific time, even worse than the Holocaust of World War II. Concerning this, the Apostle Paul said:

PEACE AND SAFETY?

"For when they shall say, Peace and safety (refers to Israel, but will, as well, characterize the world; it pertains to the Antichrist signing the seven-year pact with Israel and other nations [Dan. 9:27]); then sudden destruction comes upon them (at the mid-point of the seven-year period, the Antichrist will break his pact, actually invading Israel [Rev. 12:1-6]), as travail upon a woman with child; and they shall not escape" (I Thess. 5:3).

At the midpoint of the seven-year time frame, referred to as the *"Great Tribulation,"* the Antichrist will show his true colors and will attack Israel. In fact, at that time Israel will suffer her first military defeat since becoming a Nation in 1948. Actually, were it not for intervention by the Lord, Israel would be completely destroyed at that particular time, but, thankfully, the Lord will intervene.

THE ANTICHRIST

Concerning this very time, Daniel said, and I continue to quote from THE EXPOSITOR'S STUDY BIBLE:

"And at the time of the end shall the king of the south (Egypt) push at him: and the king of the north (the Antichrist, Syria) shall come against him like a whirlwind, with chariots, and with horsemen, and with

many ships; and he shall enter into the countries, and shall overflow and pass over. (The phrase, 'And at the time of the end,' refers to the time of the fulfillment of these Prophecies, which, in fact, is just ahead. It is known that 'the king of the south' refers to Egypt because that's who is referred to at the beginning of this Chapter, which spoke of the breakup of the Grecian Empire. As well, 'the king of the north' proves that the Antichrist will come from the Syrian division of the breakup of the Grecian Empire. So, the Antichrist will more than likely be a Syrian Jew.)

"He shall enter also into the glorious land (into Israel), and many countries shall be overthrown (those in the Middle East): but these shall escape out of his hand (escape out of the hand of the Antichrist), even Edom, and Moab, and the chief of the children of Ammon. (Edom, Moab, and Ammon comprise modern Jordan. His entering into the 'glorious land' refers to his invasion of Israel at the midpoint of his seven-year nonaggression pact with them, therefore, breaking his covenant [9:27].

"The countries listed comprise, as stated, modern Jordan, where ancient Petra is located, to which Israel will flee upon the Antichrist 'entering into the Glorious Land' [Rev. 12:6].)

"He shall stretch forth his hand also upon the countries: and the land of Egypt shall not escape. ('Egypt' refers to 'the king of the south' of Verse 40, as stated.)

"But he shall have power over the treasures of gold and of silver, and over all the precious things of Egypt: and the Libyans and the Ethiopians shall be at his steps. (The 'precious things of Egypt,' no doubt, refer to the ancient mysteries of Egypt, regarding the tombs, the pyramids, etc. He will, no doubt, claim to unlock many of these mysteries; he very well could do so, regarding the supernatural power given to him, and we continue to speak of the Antichrist, with all of this being done by the powers of darkness).

"But tidings out of the east and out of the north shall trouble him: therefore he shall go forth with great fury to destroy, and utterly to make away many. (After the

Antichrist breaks his covenant with Israel, actually 'entering into the Glorious Land,' he will be prevented from further destroying her by the 'tidings of the east and out of the north' that 'shall trouble him.' No doubt, these will be nations, probably led by Russia [north], Japan, and China [east], forming a union against him, but which will have no success)" **(Dan. 11:40-44).**

THE MUSLIM WORLD, THE ANTICHRIST, AND ISRAEL

When the Antichrist turns on Israel, actually, as stated, defeating her, no doubt, the Muslim world will be aiding and abetting the man of sin in all of his efforts. As well, every evidence is that the entirety of the Middle East, with the exception of Jordan, with all of its oil wealth, will now be in his control. In fact, Daniel 11:43, as previously quoted, in essence, tells us this. So, he will have all the money he needs in order to do what he needs to do, which is to take over the entire world. He will not succeed, however, in doing that. The Scripture says:

"And he shall plant the tabernacles of his palace between the seas in the glorious Holy Mountain; yet he shall come to his end, and none shall help him. *('And he shall plant the tabernacles of his palace,' refers to him taking over the newly-built Temple in Jerusalem and stopping the sacrifices as prophesied in Daniel 8:9-12. This speaks of the time when he will turn on Israel at the midpoint of the seven-year Great Tribulation.*

"'Between the seas in the glorious Holy Mountain,' refers to the Dead Sea and the Mediterranean Sea. The 'glorious Holy Mountain' is Mount Moriah, where the Temple is located.

"'Yet he shall come to his end, and none shall help him,' is tied to the first part of this Verse, which speaks of him desecrating the Temple. This ensures his destruction by the Lord, which will take place at the Second Coming)" **(Dan. 11:45).**

And yet, the Muslim world, who will think the Antichrist is their champion because he has turned on Israel, will themselves be rudely awakened. The Word of God is clear concerning this.

THE ANTICHRIST TURNS ON THE MUSLIMS

The Scripture says concerning this:

"And the king *(the Antichrist)* **shall do according to his will; and he shall exalt himself, and magnify himself above every god, and shall speak marvelous things against the God of gods, and shall prosper till the indignation be accomplished: for that that is determined shall be done.** *(The phrase, 'And the king shall do according to his will,' refers to the Antichrist, who will pretty much have his way until the Second Advent of Christ.*

"'And magnify himself above every god,' actually refers to him deifying himself [II Thess. 2:4]. At this time, and according to Daniel 9:27, he will take over the newly-built Temple in Jerusalem, as stated, do away with the Jewish sacrifices, which have not long since begun, and will set up an image of himself [Rev. 13:15].

"'And shall speak marvelous things against the God of gods,' means that he will literally declare war on Christ. His campaign of declaring himself 'god' will, of necessity, demand that he blaspheme the True God as no one has ever blasphemed.

"'And shall prosper till the indignation be accomplished,' means that much of the world will accept his claims, joining with him in their hatred of the God of the Bible.)

"Neither shall he regard the God of his fathers, nor the desire of women, nor regard any god: for he shall magnify himself above all. *(The phrase, 'Neither shall he regard the God of his fathers,' no doubt, refers to him being a Jew. He will not regard the God of 'Abraham, Isaac, and Jacob.'*

"'Nor the desire of women,' probably refers to him turning against the Catholic church and, thereby, the Virgin Mary.

"'Nor regard any god: for he shall magnify himself above all,' refers to all the religions of the world, which will include Islam, all of which will be outlawed, at least, where he has control, demanding that worship be centered upon him)" **(Dan. 11:36-37).**

Now the Muslims will find out, as did the Jews, that the Antichrist has no respect for anyone, and especially their religions, including Islam. While he most definitely will hate the Jews above all, still, he will have, as stated, *"no regard for any god."* The Bible actually tells us what he will honor.

THE STRANGE GOD

The Scripture says:

"But in his estate shall he honour the god of forces; and a god whom his fathers knew not shall he honour with gold, and silver, and with precious stones, and pleasant things. *(The phrase, 'And a god whom his fathers knew not shall he honour,' refers to a 'strange god' mentioned in the next Verse, who is actually the fallen Angel who empowered Alexander the Great. He is called 'the Prince of Grecia,' which does not refer to a mortal, but instead, a fallen Angel [Dan. 10:20]. This 'god,' his fathers, Abraham, Isaac, and Jacob, did not know.)*

"Thus shall he do in the most strong holds with a strange god, whom he shall acknowledge and increase with glory: and he shall cause them to rule over many, and shall divide the land for gain. *(The phrase, 'Thus shall he do in the most strong holds,' refers to the great financial centers of the world, which will be characterized by rebuilt Babylon or possibly even newly built Dubai. This 'strange god,' as stated, is a fallen Angel; therefore, he will probably think he is giving praise and glory to himself when, in reality, he is actually honoring this 'fallen Angel.'*

"'And he shall cause them to rule over many,' refers to the many nations he will conquer because of the great power given to him by this fallen Angel, instigated by Satan)" **(Dan. 11:38-39).**

RELIGION

Religion is that which is conceived by man, birthed by man, instituted by man, and carried out by man in order to reach God or else to better oneself in some way. Anything of this capacity conceived by man is unacceptable to God. This means that anything and everything that's not strictly according to the Word of God is unacceptable.

Islam, Buddhism, Hinduism, Confucianism, Shintoism, modern Judaism, Mormonism, Catholicism, etc., all and without

NOTES

exception, come under the heading of religion. This, as well, includes the part of Christianity that has been corrupted, and much of it has!

BIBLICAL CHRISTIANITY

Biblical Christianity is not a religion, but rather a relationship, and that with a Man, the Man, Christ Jesus. Yet, much of modern Christianity, as stated, has been divorced from the Bible, meaning that it is perverted and twisted and, therefore, corrupt. It too must come under the heading of religion. Perhaps the simple phrase, *"Jesus Christ and Him Crucified,"* would come closer to explaining Biblical Christianity than anything else. Concerning this, the Apostle Paul said:

"Now the Spirit *(Holy Spirit)* **speaks expressly** *(pointedly),* **that in the latter times** *(the times in which we now live, the last of the last days, which begin the fulfillment of Endtime Prophecies)* **some shall depart from the Faith** *(anytime Paul uses the term 'the Faith,' in short, he is referring to the Cross; so, we are told here that some will depart from the Cross as the Means of Salvation and Victory),* **giving heed to seducing spirits** *(evil spirits, i.e., 'religious spirits,' making something seem like what it isn't),* **and doctrines of devils** *(should have been translated, 'doctrines of demons'; the 'seducing spirits' entice Believers away from the true Faith, causing them to believe 'doctrines inspired by demon spirits')"* **(I Tim. 4:1).**

While the words *"religious"* and *"religion"* appear in James 1:26-27, the Greek words originally used would have been better translated *"spiritual"* and *"spirituality,"* making it read, *"If any man among you seem to be spiritual . . ."* and *"Pure spirituality. . . ."*

THE GREAT WHORE

The Holy Spirit, even as we shall see, takes a very dim view of religion, which, in fact, has been the nemesis of the Lord from the very beginning of time. We see religion at work in the case of Cain and Abel, the offspring of the First Family. The Lord had given instructions as to how communion with Him should be carried out, plus forgiveness of sins. It would be by the means of the slain lamb offered up in sacrifice, which would be a symbol of the coming Redeemer. Abel offered up his sacrifice accordingly and was accepted by God.

Conversely, his brother, Cain, refused to offer up that which God demanded, instead, offering up the fruit of his own hands, whatever that may have been. Please understand, Cain did not deny there was a God and did not deny the need for a sacrifice, but rather he offered a sacrifice of his own choosing, which God would not accept and, in fact, could not accept (Gen., Chpt. 4). Cain's unacceptable offering was the first evidence of *"religion."*

We know what the Lord thinks of religion by what He said in the Book of Revelation:

DECEPTION

"And there came one of the seven Angels which had the seven Vials, and talked with me *(probably is the seventh Angel; however, we actually have no way of truly knowing)***, saying unto me, Come hither; I will show unto you the Judgment of the great whore who sits upon many waters** *(the 'great whore' refers to all the religions of the world that ever have been, which are devised by men as a substitute for 'Jesus Christ and Him Crucified'; God's Way is Christ and Him Crucified Alone; as well, the 'many waters' are a symbol for multitudes of people)***:**

"With whom *(the great whore, i.e., all type of religions)* **the kings of the Earth** *(from the very beginning, most nations have been ruled by some type of religion)* **have committed fornication** *(all religions devised by men, and even the parts of Christianity that have been corrupted, are labeled by the Lord as 'spiritual fornication' [Rom. 7:1-4])***, and the inhabitants of the Earth have been made drunk with the wine of her fornication** *(proclaims the addiction of religion; the doing of religion is the most powerful narcotic there is)***" (Rev. 17:1-2).**

All of this means that all religion is devised either by demon spirits, men, or a combination of both. In any case, as stated, it is unacceptable to God. Religion is Satan's substitute for the reality of Christ.

To describe religion, the Holy Spirit used

one of the most base, descriptive phrases (the great whore) that could be used. He did this for purpose.

The simple meaning of the word is that it pertains to a woman who practices promiscuous sexual intercourse for hire. It also means, *"To pursue a faithless, unworthy, or idolatrous desire."*

Used in the spiritual sense, *"It pertains to religious favors offered for a price."* As well, it will stoop to any level, strike any bargain, and go to any length to attain its devious ends.

THE RELIGION OF ISLAM

I think I can say without fear of contradiction that the most destructive religion that's ever been birthed in the heart of evil man is the religion of Islam. In one overwhelming sense of the word, it is very much akin to the religion of Baal worship in Old Testament times. This form of worship majored in human sacrifice, and I think it is overly obvious that the religion of Islam follows suit.

This religion, as stated, made its debut in A.D. 622. It began with Muhammad of the tribe of Quraysh in Mecca. He claimed to have received a revelation that God (Allah) was *"one"* and that he (Muhammad) was to be Allah's messenger of that truth.

He began this religion by making converts of some of his family members and close friends. Due to opposition, he left Mecca and went to the town of Medina, both in present day Saudi Arabia. This particular episode, his flight from Mecca to Medina, is now viewed as year *"one"* on the Islamic calendar. But, actually, it was the year A.D. 622.

THE JEWS

In Medina, Muhammad came into contact with a large Jewish community. Evidently, his dealing with them resulted in him being influenced in that he adopted some of the Jewish practices. For example, at least at that particular time, he taught that faithful Muslims should pray facing Jerusalem. The Jews did the same thing and, in fact, had been doing the same thing for some 1,500 years. When the Jews rejected the message of Islam, which they did unequivocally, only then did he change his method of praying by directing prayers toward Mecca.

He also taught his followers to fast on the tenth day of Tishri, the same day as the Jewish fast of Yom Kippur. This was later expanded to include the entire month of Ramadan; however, it should be added that this so-called *"fast"* only includes the daylight hours. At night they can eat whatever they desire.

In his so-called revelation, he also demanded that his followers abstain from pork and, as well, that all little Muslim boys be circumcised, which, as most know, are standard Jewish practices.

He claimed to accept the Jewish Prophets of Noah, Abraham, Moses, and David. He also included Adam in this list, as well as the *"Prophet Jesus."* And yet, he strongly rejected the idea of the Deity of Christ. So, it's difficult to understand how that he could claim that Jesus was a great Prophet while, at the same time, being a liar, considering how much our Lord affirmed His Personal Deity.

MUHAMMAD

Muhammad claimed that he was personally *"the seal of Prophecy,"* meaning that he was God's final Messenger. While he accepted some of the Scriptures of the Old Testament as well as the New Testament, still, he always perverted the Text. At any rate, his *"revelations,"* embodied in the Koran, became the authoritative *"scriptures"* for his faithful followers. These followers were called and are called *"Muslims,"* from the Arabic word *"Islam,"* meaning *"submission to the one God."*

Due to his acceptance of some of the Jewish practices, he felt that surely the Jews would accept his message of *"one God."* He found to his dismay that the Jewish Rabbis gave him no credence whatsoever, ridiculing his illiteracy, and especially his confusion of Biblical traditions. But, above all, the Jewish people could not even remotely accept a non-Israelite as God's *"seal of Prophecy."*

In a rage because of the rejection of the Jews, he initiated a policy of extermination that resulted in thousands of Jews being massacred, with thousands of others being evicted from their homes and, in fact, from

northern Arabia.

THE ARAB-ISRAELI CONFLICT

To understand the Arab-Israeli conflict, we must try to understand the attitude of Islam toward the Jewish people.

The land that we presently refer to as *"Israel"* or *"Palestine"* was conquered and ruled by the Muslims from the Seventh Century to the Twentieth Century.

There was one interruption during this period of time, and that was when the *"Christian"* crusaders ruled the land for less than 100 years. Islam presently finds it unacceptable that this land, originally conquered for Allah by his followers, now be ruled by the Jews, a people who they consider to be inferior and subservient. At least, that is the way it is pictured in the Koran.

The Muslims do not consider the Bible to be the Word of God, but rather the Koran. Therefore, they find it impossible to acknowledge the historic reality that the land of Israel, according to the Bible, belongs to the Jews. This is the real key to understanding the impasse that exists in Israel presently. The Arab countries, predominantly Muslim, refuse to accept a foreign, Jewish presence in a land that is supposed to be, according to them, a part of the *"world of Islam."*

THE MODERN CONTENTION

Regrettably, most people in the world presently, and we speak of those who are not Muslim or Jewish, think that the problem in Israel, as it regards the Palestinians, is that Israel will not allow the Palestinians to have a separate state. Also, if the evil Jews, or so the world thinks, would only allow these poor Palestinians to have their own land, all the problems would then be solved. Let's look at that a little closer.

THE TRUTH

That which the world erroneously thinks has absolutely nothing to do with the problem at hand in Israel as it regards the Palestinians. In fact, Israel has tried again and again to give the Palestinians particular areas they could call their own, the Gaza Strip being an example. In fact, not so long before Yasser Arafat died, Israel agreed to all his demands regarding a separate state with the exception of one. They would not give up Jerusalem, which he demanded as the capital of the new country of Palestine. So, the talks fell apart.

The truth is, the Muslims demand two things. They are:

1. Every Jew in Israel dead; and

2. The entire land of Israel, thereby, being Muslim, with the name changed to *"Palestine."*

From the time of the inception of Israel as a state in 1948, the Muslims have initiated several wars with this view in mind. They have lost each one of those wars. And the reader should keep the following in mind.

ISRAELI COMPASSION

Even though the Muslims initiated each one of these wars against Israel, with Israel coming out victor in each one, still, the Israeli's allowed the Muslims to remain in the land. Had the scene been reversed and the Muslims having won any one of these conflicts, as stated, every Jew would have been massacred.

PALESTINIANS?

Actually, there is no such thing as a nationality of people, or even a segment of people, who can honestly be referred to as *"Palestinians."* The truth is, all the so-called Palestinians in Israel presently are actually Jordanians, Egyptians, Syrians, etc.

The word or name *"Palestinian"* actually has its roots in the name *"Philistines,"* who inhabited the area presently called Gaza in Old Testament times. To be sure, the modern Palestinians are not descendants of the ancient Philistines.

If it is to be noticed, not a single one of the Arab states in the Middle East will allow any of the Palestinians to immigrate to their country. In other words, they are forced to remain where they are in Israel in order that they be a thorn in Israel's side, and, as well, providing occasion for the world to blame Israel when, in reality, the fault is not that of Israel at all.

America has been pouring hundreds of millions of dollars into the Gaza Strip, and to the Palestinians in general, over the last

several years, all to no avail. In other words, the money seldom gets to the people but is stolen by the Muslim leaders.

As well, immediately after September 11, 2001 (9/11), the Palestinians were in the streets rejoicing over our terrible loss, despite the hundreds of millions squandered on this lost effort. They were quickly told by the Palestinian authorities, whomever that may have been, to stop their rejoicing because that may cause America to cut off the money flow. Once again, it's not Uncle Sam, but rather Uncle Sap!

JEHOVAH OR ALLAH?

Respecting what has been said, the impetus behind the Muslim determination to destroy Israel cannot be narrowly defined as a family affair, even though both entities are direct descendants of Abraham (Isaac and Ishmael), or so it is believed by some.

The conflict is much deeper than that, in fact, even beyond the comprehension and understanding of the Muslims themselves.

Yes, there is the matter of engendered jealousy over Ishmael being passed over as the recipient of the Abrahamic Covenant given to the Patriarch by the Lord. That Blessing and the Promise of perpetual ownership of the land of Israel fell to Isaac and his heirs, which are the Jews.

"And God said, Sarah your wife shall bear you a son indeed; and you shall call his name Isaac: and I will establish My Covenant with him for an Everlasting Covenant, and with his seed after him" (Gen. 17:19).

But, as well, Ishmael was also given the promise of becoming *"a great nation"* (Gen. 21:18)—a nation so great *"that it shall not be numbered for multitude"* (Gen. 16:10). That Promise has been faithfully fulfilled by God. Tiny Israel floats in the middle of a sea of Arab nations scattered across a large portion of the globe, but with the greatest concentration in the Middle East.

THE LAND OF ISRAEL

The land area of the State of Israel presently occupied by the Israelis is only about one-tenth of one percent of the entire land mass occupied by the Muslims in the Middle East. Now, think about what I've just said.

That means that the Muslims in the Middle East have approximately 1,000 times more land area than the Israelis, and yet, they're demanding this little bit as well!

It all boils down to the Muslims refusing to accept the Bible; therefore, they reject that which was stipulated by the Lord concerning this very thing, so long, long ago.

There are basically two differences between God's Covenant with the Jews and His Covenant with the Ishmaelites. Israel was specifically given the land called Palestine or Israel (Gen. 13:14-17; 17:6-8, 19-21; 28:3-4). The paramount difference, however, is discovered in these words, as stated:

"And I will bless them who bless you, and curse him who curses you: and in you shall all families of the Earth be blessed" (Gen. 12:3).

The Promise is further defined in Genesis 22:18:

"And in your seed shall all the nations of the Earth be blessed." That "Seed" of blessing delivered to the Gentile nations through the Jewish people—including Arabs—was and is "The Messiah, the Lord Jesus Christ," which the world of Islam will not recognize.

Paul said:

"Now to Abraham and his Seed were the Promises made. He said not, And to Seeds, as of many; but as of One, And to your Seed, which is Christ" (Gal. 3:16).

THE SEED

The presence and assigned mission of the Jews were, therefore, uniquely set apart in marked contrast to those described as characteristic of Ishmael's seed and national legacy. The "Seed" component in God's Program for humanity surpasses every other aspect of history. In addition to being the Saviour of men, Messiah is also the King. When His Kingdom finally arrives, He will establish and enforce stability. The One Who could so bless mankind was the exclusive province of Abraham's Seed through Isaac. The Promise is specific. The Abrahamic Covenant provides the following:

• A King for the Throne:
"And kings shall come out of you" (Gen. 17:6).

NOTES

• A land for the King:
"And I will give unto you, and to your seed after you, the land wherein you are a stranger, all the land of Canaan" (Gen. 17:8).

• A people for the King:
"And I will be their God" (Gen. 17:8).

THE BLESSING ASPECT

It was the "Blessing" aspect of the Covenant that developed the animosity in Esau's posterity because the Blessing fell to Jacob rather than to Esau, who fathered their people. Had the Arabs embraced obediently the Saviour and kingly aspect of the Blessings of the Messiah, history would have taken another course.

These residual resentments became deeply ingrained in the attitudes of the Arabs toward Israel, and those resentments spun off in manifold and discernable ways as the centuries passed. Scripture is replete with accounts of the heirs of Ishmael who warred against Israel while growling their determination to "Come, and let us cut them off from being a nation; that the name of Israel may be no more in remembrance.

"For they have consulted together with one consent . . ." (Ps. 83:4-5). Their "one consent" was the extermination of the Nation of Israel.

However, I must remind all and sundry that all who have said that and tried to bring it to pass have met, and without exception, an untimely end.

Since the days of the Psalmist, Arab determination has not wavered; however, the entrance of the new religion, Islam (Seventh Century A.D.), refined and sanctified the rationale. It then became incumbent to subjugate or exterminate Jews "in God's Name."

The whole world has witnessed the tirade of the Iranian president, Mahmoud Ahmabinejad, stating, in effect, that "the Jews should be wiped from the face of the Earth."

A man named Sheikh As'ad Tamini, who claims leadership of "Islamic Jihad Beit Al-Maqudis," focused the issue in a statement made some years ago, lauding such behavior. His statement concerned a remark having been made by the late president Hussein, as that tyrant spoke of unleashing chemical weapons against Israel. Hussein stated, *"The killing of Jews will continue – killing, killing in God's name, until they vanish." Tamini responded, "I hope he is as good as his word."*

Thus, the *"Allah"* discovered by Muhammad was a very different god from the God found in the Bible. Muhammad's religion, which, in his view, was to replace Judaism and Christianity, would have a new book (the Koran), a new look (Friday), and a new center of worship (Mecca), all brought about by wholesale murder.

JIHAD

The word *"Jihad"* is one of the great words of the Muslim vocabulary. In effect, it is a declaration of war against all and everything that's not Muslim. They claim that to die in Jihad is to be assured a place in Heaven.

THE VIEW OF HEAVEN IN THE KORAN

• Koran 44:51 through 59 says that large-eyed virgins are awaiting Muslims in Heaven.

• It says the female virgins will have large *"swelling breasts"* (Koran 78:31-35).

• In Heaven the virginity of these women, according to the Koran, will be automatically restored after each encounter (Koran 56:35).

• Men in paradise will recline on couches surrounded by fruit, meats, and beautiful women (Koran 52:16-22).

• The Koran says that Muslim men in Heaven will have a virtual assortment of sex, in other words, whatever is desired (Koran 55:62-77).

• In the Hadiph, it is said that men will have the availability of 72 virgins and, in fact, there will also be a free sex market for both men and women (Hadiph Al Hadis Vol. 4, Page 172, No. 34).

• The Koran claims that in Heaven men will enjoy a fountain of wine, which they can enjoy without ever getting drunk (Koran 37:45).

• The Koran also states that those who wish for the pleasure of young boys will find many in paradise (Koran 76:19).

HOLY WAR?

Holy?

• The Koran states that all Muslims must fight until there is no worship but that of Allah (Koran 2:193; 8:39).

• Christians and Jews must be exterminated (Koran 2:193; 9:5, 29-30).

• Those who convert to Christianity or leave the Islamic religion for any reason must be killed (Koran 4:91). Muhammad said, *"Whosoever changes his religion, kill him"* (Al-Bukhari 9:57).

• Those who criticize Islam must be killed (Koran 9:12; 45:9).

• Those who cut off the heads of infidels are guaranteed a paradise (Koran 47:4-6).

• By killing, one is following the example of Muhammad, who killed as well (Koran 33:21).

• The Prophets of Islam are to promote terrorism (Koran 17:59).

• As it regards all of this, symbolically, the modern State of Israel stands as a constant reminder to rabid fundamentalist Muslims of their humiliation before infidels—a condition that can only be remedied through conquest.

RELIGIOUS DOMINANCE

The issue of land in the Middle East, namely Israel, while very important, is not primarily the great question. The great question concerns religious dominance—the lack of which is intolerable to the Muslim, who is taught that Allah is all and is to possess all.

An abiding tenet of Islam is that all lands are to be subject to Allah. Therefore, once a territory is taken, it must remain under Muslim domination. If land is lost, holy war (Jihad) becomes necessary. Any concessions or treaties made with enemies under conditions making it impossible to restore dominion by force are observed only until means are available to remedy the situation.

For this reason, as Arab spokesmen have repeatedly avowed, any negotiated peace agreement with Israel will only provide a staging area from which to pursue total elimination of the Jewish presence from land claimed to be sacred to Allah. Hence, the negotiations and peace treaties with the Palestinians regarding the Gaza Strip, Jericho, the West Bank and Jerusalem, should be looked at accordingly. In such a perpetual state of conflict, Israelis know all too well that the western world must learn or live to regret—survival against the Muslim onslaught means having a superior strength and the will to use it.

MUSLIM EVANGELISM

The Muslims, beyond the shadow of a doubt, are bent on possessing this Planet for Allah, either by coercion or persuasion. They do not lack the will to use whatever means necessary, even to the slaughter of millions, along the way. By devious means, they are making great headway around the world.

In France, Islam ranks second only to Catholicism. England has received such a massive influx of Muslims, so many, in fact, that the face of the landscape has literally changed. In 1945, there was one mosque in England; in 2007, there were over 3,000. In fact, London is the site of the largest mosque in Western Europe. The story is the same in North America.

The first mosque in the United States was built in Cedar Rapids, Iowa, in 1934. In 1989, there were approximately 700 mosques in the United States. By 2007, there were well over 2,000.

Muslims lay claim to some 10 million adherents to Islam in North America, drawn mostly from the black population. Actually, these converts to Islam in America call Christianity *"the white man's religion,"* while Islam is called *"the black man's religion."* In 1989, the Muslims boasted that they would soon surpass the Jewish population in this country. In fact, they have reached their goal.

Some years ago, Dr. Ishmael Faruqui challenged Muslims to pursue a goal of 50 million to 75 million new American converts to Islam. He said, *"Only from massive conversion can we hope to elect Muslim politicians, appoint Muslim judges, and incorporate Shariah law into the judicial system of America. We must transcend our minority status to make Islam a dominant force in America and the West."*

Considering this, we must understand that *"Shariah Law"* is about the worst thing that can happen to anyone. It is a throwback

NOTES

to the Dark Ages. In this particular law, women are looked at as no more than cheap goods. In fact, there is no equality or freedom in this law. If the truth be known, *"Shariah Law"* was designed by demon spirits.

As well, we must understand that students from Islam countries now form the largest group of international students in North American universities and colleges.

THE ULTIMATE STRUGGLE

There is only one answer for this scourge that threatens the entirety of the world, and especially the nation of America. In fact, there is only one answer for the entirety of mankind, and that answer is the Lord Jesus Christ and what He did for us at the Cross of Calvary.

The ultimate struggle is not territory or the subjugation of people by force; it is, instead, the acceptance or rejection of the Lord Jesus Christ, Who Alone can save.

Muhammad claimed to have a revelation from God. In fact, he did have a revelation, and of that there can be no doubt; however, it was not from God, but rather from demon spirits. As a result, He has succeeded only in leading millions deeper into spiritual darkness.

When one looks at the tens of thousands kneeling around the sacred Kaba in Mecca (so-called sacred), surely he is moved with a deep sense of sadness. There is no salvation in that place or in the stone before which they kneel. The only hope of Salvation for the Muslim world and, in fact, for everyone, is to bow at the Feet of the Lord Jesus Christ, accepting Him as Saviour and as Lord (Jn. 3:3; 14:6; Rom. 10:8-9, 13).

THE LORD JESUS CHRIST

The Scripture says, and I quote from THE EXPOSITOR'S STUDY BIBLE:

"And being found in fashion as a man *(denotes Christ in men's eyes),* **He humbled Himself** *(He was brought low, but willingly),* **and became obedient unto death** *(does not mean He became obedient to death; He was always the Master of Death; rather, He subjected Himself to death),* **even the death of the Cross.** *(This presents the character of His Death as one of disgrace and* *degradation, which was necessary for men to be redeemed. This type of death alone would pay the terrible sin debt, and do so in totality.)*

"Wherefore God also has highly exalted Him *(to a place of supreme Majesty; Jesus has always been Creator, but now He is Saviour as well)*, **and given Him a Name which is above every name** *(actually says, 'The Name,' referring to a specific Name and Title; that Name, as Verse 11 proclaims, is 'Lord')*:

"That at the Name of Jesus every knee should bow *(in the sphere of the Name, which refers to all it entails; all of this is a result of the Cross, the price paid there, and the Redemption consequently afforded)*, **of** *things* **in Heaven, and** *things* **in earth, and** *things* **under the earth** *(all Creation will render homage, whether animate or inanimate)*;

"And *that* **every tongue should confess that Jesus Christ** *is* **Lord** *(proclaims 'Lord' as the 'Name' of Verse 9; it means 'Master' of all, which again has been made possible by the Cross)*, **to the Glory of God the Father.** *(The acknowledgement of the Glory of Christ is the acknowledgment of the Glory of the Father)*" **(Phil. 2:8-11).**

SOME PARTICULARS REGARDING ISLAM

• Jerusalem is the third holiest place in Islam, after Mecca and Medina—the latter two both in Saudi Arabia. Tradition has it that the prophet Muhammad journeyed at night from Mecca to Jerusalem's Al-Aqsa Mosque, and from there ascended to Heaven on a winged horse; however, there is no proof that Muhammad was ever in Jerusalem.

• About ninety percent of all Muslims are Suni's—considered the orthodox sect. Of the dissident sects of Islam, the largest and most important are Shiites—fundamentalists, as in Iran. A split came in A.D. 680 over the dreadful manner in which Suni's tortured and killed Shiite leader Caliph Yazid.

• Some 70 sects and offshoots of Islam have arisen because of doctrinal differences, which, in some cases, are irreconcilable.

• Muslims recognize the Torah (first five Books of the Old Testament), the Psalms, and the Gospels of the New Testament;

NOTES

however, they believe that only the Koran preserves the truth as it was given by God. It is, therefore, they say, the only true book.

• The Koran speaks of a line of Prophets, beginning with Adam and ending with Muhammad. Both Jesus and Moses, according to the Muslims, are part of this line although they vehemently deny the Deity of Christ.

• Muslims vehemently reject the Christian Doctrine of the Trinity as sinful and blasphemous.

• In Islam, there is no separation between the religious and the secular. All Islamic nations ostensibly declare their adherence to that concept.

• The concept of Islamic Law (Shariah Law) is all-inclusive. It embraces all aspects of human life and endeavor, both private and public, devotional and secular, civil and criminal.

• Jihad, meaning striving or struggle, is a term that has acquired the Islamic connotation of religious or holy war. Today, however, Jihad has developed into a broader context of striving for the common well-being of Islam and Muslims, and not necessarily exclusively on military terms.

• The birth rate in Islam is 42 per 1,000, while in the western world, it is only 13 per 1,000.

(Some of the information respecting Islam was derived from articles written by Elwood McQuade, Editor of *"The Friends of Israel Gospel Ministry"*, and Will Varner, Dean of the Institute of Biblical Studies of that same organization.)

THE CONTRIBUTION OF ISLAM TO THE WORLD

Before the question of Islam's contribution to the world, it should be noted that the Koran is the guidance for all that is done by the Muslims. The Koran is their guiding light. They derive, as previously stated, their terrorist activities from the Koran. They guide their daily lives and living by the Koran. They guide their business activities by the Koran.

In fact, there is no such thing as a separation of religion and state as it regards Islam and the Koran. Religion and the state are one and the same, all guided, as stated, by the Koran.

So, the question should be asked as to where the Koran has led the world of Islam. Guided by the Koran, what contributions have the Muslims made to the betterment of humanity? I think that's a good question!

THE ROLE OF WOMEN IN THE RELIGION OF ISLAM

Has the Koran bettered the lot of women? What type of place and position do they occupy as it regards this religion?

Off the bat, so to speak, Koran 4:34 states, *"Men are superior to women on account of the qualities with which God has gifted the one above the other."* So, immediately, it is known as to what the religion of Islam thinks of women. In fact, women are looked at as mere property, somewhat like a field for men to plow whenever and however they like (Koran 2:223).

Also, the Koran states that men are free to have as many as four wives at a time if they so desire (Koran 4:3).

According to the Koran, men have the right to cohabit with women before marriage (Koran 4:24). And, oh yes, the Koran states that women must hide their faces with a veil, which is obvious to all who observe women in that religion (Koran 33:59). As well, in the religion of Islam, men can have as many female slaves as they so desire, and they may feel free to have sex with them as much as they desire (Koran 4:24).

I think it should be obvious, at least, if the Koran is a guide, that women are given little shift in the religion of Islam. As stated, they are no more than property, just objects.

TOLERANCE FOR OTHER RELIGIONS

While Christianity is very evangelistic, or, at least, it should be, Evangelism is simply the telling of the Story of the Lord Jesus Christ and His Power to save. The idea of exterminating all who are not Christians is alien to the Christian Faith. The Word of God admonishes us to love all people, irrespective of whom they might be, including Muslims (Mat. 5:43; 22:39; Mk. 12:31; Lk. 10:27; Rom. 13:9). In the world of Islam, however, there is really no tolerance for

NOTES

other religions.

Evangelism, as it regards the world of Islam, is almost altogether by force. Koran 2:193 says, *"Fight therefore against them until . . . the only worship be that of Allah."* Of course, friendship with Christians and Jews are not allowed (Koran 5:51).

All religions other than Islam are merely tolerated. The reader must understand, if Islam had the power to do so, they would kill every non-Believer (those who do not believe in the religion of Islam), or, at least, make slaves of them. They do not lack the will as it regards this horror, only the way. If they had the power to do so, they would make the world one gigantic blood bath. If we fail to see that, and if we fail to understand that, we are only deceiving ourselves.

JEWS AND AFRICANS

The Koran states that Allah will not allow Africans into Heaven (Koran 3:106).

The Koran also states that all Jews are cursed by Allah (Koran 4:46). In fact, Jews are looked at by Muslims as *"subhuman apes"* (Koran 2:65). During World War II, prominent Muslims joined with Nazism in order to kill Jews. In fact, certain Muslims aided and abetted in the slaughter of tens of thousands of Jews during that period of time.

Again addressing blacks, Muhammad called blacks *"raisin heads"* (Al Bukhri, Vol. 1, No. 662, and Vol. 9, No. 256).

Our African American friends should take note of this when they claim that Islam is the black man's religion, while Christianity is the white man's religion!

To the contrary, Biblical Christianity looks at the whole human race, irrespective of the nationality, as one. The Scripture says:

"God Who made the world and all things therein (*presents God as the Creator*)**, seeing that He is Lord of Heaven and Earth** (*proclaims Him not only as Creator, but the constant Manager of all that He has created as well*)**, dwells not in Temples made with hands** (*He is bigger than that!*)**;

"Neither is worshipped with men's hands (*the Second Commandment forbids the making of any graven image of God, or the worship of any type of statue, etc.*)**, as though He needed anything** (*God needs nothing!*)**,

seeing He gives to all life, and breath, and all things (*presents His Creation needing what He provides, which is provided by no other source*);

"And has made of one blood all nations of men for to dwell on all the face of the Earth (*proclaims all having their origin in Adam*)**, and has determined the times before appointed, and the bounds of their habitation** (*pertains to particular parts of the world, and those who occupy these areas; however, the statement, 'one blood all nations of men,' eliminates any type of racial superiority*);

The Word of God then tells us what man should do. It says:

"That they should seek the Lord (*presents the chief end of all God's Dealings with men [I Pet. 2:24; II Pet. 3:9; Jn. 3:15-20; Rev. 22:17]*)**, if haply they might feel after Him, and find Him** (*Paul is appealing to the action of logic and common sense in trying to address these Athenians*)**, though He be not far from every one of us** (*speaks of the Creator being very close to His Creation*)**:**

"For in Him we live, and move, and have our being (*proclaims God as the Source of all life*) **. . ." (Acts 17:24-28).**

As the Scriptures bear out, all men in the Eyes of God are the same. In fact, the Scripture also says, *"For God so loved the world . . ."* (Jn. 3:16).

TWO CLASSES

And yet, it can be said, as well, that the Lord looks at the entirety of the human race as consisting of two classes, those who are redeemed, meaning they have accepted the Lord Jesus Christ as their Saviour and Lord, and those who are unredeemed, meaning they have not accepted Him. With God, as I think it should be overly obvious, there is no racism. As well, there is no preference regarding gender. In other words, the Lord looks at men and women in the same capacity. Concerning that, the Scripture says, and I continue to quote from THE EXPOSITOR'S STUDY BIBLE:

ALL ONE IN CHRIST JESUS

"For you are all the Children of God by Faith in Christ Jesus. (*Every person who is Saved, and every person who has ever been or ever will be Saved, is Saved only by 'Faith in Christ Jesus,' which refers to what He did at the Cross.*)

"For as many of you as have been baptized into Christ (*refers to the Baptism into His Death at Calvary [Rom. 6:3-5]; the reference is not to Water Baptism*) **have put on Christ** (*means to be clothed with Him [Jn. 14:20]*)**.**

"There is neither Jew nor Greek, there is neither bond nor free, there is neither male nor female (*all have a common life in Christ Jesus*)**: for you are all one in Christ Jesus.** (*This proclaims an end of all class, status, and social distinction. This phrase alone answers all racism.*)

"And if you be Christ's, then are you Abraham's seed (*Christ is Abraham's Seed, so my union with Christ makes me Abraham's seed as well*)**, and heirs according to the Promise** (*heirs of God and joint heirs with Jesus Christ [Rom. 8:17]*)**" (Gal. 3:26-29).**

The Death of Christ on the Cross, which atoned for all sin, lifted the status of women to that of equal with man. Since the Cross, there is no distinction as it regards place, position, race, or gender.

ISLAMIC TERRORISM

On September 11, 2001, our nation tasted Muslim terrorism. Over 3,000 were killed when the twin towers in New York City were brought down by Muslims flying hijacked airplanes into them, along with the plane that crashed into the Pentagon in Washington, D.C. Many Muslims saw this as a fulfillment of Koran 4:78 where it says, *"Wherever you be, death will overtake you—although you be in lofty towers!"* All over the world this slaughter was celebrated by Muslims because it was done in obedience to Allah's command to fight nations, which are not worshipping Allah. As stated, the Koran is the guiding light for all Muslims, and, to be sure, the Koran advocates terrorism on a grand scale.

In the Koran, war is described as *"good"* (Koran 2:216). Also, Koran 3:169 states that all who die fighting the infidels will eat with Allah in the highest level of paradise

(Koran 3:169). In fact, this, among other so-called promises, is the means by which suicide bombers are recruited. The Koran states that slaughtering their infidels, and that speaks of all who do not subscribe to Islam, will gain one great reward in the next life (Koran 8:67).

Muhammad proclaimed himself an apostle of mass murder. Some 800 Jews in a particular conflict had surrendered to him. He tied their hands behind their backs and then cut their heads off, even after they had surrendered and were defenseless. He then went and had trenches dug, which was at the marketplace in Medina, and threw the heads of the Jews into these trenches.

These individuals were not killed in battle but were slaughtered while they were unarmed and had unconditionally surrendered. They were slaughtered in cold blood in order to gain their booty. So, that should give us an understanding of what and who the founder of Islam was. To be sure, many of his followers function in the same capacity.

THE NAME ALLAH

Also, it is a known fact that those who are Muslims and then convert to another religion must be killed (Koran 4:91). In fact, Muhammad said, *"Whosoever changes his religion, kill him"* (Al-Bukhari 9:57).

Most of us have seen over television Muslims cutting off the heads of their victims. This is done because it is claimed by the Koran that cutting off the heads of infidels assures one of paradise (Koran 47:4-6).

Koran 17:59 tells its prophets to spread terrorism.

Once again, all of this comes from the Koran.

When former President Bush stated before the whole world shortly after September 11, 2001 (9/11), that the Koran was a book of love and peace, his statement was not only 180 degrees wrong, but, to be frank, it was an abomination. When Mr. Bush in London was asked the question, *"Do Muslims and Christians pray to the same God?"* and the President answered, *"Yes,"* again, he could not have been more wrong.

The name *"Allah"* came from one of the so-called Babylonian deities chosen by

NOTES

Muhammad. It has no relationship to the God of the Bible. Let all understand that this *"Allah"* is actually a demon spirit, and when Muslims pray to this so-called god, they are actually praying to a demon spirit.

It may have been politically expedient for our President to say such a thing, but politically expedient or not, the truth is the truth, and a lie is a lie! Building our policy on a lie can never come out to a good end. We must ever understand that.

CONTRIBUTIONS?

The truth is, the religion of Islam has contributed absolutely nothing beneficial for mankind—absolutely nothing! In fact, it has contributed, as we have stated, slavery, terrorism, inequality, ignorance, superstition, murder, and mayhem. If such could be called contribution, that is their contribution.

There is not a university worthy of note in the Muslim world. If they want a decent education, they must attend a university in the western world. In fact, there are probably more Muslims in our universities in America, all from Muslim countries, mostly from the Middle East, than any other group of people. We are training them to be doctors, scientists, chemists, biochemists, etc. Regrettably, some, if not many of them, will use their education to try to destroy us. As well, beginning in preschool, little Muslim children are taught daily to hate Jews and Americans. In fact, this is looked at as a great part of their education.

Most Muslim countries, despite the influx of hundreds of billions of dollars for the purchase of oil, are little more than economic basket cases.

THE ECONOMY OF MUSLIM COUNTRIES

The following is the per capita income of Muslim countries. The numbers are from 2006, with the exception of the first one, which is 2004.
- Afghanistan: $800
- Bahrain: $25,800
- Iran: $8,700
- Iraq: $2,900
- Jordan: $5,100
- Kuwait: $23,100
- Lebanon: $5,700

- Malaysia: $12,900
- Morocco: $4,600
- Oman: $14,400
- Pakistan: $2,600
- Quatar: $29,800
- Saudi Arabia: $13,600
- Syria: $4,100
- United Arab Emirates: $49,700 (most of the money going into the U.A.E. is for the building of the super city of Dubai. The truth is, the people as a whole are notoriously poor, not sharing at all in the hundreds of billions that are going into the building of this city.)
- Yemen: $1,000
- United States: $44,000

In some of these countries, hundreds of billions of dollars are going into their coffers each year from the sale of oil; however, very little of it ever reaches the common people. This means that a handful of people are obscenely rich, while the rest are abjectly poor.

It is the ambition of Islam to conquer the entirety of the world. If such a thing came to pass, it's fairly simple to tell what the world then would be like by what is taking place in modern Islamic nations. We have heard about the Dark Ages. In fact, most Muslim nations are still in the Dark Ages. If the Muslims succeeded in taking over the entirety of the world, which, thankfully, they will not, the world would be plunged into a worse time of darkness than it has ever known previously.

Islam has made no contribution whatsoever in any capacity to the betterment of humanity, but rather the very opposite.

THE PEOPLE OF AMERICA AND ISLAM

It is strange, but tens of millions of people in the great nation of America, despite September 11, 2001 (9/11), do not seem to really see the evil of the religion of Islam. It is passed off as an honorable and great religion, which has been hijacked by a few fanatics. The facts are, nothing could be further from the truth.

Regrettably and sadly, we hide our heads in the sand, and I suppose it's because we do not want to face up to the truth. The Muslim world hates us, referring to America

as the *"Great Satan,"* and Israel as the *"little Satan."* Their ambition is to kill every Jew on the face of the Earth and take over the land of Israel in totality. They see the United States of America as the greatest hindrance to the fulfillment of that ambition.

Our nation is in trouble, and it's because we are leaving the Word of God. Regrettably, the deterioration of the fabric of this country has to do with the deterioration of the church. The Scripture plainly says:

"For the time *is come* that Judgment must begin at the House of God (*Judgment always begins with Believers and pertains to their Faith, whether in the Cross or otherwise; the Cross alone is spared Judgment, for there Jesus was judged in our place*): **and if *it* first *begin* at us, what shall the end *be* of them who obey not the Gospel of God?** (*If God will judge His Own, how much more will He judge the unredeemed? The Cross alone stays the Judgment of God. Let that ever be understood.*)

"And if the Righteous scarcely be Saved (*can be Saved only by trusting Christ and what He did for us at the Cross, and nothing else*)**, where shall the ungodly and the sinner appear?** (*If the great Sacrifice of Christ is rejected and spurned, where does that leave those who do such a thing? There is no hope for their Salvation*)**" (I Pet. 4:17-18).**

WHAT SHOULD THE U.S. DO ABOUT ISLAM?

What the U.S. should do, and what the U.S. is doing, are two different things altogether. America is notorious for not seeing the obvious. Heretofore, the Lord has grandly watched over this great nation, but the modern church has drifted so far from the Biblical model that, regrettably, anything could happen. As the Church goes, so goes the nation.

A POLICY BASED ON A LIE

That policy consists of the idea, grossly erroneous, I might quickly add, that the religion of Islam is peaceable and righteous and that it has been hijacked by a few fanatics. Nothing could be further from the truth. As we have stated elsewhere in this dissertation, the religion of Islam is based entirely upon the Koran. To be sure, the Koran advocates terrorism, and even the slaughter of untold millions, if necessary, to further the cause of this religion. While all Muslims aren't murderers, still, all Muslims belong to a religion that strongly advocates wholesale murder, all in the name of Allah. As well, this wholesale murder includes mostly innocent victims.

We have spent over a trillion dollars in Iraq and have spilled the blood of over 4,000 young men and young ladies based on this false policy. We don't seem to understand that this religion is not peaceable, is not righteous, and, in fact, holds to no principles whatsoever, which are very special in our way of thinking. I speak of honor, honesty, integrity, truthfulness, etc. Those things are foreign to the religion of Islam.

THE GREATEST DANGER

America, I believe, is facing a greater danger presently than it has ever faced in the entirety of its history, greater than the Cold War, greater than Vietnam, etc. This danger is exacerbated when we realize that President Obama is a Muslim sympathizer. In fact, Muslims now head up Homeland Security. That's like putting a fox in charge of the hen house.

Technologically, it is now possible for an atomic bomb to be constructed, which is no larger than a softball. In other words, it can be easily carried in a suitcase, etc. Such a bomb could destroy much of New York City, much of Washington, D.C., or any other large American city, with literally hundreds of thousands of dead and hundreds of thousands of others dying.

The Muslims hate us. If they can get their hands on such a weapon, and knowing they have claimed they will use such, we have to take them at their word. September 11, 2001, should have been a wake-up call! Again, it is the religion of Islam as a whole that is the danger and not just a few radicals.

As we have stated, all Muslims aren't murderers! However, all Muslims are a part of a wicked system, which operates on the premise of wholesale murder.

In the 1930's and 1940's, all Germans who were members of the Nazi party were not

NOTES

murderers. Nevertheless, they were a part of the most horrifying, murderous regime that possibly the world ever knew, at least, up to that time. Incidentally, many leading Muslims were a part of the Nazi butchery because of their hatred for the Jews.

Concerning the efforts made by Muslim terrorists to set off two gasoline bombs in London in June of 2007, as well as the effort in Scotland, which was thwarted by the Mercy and Grace of God, many of our news pundits were totally confused that the culprits in these efforts were not the usual stereotype, but rather Muslim medical doctors. The same thing could be said concerning the Muslim psychiatrist at Fort Hood in Texas.

"How could they do such a thing, considering that they had a good living?" was the question asked! How could individuals of this nature, some of them extremely intelligent, attempt such a barbaric action?

Once again, these newsmen, operating from the principle of radical Islam, did not and do not understand that it is the religion of Islam, and not merely a few malcontents, that nurtures such murderous action.

Will it take an atomic bomb leveling a great part of one of our major cities, with hundreds of thousands of casualties, to wake us up to the truth?

POLITICAL CORRECTNESS

Colin Powell, the former Secretary of State, angry with me and several others who had told the truth about Islam, made the ridiculous statement, *"We need more Muslims in this country."* I wonder if our good former Secretary of State has stopped to realize what is presently taking place in Denmark, France, Germany, Great Britain, etc., who opened their doors to the Muslim world.

I'll say it again: our nation is facing a greater danger presently than it has ever faced before. Sadder yet, that danger, which could result in untold numbers of casualties, is being brought on by ignorance, blindness, or both! As someone has well said, *"There are none so blind as those who will not see."*

So-called political correctness is killing us. Almost all the time it refers to a policy that doesn't make sense because it is, in fact, nonsensical.

WHAT POLICY TOWARDS THE MUSLIMS SHOULD OUR NATION HAVE?

• This huge lie of a few radicals having hijacked the Muslim religion should be laid to rest. The truth should be told denoting the fact that it is the religion of Islam, which is the cause of virtually all the terrorism in the world today.

• We should not allow any more Muslims to immigrate into our country. Muslim students studying in our colleges and universities should be sent back to their respected countries. Training scientists, among others, who later on could very well use their knowledge to wreak havoc on this nation is not exactly wise.

• We should know what is going on in the many mosques in this nation where most of the plans for terrorism are fomented.

• Muslims who foment terroristic plans against this nation, in any capacity, should be immediately deported when found out.

• Should we outlaw the Muslim religion? No, that's not our way. However, as stated, we should know, unequivocally so, what the religion of Islam actually is and conduct ourselves accordingly.

Now, will any of this be done? Regrettably, not in a million years! Once again, it's not really Uncle Sam, but rather Uncle Sap!

I close this dissertation by once again asking the question, *"Is it going to take the destruction of one of our cities, with hundreds of thousands of casualties, before we finally come to the truth?"* Someone has stated that the only reason this has not yet happened is because the Muslims, due to the insanity of some of our leaders, are making more headway in this nation by the present means they have adopted.

Also, we must not forget that even those who refer to themselves as *"moderate Muslims"* are in sympathy with the terrorists. Once again, it is the religion that is the problem!

Muslims do not lack the will to carry out their ambition of taking over the world, only the way. We are fools if we do not understand that if they had their way, and they had the power to back it up, every non-Muslim in the world would be forced to convert to Islam or

NOTES

be killed or made slaves. In fact, if the Muslims had their way, the world would be plunged into another Dark Ages of unprecedented proportions. Actually, it is only the might and power of America at this time, and I might quickly add, the help of the Lord, that stands between this scourge and total oblivion.

"Because sentence against an evil work is not executed speedily, therefore the heart of the sons of men is fully set in them to do evil. *(The government is morally and spiritually obligated to put down all 'evil work,' whether in the hearts and lives of individuals or in entire nations. To not do so will only increase the evil)*" **(Eccl. 8:11).**

(9) "PROCLAIM YOU THIS AMONG THE GENTILES; PREPARE WAR, WAKE UP THE MIGHTY MEN, LET ALL THE MEN OF WAR DRAW NEAR; LET THEM COME UP:

(10) "BEAT YOUR PLOWSHARES INTO SWORDS, AND YOUR PRUNING-HOOKS INTO SPEARS: LET THE WEAK SAY, I AM STRONG.

(11) "ASSEMBLE YOURSELVES, AND COME, ALL YOU HEATHEN, AND GATHER YOURSELVES TOGETHER ROUND ABOUT: THITHER CAUSE YOUR MIGHTY ONES TO COME DOWN, O LORD.

(12) "LET THE HEATHEN BE WAKENED, AND COME UP TO THE VALLEY OF JEHOSHAPHAT: FOR THERE WILL I SIT TO JUDGE ALL THE HEATHEN ROUND ABOUT."

The pattern is:

1. (Vs. 9) Verses 9 through 11 picture the assembling of the mighty army which the Antichrist will lead against Jerusalem.

2. Verse 10 proclaims the nations of the world under the domain of the Antichrist preparing for war against Israel, who is now recovering herself somewhat since her defeat by the Antichrist some three and a half years before.

3. Verse 11 refers to Revelation 16:16.

4. Verse 12 pertains to the Battle of Armageddon, when the Lord will judge the nations of the world. It will not be a pretty picture (Ezek., Chpts. 38-39).

PREPARE FOR WAR

As stated, Verses 9 through 11 picture

the assembling of the mighty army, which the Antichrist is to lead against Jerusalem. Here the army is envisioned by the Prophecies; other Prophecies direct attention to its Commander. Thus, the Holy Spirit parted Prophetic facts among Prophetic Preachers.

The phrase, *"You proclaim this among the Gentiles,"* refers to the armies under the Antichrist, which are bitterly opposed to Christ as well as Israel.

This conflict is far more involved than the mere contest of one battle, as severe as it may be. It involves Gentile domination from the time of Nebuchadnezzar all the way through the Antichrist. It is the signal that such domination is coming to an end, with Israel then to be restored to her place and position as the leading Nation in the world, as promised.

While it is true that the Gentiles, at least partly, have recognized Christ as the Son of God and, therefore, the Saviour of the world, with Israel rejecting Him, still, the Church, made up mostly of Gentiles, has by now been raptured away. Consequently, the remaining Gentiles, at least, for the most part, are bitterly opposed to Christ and will gladly throw in their lot with the Antichrist.

This does not mean, however, that every nation in the world will join with the Antichrist, but it does mean that many, if not most, will.

The phrase, *"Prepare war, wake up the mighty men,"* has to do with the Lord throwing down the gauntlet, so to speak.

The Antichrist, especially during the last three and a half years of the Great Tribulation, will speak tremendous things against the Lord. Daniel said, *"And he shall speak great words against the Most High . . ."* (Dan. 7:25). Therefore, the Lord will take him up on his challenge.

The phrase, *"Let all the men of war draw near; let them come up,"* has to do with *"the way of the kings of the east being prepared"* to help the Antichrist at *"Armageddon"* (Rev. 16:12, 16).

BEAT YOUR PLOWSHARES INTO SWORDS

Isaiah, saying the very opposite of the

heading, and speaking of the Millennium, said, *"Shall beat their swords into plowshares,"* while Joel, speaking of the Battle of Armageddon, speaks of the greatest military buildup possibly of all time!

Revelation, Chapter 16 says, *"And I saw three unclean spirits like frogs come out of the mouth of the dragon, and out of the mouth of the beast, and out of the mouth of the false prophet"* (Rev. 16:13), which will be for the express purpose of mobilizing the nations at Armageddon. Then, *"Let the weak say, I am strong."*

At that time, the nations of the world will be grandly deceived by the Antichrist, and that deception will be aided and abetted by these *"unclean spirits."*

At the height of the Cold War, a million dollars a minute, 24 hours a day, 7 days a week, was being spent upon weapons. Although that has abated somewhat at the present, still, a tremendous amount of money continues to be spent in this capacity. The phraseology of this Scripture demands that the arming process of that hour will equal, or even surpass, what has been done in the past, at least, on some scale!

So, we have here Prophecies being given concerning the coming Battle of Armageddon, which actually were given approximately 2,500 years ago or more. As well, we can be certain that what the Lord has said will happen most definitely will take place.

THE ANTICHRIST AND ARMAGEDDON

All the time the Antichrist will think that the plans are his as it regards mobilization and his determination to wipe Israel, so to speak, from the face of the Earth. However, what he doesn't realize is that the Lord is leading him into a trap. As a result, the nations of the world, which throw in their lot with the man of sin, ever how many that will be, with every determination to completely annihilate Israel, will be brought to one particular place, *"the Valley of Jehoshaphat,"* with the Lord saying, *"For there will I sit to judge all the heathen roundabout."* Man is foolish, and overly so, if he thinks he can outwit God! But, regrettably, many, if not most, think just that. The Antichrist will find to his utter dismay that this battle will not turn out as he envisioned, but, in reality, it will be his destruction.

(13) "PUT YOU IN THE SICKLE, FOR THE HARVEST IS RIPE: COME, GET YOU DOWN; FOR THE PRESS IS FULL, THE FATS OVERFLOW; FOR THEIR WICKEDNESS IS GREAT.

(14) "MULTITUDES, MULTITUDES IN THE VALLEY OF DECISION: FOR THE DAY OF THE LORD IS NEAR IN THE VALLEY OF DECISION.

(15) "THE SUN AND THE MOON SHALL BE DARKENED, AND THE STARS SHALL WITHDRAW THEIR SHINING.

(16) "THE LORD ALSO SHALL ROAR OUT OF ZION, AND UTTER HIS VOICE FROM JERUSALEM; AND THE HEAVENS AND THE EARTH SHALL SHAKE: BUT THE LORD WILL BE THE HOPE OF HIS PEOPLE, AND THE STRENGTH OF THE CHILDREN OF ISRAEL."

The construction is:

1. Verse 13 has to do with Revelation 14:16, 20.

2. This *"Valley of Jehoshaphat,"* where the Battle of Armageddon, at least partially, shall be fought, is referred to in Verse 14 as *"the valley of decision."* It means that the Lord has made the *"decision"* to there meet Satan and his man, the Antichrist, which will instigate the Second Coming.

3. Verse 15 proclaims a literal happening, which will take place at the Second Advent of Christ, which will be in the midst of the Battle of Armageddon (Mat. 24:19-31).

4. Verse 16 refers to the Almighty Power of the Lord Jesus Christ, which will be used to defend Israel, which refers to the defeat of the Antichrist.

PUT IN THE SICKLE

The phrase of Verse 13, *"Put you in the sickle, for the harvest is ripe,"* has to do with Christ thrusting *"in His Sickle on the Earth; and the Earth was reaped"* (Rev. 14:16).

The phrase, *"For the press is full, the fats overflow,"* has to do with Revelation 14:20, *"And the winepress was trodden without the city, and blood came out of the winepress, even unto the horse bridles, by the space of a thousand and six hundred furlongs (184 miles)."*

This is done, *"For their wickedness is great."*

No doubt, the *"blood"* mentioned in Revelation 14:20 will be mixed with water. The Prophet Ezekiel, also describing this coming time, says of the Lord, *"And I will plead against him* (the Antichrist) *with pestilence and with blood; and I will rain upon him, and upon his bands, and upon the many people who are with him, an overflowing rain, and great hailstones, fire, and brimstone"* (Ezek. 38:22).

One can well imagine the carnage all of this will bring about. It speaks of *"great hailstones, fire, and brimstone"* being used as artillery and raining down upon the Antichrist and his armies. Along with that will be an *"overflowing rain,"* which will make a river of sorts, flowing all the way from the *"Valley of Jehoshaphat,"* to somewhere near the border of Egypt, where it will then flow into the Mediterranean. That is a distance of approximately 184 miles.

Actually, the Valley of Jehoshaphat on its western side is only about 15 miles from the Mediterranean; however, there is a range of hills between the Valley and the sea. So, water seeking the least hindrance will flow south until it comes near the border of Egypt, where there are no hills, and it will flow into the Mediterranean.

THE VALLEY OF DECISION

The term, *"The valley of decision,"* given to us in Verse 14, simply means that the Lord has made the decision to confront the Antichrist and his armies in the *"Valley of Jehoshaphat."* While the *"man of sin"* may have thought this was his decision, nevertheless, this Scripture emphatically states that it is the *"Decision of the LORD."*

THE DAY OF THE LORD

The phrase, *"The Day of the LORD,"* is mostly an Old Testament term (Lam. 2:22; Isa. 2:12; 13:6, 9; 34:8; Jer. 46:10; Ezek. 13:5; etc.).

While the term applied to a limited degree to the happenings in Old Testament times, such as Lamentations 2:22 and Jeremiah 46:10, the greater fulfillment by far pertains to the coming Great Tribulation. In fact, the *"Day of the LORD,"* will have a time frame from the Rapture of the Church to the Second Coming. Exactly how long that will be, we aren't told. We know it will not be less than seven years, but it could be as many as 15 or 20 years because every Scriptural evidence is that the Great Tribulation period will not commence immediately after the Rapture of the Church. But how long that time frame is between the Rapture and the commencing of the Great Tribulation, we aren't told. Wuest gives the following information regarding this time frame.

• *First, the Day of the Lord has to do with the nation Israel, and not with the Church, which latter was unknown to the Old Testament Prophets. In fact, Simon Peter says that the Prophets searched their writings in an effort to discover what would take place between the Cross of Christ and the Millennium, which is a timeframe of 2,000 or more years. Paul tells us that the fact that Jew and Gentile would someday be one body was unknown until it was revealed to him (Eph. 3:4-7).*

• *Second, the period designated by that term, even as it was used by Joel the Prophet, is yet future.*

• *Third, the character of the period is one of judgment upon Israel because of its sin, and as well on the Antichrist, even as revealed by the Prophet Joel.*

• *Fourth, it refers, as stated, to the period of the Great Tribulation since events predicted by the Old Testament Prophets are those which John predicts in connection with the period of the time spoken of in Revelation, Chpts. 6-19, a period of unparalleled trouble which will take place after the Church is caught up, and which is designated by the term, "the Great Tribulation" (Rev. 7:14).*

• *Fifth, it is the time of the coming to earth of the Messiah in Judgment. Hence, it cannot refer to the First Advent of Christ, since He came at that time in humiliation and offered Himself as the Sacrifice for sin, but rather, it refers to the Second Advent, i.e., "The Second Coming."*[1]

THE LORD SHALL ROAR OUT OF ZION

The phrase of Verse 16, *"The LORD also*

shall roar out of Zion," is powerful indeed! In modern vernacular it means that the Lord will *"pull off the gloves."* In other words, the Antichrist is not going to like these odds. The phrase carries the idea of pent-up emotion that's been held in check for a long, long time and then suddenly explodes. Although human terminology does little to portray the Actions and Attitude of the Lord, still, we as human beings have no means to express what is happening other than that which we know and understand. But, whatever color is put on the phrase, or whatever understanding is derived, of this one can be certain, using a favorite human euphuism, *"It's going to be a 'Bad Day At Black Rock' for the Antichrist."*

The Antichrist will think that what Haman, Herod, and Hitler tried to do but failed, now he will succeed. The Jewish people will be no more! But it's not going to turn out the way he thinks.

THE HOPE AND STRENGTH OF ISRAEL

The last phrase of Verse 16 says, *"But the LORD will be the Hope of His People, and the Strength of the Children of Israel."*

The strongest army in the world, which will characterize that of the Antichrist, is one thing; however, an army, whether weak or strong, with the Lord Jesus Christ serving as the Commander, is something else again. That's what's going to happen at the Battle of Armageddon. The Lord Jesus Christ is going to come back to this Earth, and He will come back as the *"Hope of His People,"* and the *"Strength of the Children of Israel."* The great Prophet Zechariah said, **"Then shall the LORD go forth, and fight against those nations, as when He fought in the day of battle" (Zech. 14:3).** Copying the notes from THE EXPOSITOR'S STUDY BIBLE, we find that the word *"then"* is the key.

1. "'Then': when Israel will begin to cry to God for Deliverance, knowing that He is their only Hope.

2. "'Then': when half of Jerusalem has fallen, and it looks like the other half is about to fall.

3. "'Then': when it looks like every Jew will be annihilated, with two-thirds already killed.

4. "'Then': when it looks like the Promises of God made to the Patriarchs and Prophets of old will fall down.

5. "'Then': when it looks like the Antichrist will win this conflict, which will make Satan the lord of the Earth.

"'Then shall the LORD go forth,' refers to the Second Coming, which will be the most cataclysmic event that the world has ever known. 'And fight against those nations,' pertains to the nations under the banner of the Antichrist, which have set out to destroy Israel, and actually with annihilation in mind.

"'As when He fought in the day of battle,' probably refers to the time when the Lord led the Children of Israel out of Egypt by way of the Red Sea (Ex. 14:14; 15:3). This was Israel's first battle when Jehovah Messiah 'went forth' and fought for them. Israel then passed through a valley between mountains of water; in this, their last battle, they will escape through a valley between mountains of rock, which the next Verse proclaims."

(17) "SO SHALL YOU KNOW THAT I AM THE LORD YOUR GOD DWELLING IN ZION, MY HOLY MOUNTAIN: THEN SHALL JERUSALEM BE HOLY, AND THERE SHALL NO STRANGERS PASS THROUGH HER ANYMORE."

The construction is:

1. Israel will then know that Jesus Christ is the *"LORD your God."*

2. At the Second Coming, He will make His Headquarters in Jerusalem.

3. At that time, He will, no doubt, totally rebuild Jerusalem, making it the most beautiful city on the face of the Earth, *"Then shall Jerusalem be holy."*

4. The idea of the phrase, *"And there shall no strangers pass through her anymore,"* means, *"to pass through in order to destroy"*! Never again will that happen.

I AM THE LORD YOUR GOD

The Second Advent of Christ is the Second Coming, which will result in the Antichrist being totally and completely defeated, with his army following suit. Actually, five-sixths of that army will be decimated. Upon the Second Advent of Christ, there will be no

doubt as it regards the Victory of the Lord Jesus Christ. However, at the moment of our Lord's Return, in which He will be accompanied by every Saint of God who has ever lived, along with untold thousands of Angels, Israel will not recognize Him for Who He actually is. They will, of course, know and realize that He most definitely is their Messiah, but, at first, they will not recognize Him as the One they crucified so long, long ago.

Concerning the moment when Christ will be revealed to them, the Scripture says:

"And one shall say unto Him, What are these wounds in Your Hands? Then He shall answer, Those with which I was wounded in the house of My Friends" (Zech. 13:6). They will then know full well that it is Jesus Christ, the very One they crucified. This will bring about a national mourning, and rightly so. It will be the time of Israel's great Repentance for that terrible act committed so long ago.

THE LORD WILL DWELL IN ZION

The word *"dwell"* or *"dwelling"* proclaims the fact that the Lord will change His Headquarters from Heaven to Earth. The location will be *"Zion."* Actually, Jerusalem will be the Headquarters of our Lord, with Him being the President, so to speak, of the entirety of the Earth. In fact, He will be referred to as the King of kings and Lord of lords! Concerning this, the great Prophet Isaiah said:

"And many people shall go and say, Come you, and let us go up to the mountain of the LORD, to the House of the God of Jacob; and He will teach us of His Ways, and we will walk in His Paths: for out of Zion shall go forth the Law, and the Word of the LORD from Jerusalem" (Isa. 2:3).

The *"Law,"* as referred to here, has no reference to the Law of Moses, but rather to instruction, direction, and teaching. Again, this is the coming Kingdom Age when the Messiah, *"The Greater than Solomon,"* will rule the world by Wisdom, Grace, and Love.

At that time, scientists, agronomists, chemists, in fact, individuals from every walk of life and occupation, will beat a steady path, so to speak, to Jerusalem to seek wisdom from the Lord as to how to do things, with such information being instantly given. And then Isaiah said:

NO MORE WAR

"And He shall judge among the nations, and shall rebuke many people: and they shall beat their swords into plowshares, and their spears into pruning hooks: nation shall not lift up sword against nation, neither shall they learn war anymore" (Isa. 2:4).

During the Cold War, the nations of the world were spending an average of over a million dollars a minute, 24 hours a day, on weapons of destruction. What that number is now I have no idea. However, one can be sure that much of the productivity of this present world is going for weapons of war, which, in reality, is a waste. It is admitted that we as a nation have to have such weapons, but we look forward to the time when they will no longer be needed. That time will be in the coming Kingdom Age.

Think about it! Considering that there are no more budgets for war, trillions of dollars can be spent upon productive enterprises and infrastructure for all nations.

THEN SHALL JERUSALEM BE HOLY

In the past, when the Lord resided in the Temple between the Mercy Seat and the Cherubim, it was then holy. However, Satan contested this holiness and, therefore, this site, as no place on Earth. The contention goes on even now and will actually exacerbate during the coming Great Tribulation.

However, during the coming Kingdom Age, this area, the Temple site, will be holy because Christ is present and will forever remain so! It is this *"Holiness"* that will be the strength of Israel and, thereby, the whole world.

At its beginning, Jerusalem was called *"Salem,"* with Melchizedek as its king. Whereas *"Salem"* was first spoken of in Genesis 14:18, Jerusalem is first mentioned in Scripture in Joshua 10:1. The name means, *"City of peace,"* or *"Foundation of peace."*

It is one of the ironies of history that the city with such a name has seen so little peace and for its possession, rivers of blood have been shed.

It also was originally called *"Jebus"* (Judg. 19:10-11; I Chron. 11:4; II Sam. 5:6-9). This was the old name of *"Jerus."* It is called *"Jebusi"* (Josh. 18:16, 28); *"Ariel"* (Isa. 29:1); *"the City of Righteousness"* (Isa. 1:26); and *"Holy City"* (Isa. 48:2; 52:1; Neh. 11:1).

DAVID

David captured the city from the Jebusites and made it the capital of united Israel (II Sam. 5:6-9). It remained the capital until the division of the kingdom about 1,000 B.C. Jerusalem then continued to be the capital of Judah until 605 B.C., when it was invaded by Nebuchadnezzar. It was not, however, completely destroyed until 586 B.C.

It became the capital of Israel again about 536 B.C., and remained so until the nation and city were destroyed by the Romans in A.D. 70.

Jerusalem has undergone no less than 28 sieges from Joshua's time to our day. In the period between the close of the Old Testament to A.D. 70, it was besieged 10 times. Since then, it has been besieged eight times, coming up to A.D. 1917, and nine times if we consider the last war between the Jews and the Arabs.

Also, Jerusalem, in the coming Great Tribulation, shall be the capital of the Antichrist, at least, for a short period of time (Ezek., Chpt. 37; Dan. 9:27; 11:40-45; II Thess. 2:3-4; Rev. 11:1-11).

As well, and as Verse 17 states, it will be the eternal capital in the reign of the Lord Jesus Christ, which will be during the time of the Kingdom Age.

NO STRANGERS

The phrase, *"And there shall no strangers pass through her anymore,"* as stated, means to pass through in order to destroy!

All war will forever be ended, with the exception of Satan being *"loosed out of his prison"* at the conclusion of the 1,000 year Millennial Reign, when he shall be allowed to *". . . go out to deceive the nations which are in the four quarters of the Earth . . ."* (Rev. 20:7-8).

The Scripture further says, *"And they went up on the breadth of the Earth, and compassed the camp of the Saints about, and the beloved city: and fire came down from God out of Heaven, and devoured them"* (Rev. 20:9).

What little information that is given in the Bible concerning this event is given only in Revelation, Chapter 20. Therefore, it seems that Satan will be given very little latitude at that time and will be stopped before any damage is done, with him then being *"cast into the Lake of Fire and brimstone"* (Rev. 20:10).

Then John said, *". . . the Holy City, New Jerusalem, coming down from God out of Heaven, prepared as a Bride adorned for her husband"* (Rev. 21:2).

Then the *"New Jerusalem"* will take the place of the old and will be of such grandeur that it will beggar description!

(18) "AND IT SHALL COME TO PASS IN THAT DAY, THAT THE MOUNTAINS SHALL DROP DOWN NEW WINE, AND THE HILLS SHALL FLOW WITH MILK, AND ALL THE RIVERS OF JUDAH SHALL FLOW WITH WATERS, AND A FOUNTAIN SHALL COME FORTH OUT OF THE HOUSE OF THE LORD, AND SHALL WATER THE VALLEY OF SHITTIM."

The exegesis is:

1. Verse 18 pertains to the great prosperity that will come to Israel in the Kingdom Age.

2. With Israel now in her rightful place and position, she will bless the entirety of the world, and grandly so!

3. *"And a fountain shall come forth out of the House of the LORD,"* pertains to the river that will come from the Temple in Jerusalem, as seen by the Prophet Ezekiel (Ezek. 47:1-12).

4. This will be a literal river coming out from under a literal Temple in Jerusalem, which will take place in the Kingdom Age.

5. *"And shall water the Valley of Shittim,"* refers to the Dead Sea Valley, which will now be productive.

PROSPERITY UNEQUALLED

With Israel in its right place, serving as the Priestly Nation of the world, and all under Christ, blessings will flow out all over the world in an unprecedented manner. There will be no more poverty, with a few having everything and most having little

or nothing, even as it is presently in most nations of the world. There will be no third-world countries at that time, but, in fact, every nation in the world will be equally blessed, and abundantly so.

(19) "EGYPT SHALL BE A DESOLATION, AND EDOM SHALL BE A DESOLATE WILDERNESS, FOR THE VIOLENCE AGAINST THE CHILDREN OF JUDAH, BECAUSE THEY HAVE SHED INNOCENT BLOOD IN THEIR LAND.

(20) "BUT JUDAH SHALL DWELL FOREVER, AND JERUSALEM FROM GENERATION TO GENERATION.

(21) "FOR I WILL CLEANSE THEIR BLOOD THAT I HAVE NOT CLEANSED: FOR THE LORD DWELLS IN ZION."

The synopsis is:

1. There is no contradiction concerning Egypt between Verse 19 and Isaiah, Chapter 19. The Judgment here predicted has come and gone; the Promise given by Isaiah is yet future.

2. (Vs. 20) In that day, and we speak of the coming Kingdom Age, Judah will include all the Children of Israel from all the Tribes, for all will be there (Ezek. 48:1-29). The Promise of God is that this land, *"Judah,"* and this city, *"Jerusalem,"* will last forever. It will be occupied by Jews and not by Muslims!

3. The word *"cleanse"* in Verse 21 means *"to avenge."* This Prophecy ends, like that of Ezekiel, with the fact of God living visibly on the Earth with men.

THE LORD DWELLS IN ZION

All of these glorious things will be brought to pass because of this one fact, *"The LORD dwells in Zion."*

As well, such glorious things can be brought to fruition in any life presently if one will only allow the Lord to *"dwell in the heart."*

Thus, Joel ends his great Prophecy, not with despondency, but with great joy.

He begins by saying, *"Hear this, you old men, and give ear, all you inhabitants of the land,"* and closes by saying, *"For the LORD dwells in Zion."*

It shall yet come to pass exactly as the Prophet foretold!

CONCLUSION

It is Friday, March 5, 2010, as I conclude our efforts regarding the Commentary respecting both Hosea and Joel.

I have been blessed immeasurably in compiling this work. If I have been able to open up the Word of God to you to a greater measure, then it will have been worth all the time and effort.

I love the Word of God. I have read the Bible completely through some 51 times. There is nothing of which I am aware that is more profitable, more helpful, more instructive, or more informative than the *"Word."* No wonder that Jesus said:

". . . Man shall not live by bread alone, but by every Word that proceeds out of the Mouth of God" (Mat. 4:4).

"I can see far down the mountain,
"Where I have wandered many years,
"Often hindered on my journey,
"By the ghosts of doubts and fears,
"Broken vows and disappointments,
"Thickly strewn along the way,
"But the Spirit has led unerring,
"To the land I hold today."

BIBLIOGRAPHY

CHAPTER 2

Arthur Penryhn Stanley, *The History of the Jewish Church: Vol. 2*, New York, Scribner, Armstrong, & Co., 1878, pgs. 484-486.

CHAPTER 3

Kenneth S. Wuest, *In These Last Days*, Eerdman's Publishing Co., Grand Rapids, Michigan, 1954.

REFERENCE BOOKS

Atlas Of The Bible — Rogerson
Expository Dictionary of Bible Words — L.O. Richards
Matthew Henry Commentary On The Holy Bible — Matthew Henry
New Bible Dictionary — Tyndale
Strong's Exhaustive Concordance Of The Bible
The Complete Word Study Dictionary
The Essential Writings — Josephus
The Interlinear Greek — English New Testament — George Ricker Berry
The International Standard Bible Encyclopedia
The Pulpit Commentary — H.D.M. Spence
The Student's Commentary On The Holy Scriptures — George Williams
The Zondervan Pictorial Encyclopedia Of The Bible
Vine's Expository Dictionary Of New Testament Words
Webster's New Collegiate Dictionary
Word Studies In The Greek New Testament, Volume I — Kenneth S. Wuest
Young's Literal Translation Of The Holy Bible

NOTES

THE
BOOK OF AMOS

INTRODUCTION

It is June 2, 2010, as I begin Commentary on the Book of Amos.

Amos is said to have been relatively uneducated due to his occupation of being a herdsman and a gatherer of sycamore fruit (cultivator of sycamore trees). However, the Prophet's acrid acquaintance with the Law of Moses denotes much more than a familiarity with the national traditions. His knowledge of the Pentateuch appears not only in general allusions to history, ritual, and ceremony, but in the actual use of verbal forms and expressions, which belong to the Mosaic writings.

QUOTATIONS

The quotes used by the Prophet throughout his Book prove his knowledge of history and ritual of the Mosaic Books. As well, his threats and promises are often couched in Mosaic language.

In fact, Hosea and Jeremiah seem to have borrowed from or, at least, been well acquainted with his writings.

Therefore, to call Amos uneducated may hold true regarding certain particulars, such as his occupation or his lack of formal training. However, that he was well versed in the Word of God is obvious and evident and, in reality, constitutes the greatest education of all by far!

That which men refer to as educated or uneducated is one thing. Those designations as applied by the Lord are quite another. Consequently, it is obvious that the Lord considered Amos to be very educated, at least, in the things that really mattered,

for He called him to deliver a very important Message to the northern kingdom of Israel, as well as other nations. Even though he did not refer to himself as a Prophet, still, the Lord definitely did!

PROSPERITY?

At the time when Amos prophesied, both the northern kingdom of Israel and the southern kingdom of Judah stood high in prosperity and wealth. Israel, secure from outward enemies and strong in inward resources, was very far from expecting ruin and destruction. Prosperity in both kingdoms (Judah and Israel) had produced its too common fruits—pride, luxury, selfishness, and oppression. In Judah, such sins were rife, but in the northern kingdom, they were accentuated and increased by the calf-worship, which was still practiced there.

BETH-EL

To Beth-el, the central seat of this idolatry, Amos was sent from Jerusalem. His mission was to rebuke this iniquity and to announce to these careless sinners the approach of Divine Judgment.

As well, and as briefly alluded to, though his special mission was directed to Israel, Amos does not confine himself altogether to denunciations of this kingdom. His cry extended to Judah and even unto the hostile nations, which surrounded the Covenant people.

AMOS

Amos is the third of the *"Minor Prophets,"* minor only in the sense that their Books are shorter than those referred to as the

"Major Prophets." His name is usually taken to signify *"Carrier,"* but is better interpreted *"Heavy"* or *"Burdened,"* and actually corresponds to the grievous Message, which he had to deliver.

Amos seemed to have lived and ministered approximately 50 to 75 years before Joel. However, there are some who claim, and with some conviction, that he followed Joel because he takes up this Prophet's words in the commencement of his own prediction (compare Amos 1:2 with Joel 3:16). However, it is unwise to speculate on dates due to similarity of Texts simply because the Holy Spirit, Who is the Author of all the Word of God, could easily have given the same words, or even the same phraseology, to different writers, which He, at times, no doubt did!

It is not too difficult to pinpoint the time frame of Amos' Prophecies due to their being somewhat dated; however, the difficulty comes with Joel, which was undated.

The Ministry of Amos probably lasted only about two years or, at the most, four or five.

CHAPTER 1

(1) "THE WORDS OF AMOS, WHO WAS AMONG THE HERDMEN OF TEKOA, WHICH HE SAW CONCERNING ISRAEL IN THE DAYS OF UZZIAH KING OF JUDAH, AND IN THE DAYS OF JEROBOAM THE SON OF JOASH KING OF ISRAEL, TWO YEARS BEFORE THE EARTHQUAKE."

The construction is:

1. *"The words of Amos, who was among the herdmen of Tekoa,"* specifies him as a shepherd.

2. The phrase, *"Which he saw concerning Israel,"* could very well have been a Vision. Man's words cannot be *"seen,"* only God's Words.

3. *"In the days of Uzziah king of Judah, and in the days of Jeroboam the son of Joash king of Israel,"* concerns the time of the Moving of the Holy Spirit upon Amos, and the delivering of his Prophecy. Incidentally, this was Jeroboam II.

4. *"Two years before the earthquake,"* is said by Josephus, the Jewish historian, to be attributed to God's Displeasure at Uzziah's usurpation of the Priest's office (II Chron. 26:16).

RICH?

Some have attempted to conclude that Amos was a rich possessor of flocks; however, his own words (Amos 7:14-15) decide his position as that of a poor, laboring man. Incidentally, his name does not occur elsewhere in the Old Testament.

"Tekoa" was the home of Amos, a small town of Judah, situated on a hill about five miles south of Bethlehem, lying in a pastoral district.

It was on these hills surrounding this small village where Amos tended sheep and was a cultivator of sycamore trees. As well, it was here that he received the Divine Call. Untrained in the schools, no Prophet or Prophet's son, he was sent to prophesy against Israel. So, like an Apostle, he left all at his Master's Word and traveled from Judah. He came to Beth-el, the temple and summer palace of the king of the northern kingdom of Israel, to raise his voice against the worship of the calf, which prevailed there in profane union with the service of Jehovah.

A PERSONAL EXPERIENCE

On one of our trips to Israel, the mayor of modern Tekoa called our hotel in Jerusalem and invited us to come visit his small town.

I was appreciative of the invitation for several reasons, not the least being that this was the birthplace and home of the Prophet Amos.

The next morning, with the help of a guide, we drove the some 10 or 12 miles to this pastoral district. Here, at least at that time, the Palestinians and Israelis were living side by side, seemingly, without incident.

The mayor greeted us warmly. I soon found out that he was a native of Detroit, Michigan.

There really wasn't much in the way of a town, mostly a commune, where the Israelis were attempting to bring this area back to cultivation and prosperity.

The area, approximately 10 to 12 miles

south of Jerusalem, consisted of a rolling landscape that was suited for flocks of sheep. In fact, from my vantage point I could see several flocks being tended by their shepherds.

As this was only about five miles south of Bethlehem, no doubt, David, in his tending of the sheep, ranged this far south. Therefore, about 250 years before Amos, David served in the same occupation and in the same area.

As I stood there that day on one of the highest points, observing the sweeping landscape, I wondered on which of these hills did the Spirit of God speak to Amos, giving him the Message that he must deliver.

Spending days on end in solitude, Amos, no doubt, sought the Lord intensely, with the Spirit of God having the opportunity to gradually mold his mind, heart, and thinking, until he became a fit vessel to be used for the Master's Service. How many times, walking these lonely hills, leading the sheep, and in prayer to the Lord, did the tears course down his cheeks as the burden for the northern kingdom of Israel became heavier and heavier?

CONCERNING ISRAEL

The phrase, *"Which he saw concerning Israel,"* could very well have been a Vision. Man's words cannot be *"seen,"* only God's Words. Hence, the Apostle John said, *"I turned to see the Voice . . ."* (Rev. 1:12).

A PERSONAL EXPERIENCE

Just last night in prayer, the Spirit of God moved exceedingly upon me, as about 15 or 20 of us gathered to seek the Lord.

I suppose I had prayed for about 15 or 20 minutes, with only a small Anointing, but then the Spirit of God began to Move mightily. Consequently, I have at least some small knowledge of what Amos was speaking of when he spoke of seeing the *"Words of God."*

In this prayer meeting the Spirit of God brought to my mind Paul's statement, *"So then Faith comes by hearing, and hearing by the Word of God"* (Rom. 10:17).

More particularly and directly, the Spirit of the Lord began to impress upon my mind

and spirit the Words, *"Faith cometh,"* actually repeating them over and over!

In that context, and for a few minutes, I literally *"saw"* that which Faith in the Word of the Lord would bring. Even though I will not go into detail as to exactly what I *"saw,"* still, it was so real as to be implanted indelibly upon my mind. It concerned this Ministry and the Call of God upon my life respecting world Evangelism.

UZZIAH AND JEROBOAM II

The phrase, *"In the days of Uzziah king of Judah, and in the days of Jeroboam the son of Joash king of Israel,"* concerns the time of the Moving of the Holy Spirit upon Amos and the delivering of his Prophecy.

At this time, Jeroboam had overcome the Syrians and recovered the original territory of his kingdom from Hamath in the extreme north to the Dead Sea on the south (II Ki. 14:25, 28).

As well, Uzziah, king of Judah, had subdued the restless Edomites and Philistines and reduced the Ammonites to subjection. Also, he had raised a powerful army and strongly fortified Jerusalem (II Chron., Chpt. 26).

As stated, at this particular time, both kingdoms were prosperous, strong, and were very far from expecting ruin and destruction.

Even though *"Judah"* is mentioned, still, the Message of Amos was primarily to the northern kingdom of Israel.

The phrase, *"Two years before the earthquake,"* gives us no clue as to its time frame as no mention is made of this event in the historical books.

Amos mentioned this possibly because he felt it was a token of the Judgment, which was coming upon the northern kingdom and even the southern kingdom of Judah some time later!

Josephus, the Jewish historian, attributed this earthquake to God's Displeasure at Uzziah's usurpation of the Priest's office (II Chron. 26:16).

(2) "AND HE SAID, THE LORD WILL ROAR FROM ZION, AND UTTER HIS VOICE FROM JERUSALEM; AND THE HABITATIONS OF THE SHEPHERDS

SHALL MOURN, AND THE TOP OF CARMEL SHALL WITHER."

The composition is:

1. *"The LORD will roar from Zion,"* portrays Jerusalem. Here was Jehovah's Throne. The kings of the nations uttered their feeble voices from their governmental centers, but Jehovah roared as a lion from out of Zion.

2. The phrase, *"And the habitations of the shepherds shall mourn,"* refers to the coming Judgment of the Lord to be so severe that it would affect every part of Israel, even the peaceful pastures of the shepherds, even to *"the top of Carmel."*

3. Whatever the Lord says, to be sure, it will most definitely come to pass.

JERUSALEM

The phrase, *"The LORD will roar from Zion,"* as stated, refers to Jerusalem.

The beginning phrase, *"And he said,"* is actually the commencement of *"the Words"* of Amos.

The following phrase, *"To roar out of Zion,"* is almost the same as Joel 3:16, showing that Joel would utter the same words at a later date, at least, if our tabulations are correct that Joel followed Amos.

This would show that God's Punishments are not directed exclusively on heathen nations.

The word, *"roar,"* signifies the thunder of the Voice of God, at least, in the Spiritual sense, announcing coming Judgment.

As well, the words, *"from Zion,"* denote that the Lord was not in Dan or Beth-el, the seats of idolatrous worship, but in Jerusalem, the abode of His Presence, that is, His Dwelling between the Mercy Seat and the Cherubim in the Temple.

Even though we know the Lord is omnipresent, meaning that He is everywhere, still, in a sense of the word, He had confined Himself to the Holy of Holies in the Temple in Jerusalem. At that time, Judah was the only Nation in the world where the Presence of God dwelt. In fact, and more than likely, it was God the Holy Spirit Who dwelt in the Temple in Jerusalem. Concerning the New Covenant, Paul said, **"Know you not that you are the Temple of God** (where

NOTES

the Holy Spirit abides), **and *that* the Spirit of God dwells in you?** *(That makes the Born-Again Believer His permanent Home)"* **(I Cor. 3:16).**

THE CROSS OF CHRIST

Before the Cross, the Holy Spirit could not abide in the hearts and lives of anyone except for a special few who were called to perform a Special Service, such as Prophets of the Lord, etc. And even then, the Holy Spirit only helped them to carry out their task, with no mention in the Old Testament of the Holy Spirit involving Himself in the Sanctification process of the Saint.

Why not?

The reason the Holy Spirit could not abide in the hearts of all, or anyone, permanently was because animal blood was woefully insufficient to remove the sin debt, which was characteristic of every human being (Heb. 10:4). While animal sacrifices did serve as a stopgap measure until the First Advent of Christ, still, it was only a temporary measure.

JOHN THE BAPTIST

If it is remembered, when John the Baptist introduced Christ, he said, **". . . Behold the Lamb of God** *(proclaims Jesus as the Sacrifice for sin, in fact, the Sin-Offering, Whom all the multiple millions of offered lambs had represented),* **which takes away the sin of the world** *(animal blood could only cover sin, it could not take it away; but Jesus offering Himself as the Perfect Sacrifice took away the sin of the world; He not only cleansed acts of sin but, as well, addressed the root cause [Col. 2:14-15])"* **(Jn. 1:29).**

When Jesus died on the Cross of Calvary, He, in effect, offered Himself as a Sacrifice. In fact, He was the only One in history Who could do such a thing inasmuch as He was Perfect. Not being born of normal procreation, meaning that He did not have an earthly father, born of the Virgin Mary, the sin of Adam did not pass to Him as it had to all others.

Jesus Christ came to this world for many reasons, but the major reason of all was the Cross. From before the foundation of the world, before the creation of man, through foreknowledge, God knew He would make the Universe, would make this Planet called Earth, and would create man. He also knew that man would fall. Therefore, it was deemed desirable by the Godhead that man would be redeemed by God becoming Man and going to the Cross, where there the price would be paid for the terrible sin debt. It was a price that man could not pay. So, if man was to be redeemed, Salvation would have to come wholly from without man, which it did, in the Person of the Lord Jesus Christ, God's Son.

In His Life and Living, He kept the Law of God perfectly, never sinning even one time in word, thought, or deed. And He did it all for us as our Representative Man. Then, to address the broken Law, of which all were guilty, He went to the Cross and offered Himself as a Perfect Sacrifice, which God accepted as payment in full. Now, in order to be Saved, to be cleansed from all sin, and to be declared perfect in the Eyes of God, all a human being has to do is simply exhibit Faith in Christ. He must believe Who He was and is, meaning that He is God, and What He did, which pertains to the Cross of Calvary. Simple childlike Faith will guarantee Salvation to anyone who so believes (Jn. 3:3, 16).

Now that all sin is atoned, the moment the person is Saved, the Holy Spirit comes into his heart and life to abide forever (Jn. 14:16-17). As stated, all of it is made possible by the Cross.

In fact, the following formula may help us to understand it a little better:

• Jesus Christ is the Source of all things we receive from God (Jn. 1:1-2; Col. 2:10-15).

• The Cross of Christ is the Means, and the only Means, by which everything is given to us (Rom. 6:1-14; I Cor. 1:17-18, 23; 2:2).

• Inasmuch as the Cross of Christ is the only Means by which the Lord deals with man, the Cross of Christ without fail must be the Object of our Faith (I Cor. 2:2; Gal. 6:14; Col. 2:14-15).

• The Holy Spirit superintends all of this inasmuch as He Works entirely within the parameters, so to speak, of the Cross of Christ. In other words, it is the Cross which

NOTES

gives the Holy Spirit the legal means to do all that He does (Rom. 8:1-2, 11).

As the Lord was only in Jerusalem under the Old Covenant, presently, He is only in the hearts and lives of Believers who have trusted Christ for Salvation and Redemption.

JUDGMENT

The phrase, *"And the habitations of the shepherds shall mourn,"* refers to the coming Judgment of the Lord, which would be so severe that it would affect every part of Israel, even the peaceful pastures of the shepherd.

As well, the phrase, *"And the top of Carmel shall wither,"* refers to Mt. Carmel, which stretches boldly into the sea on the south of the Bay of Acre, and is remarkable for its extreme fertility, its rich pastures, its vines, olives, fruits, and flowers. The very name *"Carmel"* means *"the Vineyard of God."* As well, it was on its promontory heights that, some years earlier, Elijah had called fire from Heaven (I Ki. 18:38).

Consequently, the very first announcement by Amos against Israel was of coming Judgment, which was startling, to say the least! It was designed thusly by the Holy Spirit to get the attention of the wicked northern kingdom. However, it did not seem plausible to Israel at all, especially considering that they, at that particular time, were strong, rich, and prosperous. Hence, the very worst thing that can happen to an individual is for his self-made plans to succeed.

GOD'S APPROVAL?

Many conclude that if their plans of self-will are prosperous, this must signify God's Approval! However, God can never bless error or sin. Therefore, the prosperity of such plans only tends to deepen the deception, making it even harder, if not impossible, for the individual or nation to come back to God.

Thus was Israel and thus are many modern Christians!

Israel, and especially at that time of her strength and prosperity, would pay no heed to Amos. He was rebuked, lampooned, and caricatured! Nevertheless, the Words he spoke were from God and would come to pass in a terrible finality.

It would have been better at that time if Israel had suffered adversity. Perhaps she would have been more inclined to have listened to the Prophet. As it was, she desired that nothing disturb her complacency; therefore, she continued in her calf-worship, which would lead to her doom in a little over 50 years.

Sometime ago, actually in the early 1990's, a leading Pentecostal denomination boasted of its large churches and prosperous congregations. It equated such with the Blessings of God; however, such, at least for this denomination, was anything but the Blessings of God. Presently (2010), this denomination is following after *"strange fire."* As a result, there is very little of true spirituality left.

As stated, sometimes prosperity is the worst thing that can happen to us.

(3) "THUS SAYS THE LORD; FOR THREE TRANSGRESSIONS OF DAMASCUS, AND FOR FOUR, I WILL NOT TURN AWAY THE PUNISHMENT THEREOF; BECAUSE THEY HAVE THRESHED GILEAD WITH THRESHING INSTRUMENTS OF IRON."

The exegesis is:

1. *"For three transgressions of Damascus, and for four,"* portrays an abrupt change by the Holy Spirit from His Pronouncement of Judgment on Israel to the Proclamation of Punishment on neighboring heathen nations for their injurious treatment of His Own People.

2. While the People of the Lord have to be chastised at times, to be sure, it is the Lord Who will do this and not man. While He may use man to do so, they will be an unwitting instrument in His Hands.

3. Every nation in the world is under the control of the Lord, even though they do not even believe in Him.

DAMASCUS

The phrase, *"For three transgressions of Damascus, and for four,"* portrays an abrupt change by the Holy Spirit from His Pronouncement of Judgment on Israel to the Proclamation of Punishment on neighboring heathen nations for their injurious

treatment of His Own People. The abrupt change in direction by the Holy Spirit was by design. The reasons are severalfold:

• Even though God's Own People had gone into deep sin, still, His watchful care over them never slacked, portraying to all that God keeps His Covenants even if man does not. In other words, *"He abides faithful."*

• The announcement of coming Judgment upon Israel, at least, if they didn't repent, coupled with the announcement of Judgment upon surrounding heathen nations, is meant to impress upon Israel that God is impartial towards sin irrespective of where it is found. In other words, sin will be punished (unless repented of) wherever it is found.

JUDGMENT AND THE CROSS OF CHRIST

The only thing standing between man and the Wrath of God is the Cross of Christ. In fact, it has always been that way. Due to man's fallen condition, were it not for the Cross, the Lord could not even look at us, much less have communion with us.

Immediately after the Fall, with Adam and Eve being driven from the Garden, the Lord told the First Family that despite their fallen condition, they could still have forgiveness of sins and communion with Him. However, it would have to be by virtue of the slain lamb, which was a substitute for Christ until He would come. Outside of the slain lamb, man had no access with God, and God had not access to man. Of course, when Jesus came, and the Cross became a reality, this opened up the way for God to extend Grace (good things) to all who would believe Him.

Our Ministry (Jimmy Swaggart Ministries) specializes in the Message of the Cross. The Bible teaches that this Message is the Gospel (I Cor. 1:17). Paul said:

"For Christ sent me not to baptize *(presents to us a Cardinal Truth)***, but to preach the Gospel** *(the manner in which one may be Saved from sin)***: not with wisdom of words** *(intellectualism is not the Gospel)***, lest the Cross of Christ should be made of none effect.** *(This tells us in no uncertain terms that the Cross of Christ must always* *be the emphasis of the Message. In fact, this one Scripture tells us as to exactly what the Gospel of Jesus Christ actually is. It is the Cross of Christ)"* **(I Cor. 1:17).**

BELIEVERS AND THE CROSS OF CHRIST

Unfortunately, the modern church is not too very much preaching the Cross. A Baptist Preacher wrote me the other day stating, *"Brother Swaggart, had you preached the Cross some fifty years ago as you are now doing, most of the Churches would have wholeheartedly accepted this Message."* He went on to say, *"But it's been so long since the Church has preached the Cross as the only solution for mankind, that any more, what you are preaching sounds like a new Message to them, when in reality, it is older than time."*

By radio, television, the Internet, and our publications, I have relayed the word to those who hear us that they just might be the only thing standing between this nation and the Wrath of God. I am meaning those who have accepted the Cross of Christ and understand that it alone is the solution for sin. Let me say it in a different way.

It doesn't matter who they may be or where they may be, it is the Preacher who preaches the Cross, and the Believer who understands and accepts the Message of the Cross, who holds back the Judgment of God. That is quite a statement, but I know it to be true.

In the last 50 or so years, the modern church has all but abandoned the Cross of Christ. As a result, our nation presently has never been in more danger than it is at this moment. If you trace it back far enough, you will find what I say is true. Thank God that He has given this Ministry a worldwide platform to proclaim this Message. It is the Gospel, and it alone is the Gospel.

A PERSONAL EXPERIENCE

A few weeks ago while in prayer, the Lord spoke the following to my heart:

He related to me as to how the Evil One had tried to close the door respecting this Ministry, but that the Lord kept it open about ten percent, as it regards the coverage we had in the 1980's. But then He said to

NOTES

me, *"I am going to open the door wide, and what I open, no man can close."*

THE HARVEST AND THIS MINISTRY

The other night I awakened sometime close to midnight. I was to preach that morning at Family Worship Center. My subject had to do with Joseph and his interpretation of Pharaoh's Dream.

As all Bible students know, the Lord gave a most startling Dream to Pharaoh, which troubled the monarch greatly, simply because he did not know what it meant. No doubt, his prognosticators, his fortunetellers, his astrologers, etc., tried to interpret the Dream for him, but whatever they would have told him did not satisfy him because he knew this was not the interpretation. Then the chief butler told the monarch of Joseph, who was then in prison, and his ability to interpret dreams. They sent for Joseph, and he came and stood before the most powerful monarch on the face of the Earth.

Pharaoh then related his Dream to Joseph. He told the young man how that he dreamed that seven fat cattle came up out of the river and fed in a meadow. He then said that seven other cattle came up after them, poor and lean fleshed, and then the lean cattle ate up the first seven fat cattle.

He then related how that he saw seven ears of grain on one stalk, full and good, and how that seven other ears that were withered came up and devoured the seven good ears.

Pharaoh's Dream was double, referring to the cattle and the stalks of grain. As a result, it also had a double meaning that, more than likely, even Joseph did not know.

The seven fat cattle and the seven fat ears of grain represent seven years of harvest that would come to Egypt, which would begin immediately, and would be the greatest harvest that nation had ever known. In fact, it would be so bountiful that granaries would have to be built all over Egypt to take care of the surplus.

The seven lean cattle and the seven lean ears of grain represented seven years of famine that were going to come upon the Middle East. In fact, Egypt would have to be the breadbasket for most, if not all, of these nations.

The meaning was that the seven years of famine would be what it took to bring Jacob to Joseph, and that's exactly what happened. But there is a second meaning, as stated, because the Dream was doubled.

MODERN TIMES

Looking at the lean cattle and the wasted ears of grain first, this represents the seven years of Great Tribulation that's coming upon this world very soon, which Jesus said would be the worst the world has ever known (Mat. 24:21). And as the famine of 3,700 years ago brought *"Jacob to Joseph,"* likewise, the coming Great Tribulation called, *"the time of Jacob's Trouble,"* will serve to bring *"Jacob to Jesus."* That time is soon to come upon this world.

THE HARVEST

It is the first part of the Dream that I wish to bring to your attention now. As it signaled the greatest harvest that Egypt had ever known, likewise, I believe that it portrays a Harvest of souls that's about to take place in this world, which will immediately precede the coming Great Tribulation. As stated, inasmuch as the Dream was doubled, this means that it had a great meaning for the immediate future regarding Joseph, as it did, and, as well, it refers to that which is soon to come upon this world.

Modern technology has made it possible to reach untold millions with a single Service. I believe the Lord said this to me that night when I awakened as He brought all of this to my mind and spirit.

He said to me, *"This Ministry (Jimmy Swaggart Ministries) is going to have a part in fulfilling the Dream given to this heathen monarch some 3,700 years ago, as it regards the coming Harvest."* I believe that we're going to see hundreds of thousands, if not millions, of souls brought to a Saving Knowledge of Jesus Christ. The Message of the Cross, which the Lord has given to us, addresses itself not only to the Church but, as well, to a lost and dying world. This means that all who are associated with this Ministry, even to the slightest degree, will

have a part in this great Harvest. The Lord said one other thing to me that night.

JUST BELIEVE!

He told me to tell the people simply to believe.

• They are to believe that this Harvest is coming.

• They are to believe that God has given us the Message for this time and place, the Message of the Cross.

• They are to believe that He has called us for this task.

• They are to believe that they are themselves an integral part of this Move of God. Let me say it again:

The only thing standing between mankind and the Judgment of God is the Cross of Christ.

FALSE WORSHIP

As stated, evidently Israel, despite their calf-worship, somehow felt that their present prosperity denoted the Blessings of God and, consequently, God's Approval.

In their minds, they were not idol-worshippers inasmuch as these calves represented Jehovah, at least in their thinking. They even kept particular Feast Days, as in Judah, and offered sacrifices on their man-made altar (I Ki. 12:28-33).

This form of worship, however, which equated idols with Jehovah, was an abomination in the Eyes of God. But that type of worship did not die with the Israelites of so long ago. For instance, Catholics equate the *"church"* with Christ. In other words, if they are faithful to their church and obey its demands, whatever they might be, and no matter how unscriptural they might be, they equate the church and Christ as one in the same. But, of course, the church has preeminence. Actually, they teach that the Bible is whatever the church says it is. So, they feel free to change things as they so desire. In the Eyes of God, this is the same as the idol-worship of Israel of old.

As well, there are millions of Protestants who, in one sense of the word, pay the same allegiance to their church or denomination as Catholics do theirs. In other words, their faith is not so much in Christ and the Cross as it is their particular church.

Please note the following carefully:

Religion is the greatest idol in the world today and, in fact, ever has been. Please understand this also, religion is that which is conceived totally by man, birthed by man, and instituted by man. This means it's not of God, and it also means it's that which God cannot accept. Let us say it this way:

Any type of worship, which does not have the Cross of Christ as its foundation, is looked at by God as religion. In other words, it is unacceptable. Jesus plainly said, *"God is a Spirit: and they who worship Him must worship Him in spirit and in truth"* (Jn. 4:24).

This doesn't mean that each worshipper has to understand all about the Cross in order for the Lord to accept our worship. It simply means that we must understand that it is the Cross of Christ which gives us access to God and God access to us. Paul said:

"For through Him (through Christ and what He did for us at the Cross) **we both** (Jews and Gentiles) **have access by One Spirit unto the Father.** (If the sinner comes by the Cross, the Holy Spirit opens the door, otherwise, it is barred)" **(Eph. 2:18).**

John wrote, **"Verily, verily, I say unto you, He who enters not by the door into the sheepfold** (proclaims to us that there is a 'door,' and, in fact, only one 'door!'), **but climbs up some other way, the same is a thief and a robber** (using a 'way' other than Christ; He Alone is the Door).

"But he who enters in by the Door (Way) **is the Shepherd of the Sheep.** (Jesus Alone is the True Shepherd)" **(Jn. 10:1-2).**

A BLOOD SPLATTERED DOOR

The Lord through Moses said:

"And you shall take a bunch of hyssop (the 'hyssop' was not connected with the 'lamb,' but with the application of its blood; it speaks, then, not of Christ, but of the sinner's appropriation of the Sacrifice of Christ; 'hyssop' was a type of grass which grew in crevices between the rocks), **and dip it in the blood that is in the bason, and strike the lintel and the two side posts with the blood that is in the bason** (in fact, the blood applied to the header [lintel] and

two side posts formed a perfect cross; we are to never regard the Cross of Christ as a mere circumstance in the Life of Christ referring to His sin-bearing; it was the grand and only scene of sin-bearing; He did not bear our sins anywhere else; He did not bear them in the manger, nor in the wilderness, nor in the Garden, but 'only on the Tree' [I Pet. 2:24])**; and none of you shall go out of the door of his house until the morning.** (The death Angel was to come through at night and, beyond the protection of the Blood of the Lamb, there was no assurance of safety. In fact, there was no safety outside of this application, just as there is no safety presently outside of this application)" **(Ex. 12:22).**

TRANSGRESSIONS

The expression, *"For three transgressions . . . and for four,"* is a Hebrew idiom expressive of *"many."*

"Damascus" had been an active enemy of Israel since the time that Razon threw off his allegiance (I Ki. 11:23), and seized Damascus, which had been tributary to David (II Sam. 8:5). Consequently, there was almost constant war between Syria and Israel.

They had repeatedly come against God's People and now would suffer the Judgment of God.

It should be understood that any hand laid in anger on God's People, whether past or present, and irrespective of their spiritual condition, as Israel, will always incur the Wrath of God. To touch that which belongs to God is to touch God!

One of the reasons that God has blessed America so abundantly is because of the separation of Church and state and the freedom to worship as one's conscience leads. But, I might quickly add, if a religion, any religion, calls for the overthrow of the government by wholesale murder, even as the religion of Islam, that's where the freedom ends.

PUNISHMENT

The phrase, *"I will not turn away the punishment thereof,"* simply means, *"I will not reverse it."* Amos does not expressly say what, but he means the sentence of

Judgment. The phrase can, as well, mean, *"I will no longer disregard their sins."*

CRUEL TREATMENT

The phrase, *"Because they have threshed Gilead with threshing instruments of iron,"* is the culminating offense of the Syrians. The phrase is symbolic of extremely cruel treatment carried out on Israel by Syria. Damascus was the capital of Syria and, in fact, still is.

This cruel treatment referred to in the Text probably refers to the time of Hazael during the reign of Jehu (II Ki. 10:32).

During this time, and in one of the invasions of Israel by Syria, the Septuagint said, *"Because with iron saws they sawed asunder women with child."*

This is probably what Elisha was speaking of in his words to Hazael, when he said, *". . . Because I know the evil that you will do unto the Children of Israel: their strongholds will you set on fire, and their young men will you kill with the sword, and will dash their children, and rip up their women with child"* (II Ki. 8:12).

(4) "BUT I WILL SEND A FIRE INTO THE HOUSE OF HAZAEL, WHICH SHALL DEVOUR THE PALACES OF BEN-HADAD."

The structure is:

1. Verse 4 probably refers to *"Ben-hadad III,"* the son of Hazael, who was a monarch of small ability.

2. Under the sway of Ben-hadad III, Syria sank into insignificance (II Ki., Chpt. 13).

3. Incidentally, *"Ben-hadad"* is a title corresponding to Pharaoh, Caesar, etc.

JUDGMENT

The phrase, *"But I will send a fire into the house of Hazael,"* is meant to be both literal and symbolic.

The statement, *"Which shall devour the palaces of Ben-hadad,"* speaks of the fortresses. In other words, such fortifications would not hinder or serve as a bulwark against the Judgment of God. Man may attempt to defend himself against such, but his attempts are futile, to say the least!

(5) "I WILL BREAK ALSO THE BAR OF DAMASCUS, AND CUT OFF THE

INHABITANT FROM THE PLAIN OF AVEN, AND HIM WHO HOLDS THE SCEPTRE FROM THE HOUSE OF EDEN: AND THE PEOPLE OF SYRIA SHALL GO INTO CAPTIVITY UNTO KIR, SAYS THE LORD."

The exegesis is:

1. *"And the people of Syria shall go into captivity unto Kir, says the LORD,"* no doubt, pertains to the invasion some 50 years later of the Assyrian, Tiglath-Pileser, who killed Rezon and sacked Damascus, as well as leading multiple thousands of Syrians *"into captivity unto Kir,"* exactly as prophesied.

2. The Lord said, *"I will!"* To be sure, whatever the Lord says that He will do, one can be confident that it will be done.

3. No matter how strong a nation or empire might be, it is nothing in the Eyes of God.

I WILL

The phrase, *"I will break also the bar of Damascus,"* refers to the securing of the gate of the city. In other words, when the Judgment came, as surely it did, Syria's efforts at defending herself were in vain.

The phrase, *"And the people of Syria shall go into captivity unto Kir, says the LORD,"* as stated, no doubt, refers to the invasion, which took place some 50 years later by the Assyrian, Tiglath-Pileser, who killed Rezon and sacked Damascus. As well, he led multiple thousands of Syrians into captivity and *"unto Kir,"* exactly as prophesied.

"Kir" has been identified with the country on the banks of the River Kir, which flows into the Araxes on the southwest of the Caspian Sea.

It is interesting in this Scripture that the Holy Spirit uses the phrase, *"The house of Eden."* The phrase means, *"House of delight, or pleasure,"* and was located in the general area of Haran. This city was the northern extremity of Syria and is where Abraham lived for a period of time (Gen. 11:31). In those days, some concluded it to be the original site of the Garden of Eden, and, hence, it was called the *"House of pleasure."* However, there is greater evidence, I think, that the site of original Eden was in the vicinity of Babylon.

(6) "THUS SAYS THE LORD; FOR THREE TRANSGRESSIONS OF GAZA, AND FOR FOUR, I WILL NOT TURN AWAY THE PUNISHMENT THEREOF; BECAUSE THEY CARRIED AWAY CAPTIVE THE WHOLE CAPTIVITY, TO DELIVER THEM UP TO EDOM."

The overview is:

1. The phrase, *"Three transgressions . . . and for four,"* is a Hebrew idiom expressive of *"many."*

2. The phrase, *"To deliver them up to Edom,"* speaks of the Philistines handing over the captive Israelites to their bitterest enemies, the Edomites, as slaves.

3. God's Anger, as is obvious here, burns against such treachery and slavery, hence, the Judgment on Gaza.

THE PUNISHMENT OF GAZA

As the word of Judgment against Damascus was prefaced by *"Thus says the LORD,"* likewise, the Prophecy now changes from Damascus to Philistia, and is prefaced, as well, with *"Thus says the LORD,"* ensuring its fulfillment.

"To deliver them up to Edom," refers to the Philistines handing over the captive Israelites to their bitterest enemies, the Edomites, making slaves of them. God's Anger, as is here obvious, burns against such activity.

The short phrase, *"The whole captivity,"* means that neither age nor sex was spared.

It is not exactly known as to what transgression is spoken of, unless it was the invasion of Judah by the Philistines and Arabians in the time of Jehoram, mentioned in II Chronicles 21:16.

ISRAEL AND MODERN GAZA

As is presently known, modern Gaza is a strip of land at the southwest part of Israel, occupied by over one million so-called Palestinians. Actually, there is no such thing as a Palestinian, these people being Egyptian, Syrian, Jordanian, etc.

When this area was turned over to the Palestinians several years ago by Israel, Benjamin Netanyahu, the present Prime Minister of Israel, then said to the Prime Minister at that time that the Palestinians

NOTES

would use this area as a staging ground to lob rockets over into Israel. That's exactly what has happened. Over a thousand rockets a year are lobbed into Israel, which is something that is not exactly to be desired, to say the least. That's the reason that Israel has blockaded that area from the sea; it is to stop weapons from coming in. Israel has no problem whatsoever with foodstuff and suchlike coming in, only weapons, which reason ought to be obvious.

If it is to be noticed, not a single Arab country, which surrounds Israel, will allow any Palestinian to immigrate, even though there is plenty of room. Why?

They want these people to remain there in order to be a thorn in Israel's side and, as well, to garner sympathy from the rest of the world.

Many people think that if Israel would just give half of Jerusalem to the Palestinians, where they could establish it as their capital, and also the West Bank, in connection with Gaza, then everything would be satisfactory. Nothing could be further from the truth.

The Muslim world wants every Jew dead and every foot of ground in Israel to be taken over by Islam. Actually, they hate Israel, the contention going back to the time of Abraham, calling her *"little Satan."* America is referred to by the Muslim world as *"the great Satan."* They hate us no less, and it's because of Jesus Christ!

The Koran is their Bible, and the Koran calls for the overthrow of every government in the world that is not Muslim, and to do so either by diplomacy or violence. To be sure, they do not lack the will, only the way.

While only a few Muslims are murderers, the truth is, every single Muslim is in sympathy with the murderers. Unfortunately, the policy of the United States is the exact opposite as to what it ought to be concerning Islam. It is not a peace loving religion, with a few fanatics that cause all the problems. It is their Bible, the Koran, that draws the blueprint, which, if successful, would throw the world into Dark Ages worse than anything that's ever been seen. In fact, because of its aspect of violence, this religion is of greater danger to America than anything we've ever faced.

(7) "BUT I WILL SEND A FIRE ON THE WALL OF GAZA, WHICH SHALL DEVOUR THE PALACES THEREOF."

The synopsis is:

1. "Gaza" is used here as the representative of the five cities of the Philistines.

2. Despite their supposed strength, the Holy Spirit here says, in essence, "You will be brought down."

3. It is ironic, these were enemies of Israel nearly 2,800 years ago. They still are!

I WILL SEND A FIRE

Each guilty city, and we speak of the five largest cities of Gaza at that time, was to have its own special punishment, though, probably, the calamity of each is common to all.

Gaza was conquered by Sennacherib when he invaded Judah in the time of Hezekiah. It was, as well, invaded by Pharaoh—Necho (Jer. 47:1), and by Alexander the Great, who spent more than two months in its siege.

(8) "AND I WILL CUT OFF THE IN-HABITANT FROM ASHDOD, AND HIM WHO HOLDS THE SCEPTRE FROM ASHKELON, AND I WILL TURN MY HAND AGAINST EKRON: AND THE REMNANT OF THE PHILISTINES SHALL PERISH, SAYS THE LORD GOD."

The pattern is:

1. Exactly as prophesied, there is no trace of "Philistines" left at this time.

2. This area is now presently occupied by the modern Palestinians, who are actually Egyptians, Syrians, Jordanians, etc.

3. What the modern Palestinians do not seem to know, or the balance of the world, for that matter, is that while Israel presently is a long way from God, still, the Prophets of old have predicted her Restoration as a mighty Nation in the Earth. This will take place at the Second Coming of the Lord. That will be the time that Israel will accept Jesus Christ as their Saviour and their Lord.

ASHKELON

It is said that "Ashkelon" was one of the most beautiful cities of Gaza, situated close to the sea. It was said that its position was one of the fairest along that part of the Mediterranean coast. When the interior of the amphitheatre was adorned with splendid

temples and palaces, ascending, rank above rank, from the shore to the summit, the appearance from the sea must have been very imposing.

Even though it did not have a great harbor, still, it carried on a lucrative foreign commerce, which was the chief cause of its power and importance. It was about 50 miles from Jerusalem.

All of these cities, Ashdod, Ashkelon, and Ekron, suffered terrible Judgment exactly as, "Thus says the LORD."

The phrase, "And the remnant of the Philistines shall perish," refers to those who had as yet escaped destruction. It is here said that they "shall perish," and confirmed, "Says the LORD."

(9) "THUS SAYS THE LORD; FOR THREE TRANSGRESSIONS OF TYRUS, AND FOR FOUR, I WILL NOT TURN AWAY THE PUNISHMENT THEREOF; BECAUSE THEY DELIVERED UP THE WHOLE CAPTIVITY TO EDOM, AND REMEMBERED NOT THE BROTHERLY COVENANT."

The construction is:

1. Evidently, to warrant the Judgment by God, Tyre, in some way, had gotten its hands on some Jewish prisoners, whom they delivered over to the Edomites. This cruel conduct was quite unprovoked, as no Jewish king had ever made war against Phoenicia or its capital.

2. "And remembered not the brotherly covenant," refers to the original covenant made with Tyre by David and Solomon (II Sam. 5:11; I Ki. 5:1, 7-11; 9:11-14; II Chron. 2:11).

TYRUS

Now the Prophecy is directed against the princely city of "Tyrus." The sin of Tyre, the great Phoenician merchant city, was committed in concert with the Philistines (Ps. 83:7), and was of the same character, except that she is not accused of carrying away captives, but only of handing them over to the Edomites. As to how these Jewish captives fell into the hands of Tyrus, we aren't told.

(10) "BUT I WILL SEND A FIRE ON THE WALL OF TYRUS, WHICH SHALL DEVOUR THE PALACES THEREOF."

The pattern is:

1. The punishments by Sargon of Assyria, and later by Nebuchadnezzar, who besieged the city for thirteen years, as well as its capture and destruction by Alexander the Great, are well-known.

2. Tyrus was one of the most powerful cities in that part of the world. But yet, the Lord predicts its destruction, which came to pass exactly as predicted.

3. Would Tyrus or any of the heathen cities, for that matter, pay any attention to these pronounced Judgments given by an obscure Prophet and, as well, a common laborer?

THE WAYS OF THE LORD

When these Prophecies were given by Amos, Judah was the only Nation on the face of the Earth that was monotheistic, which meant they worshipped one God, Jehovah. All the other nations of the world were polytheistic, meaning they worshipped many gods, actually, demon spirits. So, the only Light on the face of the Earth at that time was Judah.

Due to the fact that Israel had split asunder, with the northern kingdom being referred to as Samaria or Israel and the southern kingdom referred to as Judah, the proud strength of this Nation, which was indeed great under David and Solomon, had now been weakened and had lost most of its glory. But yet, due to the fact that some of these Israelites were the only people on the face of the Earth who served God, the Lord would use His Prophets not only to speak to Judah and Israel but surrounding nations as well. Would these heathen nations heed these Prophecies?

The truth is, not even Judah and Israel heeded the Prophecies too very much, much less these heathen nations!

WHY WOULD THE LORD WARN THESE HEATHEN NATIONS?

Of course, the Lord knew that these Prophecies, uttered sometimes 40 and 50 years, or even longer, before their fulfillment, would be heeded not at all. But yet, He moved upon the Prophets to give them nevertheless.

Why will the Lord deal with people about

their eternal soul when He already knows they will not respond favorably?

The only way that one can answer these questions is that God is Merciful. As well, He looks ahead to the coming Great White Throne Judgment where, in proverbial black and white, each person and each city or nation will see the Mercy extended to them by warnings given, so they will have no excuse.

The Lord has given to this Ministry (Jimmy Swaggart Ministries) a Revelation of the Cross, which I fully believe is what the Spirit is saying to the churches. Will most preachers or even most Christians heed this Message? No, most will not even bother to hear it, even though it is available. At the Judgment Seat of Christ, however, these Believers will not be able to say, *"I did not know."*

(11) "THUS SAID THE LORD; FOR THREE TRANSGRESSIONS OF EDOM, AND FOR FOUR, I WILL NOT TURN AWAY THE PUNISHMENT THEREOF; BECAUSE HE DID PURSUE HIS BROTHER WITH THE SWORD, AND DID CAST OFF ALL PITY, AND HIS ANGER DID TEAR PERPETUALLY, AND HE KEPT HIS WRATH FOR EVER."

The composition is:

1. Now, the Prophet commences his denouncements against the three nations that were more kindred to Israel: Edom, Ammon, and Moab.

2. *"And he kept his wrath forever,"* refers to Edom's relentless persecution, inhumanity, savage fury, and persistent anger against Israel.

3. Edom sprang from Esau and, in effect, is a brother of Israel, i.e., *"Jacob."*

HIS BROTHER

The phrase, *"Because he did pursue his brother with the sword,"* goes all the way back to the time of Esau, from whom Edom sprang, and was consistent in its unbrotherly conduct, rather than any specific outrages.

The word, *"brother,"* pertains to Jacob and the animosity that existed between him and his brother Esau.

"And he kept his wrath forever," refers to Edom's persecution, inhumanity, savage fury, and persistent anger against Israel.

This means that Edom kept up his grudge (Gen. 25:24). God's Anger burns, as well, against hatred (Num. 20:14-21; II Chron. 28:17; Ps. 137:7; Obad. 10:14).

(12) "BUT I WILL SEND A FIRE UPON TEMAN, WHICH SHALL DEVOUR THE PALACES OF BOZRAH.

(13) "THUS SAYS THE LORD; FOR THREE TRANSGRESSIONS OF THE CHILDREN OF AMMON, AND FOR FOUR, I WILL NOT TURN AWAY THE PUNISHMENT THEREOF; BECAUSE THEY HAVE RIPPED UP THE WOMEN WITH CHILD OF GILEAD, THAT THEY MIGHT ENLARGE THEIR BORDER:

(14) "BUT I WILL KINDLE A FIRE IN THE WALL OF RABBAH, AND IT SHALL DEVOUR THE PALACES THEREOF, WITH SHOUTING IN THE DAY OF BATTLE, WITH A TEMPEST IN THE DAY OF THE WHIRLWIND:

(15) "AND THEIR KING SHALL GO INTO THE CAPTIVITY, HE AND HIS PRINCES TOGETHER, SAYS THE LORD."

The pattern is:

1. (Vs. 13) *"Ammon"* was connected with Israel by being an offspring of Lot, which *"Moab"* was, as well!

2. (Vs. 13) *"That they might enlarge their border,"* concerns their greed for more territory, especially in later years when they seized the possessions of the Tribe of Gad—a proceeding that brought upon them the denunciation of Jeremiah (Jer. 49:2-6).

3. (Vs. 14) *"Rabbah"* was the capital of Ammon, about 25 miles northeast of the Dead Sea, and is the same as present-day Ammon, Jordan.

4. (Vs. 15) All these Judgments were occasioned by the persecution inflicted by these heathen nations on God's People, Israel.

AMMON

The birth of Ammon and Moab was incestuous in that Lot's two daughters became pregnant by him as a result of his drunkenness. Consequently, the seed of that offspring retained the stamp of its birth in habits, character, and worship (Gen. 19:30).

Ammon's hostility toward Israel was shown in their participation with Moab in the affair of Balaam (Deut. 23:4). There

were other incidents as well!

The phrase, *"Because they have ripped up the women with child of Gilead,"* is referred to in Hosea 13:16; and II Kings 8:12; 15:16.

RABBAH

"Rabbah," as stated, was the capital of Ammon, about 25 miles northeast of the Dead Sea, and is the same as present-day Ammon, Jordan.

Considerable archeological remains exist in the vicinity of Ammon today. At the airport, a building of the Thirteenth Century B.C. has been unearthed. It was used as a depository for cremated human remains, many of them of young children, perhaps sacrificed to the idol god, *"Molech."*

CAPTIVITY

The *"captivity"* referred to in Verse 15 pertained not only to *"their king,"* but, as well, to their god, *"Molech."*

All of these Judgments, as stated, were occasioned by the persecution inflicted by these heathen nations on God's People.

As well, it seems that the animosity was even more intense among Israel's kindred, namely *"Edom," "Ammon,"* and *"Moab."*

It has often been observed that no anger is so savage as the anger which springs up between relations of blood. A brotherly hate is the chief of hates.

As well, it may be truly said that there is no animosity that burns with a more hellish heat than that connected with religion. Gibbon, the Roman historian, referring to the cruelties inflicted upon the early Christians, says:

"They died in torments, and their torments were embittered by insult and derision. Some were nailed on crosses, others sewn up in the skins of wild beasts and exposed to the fury of dogs; others, again, smeared over with combustible material, were used as torches to illuminate the darkness of the night. The gardens of Nero were destined for the melancholy spectacle, which was accompanied by a horse race and honored with the presence of the Emperor, who mingled with the populace in the dress and attitude of a charioteer."[1]

It has been well said that, *"The blood of*

the martyrs is the seed of the Church."

"A blameless Faith was all the crime,
"The Christian martyr knew;
"And when the crimson current flowed,
"Upon that barren sand,
"Up sprang a tree, whose vigorous boughs,
"Soon overspread the land;
"O'er distant isles its shadow fell, nor knew,
"Its roots decay,
"E'en when the Roman Caesar's throne and,
"Empire passed away."

CHAPTER 2

(1) "THUS SAYS THE LORD; FOR THREE TRANSGRESSIONS OF MOAB, AND FOR FOUR, I WILL NOT TURN AWAY THE PUNISHMENT THEREOF; BECAUSE HE BURNED THE BONES OF THE KING OF EDOM INTO LIME."

The exegesis is:

1. Amos now denounces Moab, also connected by ties of blood with Israel.

2. The phrase, *"Because he burned the bones of the king of Edom into lime,"* shows that God's Anger burns against unnatural and cruel crimes, even though their victims be as cruel and wicked as was the king of Edom.

3. One can be certain that the prefix, *"Thus says the LORD,"* guarantees its fulfillment.

MOAB

Amos now denounces Moab, which is also connected by ties of blood with Israel.

As stated, Moab's hostility many years before had been shown in the hiring of Balaam to curse the Israelites and in seducing them to idolatry (Num., Chpts. 22-25).

As well, David had to take most stringent measures against Moab (II Sam. 8:2). In other words, albeit kindred to Israel, they were, as well, bitter enemies!

The phrase, *"Because he burned the bones*

NOTES

of the king of Edom into lime," shows that God's Anger burns against unnatural and cruel crimes.

NATIONS NEAR JUDAH

If it is to be noticed, all of these pronounced Judgments by the Lord concerned the Middle East. Why the Middle East? And why only the Middle East?

Other parts of the world, in fact, the entirety of the world of that day, was of interest to God, as would be obvious; however, only with small exception is this part of the world mentioned in the Old Testament. It broadens somewhat in the New Testament, including all that was in the Roman Empire, but yet, Rome was addressed only as it impacted the People of God.

A PERSONAL EXPERIENCE

Standing on top of Masada once with a Jewish guide, he was pointing out to me the remains of the ruins of the Roman encampment when they overthrew Masada nearly 2,000 years ago.

I made mention to him that mighty Rome, which ruled the world for nearly 1,000 years, is now but a distant memory, and, to the contrary, Israel is now a thriving Nation.

He stood there for a moment locked in his own thoughts at the import of the statement. He then said to me, *"I've never thought of that!"*

Nations without God, no matter how powerful, rich, and prosperous they might be, will ultimately perish. Those who know the Lord, in one way or the other, abide forever.

As it regards Old Testament times, Jehovah dwelt in the Holy of Holies in the Temple in Jerusalem, actually, between the Mercy Seat and the Cherubim. While, of course, the Lord is Omnipresent, meaning everywhere, still, as it regards Earth and the place of His Attention, then, it was Jerusalem. Now, it is the heart of every Believer.

Before the Cross, and due to the fact that the blood of animals could not take away sins, this meant that the sin debt remained. Consequently, the Lord could not abide within the hearts and lives of Believers, only in those with whom He had appointed to a particular task, and then only until the task was completed. Since the Cross, referring to the fact that all sin was there atoned, past, present, and future, at least for those who will believe (Jn. 3:16), the Holy Spirit can and, in fact, does abide in the hearts and lives of all Believers, and does so permanently (Jn. 14:16-17).

The Moabites showed the spirit of revenge under which they acted. It is noticed by the Lord and will ultimately bring Divine Judgments upon them. Expositors say, *"The evil passions of the heart break out in various forms, but the Lord keeps an account of motives as well as of conduct. Those who deal cruelly, shall be cruelly dealt with."*

(2) "BUT I WILL SEND A FIRE UPON MOAB, AND IT SHALL DEVOUR THE PALACES OF KIRIOTH: AND MOAB SHALL DIE WITH TUMULT, WITH SHOUTING, AND WITH THE SOUND OF THE TRUMPET."

The pattern is:

1. The phrase, *"And Moab shall die with tumult,"* refers to her destruction beginning with Nebuchadnezzar.

2. In fulfillment of this Verse, the Moabites ultimately ceased to have independent existence as a nation. In fact, that area is now a part of modern Jordan.

3. Strangely enough, the country of Moab was kin to Israel, so to speak, being the offspring of Lot, Abraham's nephew.

MOAB ULTIMATELY CEASED TO EXIST AS A NATION

The phrase, *"And Moab shall die with tumult,"* refers to her destruction beginning with Nebuchadnezzar and finally falling under the control of the Persians and various Arab groups. Ultimately, the Moabites, in fulfillment of this Passage, ceased to have independent existence as a nation.

(3) "AND I WILL CUT OFF THE JUDGE FROM THE MIDST THEREOF, AND WILL SLAY ALL THE PRINCES THEREOF WITH HIM, SAYS THE LORD."

The exegesis is:

1. The six nations concerned in the Prophecies, *"Syria, Philistia, Tyre, Edom, Ammon, and Moab,"* defiled Immanuel's Land, for they lived within its original

boundaries. Judgment, therefore, expelled them.

2. These nations opposed Israel, and to oppose that which belongs to God, opposes God!

3. They forgot, or else they ignored, the Promise made to Abraham. It said:

"And I will bless them who bless you, and curse him who curses you: and in you shall all families of the Earth be blessed" (Gen. 12:3).

THE WORD OF THE LORD

Regrettably and sadly, not only did the heathen nations defile Immanuel's Land, but Judah and Israel, heirs of that inheritance, also defiled it, and, consequently, a similar Judgment struck them. It is very solemn when God's professing People are condemned with the ungodly.

As we shall see, the distinctions between the causes of the Judgment respecting Judah and Israel are significant and instructed. The one was doctrinal; the other, moral. Judah claimed to be orthodox; Israel, to be progressive.

DOCTRINE AND MORALITY

Judah's sin was despising the Bible and accepting the lies of man's religious teaching. Such is the feature of Protestantism today. There is a profession of loyalty to the Bible, but it is really despised and the religious teaching of prominent men preferred. In fact, to call these teachings *"lies,"* as Amos did, would be denounced today as rude and violent language and an affront to unity.

Israel was addressed as having at least a smattering of knowledge of Truth, but the main charge against the northern kingdom was a moral one. Their conduct was in question. To have spoken to them as professing keepers of the Law was impossible, but their conscience could not repel an accusation as to their actions.

They sold the righteous and poor into slavery for a trifle; they crushed the head of the poor into the very dust; they perverted justice; a man and his son debased themselves with the same unhappy victim of the idolatrous and obscene worship of Astarte; they took the garments of the poor as collateral for small loans and kept them, which God commanded should be restored before sunset (Ex. 22:26). They then took the money, which they had bled from the poor, and used it for feasts before *"every altar"*—God having ordained but one Altar, and that was at the Temple in Jerusalem; and the money the Judges bled from the poor and the unfortunate, with them being unjustly condemned in their courts, they spent on wine to be drunk at these idol banquets.

DIVINE LOVE

In contrast with this sad recital, Divine Love recalls its action toward them in delivering them out of Egypt; in totally destroying the Amorites; and in raising up Prophets and Nazarites so as to maintain relationship between God and them when the Ceremonial law had failed.

Judgment, therefore, was inevitable; and its action was committed shortly afterwards to the Assyrians, who slaughtered the men of Israel in thousands and carried the residue into captivity, which, in a sense, they have not yet escaped even unto this day.

(4) "THUS SAYS THE LORD; FOR THREE TRANSGRESSIONS OF JUDAH, AND FOR FOUR, I WILL NOT TURN AWAY THE PUNISHMENT THEREOF; BECAUSE THEY HAVE DESPISED THE LAW OF THE LORD, AND HAVE NOT KEPT HIS COMMANDMENTS, AND THEIR LIES CAUSED THEM TO ERR, AFTER THE WHICH THEIR FATHERS HAVE WALKED."

The composition is:

1. As God pronounced Judgments upon heathen nations, which Judah and Israel no doubt thought were amply deserved, likewise, the thrust is now turned toward Judah, even the people who retained the Temple and its worship.

2. This amply portrays that God cannot abide sin in His Own any more than He can those who are not His private Possession.

3. Actually, sin is worse in those who belong to Him than in the heathen. *"To whom much is given much is required"* (Lk. 12:48).

JUDAH

As previously stated, the statement, *"For three transgressions of Judah, and for four,"*

is a Hebrew idiom, denoting unnumbered times and, actually, *"many times."*

As it runs like a single thread throughout the entirety of the Bible, such Passages as Verse 4 completely *"debunk"* the erroneous doctrine of *"Unconditional Eternal Security."* The idea that one, after coming to Christ, can live any way he desires, even denying Christ and His Way of Salvation, which is the Cross, and doing so without fear of the loss of Salvation, is specious indeed! And yet, millions pin the hope of their Eternal Salvation on a specious doctrine, which has no Scriptural validity. Unconfessed sin in the life of the Believer is the same, or even worse, much worse, than sin in the life of the unbeliever.

While it is certainly true that God took care of the sins of the Believer at Calvary, still, unconfessed sin makes a mockery of that Sacrifice (I Jn. 1:9).

In the Old Economy, God could not forgive sin, even in His Chosen People, without the required sacrifice, except in certain circumstances. As well, under the New Covenant, the Lord demands that proper confession of known sin be made to God (I Jn. 1:9). Provision is made on that account, and that alone.

ONLY IN CHRIST

While it is true that a Perfect God demands perfection in His Children, as He only can command, and which is found only in Christ, still, to avail oneself of such perfection, the Scriptural admonitions must be properly followed. Christians, who do not properly confess their sins to the Lord and then turn away from those sins, or, at least, make every attempt to do so, need not expect proper cleansing from sin.

THE CROSS OF CHRIST

Sin is the problem! Say what you may or claim what you will, sin is the problem! It doesn't matter if it's the Believer or unbeliever, sin is the problem! And there is only one solution to this problem, one answer to this problem, and only one, and it is *"the Cross of Christ."* Paul wrote:

"But this Man (this Priest, Christ Jesus), **after He had offered One Sacrifice for sins**

forever *(speaks of the Cross)*, **sat down on the Right Hand of God** *(refers to the great contrast with the Priests under the Levitical system, who never sat down because their work was never completed; the Work of Christ was a 'Finished Work' and needed no repetition)*" **(Heb. 10:12).**

The great Apostle also said, **"So Christ was once offered to bear the sins of many** *(the Cross was God's Answer to sin and, in fact, the only answer)* . . ." **(Heb. 9:28).**

Many, if not most, preachers presently won't even mention sin or the Cross. They claim that it may offend people. Well, if the preacher will not mention the problem, which is sin, or the Cross, which is the solution, such a preacher is an abomination in the Sight of God. Let's say it this way:

The only answer for sin is the Cross of Christ. When we understand the price attached to the Cross that was paid by Christ, and when we understand, at least as much as a poor human being can understand, the enormity of what Jesus did at Calvary, but then we refuse to portray this one and only solution to the people, such a preacher is an abomination in the Eyes of God.

THE HOLY SPIRIT

When the believing sinner comes to Christ and is Born-Again, the Holy Spirit immediately takes up His Residence in the heart of such a person (I Cor. 3:16). While the Holy Spirit, Who is God, abides in our hearts and lives for many purposes and reasons, the primary purpose is to help us overcome sin in every capacity. While the Bible does not teach sinless perfection, it most definitely does teach that sin is not to have dominion over us (Rom. 6:14).

To oversimplify an extremely complex matter, perhaps the following will help:

• As a Believer, we must first understand that even though we are a new creation in Christ Jesus, still, within ourselves, we cannot develop the Fruit of the Spirit or anything else that pertains to the Lord. The Fall has rendered the human body ineffective, and that goes for the human mind as well (Rom. 8:10).

• What must be done in our hearts and lives as Believers, as it regards growing in

Grace and the Knowledge of the Lord, is that we understand that the Holy Spirit Alone can make us what we ought to be. While every Believer has a position of perfection in Christ, the truth is, our *"condition"* is not exactly up to our *"position."* It is the business of the Holy Spirit to bring the two together (Rom. 8:1-2, 11).

• We must, as well, understand that the Holy Spirit Works exclusively within the parameters, so to speak, of the Finished Work of Christ. In other words, it is the Cross of Christ that has given the Holy Spirit the legal means to do all that He does (I Cor. 1:17, 18, 23, 2:2).

• While the Holy Spirit doesn't require very much of us, He most definitely does require, even demand, that our Faith be exclusively in Christ and what Christ has done for us at the Cross. In other words, the Cross of Christ must ever be the Object of our Faith (Rom. 6:3-5; I Cor. 1:17).

• With our Faith properly placed and properly maintained, the Holy Spirit will then function in our hearts and lives as He Alone can do (Jn. 16:13-15).

GOD'S PRESCRIBED ORDER

In brief, His Prescribed Order is *"Jesus Christ and Him Crucified"* (I Cor. 1:23). If we separate Christ from the Work that He did at the Cross, we are left with *"another Jesus"* (II Cor. 11:1-4). That doesn't mean putting Jesus back on the Cross. Our Lord is today seated by the Right Hand of the Father. His Work on the Cross is complete; however, we must remember the following:

• The Cross of Christ is a Work that has been finished in the past (Heb. 9:28).

• The Work that was accomplished at the Cross has continuing results (Lk. 9:23; 14:27).

• The results of the Cross, what Jesus there did, will never be discontinued (Heb. 13:20).

FOUR THINGS ARE SAID RESPECTING THE FAILURE OF JUDAH

The Word of the Lord is crystal clear as it regards the reason for the Judgment of God, which would ultimately come upon Judah. And please understand, the problem that persisted then is the same problem that persists now.

BECAUSE THEY HAVE DESPISED THE LAW OF THE LORD

Judah's sin was despising the Bible and accepting the lies of man's religious teaching.

The other nations are denounced for their offenses against God's People; Judah is sentenced for her offenses against God Himself.

The former had offended against the Law of Conscience or, in other words, man's religion, while the latter offended against the written Law, which was Revelation from God.

The tragedy is that the modern church has little learned, as Judah of old! The Bible, at least, in too many churches, is merely window dressing. Sadly, this includes virtually all churches.

The trend yesterday was modern thought, hence, the denial of the Word of God as little more than fables and rife in old-line churches.

Satan has taken a different tack with Pentecostals, Holiness, and Charismatics, who profess to believe all of the Word of God. He has quietly substituted psychology, which is humanistic in origin and humanistic in practice, as the panacea for the ills of modern man. Irrespective of the efforts of modern preachers to combine the two, still, they are inimical, meaning hostile to one another. And, there is no way that the two, humanistic psychology and the Bible, can be reconciled.

So, even though the Bible is not verbally denied by these practitioners, it is definitely denied in practice; consequently, the problem with the modern church is doctrinal as it was with Judah of old.

AND HAVE NOT KEPT HIS COMMANDMENTS

The Law, of course, was full of Commandments of the Lord, even though the Lord knew that Israel could not keep them, and yet, they were to try with all their strength to do so. The Sacrificial system was, in essence, a fallback as it regarded Israel. In fact, had it not been for the Sacrificial system, Israel would have been totally destroyed.

NOTES

Let's say it in this manner:

The Cross of Christ portrayed in the Sacrificial system before Christ, and a concluding fact after Christ, is the only thing which stands between man and the Judgment of God. Now, if we believe that to be true, and it most definitely is, then the Preacher had better *"preach the Cross,"* and the Believer had better place his or her Faith exclusively in Christ and the Cross.

Under the New Covenant, there are really no Commandments, but rather Faith; however, the Faith of which we speak is that which has the Cross of Christ as its sole Object.

But yet, due to the fact that they are moral, the moral Law of God, ensconced in the Ten Commandments, must be kept. Under the New Covenant, the question is not that we keep them, but rather how they are to be kept.

Under the New Covenant, if the Believer attempts to live this life by Commandments, he will fail. Paul said:

". . . If Righteousness come by the Law, then Christ is dead in vain" (Gal. 2:21). So, the way they are kept is according to the following:

• The Believer is to place his or her Faith exclusively in Christ and the Cross (Rom. 6:1-14; I Cor. 1:17-18; Gal. 6:14).

• The Holy Spirit, Who is God, and Who Works exclusively within the parameters of the Finished Work of Christ, will then Work mightily on behalf of the Believer (Rom. 8:1-2, 11).

• With our Faith properly placed, the Holy Spirit will keep the Commandments for us, meaning that we will do such without even giving it a thought.

Jesus Christ is the end of the Law, meaning He has fulfilled it in every respect, including the keeping of the Ten Commandments, and doing so perfectly. Our Faith in Him and what He did for us at the Cross puts us in the position of Law-keeper instead of the position of Lawbreaker, which we were and are before Faith in Christ. Ideally, the Believer is to allow Christ to live this life within us. Hence, Paul said, **"I am crucified with Christ** (*as the Foundation of all Victory; Paul, here, takes us back to Rom. 6:3-5*)**: nevertheless I live** (*have new life*);

yet not I (*not by my own strength and ability*), **but Christ lives in me** (*by virtue of me dying with Him on the Cross and being raised with Him in Newness of Life*)**: and the life which I now live in the flesh** (*my daily walk before God*) **I live by the Faith of the Son of God** (*the Cross is ever the Object of my Faith*), **Who loved me, and gave Himself for me** (*which is the only way that I could be Saved*)" **(Gal. 2:20).**

But once we attempt to live for God by the keeping of Commandments, that's when we have just failed.

The reason is, the Fall in the Garden of Eden made us ineffective in that capacity (Rom. 8:10). So, for this to be done, it must be done another way, and that other way is Jesus becoming our Representative Man, which He did. We must ever understand, every single thing He did was for you and me. Our simple Faith in Him, which pertains to His Life and Living, and, above all, the price He paid at Calvary's Cross, guarantees us all of that for which He died. If it is to be noticed, in Galatians 2:20, which was just quoted, Paul begins with the Cross and ends with the Cross.

AND THEIR LIES CAUSED THEM TO ERR

These *"lies"* referred to false doctrine, which was rampant under the Old Covenant as it is rampant under the New Covenant. Under the New Covenant, Paul referred to such as *"another gospel"* (Gal. 1:6).

He went on to say, *"Which is not another."* The problem is, false doctrine abounds, and most Christians are so unlearned in the Bible that they do not know the difference. The Cross of Christ and our understanding of that Finished Work is what gives us a defense against false doctrine. In fact, that's the reason that the church presently is filled up and running over with false doctrine. It is because the Message of the Cross has been ignored. Let's say it another way:

The Cross of Christ is the dividing line between the true Church and the apostate church. In fact, that's not new, having always been that way. It began in the Fourth Chapter of Genesis, regarding Cain and Abel.

The Message of the New Covenant is, *"Jesus*

NOTES

Christ and Him Crucified" (I Cor. 1:23).

It would be quite easy to innumerate particular false doctrines, and there are many. However, suffice to say, if the church is not preaching Christ and Him Crucified, then whatever it is that is being preached is not truly the Gospel of Jesus Christ and will do the listener precious little good, if any at all.

WHAT DOES IT MEAN TO PREACH THE CROSS?

It means that the Preacher must understand that Jesus Christ is the Source of all things we receive from God, and the Cross of Christ is solely the Means by which these things are given to us. The latter part of this sentence is where the problem arises.

While most will agree that Jesus Christ is the Source, many do not want to agree that the Cross of Christ is the only Means by which these things are given, whatever they might be, and the only Means by which we receive them. This means that our Faith must be exclusively in Christ and the Cross, and when I say exclusively, I mean exclusively (Lk. 9:23; 14:27).

FALSE PROPHETS

Jesus said, *"You shall know them by their fruits . . ."* (Mat. 7:16).

What *"fruits"* is He speaking of?

Primarily, He is speaking of souls being Saved, lives being changed, the sick being healed, and demons being cast out (Mat. 10:7-8).

However, it must be quickly added that *"false prophets"* claim all of these things and more! Concerning people being Saved, huge numbers are advertised, as well as all types of Miracles, with Signs and Wonders heralded constantly. However, mere claims, irrespective of their size and fanfare, are not enough.

Where is the proof?

If souls are truly being Saved, obviously, they can be found somewhere. If lives are truly being changed, certainly the evidence of these changed lives will be obvious. As well, claims of the sick being healed and Miracles performed will not always be confined to that which is not obvious to the eye.

Sadly, too many Christians believe

whatever they are told without any proof to validate the claims.

Tragically, modern Christianity, in too many circles, has sunk to the level of *"show business."* Consequently, if there is no plain Biblical injunction to validate any and all claims, they should be rejected out of hand.

Inasmuch as this subject is so important, perhaps the following, although going into some detail concerning various subjects, will be helpful.

SIGHTINGS OF THE VIRGIN MARY?

For instance, many Catholics claim sightings of the Virgin Mary, with many Protestants believing these claims.

Is such genuine?

In a word, *"No!"*

In fact, there have been scores of alleged sightings of the Virgin Mary virtually all over the world. The frequency of the alleged sightings has risen and fallen throughout the many, many years in which they have been reported.

In 1992, there was a report of an alleged sighting of the Virgin Mary in a Catholic church in a small town in Kentucky. The mayor of the town, as I heard the news report, was making plans to handle the crowds as a result of this event. They were receiving phone calls about it from all over America.

In the same year, someone reported seeing a vision of the Virgin Mary in one of the south Louisiana parishes. Thousands of cars converged on the area as people went to ogle the place of the alleged sighting.

I am sure that some of you are acquainted with the place that was formerly known as Medjugorje, Yugoslavia, where, over a period of time, several little girls are supposed to have held conversations with the Virgin Mary. Until warfare erupted in that area, it was visited by hundreds of thousands of people. Actually, a number of tours originated from our city of Baton Rouge as well as New Orleans, with Catholics traveling to the area, climbing the hill, and seeing the place where Mary is supposed to have appeared numerous times to these young girls.

As well, scores of tours originated from other parts of the world, concerning this phenomenon.

POPE JOHN PAUL II

Pope John Paul II said that he owed his position as Pope to the Virgin Mary. He claimed to have been visited by her sometime in the past and given varied instructions. He claimed that in one of these appearances the Virgin Mary told him that he would be Pope. As a result, he strongly supported the Mary cult, even at one point suggesting that she be made co-redemptress with the Lord Jesus Christ. Wiser heads in the Vatican finally talked him out of this. From his appointment as Pope, these alleged sightings have, in fact, multiplied. Did he really have a vision of the Virgin Mary?

Yes, I believe he had a vision, but it was not the Virgin Mary that he saw, which I will explain momentarily.

The Catholic church has always venerated Mary in an unscriptural manner, such as the *"Immaculate Conception," "praying to Mary," "looking to her as an intercessor,"* and in other ways. However, this unscriptural conduct has multiplied manyfold since John Paul II. Today, Mary is basically deified in the Catholic church.

UNSCRIPTURAL

I realize that many will take offense with me regarding my flat denial of the genuineness of these alleged sightings. It is not my intention to impugn anyone's Spiritual experience; however, any Spiritual experience must be judged in the light of the Word of God. The Bible plainly says:

"Beloved, believe not every spirit, but try the spirits whether they are of God: because many false prophets are gone out into the world" (1 Jn. 4:1).

The validity of any *"spiritual experience"* must be established by the Word of God. It cannot be established by the Pope, a church denomination, the actual fact of the Vision itself, a preacher, or anything, or anyone else. I repeat, it must be established by the Word of God, or else it is specious.

There is not one single instance in the Word of God of Mary or any of the Apostles appearing to anyone after their deaths. On the Mount of Transfiguration, Moses and Elijah appeared to Christ, with Peter,

James, and John present. They viewed the event, but they were not included in the exchange of conversation (Lk. 9:27-36).

Actually, when Peter suggested that they *"make three tabernacles; one for Christ, and one for Moses, and one for Elijah,"* the Scripture says he didn't even know what he said.

Then the Word says, *"And there came a Voice out of the cloud, saying, This is My Beloved Son: hear Him"* (Lk. 9:35).

HEAR HIM!

The purpose of the statement is clear. Peter was placing Moses on the same par with the Lord Jesus Christ, and the Heavenly Father was quick to correct his presumption. Jesus was the One they were to listen to and no other.

As stated, there is no record in the Word of God of any appearance of Mary to anyone after her death. Therefore, if the precedent is not established in the Word of God, then the alleged appearances are not Scripturally valid, and, consequently, it is not actually Mary who is appearing to these individuals. If it is not Mary, then who or what is it?

FAMILIAR SPIRITS

Most of the sightings are probably fabrications; however, the possibility definitely exists that some could be real. Nevertheless, it is not Mary but demon spirits (familiar spirits) impersonating Mary.

Paul said, *"And no marvel; for Satan himself is transformed into an Angel of light"* (II Cor. 11:14).

There are many *"Angels of light"* impersonating that which appears to be of God.

Visions, Dreams, and actual Visitations by the Lord are real because they are Scriptural. Still, we must be careful not to arbitrarily accept everything that claims to be of God, but we must *"try the spirits"* to determine their Scriptural validity. If it's not Scriptural, it is a *"lie."*

What is a familiar spirit?

It is a demon spirit that makes itself familiar with the individual in question, whoever he may be, and then appearing to someone in the form of the person impersonated. That is what John Paul II saw. A demon

NOTES

spirit, and not Mary, appeared to him.

The Prophet Isaiah said:

"And when they shall say unto you, Seek unto them that have familiar spirits, and unto wizards that peep, and that mutter: should not a people seek unto their God? for the living to the dead?"

The Prophet then said, *"To the Law and to the Testimony: if they speak not according to this Word, it is because there is no light in them"* (Isa. 8:19-20).

THE CHURCH WORLD

Most of the alleged Mary sightings or visions are associated with the world of Catholicism. However, the Protestant world, especially the Pentecostal (and I am Pentecostal) and Charismatic segments, are little better. By and large, the Christian church world is so Scripturally illiterate that if anything is claimed to be a Miracle, it is eagerly embraced.

We who are Protestant smile at the unscriptural claims of the sightings of Mary and other phenomenon, yet, at the same time, we often follow and loudly proclaim that which purports to be a Miracle from God when, in reality, many times, it is not. Yes, God performs Miracles today, but He needs no false claims or false miracles to validate His Miracle-working Power. Too often the claims are not meant to praise the Lord at all but to praise man.

Consequently, the same scrutiny must be applied to all other apparent Miracles as is applied to the alleged sightings of Mary. They must have Scriptural validity.

SCRIPTURAL VALIDITY

• There is Scriptural validity for *"anointing with oil"* and *"praying for the sick"* (James 5:14).

• There is Scriptural validity for the use of *"handkerchiefs or aprons,"* taken from the person of a man or woman of God, regarding the healing of the sick or evil spirits being cast out (Acts 19:11-12).

• There is Scriptural validity for using the Name of Jesus and casting out demons, speaking with new Tongues, putting away demon spirits, and the drinking of any deadly thing without hurt, with the latter never referring to presumptuous exhibitionism but to accidental ingestion (Mk. 16:17-18).

• There is Scriptural validity for *"falling out"* under the Power of God, for the Apostle John said, *". . . I fell at His Feet as dead . . ."* (Rev. 1:17).

Also, at the dedication of Solomon's Temple, *". . . the Priests could not stand to minister because of the cloud . . ."* (I Ki. 8:11).

• There is Scriptural validity for the laying on of hands for healing (Acts 28:8).

• There is Scriptural validity for taking someone by the hand and lifting him up after prayer (Acts 3:7).

• There is Scriptural validity for the *"place being shaken"* as a consequence of prayer and the Moving of the Holy Spirit (Acts 4:31).

• There is Scriptural validity for one's shadow passing over someone and his being healed (Acts 5:15).

• There is Scriptural validity for mixing spittle and clay and anointing the eyes of the blind with the mixture that they might be healed (Jn. 9:6).

However, it should be noted that the Lord Jesus Christ is the only One Who ever did this, with no record in the Word of the Apostles or anyone else ever attempting to do so.

• There is Scriptural validity for praying for the dead to be raised (Acts 9:36-41).

• There is Scriptural validity for one being miraculously transported from one place to another without any means of transportation or conveyance (Acts 8:39-40).

• There is Scriptural validity for the visitation of Angels (Acts 5:19); however, as stated, we must make certain it is an Angel from the Lord and not an *"Angel of light."*

• John 20:22 speaks of Jesus breathing on the Disciples saying, *". . . Receive you the Holy Spirit."* However, there is no record that He did this at any other time or in any other capacity. I feel it would be a serious presumption, or even sin, to think that any frail mortal could breathe on anyone and have him receive the Holy Spirit.

THE LAST DAYS

In these last days proceeding toward the advent of the Antichrist and the Great

NOTES

Tribulation, miracles from the spirit world are going to become more numerous. When the Antichrist makes his debut, it will not only be political but also spiritual. He will be accompanied by the False Prophet, who will perform miracles. The apostate church will, no doubt, fall in with him, claiming, as Israel, that the Antichrist is the Messiah. The Antichrist will come with *". . . power and signs and lying wonders"* (II Thess. 2:9).

His tactics will be amazingly successful. He will deceive many *". . . because they received not the love of the Truth, that they might be Saved"* (II Thess. 2:10). As these days swiftly approach, we must be very careful that what we accept is totally Scriptural. The Bible is the foundation; it is the criteria; there is no other.

Just because something purports to be a Miracle (or actually seems to be one) does not necessarily mean it is Scriptural.

As the Prophet of old said, *"To the Law and to the Testimony . . ."* (Isa. 8:20).

AFTER THE WHICH THEIR FATHERS HAVE WALKED

There is a tremendous push in the modern church to follow the lead of recognized so-called spiritual leaders and to place oneself under the *"covering"* of these individuals. The same is said for religious denominations, implying that if one doesn't belong to a particular denomination, then one is trying to hide something, which is the reason he or she doesn't want this denomination for their covering, etc.

There is absolutely nothing in Scripture that validates such practice. Actually, it is blatantly unscriptural.

Jesus said, *"Follow Me,"* (Mat. 4:19), and not some poor, frail mortal.

Paul said, *"Be you followers of me, even as I also am of Christ"* (I Cor. 11:1).

Even Paul did not follow the Apostles, even though he loved them, respected them, and held them in high regard! He followed Christ, as all men should do.

The Prophet Isaiah said, *"Woe to the rebellious children, says the LORD, who take counsel, but not of Me; and who cover with a covering, but not of My Spirit, that they may add sin to sin"* (Isa. 30:1).

In Isaiah, Chapter 29, the design of the Jewish rulers to seek the alliance of Egypt was covertly looked at and condemned; now it is openly declared and rebuked.

"Counsel," which is not of the Word of God, is also not from God.

As well, only the Spirit of God can cover someone, which He does through the Word, which speaks of what Jesus did for us at the Cross. Actually, the *"covering"* comes for each Believer through Christ, Who Alone can actually cover. And He does so by the Spirit through the Cross. Christ is the Source while the Cross is the Means.

Any poor mortal who thinks he can be the *"covering"* for another presents spiritual and Scriptural ignorance.

ONE CAN LIE TO MEN; ONE CANNOT LIE TO THE HOLY SPIRIT

One cannot successfully lie to God, but one can lie to men, and many often do. The idea that one is safe if he has some type of man-made covering is foolishness. This teaching stems from psychology, which denies the Word of God as our Source of strength and direction, and, instead, calls for leaning on the frail arm of man. What difference does it make if all the men in the world vouch for an individual, and God doesn't? Conversely, what difference does it make if all the men in the world will not vouch for an individual, and God does?

We should seek earnestly the well-wishes, counsel, and approval of our brethren in the Lord. However, it is not man's approval or well-wishes that make the difference; it is God's Approval and His Alone. Paul said:

"Do we begin again to commend ourselves? or need we, as some others, Epistles of commendation to you, or letters of commendation from you?" (II Cor. 3:1).

Paul also said:

"For not he who commends himself is approved, but whom the Lord commends" (II Cor. 10:18).

Some time ago in a so-called Christian magazine, there was a write-up by one of the editors concerning a particular Evangelist. He had submitted himself to a group of men,

and they became his covering. It was ballyhooed as an example of an honest Minister.

However, it is very easy to submit oneself to individuals or denominational leaders who live a half continent away and are seen perhaps once a year, if that. This type of submission may sound good to the carnal mind, but it is not spiritually valid. Sadly, great numbers of preachers have fallen for this carnal foolishness.

The truth is, there are many who are trying to get away with sin, and doing so by submitting themselves to some man or denomination. This makes them look good outwardly, but the truth is, they are hiding behind other men so as to impress others.

FIG LEAVES

Concerning the Fall of Adam and Eve, the Word says, **". . . and they sewed fig leaves together, and made themselves aprons" (Gen. 3:7).** The notes from THE EXPOSITOR'S STUDY BIBLE say, *"Sinners clothe themselves with morality, sacraments, and religious ceremonies; they are as worthless as Adam's apron of fig leaves."*

And then Moses wrote, **"Unto Adam also and to his wife did the LORD God make coats of skins, and clothed them" (Gen. 3:21).** THE EXPOSITOR'S says, *"In the making of coats of skins, God, in effect, was telling Adam and Eve that their fig leaves were insufficient; as well, He was teaching them that without the shedding of blood, which pertained to the animals that gave their lives, which were Types of Christ, is no remission of sin; in this first sacrifice was laid the foundation of the entirety of the Plan of God as it regards Redemption; also, it must be noticed that it is the 'LORD God' Who furnished these coats, and not man himself; this tells us that Salvation is altogether of God and not at all of man; the Life of Christ given on the Cross, and given as our Substitute, provides the only covering for sin; everything else must be rejected."*

THE LORD OR MAN

We can either have the covering of the Lord or the covering of man; we cannot have both. If we opt for man's covering, then we will receive no covering at all. The Holy

Spirit will simply step aside and allow us to trust the ways of Egypt. I love my brethren in the Lord. I seek their counsel and their help—and I need all the help I can get. But to proclaim some poor, frail individual, or poor, frail denominational head as my *"covering"* is foolishness indeed because it is blatantly unscriptural.

To be frank, millions are in Hell today because they followed this pernicious teaching and trusted in *"fathers"* who did not follow the Lord.

One day all of us will stand before God, and in that hour, we will not be able to point to someone else and say, *"He was my covering, and, therefore, he is responsible."*

It should be readily obvious that the Lord is going to hold each person responsible for his own actions; consequently, the Catholic will not be able to point to the Priest and say, *"But he said. . . !"* Neither will the Protestant be able to point to some preacher or *"father"* and shift responsibility!

Every person is responsible for his own actions, and when standing before the Lord, will have to personally give account.

How far has the church drifted from the Ways of God! Today one is ridiculed if he says, *"The Lord is my Covering."* He is praised if he says, *"Man is my covering."*

I will say as Joshua said a long time ago, *". . . as for me and my house, we will serve the LORD"* (Josh. 24:15).

(5) "BUT I WILL SEND A FIRE UPON JUDAH, AND IT SHALL DEVOUR THE PALACES OF JERUSALEM."

The synopsis is:

1. And that's exactly what happened! Not too many years later, the Nation and city were completely destroyed by the Babylonians.

2. The Lord expects no less from His Own than He does from the heathen. In fact, He expects much more from His Own because, as previously stated, *"To whom much is given, much is required."*

3. Judah had forsaken the Cross, so to speak, or else looked at it merely as a ceremony. Considering that it is the Cross alone which holds back the Judgment of God, the Cross being ignored or denied leaves nothing but Judgment.

THE ONLY THING STANDING BETWEEN MAN AND THE JUDGMENT OF GOD IS THE CROSS OF CHRIST

We have already said this in this Volume; however, this is so important, so very important, actually, a matter of life and death, that we dare not say it too little.

Not long before their destruction, Judah came to the place that she either ignored the sacrifices altogether or else attended to them wrongly.

What do we mean by that?

In other words, they thought they could offer up sacrifice at the end of the week, and that would cover all of their sins of that week, and then they were free to sin more during the next week.

It should be understood, the Cross of Christ, whether symbolized by the sacrifices of the Old Testament or the actual fact of the New, is meant to rid us of sin and not that we may keep sinning.

At this present time (2010), the modern church has all but abandoned the Message of the Cross. The Word of Faith people, which, in reality, is no faith at all that God will recognize, openly repudiates the Cross, referring to it as *"past miseries."* They, as well, call it, *"the greatest defeat in human history."* One of their brightest lights also stated, *"If the Preacher preaches the Cross, he is preaching death."* He went on to say, *"He should preach the Resurrection and the Exaltation of Christ."*

Most definitely the Preacher should preach the Resurrection and the Exaltation of Christ; however, it was the Cross of Christ that made the Resurrection of Christ possible, as well as His Exaltation at the Right Hand of God.

Paul said, *"For the preaching of the Cross is to them who perish foolishness; but to we who are Saved it is the Power of God"* (I Cor. 1:18). He did not say, *"For the preaching of the Resurrection. . . ."* He also stated, *"God forbid that I should glory save in the Cross of our Lord Jesus Christ . . ."* (Gal. 6:14). He did not say, *"God forbid that I should glory save in the Resurrection . . ."* and we could go on and on with many more Scriptures in that particular direction. But I think the reader gets the point.

Then there is a great segment of the modern church who will not even mention the Cross, will not sing songs about the Blood, etc., simply because they claim, *"It may offend people."* Listen again to Paul:

"But we Preach Christ Crucified (this is the Foundation of the Word of God and, thereby, of Salvation)**, unto the Jews a stumblingblock** (the Cross was the stumblingblock)**, and unto the Greeks** (Gentiles) **foolishness** (both found it difficult to accept as God a dead Man hanging on a Cross, for such Christ was to them)**" (I Cor. 1:23).**

In other words, the great Apostle said, *"I know that the preaching of the Cross doesn't sit well at all with the Jews, and, as well, that the Gentiles think of it as foolish; nevertheless, 'we preach Christ Crucified.'"*

In other words, he was not trying to get the plaudits of man, but rather trying to please God.

Why did Paul preach the Cross even as he did?

He did so because there was no other answer to the human dilemma, as there is no other answer to the human dilemma.

(6) "THUS SAYS THE LORD; FOR THREE TRANSGRESSIONS OF ISRAEL, AND FOR FOUR, I WILL NOT TURN AWAY THE PUNISHMENT THEREOF; BECAUSE THEY SOLD THE RIGHTEOUS FOR SILVER, AND THE POOR FOR A PAIR OF SHOES."

The construction is:

1. As the northern kingdom of Israel sank lower and lower into sin and depravity, all justice flew out the window.

2. They sold the *"righteous"* and the *"poor"* into slavery, and for a pittance.

3. As we have previously stated, the phrase, *"For three transgressions of Israel, and for four,"* actually refers to many transgressions.

ISRAEL

In Biblical Israel, when an individual sold a piece of land, to seal the purchase, the seller would pull off his shoes and give them to the man who had bought the land, etc.

The idea here is, when the poor had to borrow money, they were charged a ruinous

amount of interest, which itself was illegal. At any rate, the interest would be so high that the poor could not pay it and would have to give over their property to the lender. And, for a bribe, the judges would make the conspiracy possible.

But, in all of this injustice, we here see plainly that the Lord observed everything that was taking place.

(7) "THAT PANT AFTER THE DUST OF THE EARTH ON THE HEAD OF THE POOR, AND TURN ASIDE THE WAY OF THE MEEK: AND A MAN AND HIS FATHER WILL GO IN UNTO THE SAME MAID, TO PROFANE MY HOLY NAME."

The pattern is:

1. These Passages portray the fact that Israel had laid aside the Word of God for their own inventions.

2. In other words, they had made up their own laws and concocted their own salvation. It was very similar to what is happening in much of the modern church world presently.

3. Now, they were progressive, liberal, and unrestricted by the old-fashioned ideas of the Bible.

4. The Lord was carefully observing all they did. Upon refusal to repent, they would face Judgment, and terrible Judgment at that!

IMMORALITY

Verse 7 pertains to iniquity in two directions, both immoral. They are as follows:

• As a nation or a people turn from God, the rights of the poor, dispossessed, downtrodden, and helpless are abrogated, to say the least! Every *"right"* and protection of the poor and helpless have come about, wherever it is practiced, because of the Word of God. Where God is given no place and position, likewise, no consideration is given to these unfortunates.

When the Lord is followed, He Who considers even a *"bird's nest,"* can be relied upon in all matters of life, and, especially, those who cannot protect themselves (Deut. 22:6-7).

Israel had strayed from God, and now Israel gave no consideration to the poor.

• *"And a man and a father will go in unto the same maid, to profane My Holy Name."*

These Passages portray the fact that Israel

had laid aside the Word of God for their own inventions.

The further away from God a person, a Church, or even a nation, gets, the more immoral it becomes. The fall of every empire of the past was characterized by three gross sins that became pandemic. They were and are:

1. Homosexuality;
2. Pedophilia; and,
3. Incest.

When a nation begins to lose its way, homosexuality becomes rampant.

HOMOSEXUALITY

"**Wherefore God also gave them up to uncleanness through the lusts of their own hearts** (*not merely permissive, but God judicially delivered them over*), **to dishonour their own bodies between themselves** (*speaks of every type of immorality*):

"**Who changed the Truth of God into a lie** (*refers back to Verse 23, which speaks of spiritual and sexual uncleanness*), **and worshipped and served the creature more than the Creator** (*this refers to man worshiping the creation of his own hands, which means that he is worshiping something less than himself*), **Who is blessed forever. Amen** (*should have been translated 'Bless-ed' [two syllables], because it refers to the One doing the blessing, in this case, the Lord*).

"**For this cause God gave them up unto vile affections** (*the Lord removed His Restraints and, therefore, gave them unimpeded access to their desires*): **for even their women did change the natural use into that which is against nature** (*in short, speaks of Lesbianism*):

"**And likewise also the men** (*homosexuality*), **leaving the natural use of the woman** (*speaks of the sex act which is performed between the man and his wife*), **burned in their lust one toward another** (*raging lust*); **men with men working that which is unseemly** (*specifies its direction, which is total perversion*), **and receiving in themselves that recompense of their error which was meet** (*refers to the penalty attached to wrongdoing*).

"**And even as they did not like to retain God in *their* knowledge** (*carries the idea of*

the human race putting God to the test for the purpose of approving or disapproving Him), **God gave them over to a reprobate mind** (*Light rejected is Light withdrawn*), **to do those things which are not convenient** (*which are not fitting*)" (**Rom. 1:24-28**).

THE CROSS OF CHRIST AND THE JUDGMENT OF GOD

God is unalterably opposed to sin; consequently, the only place that God can meet with sinful man is at the Cross. There is no other! As previously stated, the only thing standing between man and the Judgment of God is the Cross of Christ. All of this means that if the church is not preaching the Cross, this opens up the nation to the Judgment of God. That is why this Ministry (Jimmy Swaggart Ministries) is so important. And, by that, I am not speaking of our persons, but rather the Message that God has given us to give to this nation and the world. It is the Message of "*Jesus Christ and Him Crucified.*" Those of you who embrace this Message, which is the Gospel, are, in effect, standing in the gap. This means that when the Church stops preaching the Cross, then Judgment comes. Let us say it again:

The Cross alone stands between mankind and the Wrath of God. God is unalterably opposed to sin in any form, and there is only one thing that deals with sin, and that is the Cross of Christ.

The modern church is trying to function without an admittance of sin. The "*Seeker-Sensitive*" and the "*Purpose Driven Life Group,*" claim that sin should not even be mentioned behind the modern pulpit because it may offend someone. Those two groups together make up a large portion of the modern church. And, we have the "*Word of Faith Group,*" which claims that the way to stop people from sinning is for the preacher to never mention it. They claim that when sin is mentioned, it creates a sin consciousness in the lives of the hearers, and then they will go out and sin. So, according to them, just never mentioning sin will solve the problem.

That's strange when we consider that Paul mentioned sin seventeen times in the Sixth Chapter of Romans alone.

No, the problem is sin, whether the unredeemed or the redeemed. And there is only one answer for it. As stated, the answer is the Cross.

(8) "AND THEY LAY THEMSELVES DOWN UPON CLOTHES LAID TO PLEDGE BY EVERY ALTAR, AND THEY DRINK THE WINE OF THE CONDEMNED IN THE HOUSE OF THEIR GOD."

The exegesis is:

1. As is obvious here, the Lord observed all that was being done.

2. As well, the Lord places in a Book in Heaven all the deeds done by every individual, whether good or bad (Rev. 20:11-15). The only way that bad deeds can be erased is by the person accepting Christ, Whose Blood cleanses from all sin (I Jn. 1:7).

3. This concerned the loan of money to the very poor, who gave their clothes on their backs as a *"pledge"* or collateral. According to the Word of God (Ex. 22:26; Deut. 24:13-17), the clothing was to be returned before nightfall.

4. The phrase, *"By every altar, and they drink the wine of the condemned in the house of their god,"* proclaims many altars, whereas, the Law of Moses specified only one Altar and one place of sacrifice. That was at the Temple in Jerusalem.

ONE PLACE OF SACRIFICE

The Lord specifically directed that there was to be one place of sacrifice, which was to be the Tabernacle in the wilderness, and, as well, in Israel, and also the Temple when it was built (Lev. 17:1-4).

Concerning this, Mackintosh says, *"A man might say, can I not offer a Sacrifice in one place as well as another? The answer is, Life belongs to God, and His claim thereto must be recognized in the place where He has appointed – before the Tabernacle of the Lord. That was the only meeting-place between God and man. To offer elsewhere proved that the heart did not want God.*

"The Moral of this is plain. There is one place where God has appointed to meet the sinner, and that is the Cross – the antitype of the Brazen Altar. There and there alone has God's claims upon the life been duly recognized. To reject this meeting-place is

to bring down judgment upon one's self – it is to trample underfoot the just claims of God, and to arrogate to one's self a right to life which all have forfeited."[1]

(9) "YET DESTROYED I THE AMORITE BEFORE THEM, WHOSE HEIGHT WAS LIKE THE HEIGHT OF THE CEDARS, AND HE WAS STRONG AS THE OAKS; YET I DESTROYED HIS FRUIT FROM ABOVE, AND HIS ROOTS FROM BENEATH."

The construction is:

1. The name *"Amorite"* (Josh. 24:18) is meant to serve as a representative of the seven nations of Canaan, who were dispossessed by the Israelites (Gen. 15:16; Ex. 23:27; 24:11).

2. The Lord left these heathen tribes in the land of Israel for a purpose. He could easily have removed them before the arrival of the Israelites; however, He wanted His People to learn trust.

3. All of this is a type, if you will, of the spiritual conflicts which face us as Believers. The Lord could easily remove all such things; however, He allows Satan certain latitude, which the Victory over him will occasion our Spiritual Growth.

THE BLESSINGS

In Verse 9 and the following two, the Holy Spirit through the Prophet cites three former blessings given to Israel but, seemingly, little appreciated. This Verse contains the first account.

The phrase, *"Yet destroyed I the Amorite before them,"* is meant to personify the personal pronoun *"I,"* which is continually repeated, in order to contrast God's Faithfulness and the people's unthankfulness.

The manner in which the phrase is used is meant to show Israel's inability to cope with such an enemy and their entire dependence on the help of the Lord.

The phrase, *"Yet I destroyed his fruit from above, and his roots from beneath,"* is meant to express the posterity of these heathen nations. In other words, the victory was complete!

(10) "ALSO I BROUGHT YOU UP FROM THE LAND OF EGYPT, AND LED YOU FORTY YEARS THROUGH THE WILDERNESS, TO POSSESS THE LAND OF THE AMORITE."

The pattern is:

1. The Lord not only defeated the *"Amorite,"* but also gave their land to Israel as an inheritance.

2. *"And led you forty years through the wilderness,"* is meant to bring to mind that terrible odyssey, which, by all rights, should have forfeited the Blessings, but instead the Grace of God gave them everything.

3. Actually, Israel was meant to stay in the wilderness only about two years. The thirty-eight extra years was because of their unbelief. How much *"wilderness"* do we have to go through because of unbelief?

DELIVERANCE

The deliverance from Egypt and the guidance through the desert, though chronologically first, are mentioned last, as the great and culminating example of the Favor and Protection of God.

First, God prepared the land for Israel and then trained them for possession of it.

All of the Lord's Dealings with us come under the heading of training. In essence, one might say, every single thing is a test. How will we act? How will we react? All of it is meant for our growth, but yet, I'm afraid that as Israel stayed far too long in the wilderness, sometimes, if not many times, we do the same.

(11) "AND I RAISED UP OF YOUR SONS FOR PROPHETS, AND OF YOUR YOUNG MEN FOR NAZARITES. IS IT NOT EVEN THUS, O YOU CHILDREN OF ISRAEL? SAYS THE LORD."

The overview is:

1. *"Nazarites"* were those who took a special vow, whether temporary or lifelong.

2. Of perpetual Nazarites, we have as instances Samson, Samuel, and John the Baptist.

3. The question, *"Is it not even thus, O you Children of Israel? says the LORD,"* is meant to specify that these things stated are undeniable, thereby, signaling favor from God, making Israel separate from other nations, and binding them to be a holy people.

PROPHETS AND NAZARITES

The phrase, *"And I raised up of your sons for Prophets, and of your young men*

for Nazarites," proclaims the *"Prophet"* and the *"Nazarite"* alike as Miracles of Grace. The former gave heavenly teaching, the latter exhibited holiness of life.

Looking at Prophets first, Samuel was the first one to stand in the Office of the Prophet. He was also the last Judge of Israel. While there definitely were Prophets before Samuel, the Office before Samuel had not actually been established. It was established with Samuel simply because Israel had now become a Nation. Saul was its first king, although not of the Will of God, but rather the people. At any rate, the Lord began to deal with Israel from that time forth as a cohesive Nation, even though it did not come into full flower before David.

The Prophet was used by the Lord not only to foretell futuristic events but, most of all, to be a Preacher of Righteousness, which was meant to whip the Nation into shape. In other words, the Lord guided the Spiritual temperature of the Nation, so to speak, by the Message of the Prophet. Regrettably, the Message was seldom heeded; nevertheless, the Lord was faithful in giving it.

APOSTLES

While the Office of the Prophet continues under the New Covenant, a new Office was established with the First Advent of Christ. It was and is the Office of the Apostle.

The identifying mark of the true Apostle of the Lord, one might say his characteristic, is the Message which the Lord gives him in order to guide the Church. And please understand, this is not an elected Office and neither are Apostles appointed by men; it is strictly a Call of God. The Holy Spirit knows what the Church needs and gives the Apostle the emphasis of the Message intended. While others may be Called of God to preach the same Message, and do it with success, still, the Apostle will minister somewhat with greater authority, at least, as it regards the subject at hand.

NAZARITES

"Nazarites" were those who took a special vow, whether temporary or lifelong. Of perpetual Nazarites, we have, as stated, as examples, Samson, Samuel, and John the Baptist.

No doubt, there were many others whose names were not given in the Word of God.

The *"Nazarite"* had to abstain from wine and intoxicating drinks, vinegar, and raisins, in other words, those things from which alcoholic beverage could be made. This was aimed at safeguarding the integrity and holiness of the Nazarite from possession by a spirit other than that of Jehovah (Prov. 20:1).

As well, he must not cut his hair during the time of consecration.

Also, he must not go near a dead body, even that of his nearest relation, a prohibition which applied also in the case of the High Priest.

Relative to the touching of a dead body, if this rule was broken, the Nazarite had to undergo closely detailed purificatory rites and to begin all over again his vow. If his vow was temporal, he had to offer various prescribed sacrifices when it was completed and, thereafter, cut his hair and burn it on the Altar. Then, after certain ritual acts by the Priests, the Nazarite was freed from his vow (Num., Chpt. 6).

The question, *"Is it not even thus, O you Children of Israel? says the LORD,"* is meant to specify that these things stated are undeniable and, thereby, signal favor from God, making Israel separate from other nations and, thus, bound to be a holy people. At least, that was the intention!

(12) "BUT YOU GAVE THE NAZARITES WINE TO DRINK; AND COMMANDED THE PROPHETS, SAYING, PROPHESY NOT."

The overview is:

1. The idea of Verse 12 is: this ungrateful Nation systematically tried to silence the voices which were a standing rebuke to them.

2. The action of Israel at this time was to silence the Voice of God.

3. It was a deliberate action against the Word of the Lord, and done with contempt.

WINE TO DRINK

Whenever a nation or religious denomination strays from the Bible, they desire no reminders of their erroneous action; consequently, two things are done:

"But you gave the Nazarites wine to drink." This speaks of Israel abrogating God's Way of Holiness and substituting their

NOTES

own! The *"Nazarite"* spoke of separation, of which Paul also spoke, at least, in the spiritual sense, when he said, *"Wherefore come out from among them, and be you separate, says the Lord, and touch not the unclean thing; and I will receive you"* (II Cor. 6:17).

Tragically, there is very little *"separation"* from the world left in the modern church.

Religious man's carnal instinct is always to attempt to legislate Holiness, which, by its nature, is impossible. Seeing that doesn't work, by and large, it is then ignored, as presently.

True Holiness is an inward work and can only be given by God. By its very nature, it cannot be earned or merited.

Holiness becomes a part of the Believer when such a person places his Faith exclusively in Christ and the Cross, which, in effect, states that what Christ did at the Cross makes it possible for man to be holy. Please understand, God can only meet sinful man at the Cross. There is no other way.

Unfortunately, if Holiness in the modern church is thought of at all, it is an attempt at such through works, which God can never accept. We are what God wants us to be only by placing our Faith exclusively in Christ and what He did for us at the Cross, understanding that Jesus is the Source of all things we receive from God, while the Cross is the Means by which all is given to us. This requires and even demands that the Cross of Christ ever be the Object of our Faith.

WHAT DO WE MEAN BY THE CROSS BEING THE OBJECT OF OUR FAITH?

The Cross of Christ is so little understood in the present church that, anymore, the Faith of Believers is misplaced in every direction. When we place our Faith exclusively in the Cross of Christ, this means that we understand, at least as far as a poor human can understand, what Jesus did for us at the Cross. It means that we also understand that within ourselves, by the means of the flesh, we cannot hope to bring about what is needed. We also understand that when our Faith is properly placed, the Holy Spirit, Who Works exclusively within the parameters of the Finished Work of Christ, can then Work in our lives, bringing about that which He Alone can do.

All of this means that our Faith is not in our church, not in preachers, not even in ourselves, but altogether in Christ and the Work He accomplished at Calvary. And that's where the problem comes.

THE OFFENSE OF THE CROSS

Paul mentioned in the Fifth Chapter of Galatians that there would be an offense to the Cross of Christ.

Why?

The Cross of Christ lays waste all of man's works, efforts, plans, and schemes as it regards Righteousness and Holiness. It exposes all of that for what it is, meaning that no matter how many Scriptures we load on, the fact is, it is still flesh. Man, and especially religious man, does not enjoy being told that his grand scheme, whatever it is, simply won't work. He's not happy hearing that. That is the offense. Abraham is a perfect example.

Ishmael was a work of the flesh. Never mind that Abraham and Sarah were trying to bring about the great Promise of God, still, what they did and what they brought forth, God could never accept.

Nevertheless, the time came that Ishmael had to go. The evidence is, he was making every attempt to kill Isaac, who was about 15 years younger than he was, and make it look like an accident. The flesh will always war against the Spirit. We must never forget that.

When the Lord told Abraham that Ishmael had to go, even along with his mother, this was not something that Abraham desired to hear. Ishmael was a product of his own scheming and manipulation, so he wasn't happy about having to give him up. But, thankfully, he obeyed the Lord. That to which religious men give birth, they are bound to protect. That's the reason that the Message of the Cross is not popular.

STOP THE MOUTH OF THE PROPHETS

The Scripture says, *"And commanded the Prophets, saying, Prophesy not."* Once Holiness is ignored or else changed to other than God's Standards, the Word of God then becomes a rebuke, and, consequently,

NOTES

there is no desire for it to be heard. As well, the *"Prophets"* will be ordered to trim their message.

Of course, true Prophets cannot do that, and, therefore, they are killed, and that, either literally or by character assassination.

At the present time and in the modern church, God's Order of Ministerial Authority, found in Ephesians 4:11, has been abrogated in favor of denominational authority. In other words, man's way has been substituted for God's Way. Consequently, religious *"denominationalism"* is probably the greatest sin of the modern church.

Even though there was no such thing as *"denominationalism"* in the Old Covenant, at least, as we think of such today, still, its principle was rampant then as now! Since the principle is the same, I think it would be wise to include a statement regarding modern denominationalism.

DENOMINATIONALISM

Webster defines the word as, *"devotion to denominational principles or interest"* and *"the emphasizing of denominational differences to the point of being narrowly exclusive."*

Denominationalism carries the idea, whether realized or not, that association with some particular religious denomination plays a part in one's Salvation. In other words, in the minds of some people, in order to be Saved, one must accept Christ plus be a member of the Catholic church, the Baptist church, the Church of God, etc. Such thinking constitutes *"Christ plus,"* which the Lord can never accept. It also nullifies one's Salvation. That is, if a person believes that, then he is not saved. Paul, in effect, said as much:

"Christ is become of no effect unto you, whosoever of you are justified by the Law; you are fallen from Grace" (Gal. 5:4).

Some Christians would argue that their extreme devotion to a denomination has nothing to do with the Law of Moses. While, in fact, it doesn't, still, in principle, it does! As the people in Paul's day were trusting in *"Law"* as well as Christ to save them, millions are doing the same today by attempting to trust Christ plus a *"Law"* of their own making. In principle, it is the same as what Paul was addressing. Consequently, multiple hundreds of millions of people are in Hell right now because of such actions, which makes it extremely serious indeed!

IS IT A SIN TO BELONG TO A RELIGIOUS DENOMINATION?

No! It is not a sin to belong to a religious denomination as long as one realizes what it is. Unfortunately, many Christians have the idea that their particular religious denomination is *"God's Denomination."* In other words, one does not truly belong to the Body of Christ until one belongs to that particular denomination. That, in a nutshell, is the meaning of *"denominationalism."* It is also Satanic inasmuch as it places a work of man on a par with the Work of God.

God has no denominations. However, He does have a *"Body,"* which is made up of all Born-Again Believers, irrespective of whom they may be, where they may be, or what church or denomination they may be associated with (Eph. 1:22-23; 2:16, 22; Col. 1:18).

All denominations are man-made structures. They are not inherently wrong or inherently right. There is little harm in associating with one, providing one understands that they are man-made and that associating with them or disassociating oneself from them has nothing to do with one's Salvation.

The moment one begins to believe that one's man-made denomination is favored by God more than others, then one is beginning to lean toward denominationalism. This will ultimately lead to *"Salvation by works,"* which God will not and, in fact, cannot accept.

Ideally, a religious denomination is supposed to be a tool—just as a computer, an automobile, a printing press, and a television camera are tools—to be used for the Work of God. Denominations embrace a doctrinal structure and are supposedly designed for fellowship and the propagation of the Gospel. It should be no more and no less!

However, if one reads these words and thinks of his religious denomination as something more, then the seed of denominationalism has already been planted.

NOTES

None of these things (denominations) constitute wrongdoing, but man, even converted man, due to the corruption of the human heart, has a tendency to resort to idols. Hence, John the Beloved warned, *"Little children, keep yourselves from idols"* (I Jn. 5:21).

Millions of Christians have made an *"idol"* out of their religious denomination and, as such, have fallen from Grace.

WERE THERE ANY RELIGIOUS DENOMINATIONS IN THE EARLY CHURCH?

No! The Holy Spirit laid down the guidelines in the Book of Acts and in the Epistles concerning church structure and organization, and there is not even a hint of a religious denomination. In the Early Church structure, as designed by the Holy Spirit and, therefore, meant to be the standard for all time, the local Church is the highest Church body, Church structure, and authority. In other words, nothing is to supersede the authority of the local Church.

Notice that none of the Books of the New Testament were written by a denominational headquarters, instead, they were written by individuals, such as the Apostle Paul or Simon Peter, etc., and then sent to the local Churches. In every case, God used a man instead of a Church denomination. In fact, He has never used a Church denomination, as such, in any capacity.

Some time back, a brother said to me, *"God is working in the Catholic church."*

I turned to him and said, *"No, God is not working in the Catholic church or any other denominational structure; He works in the hearts of men and women."* It has nothing to do with a religious denomination; it has to do with the condition of the heart of the individual to whom God speaks.

In other words, when God begins to Move, He doesn't search out a denomination to work through; He looks for men and women with hungry hearts, reaching out toward Him. Who they are, where they are, or what denomination, organization, or church they may be associated with is incidental and has no bearing on the matter.

So the question must be asked, *"If the*

Holy Spirit did not design a Church denomination in the New Testament, is it improper to have one now?"

It's not improper, provided it is kept Scriptural, in other words, that denominational authority never supersede the authority of the local Church. However, I am not aware of any religious denomination, at least, in the Pentecostal realm, that does not supersede the authority of the local Church. Presently, the word of the denomination, not the local Church, is final. That is unscriptural and as leaven, will eventually corrupt the whole.

NO ONE EXCEPT THE LORD

No one except the Lord has the right to tell a local Pastor what He can or cannot do with respect to the leading of his local congregation. There is no higher God-given authority than the Pastor of a local Church. All the other man-made designations, such as superintendents, overseers, moderators, presidents, etc., are just that, man-made, and, as such, have no Scriptural or spiritual authority with God.

While it is certainly true that some individuals occupying these offices are godly and, as such, are a great blessing to the Work of God, still, it is Scripturally wrong for a local Pastor to acquiesce to unscriptural demands made by men filling unscriptural positions, that is, if such actually is the case. To do so is to abrogate the Headship of Christ over the local Body.

Then we wonder why churches are dead, lifeless, and have no Moving of the Holy Spirit, resulting in precious few, if any, being Saved, baptized with the Holy Spirit, or healed by the Power of God! It is because, in many cases, the Headship of Christ has been abrogated by man, and the church is now answering to man instead of God. The Lord will never serve in a subordinate role; He will simply vacate the premises.

Now, this is not meant to say that the offices of superintendent, president, moderator, etc., are wrong spiritually. If godly men occupy these positions, they can be a tremendous blessing to the Work of God. When it comes to authority, however, their contribution should be limited to advice and godly

counsel, which should be readily appreciated. Dictatorial authority, however, is not Biblical and should be understood thusly.

Jimmy Swaggart Ministries has an organization called *"World Evangelism Fellowship."* If asked, we will give counsel to the Pastors of the Churches in this fellowship; however, we will not abrogate the authority of the local Pastor and his congregation. Now, if there is a matter that becomes very serious, in other words, where sin is involved and Repentance is refused, we would then have to tell such a person that their church is no longer in this Fellowship. I don't recall that we've ever had to do that, and I pray that we never have to. But, if so, it would only be after all other measures had failed.

WHAT ARE THE SIGNS OF DENOMINATIONALISM?

Whenever individuals attend a particular church just because it is in their denomination, irrespective of its spiritual deadness, this is a sign of *"denominationalism."* It means that the person, whether realized or not, is looking to that denomination instead of God.

A person should attend a Church because the Word of God is interpreted correctly and preached under the Anointing of the Holy Spirit, thereby, done so without compromise or favoritism. The Spirit of God should be Moving there, resulting in souls being Saved, lives being changed, and Believers being baptized with the Holy Spirit. That and that alone should be the criteria!

When denominations become so sacrosanct that they cannot be corrected or their faults pointed out, then *"denominationalism"* has already set in. The idea is that if you criticize the denomination, then you are criticizing God. Such thinking is foolish at best and blasphemy at worst!

DENOMINATIONALISM AND HIERARCHY GO HAND IN HAND

The word *"hierarchy"* means, *"a ruling body of clergy organized into orders or ranks each subordinate to the one above it."*

You will look in vain in the New Testament for a *"hierarchy."* One does not exist!

Denominationalism   always   includes

hierarchy. The demand is that preachers submit themselves and their ministries to the hierarchy above them. Little by little, the hierarchy begins to believe and teach that when God speaks, He will speak to the top of the hierarchy, and they will filter it down to their subordinates, with it finally reaching the local Pastors.

That is blasphemy! But, sadly, many Christians, including pastors, feel that the process is Scriptural because they do not know the Bible. All Scriptural submission is horizontal, not vertical. Paul said, *"Submitting yourselves one to another in the fear of God"* (Eph. 5:21).

Notice that submission is to be *"one to another."* In other words, I am to submit to you, and you are to submit to me. It is horizontal!

Vertical submission, which is rampant in denominationalism, teaches, in effect, that one cannot hear from God oneself but must submit to someone above in the hierarchical order who can hear from God on one's behalf and pass it on. That abrogates the Headship of Christ!

Within the framework of the local Church, it is certainly true that younger individuals, even younger Church leaders, are to submit to their senior Pastor as long as he remains Scriptural, but that is as far as it goes (I Pet. 5:5).

Incidentally, the titles, such as *"Pastor, Elder, Presbyter, Bishop, or Shepherd,"* all mean one thing: Pastor. None of these titles designate any higher Calling from God than Pastor. In other words, nothing is to usurp authority over the local Pastor.

Hence, the idea of the title *"Bishop,"* referring to a Spiritual Leader over certain areas or numbers of churches, did not come from the New Testament. It came from men who, desiring place and position, simply created such place and position.

It is tragic how far we stray from the Bible; when we do, disaster is always the result!

Paul said, *"Examine yourselves, whether you be in the Faith; prove your own selves. Know you not your own selves, how that Jesus Christ is in you, except you be reprobates?"* (II Cor. 13:5).

Almost exclusively, it is religious denominations that say to the true God-called Prophets, *"Prophesy not."*

(13) "BEHOLD, I AM PRESSED UNDER YOU, AS A CART IS PRESSED THAT IS FULL OF SHEAVES."

The overview is:

1. The sense of Verse 13 is that God is burdened and wearied with their sins.

2. God is patient, very patient; however, there is a limit to that patience.

3. We must never forget, God is a God of Mercy, but He is also a God of Judgment.

THE CROSS OF CHRIST ALONE HOLDS BACK JUDGMENT

God is unalterably opposed to sin in any form. In fact, sin must be judged, and sin must always be judged. The only thing that can stop the Judgment of God, and has been from the very beginning, is the Cross of Christ. In fact, God can meet man only at the Cross. He expects man to avail himself of that which Jesus did at Calvary. That being done, Judgment is stopped simply because Jesus has taken the Judgment that should have come upon us, and will come upon us, if we reject God's Way of Salvation.

Our heading, in essence, states that the only thing standing between mankind and Judgment is the Cross of Christ. If that, in fact, is true, and it most definitely is, then it's imperative that the Church preach the Cross. Is that, in fact, being presently? No!

The Cross of Christ was once preached strongly for Salvation, and rightly so; however, even that is going by the wayside. At this time (2010), the Cross of Christ is being preached less than at any time in the history of the Church since the Reformation. This opens this nation, and even the other parts of the world, to the Judgment of God. Inasmuch as the Cross of Christ is the only thing that holds back Judgment, then it's imperative that it be preached.

The Lord has given to this Ministry the responsibility and the burden that we hold up the Cross of Christ not only for Salvation but, as well, for Sanctification. There is no other answer! That is our Message, *"The Cross of Christ."* And once we understand that, we realize that this is the story of the Bible, *"Jesus Christ and Him Crucified"*

(I Cor. 1:23). In fact, if one properly understands the Cross of Christ, then one properly understands the Word of God. And, as well, it can be said, and must be said, that if one doesn't properly understand the Message of the Cross, then one doesn't properly understand the Word of God. In fact, without exception, all false doctrine stems from a misunderstanding or misinterpretation of the Message of the Cross, i.e., *"the Atonement."*

THE FIRST CHAPTER OF THE GOSPEL OF JOHN

In a sense, the First Chapter of the Gospel of John is a compendium of the First Chapter of Genesis. In this Chapter, we will easily find the purpose of the entirety of the Word of God or, one might say, the Plan of God. The Holy Spirit inspired John to write the following:

"In the beginning *(does not infer that Christ as God had a beginning because, as God, He had no beginning, but rather refers to the time of Creation [Gen. 1:1])* **was the Word** *(the Holy Spirit through John describes Jesus as 'the Eternal Logos')***, and the Word was with God** *('was in relationship with God,' and expresses the idea of the Trinity)***, and the Word was God** *(meaning that He did not cease to be God during the Incarnation; He 'was' and 'is' God from eternity past to eternity future)*.

"The same was in the beginning with God *(this very Person was in eternity with God; there's only one God, but manifested in three Persons – God the Father, God the Son, God the Holy Spirit)*" **(Jn. 1:1-2).**

THE INCARNATION

"And the Word was made flesh *(refers to the Incarnation, 'God becoming man')***, and dwelt among us** *(refers to Jesus, although Perfect, not holding Himself aloft from all others, but rather lived as all men, even a peasant)***, (and we beheld His Glory, the Glory as of the Only Begotten of the Father,)** *(speaks of His Deity, although hidden from the eyes of the merely curious; while Christ laid aside the expression of His Deity, He never lost the possession of His Deity)* **full of Grace and Truth** *(as 'flesh,'*

proclaimed His Humanity, 'Grace and Truth' His Deity)" **(Jn. 1:14).**

THE CROSS

The purpose for God becoming Man was to go to the Cross. The Scripture says:

"The next day *(refers to the day after John the Baptist had been questioned by the emissaries from the Sanhedrin)* **John sees Jesus coming unto him** *(is, no doubt, after the Baptism of Jesus and the temptation in the wilderness)***, and said, Behold the Lamb of God** *(proclaims Jesus as the Sacrifice for sin, in fact, the Sin-Offering, Whom all the multiple millions of offered lambs had represented)***, which takes away the sin of the world** *(animal blood could only cover sin, it could not take it away; but Jesus offering Himself as the Perfect Sacrifice took away the sin of the world; He not only cleansed acts of sin but, as well, addressed the root cause [Col. 2:14-15])*" **(Jn. 1:29).**

(14) **"THEREFORE THE FLIGHT SHALL PERISH FROM THE SWIFT, AND THE STRONG SHALL NOT STRENGTHEN HIS FORCE, NEITHER SHALL THE MIGHTY DELIVER HIMSELF."**

The diagram is:

1. Upon hearing the Message as given by Amos, the people seemingly made light of his Prophecy, even as Verse 12 did outline.

2. Their attitude was that such could not happen; and, if such a preposterous thing somehow actually did happen, they certainly would be able to properly defend themselves.

3. The Holy Spirit, knowing their thoughts, addresses them forthwith by implying that He will fight for the enemy and against them.

WHEN GOD IS AGAINST US

Israel, as previously stated, was addressed as having some knowledge of truth, but the main charge against the northern kingdom was a moral one. Their conduct was in question. To have spoken to them as professing keepers of the law was impossible, but their conscience could not repel an accusation as to their actions. They sold the righteous and the poor into slavery for a trifle; they crushed the head of the poor into the very dust; they perverted justice; a man and his son debased themselves with the same unhappy victim of the idolatrous and obscene worship of Astarte; the pledged clothes, which God commanded should be restored before sunset (Ex. 22:26), were used as a couch of feasting before *"every altar"*— God having ordained but one Altar; and the money which they fined those unjustly condemned in their courts, they spent on wine to be drunk at these idol banquets.

In contrast with this sad recital, Divine Love recalls its action toward them in delivering them out of Egypt, in totally destroying the Amorites, and in raising up Prophets and Nazarites so as to maintain relationship between God and them when the Ceremonial law had failed.

Judgment, therefore, was inevitable; and its action was committed shortly afterward to the Assyrians, who slaughtered the men of Israel in thousands and carried the residue into captivity; from which they have not yet escaped (Williams).[2]

(15) "NEITHER SHALL HE STAND WHO HANDLES THE BOW; AND HE WHO IS SWIFT OF FOOT SHALL NOT DELIVER HIMSELF: NEITHER SHALL HE WHO RIDES THE HORSE DELIVER HIMSELF."

The structure is:

1. By their sins and rebellion, the people of Israel no longer desired God's Deliverance, but claimed they could deliver themselves. However, the Holy Spirit says otherwise!

2. If God is against us, there is no escape.

3. The mills of God grind slowly, but they grind exceedingly fine, meaning they miss nothing!

REHABILITATION?

By their sins and rebellion, the people of Israel no longer desired God's Deliverance but claimed they could deliver themselves. However, the Holy Spirit through the Prophet says that the warrior will not be able to war, the runner shall not be able to run, and the rider shall not be able to ride!

The modern church has likewise opted for its own deliverance; however, in reality, it doesn't even believe in the Word. Whereas the Biblical word is *"deliverance,"* the psychological word presently used by most of

the church is *"rehabilitation."*

Let it be understood that such a word does not exist in the Bible because the very nature of the word means that man can rehabilitate or restore to a condition of health and useful constructive activity.

God says that man cannot do that, hence, Jesus had to come from Heaven and pay a terrible price in order that man could be delivered from the terrible plague of sin. It is sad when the modern church thinks it can do such within itself or, at the most, by paying lip service to God.

The truth is, the modern church can no more deliver itself than Israel of old.

Only God can deliver!

(16) "AND HE WHO IS COURAGEOUS AMONG THE MIGHTY SHALL FLEE AWAY NAKED IN THAT DAY, SAYS THE LORD."

The pattern is:

1. The word *"naked"* means to be *"weaponless."*

2. When the soldier runs away, he throws aside his armor and weapons in order to more easily escape. This would be the plight of Israel—so says the Lord!

3. How foolish was Israel to ignore the Word of the Lord. It is no less foolish presently!

PROPHESY NOT

Israel's future, barring Repentance, was dire indeed! And yet, their answer to Amos was, *"Prophesy not!"*

They seem to have had the idea that by not hearing these words, ignorance would protect them, consequently, abrogating these dire predictions.

In the natural sense, if an automobile is speeding down a highway on a dark night in the midst of a storm, and somebody goes to the trouble of flagging down the occupants, telling them that just ahead the bridge is out and that they must stop, such information is appreciated, and greatly so! However, in the Spiritual sense, the opposite is the case. Even though plunging headlong to certain destruction, men, as Israel of old, desire no one to warn them of the disaster which lies just ahead!

"He looked for a City and lived in a tent,

*"A pilgrim to Glory right onward he
    went;
"God's Promise His Solace, so royal
    his birth,
"No wonder he sought not the glories
    of Earth."*

*"He looked for a City his God should
    prepare,
"No mansion on Earth could he covet
    or share.
"For had not God told him that royal
    abode,
"Awaited His Pilgrims on ending the
    road."*

*"He looked for a City; if sometimes he
    sighed,
"To be trudging the road, all Earth's
    glory denied,
"The thought of that City changed
    sighing to song,
"For the road might be rough, but it
    could not be long."*

*"He looked for a City; his goal, Lord,
    we share,
"And know that bright City which You
    do prepare,
"Is ever our portion, since willing to
    be,
"Just pilgrims with Jesus, our roof a
    tent tree."*

CHAPTER 3

(1) "HEAR THIS WORD THAT THE LORD HAS SPOKEN AGAINST YOU, O CHILDREN OF ISRAEL, AGAINST THE WHOLE FAMILY WHICH I BROUGHT UP FROM THE LAND OF EGYPT, SAYING."

The diagram is:

1. Having addressed several nations dwelling near the Promised Land, God now continues to address the whole family of Israel redeemed from the land of Egypt.

2. This family alone He recognized *"known"* as His. For this reason, He would punish them for their iniquities, of which they refused to repent.

3. God cannot abide sin in anyone, even

His Own, and especially His Own!

HEAR THIS WORD THAT THE LORD HAS SPOKEN

Williams says, *"This is a solemn principle. Relationship to God compromises the Name of God. It is a great privilege to be a testimony for God, but that testimony must accord with the Holiness of God and must not falsify His Character.*

"If the testimony becomes corrupted, its professors must be judged, for God must vindicate His moral glory; hence, if calamity and suffering, and because of sin occurs, they were not accidental but from God. There was a cause, as we shall see."[1]

The phrase, *"Hear this Word that the LORD has spoken against you,"* is dire indeed!

This *"Word"* is actually *"against the whole family,"* referring to all the Tribes, which were brought out of Egypt. Even though the northern kingdom of Israel would be judged separately from the southern kingdom of Judah, still, both would be judged, although not at the same time. In fact, Judah, the southern kingdom, suffered the Judgment of God a little over 130 years after Judgment came on the northern kingdom of Israel. It may take awhile for the Prophecy to be fulfilled, but, if it's from the Lord, one can be doubly certain that it most definitely will be fulfilled.

(2) "YOU ONLY HAVE I KNOWN OF ALL THE FAMILIES OF THE EARTH: THEREFORE I WILL PUNISH YOU FOR ALL YOUR INIQUITIES."

The pattern is:

1. Of all the nations in the world, Israel and Judah alone belonged to the Lord.

2. *"You only have I known,"* means loved, acknowledged, and chosen.

3. *"Therefore I will punish you for all your iniquities,"* means that they must not presume upon their privileges.

4. Their retention of God's Favor depended upon obedience to His Word (Ex. 19:5). The nearer they were brought to God, the greater their guilt if they fell from God.

SINNING AGAINST LIGHT

Unlike the heathen nations denounced

in the former Chapters, Israel had sinned against light, knowledge, and love, therefore, the sentence on her must be heavier. To whom much is given, much is required!

In fact, Israel, and putting both the northern kingdom and the southern kingdom into one, was the only Nation on Earth that truly knew God and had a relationship with Him. All the other nations were idol-worshippers.

Consequently, the Lord dealt with all the other nations of the world as they dealt with Israel. If one is to notice, certain nations or areas of the world are not even mentioned in the Bible because they had no relationship with God's People. This did not mean that God did not love them, for He did! He loved them so much, in fact, that *"He would send His Only Begotten Son, that whosoever believes in Him should not perish, but have Everlasting Life"* (Jn. 3:16).

Actually, Israel was supposed to evangelize all of these nations but, tragically, failed in that they not only did not evangelize them, but, in fact, became like them.

In truth, God's major Interest, as related in His Word, has always been, and is now, His People, whether Israel of old or the New Testament Church, which includes the modern church.

If one is to notice, the Lord dealt with the mighty Roman Empire only as it dealt with His Body, the Church. Therefore, that, and that alone, with some exceptions, is His Interest.

(3) "CAN TWO WALK TOGETHER, EXCEPT THEY BE AGREED?"

The construction is:

1. Companionship with God can only be enjoyed upon the basis of separation from evil.

2. The old adage, *"Birds of a feather flock together,"* is pretty much the same as this Verse.

3. The Lord will walk with us only on the basis of us agreeing with His Word, and doing so to the best of our ability.

IN AGREEMENT

Verse 3, even though having far reaching consequences, actually pertains to Amos as a Prophet and the Lord as his Sponsor.

NOTES

Evidently, Amos is now at Beth-el, where one of the golden calves is located, and where, no doubt, a magnificent temple of worship had been erected. Upon hearing his words, the people do not believe him and in answer to their response, Amos claims, and rightly so, that he and the Lord are *"walking together,"* and that such would not be possible except *"they be agreed."*

Therefore, his Prophecies are from the Lord and, in effect, are the very Words of the Lord.

Consequently, his following statements portray him giving a series of Parables or comparisons, which established his right to prophesy. He illustrates the truths that all effects have causes and that from the cause, one can infer the effect.

In other words, there is a cause for every action.

As well, and from this Verse, one has the reason for all the denominational splinters in the world of Christendom. They do not *"agree,"* therefore, they cannot *"walk together,"* hence, the Baptist church, the Methodist church, the Church of God, the Nazarenes, etc.

IS CHRIST DIVIDED?

Paul would address all of this by saying, *"Now I beseech you, brethren, by the Name of our Lord Jesus Christ, that you all speak the same thing, and that there be no divisions among you; but that you be perfectly joined together in the same mind and in the same judgment"* (I Cor. 1:10).

He also asked, *"Is Christ divided?"* (I Cor. 1:13).

Of course, the answer is obvious, Christ is not divided; therefore, the *"divisions among us,"* is because we *"all do not speak the same thing,"* i.e., the Bible.

This becomes even more serious when one considers that there is only one Gospel and one Christ. Paul further says, *"But though we, or an Angel from Heaven, preach any other gospel unto you than that which we have preached unto you, let him be accursed"* (Gal. 1:8).

Therefore, all the various church denominations are not the Will of God; consequently, the seeker must find the one that is closest to the Word of God, for that alone is the criteria!

Regrettably, it is not the criteria for most professing Christians! For most, the criteria are many and varied, social activities, entertainment, nearness, particular denomination, etc.

WHAT CHURCH SHOULD I ATTEND?

The Church you should attend is the one that is rightly and correctly preaching the Gospel, which occasions the feeding of one's soul.

Even though I do not at all enjoy making the following statement, still, I feel it must be made. The modern church is in worse condition spiritually than at any time since the Reformation. That's quite a statement, but I believe it to be true. Sadly and tragically, fewer people are being Saved at this time (2010) than at any time since the Reformation. Fewer Believers are being baptized with the Holy Spirit with the evidence of speaking with other Tongues than at any time since the turn of the Twentieth Century.

We (Jimmy Swaggart Ministries) are doing something presently, because we believe the Lord has told us to do so, which I don't think the Lord would have recommended even 10 years ago. Let me explain.

Regardless of what we think that Church actually is, at least, what it has become in these modern times, the truth is, Church is the Message that is preached from behind the pulpit. Everything else is elementary, if holding any place at all. So, we are encouraging those who follow our Ministry to make Family Worship Center and our Media Ministry their Church, irrespective as to where they might live in the world. In effect, Believers can join us by the Internet, by our telecast, or by our radio stations, and worship with us although in different parts of the world. Once again I make this statement:

The single most important thing is the Gospel that is preached. As stated, anything else and everything else is incidental. If the wrong gospel is attended, it can cause untold problems, even the loss of the soul. The greatest effort on the part of the Evil One is to compromise the Gospel, to rob it of its power, and to make it less than what

NOTES

it is. Unfortunately, he has been all too successful. Paul said the following:

ANOTHER GOSPEL

"I marvel that you are so soon removed from Him (the Holy Spirit) Who called you into the Grace of Christ (made possible by the Cross) unto another gospel (anything which doesn't have the Cross as its Object of Faith):

"Which is not another (presents the fact that Satan's aim is not so much to deny the Gospel, which he can little do, as to corrupt it); but there be some who trouble you, and would pervert the Gospel of Christ (once again, to make the object of Faith something other than the Cross)."

ACCURSED

"But though we (Paul and his associates), or an Angel from Heaven, preach any other gospel unto you than that which we have preached unto you (Jesus Christ and Him Crucified – I Cor. 1:23), let him be accursed (eternally condemned; the Holy Spirit speaks this through Paul, making this very serious).

"As we said before, so say I now again (at some time past, he had said the same thing to them, making their defection even more serious), If any man preach any other gospel unto you (anything other than the Cross) than that you have received (which Saved your souls), let him be accursed ('eternally condemned,' which means the loss of the soul).

"For do I now persuade men, or God? (In essence, Paul is saying, 'Do I preach man's doctrine, or God's?') or do I seek to please men? (This is what false apostles do.) for if I yet pleased men, I should not be the Servant of Christ (one cannot please both men and God at the same time)" (Gal. 1:6-10).

WHAT IS THE GOSPEL?

Pure and simple, the Holy Spirit through the Apostle Paul told us what the Gospel of Jesus Christ actually is. He said:

"For Christ sent me not to baptize (presents to us a Cardinal Truth), but to preach the Gospel (the manner in which one may be Saved from sin): not with wisdom of words *(intellectualism is not the Gospel)*, **lest the Cross of Christ should be made of none effect.** *(This tells us in no uncertain terms that the Cross of Christ must always be the emphasis of the Message)*" **(I Cor. 1:17).**

In plain and simple words, the great Apostle here gives us a definition of the Gospel of Jesus Christ. It is *"Jesus Christ and Him Crucified."* In fact, the meaning of the New Covenant is the Cross of Christ, i.e., what Jesus there did. When we speak of the *"Cross,"* I'm certain that the reader understands we're not talking about a wooden beam but what Jesus there accomplished in the giving of Himself as a Perfect Sacrifice, thereby, becoming the Sin-Offering, which satisfied the demands of a thrice-Holy God. In other words, at the Cross, Jesus atoned for all sin, past, present, and future, at least, for all who will believe (Jn. 3:16).

Paul also said, **"For the preaching** *(Word)* **of the Cross is to them who perish foolishness** *(Spiritual things cannot be discerned by unredeemed people, but that doesn't matter; the Cross must be preached just the same, even as we shall see)*; **but unto us who are Saved it is the Power of God.** *(The Cross is the Power of God simply because it was there that the total sin debt was paid, giving the Holy Spirit, in Whom the Power resides, latitude to work mightily within our lives)*" **(I Cor. 1:18).**

WHAT DOES IT MEAN TO PREACH THE CROSS?

The Preacher must understand that Jesus Christ is the *"Source"* of all things we receive from God. But, at the same time, he has to also understand that the Cross of Christ is the *"Means"* by which these things are given to us. In fact, I have already said that in this Volume and, no doubt, will say it again because it is so very, very important.

It is the Cross of Christ that has made possible everything we receive from the Lord. As we've also said, God cannot meet with sinful man anywhere except at the Cross. It is the Cross of Christ that makes it all possible.

This doesn't mean that every time the Preacher preaches, he has to preach about the Cross of Christ. However, it does mean

that he must understand and believe totally and completely that the Cross of Christ, and nothing else, is the Means by which the Lord deals with the human race. In fact, *"Jesus Christ and Him Crucified"* is the Story of the entirety of the Bible.

As we as Believers pray, our Lord told us that we should pray to the Father in His Name, and, of course, we're speaking of the Name of Jesus. This means that we would have no audience at all and could not approach the Father whatsoever, at least, that He would take notice of us, other than we come to Him in the Name of Jesus. This speaks of what our Lord did at the Cross. In fact, the very Name *"Jesus"* means *"Saviour,"* and He is Saviour by virtue of the Cross and the price He there paid.

(4) "WILL A LION ROAR IN THE FOREST, WHEN HE HAS NO PREY? WILL A YOUNG LION CRY OUT OF HIS DEN, IF HE HAS TAKEN NOTHING?"

The pattern is:

1. As the lion roars when it has found its prey, God, therefore, makes the Prophet utter his voice because He is ready to execute vengeance.

2. There is a cause for every action.

3. These Parables are given in order to show Israel the Mind of God. They constitute a warning, a stern warning! Unfortunately, it was all to no avail.

A CAUSE FOR EVERY ACTION

As it regards this Verse, the Lord is saying that one can look at the nature of wild animals, which gives us a clue as to what the Lord is doing.

If the lion roars, he has found a prey. This means that the Lord does nothing capriciously. He always has a reason for everything that He does. The reason for the coming Judgment upon Israel is their sin and refusal to hear the warning, even though it is given to them by the Prophet over and over again. The manner of man to resist the Lord is a marvel to behold. Let's look for a few moments at the New Covenant:

Due to the Fall, man without God is totally depraved. This means that he can have no correct thought about God whatsoever. So, if he is to be Saved, Salvation will have to come from the Lord in every capacity.

The Gospel is preached in some manner, whether by word, action, or song. The Holy Spirit uses the Word to convict the sinner of his or her lost condition. He then gives the sinner the Faith to believe, for on his own, he can have nothing of God of himself. Thankfully, a few respond favorably. Sadly, most don't!

At any rate, at the moment the sinner registers belief in the Lord, using the Faith that the Holy Spirit has given him, the person is Saved.

CHRIST AND THE CROSS

All of this seems easy; however, the Lord has paid a terrible price that we might be Saved. Knowing that due to the Fall, man could not do anything about his lost condition, God became Man, the Man Christ Jesus, which means that He is now not only very God but, as well, very Man. It's called the Incarnation, God becoming Man. He did that for many reasons, but the primary reason of all is that He would go to the Cross, giving Himself in Sacrifice, which God would accept as payment in full, which He did. So, Salvation began with God and was carried out by God.

To receive this wonderful Salvation, this wonderful Eternal Life, and to become an Heir of God, a joint-Heir with Jesus Christ, which proclaims riches beyond comprehension, all the believing sinner has to do is just have Faith in the Lord, which simply means to believe. At that moment, he is Born-Again (Jn. 3:16).

THE LOVE OF GOD

When one thinks about this, it becomes incomprehensible. Why would God do such a thing, especially considering that the ones for whom He has done this have no love for Him whatsoever but, actually, have hate? It is because God is Love. It was Love that created man, not of necessity, and so Love must redeem man.

THE CROSS AND SANCTIFICATION

The Lord, as would be obvious, demands nothing of the believing sinner, as it regards being Born-Again, except simply to believe.

That being done, the great Work of Redemption is instantly accomplished, with the Lord at that moment imputing a perfect Righteousness to such an individual. After one comes to Christ, now having a new nature, such a one falls in love with the Bible, and falls in love with anything and everything pertaining to the Lord. So, the Lord now expects us to learn what is in His Word. He has a way for us to live for Him, which is the Way of the Cross. He doesn't require much of us, but He does require one thing, and that is that the Believer's Faith be placed exclusively in Christ and the Cross, and remain exclusively in Christ and the Cross. That being done, the Holy Spirit will then grandly use His Almighty Power in our hearts and lives, conforming us to the Image of Christ.

Now, as should be obvious, that's very simple. But yet, Satan does everything to keep us from doing that which is given to us in the Word (Rom. 6:1-14; 8:1-2, 11; I Cor. 1:17-18, 23; 2:2; Gal., Chpt. 5; 6:14; Eph. 2:13-18; Col. 2:10-15).

There is an offense to the Cross. Why?

THE OFFENSE OF THE CROSS

Paul mentioned this in the Fifth Chapter of Galatians. He said:

"And I, brethren, if I yet preach Circumcision, why do I yet suffer persecution? *(Any message other than the Cross draws little opposition.)* **then is the offense of the Cross ceased.** *(The Cross offends the world and most of the Church. So, if the preacher ceases to preach the Cross as the only way of Salvation and Victory, then opposition and persecution will cease, but so will Salvation!)* **"(Gal. 5:11).**

Why in the world is the Cross of Christ an offense?

How in the world could the Cross of Christ be an offense?

The life in Christ is no longer a self-centered life that one lives but a Christ-centered one. One's new life is a Person, the Lord Jesus. Through the Person and Ministry of the Holy Spirit, the Lord Jesus is manifest in one's life. The new life is no longer like the former one, dependent upon the ineffectual efforts of a man attempting to draw near to God by his own works. The new life is a Person, namely Christ, within a person, living out His Life in that person. Instead of attempting to live one's life in obedience to a set of rules in the form of the legal enactments of the Mosaic Law, one now yields to the indwelling Holy Spirit and cooperates with Him in the production of a life pleasing to God. He is energized by the Divine Life resident in him through the regenerating Work of the Spirit, which is all made possible by the Cross.

However, man, even believing man, somewhat balks at this position made possible by the Cross and given to us by the Holy Spirit. Herein lies the problem. Man likes to have some credit and some position. He likes that which he can see and handle. He refuses to be treated as vile and incapable of good and is angered that he and his religious efforts should be condemned to annihilation.

Oh yes! He will willingly practice efforts to annihilate himself, for that ministers to his own importance. However, to accept the absolute Judgment of death upon his nature, his religious energies, and his moral virtues, is distasteful and repelling. To be commanded to be silent and, as a dead sinner, to trust the Life-giving Saviour, finding in Him all that is needful for Righteousness and worship, is repugnant to carnal man, hence, the offense of the Cross.

THE MODERN WAY OF WORKS

The modern church is the busiest church that has ever been. It is up to its neck, proverbially speaking, in works of every nature. The thousands, and even millions, participating in all of these works think somehow that this brings about Righteousness and Holiness. It doesn't, even as it can't! In fact, in the modern church, there is little mention of the Cross at all, claiming that such might offend people. So the Seeker Sensitive model is that no one be offended. Consequently, sin is not mentioned, the Cross is not mentioned, the Blood is not mentioned, and Calvary is not mentioned!

At any rate, for a great deal of time, I wondered how in the world that preachers could get people to deprive their families, working nearly day and night, almost like slaves.

The reason I came to know was in the

statement just previously made. Let me state it again, please:

Christians will willingly practice efforts to annihilate themselves, for that ministers to their own importance, and that's the answer. Look what I have done! And look what I am doing! When you tell that person that all of those efforts constitute nothing in the Eyes of God, but rather Faith exclusively in Christ and what Christ did for us at the Cross, that is an offense to that individual. So, please allow us to say it again:

The Lord has but one Way of Salvation. That one Way is *"Jesus Christ and Him Crucified"* (I Cor. 1:23).

As well, our Lord has but one Way of Sanctification, and that is *"Jesus Christ and Him Crucified"* (I Cor. 1:123).

THE MODERN MESSAGE IS MORALITY AND GOOD WORKS

In other words, we are to be good and, therefore, to do good.

Now, as every false direction, there is some truth in that statement. Of course, we as Believers are to be good and to do good, but the great question is, *"How do we come to that place?"*

The modern church is teaching and preaching that one can be good without our Lord and His Cross. In other words, being good is just simply a matter of changing one's habits. And then we are to do good, which is believed to bring about Righteousness and Holiness. It doesn't!

God honors nothing but Faith in His Son, the Lord Jesus Christ, and what He did for us at the Cross. In fact, and as previously stated, the only place that a thrice-Holy God can meet with sinful man is the Cross of Christ. One will always find that the Lord is absent from any other proposed place of meeting.

(5) "CAN A BIRD FALL IN A SNARE UPON THE EARTH, WHERE NO GIN IS FOR HIM? SHALL ONE TAKE UP A SNARE FROM THE EARTH, AND HAVE TAKEN NOTHING AT ALL?"

The construction is:

1. The idea is: the bird is caught because it is too close to the trap.

2. The trap which the sinner sets for himself is sin.

3. Sin is a trap, and the only answer for this destruction is the Cross of Christ.

SIN IS A TRAP

Verse 5 states that the trap will not be sprung unless its spring is touched.

The idea is that sin is a trap, and it always catches those who engage in it. No one can beat the game, and none shall escape.

The idea continues; when God appoints retributive punishments for the guilty and announces the same by His Prophets, they must be expected with absolute certainty.

When Amos is through with these simple narratives, he will have laid to rest the arguments of the people, whether they care to admit it or not!

(6) "SHALL A TRUMPET BE BLOWN IN THE CITY, AND THE PEOPLE NOT BE AFRAID? SHALL THERE BE EVIL IN A CITY, AND THE LORD HAS NOT DONE IT?"

The pattern is:

1. Two great principles—one of Law, and the other of Grace—appear in Verses 6 through 8.

2. First: God will judge evil. Second: He forewarns those whom He is about to judge.

3. There is just cause when He should judge evil, but love intervenes with her warning.

LAW AND GRACE

Just as trembling is caused by a lion's roar, so is prophesying by Jehovah's Voice. When the Lord speaks, the Prophet cannot be silent; however, men may demand his silence. The Prophet is saying that as a *"trumpet is blown in the city,"* which is meant to arouse alarm in the minds of the people, likewise, surely, they will consider that his Prophecies are cause for alarm. As they would be *"afraid"* for the former, they, surely, should be afraid of the latter.

The question, *"Shall there be evil in a city, and the LORD has not done it?"* refers to the people claiming that if calamities did actually come, it would have nothing to do with the Lord. Amos says otherwise!

He is saying that, in their case, all calamities may be rightly regarded as the punishment of sin and their refusal to repent. Thus, the ruin impending on Israel was sent

by the Lord, Whose agent was the enemy now approaching.

This is a startling statement and actually applies to any and all, at least, where sin is concerned.

Therefore, every calamity of nature, which is rightly referred to as *"an act of God,"* is sent or allowed by God, mostly because of sin. Admittedly, Satan is the *"prince of the powers of the air,"* and the *"god of this world,"* still, whatever he does can only be done with the permission of the Lord. To believe otherwise places God in a subservient position to the Evil One, which, of course, is facetious!

The word, *"evil,"* in the Text, at least, in this sense, refers to affliction or calamity.

WHAT PART DOES THE LORD PLAY IN ALL CALAMITY AND AFFLICTION?

In a sense, the Lord has everything and anything to do with all happenings on this Earth. As stated, while Satan *"steals, kills, and destroys,"* still, he can only do what the Lord allows him to do. But it's not as simple as all of that!

When Adam and Eve fell in the Garden of Eden, in essence, they gave their dominion to the Evil one, Satan. They, no doubt, did not realize they were doing this when it happened, but that is exactly what happened. Consequently, even as the Holy Spirit says, and just quoted, Satan is the *"prince of the powers of the air"* (Eph. 2:2). As well, he is the *"god of this world"* (II Cor. 4:4).

Sin is always a factor in Judgment coming upon any nation, any city, or even any person. God is always longsuffering; however, even longsuffering has an end to it. If there is no repentance, at least, as it regards some of the people, Judgment is forthcoming. As well, at times the Lord allows calamity to come, and we speak of Believers, in order to build trust and Faith in that person, whomever he might be. Job is a perfect example! Job had not sinned, but yet, he underwent a terrible trial, which the Lord played out, not only for Job's sake, but for every other Believer who has ever lived.

As well, the Lord expects more of nations where there is a goodly number of Believers than He does those who are embedded in heathenistic religions. As we've already stated, to whom much is given, much is required!

And yet, in all of this, we must understand that no sickness, even death, or trouble, calamity, or turbulence in the elements is in the Will of God. It is all because of the Fall. We are now coming down to the close of the Church Age, when the Lord is going to usher in a thousand years of peace and prosperity such as the world has never known before. And yet, before that time comes, seven years of great tribulation will come upon this world, which will be worse than the world has ever seen before in its history. Jesus said so (Mat. 24:21).

It is true that God is omnipotent, meaning He is all-powerful, and there is nothing beyond His Capabilities. As well, He is omniscient, meaning that He knows all things, past, present, and future. In addition, He is omnipresent, meaning that He is everywhere. Still, even though God is all of this, He will not do anything that violates His Nature and His Character.

For instance, He had the Power, and has the Power, to merely state, *"All sin is reconciled,"* and He could have done so without Jesus having to go to the Cross. However, to do that would violate His Nature, which is of Perfect Justice, Perfect Character, in fact, perfection in every capacity. So, His Nature demanded that sin be addressed in that the Law was to be kept in every respect. To do that, God would have to become man and go to the Cross in order that sin might be addressed and, thereby, paid in full.

JUST

John wrote, *"If we confess our sins, He is faithful and just to forgive us our sins, and to cleanse us from all unrighteousness"* (I Jn. 1:9).

I want to call your attention to the two words, *"faithful and just."*

The first word means simply that if we truly confess our sins before the Lord, irrespective as to how many there may be, or how bad they may be, He will always forgive. But, as well, He used the word *"just."*

This means that God is not forgiving these sins merely on the basis of a system,

but the word *"just"* proclaims the fact that the price has been paid, and paid in full. In other words, no shortcuts were taken. Our Lord suffered the full brunt of the Judgment of God in His Dying and Death in order to serve as the Sin-Offering, thereby, making doubly certain that the payment for sin was fully paid. So, when you as a Believer ask the Lord to forgive you for something you have done that is wrong, He will always be faithful to do that. But, as well, no Angel, no demon, or even Satan himself will ever be able to say that what was done and is done constantly by our Lord is any way illegal. The full Power of a total and completed Redemption Plan is behind every act of forgiveness. Oh, how I sense the Presence of God even as I utter these words. How much is this grand Plan so Perfect, so all-inclusive, so total, and so complete that it will never be questioned in time or eternity. While there are any number of Greek words in the New Testament that speak of Redemption, the following three are perhaps used more than all. They are:

1. Garazo: it means to be purchased out of slavery.

2. Exgarazo: it means to be purchased, never to be put up for sale again.

3. Lutroo: it means that such a price was paid for our Redemption, as it regards the Cross of Christ, that Angel, demon spirit, or Satan himself, will never be able to say in eternity future that the price paid was insufficient.

(7) "SURELY THE LORD GOD WILL DO NOTHING, BUT HE REVEALS HIS SECRET UNTO HIS SERVANTS THE PROPHETS."

The pattern is:

1. Verse 7 proclaims the Grace of God.

2. The Lord forewarned those whom He is about to judge.

3. Such is done to provoke Repentance, that is, if possible, that the Judgment be halted.

THE REVELATION OF HIS SECRET

If Grace is rejected, then the people become candidates for Judgment.

"Prophets" were used then to *"foretell,"* and, as well, *"Prophets"* are used thusly today, but not nearly as much. The reason

is the Bible.

Under the Old Economy of God, the people had a part of the Word of God, but only a part. Therefore, the *"Prophets"* were used to give guidance, instruction, and direction, which, within itself, at least, many times, actually became the written Word, which we know today as the Bible.

With John on the Isle of Patmos, the Canon of Scripture was completed with the Book of Revelation; consequently, between Genesis and Revelation, *"The Lord has revealed His Secrets."* As stated, it was *"unto His Servants the Prophets,"* i.e., Moses, Joshua, Samuel, David, Solomon, Isaiah, Jeremiah, Ezekiel, etc., Matthew, Mark, Luke, John, Paul, James, and Peter.

Nevertheless, and along with His written Word, He also continues to reveal *"secrets"* to *"His Servants the Prophets."* An example is found in Acts, Chapter 21, where *"a certain Prophet named Agabus,"* gave Paul certain information respecting that which would happen to him in the near future. As well, the Lord has continued to reveal many and varied things down through the centuries and even at present, respecting leading, guidance, direction, and the impartation of certain information.

He still uses the same methods now as in the Bible, i.e., Dreams, Visions, Prophecies, or Tongues and interpretation of Tongues. However, anything that we have that's truly from the Lord will always coincide perfectly with the Word of God. If not, then whatever it is, it is not of God.

However, as in the Old (Deut. 13:1-4), so in the New, we are reminded to *". . . try the spirits whether they are of God: because many false prophets are gone out into the world"* (I Jn. 4:1).

(8) "THE LION HAS ROARED, WHO WILL NOT FEAR? THE LORD GOD HAS SPOKEN, WHO CAN BUT PROPHESY?"

The overview is:

1. The idea is: as the lion's roar causes fear, likewise, when the Lord speaks, the Prophet must be fearful not to prophesy.

2. When people ignore the Word of the Lord, this shows they are in a hardened condition, which means that Judgment is inevitable.

3. It is not always easy for the Prophet to speak the Word of the Lord. Many times the Word from the Lord is not positive; consequently, such generates anger. In fact, that's why many Prophets in Old Testament times were maltreated and even killed.

PROPHESY

The true God-called Preacher will preach, irrespective of the demands for his silence. And, to be sure, those demands will come!

Satan makes his greatest efforts to silence the true Prophet of God because only such has the True Word of God. Remarkably, the Evil One uses religion as he uses nothing else in his attempt to silence the Man of God.

One of the greatest examples is denominational leaders, who take it upon themselves, and unscripturally so, to tell men where they can preach, what they can preach, when they can preach, and why they can preach. Those who allow such to happen, and under any circumstances, either have not been truly called by God, or they are truly failing God.

An example is Peter and John, who were commanded by the *"Rulers, Elders, and Scribes,"* not to speak at all or teach in the Name of Jesus.

"But Peter and John answered and said unto them, Whether it be right in the Sight of God to hearken unto you more than unto God, you judge.

"For we cannot but speak the things which we have seen and heard" (Acts 4:18-20).

But unfortunately, there aren't many modern Preachers of the caliber of Peter and John.

(9) "PUBLISH IN THE PALACES AT ASHDOD, AND IN THE PALACES IN THE LAND OF EGYPT, AND SAY, ASSEMBLE YOURSELVES UPON THE MOUNTAINS OF SAMARIA, AND BEHOLD THE GREAT TUMULTS IN THE MIDST THEREOF, AND THE OPPRESSED IN THE MIDST THEREOF."

The overview is:

1. Strangely enough, the Philistines and the Egyptians are invited to behold the great evils and oppressions in the midst of Samaria (Israel) and to recognize the Justice of God in sending them.

2. This principle appears frequently in the Scriptures: the heathen are oftentimes righteous judges of the professing People of God.

3. The implication is: it was the eternal disgrace of Israel that there were doings in her cities which the very heathen would condemn.

BEHOLD!

The word *"behold"* is extended to any and all. Even though the Philistines and Egyptians would not do such a thing, still, the analogy is well taken!

It was said by a newsman the other day over one of the networks, *"America has become like nations where we once sent Missionaries."*

How right that newsman was and is. Our country is in a terrible condition simply because the church is in a terrible situation. Less people are being truly Born-Again today than at any time since the Reformation. Fewer Believers are being baptized with the Holy Spirit with the evidence of speaking with other Tongues than at any time since the turn of the Twentieth Century. Whatever problems there are in this nation, the fault can be laid at the doorsteps of the church.

We fuss about the present Administration and, admittedly, it could not be much worse, if at all! But the following must be noted:

People elect to office what they are, whether it be religious office, or secular office.

(10) "FOR THEY KNOW NOT TO DO RIGHT, SAYS THE LORD, WHO STORE UP VIOLENCE AND ROBBERY IN THEIR PALACES."

The structure is:

1. Persistence in the evil of covetousness and the love of money deadens moral consciousness.

2. God's People can push so far away from Him that, anymore, they do not know the difference in right or wrong.

3. The only thing standing between a thrice-Holy God and sinful man is the Cross of Christ. But, regrettably, the Cross is little being preached anymore at present.

SIN

As it regards the modern church, sin takes on a brand-new definition almost every day. Little by little, the standards are lowered until there is no standard left. In today's modern church climate, at least in the far greater number of churches, alcohol is tolerated, and homosexuality is tolerated as an alternate lifestyle, in fact, the list is long. In other words, in the modern church, nothing is wrong anymore.

We must remember, the Lord saves us from sin and not in sin.

(11) "THEREFORE THUS SAYS THE LORD GOD; AN ADVERSARY THERE SHALL BE EVEN ROUND ABOUT THE LAND; AND HE SHALL BRING DOWN YOUR STRENGTH FROM YOU, AND YOUR PALACES SHALL BE SPOILED."

The overview is:

1. *"An adversary there shall be,"* at least in this case, refers to Sennacherib, the Assyrian king.

2. He emptied the palaces in Israel filled with the spoils robbed from the poor, etc.

3. What we sow, we reap!

THE SPOILING OF ISRAEL

"An adversary," will follow all who traffic in that which is not sanctioned by the Lord and His Word. It may be awhile in coming, but come it shall!

Money made in any manner that is not Scriptural, no matter the attempts at self-justification, will ultimately bring the ruin here mentioned. Two statements:

1. *"He shall bring down your strength from you."*

2. *"And your palaces shall be spoiled."*

These two things find their fulfillment in wrecked lives, children who do not know God, and misery, which accompanies the failure to obey the Word of God.

(12) "THUS SAYS THE LORD; AS THE SHEPHERD TAKES OUT OF THE MOUTH OF THE LION TWO LEGS, OR A PIECE OF AN EAR; SO WILL THE CHILDREN OF ISRAEL BE TAKEN OUT WHO DWELL IN SAMARIA IN THE CORNER OF A BED, AND IN DAMASCUS IN A COUCH."

The overview is:

1. So thorough would be the action of Sennacherib that the few people left alive would only be comparable to a piece of an

ear of a sheep taken out of the mouth of a lion to prove to the owner that it was killed.

2. *"In Samaria in the corner of a bed, and in Damascus in a couch,"* denotes the luxurious rich; but Israel would find that such riches would not save them.

3. The Holy Spirit through the Prophet is speaking here of total destruction. But yet, it seemed to have no positive effect on the people.

THE PROPHECIES OF AMOS

These Israelites at this time were very confident in their riches and, as well, had become very friendly with the Syrians, as well as their idol-worshipping ways. Consequently, the Prophecies of Amos seemed preposterous, or even as mindless drivel, and so does the Word of God preached by faithful Ministers, who warn of Judgment to come. The *"lifestyles of the rich and the famous"* have no place or program for such thinking.

America basked in the idea that after the fall of the former Soviet Union, we were the only super power left in the world. But this nation has forsaken the Lord. As such, the blood of multiple thousands of young men and young women has been shed on foreign battlefields for little purpose, if any at all. The riches of this nation have gone down that drain as well! Without God, deterioration rapidly increases, and this nation, for all practical purposes, is presently without God.

(13) "HEAR YOU, AND TESTIFY IN THE HOUSE OF JACOB, SAYS THE LORD GOD, THE GOD OF HOSTS."

1. To the insults and denials of these individuals in Samaria, Amos claims, and rightly so, that his words are really the Words of the *"Lord GOD,"* the *"Almighty God."*

2. The people are implored to *"hear!"*

3. What Amos was prophesying was given to him by *"Almighty God."*

ALMIGHTY GOD

The manner in which Amos makes this statement leaves absolutely no room for doubt. As well, as he delivered the Word, the Anointing of the Holy Spirit must have powerfully moved upon him to utter these words, which should have definitely struck fear in the hearts of the listeners.

In other words, it was impossible to have a higher authority than that had by Amos, *"Almighty God."*

(14) "THAT IN THE DAY THAT I SHALL VISIT THE TRANSGRESSIONS OF ISRAEL UPON HIM I WILL ALSO VISIT THE ALTARS OF BETH-EL: AND THE HORNS OF THE ALTAR SHALL BE CUT OFF, AND FALL TO THE GROUND."

The structure is:

1. The word *"altars"* is plural of magnitude, for the great altar erected at Beth-el by Jeroboam I for the worship of the golden calf.

2. *"And the horns of the altar shall be cut off, and fall to the ground,"* referred to the altar of the golden calf.

3. The *"horns"* represented the most sacred of this heathen altar. The prediction is that when Judgment comes, these *"horns"* will be broken off, signifying God's Rejection of this man-made altar as an Atonement for sin.

4. Be it known: Just as in this prediction, the *"horns"* of every man-made altar (which attempts to take the place of Calvary) shall ultimately be cut off and *"fall to the ground."*

THE ALTARS OF BETH-EL

"Beth-el" had been chosen by Jeroboam I, at least partially, for its proximity to the southern border of Israel; however, Satan had other reasons for the erection of the golden calf at this location. The very word, *"Beth-el,"* means *"House of God."* Therefore, the Evil One would seek to demean that, and greatly so, which was God's.

It was here at Beth-el that Jacob had the Vision of God (Gen. 31:13; 35:7).

Beth-el was allotted to Ephraim who captured it. It bordered the territory of Benjamin (Josh. 18:13).

Many years before, when it was necessary for Israel to punish the Tribe of Benjamin, the people sought advice on the conduct of the battle and worshipped at Beth-el *"for the Ark . . . was there"* (Judg. 20:18-28; 21:1-4).

It was a Sanctuary, too, in the time of Samuel, who visited it annually (I Sam. 7:16; 10:3).

As stated, it was here where Jeroboam I proposed his rival cult of the golden calf. It was, as well, condemned by a Man of God from Judah (I Ki. 12:28-13:32).

At the present (2010), modern Israel has an army camp at this site.

Let it be known that, as the horns of this altar were broken off, and rightly so, likewise, every altar that is not *"Christ and Him Crucified"* shall be broken off and cast down to the ground.

(15) "AND I WILL SMITE THE WINTER HOUSE WITH THE SUMMER HOUSE; AND THE HOUSES OF IVORY SHALL PERISH, AND THE GREAT HOUSES SHALL HAVE AN END, SAYS THE LORD."

The overview is:

1. Verse 15 speaks of the obvious prosperity of Samaria, where luxury, ease, and comfort, among other things, had sapped all Spiritual Strength from God's People.

2. The phrase, *"And the great houses shall have an end, says the LORD,"* refers to every house in this world which is built on sand. They will ultimately fall (Mat. 7:26).

3. Everything that's not of God will ultimately crash.

"O Lamb of God, still keep me,
"Close to Your wounded Side;
"'Tis only there in safety,
"And peace I can abide."

CHAPTER 4

(1) "HEAR THIS WORD, YOU KINE OF BASHAN, THAT ARE IN THE MOUNTAIN OF SAMARIA, WHICH OPPRESS THE POOR, WHICH CRUSH THE NEEDY, WHICH SAY TO THEIR MASTERS, BRING, AND LET US DRINK."

The overview is:

1. The phrase, *"Hear this word, you kine (cattle) of Bashan,"* pertains to the rich pastureland east of Jordan, where cattle there fed became strong and fat. The nobles of Samaria are compared to them here.

2. *"Which oppress the poor, which crush the needy,"* registers God's Love for the poor and His Indignation against oppression, which is a feature of the Book of Amos.

3. The phrase, *"Which say to their masters, Bring, and let us drink,"* refers to the

nobles appealing to Jeroboam II to provide them with luxurious banquets furnished by money robbed from the poor.

HEAR THIS WORD

The *"Word"* that was uttered by Amos was the Word of the Lord, which puts it in a class by itself. It is amazing, this *"Word"* was given to Amos nearly 2,800 years ago, and yet, it is still just as viable today as it was then because it is the Word of the Lord. That's the reason the Bible is of such moment and such magnitude; it is the Word of the Lord. In fact, there is no Word of the Lord in the world today other than the Bible. There are some that claim such, such as the Book of Mormon and the Koran, but, to be sure, these so-called words have their origination in demon spirits. They have absolutely nothing to do with the Lord. The Bible alone, and a word for word translation, at that, such as the King James Version, holds that distinction. In fact, in many circles the Bible has been corrupted by paraphrases, such as the so-called Message Bible. That's the reason we say that a word for word translation is absolutely necessary, and, even then, it must be inspected very carefully. That's the reason we recognize the King James. The translators, who were some of the best Hebrew and Greek scholars in the world of that day, had instructions from King James to obtain the most accurate translation that was possible. This they did. They did not have a religious ax to grind, so to speak, meaning that they were partial to certain doctrines and impartial to others. They only had one driving force and that was to translate it correctly. I personally believe they did a tremendous job, and that's the reason I totally recommend the King James Version.

TRANSLATION

And yet, there are some things that should be understood about translation. There are many words in the King James translation that are no longer used in modern English, such as *"hast,"* *"thou,"* *"thee,"* etc. These words, and many others similar, were used in Elizabethan English nearly half millennia ago. They are no longer used at present.

As well, it may come as a shock to most

Christians, but the Prophets of old and the Apostles of the New Testament, and our Lord, as well, did not use words such as *"hast,"* etc. As stated, these are Elizabethan words, which are no longer in vogue. Other words have taken their place, which mean the same thing.

WHAT WAS THE WORD OF THE LORD THAT AMOS WAS GIVING TO THE PEOPLE?

In this case, it pertained to the manner in which the poor of Israel were being treated by those in authority. What little they had was being taken from them by corrupt judges and others who held power. To be sure, all of this was coming up to the Eyes of the Lord, and now through the Prophet, He cries out against it.

The idea is, these authorities, whoever they may have been, were going to face the Judgment of God for their sins. This tells us that God sees all, and, ultimately, all will give account.

This didn't mean that the poor were godly, and the rich were ungodly. The truth is, at least for the far greater part, all were ungodly; nevertheless, stealing from the ungodly continues to be *"stealing"* in the Eyes of God.

Some Christians may think that no wrongdoing is involved when we lie to the Internal Revenue Service (I.R.S.). No, a lie is a lie, and cheating is cheating, irrespective as to whom it might be. Jesus said:

". . . Render to Caesar the things that are Caesar's, and to God the things that are God's . . ." (Mk. 12:17). In other words, Christians are obligated before God to pay taxes and to pay the correct amount. While it's not wrong to avoid taxes regarding all legal means, it is wrong to evade taxes.

(2) "THE LORD GOD HAS SWORN BY HIS HOLINESS, THAT, LO, THE DAYS SHALL COME UPON YOU, THAT HE WILL TAKE YOU AWAY WITH HOOKS, AND YOUR POSTERITY WITH FISHHOOKS."

The pattern is:

1. Verse 2 addresses the Assyrian monarch, who, upon subjugating an enemy, passed hooks through the lower lips of their captives and thus led them away to slavery.

NOTES

This would happen to Israel!

2. Those who heard Amos knew exactly what he was talking about but simply did not believe him. Nevertheless, irrespective of their unbelief, it ultimately came to pass exactly as the Lord said through the Prophet.

3. God's Holiness demands certain things. It demands that sin be repented of and put out of our lives.

THE HOLINESS OF GOD

The New Testament terminology suggests the distinction between the Holiness, which is God's very Being, and the Holiness, which marks out the character of His People.

The Greek words that denote Holiness, as it regards God's People, leave the impression, and rightly so, that man within himself is not holy and cannot be holy, all as a result of the Fall. The Holiness we have is imputed to us by the Lord and given freely upon Faith; however, it must be Faith in Christ and what Christ has done for us at the Cross.

Even though the Holiness within itself is Perfect, because it comes from God, this doesn't mean that the individual is perfect. In fact, none of us are.

As it regards the Holiness of God, not only is that Holiness Perfect, but, as well, God is Perfect, and in every respect. Holiness with God denotes a character that is an absolute antithesis to that of the world.

It is clear that in Scripture, generally, Holiness means separation, and the term is used with reference to persons or things that have been separated or set apart for God and His Service. In many cases, the word Holiness does not directly imply ethical attributes but mainly consecration to the Lord and His Service and, so, separation from the common sphere. It is God Who causes the separation and, so, conveys the Holiness that may be implied by the separation.

Holiness means not only living a separate life but bearing a character different from that of the ordinary man. Thus, the word attained a distinct ethical implication. Holiness is, therefore, recognized as belonging to what has been chosen and set apart by God and given a character that conforms to God's Law.

CHRIST AND HOLINESS

Christ in His Life and Character is the supreme example of Divine Holiness. In Him, it consisted in more than mere sinlessness: it was His entire Consecration to the Will and Purpose of God, and to this end, Jesus sanctified Himself (Jn. 17:19). The Holiness of Christ is both the Standard of the Christian character and its guarantee: *"He Who sanctifies and those who are sanctified have all one origin"* (Heb. 2:11).

The New Testament emphasizes the ethical nature of Holiness in contrast to all uncleanliness. It is represented as the supreme vocation of Christians and the goal of their living. In the final assessment of human destiny, the two categories known to Scripture are the righteous (the Holy) and the wicked (unholy).

(Some of the material on Holiness has been derived from the New Bible Dictionary.)

HOLINESS AND THE CROSS OF CHRIST

As we have previously stated, there is no way that man within himself, irrespective of his ethical standards, can attain to Holiness. Due to the Fall, such does not lie within the grasp of the human being. So, if man is to be Holy, such an attribute must be ascribed to him solely by God. This is where the Cross of Christ comes in, making such possible between a thrice-Holy God and sinful man.

At the moment of Conversion, due to a person's Faith in Christ and the Cross, the Lord pronounces such a person as Holy. The Holy Spirit could not dwell in such a person were that not the case (I Cor. 3:16-17).

All of this means that we are *"Holy"* by virtue of being *"in Christ."* We remain Holy by the Work of the Holy Spirit, Who demands that our Faith ever be in the Cross, which has made all of this possible.

In the Eyes of God, those who place their Faith and trust in Christ and what He has done for us at the Cross, in a sense, cannot be less than the One in Whom we have believed.

UNHOLY THINGS

Now, it is quite possible for the Believer who is Holy, at least, in the Eyes of God, Whose Eyes Alone matter, to do things

which are unholy. While such does not affect our standing with God, it does grieve the Holy Spirit and can cause the Believer tremendous problems (Eph. 4:30).

It is very difficult for religious man to understand that he cannot attain to Holiness in any capacity by works, and we speak of works of any nature. Holiness is a *"standing"* or *"position"* that one is given in Christ upon the acceptance of Christ (Rom. 5:1-2; 6:1-14; I Cor. 2:2). It is totally and completely a Gift of God and from God. It is hard for us to look at some people, or even ourselves, for that matter, and conclude such to be Holy. But yet, God does conclude us to be Holy but strictly on the merit of the Lord Jesus Christ and what He has done for us at the Cross. It is a matter of Faith on the part of the believing sinner but, as well, a matter of Faith in the correct Object, which must always be in the Cross of Christ, which makes it all possible (Eph. 2:13-18; Gal. 6:14).

THE UNHOLY

Actually, the only way the Believer can be judged by God as unholy is when he ceases to be a Believer.

The Scripture says, *"Of how much sorer punishment, suppose you, shall he be thought worthy, who has trodden under foot the Son of God, and has counted the Blood of the Covenant, wherewith he was sanctified, an unholy thing, and has done despite unto the Spirit of Grace?"* (Heb. 10:29).

This Passage speaks of a Believer who, in fact, has ceased to believe, meaning that the Cross of Christ is of no consequence to him. He has judged *"the Blood of the Covenant, wherewith they were sanctified, as an unholy thing."* Consequently, he then becomes unholy, which means that if he remains in that condition, he has lost his soul. In fact, this is the only way that a Christian can lose his or her way with God. It is Faith in Christ and what He did for us at the Cross, which gets us in, even though the believing sinner may understand little of that of which he has believed. As well, it is Faith in Christ and the Cross that keeps one in, of which we are to fully understand, and which can be understood after one comes to Christ. Ceasing to believe in that which got us in, and we speak of the Cross of Christ, abrogates one's place and position in Christ. In other words, they are no longer in Christ!

Some claim that if one is truly Saved, that one would not do such a thing. However, the entirety of the Book of Hebrews was written by Paul simply because many Jews, who had been wondrously Saved and filled with the Spirit, were turning their backs on Christ and going back into Judaism, and many others were contemplating doing so (Heb. 5:11-14; 6:1-6).

VICTORY IN JESUS

While failure on the part of the Believer does not abrogate one's place and position in Christ, it must ever be remembered that the Holy Spirit is given to us for many things, but the main thing is to rid us of all sin. While the Bible does not teach sinless perfection, it most definitely does teach that *"sin is not to have dominion over us"* (Rom. 6:14). The Lord does not save us in sin, but rather from sin. And the Lord has made a way for us to live a life that's not dominated in any way by the sin nature. As stated, this does not mean that the person is sinlessly perfect, for that is not to be until the Trump sounds (I Cor. 15:53).

God's Way of Life and Living, His Way of Victory, which is the same for every Believer, is that we understand the following:

• Jesus Christ is the Source of all things we receive from God (Jn. 1:1-2, 14, 29; Col. 2:10-15).

• The Cross of Christ is the Means by which all of these things are given to us (Rom. 6:3-5; I Cor. 1:17-18, 23; 2:2).

• With the Cross of Christ being the Means by which these things are given to us, this demands that the Cross of Christ ever be the Object of our Faith (Rom. 6:3-5, 11, 14; I Cor. 1:23).

• The Holy Spirit superintends all of this and actually functions according to the Finished Work of Christ. In other words, it is the Cross of Christ that has given the Holy Spirit the legal means to do all that He does for us (Rom. 8:1-2, 11; Eph. 2:13-18).

God in His Holiness cannot tolerate sin in any form. So, the only way that He can accept us is that our Faith be evidenced in the

NOTES

One Who has paid the price for us, namely Christ. And, please understand, it is altogether by Faith, but that Faith must have as its Object the Cross of Christ. The Lord will accept no other kind of Faith.

"By Faith Enoch was translated that he should not see death *(refers to God transferring Enoch to Heaven in his physical body while he was yet alive)*; **and was not found, because God had translated him** *(refers to his translation being well-known at that time)*: **for before his translation he had this testimony, that he pleased God.** *(He pleased God because he placed his Faith exclusively in Christ and the Cross.)*

"But without Faith *(in Christ and the Cross; anytime Faith is mentioned, always and without exception, its root meaning is that its Object is Christ and the Cross; otherwise, it is faith God will not accept)* **it is impossible to please** *Him* *(Faith in anything other than Christ and the Cross greatly displeases the Lord)*: **for he who comes to God must believe that He is** *(places Faith as the foundation and principle of the manner in which God deals with the human race)*, **and** *that* **He** *(God)* **is a rewarder of them who diligently seek Him** *(seek Him on the premise of Christ and Him Crucified)*" **(Heb. 11:5-6).**

(3) "AND YOU SHALL GO OUT AT THE BREACHES, EVERY COW AT THAT WHICH IS BEFORE HER; AND YOU SHALL CAST THEM INTO THE PALACE, SAYS THE LORD."

The overview is:

1. Verse 3 proclaims the fact that Israel, that is if no Repentance was forthcoming, would be taken over by the Assyrians, and it would not be a pleasant time.

2. They would be led forth, not through the gates of the city of Samaria, but through its broken walls. They would go quietly and in a straight line so as to mitigate the pain of their tortured lips.

3. The last phrase could be better said, *"You shall be cast as slaves into the palace of Sennacherib."* In other words, the luxury of Samaria would be reduced to slavery.

THE PREDICTION OF THE HOLY SPIRIT

Verse 3 proclaims the expressed contrast between their reclining as luxurious nobles in the palaces of Samaria and their groveling as slaves in the palaces of Nineveh.

The phrase, *"Every cow at that which is before her,"* refers to these women of Verse 1, the wives of the upper class, who now are reduced to the lowest form of servitude. They have fishhooks piercing their lower lips, with a line attached to the person immediately in front of them, with hundreds, or even thousands, led in single file before them.

The Message that Amos delivered surely would not have seemed strange to the ears of the hearers simply because all knew of the extreme cruelty of the Assyrians.

In fact, it is said that just before the gate was reached on the main thoroughfare leading into the capital city of Assyria, Nineveh, a mountain of human skulls by the side of the road greeted every visitor. In effect, this was telling all and sundry of the power of Nineveh, and if that power was opposed, death would be the result, typified by the mountain of skulls.

One would think that such a prediction, and given by the Power of the Holy Spirit, at that, would surely bring a city or a nation to Repentance; however, Amos' Message was, instead, met with ridicule and outright derision.

THE MODERN CHURCH

The Bible teaches us that *"in the last days perilous times shall come"* (II Tim. 3:1). As well, Jesus said, **"For then shall be great tribulation** (the last three and one half years of the Great Tribulation)**, such as was not since the beginning of the world to this time, no, nor ever shall be** (the worst the world has ever known, and will be so bad that it will never be repeated).

"And except those days should be shortened, there should no flesh be saved (refers to Israel coming close to extinction)**: but for the elect's** (Israel's) **sake those days shall be shortened** (by the Second Coming)**" (Mat. 24:21-22).**

The truth is, the modern church as a whole has little understanding of Biblical eschatology, which is the study of Endtime events according to the Word of God. The Bible, we believe, outlines the following and

in the order given:

• The Rapture of the Church, or could be referred to as the Resurrection (I Thess. 4:13-18; I Cor., Chpt. 15).

• The advent of the Antichrist: the Scripture plainly tells us that the Antichrist will not come on the scene until after the Rapture of the Church (II Thess. 2:6-12). Actually, the Bible tells us that the Antichrist will come out of one of the countries in the Middle East (Dan. 7:8; 8:9, 23-25; 11:35-45).

• The Great Tribulation lasting for seven years (Mat. 24:21; Dan. 9:27).

• The Battle of Armageddon: this Battle will take place at the conclusion of the Great Tribulation, with the Antichrist attempting to annihilate Israel (Rev. 14:14-20; Zech. 12:1-8; 14:1-3; Ezek., Chpts. 38-39).

• The Second Coming of the Lord (Rev. 19:11-14; Mat. 24:27-31; Ezek., Chpts. 38-39).

• The Kingdom Age when Jesus will reign Personally from Jerusalem, which will last 1,000 years, with the world seeing peace, freedom, and prosperity, as it has never known before (Isa. 2:2-4; 4:1-6; 11:1-16; 12:1-6; 14:1-8; 25:1-12; 26:1-9; 30:18-26; 32:1-8; 33:17-24; 35:10; Rev. 20:4-6).

• The Perfect Age, which will last forever: at this time, God will bring His Headquarters down from Heaven to Earth, where it will abide here forever. As stated, this will be a Kingdom with no end, in other words, it will last forever (Rev., Chpts. 21-22).

DOMINION TEACHING

There are some who teach that all of these Prophetic words just given will not come to pass, at least, not in the order given. They claim that Revelation and Daniel were fulfilled immediately before Christ and immediately after Christ. In fact, they claim that the world is getting better and better, with Christianity gaining the ascendancy, and soon they will be able to tell Christ when He can come back.

What presumption! What arrogance! The idea that some poor mortal is going to tell the Lord when He can come back is ludicrous, to say the least!

These individuals appoint men as Apostles, claiming they have dominion over the Earth, when, in reality, precious few, if any, are Saved under their Ministry; precious few, if any, are baptized with the Holy Spirit under their Ministry; in fact, there is much of nothing that happens under their Ministry.

THE MESSAGE OF THE CROSS

It is my personal belief that the Message of the Cross has got to be preached to the Church once again, for a church without the Cross is no church at all. Please understand this:

A thrice-Holy God can meet with sinful man only at one place, and that is the Cross of Christ. As well, the only thing standing between mankind and the Judgment of God is the Cross of Christ. The Cross alone holds back Judgment, and yet, presently, the modern church preaches the Cross almost none at all. As such, this nation is now open to the Judgment of God, which has already begun to take place. Witness the terrible turbulent weather, the oil spill in the Gulf, and the erroneous directions of this Muslim-leaning Administration in Washington.

The Lord has raised up this Ministry (Jimmy Swaggart Ministries) for the express purpose of taking the Message of the Cross to the modern church and, in fact, to the entirety of the world. The Message of the Cross is what the Spirit is saying to the churches (Rev. 3:22). I personally feel this is the last presentation that the Holy Spirit is going to make to the church and the world. Even though it will be rejected by most of the church, still, I personally believe that hundreds of thousands, if not millions, are going to come to Christ, with possibly the greatest Move of God the world has ever known. Truly, He is saving the best unto the last (Jn. 2:10).

(4) "COME TO BETH-EL, AND TRANSGRESS; AT GILGAL MULTIPLY TRANSGRESSION; AND BRING YOUR SACRIFICES EVERY MORNING, AND YOUR TITHES AFTER THREE YEARS:

(5) "AND OFFER A SACRIFICE OF THANKSGIVING WITH LEAVEN, AND PROCLAIM AND PUBLISH THE FREE OFFERINGS: FOR THIS LIKES YOU, O YOU CHILDREN OF ISRAEL, SAYS THE LORD GOD."

The overview is:

NOTES

1. (Vs. 5) The invitation of Verses 4 and 5 is meant to portray irony.

2. (Vs. 5) *"Go up to Beth-el – but not to worship Me – to transgress against Me!"*

3. (Vs. 5) Israel professed to be God's Worshippers, but they adored Him under the similitude of the golden calf—as multitudes do today under the similitude of man-made directions other than the Cross of Calvary.

4. (Vs. 5) God denounces as *"idolatry"* all worship that is not based on the Atoning Work of Calvary.

IDOLATRY

In these two Verses, there is an imitation of the Divine Worship commanded in Leviticus, yet corrupted—for *"leaven"* was forbidden. It was will-worship (*"for this likes you"*).

The phrase, *"And bring your sacrifices every morning,"* portrays that they were careful to maintain the outward semblance of the regular Levitical worship, and even beyond the letter of the Law in some respects, though their service was all the time idolatry.

The idea is, these people felt very secure in their present position. They were prosperous and, thereby, wealthy, albeit from the oppression of the poor, but they still called this the Blessings of God.

They felt smug in their religious position because of the tremendous amount of religious activity.

They were so deceived that they did not realize they were only increasing their apostasy and, thereby, angering God. They *"loved these things,"* and their whole heart was set on this will-worship, i.e., a religion of their own making.

The modern *"greed message"* is not totally unlike this ancient travesty.

These preachers, whoever they might be, claim great financial prosperity for those who will freely, or even sacrificially, give, when all the time, the only ones who will be prosperous are the preachers because the motivation is wrong.

In this erroneous message, the poor are *"oppressed"* exactly as in this account, with the only difference being that the money was forcibly taken in the former, while, in the latter, it is taken by false promises of great blessing from God.

It just might be possible that this modern form of extortion is even worse than that done by the oppressors of the poor in ancient Israel. The modern effort is done in the *"Name of the Lord,"* thereby, making Him a party to this nefarious activity.

As Israel of old, the modern *"faith message,"* which, in reality, at least for the most part, is no faith at all, has made up its own religion.

While it is certainly true that God blesses those who give to Him, and He blesses abundantly, still, to make that the motivation for giving totally contradicts the true reason for giving to God, which should be *". . . to prove the sincerity of your love"* (II Cor. 8:8).

People give to God for one of several reasons here listed. Only the last two are valid:

• Fear;
• Greed;
• Duty; and,
• LOVE.

For what reason do you give to God?

(6) "AND I ALSO HAVE GIVEN YOU CLEANNESS OF TEETH IN ALL YOUR CITIES, AND WANT OF BREAD IN ALL YOUR PLACES: YET HAVE YOU NOT RETURNED UNTO ME, SAYS THE LORD."

The structure is:

1. In Verse 6 and the following Verses, the Holy Spirit through the Prophet sets forth instances of Judgment, which He had sent at various times to correct Israel.

2. The phrase, *"Yet have you not returned unto Me, says the LORD,"* proclaims God's unwearied Love, which had not conquered their rebellion.

3. The Lord deals with wayward Believers in various and different ways, all, hopefully, to bring the person back to the rightful place. The worst thing is when the Holy Spirit no longer makes the effort. Such a person is then on very dangerous ground.

YET HAVE YOU NOT RETURNED UNTO ME

The phrase, *"Yet have you not returned unto Me,"* in the Hebrew, does not imply that they returned not at all, but that they did after a fashion return. However, it was

not so as to reach God, as their Repentance was a half-hearted Repentance and their worship a half-hearted worship and, therefore, unacceptable.

In other words, it seems that they did recognize that the Lord was the Author of these Judgments (famine, drought, blight, pestilence, and earthquakes), and they knew what they implied! But, still, they were so loath to leave their sins that they only went through the motions regarding a return to Him.

In 1989, I believe it was, the leader of a major Pentecostal denomination encouraged the pastors to *"preach on the Holy Spirit,"* because it was being called to the attention of the leadership that very few people were being baptized with the Holy Spirit in these respective churches.

While the recognition of the problem is commendable, still, the actual solution entails far more than here suggested.

Such was Israel of old! They threw God a crumb, so to speak, seemingly oblivious to the true need.

Regarding the Pentecostal denomination mentioned, and I might quickly add, Pentecostal in name only, an inquiry as to why the Holy Spirit was offended in the first place might be the better course of action. However, that would be an admittance that a wrong course had been taken (the psychological way), and that Repentance was required, which is anathema to self-righteousness. Therefore, the situation, at least, in that particular denomination, has gone from bad to worse.

CLEANNESS OF TEETH IN ALL YOUR CITIES

The phrase, *"Cleanness of teeth in all your cities,"* referred to famine. Here it is want of *"bread,"* and in the denomination mentioned, it is the want of *"spiritual bread,"* which characterizes, as well, almost all of Christendom. I don't mean to be negative, but there is less true Gospel presently being preached around the world than at any time since the Reformation. And please understand, it was to the Apostle Paul that the meaning of the New Covenant was given, which, in effect, is the meaning of the Cross. Paul preached the Cross! If we claim to preach the Gospel presently, we must preach the Cross as well. That means the following:

• We must understand that Jesus Christ is the Source of all things we receive from God.

• Jesus is the Source through His Cross. In other words, the Cross of Christ is the Means by which these things are given to us. And I speak of anything and everything that we receive from God.

• Understanding that the Cross of Christ is the Means by which we receive all these things, this means that the Cross of Christ must ever be the Object of our Faith, and that alone!

• This being done, the Holy Spirit, Who Works entirely within the framework of the Finished Work of Christ, i.e., *"the Atonement,"* will then work mightily on our behalf. However, if we place our faith in anything other than the Cross of Christ, understanding that it is by this Means and this Means alone that we receive from God, we are then committing spiritual adultery (Rom. 7:1-4).

SPIRITUAL ADULTERY

In the first four Verses of Romans, Chapter 7, Paul uses the analogy of a woman who is married to a man and then goes and marries another man, meaning she now has two husbands. No death is mentioned, etc. Paul bluntly says that she shall be called *"an adulteress,"* and rightly so.

This analogy is used, and it is quite an analogy, meaning that we are married to Christ. He is our Husband. As such, He is to meet our every need, and, in fact, He Alone can meet our every need. However, if we go out and place our faith in something other than Christ and the Cross, we are being unfaithful to Him, which means that we then are like the woman of Paul's analogy, living in a state of spiritual adultery. In other words, we are being unfaithful to our Husband, Christ (II Cor. 11:1-4).

The truth is, and I do not say this with any joy, as should be obvious, almost the entirety of the modern church, and we speak of those who are truly Born-Again, is living in a state of *"spiritual adultery."* It is not that they have willfully rejected the

Ways of the Lord but mostly because they simply do not know the Ways of the Lord. In other words, while many understand the Cross of Christ as it relates to Salvation, they have no understanding at all as it relates to Sanctification. As a result, every type of scheme that one can imagine is proposed to the modern church regarding how to live for God. Every modern scheme, I might quickly add, other than the Cross of Christ.

Without a proper understanding of the Cross of Christ, there is no Victorious Living. While one can be Saved and not understand the Message of the Cross, one most definitely cannot live a Victorious Life without this understanding. That's why Paul kept saying, *"Know you not"* (Rom. 6:3), *"knowing this"* (6:6), *"knowing"* (6:9), *"know you not"* (6:16), and *"know you not, brethren"* (Rom. 7:1). Actually, Paul mentions *"know"* or *"knowing"* some nine times in Romans, Chapters 6, 7, and 8. But, regrettably, most modern Believers simply don't know because the Cross of Christ, as it regards Sanctification, is seldom preached behind modern pulpits, if any at all. *"Faith comes by hearing and hearing by the Word of God,"* and if it's not preached, the people cannot hear. That is tragic when we realize that virtually ninety-nine percent plus of the entirety of the Bible is given over to telling us how to live for God. Preachers by the thousands are telling people how to be Saved, which is by trusting Christ, which is exactly what they should do. Thank God a thousand times over for that. However, then they are telling Believers all the wrong things, at least, for the most part, as to how we live this life. And yet, and, as stated, this subject makes up almost the entirety of the Word of God.

(7) "AND ALSO I HAVE WITHHELD THE RAIN FROM YOU, WHEN THERE WERE YET THREE MONTHS TO THE HARVEST: AND I CAUSED IT TO RAIN UPON ONE CITY, AND CAUSED IT NOT TO RAIN UPON ANOTHER CITY: ONE PIECE WAS RAINED UPON, AND THE PIECE WHEREUPON IT RAINED NOT WITHERED."

The structure is:

1. All of this proclaims the Lord having

total control, as should be obvious!

2. The Lord is able to make it rain or to withhold the rain.

3. For Someone Who has that kind of Power, don't you think it makes good sense to serve Him, especially considering that He wants to do us good?

MINUTE DETAIL

So as the people could not attribute this drought mentioned in Verse 7 to the blind laws of nature, the Lord caused it to be a partial drought, giving rain to one city while He withheld it from another.

He even went so far as to cause the rain to fall on a particular piece of ground, with that adjoining it having no rain whatsoever!

Such proclaims a total control down even to the most minute detail, but, still, the people would not favorably respond.

The implication is that if He could do this, He, as well, could bless abundantly, if the people would only serve Him.

The heart that truly loves God relishes in this type of involvement by the Heavenly Father; however, the heart that has no desire to serve Him cringes at the very idea of such minute detail.

BELIEVERS

As it regards Believers, the Lord is involved and, in fact, has to be involved, in every single detail of our lives. This we must believe, and this we must understand. He wants us to seek His Face regarding every single thing that we do, not just the large things, whatever they might be, but even that which we consider to be insignificant. The Lord, as we certainly should know, knows everything, past, present, and future. And, as well, He desires to do beautiful and wonderful things for us. That's why He said, "... *I am come that they might have life, and that they might have it more abundantly*" (Jn. 10:10). All of this is referred to as *"Grace."* It simply means the Goodness of God. So, how do I as a Believer ensure that all of these good things that the Lord wants to do for me are, in fact, brought to pass?

This is for Believers who are mature in the Lord. This means that you have come to the place in your Christian experience that

you want nothing but that which the Lord wants you to have. In other words, we want His Perfect Will in all things regarding our life and living. We know that He knows best, and in every capacity. So, how do we bring about all of these Blessings?

THE CROSS OF CHRIST

We must ever understand the following. It is that which I have already given several times in this Volume and will do so several more times. The repetition is because it is so very, very important. In fact, if we do not understand that which I am about to give again, we will then forfeit so much of what the Lord wants to do for us.

• Jesus Christ is the Source of all things we receive from God. He is the One Who has paid the price. He is the One Who has made everything possible. He is the One Who has satisfied the demands of a thrice-Holy God (Jn. 1:1-2, 14, 29; 3:16; Col. 1:10-15).

• The Cross of Christ is the Means by which He gives us all things. This means that the Fruit of the Spirit is made possible only through the Cross. This means that Salvation and the Baptism with the Holy Spirit, all and without exception, are made possible by the Cross. This means that all Healing comes by Means of the Cross. This means that every Blessing and all prosperity are made possible by the Cross. In other words, for every single thing we receive from Christ, it is the Cross of Christ which has made it possible (Rom. 6:3-5; I Cor. 1:17-18, 21, 23; 2:2; Gal., Chpt. 5; 6:14; Col. 2:14-15).

• With the Cross of Christ being the Means by which all things are given to us, this means that the Cross must ever be the Object of our Faith. Of course, I'm sure you understand, we aren't speaking of a wooden beam, but rather what Jesus there did. The Cross of Christ is something, which took place nearly 2,000 years ago, but has continuing benefits and, in fact, benefits, which will never be discontinued. That's the reason that Paul referred to it as the *"Everlasting Covenant"* (Heb. 13:20). It is absolutely imperative that our Faith be anchored in the Cross and the Cross alone (Gen. 3:21; 4:4; 8:20; 13:4; Ex. 12:13; Jn. 6:53-56; Rom. 6:3-5; I Cor. 1:17-18, 23; 2:2; Col. 2:14-15).

• It is the Holy Spirit, Who Works exclusively within the parameters of the Finished Work of Christ, Who oversees this great Plan of God. In other words, if we try to come to the Lord by any means other than the Finished Work of Christ, i.e., *"the Cross,"* the Holy Spirit will bar the entrance. It is the Holy Spirit Who carries out all of this for which Jesus has paid such a price (Rom. 8:1-2, 10; Eph. 2:13-18).

This given above is God's Divine Order of Life and Living. It's very simple, so simple, in fact, that a child can understand it. However, the truth is, most all of us have learned so many wrong things that before the Truth can finally begin to penetrate our hearts and lives, the Holy Spirit must rid us of all the false doctrine and the false direction. Unfortunately, that takes time!

God's Prescribed Order of Life and Living, of all Victory, and we speak of Victory in every capacity of life, and especially over sin, is found exclusively in Christ Jesus and what He did for us at the Cross, which demands that the Cross of Christ ever be the Object of our Faith.

(8) "SO TWO OR THREE CITIES WANDERED UNTO ONE CITY, TO DRINK WATER; BUT THEY WERE NOT SATISFIED: YET HAVE YOU NOT RETURNED UNTO ME, SAYS THE LORD."

The overview is:

1. The phrase used again, *"Yet have you not returned unto Me, says the LORD,"* has reference to the fact that while they were staggering from one city to another in order to find water, still, their hearts were so hard that their acute circumstances were not enough to bring them to Repentance.

2. It is amazing at the insistence of men to reject the Ways of the Lord.

3. Everything the Lord did to these people was in order to bring them to Himself, where He could bless them but, regrettably, to no avail.

THE WAYS OF THE LORD

The idea of this Verse is that the drought in certain areas was so severe, the people in these areas were forced to go to the cities which had water, even with great discomfort.

The phrase, *"But they were not satisfied,"*

means that their efforts brought no permanent relief.

The exhaustive efforts of the Lord in dealing with these people, attempting to bring them to a place of Repentance, are remarkable, to say the least! And yet, at this very moment, He is dealing with many souls in the same remarkable manner, trying to bring them to where they ought to be before God. With some few, He has success, but with most, they are as Israel of old, determined to go their own way and, thereby, to be destroyed.

WHY WILL SOME ACCEPT THE LORD, BUT MOST WON'T?

The Lord Alone knows the answer to the question of our heading.

Why will Jacob say *"yes"* to the Lord, and his twin brother, Esau, say *"no"*? Why will Isaac love the Lord, and Ishmael, raised in the same family, have no desire for the Lord at all? Why would Abel obey the Lord regarding the sacrifices, and his brother Cain rebel against the Word of the Lord?

Some claim that all are born predestined to either Heaven or Hell, and there's nothing they can do about it. That isn't true at all!

In fact, the questions I have posed proclaim to us the free moral agency of the human heart. In other words, every person is born with the ability to say *"yes"* or *"no"* to the Lord. There is no record in the Word of God that the Lord tampers with anyone's free moral agency. He will deal with people, speak to people, and move upon people, but He will not force the issue. One way or the other, the human being has to make that decision himself.

(9) "I HAVE SMITTEN YOU WITH BLASTING AND MILDEW: WHEN YOUR GARDENS AND YOUR VINEYARDS AND YOUR FIG TREES AND YOUR OLIVE TREES INCREASED, THE PALMERWORM DEVOURED THEM: YET HAVE YOU NOT RETURNED UNTO ME, SAYS THE LORD."

The pattern is:

1. The Lord dealt with Israel with famine, drought, and now blight, but to no avail!

2. All of this tells us that the Lord has complete control over everything. He can bring the rain or withhold the rain. The

same holds true for everything else of which we might think.

3. All of this is done out of Love to try to bring Israel to her spiritual senses and to try to bring Israel to Himself, but, as stated, all to no avail.

THE POWER OF THE LORD

So, as is obvious here, the Lord Commands even the *"palmerworm,"* with a small insect obeying Him, to carry out His Design.

Therefore, if He has such minute control on the negative side, He, as well, has the same type of control on the positive side.

This portrays the fact that God is minutely involved in every aspect of the life of the Believer, down to even the most minute detail. As stated, the consecrated heart eagerly seeks and desires this, while the carnal heart is repelled. Inasmuch as God is Omniscient (all-knowing), Omnipotent (all-powerful), and Omnipresent (everywhere), this presents for Him no difficulty!

(10) "I HAVE SENT AMONG YOU THE PESTILENCE AFTER THE MANNER OF EGYPT: YOUR YOUNG MEN HAVE I SLAIN WITH THE SWORD, AND HAVE TAKEN AWAY YOUR HORSES; AND I HAVE MADE THE STINK OF YOUR CAMPS TO COME UP UNTO YOUR NOSTRILS: YET HAVE YOU NOT RETURNED UNTO ME, SAYS THE LORD."

The overview is:

1. *"I have sent among you the pestilence after the manner of Egypt,"* has no reference to the plague of Exodus 9:3, etc., but was an allusion to the plague which was reckoned to be epidemic in Egypt and other loathsome diseases for which that country was notorious.

2. No Judgments seemed to be enough to bring Israel back to the Lord!

3. To be sure, the Lord holds the same type of control over His People presently as He did then.

I HAVE SENT AMONG YOU

The Lord had promised Israel when they were brought out of Egypt that He would *". . . put none of these diseases upon you, which I have brought upon the Egyptians."* He then said, *"For I Am the LORD Who*

NOTES

heals you" (Ex. 15:26).

However, this Blessing promised was dependent upon their following the Lord and not sinful ways, as here proclaimed.

Therefore, the Child of God, whether under the Old Covenant, or presently under the New, is protected from many things that come upon the world, providing obedience to the Lord is rendered.

The phrase, *"Your young men have I slain with the sword,"* probably refers to the wars with Assyrians, wherein the Israelites suffered heavy losses (II Ki. 6:25; 8:12; 13:3, 7, 22).

YET HAVE YOU NOT RETURNED UNTO ME, SAYS THE LORD

Over and over again, the phrase of our heading is used by the Lord, proving that He went to all lengths to get Israel to repent, but all to no avail.

Does the Lord deal with modern Believers in the same way?

Yes, He does!

The Lord loves us. He loves us enough to go to all kinds of trouble to bring us to our spiritual senses if, in fact, there is a problem. So, the question may well be asked, *"Doesn't the Lord know what our reaction will be beforehand?"* And if He knows that Israel, or even modern Believers, will not do right, despite His Actions, why does He even bother?

Yes, the Lord knows exactly what we will do before it is ever done. But yet, He deals with us anyway.

He does so, so that we will have no excuse. One day every unsaved person who has ever lived will stand before Christ at the Great White Throne Judgment. It will be shown them in proverbial black and white exactly who they are and what they did. In other words, they will have no argument.

When it comes to Believers, we will stand at the Judgment Seat of Christ. To be sure, no sins will be mentioned there simply because all of that was taken care of at Calvary. However, we will definitely answer for our motives and our faithfulness, or the lack thereof, and rewards will then be handed out accordingly!

It's very difficult for human beings to try to understand God in every capacity. We cannot contemplate Someone Who knows everything past, present, and future, and, as well, is Almighty, meaning that He can do anything. We can go so far in relationship to understanding that but no further. But one thing we do know, the *"Judge of all the Earth will do right"* (Gen. 18:25).

(11) "I HAVE OVERTHROWN SOME OF YOU, AS GOD OVERTHREW SODOM AND GOMORRAH AND YOU WERE AS A FIREBRAND PLUCKED OUT OF THE BURNING: YET HAVE YOU NOT RE-TURNED UNTO ME, SAYS THE LORD."

The construction is:

1. *"And you were as a firebrand plucked out of the burning,"* refers to the fact that it was only the Mercy of God which stopped the destruction short of total.

2. But impenitence was the unchanging response to each stroke—*"yet have you not returned unto Me."*

3. All of these Passages tell us that while men may rule, God often overrules!

THE MERCY OF GOD

The phrase, *"I have overthrown some of you, as God overthrew Sodom and Gomorrah,"* probably refers to an earthquake that came on some of their areas because this is the word used to describe the destruction of Sodom and Gomorrah in Genesis 19:25. However, there is no information given respecting this particular earthquake to which the Prophet alludes, providing there actually was one.

The phrase, *"As God overthrew,"* proclaims the substitution of the Name of God for the personal pronoun when the Lord Himself is speaking and is not uncommon at all in the Hebrew language.

The phrase, *"And you were as a firebrand plucked out of the burning,"* refers to the fact that it was only the Mercy of God which stopped the destruction short of total, but a refusal to repent was their response to each stroke—*"yet have you not returned unto Me."*

In reading the Text, beginning with Verse 6 through Verse 11, one is struck with God's personal Involvement. *"I have also given"* (Vs. 6), *"also I have withheld"* and *"I caused"* (Vs. 7), *"I have smitten"* (Vs. 9), *"I*

have sent" and *"I have made"* (Vs. 10), and *"I have overthrown"* (Vs. 11), denoting every effort being made that could be made!

As the Lord was involved then, He, as well, is involved now in the same capacity, attempting to bring recalcitrant Believers back to His Side.

(12) "THEREFORE THUS WILL I DO UNTO YOU, O ISRAEL: AND BECAUSE I WILL DO THIS UNTO YOU, PREPARE TO MEET YOUR GOD, O ISRAEL."

The overview is:

1. As a consequence, Israel is now warned of a Supreme Judgment—that is, to meet God Himself.

2. *"Prepare to meet your God, O Israel,"* means to make ready to meet God in Judgment, turning to Him with changed heart, praying that He will forgive and withdraw His heavy Hand.

3. Is the Lord presently saying to America, *"Prepare to meet your God, O America?"*

PREPARE TO MEET YOUR GOD

As stern as this Text is, within the Command is an extension of Mercy.

In effect, the Lord is saying, *"Inasmuch as all previous Judgments have been in vain, therefore, will I send upon them something more terrible still."* However, He does not really say what this Judgment actually is.

And then He says, *"And because I will do this unto you,"* which actually refers to the bringing on of heavier punishment, He tells them to *"prepare to call upon your God,"* which is actually the meaning of *"Prepare to meet your God."*

PRESENT CIRCUMSTANCES

Is the Lord saying the same thing to America today?

I believe He most definitely could be. In the last several years, the nation has experienced worse weather than it has known in its history. And now we have the terrible debacle in the gulf, with thousands of barrels of oil spewing out every day into the water, which, if not stopped quickly, could totally destroy the fishing industry in this part of the world.

We have an Administration in office, which doesn't know God at all. And, in fact, if the truth be known, is totally antagonistic to the Lord and His Ways. And, of course, tragically so, they do not stand alone. Great parts of the intelligentsia of this nation literally hate the Lord Jesus Christ and, especially the Bible. Little by little, the freedoms that Christians have enjoyed and now enjoy are being eroded. More and more, evil is becoming predominant. There are three major sins which have characterized empires of the past, which became dominant immediately before their fall. Those sins are:

1. Homosexuality;
2. Incest; and,
3. Pedophilia.

These things are rampant in America presently.

IS THERE ANY HOPE?

Yes, there is hope!

In 1997, the Lord gave me a Revelation of the Cross, which was actually that which the Lord had given to the Apostle Paul. In other words, it was not something new. As a result of Family Worship Center and all of our media dedicated to the teaching and preaching of this Message, thank the Lord, many more are accepting it. As stated, it's not something new, but it's actually the Gospel (I Cor. 1:17).

The only thing standing between mankind and the Judgment of a thrice-Holy God is the Cross of Christ. And, once again, that's not new, having always been the case. So, what am I saying?

I am saying that the number of people who adhere to the Message of the Cross, as small as that number might be, at least, as it regards the whole, just might be the only thing that can stop the Judgment of God on this nation.

The Cross of Christ is the only place that a thrice-Holy God and sinful man can meet. There *"Mercy and Truth are met together; Righteousness and Peace have kissed each other"* (Ps. 85:10).

Under the Law, *"Mercy"* and *"Truth"* could not meet. *"Righteousness"* and *"Peace"* could not kiss or greet each other; however, in Christ, the two have met.

Jesus satisfied the Law and did so in every

capacity. He did so at the Cross. Christ is the Source, and the Cross is the Means.

(13) "FOR, LO, HE WHO FORMS THE MOUNTAINS, AND CREATES THE WIND, AND DECLARES UNTO MAN WHAT IS HIS THOUGHT, WHO MAKES THE MORNING DARKNESS, AND TREADS UPON THE HIGH PLACES OF THE EARTH, THE LORD, THE GOD OF HOSTS, IS HIS NAME."

The overview is:

1. The Majesty of God is set forth in this Scripture.

2. The mountains may be seen; the wind, unseen; man's thought, unread; day and night, unchangeable; and the revolution of the Earth in its orbit, invariable. But all was in the Power of this dread Judge—*"Jehovah Elohim Sabaioth"* is His Name!

3. The greatest privilege on the face of the Earth is for one to have the opportunity to know the Lord and to serve Him.

THE LORD, THE GOD OF HOSTS, IS HIS NAME

The Holy Spirit here appeals to Israel on the same level of their sin, which is pride, and which expressed itself in their progressive thought, as stated! Consequently, in His Statement, He says several things:

• He proclaims His Greatness to them and, at the same time, their lack of greatness.

• If He has the Power to do all these things, and He definitely does, then He has the Power to do with them as He desires.

• Should they not want to serve One Who is so great and powerful and, as well, so greatly beyond these foolish idols they are worshipping?

• Do they not realize how privileged they are to serve God and, especially, to have Him deal with them in a fashion that denotes His tremendous Concern for their welfare?

• In view of Who He is and who they are, why would they not desire to fall at His Feet and ask for His Mercy and Grace, which would be freely given?

IS IT WHO HE IS OR WHAT HE DID?

It is both!

Jesus Christ is God. Even though He was manifest in the flesh, still, He never ceased to be God, not even for one moment. As someone has said, *"While He laid aside the expression of His Deity in the Incarnation, not for a moment did He lay aside the possession of His Deity."*

So, what God demanded to be done, as it regards the Redemption of humanity, only the Lord Jesus Christ could have done such a thing. To carry out Redemption, one had to be perfect. That means perfect in word, thought, and deed. To be sure, God is Perfect. However, whenever God became Man, He, in a sense, reduced Heaven, all the attributes of the Throne of God, to Jesus Christ as a Man, *"The Man, Christ Jesus."* In other words, everything was riding on Him, not only the Salvation of mankind but the very existence of the Throne of God itself.

However, I remind all and sundry that Who He was, the Son of the Living God, within itself, could not save anyone had it stopped there. As God, our Lord has always existed, but as God, that fact alone could not save anyone. For mankind to be redeemed, then God would not only have to become Man but would have to go to the Cross.

So, in the final alternative, it was not only Who He was but what He did, i.e., *"the Cross,"* which redeemed fallen humanity. Let's say it another way:

• While the Virgin Birth of Christ was absolutely necessary, had it stopped there, not a single soul would have ever been Saved.

• While His Perfect Life and Living was absolutely necessary, never sinning even one time in word, thought, or deed, still, had it stopped there, not one single soul would have ever been Saved.

• While His Healings and Miracles were absolutely necessary, still, had it stopped there, not a single soul would have been Saved.

For man to be Saved, God would have to become Man and, thereby, go to the Cross, where there the price was paid, and paid in full! That's why the Scripture can say and, in fact, does say:

"And the Spirit and the Bride say, Come. *(This presents the cry of the Holy Spirit to a hurting, lost, and dying world. What the Holy Spirit says should also be said by all Believers.)* **And let him who hears say, Come.**

(It means if one can 'hear,' then one can 'come.') **And let him who is athirst come** *(speaks of spiritual thirst, the cry for God in the soul of man).* **And whosoever will, let him take the Water of Life freely** *(opens the door to every single individual in the world; Jesus died for all, and, therefore, all can be Saved, if they will only come)"* **(Rev. 22:17).**

"Breathe on me, Breath of God,
"Fill me with life anew,
"That I may love what You do love,
"And do what You would do."

"Breathe on me, Breath of God,
"Until my heart is pure;
"Until my will is one with Thine,
"To do and to endure."

"Breathe on me, Breath of God,
"Till I am wholly Thine;
"Until this earthly part of me,
"Glows with Your Fire Divine."

"Breathe on me, Breath of God,
"So shall I never die,
"But live with You the Perfect Life,
"Of Your Eternity."

CHAPTER 5

(1) **"HEAR YOU THIS WORD WHICH I TAKE UP AGAINST YOU, EVEN A LAMENTATION, O HOUSE OF ISRAEL."**

The exegesis is:

1. *"Hear you this word which I take up against you,"* refers to the certitude of the coming Judgment because Israel would not repent, because they saw no need to repent.

2. The phrase, *"Even a lamentation, O House of Israel,"* is the same as a funeral dirge.

3. Unfortunately, the people of Israel paid little attention to the Prophet Amos. He was completely ignored, and yet, he ultimately predicts that Israel will be restored; however, it will be after the Second Coming.

A LAMENTATION

The word, *"against,"* should have been translated *"over."* Therefore, this lamentation the Prophet took up as a heavy burden *"over,"* and not *"against,"* the House of Israel.

The true Preacher's heart is burdened with the sinner's doom; and he pleads with him and not against him. Elijah erred in pleading against Israel (Rom. 11:2), and was superseded by Elisha.

The phrase, *"Even a lamentation, O House of Israel,"* proclaims the closeness of the coming doom, but, again, Israel would not hear.

SIN

As far as is known, sin originated with Lucifer, and that was when he led his revolution against God some time in eternity past. All sin is a disobedience of God's Word or a rebellion against God's Word. That's the reason the Bible is so important; it is the Word of God. This means that it doesn't merely contain the Word of God but, in fact, is the Word of God.

There is only one solution for sin and one answer for sin, and that is the Cross of Christ. Concerning this very thing, Paul said:

"So Christ was once offered to bear the sins of many *(the Cross was God's Answer to sin and, in fact, the only answer)*; **and unto them who look for Him shall He appear the second time without sin unto Salvation.** *(This refers to the Second Coming. 'Without sin' refers to the fact that the Second Coming will not be to atone for sin, for that was already carried out at the Cross at His First Advent. The Second Coming will bring all the results of Salvation to this world, which refers to all that He did at the Cross. We now only have the 'Firstfruits' [Rom. 8:23])"* **(Heb. 9:28).**

Paul also said:

"But this Man *(this Priest, Christ Jesus),* **after He had offered one Sacrifice for sins forever** *(speaks of the Cross),* **sat down on the Right Hand of God** *(refers to the great contrast with the Priests under the Levitical system, who never sat down because their work was never completed; the Work of Christ was a 'Finished Work,' and needed no repetition)"* **(Heb. 10:12).**

And then, **"And their sins and iniquities will I remember no more.** *(He has taken them all away, and did so by the Cross.)*

"Now where remission of these *is (with all sins atoned, the argument is settled),* **there is no more offering for sin.** *(No more offering is necessary, for Christ paid it all)"* **(Heb. 10:17-18).**

And finally, **"For if we sin wilfully** *(the 'willful sin' is the transference of Faith from Christ and Him Crucified to other things)* **after that we have received the knowledge of the Truth** *(speaks of the Bible way of Salvation and Victory, which is 'Jesus Christ and Him Crucified' [I Cor. 2:2]),* **there remains no more sacrifice for sins** *(if the Cross of Christ is rejected, there is no other sacrifice or way God will accept)"* **(Heb. 10:26).**

Unfortunately, the modern church has all but rejected the Cross of Christ. That being the case, and it most definitely is, sins committed remain because there is no remission of sins other than by and through the Cross of Christ.

(2) "THE VIRGIN OF ISRAEL IS FALLEN; SHE SHALL NO MORE RISE: SHE IS FORSAKEN UPON HER LAND; THERE IS NONE TO RAISE HER UP."

The overview is:

1. The northern kingdom is here compared to a virgin because never hitherto conquered.

2. *"She shall no more rise,"* means that she will never again be restored as a separate nationality.

3. Later, the southern kingdom, Judah, would fall as well; however, Judah was restored, at least, after a fashion. The Twelve Tribes were represented in Judah. They will be restored to full bloom in the coming Kingdom Age, which is after they recognize Christ and accept Him as Saviour and Lord.

THE VIRGIN OF ISRAEL

Had both the northern kingdom of Israel and the southern kingdom of Judah lived in obedience to the Lord, no other nation or combination of nations in the world could have ever defeated them. The Power of God, which was and is unlimited, would have always been on their side, and nothing can overcome that!

However, Israel and Judah didn't do that. Instead of being a testimony and a witness for the Righteousness of God to the surrounding nations, they instead became more and more like the heathen nations until there was no remedy. Despite the fact that the Lord knew that all His Overtures to them would be repelled, still, He sent the Prophets and dealt with them in every way possible, all in order to try to get them to turn. But it was all to no avail! Only love could do such a thing, knowing that it was all futile.

SHE SHALL NO MORE RISE

Under David and his son, Solomon, Israel became one of, if not the mightiest Nation on the face of the Earth of that day. David was a Type of the conquering Christ, meaning that God helped him to subdue all enemies, while Solomon was a Type of the Millennial Christ. Regrettably, Solomon lost his way in the last years of his reign. When he died, his son Rehoboam became king (I Ki. 12). Rehoboam played the fool and turned Israel against him, which occasioned Ten Tribes breaking off and forming their own Nation, referred to as Israel, Samaria, or Ephraim. Two Tribes were left, which formed Judah, the two being Benjamin and Judah. However, the Temple was in Jerusalem, which meant the Brazen Altar, a Type of the Cross, was there as well. Jeroboam, the first king of Israel, led the Nation into deep idolatry (I Ki. 12:25-33). In truth, the northern kingdom of Israel didn't have one godly king. They were all antagonistic to the Lord, some worse than others, but all ungodly. The Nation lasted approximately 250 years before it was finally destroyed by Assyria. Judah lasted about 130 odd years longer before being destroyed by the Babylonian Empire (II Chron. 36:13-21).

(3) "FOR THUS SAYS THE LORD GOD; THE CITY THAT WENT OUT BY A THOUSAND SHALL LEAVE AN HUNDRED, AND THAT WHICH WENT FORTH BY AN HUNDRED SHALL LEAVE TEN, TO THE HOUSE OF ISRAEL."

The overview is:

1. So great would be the destruction of the army of Israel in the battles with the Assyrians that battalions a thousand strong, or companies a hundred strong, would come out of these conflicts with only about

NOTES

ten percent as survivors.

2. Now the reader must remember that all of this was prophesied some 60 odd years before it came to pass. The evidence is, however, Israel believed little or not any at all of what the Prophet Amos said.

3. I'm afraid the modern church falls into the same category. It little believes in the coming Rapture of the Church. It little believes that the man of sin will be revealed, which will usher in the worst tribulation the world has ever known. Nevertheless, it most definitely is going to happen (Mat. 24:21).

THE COMING DESTRUCTION

To say the least, the prediction given here in this Verse is dire indeed! To have ninety percent of the men killed in battle would completely denude entire villages and cities. The suffering incurred is unimaginable, and yet, this is exactly what happened!

One wants to ask, "How?" and "Why?" especially considering the tremendous warnings given by the Holy Spirit through the Prophet.

MANY VOICES

Every preacher in the world claims to be right! Every church claims to be right! And yet, what is being preached and taught oftentimes is diametrically opposite of the Word of God. So, we know that all cannot be correct, especially when the messages are so diverse. So, what is right?

This is the reason that Jesus constantly stated, "He who has ears to hear, let him hear" (Mat. 11:15; 13:9; 13:43; Mk. 4:23; Lk. 8:8). To be frank, this problem has always been, and will be, unto the return of our Lord.

Paul tells us what the Gospel actually is. He said:

"For Christ sent me not to baptize, but to preach the Gospel: not with wisdom of words, lest the Cross of Christ should be made of none effect" (I Cor. 1:17).

Plain, pure, and simple, Paul here tells us that the Message of the Cross is actually the "Gospel."

He then said, "But we preach Christ Crucified, unto the Jews a stumblingblock, and unto the Greeks foolishness" (I Cor. 1:23).

He also stated:

"For I determined not to know anything among you, save Jesus Christ, and Him Crucified" (I Cor. 2:2).

The great Apostle tells us in these Passages, and many more that we could name, that the Gospel is, *"Jesus Christ and Him Crucified."* In essence, he says, *"Of a truth, that is a stumblingblock to the Jews, and foolishness to the Gentiles"*; nevertheless, he preached the Cross because it is the only solution.

Man has one problem and that is sin, and there is one solution, and that is the Cross of Christ. Let us say it again:

A thrice-Holy God can only meet with sinful man at the Cross of Christ.

That is the voice that you as a Believer must hear. Anything else, while it may be educated, glib, smartly produced and delivered, still, if it's not the Cross of Christ, whatever it is, it's not the Gospel of Jesus Christ.

(4) "FOR THUS SAYS THE LORD UNTO THE HOUSE OF ISRAEL, SEEK YOU ME AND YOU SHALL LIVE."

The exegesis is:

1. This is a pure and plain offer to repent, which would avoid the Judgment, but sadly, all to no avail!

2. *"Seek you Me, and you shall live,"* means for the individual to seek the Lord in the appointed way and, consequently, be Saved from destruction.

3. *"He who has the Son has life . . ."* (I Jn. 5:12); for, apart from Christ, there can only be death.

SEEK ME AND LIVE

In effect, as the Call was given to Israel so long ago, it is given to any and all presently! As Israel rejected the royal impartation, as well, the present far greater majority follows suit.

Israel, no doubt, reasoned that if these dire predictions really were from the Lord, why would He have sent someone such as Amos to deliver the message? It was obvious to the religious and secular leaders of Israel that Amos was not of the landed gentry or of the aristocracy; therefore, such an important message surely would not have been sent by such a one, or so they reasoned.

Fault found with the messenger has always been the conduct of Christ-rejecters. He is not up to their expectations either intellectually, physically, or even spiritually in some cases. Therefore, they reject his message.

Accordingly, they rejected Christ! He was not recognized by the Pharisees or the religious leaders of Israel, and, as was obvious, He was not of the aristocracy. So, at least in their reasoning, how could He be the Messiah?!

To reject God's Messenger is to reject God's Message!

A PERSONAL EXPERIENCE

In 1997, the Lord gave to me the Revelation of the Cross. It was not something new but, actually, that which had already been given to the Apostle Paul and possibly others, as well, down through the centuries. But knowing of the animosity that most of the church world holds against my person, I reasoned that if the Lord had given this great Truth to someone else, quite possibly, the church would more readily accept it.

It was some time during the wee hours of the morning. I awakened, and to be frank, none of this was on my mind. I got up out of bed to get something, and all of a sudden, I sensed the Presence of God. The Lord then spoke to my heart saying, *"You have thought that had I given this Word to someone else, it would have been more readily accepted; however,"* the Lord continued, *"it would not have made any difference as to whom I would have given this Message. It would have been met in the same manner as with you."*

While, of course, the messenger is always held up to ridicule, still, the real rejection goes far deeper. It is a rejection of God and His Word. I think it can be summed up in the following:

THE FINISHED WORK

What Jesus did at Calvary is a Finished Work. It left nothing hanging. The price was paid in totality. This means, if we try to add anything to what He did, we sin and sin greatly. But this is the major problem.

Man, and especially religious man, takes

no delight in freely admitting what he actually is, and that his only means of Righteousness is to place his Faith exclusively in Christ and what Christ did at the Cross. That brings man no glory at all. It does not minister at all to his ego; consequently, the Cross of Christ is actually an offense to him (Gal. 5:11). Nevertheless, this is God's Way, and I speak of total Faith in Christ and what Christ did at the Cross, and He will not change His Way. It's either His Way or it is wreckage.

(5) "BUT SEEK NOT BETH-EL, NOR ENTER INTO GILGAL, AND PASS NOT TO BEER-SHEBA: FOR GILGAL SHALL SURELY GO INTO CAPTIVITY, AND BETH-EL SHALL COME TO NOUGHT."

The overview is:

1. Beth-el was the great center of the worship of God under the similitude of a calf.

2. But that idol could not quench the fire that broke out in the house of Joseph.

3. Gilgal, Beer-sheba, and Beth-el are in Judah. The idea is: those from the northern kingdom who tried to escape to the southern kingdom, that is, when Judgment came, would not succeed. Whatever their plans were, they "shall surely go into captivity."

THE WAYS OF MAN
WOULD NOT WORK

As both "Gilgal" and "Beer-sheba" were in the land of Judah, it is not clear as to what role they played in this scenario, if any. However, all three, "Beth-el, Gilgal, and Beer-sheba," had once been places where God had wondrously moved.

"Beth-el" was connected with Jacob because it was here that he had the Vision of the ladder with the Lord above it (Gen. 28:12-13).

"Gilgal" was where Israel made her first headquarters after crossing the Jordan into the Promised Land, and where the Ark of the Covenant was, no doubt, kept for a period of time (Josh. 5:10).

"Beer-sheba" was where Isaac was born to Abraham and Sarah (Gen. 21:2-3, 31). However, it seems that this area, as well as "Gilgal," had now become a shrine of idolatrous worship, to which the Israelites resorted, though it lay far out of their territory (Amos 8:14).

NOTES

The phrase, "For Gilgal shall surely go into captivity," ultimately came to pass with the fall of Judah nearly 200 years later.

As well, the phrase, "Beth-el shall come to naught," really means that "Beth-el," the "House of God," had become "Beth-aven," the "House of Vanity" (Hos. 4:15), or, in other words, the temple of an idol.

(6) "SEEK THE LORD, AND YOU SHALL LIVE; LEST HE BREAK OUT LIKE FIRE IN THE HOUSE OF JOSEPH, AND DEVOUR IT, AND THERE BE NONE TO QUENCH IT IN BETH-EL."

The construction is:

1. The idea is: "Turn to the Lord, or suffer the fire of Judgment!"

2. As clearly as it was given, still, Israel would not turn.

3. All they had to do was "seek the LORD," which is all anyone has to do, and if done with a sincere heart, the Lord will definitely hear and answer.

THE ADMONITION

I personally feel that America is in the same situation presently as was Israel of old as it regards the prophesying of Amos. And yet, I'm afraid there are few Prophets today in America such as Amos was in Israel of old. If Repentance is to be forthcoming, it has to begin with the Church. Peter said:

"For the time is come that Judgment must begin at the House of God (Judgment always begins with Believers, and pertains to their Faith, whether in the Cross or otherwise; the Cross alone is spared Judgment, for there Jesus was judged in our place): and if it first begin at us, what shall the end be of them who obey not the Gospel of God? (If God will judge His Own, how much more will He judge the unredeemed? The Cross alone stays the Judgment of God. Let that ever be understood.)

"And if the Righteous scarcely be saved (can be Saved only by trusting Christ and the Cross and nothing else), where shall the ungodly and the sinner appear? (If the great Sacrifice of Christ is rejected and spurned, where does that leave those who do such a thing? There is no hope for their Salvation)" (I Pet. 4:17-18).

THE CHURCH AND THE NATION

We are plainly told here that Judgment must begin in the House of God. This is speaking of Believers, for we are the *"House."* For the church to repent, it has to come back to the Cross. The only Sacrifice for sin was offered at the Cross. So, if there be any type of Repentance, any type of acknowledgement of false direction, it must be at the Cross. Let us say it again:

A thrice-Holy God can meet with sinful man only at the Cross of Christ. Only then does the nation stand a chance!

Regarding our Text, the implication is that the *"House of Joseph"* would be consumed, as well as the great temple of idols at *"Beth-el."* With the advent of the Assyrians a short time later, it happened exactly as the Prophet had predicted.

(7) "YOU WHO TURN JUDGMENT TO WORMWOOD, AND LEAVE OFF RIGHTEOUSNESS IN THE EARTH."

The exegesis is:

1. God can have no fellowship either with falsehood in doctrine or evil-doing in conduct, as is described in this Verse.

2. The latter phrase of Verse 7 denounces bribery and injustice.

3. Justice was cast to the ground and perverted to most bitter wrong.

RIGHTEOUSNESS

To very much simplify the issue, Righteousness is simply that which is right; however, it is not right as defined by man, but rather by God. Man's definition is generally subjective, meaning it changes with the individual; however, God's definition does not change. It is the same now as it was 2,000 years ago, etc. In other words, it is objective Righteousness.

The truth is, man cannot produce anything that God will label as righteous. It doesn't matter what he does; if man puts his hand to it, it is polluted.

All of this means that the only Righteousness that God will accept is that which He freely imputes.

GOD'S WAY OF RIGHTEOUSNESS

The Lord is ready and willing to impute

a perfect Righteousness to man, and that means any man or woman who meets His Conditions.

What does He demand?

It's very simple what God demands. He demands that we understand that Jesus Christ is the Son of the Living God, and that He died on Calvary for us that we might be Saved. Expressing Faith in Him and what He did for us at the Cross, and being totally sincere in our hearts, guarantees a spotless, pure, perfect Righteousness, the Righteousness of God, instantly given to us (Gal. 3:6; Rom. 3:22, 25, 26; 4:3, 5, 11, 13).

(8) "SEEK HIM WHO MAKES THE SEVEN STARS AND ORION, AND TURNS THE SHADOW OF DEATH INTO THE MORNING, AND MAKES THE DAY DARK WITH NIGHT: WHO CALLS FOR THE WATERS OF THE SEA, AND POURS THEM OUT UPON THE FACE OF THE EARTH: THE LORD IS HIS NAME."

The exegesis is:

1. The *"seven stars"* refer to the *"Pleiades."*

2. *"Orion"* is the constellation commonly known as *"the Giant."* The space in the sword of the Giant alone is estimated to be 2,200,000,000,000,000,000 (two quintillion, two hundred quadrillion) times larger than the sun. Therefore, what is here discussed, referring to God's Creation, is so large that it beggars description.

3. The entirety of the phrase, *"The shadow of death into the morning,"* pertains to the coming Resurrection of Life. As well, *"And makes the day dark with night,"* refers to the coming Resurrection of Damnation (Jn. 5:29).

GOD'S CREATION

The phrase in Verse 8, *"The shadow of death,"* refers to deep darkness. The Hebrew word occurs 10 times in the Book of Job, four times in the Psalms, and occasionally in other Books of the Bible. Yet, men who profess to be scholars declare it to be a comparatively modern word.

The phrase, *"Who calls for the waters of the sea, and pours them out upon the face of the Earth,"* refers to the fact that the rain that waters the Earth is produced by the action of the sun upon the sea. This supposed discovery of science a little over a hundred years ago was a matter of common knowledge 3,000 years ago, at least, to those who studied the Word of God.

As it regards Creation, the following may be noted:

THE EARTH

• The Earth free-floats in space (Job 26:7), affected only by gravity. While other sources declared the Earth sat on the back of an elephant or a turtle, or was held up by Atlas, the Bible alone states what we now know to be true—*"He hangs the Earth on nothing."*

CREATION

• Creation is made of particles, indiscernible to the eyes (Heb. 11:3). Not until the Nineteenth Century was it discovered that all visible matter consists of invisible elements.

SHIPS

• The Bible specifies the perfect dimensions for a stable water vessel (Gen. 6:15). Shipbuilders today are well aware that the ideal dimension for ship stability is a length six times that of the width. Keep in mind, God told Noah the ideal dimensions for the Ark about 4,500 years ago.

RUNNING WATER

• When dealing with disease, clothes and the body should be washed under running water (Lev. 15:13). For centuries people naively washed in standing water. Today we recognize the need to wash away germs with fresh water.

SPRINGS

• Oceans contain springs (Job 38:16). The ocean is very deep. Almost all of the ocean floor is in total darkness and the pressure there is enormous. It would have been impossible for Job to have explored the *"springs of the sea."* Until recently, it was thought that oceans were fed only by rivers and rain. Yet, in the 1970's, with the help of deep diving, research submarines that were constructed to withstand 6,000 pounds-per-square-inch pressure, oceanographers

discovered springs on the ocean floors!

BLOOD

• Blood is the source of life and health (Lev. 17:11, 14). Up until about 120 years ago, sick people were *"bled"* and many died as a result. Today we know that healthy blood is necessary to bring life-giving nutrients to every cell in the body. God declared that *"the life of the flesh is in the blood"* long before science understood its function.

KINDS

• The Bible states that God created life according to *"kinds"* (Gen. 1:24). The fact that God distinguishes kinds agrees with what scientists observe—namely that there are horizontal genetic boundaries beyond which life cannot vary. Life produces after its own kind. Dogs produce dogs and roses produce roses. Never have we witnessed one kind changing into another kind as evolution supposes. There are truly natural limits to biological change.

CHICKEN

• Chicken or egg dilemma solved (Gen. 1:20-22). Which came first, the chicken or the egg? This question has plagued philosophers for centuries. The Bible states that God created birds with the ability to reproduce after their kind. Therefore, the chicken was created first with the ability to make eggs! Yet, evolution has no solution for this dilemma.

PHYSICAL BODIES

• Our physical bodies are made from the dust of the ground (Gen. 2:7; 3:19). Scientists have discovered that the human body is comprised of some 28 base and trace elements—all of which are found in the Earth.

FINISHED

• The first law of thermodynamics established (Gen. 2:1-2). The first law states that the total quantity of energy and matter in the Universe is a constant. One form of energy or matter may be converted into another, but the total quantity always remains the same. Therefore, the Creation is *"finished"* exactly as God said way back in Genesis.

TIME, MATTER, ENERGY

• The first three Verses of Genesis accurately express all known aspects of the Creation (Gen. 1:1-3). Science expresses the Universe in terms of time, space, matter, and energy. In Genesis, Chapter 1, we read: *"In the beginning (time) God created the heavens (space) and the Earth (matter)...."* Then God said, *"Let there be light (energy)...."* No other Creation account agrees with the observable evidence.

UNIVERSE

• The Universe had a beginning (Gen. 1:1; Heb. 1:10-12). Starting with the studies of Albert Einstein in the early 1900's and continuing today, science has confirmed the Biblical view that the Universe had a beginning. When the Bible was written, most people believed the Universe was eternal. Science has proven them wrong but the Bible correct.

SPHERE

• The Earth is a sphere (Isa. 40:22). At a time when many thought the Earth was flat, the Bible told us that the Earth is spherical.

REVOLVING EARTH

• Scripture assumes a revolving (spherical) Earth (Lk. 17:34-36). Jesus said that at His Return, some would be asleep at night while others would be working during the day, concerning activities in the field. This is a clear indication of a revolving Earth, with day and night occurring simultaneously.

LIGHT

• Light can be divided (Job 38:24). Sir Isaac Newton studied light and discovered that white light is made of seven colors, which can be *"parted"* and then recombined. Science confirmed this four centuries ago— God declared it 4,000 years ago!

(The information above on Creation was derived from the booklet, *"101 Scientific Facts and Foreknowledge,"* printed by Eternal Productions.)

(9) "WHO STRENGTHENS THE SPOILED AGAINST THE STRONG, SO THAT THE SPOILED SHALL COME AGAINST THE FORTRESS."

The overview is:

1. The idea is that God can smite the strongest. No fortress is a refuge from Him.

2. Men are foolish if they think they can outwit God!

3. God is *"Omnipotent"* (all-powerful), *"Omniscient"* (all-knowing), and *"Omnipresent,"* meaning that He is everywhere.

(10) "THEY HATE HIM WHO REBUKES IN THE GATE, AND THEY ABHOR HIM WHO SPEAKS UPRIGHTLY."

The structure is:

1. The pronoun *"they"* refers to the Judges of Israel.

2. The pronoun *"him"* refers to Amos, who was hated because he *"spoke uprightly."*

3. He, no doubt, stood in the *"gate of the city"* and rebuked the worshippers who were coming to Beth-el. If so, this would have been extremely annoying to the religious leaders!

THE RESPONSE

Israel's response to the pleadings of Verses 4 through 6 was the cruel wrong of Verse 7; and her response to the loving entreaty of Verses 8 and 9, the anger and hatred of Verse 10.

The pronoun, *"they,"* as stated, referred to Judges who hated a truthful witness, for his honesty rebuked their wickedness.

Even though Amos was, no doubt, speaking of all who *"spoke uprightly"* and were hated accordingly, as well, he, no doubt, was referring particularly to himself.

THE GOSPEL

The world doesn't care for the Gospel at all, and, in fact, it hates the Gospel. There is a reason, which we will momentarily address.

What I'm going to say is very strong, but I know it to be true.

Despite the fact of over 3,000 people murdered by the Muslims on September 11, 2001, in effect, more killed than at Pearl Harbor, still, as it regards great segments of society in this country, there is a greater hatred for Biblical Christianity even than it is for Islam.

How could that be?

The Lord through Moses told us how that could be. He said, **"And I will put enmity** *(animosity)* **between you and the woman** *(presents the Lord now actually speaking to Satan, who had used the serpent; in effect, the Lord is saying to Satan, 'You used the woman to bring down the human race, and I will use the woman as an instrument to bring the Redeemer into the world, Who will save the human race'),* **and between your seed** *(mankind which follows Satan)* **and her Seed** *(the Lord Jesus Christ)***; it** *(Christ)* **shall bruise your head** *(the Victory that Jesus won at the Cross [Col. 2:14-15]),* **and you shall bruise His Heel** *(the sufferings of the Cross)"* **(Gen. 3:15).**

The reason is simple: the animosity toward the Lord Jesus Christ and the Word of God is present because it is real. All other religions of the world are figments of men's imagination but actually conceived by demon spirits. So, individuals without God in this nation, or anywhere, have much more in common with the religion of Islam, despite the fact that it is a religion of bloodshed, murder, torture, enslavement, ignorance, and superstition, than they do with Biblical Christianity. While some few unredeemed individuals will see the danger of Islam, the truth is, most don't. That's the reason for our ridiculous policies in this nation as it regards the religion of Islam.

Our government spends hundreds of billions of dollars and sheds the blood of thousands of our young men and young ladies, claiming they're going to make a democracy out of Iraq and Afghanistan. They refuse to admit that it's a religion that we are up against and, as such, Islam and democracy are light years apart. As long as we keep tens of thousands of soldiers in these countries and keep pouring in hundreds of billions of dollars, we can keep the bombings down somewhat. However, the moment we leave, whether it's next year or 50 years from now, these two countries will revert back to what they were before despite all the blood and money wasted.

They openly state that they hate us, and they're going to destroy this nation and turn it into a sea of Islam. And they are prepared to use any means to do it. But we hide our heads in the sand, claiming that this religion is a very peaceable religion, and that

it's only a few fanatics causing the problem. While all Muslims aren't murderers, to be sure, all Muslims are in sympathy with the murderers, whomever they might be. Of course, there is an exception here and there, but rare indeed!

They hate the United States and they hate Israel. They hate us because of Jesus Christ, and their hatred of Israel goes back some 4,000 years, all the way to Abraham. They claim that Ishmael is the promised seed, while the Bible proclaims the fact that Isaac was and is the Promised Seed, meaning that through him the Redeemer would come, Who was the Lord Jesus Christ.

We are allowing some 2,000 Muslims a month into our country, which is an invitation to destruction. We even allow them to serve in our armed forces, which is tantamount to high treason because they swear our destruction. Worse yet, the Obama Administration is totally antagonistic to Biblical Christianity and totally favorable toward the religion of Islam. In fact, the President, if not a card-carrying Muslim, so to speak, is most definitely a Muslim sympathizer. This is catastrophic for our nation.

And yet, if we as Believers *"will humble ourselves and pray, and turn from our wicked ways, then the Lord will hear from Heaven, will forgive our sins, and will heal our land."* He is still able to do such!

(11) "FORASMUCH THEREFORE AS YOUR TREADING IS UPON THE POOR, AND YOU TAKE FROM HIM BURDENS OF WHEAT: YOU HAVE BUILT HOUSES OF HEWN STONE, BUT YOU SHALL NOT DWELL IN THEM; YOU HAVE PLANTED PLEASANT VINEYARDS, BUT YOU SHALL NOT DRINK WINE OF THEM."

The overview is:

1. God's Anger burns against exactions (*"burdens"*) upon the poor.

2. The luxury obtained by such oppression is short-lived.

3. The Lord knows the multitude and magnitude of such cruel deeds. His Word is, *"Vengeance is Mine; I will repay, says the Lord"* (Rom. 12:19).

(12) "FOR I KNOW YOUR MANIFOLD TRANSGRESSIONS AND YOUR MIGHTY SINS: THEY AFFLICT THE JUST, THEY

TAKE A BRIBE, AND THEY TURN ASIDE THE POOR IN THE GATE FROM THEIR RIGHT.

(13) "THEREFORE THE PRUDENT SHALL KEEP SILENCE IN THAT TIME; FOR IT IS AN EVIL TIME."

The overview is:

1. (Vs. 13) The pronoun *"they"* in Verse 12 refers to evil Judges.

2. (Vs. 13) *"Turn aside"* addresses the perversion of justice.

3. (Vs. 13) Prudent men suffered wrong in silence and did not prosecute those who injured them, knowing it to be useless, because of the corruption of the courts of law of that day.

AN EVIL TIME

If one is to notice, the Commands by the Holy Spirit lay heavily in the Word of God regarding fair and just treatment afforded the poor and helpless. And yet, this characterizes almost all of the world presently.

Communism claimed that it would address itself to this injustice and provide equal justice for all; however, this corrupt philosophy, which denies God and His Word, proved to be the biggest offender of all. Instead of providing a classless society, as promised, it very much provided the opposite. Those in the upper elite of the Communist Party lived in the lap of luxury, supported by the toil and sweat of those beneath them.

The moral is, without God and an adherence to His Word, there is no justice or righteous judgment.

America has probably come closer to achieving this goal than most but still falls far short. The reason is, the Word of God is only followed by a few.

Anytime the Bible is ignored, it is always *"an evil time,"* and in modern America, it is being ignored more and more, not only by the country as a whole but by the church as well. And, as the church goes, so goes the nation!

(14) "SEEK GOOD, AND NOT EVIL, THAT YOU MAY LIVE: AND SO THE LORD, THE GOD OF HOSTS, SHALL BE WITH YOU, AS YOU HAVE SPOKEN.

(15) "HATE THE EVIL, AND LOVE THE

GOOD, AND ESTABLISH JUDGMENT IN THE GATE: IT MAY BE THAT THE LORD GOD OF HOSTS WILL BE GRACIOUS UNTO THE REMNANT OF JOSEPH."

The construction is:

1. The prescription for the avoidance of terrible Judgments is given in Verses 14 and 15.

2. (Vs. 15) In effect, the Holy Spirit condescends to give another Altar Call by saying, *"Seek good, and not evil, that you may live."*

3. In a moment's time, God can turn good to evil or evil to good. If we ignore His Word, the good can be turned to evil and, in fact, will be turned to evil. If we adhere to His Word, He can and will turn the evil to good.

THE ALTAR CALL

The Way of the Lord is not a complicated Way. It is very simple to simply obey His Word. In fact, in these two Verses, the Holy Spirit lays it out perfectly as to what the individual is to do in order to stop Judgment and to have the Blessings of the Lord. The admonitions are as follows:

SEEK GOOD, NOT EVIL, THAT YOU MAY LIVE

The heart, which has no desire to seek God, would sarcastically ask as to, *"What exactly is good and evil?"*

That question is asked because man-made definitions change constantly. There is only one Standard for *"good and evil,"* and that is the Bible.

God's Standard never changes, whereas, man's standards change with the next court.

At that time, Israel had the Bible, which consisted of all the Books through II Samuel, as well as most of the Psalms and all of the Wisdom Books. Therefore, they were without excuse, for they knew what to seek for and to turn from.

SATAN'S ATTACK AGAINST THE WORD OF GOD

The Evil One seemingly has grown smarter in these last few decades than ever before. When I was a young Preacher getting started, he made his attacks against the Bible from a frontal position. He claimed it wasn't true, etc., but in the last few decades, he has changed his tactics.

Instead of a frontal attack on the Word of God, he is doing something else entirely. He is producing scores of paraphrases of the Bible, such as the Message Bible, which, in reality, is no Bible at all, and inducing Believers to accept it as the Word of God. Jesus said:

"*. . . Man shall not live by bread alone, but by every Word that proceeds out of the Mouth of God*" (Mat. 4:4). Jesus was quoting Deuteronomy 8:3.

If the Believer doesn't have a *"word-for-word"* translation, then whatever it is he does have may be a religious book, but it's not the Bible. The King James is a word-for-word translation, and that which I unreservedly recommend.

The King James translators were the greatest Hebrew and Greek scholars in the world of that day. They were given instructions by King James that they were to translate the Bible from the original languages (Hebrew for the Old Testament and Greek for the New), and to stay impeccably true to the Original Text. In fact, these men had no prejudice either way, but only one overwhelming command, and that was to stay true to the Original Text, which they did. The Bible is the Word of God and, in fact, there is no other. This means that the Book of Mormon, the Koran, and other so-called sacred writings, have no validity at all. All of these other *"works"* were devised by men, and if the truth be known, had their origination with demon spirits. The Bible alone is the Word of God and is, therefore, by far the single most important collection of Books on the face of the Earth. Because it is the Word of God, and is the only Word of God, this makes it so very, very important. In fact, one might say that the Bible is the road map for life and living and the blueprint for eternity. As we have stated, there is no other.

THE EXPOSITOR'S STUDY BIBLE

Back in the mid 1980's, the Lord began to deal with me about developing a Study Bible. Thinking it was something out of my own mind and knowing my gross inadequacy,

I immediately dismissed it; however, the Holy Spirit kept dealing with me about the matter. But looking back, the Lord did not allow this to come to fruition until He first gave me the Revelation of the Cross. When I say *"Revelation,"* more than likely the word, *"illumination,"* would be a better term. What He gave me was not new, by any means, but that which had already been given to the Apostle Paul. At any rate, and looking back, I firmly believe that unless one has a working knowledge of the Cross of Christ, then one cannot have a correct understanding of the Word of God (Jn. 1:1-2, 14, 29; Col. 2:10-15). The Cross of Christ is the meaning of the New Covenant, and the New Covenant is Christ and Christ Alone, which is that which was given to the Apostle Paul.

While looking at other Study Bibles, I discovered that some had material that was well worth one's study, but the physical layout of these Bibles was a hindrance instead of a help to me. One brother wrote me and basically stated that the notes explaining the Scriptures were at times so hard to find in most Study Bibles that by the time he finally found it, he had lost his train of thought.

At any rate, one day in 2004, if I remember correctly, while I was working on one of the Commentaries and attempting to make particular Passages of Scripture easier to understand, the Lord spoke to my heart and stated, *"This is the way that I want you to develop the Study Bible. Put the explanation in with the Text."* I then had no more excuses; I had to do what the Lord was impelling me to do.

In developing this Bible, I think I can say without fear of exaggeration or contradiction that I sensed the Presence of the Lord in helping me as never before. Over and over again, I mentioned to Frances that I believed the Lord was going to greatly use this Bible to help others understand its Sacred Content. That He has done and is doing.

In fact, I sought the Lord earnestly as to every part of what was done, even down to the color of the Text and the notes. I feel that the Lord most definitely led us in everything that was done. At any rate, we give Him all the praise and all the glory.

AND SO THE LORD, THE GOD OF HOSTS, SHALL BE WITH YOU, AS YOU HAVE SPOKEN

The idea is, God cannot be with those who have unconfessed sin within their lives, irrespective of whom they may be.

The implication also weighs heavily that the Lord desires to be with His People and only asks that they *"seek good."*

When we use the term *"unconfessed sin,"* we are speaking of that which is an unscriptural direction, and the Believer, irrespective of wrong direction, insisting upon going that way, whatever it might be. We aren't speaking of Believers who are struggling with something in their lives, and who ask forgiveness every time the sin is committed. The truth is, unless the Believer understands what the Lord gave to the Apostle Paul as it regards the meaning of the New Covenant, which is the meaning of the Cross of Christ, such a Believer will be dominated by the sin nature and will not be able to live a victorious life. Such a person is not living in sin even though he is living a life of spiritual failure. The truth is, he hates the sin within his life, even as Paul said. His words are:

"For that which I do *(the failure)* **I allow not** *(should have been translated, 'I understand not'; these are not the words of an unsaved man, as some claim, but rather a Believer who is trying and failing)*: **for what I would, that do I not** *(refers to the obedience he wants to render to Christ, but rather fails; why? as Paul explained, the Believer is married to Christ but is being unfaithful to Christ by spiritually cohabiting with the Law, which frustrates the Grace of God; that means the Holy Spirit will not help such a person, which guarantees failure [Gal. 2:21])*; **but what I hate, that do I** *(refers to sin in his life, which he doesn't want to do and, in fact, hates, but finds himself unable to stop; unfortunately, due to the fact of not understanding the Cross as it refers to Sanctification, this is the plight of most modern Christians)*" **(Rom. 7:15).**

CAN SATAN OVERRIDE THE WILL OF A BELIEVER?

Yes, he can!

If the Believer doesn't have his or her faith exclusively in Christ and the Cross but is rather depending on willpower or something else, Satan will definitely override that person's will. In fact, it is happening millions of times each and every day. Look at your own life.

The last time you failed the Lord, is that what you wanted to do? Of course not! Every true Believer hates sin. While the flesh may want something that is wrong, *"the inward man"* doesn't want it because we have been transformed by the Power of God.

While the willpower is definitely important, it, within itself, is not enough to hold back the powers of darkness.

When the Believer places his or her Faith exclusively in Christ and the Cross, and maintains it exclusively in Christ and the Cross, the Holy Spirit, Who is God, and Who can do anything, will then help the Believer, which will ultimately guarantee Victory (Rom. 6:14).

HATE THE EVIL, AND LOVE THE GOOD, AND ESTABLISH JUDGMENT IN THE GATE

To enjoy God's Companionship, which Israel proudly claimed to posses, *"as you have spoken,"* there must be a definite separation from evil, attachment to the good, and an abolition of all things dishonest.

The truth is, Israel had the Law of God, which was the most fair and equitable legislation the world had ever known, and by far. In fact, it was light years ahead of anything else because it was totally of the Lord. In other words, this Law gave Israel a tremendous advantage over other nations. Actually, the Law of Moses came in three parts. They are:

1. Civil Law: this pertained to how the Israelites were to treat each other, in other words, one's disposition toward his fellowman and, also, how Gentiles were to be treated.

2. The Ceremonial Law: this addressed the Sacrificial system, Sabbath keeping, the Feast Days, Circumcision, etc.

3. The Moral Law: this pertained to the Ten Commandments (Ex. 20).

The Law was given to show man what

God's Standard of Righteousness actually was. It was given, as well, and despite its simplicity, to show that man, due to the Fall, was simply unable to keep its precepts. That was the main reason for the Sacrificial system. In fact, were it not for that system, Israel would have been destroyed long before. As is obvious, the Sacrificial system was a Symbol or a Type of the Lord Jesus Christ and what He would do at the Cross when, in fact, He did come to this world. As we have stated repeatedly, a thrice-Holy God and sinful man can only meet at the Cross.

WHY DIDN'T GOD GIVE MAN POWER TO KEEP THE LAW?

Someone has well said that the Law of God was and is like a mirror that shows man what he is but gives him no power to change it.

If God had, in fact, given man the power to keep the Law, the end result would not have been what one thinks. Man's problem is pride and giving man such power would have only exacerbated the problem. In other words, the pride would have become worse. So, the Lord, by the giving of the Law, showed man how incapable he was, and it was meant to push him toward the Cross of Christ, i.e., the Sacrificial system. Please understand the following:

THE MODERN BELIEVER'S INCAPACITY

Even now, with the Holy Spirit abiding constantly in our hearts and lives, unless we function God's Way, the modern Believer still cannot live a victorious life.

What is God's Way?

His Way is the Cross of Christ. Please note the following diagram. It is very much abbreviated, but I believe will direct the Believer in the right direction.

• FOCUS: The Lord Jesus Christ (Jn. 1:1-2, 14, 29; 14:6; Col. 2:10-15).
• OBJECT OF FAITH: The Cross of Christ (Rom. 6:1-3; I Cor. 1:17-18, 23; 2:2; Col. 2:14-15).
• POWER SOURCE: The Holy Spirit (Rom. 8:1-2, 10-11).
• RESULTS: Victory (Rom. 6:14).

Using the same formula, the following, however, is the way that most modern Believers are trying to live for God.

NOTES

• Focus: Works.
• Object of Faith: One's performance of these works.
• Power Source: Self.
• Results: Defeat.

GOD'S PRESCRIBED ORDER OF LIFE AND LIVING

Let's say it another way and, actually, it's that which we've already given several times. However, it's so important that I will keep saying it until the Believer has it in his or her spirit.

• Jesus Christ is the Source of all things we receive from God (Col. 2:10, 15).
• The Cross of Christ is the Means by which these things are given to us (I Cor. 1:17-18, 23; 2:2).
• The Cross of Christ must ever be the Object of our Faith (Rom. 6:1-14; Gal., Chpt. 5; 6:14).
• The Holy Spirit superintends all of this (Rom. 8:1-2, 10-11; Eph. 2:13-18).

With our focus on the Cross of Christ exclusively, referring to what He there did for us, the Holy Spirit, Who Works only within the parameters of the Finished Work of Christ (Rom. 8:1-2), will then work mightily on our behalf, developing in us His Fruit and, thereby, giving us power to live an overcoming, Victorious Life (Eph. 2:13-18).

IT MAY BE THAT THE LORD GOD OF HOSTS WILL BE GRACIOUS UNTO THE REMNANT OF JOSEPH

The words in the heading, *"it may be,"* do not declare uncertainty respecting God's Readiness to pardon but relate to man's unwillingness to repent and be pardoned.

Sadly, Israel would not repent, as most will not repent!

In this Passage, the Lord refers to the entirety of the northern kingdom of Israel as *"Joseph,"* because Joseph was the father of Ephraim, by which the northern kingdom is sometimes called. Of the two sons of Joseph, Manasseh and Ephraim, the latter was the youngest. And yet, when Jacob was blessing the boys so long, long before, he placed his right hand on the head of Ephraim and blessed him first, even though he was the younger (Gen. 48:13-16).

Joseph, noting that his father had laid his right hand on the head of Ephraim, signifying the greater blessing, he mentioned it to his father. But Jacob answered and said, *". . . I know it, my son, I know it: he also* (Manasseh) *shall become a people, and he also shall be great: but truly his younger brother* (Ephraim) *shall be greater than he, and his seed shall become a multitude of nations"* (Gen. 48:19).

(16) "THEREFORE THE LORD, THE GOD OF HOSTS, THE LORD, SAYS THUS; WAILING SHALL BE IN ALL STREETS; AND THEY SHALL SAY IN ALL THE HIGHWAYS, ALAS! ALAS! AND THEY SHALL CALL THE HUSBANDMAN TO MOURNING, AND SUCH AS ARE SKILFUL OF LAMENTATION TO WAILING.

(17) "AND IN ALL VINEYARDS SHALL BE WAILING: FOR I WILL PASS THROUGH YOU, SAYS THE LORD."

The overview is:

1. (Vs. 17) *"Wailing shall be in all streets,"* refers to the coming invasion of the Assyrians because Israel refused to seek the Lord. Such speaks of terrible suffering.

2. (Vs. 17) *"And in all vineyards shall be wailing,"* portrays the fact that the carnage would be not only in the cities but the countryside as well!

3. This speaks of the entire Nation of Israel coming under the same Judgment. In other words, in the coming day when Judgment would come because of a lack of Repentance, there would be no safe spots in Israel.

JUDGMENT

The phrase, *"Wailing shall be in all streets,"* speaks of terrible suffering.

The phrase, *"For I will pass through you, says the LORD,"* is an echo of the last plague of Egypt (Ex. 12:12), when God will not *"pass over"* Israel, as He did then, but will treat them as Egypt and *"pass through"* to smite and punish. The implication is terrible!

Inasmuch as the Judgment did not come immediately and, in fact, was some 25 years or more in coming, no doubt, Amos' Prophecies were forgotten in short order, as men are wont to do!

Most mistake the delay for what it actually

NOTES

is, the Mercy of God, in order that men may repent. Therefore, if they did not repent immediately upon hearing the message from the lips of Amos, it is almost guaranteed that they would not repent later, which they did not.

It is the same with any individual heart dealt with by the Holy Spirit! If they don't yield then, they seldom yield later.

A GOD OF LOVE?

Many modern so-called Christians deny the Judgment of God. It is because they do not understand the Love of God.

In fact, God doesn't merely have love as we have love but, in reality, is Love (I Jn. 4:8).

As such, this, at the same time, means that God hates everything that steals, kills, and destroys (Jn. 10:10).

All parents, who truly love their children, hate drugs, which they know will destroy their children if used wrongly. In fact, if they are true parents, they hate anything that will steal, kill, and destroy, as it regards their children, even as they should.

When it comes to people who do not serve God and are not His Children, the Lord pretty well allows them to go their own way, doing what they desire, until they begin to impact His Work and His People, or until Believers begin to pray for them.

But when it comes to those who follow the Lord, He chastises us at times because it is necessary. In fact, concerning this, the Scripture says, *"For whom the Lord loves He chastens, and scourges every son whom He receives"* (Heb. 12:6).

Paul then said, *"But if you be without chastisement, whereof all are partakers, then are you bastards, and not sons"* (Heb. 12:8).

Chastisement is not Judgment. Judgment is punishment while chastisement is correction.

But yet, if a Believer insists upon going in a direction opposite of the Word of God after the Lord has dealt with them, spoken to them, and moved upon them, then Judgment can most definitely be forthcoming. It is the final alternative and is carried out by the Lord as the last resort to bring an individual or even a nation, such as Israel, to its spiritual senses.

THE CROSS AND CHASTISEMENT

Christians go wrong when they ignore the Cross of Christ, or else they are ignorant of the Cross of Christ. I think one can say without fear of contradiction that all spiritual failure and all wrong direction is because of an improper interpretation of the Cross of Christ, an ignoring of the Cross of Christ, or an outright denial of the Cross of Christ.

One comes into Salvation by simply evidencing Faith in Christ and what Christ did for us at the Cross. While the believing sinner understands almost nothing about that, still, if he calls on the Name of the Lord, in whatever capacity, meaning that he is sincere, such a person is assured of instant Salvation (Rom. 10:13). However, after one is Born-Again, one is totally and completely changed by the Power of God. That's why Jesus referred to it as *"Born-Again"* (Jn. 3:3; II Cor. 5:17). Consequently, one then falls in love with the Bible and anything and everything as it pertains to the Lord. The Lord then, with His Help, expects the Believer to begin to learn His Word. He is to learn that as he got in by Faith, he is to stay in by Faith; however, it must be Faith in Christ and what Christ did for us at the Cross. If one tries to separate Christ from the Cross, then Paul labels such as *"another Jesus"* (II Cor. 11:4).

When we speak of the Cross, we aren't speaking of a wooden beam, but rather that which Jesus there did. As someone explained the Cross of Christ, let us repeat it:

"The Cross of Christ is something that happened now nearly 2,000 years ago, and will never need to be repeated. It has continuing results, and results, in fact, which will never be discontinued."

To try to separate Christ from what He did at the Cross leaves a person really not knowing Who Jesus actually is. The great statement of the Gospel is, *"Who He is and what He has done."*

He is the Son of the Living God, God manifest in the flesh. What He did was to afford Redemption for all who will believe. He did so by going to the Cross, which was foreordained before the foundation of the world (I Pet. 1:18-20). There He paid the price demanded by God, which man could not pay. The Work at the Cross satisfied the demands of a thrice-Holy God, making it possible for man to be redeemed.

SOWING AND REAPING

The Scripture plainly tells us that what *". . . a man sows, that shall he also reap"* (Gal. 6:7).

The Law of Sowing and Reaping, regarding that which is negative, can only be stopped by one thing, and that is the Cross of Christ and our Faith in that Finished Work. Let us not understate that.

Were it not for the Cross of Christ, there would be very little, if anything, left. Man has sinned and does sin so terribly that if reaping was done solely on that basis, God would have no choice but to destroy the whole of humanity. But it is the Cross of Christ which holds back Judgment. In fact, for those who place their Faith accordingly, all Judgment and negative reaping are stopped.

As it regards people, there are some things set in motion as a result of sin and failure, which the Lord seldom stops. However, as far as He is concerned, Faith in Christ and the Cross brings all reaping in a negative sense to a halt (Heb. 4:16; 85:10; I Jn. 1:9; 2:1-2; Heb. 7:25; 9:28).

(18) "WOE UNTO YOU WHO DESIRE THE DAY OF THE LORD! TO WHAT END IS IT FOR YOU? THE DAY OF THE LORD IS DARKNESS, AND NOT LIGHT."

The exegesis is:

1. A double *"woe"* is the burden of this message. The first was pronounced upon false profession (Vss. 18-27); the second, upon false peace (Chpt. 6).

2. *"Woe unto you who desire the Day of the LORD!"* professes Israel's claim of readiness to welcome the establishment of the Messiah's Kingdom, which would commence with the Coming of the Lord.

3. The idea of Verse 18, and which precipitated their audacious reply concerning the *"Day of the LORD,"* is in answer to Amos' demand, *"prepare to meet your God, O Israel"* (4:12).

In other words, they were boldly declaring that they were ready to meet the Lord! Therefore, they were rejecting what God said about them and, as well, they were rejecting their need for Repentance.

How so like modern man, and even the modern church!

(19) "AS IF A MAN DID FLEE FROM A LION, AND A BEAR MET HIM; OR WENT INTO THE HOUSE, AND LEANED HIS HAND ON THE WALL, AND A SERPENT BIT HIM."

The synopsis is:

1. The idea of Verse 19 is: Israel, because of refusal to repent, is destined for death. It cannot be avoided!

2. The idea is, it doesn't matter what Israel does, they will suffer the fate of which the Lord has spoken.

3. Using an illustration, the Holy Spirit says that if a man did flee from a lion, he is not safe because he is about to meet a bear. He may flee into a house, but when he leans his hand on the wall, a serpent will bite him. As stated, Israel is destined for destruction!

ESCAPE?

When the *"Day of the LORD"* actually did come, there would be no way to escape.

Verse 19 lends credence to the thought that upon hearing the words of Amos concerning these dire predictions, in their minds, they thought that such a thing was impossible. However, if in the one chance in a thousand it did happen, surely they could escape.

Consequently, the Holy Spirit likens their foolish thoughts to a man fleeing from a lion and about the time he thinks he has escaped, he meets a *"bear."*

Or, running from the lion, he escapes *"into the house,"* and pausing to rest, he leans his hand on the wall and is bitten by a snake.

In other words, he is destined for death, and by using this type of illustration, the Holy Spirit is saying that Israel is destined for death!

What must have been the further thoughts of these people when Amos addresses the very thoughts that come into their minds?

Surely, such brought Conviction, and great Conviction at that! But, still, they would not yield.

(20) "SHALL NOT THE DAY OF THE LORD BE DARKNESS, AND NOT LIGHT? EVEN VERY DARK, AND NO BRIGHTNESS IN IT?"

The overview is:

1. Amos further appeals to them by asking the question, *"Do you not feel in your inmost hearts that, in the case of such guilt as yours, the Lord can visit but to punish?"*

2. The Prophet is saying that the *"Day of the LORD"* will hold no Mercy, only Judgment!

3. God is a God of love, and because He is a God of love, He must at the same time be a God of Judgment. Sin cannot be left unaddressed.

ANSWER TO JUDGMENT OR ANSWER TO THE CROSS

I don't want to overstate the case, that is, if it's possible to do such; however, the Truth, which I am attempting to bring out, is not normally known or thought of by most Believers. It is that the Cross of Christ is the only thing that can keep back the Judgment of God. Nothing else will stay His Hand of Judgment.

As we've already stated, God is unalterably opposed to sin, even as He should be. That being the case, and considering the sinful condition this world is in, the only thing that stops destruction, and we mean total destruction, is the Cross of Christ.

The Cross is where our Lord took the Judgment upon Himself that should have come upon us, and when we say us, in this case, we are speaking of the whole of humanity. Now, how is it that, out of the entirety of the world's population, a few people trusting in Christ can have a positive effect on the entirety of humanity? Some of the reasons are as follows:

• The Work that Christ did at the Cross was of such magnitude as to defy all description.

• We must consider that what Jesus did at the Cross has the potential to save every human being on the face of the Earth if they would only believe Him. Regrettably, most won't; nevertheless, the price has been paid.

• As we have previously stated, the Cross of Christ is a Work that was accomplished some 2,000 years ago and will never have to be repeated. However, it is a Work that has continued results, in fact, results that will never be discontinued.

• Everything we receive from the Lord Jesus Christ, and I mean everything, comes to us by the Means of the Cross of Christ. And yet, no matter how many draw upon this reservoir, still, the supply is never limited.

• While Believers are the light of the world and the salt of the Earth, still, we are that by and through the Cross of Christ. So, everything is dependent on the reaction of Believers to the Cross of Christ. But sadly, the Cross is of little consequence to the modern church. That's one reason our nation is in the condition it's presently in.

(21) "I HATE, I DESPISE YOUR FEAST DAYS, AND I WILL NOT SMELL IN YOUR SOLEMN ASSEMBLIES."

The construction is:

1. Regarding their man-made religion, even though it closely resembled God's True Way of Salvation, still, the Lord's Response is, *"This I hate."* Let it be understood: God *"hates"* every proposed form of *"atonement"* other than the Cross of Christ (Gal. 5:2).

2. The phrase, *"And I will not smell in your solemn assemblies,"* pertains to the *"sweet savor,"* which ascended to the Lord upon proper *"Burnt Offerings"* being offered unto Him (Ex. 29:18).

3. The Lord is saying that no sweet savor ascends to God from these sacrifices offered by Israel on heathen altars. So the phrase is equivalent to *"I will not accept"* and *"I will take no delight in"* (Gen. 8:21; Ex. 29:18; Lev. 26:31).

ANOTHER JESUS

Concerning Believers in Paul's day who had separated Christ from the Cross, the great Apostle said:

"For if he who comes preaching another Jesus *(a Jesus who is not of the Cross)***, whom we have not preached** *(Paul's message was 'Jesus Christ and Him Crucified'; anything else is 'another Jesus')***, or if you receive another spirit** *(which is produced by preaching another Jesus)***, which you have not received** *(that's not what you received when we preached the True Gospel to you)***, or another gospel, which you have not accepted** *(anything other than 'Jesus Christ and Him Crucified' is 'another gospel')***, you**

might well bear with *him.* *(The Apostle is telling the Corinthians they have, in fact, sinned because they tolerated these false apostles who had come in, bringing 'another gospel', which was something other than Christ and the Cross)"* **(II Cor. 11:4).**

At this present time (2010), the modern church is, by and large, preaching *"another Jesus."* In fact, in the last few decades, the Cross of Christ has been so little preached that any more the modern church doesn't know where it's been, where it is, or where it is going. It is rudderless, so to speak!

If the Cross is removed from the Gospel, you have nothing but a vapid philosophy, and that's what most modern Christians are now getting.

WHY IS THE CROSS OF CHRIST IGNORED?

For many reasons!

It is ignored mostly because of ignorance. *"Faith comes by hearing, and hearing by the Word of God"* (Rom. 10:17). While the Cross of Christ is preached for Salvation in some few circles, and even that is falling by the wayside, it is preached not at all as it regards Sanctification. And when we consider that virtually the entirety of the Bible is given over to telling us how to live for God, then, surely, we should understand how important this is. In fact, it was to Paul that the meaning of all of this was given, and rightly so. In his fourteen Epistles, almost all of it is given over to telling Believers how to live for God. That should be simple to understand. The Bible is not given to unbelievers, but rather to Believers.

At present, the modern church is pointing to everything in the world regarding victory over sin, except the Cross of Christ, which alone holds the answer.

It may look in some circles as if the Church is ignoring sin, but when one considers that it is proposing every type of solution that one can think as it regards this problem, it quickly becomes obvious that it's not ignoring the problem. However, irrespective of what it pronounces, if it's not the Cross of Christ, it will be of little consequence. Actually, what is being promoted, irrespective as to what it might be called, pure and simple, it is promoting *"another Jesus."* What Paul means by this statement is that anything, which is proclaimed as the solution and the answer for man's dilemma, other than the Cross of Christ, presents *"another Jesus."*

Presently, we have the healing Jesus, the money Jesus, the social Jesus, the prosperity Jesus, the fasting Jesus, etc. The amazing thing about all of this is, once our Lord and the Cross are properly understood, He becomes all of these things, but, above all, He becomes the Victory over sin.

(22) "THOUGH YOU OFFER ME BURNT OFFERINGS AND YOUR MEAT OFFERINGS, I WILL NOT ACCEPT THEM: NEITHER WILL I REGARD THE PEACE OFFERINGS OF YOUR FAT BEASTS."

The overview is:

1. Verse 22 proclaims the fact that they maintained the formal ritual of the Mosaic worship in their idolatry.

2. It is the same presently as it regards *"Christ and the Cross."* Such are mentioned by the modern church; however, as Israel of old, the object of faith is something else entirely.

3. These sacrifices in Israel were being offered on altars that God did not recognize. He only recognized one Altar, i.e., *"one Calvary,"* and that was at the Temple in Jerusalem. Likewise, it is one Cross presently, and that's all.

ONE CROSS

Under the old Mosaic Law, the Lord gave instructions that there was to be one place of sacrifice. It typified one Cross, i.e., *"one Calvary."* The Scripture says:

"And the LORD spoke unto Moses, saying *(if it is to be noticed, over and over again this phrase is used, signifying that all was of God and nothing at all of man; in other words, Moses must not deviate from what the Lord had told him; this is a lesson that religious man finds very difficult to obey),*

"Speak unto Aaron, and unto his sons, and unto all the Children of Israel, and say unto them; This is the thing which the LORD has commanded, saying,

"What man soever there be of the house of Israel, who kills an ox, or lamb, or goat,

in the camp, or who kills it out of the camp *(should have been translated 'sacrifices' in the place of 'kills'),*

"And brings it not unto the door of the Tabernacle of the congregation, to offer and Offering unto the LORD before the Tabernacle of the LORD; blood shall be imputed unto that man; he has shed blood; and that man shall be cut off from among his people."

ONE MEETING PLACE
BETWEEN GOD AND MAN

"(Mackintosh says: 'A man might say, Can I not offer a Sacrifice in one place as well as another? The answer is, Life belongs to God, and His claim thereto must be recognized in the place where He has appointed – before the Tabernacle of the Lord. That was the only meeting-place between God and man. To offer elsewhere proved that the heart did not want God.

"The moral of this is plain. There is one place where God has appointed to meet the sinner, and that is the Cross – the antitype of the Brazen Altar. There and there alone has God's claims upon the life been duly recognized. To reject this meeting-place is to bring down judgment upon one's self – it is to trample underfoot the just claims of God, and to arrogate to one's self a right to life which all have forfeited')."

THE BLOOD OF JESUS CHRIST

"To the end that the Children of Israel may bring their sacrifices, which they offer in the open field *(which they have been offering in the open field),* even that they may bring them unto the LORD, unto the door of the Tabernacle of the congregation, unto the Priest, and offer them for Peace Offerings unto the LORD *(in essence, some three times the warning is given concerning the offering up of sacrifices in places except the Tabernacle, or Temple, that is, when the Temple would be built [Vss. 4, 7, 10]).*

"And the Priest shall sprinkle the blood upon the Altar of the LORD at the door of the Tabernacle of the congregation, and burn the fat for a sweet savour unto the LORD" (Lev. 17:1-6).

Expositors say:

"The Blood of Christ is the foundation of everything. It is the ground of God's Righteousness in justifying an ungodly sinner who believes on the Name of the Son of God; and it is the ground of the sinner's confidence in drawing near to a Holy God, Who is of purer eyes than to behold evil. God would be just in the condemnation of the sinner; but through the Death of Christ, He can be just and the Justifier of him who believes – a Just God and a Savior.

"The Righteousness of God is His consistency with Himself – His acting in harmony with His revealed character. Hence, were it not for the Cross, His consistency with Himself would, of necessity, demand the death and judgment of the sinner: but in the Cross, that death and judgment were born by the sinner's surety, so that the same Divine consistency is perfectly maintained, while a Holy God justifies an ungodly sinner through Faith. It is all through the Blood of Jesus – nothing less, nothing more, and nothing different."[1]

THE MODERN SIN

When Faith is placed in anything except Christ and the Cross presently, it is the same as offering sacrifices of old in places except the Tabernacle or the Temple. As God would not recognize such then, He will not recognize such now. The Object of Faith must, and without fail, be the Cross of Christ. It must not be anything else, no matter how good and Scriptural the other thing might be in its own right. This is imperative!

It was on the Cross where the price was paid, a price, incidentally, so staggering that it defies description, which won the Victory in every capacity. As important as our Lord's Resurrection was, the Resurrection was not the place of victory. As wonderful as His Ascension was, the Ascension was not the place of victory. As wonderful as His Exaltation before the Throne of God was, that was not the place of victory. All of these things are the result of the Victory that was won at the Cross, and that we must never forget.

(23) "TAKE YOU AWAY FROM ME THE NOISE OF YOUR SONGS; FOR I WILL NOT HEAR THE MELODY OF YOUR VIOLS."

The diagram is:

NOTES

1. The idea is: while the sacrifices were being offered before the golden calf, Psalms and Hymns of praise were being offered to God, accompanied by exquisite sacred music.

2. But the Lord would have none of this! Why? The object of their faith was in the ritual and not at all in what the sacrifices were supposed to represent, namely, the Coming Redeemer, Who would give His Life on the Cross!

3. The Lord will accept no worship that is not anchored in the Cross of Christ.

WORSHIP?

Israel was offering up sacrifices before the golden calf, and they were singing Psalms and Hymns in their so-called worship. Therefore, the thought was, at least, in their response to Amos, *"What do you mean that we need to repent?"*

The idea that God would not accept their elaborate religious ritual, and especially considering its excellent ceremony, was preposterous to them.

Regrettably, that which characterized Israel of so long ago characterizes much of the modern church.

Too many choir members render elaborately prepared presentations from hearts that have never been changed by the Power of God. Ceremony is rampant in the modern church, and refined elaborately so, but with its participants never realizing that *"ceremony"* cannot save! Whether it is Catholic ceremony or Protestant ceremony, the response of the Lord is, *"Take you away from Me."* He says, *"I hate," "I will not accept," "I will not regard,"* and *"I will not hear. . . ."* Let us say it again:

If our worship is not anchored in the Cross of Christ and centered in the Cross of Christ, then it's worship that God will not accept. He told the woman at the well, **"God *is* a Spirit** *(simply means that 'God is a Spirit Being')***: and they who worship Him must worship *Him* in spirit and in truth"** (Jn. 4:24).

WHAT IS TRUTH?

- Christ is Truth (Jn. 14:6).
- The Word of God is Truth (Jn. 17:17).
- The Holy Spirit is Truth (I Jn. 5:6).

Jesus said, *"And you shall know the Truth, and the Truth shall make you free"* (Jn. 8:32). This is the secret of all Abundant Life in Christ; the *"Truth"* is *"Jesus Christ and Him Crucified,"* which alone is the answer to the problems of man (I Cor. 1:23).

(24) "BUT LET JUDGMENT RUN DOWN AS WATERS, AND RIGHTEOUSNESS AS A MIGHTY STREAM."

The overview is:

1. Improper faith always results in improper justice.

2. Proper Faith, which is Faith in Christ and what He has done for us at the Cross, always results in *"Righteousness"* (Gal. 2:20-21).

3. The Righteousness of God is automatically given to the believing sinner upon Faith evidenced in Christ and the Cross. That alone guarantees the Righteousness of God.

JUDGMENT AND RIGHTEOUSNESS

Once again, burning words of indignation denounce the prostitution of the Courts of Justice and the consequent oppression of the poor and innocent; for at that time, as now, rich ceremonial religion accompanied gross corruption, oppression, and debauchery.

In effect, the Lord is saying that if Israel truly knows the Lord and is not hiding behind their fake religiosity, then *"let righteous Judgment run down as waters,"* concerning the fair treatment of all. In other words, let their walk match their talk.

In the midst of the denunciation of their formal worship, the Prophet announces their duty in the present crisis, attention to which could alone win God's Favor. Judgment in Righteousness, long neglected and forgotten, should permeate the land like refreshing streams of water—a symbol of special signification in any eastern country, where a perennial stream was as delightful as it was unusual.

"Judgment" refers to the Word of God being properly interpreted and, thereby, applied. Such will always bring Righteousness, and *"as a mighty stream."*

WHAT IS RIGHTEOUSNESS?

In over simplistic terms, Righteousness is simply *"that which is right."* However, the definition of what is right is given by God Alone and not man. Man's definition changes with the wind, while God's Definition remains the same forever.

All self-righteousness is subjective righteousness, meaning that it changes with whoever is giving the definition. God's Righteousness is objective, meaning that it never changes. What His Definition was 3,000 years ago, it is the same presently.

God's Righteousness can be attained in only one way. It cannot be earned, bought, or sold. God merely requires that the believing sinner place his or her Faith exclusively in Christ and what Christ has done for us at the Cross, which will be the occasion that God will instantly impute His Perfect Righteousness to such an individual. Anything else and everything else is self-righteousness. Let's say it another way:

Faith placed in anything other than Christ and the Cross results in self-righteousness. That's the reason, sadly said, that the modern church is possibly the most self-righteous church the world has ever known, at least, since the Reformation. How do I know that?

I know that simply because the object of faith in the modern church, by and large, is anything but the Cross of Christ.

(25) "HAVE YOU OFFERED UNTO ME SACRIFICES AND OFFERINGS IN THE WILDERNESS FORTY YEARS, O HOUSE OF ISRAEL?"

The diagram is:

1. Verses 25 through 27 reveal that the evil of associating idols with God had been their rule from the beginning, and now reappeared in the calf of Beth-el.

2. This was the resurrection of the golden calf.

3. In other words, Israel was without excuse!

IDOLATRY

Israel copied the crimes of their forefathers. Stephen refers to this in Acts 7:42 through 43. They had little reason to expect their sacrifices should be acceptable to God when, all along, they and their fathers had been addicted to the worship of other gods.

Did you offer to Me sacrifices, to Me only? No; therefore, not at all to Me acceptably; for the Law of worshipping the Lord our God is, Him only we must serve (Mat. 4:10). Though the ceremonial sacrifices may thus be dispensed with, Spiritual sacrifices must not be set aside.

None of these sacrifices were to God, though they professed they all were so. But they attended not to His Worship in faith or to His Glory, and He despised their efforts. Let us say it again:

Anything that's not of Christ and the Cross is despised by our Lord!

(26) "BUT YOU HAVE BORNE THE TABERNACLE OF YOUR MOLOCH AND CHIUN YOUR IMAGES, THE STAR OF YOUR GOD, WHICH YOU MADE TO YOURSELVES."

The structure is:

1. God did not question the fact that they did offer sacrifices in the wilderness. His Objection was that the sacrifices were not always to Him.

2. The *"unto Me"* is emphatic. If God is not served Alone, and with the whole heart, He is not served at all.

3. If the Offering is accepted, then the offerer is accepted. If the offering is rejected, then the offerer also is rejected. Israel's offering was rejected! (Gen., Chpt. 4).

IDOL GODS

The Verses above may be thus paraphrased:

"Did you offer Me sacrifices and Offerings forty years in the wilderness, O House of Israel?" (You certainly did, outwardly.) *"But, at the same time, you bore aloft the Tabernacle of Moloch and the image of Chiun, your star-god, which you made to yourselves, therefore,"* etc.

They could hide these gods behind the back of Moses when marching through the wilderness, but they could not hide them from the Eye of God. Even Joshua suspected them (Josh. 24:14). It is easy to make an outward profession of loyalty to Christ and, at the same time, enthrone idols in the heart.

(Moloch was the national god of Ammon, the same as Chemosh of Moab.) It was supposed to be the sun god. Its image was a hollow brazen figure, with the head of an ox and outstretched human arms.

It was heated red hot by fire within, and little children were placed in its arms to be slowly burned to death. To prevent the parents from hearing the dying screams, the priests would beat drums.

Chiun was the star-god of Babylon. It was customary for idolaters of all nations to carry small images of their gods on their journeys and in war. They were enclosed in miniature temples called tabernacles or shrines.

Israelites carried these, imitating their neighbors, the Moabites, Amorites, Ammonites, etc.

Because they carried these idols, God predicted by Amos that they, themselves, would go into captivity beyond *"Damascus"* and *"Babylon."* This was done, and they were carried into Assyria and Media (II Ki. 17:6).

(27) "THEREFORE WILL I CAUSE YOU TO GO INTO CAPTIVITY BEYOND DAMASCUS, SAYS THE LORD, WHOSE NAME IS THE GOD OF HOSTS."

The overview is:

1. Enemies of Inspiration affirm that Stephen erred in saying, *"Babylon"* and not *"Damascus"* (Acts 7:43). However, there are two replies to this:

2. First, Babylon is beyond Damascus. Second, Stephen did not say, *"As it is written in the Book of the Prophet,"* but rather, *"in the Book of the Prophets,"* i.e., the Scriptures.

3. The Prophets more than once predicted a captivity beyond Babylon. And so it fell out. The Ten Tribes were carried beyond Damascus and the Two Tribes beyond Babylon.

"The God of Abraham prays,
"Who reigns enthroned above;
"Ancient of everlasting days,
"And God of love:
"Jehovah; Great I am!
"By Earth and Heaven confess;
"I bow and bless the Sacred Name,
"Forever blest."

"The God of Abraham prays,
"At Whose supreme Command,
"From Earth I rise, and seek the joys,
"At His Right Hand:

"I all on Earth forsake,
"Its wisdom, fame, and power;
"And Him my only portion make,
"My Shield and Tower."

"He by Himself has sworn,
"I on His Oath depend;
"I shall, on eagle's wings upborne,
"To Heaven ascend:
"I shall behold His Face,
"I shall His Power adore,
"And sing the wonders of His Grace,
"Forevermore."

"The goodly land I see,
"With peace and plenty blest,
"A land of sacred liberty,
"And endless rest;
"There milk and honey flow,
"And oil and wine abound,
"And trees of life forever grow,
"With Mercy crowned."

"There dwells the Lord our King,
"The Lord our Righteousness,
"Triumphant o'er the world and sin,
"The Prince of Peace,
"On Zion's sacred height,
"His Kingdom still maintains,
"And glorious with His Saints in light,
"Forever reigns."

"The whole triumphant host,
"Give thanks to God on high;
"Hail, Father, Son, and Holy Ghost!
"They ever cry:
"Hail, Abraham's God and mine!
"I join the heavenly lays;
"All might and majesty are Thine,
"And endless praise."

CHAPTER 6

(1) "WOE TO THEM WHO ARE AT EASE IN ZION, AND TRUST IN THE MOUNTAIN OF SAMARIA, WHICH ARE NAMED CHIEF OF THE NATIONS, TO WHOM THE HOUSE OF ISRAEL CAME!"

The overview is:

1. The phrase, *"Woe to them who are at ease in Zion,"* is the second *"Woe"* pronounced, and it denounces a false peace.

NOTES

2. The first *"Woe,"* found in 5:18, addresses itself to the insulting sarcasm of Israel's self-righteousness.

3. The word *"Woe"* signifies coming Judgment, and one might say, Judgment unparalleled.

WOE TO THEM WHO ARE AT EASE IN ZION

At that time, both countries, Judah and Samaria, were prosperous, strong, and confident of the future. All of this was at the very time Amos was pronouncing Judgment.

When men compare themselves by others, their holiness seems to be sufficient, or even superior, hence, the attitude of both Judah and Samaria. However, when compared to God, only one word is sufficient, *"Woe!"*

Individuals, and even religious denominations, begin to lose their way when they take their eyes off the Lord and, instead, onto themselves. At this stage, they begin to make rules and regulations, which have little authority from the Word of God, and which they change frequently. Accordingly, they enjoy placing the label of *"righteous"* or *"unrighteous"* on whomsoever they desire. And all *"Righteousness"* and *"unrighteousness"* are judged according to those rules and not according to the Bible. As such, it becomes more and more political.

When true revival comes, and men are pulled back to the Cross, then Christ becomes the measurement, with the pronouncement of *"Woe"* on all! Beneath the searing light of His Righteousness, all self-righteousness pales into nothingness.

A FALSE TRUST

The phrase, *"And trust in the mountain of Samaria,"* presents Samaria as an impregnable military fortress. In fact, the city was so impregnable that it kept the Assyrians at bay for three years before it was finally taken (II Ki. 18:9).

"Zion" was the seat of orthodox religion and was actually the mountain in Judah on which the Temple was built. Up beside that, Samaria was esteemed impregnable; therefore, the joining together of material force and traditional religion made a grateful foundation for the natural heart and begat

a false peace.

In a slightly different way the same maladies affect the modern church. They are steeped in orthodox religion and have economic force. As such, it, as well, begets a false peace. Therefore, all the time the modern church is touting its impregnable position, the Holy Spirit is saying, *"Woe!"*

CHIEF OF THE NATIONS

The phrase, *"Which are named chief of the nations,"* represents both Judah and Israel because both are addressed in this Verse.

In fact, they had this proud title because they were the beloved and elect of God and were meant to set an example to the rest of the world (Ex. 19:5; Num. 1:17; Deut. 4:20; II Sam. 7:23).

This Nation Israel (using *"Israel"* for both Judah and Israel) was meant by God to be the premier Nation in the world. They were meant to guide the nations of the world to Jehovah; however, their strength was measured not in the size of their standing army, etc., but in the Blessings of God upon their people. These Blessings were predicated upon them adhering to His Law.

When in Covenant with Him, no nation, or series of nations, could hope to overcome them simply because the Power of God, which knew no limitations, was at their beck and call. As well, history is replete with God using His Power in astounding ways to help Israel overcome mighty foes. In fact, in just a few years, the Lord would send one Angel, who, in one night, would destroy 185,000 choice men of the mighty Assyrian army, forcing Sennacherib to give up his plans for a siege of Jerusalem and return to his own land where he was killed by his own sons (II Chron., Chpt. 32).

However, in a short time, some 30 to 50 years, Israel would fall to the Assyrians, never to be restored, at least, as far as nationhood was concerned. Judah fell a little over 130 years after Samaria.

THE TIMES OF THE GENTILES

Consequently, the Lord would take the scepter of power from the faltering hands of Judah and place it into the heathen hands of Nebuchadnezzar, where it has remained

NOTES

ever since. It was called by Christ, *"The times of the Gentiles"* (Lk. 21:24).

They fell because of sin, and they will not be restored until there is Repentance for that sin!

The phrase, *"To whom the House of Israel came,"* refers to the nobles of both Judah and Israel understanding their place and position in God, but yet, failing to serve Him.

Maintaining religion while being exalted in pride always leads to self-righteousness, which, in its evil, would ultimately crucify the Lord of Glory and, consequently, totally destroy them. In this one Verse is so much promise, and yet, so much grief!

(2) "PASS YOU UNTO CALNEH, AND SEE; AND FROM THENCE GO YOU TO HAMATH THE GREAT: THEN GO DOWN TO GATH OF THE PHILISTINES: BE THEY BETTER THAN THESE KINGDOMS? OR THEIR BORDER GREATER THAN YOUR BORDER?"

The diagram is:

1. The cities mentioned in Verse 2 were great and prosperous at this particular time.

2. But yet, both Judah and Israel are invited by the Holy Spirit to go and compare their condition with that of other countries, from the furthest east to the north and to their own neighbors, and they will see that God has done so much more for them than these others.

3. Israel is bidden to remember that she is much more favored than all these.

SERVING GOD

In a flat out posture, the Holy Spirit through the Prophet asked the question, *"Be they better?"* referring to these heathen cities being better than Judah or Samaria.

In other words, had these others received more earthly prosperity at God's Hands than Judah and Samaria? As well, was their territory greater than the twin kingdoms?

The answer is an unqualified, *"No!"*

Amos attempts to appeal to their Blessings given by God. In view of these Blessings, which are greater than all the surrounding nations, would they not want to serve God, the Author of such?

As well, would they not be afraid of losing

all these Blessings if they failed to serve the Lord?

It is a powerful argument, or else the Holy Spirit would not have urged the Prophet to deliver such!

GOD'S BLESSINGS ARE MANYFOLD

The same questions asked of Judah and Samaria can also be asked and, in fact, must be asked of all modern Christians!

Satan delights in making the Christian believe that he *(the Christian)* is not nearly as well off as his non-Christian counterparts. To buttress his argument, he will select one particular thing, magnifying it all out of proportion, in order to pull the Christian away from Faith.

What every Believer needs to remember is that God's Blessings are manyfold. They cover every aspect of human endeavor and reach much further than financial prosperity. They include physical health, and even more importantly, peace of mind, well-being, fulfillment, sense of purpose, etc.

As well, the Power of God is available to all Believers in order that sins of the flesh, such as jealousy, envy, greed, etc., might be overcome. It only remains for the Believer to place his or her Faith exclusively in Christ and the Cross. That being done and maintained in that fashion, the Holy Spirit will then mightily help the Believer to overcome the world, the flesh, and the Devil. That is God's Prescribed Order of Victory. That is His Blueprint for life and living (Rom. 6:1-14; I Cor. 1:17-18, 23; 2:2).

Satan can offer none of this and, in fact, only exacerbates it. Consequently, the well-being of the Child of God on every front is light years ahead of all that the Evil One can offer.

Therefore, every Believer should thank the Lord constantly for these never-ending streams of Blessings. This is in order that we understand that such is given, not because we are good, but because He is Good; not because we are righteous, but because He is Righteous; not because we are worthy, but because He is Worthy.

(3) "YOU WHO PUT FAR AWAY THE EVIL DAY, AND CAUSE THE SEAT OF VIOLENCE TO COME NEAR."

NOTES

The diagram is:

1. *"You who put far away the evil day,"* addresses the approaching day of God's Wrath.

2. The *"seat of violence"* refers to the corrupt Court of Justice.

3. Upon hearing Amos' stern words, the religious leaders of Samaria assigned a distant date to the time of punishment and calamity, that is, if it should come at all!

THE SEAT OF VIOLENCE

The *"seat of violence,"* as stated, refers to the corrupt Courts of Justice. These luxurious revelers of Verses 4 through 6 ridicule the Prophet's announcement of the coming Wrath of God. As well, they falsely claim their music to be like David's, and they feasted upon food violently taken from the helpless. Like their forefathers, who sat down to eat and to drink while their brother was in the pit, they were indifferent to, and insensible of, the sufferings of God's true People, the Spiritual Joseph. Therefore, they should be the first to go into captivity. And so it fell out.

Upon hearing Amos preach and deliver that which God had told him to deliver, the religious leaders of Samaria met his words with their own interpretation. They said, *"There may come an "evil day," but it will be far, far away. So, why worry about it?!"*

(4) "WHO LIE UPON BEDS OF IVORY, AND STRETCH THEMSELVES UPON THEIR COUCHES, AND EAT THE LAMBS OUT OF THE FLOCK, AND THE CALVES OUT OF THE MIDST OF THE STALL."

The exposition is:

1. *"Who lie upon beds of ivory,"* is meant to portray their spiritual insensibility.

2. It was a result of their prosperity; however, their gain was ill-gotten.

3. One should never take prosperity as a sure sign of the Blessings of God. While it most definitely might be, it's not necessarily so! It definitely wasn't with Israel.

BEDS OF IVORY

In the last 50 years, that which has probably hurt the Work of God more than anything else has been and is the so-called *"Word of Faith"* doctrine! It began primarily as a healing ministry, and while the Lord most definitely does heal, still, their formulas caused the lives of many to be cut short. In other words, they were confessing they were healed when they really were not. This quickly degenerated into money. And, presently, almost the entire thrust of this effort is *"money."*

Now, at least in those circles, faith is judged according to the worth of the suit that one wears or the make and model of the car that one drives. This is so bad that, on the way to some of their gatherings, some of their preachers will stop 20 or 30 miles away and rent the highest priced luxury car they can find. They dare not drive anything less because their compatriots would think that they didn't have faith.

People are told constantly how to get rich, but it's always by giving these particular preachers money. In fact, the preachers grow rich, but the only thing the people get is a separation from their funds.

To be sure, God will definitely not bless a lie, and this presentation is a lie. God will not bless that which is crooked, and the whole presentation is crooked.

However, there is an element of greed, I suppose, in all of us. As such, that particular gospel, which is no gospel at all, is heady and, therefore, has a ready audience.

The Bible most definitely teaches that God loves a cheerful giver and if we sow bountifully, we shall reap bountifully, etc. However, money must never be the motivation of our efforts. If so, we miss entirely what the Word of God is trying to tell us.

Some people have called this the *"prosperity message."* It isn't! It is the greed message. To be sure, the Lord's Will is His Prosperity for His People in every capacity. John said it:

"Beloved, I wish above all things that you may prosper (refers to financial prosperity, and should be the case for every Believer) **and be in health** (speaks of physical prosperity), **even as your soul prospers** (speaks of Spiritual Prosperity; so we have here the whole Gospel for the whole man)**" (III Jn., Vs. 2).**

As an aside, this particular brand of gospel, which, in reality, as stated, is no gospel at all, denigrates the Cross of Christ. They

refer to the Cross as *"past miseries,"* and *"the worst defeat in human history."* In fact, they state that if one preaches the Cross, one is preaching death. They claim the preacher should preach the Resurrection, etc. Now, that's strange when one considers the words of the Apostle Paul. He said:

"For Christ sent me not to baptize, but to preach the Gospel: not with wisdom of words, lest the Cross of Christ should be made of none effect" (I Cor. 1:17). He did not say, *". . . lest the Resurrection should be made of none effect."*

He also said, *"For the preaching of the Cross is to them who perish foolishness; but unto us who are Saved it is the Power of God"* (I Cor. 1:18).

He did not say, *"For the preaching of the Resurrection is to them who perish foolishness. . . ."*

He most definitely preached the Resurrection, but in its proper context.

He said, *"For I determined not to know anything among you, save Jesus Christ, and Him Crucified"* (I Cor. 2:2).

He did not say *"For I determined not to know anything among you, save Jesus Christ, and Him Resurrected."*

So, which are you going to accept, that which Paul gave us or some of the modern greed preachers?

(5) "WHO CHANT TO THE SOUND OF THE VIOL, AND INVENT TO THEMSELVES INSTRUMENTS OF MUSIC, LIKE DAVID."

The diagram is:

1. As is obvious here, prosperity, producing ease and luxury, was coupled with entertainment.

2. This is not so much different than the modern church.

3. As Nero fiddled while Rome burned, likewise, these Israelites were playing their own funeral dirge, but they didn't know it.

MUSIC

Music, when it is anointed by the Lord, is the highest form of praise and worship. We know this because the longest Book in the Bible is Psalms, which contains 150 songs. For the Holy Spirit to delegate this much space to music and singing shows us how important it is in the Work of God, i.e., *"our praise and worship."*

When I was eight years old, and I will never forget that moment, I asked the Lord to give me the talent to play the piano. I promised Him that I would never use it in the world or for the world but only for Him and His Glory. The Lord heard that child-like prayer and granted me that for which I asked. As well, He gave me an understanding of music as it regards that which the Holy Spirit desires, which has helped me to touch the world for Christ.

A PERSONAL ILLUSTRATION

Frances and I began in evangelistic work in 1956. If I remember correctly, that which I am about to relate took place in 1958.

We were preaching a meeting at our little home Church in Ferriday, Louisiana. After the Service that Sunday morning, there was a dinner on the ground, which took place at the back of the Church. There weren't many present that day, possibly 25 or 30. At any rate, as we were all standing and having fellowship one with another, a brand-new Cadillac drove up on the little side road that ran right beside the Church. My Uncle got out of the car, the father of Jerry Lee Lewis, my first cousin.

Of course, I was glad to see him. Uncle Elmo was a tall, gangly man, about six feet, four inches tall. He had a tremendously winsome personality, in fact, a man who just about everyone liked.

We exchanged small talk for just a few moments, and then he said to me:

"Jimmy, I have the best news in the world. Sam Phillips has just sent for you. He's starting a Gospel line with Sun Records, and you are to be the first artist."

He went on to say to me how that in 30 days I could buy a brand-new Cadillac just like Jerry Lee had just bought him.

I opened my mouth to say, *"Uncle Elmo, I'm ready to go right now."*

But, all of a sudden, the Spirit of God stopped me, and did so instantly. I stood there, saying nothing, with, I'm positive, a blank look on my face. My Uncle looked at me and said, *"Jimmy, did you hear what I said?"*

The Holy Spirit had spoken to my heart and said, *"You are not to do this."*

I finally answered my Uncle, telling him how much I appreciated the offer, but I felt I could not do it at that time.

"But Jimmy," he retorted, *"It's Gospel music!"*

"I know it," I said! *"But I can't go."*

He laid his hand on my shoulder and said, *"Jimmy, I think I understand."*

I watched him get in that big Cadillac and drive away.

I overheard one of the ladies standing nearby. She said, *"Did you just hear what he did?"* She was referring to the fact that I had turned down the offer. Had anyone asked me at that time to explain myself, I would not have been able to do so.

TRUST ME

I walked away from the small gathering that day and went into the Church. There was a small broom and mop closet there, and I went into that closet and closed the door. I said, *"Lord, I don't understand. This is Gospel music, and why would not You allow me to do this?"*

To say we needed the money would have been a gross understatement. My car was falling apart, and, if I remember correctly, I had two suits of clothes, and that was it.

And then, in answer to my question, the Lord moved greatly upon me and said to me, *"You have asked Me as to why I won't allow you to do this. My answer to you is, 'Trust Me.'"*

I remember standing there with those two words in my heart, *"Trust Me."* I then said, *"Lord, I don't understand it, but I will do exactly as You have asked, I will trust You."*

SIXTEEN MILLION RECORDINGS

In a short period of time, the Lord helped us to put out our first Album. From that day until now, which is really the life of this Ministry, we have sold over 16 million Recordings. At a point in time, the Lord told me what to do regarding the music and how to do it, and that He would bless it. He most definitely did!

We have seen millions of people touched for the Lord by our music, and, as should be obvious, we must give all the credit and all the praise and glory to the Lord.

THE PERFECT WILL OF GOD

When we first went on radio and television, our record sales were small, to say the least. With us beginning in the media, there came a point in time when the Lord spoke again to my heart about our music. He told me that He wanted all the profits from the sale of the Recordings. I remember trying to bargain with the Lord, asking Him if I could take fifty percent and He take fifty percent. There was no answer!

I finally got down to the place that I stated, *"Would You take ninety percent, and give me ten percent?"* And then the Lord spoke again to my heart.

He said to me, *"You can have all of it if you want it, but if you want My Perfect Will, you will do as I have asked."*

I called our lawyer and had him draw up the necessary papers, doing exactly what the Lord told me to do. That means that all the money that has come in from the sale of our Recordings has gone to build churches all over the world, radio and television programming all over the world, etc. In other words, it has all gone for the Lord and His Work. He gave me the talent, so He had the right to ask what He did.

SATAN AND MUSIC

Satan has used music as he has used nothing else to drag down several generations of young people to the place of destruction. As well, in many cases, he has corrupted the music of the Church also. Concerning this fallen Angel, the Scripture says:

"You have been in Eden the Garden of God; every precious stone was your covering, the sardius, topaz, and the diamond, the beryl, the onyx, and the jasper, the sapphire, the emerald, and the carbuncle, and gold: the workmanship of your tabrets and of your pipes was prepared in you in the day that you were created" (Ezek. 28:13). The notes on this Scripture from THE EXPOSITOR'S STUDY BIBLE are as follows:

"'You have been in Eden the Garden of God,' does not actually refer to the 'Eden' of Genesis, Chapter 3, but rather to the 'Eden', which existed on this Planet before Adam and Eve, which evidently was ruled

by Lucifer before his rebellion.

"'Every precious stone was your covering,' presents itself as very similar to the dress of the High Priest of Israel (Ex. 28:19).

"'The workmanship of your tabrets and of your pipes,' has to do with music. There is every indication that Lucifer's leadership had something to do with the worship of God. As well, he is called, 'O Lucifer, son of the morning' (Isa. 14:12). When the Earth was originally created, the Scripture says, 'The morning stars sang together, and all the Sons of God shouted for joy' (Job 38:4-7). So, if the idiom, 'son of the morning,' can be linked to the 'morning stars,' these Passages tell us that Lucifer, at least before his fall, was greatly used in leading the worship of God.

"In fact, this is the reason that Satan has done everything within his power to corrupt the music of the world, and to corrupt the music of the Church above all. Inasmuch as the Book of Psalms is the longest Book in the Bible, we learn from this that music and singing constitute the highest form of worship to the Lord."

(6) "WHO DRINK WINE IN BOWLS, AND ANOINT THEMSELVES WITH THE CHIEF OINTMENTS: BUT THEY ARE NOT GRIEVED FOR THE AFFLICTION OF JOSEPH."

The diagram is:

1. *"Who drink wine in bowls,"* actually referred to the sacrificial bowls, which were used in libations of wine and in the sprinkling of blood, regarding the sacrifices.

2. *"And anoint themselves with the chief ointments,"* could very well have referred to the *"holy ointment,"* as described in the Law of Moses, which was to be used only to anoint *"the Ark," "the Table," "the Candlestick,"* etc. It was definitely not to be put on one's flesh (Ex. 30:32-33).

3. It is one thing to sin but quite another to try to bring God into your sin.

BLASPHEMY

It cannot be proven from the Text if the words, *"chief ointments,"* had to do with the holy ointment, which had been designed by the Holy Spirit; however, it probably did.

In the Thirtieth Chapter of Exodus we are

told how this ointment was to be made, and what it was to be. Then Moses wrote:

"And you shall anoint Aaron and his sons, and consecrate them, that they may minister unto Me in the Priest's office.

"And you shall speak unto the Children of Israel, saying, This shall be an holy anointing Oil unto Me throughout your generations (or at least until the Cross was a fact, and the Holy Spirit could then come in a new dimension; then, these things would no longer be needed).

"Upon man's flesh shall it not be poured, neither shall you make any other like it, after the composition of it: it is holy, and it shall be holy unto you. (This ointment was not to be imitated, nor poured upon man's flesh. Spiritual graces cannot be imitated, nor can they be given to men 'in the flesh.')

"Whosoever compounds any like it, or whosoever puts any of it upon a stranger (Gentile), shall even be cut off from his people (meaning that this particular Israelite would lose his soul; the Holy Spirit, Who glorifies Christ, must not be trifled with [Mat. 12:31-32])" (Ex. 30:30-33).

MODERN BLASPHEMY!

These individuals in the northern kingdom of Samaria, who were supposed to be God's People, were doing things in the Name of the Lord, which, in essence, was tempting God. The modern counterpart is no different.

When preachers lie to their congregations, especially, in the realm of money, claiming that the Lord has told them certain things, this brings God into their wickedness. It is a serious thing and can be looked at as none other than blasphemy. I'll give you an example!

The preacher steps before the television camera and tells people that if they give a thousand dollars, or some such number, at the end of the year, every bill they have is going to be paid. In other words, they are told that their house will be free and clear, their car will be paid off, and they will owe no one anything, all because God is going to bless them so abundantly for giving that thousand dollars, etc.

Now, there is always some truth in every

NOTES

lie. Most definitely the Lord will grandly and gloriously bless His People for giving of their financial resources to His Work. However, we must make certain that what we are supporting is actually the Work of God. If it is truly His Work, He most definitely will bless those who support it. However, to get up and claim that everybody who gives a certain amount of money is going to have every bill paid by the end of the year, and to claim that the Lord has told them thus and so, is a sin of the worst kind. The Lord is not going to do something of that nature, and, as well, to bring His Name into our lie is a most grievous sin.

Better for the perpetrator to get a 38-revolver and go downtown and hold up a store, which would be much less worse in the Eyes of God, than to make the Lord a part of one's scheme, a part of one's lie.

THE BOWLS

The phrase, "That drank wine in bowls," actually referred to the sacrificial bowls, which were used in libations of wine and in the sprinkling of blood regarding the sacrifices.

Consequently, they had mixed the rituals of the Law of Moses in with their entertainment and feasting. Somehow, in their warped minds, this made it acceptable to God.

Israel of old surrounded herself with holy things but used them improperly, thinking all the time that it would make them holy.

Every Sunday morning, millions of people go to church and engage in the Lord's Supper, thinking somehow that such atones for their week of sinning. Most are not Born-Again, and, in fact, most have never been Born-Again but have, in reality, embraced a philosophy of Christianity without really knowing Christ.

(7) "THEREFORE NOW SHALL THEY GO CAPTIVE WITH THE FIRST WHO GO CAPTIVE, AND THE BANQUET OF THEM WHO STRETCHED THEMSELVES SHALL BE REMOVED."

The structure is:

1. "Therefore now shall they go captive with the first who go captive," speaks of Israel falling to the Assyrians about 130 years before the southern kingdom of Judah

fell to the Babylonians.

2. The last phrase of the Seventh Verse refers to the nobles of Israel being *"removed,"* which is a gross understatement, to say the least! They would be *"removed"* as slaves, at least the ones who were not killed.

3. What did these Jews think when they heard Amos prophesying these coming events?

INTO CAPTIVITY

The phrase, *"Therefore now shall they go captive with the first who go captive,"* refers to an event that would take place a little over 130 years before the southern kingdom of Judah fell to the Babylonians. All of this proclaims the fact that the Lord has total control over everything. He can bless, or He can curse. In fact, what He does is according to what we do.

THE BANQUET THAT
WILL BE REMOVED

In other words, their luxury would not be too long in coming to an end.

The phrase, *"Shall be removed,"* as stated, presents itself as a gross understatement, to say the least! Even the most noble of them, at least, the ones who were not killed, would be *"removed"* as slaves, with hooks in their lower lips, with a string tied to the individual immediately in front. This, as is obvious, would cause tremendous pain.

From this Passage of Amos, St. Augustine takes occasion to show that the most untrained of the Prophets possessed eloquence and literary skill.

This much is certain, even though the Holy Spirit in all of these occasions used the personality and demeanor of the Prophet in question, still, it is remarkable that in all the Texts there were no grammatical errors, at least, according to the grammar of that day. And, to be sure, the Text was not edited even in the slightest. In fact, great caution was taken that not one single word was changed in the slightest by the copyist, even though at times a copyist did make a mistake. However, that had no bearing on the authenticity of the Original Text.

As well, and as most know, there was no punctuation whatsoever in the Original Text.

NOTES

In other words, there was no such thing as periods, commas, colons, semi-colons, question marks, quotations, or paragraphs.

Therefore, the original translators had the tremendous difficulty of translating from one language to another. As well, they had to insert proper punctuation, which, within itself, was no light task, and Chapters and Verses.

(8) "THE LORD GOD HAS SWORN BY HIMSELF, SAYS THE LORD THE GOD OF HOSTS, I ABHOR THE EXCELLENCY OF JACOB, AND HATE HIS PALACES: THEREFORE WILL I DELIVER UP THE CITY WITH ALL THAT IS THEREIN."

The exegesis is:

1. *"The Lord GOD has sworn by Himself,"* speaks of the threat proceeding directly from Him. It is, therefore, immutable.

2. The balance of Verse 8 does not mean that God hates prosperity, but that He hates prosperity that is not gained by His Hand.

3. The idea is, at this time, the time of the Prophecies of Amos, Israel claimed that all was well with the Lord when, in reality, nothing was well!

THE HATRED OF THE LORD

The Lord hates all things that do not originate with Him. I think that can be said without fear of contradiction.

For the Lord to accept a thing, whatever that thing might be, it first of all must be originated by Him. It then must be given birth by Him, instituted by Him, and carried out by Him. Man can only be a willing instrument. In fact, he cannot originate anything within himself and think that it is the doings of the Lord.

All of this means that all Salvation, that is, if it's truly Salvation, comes totally and completely from the Lord. The same can be said for all Sanctification.

SANCTIFICATION

Most Christians would readily agree that all Salvation must come from the Lord; however, when it comes to Sanctification, most of the church seeks to sanctify themselves.

We must understand that the entirety of the Epistle to the Galatians was written by Paul to address this lie. Due to the false gospel of the Judaizers, the Galatians had now been brought to the place that they believed that their *"Salvation"* was by Grace, but their *"Sanctification"* was by self. Nothing could be further from the truth as it regarded Sanctification by self.

Let us say it again because it is so very, very important.

Everything we receive from the Lord comes from the Lord Jesus Christ as the Source and the Cross as the Means. In other words, everything that the Lord gives us, all and without exception, is made possible by the Cross of Christ. This necessitates, even demands, that our Faith be exclusively in Christ and the Cross and in nothing else. This is the road to Sanctification, prosperity, and all Blessing. When we place our Faith exclusively in Christ and the Cross, and maintain it in Christ and the Cross, then the Holy Spirit, Who is God, and Who can do anything, will work mightily on our behalf (Rom. 8:1-2, 10-11; I Cor. 1:17-18, 23; 2:2).

(9) "AND IT SHALL COME TO PASS, IF THERE REMAIN TEN MEN IN ONE HOUSE, THAT THEY SHALL DIE."

The structure is:

1. Verse 9 tells us that pestilence would accompany captivity, or follow it, so deadly that even a large family of ten persons should have but one survivor, if that!

2. There is no record that the people, upon hearing these words given by Amos, gave them any serious consideration. It is amazing at the ability of man to resist the Holy Spirit. It is because of the Fall.

3. Despite ignoring the Word of the Lord, still, the Lord, even though He knows what their reaction will be, continues to give warning.

THE JUDGMENT

The degree of the Judgment was to be so severe as to literally annihilate the kingdom as a Nation. Whereas, some few of the people would survive, enough to keep alive the various Tribes, still, that which was coming was beyond their wildest imagination. In fact, they simply did not believe Amos, as the world today does not believe there is a Judgment coming.

But, come it shall!

THE MODERN CHURCH

Tragically, the modern church little believes anymore that a Great Tribulation is coming, even as given by Christ (Mat. 24:21).

The entirety of the Book of Revelation spells out exactly what is coming upon this world (Chpts. 6-19). However, the modern church attempts to explain it away or deny it altogether. Nevertheless, and to be sure, a Great Tribulation, some seven years in duration, is coming upon this world. When it is concluded, even as the Word of God relates to us, possibly one half of the entirety of the population, or even more, will die. One thing is certain, however, what the Bible says is going to come to pass most definitely is going to come to pass.

Why is it that men, even those who claim to be Believers, disbelieve the Word of God?

Religious men devise their own religious schemes, diverse from the Word of God, and they are loath to admit that what they are claiming is not Scriptural. So, they ignore the Word of God altogether or else try to twist the Scriptures to mean something that they never intended.

Religious men love to give birth to their own religious predictions, little caring what the Word of God actually says. In fact, at this present time (2010), the modern church is all but Biblically illiterate. In other words, the Bible, the Word of God, has less place in the modern church than at any time in its existence, at least, since the Reformation. That is tragic but true.

(10) "AND A MAN'S UNCLE SHALL TAKE HIM UP, AND HE WHO BURNS HIM, TO BRING OUT THE BONES OUT OF THE HOUSE, AND SHALL SAY UNTO HIM WHO IS BY THE SIDES OF THE HOUSE, IS THERE YET ANY WITH YOU? AND HE SHALL SAY, NO. THEN SHALL HE SAY, HOLD YOUR TONGUE: FOR WE MAY NOT MAKE MENTION OF THE NAME OF THE LORD."

The structure is:

1. The phrase, *"For we may not make mention of the Name of the LORD,"* refers to the fact that so conscious would be the survivors that it was a Divine Judgment, they would feel that they dare not use the

ordinary language of Spiritual consolation uttered at funerals.

2. Consequently, when this Judgment would come, it would be too late to call upon God. It will be the time of vengeance. They rejected Him in life and may not cry to Him in death.

3. The idea is that such a fear will rest within their hearts that by the invocation of the Name of God, His Eye should be drawn toward this last remaining one, and he, also, should fall a victim to the Judgment of death.

THE PRECIOUS FEW

As an Evangelist, and as I read these words, a great sadness fills my heart. It is a sadness for Israel of old and a sadness for the modern church as well!

As Charles Finney said in his day, and sadly, it was true, only a small fraction of the people who claimed to live for God actually did so! Sadder still, such is true presently!

In too many lives, the Lord is merely an asterisk or an addendum. In other words, just a small add-on.

Sometime ago, a dear brother, who travels from church to church, said to me, *"Brother Swaggart, for the most part, the people do not want revival. They are satisfied to take care of their religious obligation by attending church once a week, if that, but have little or no relationship with Christ."*

He then went on to say that there were some few exceptions, but precious few!

However, if that *"precious few,"* which the Bible calls a *"Remnant,"* will *"humble themselves, and pray, and seek God's Face, and turn from their wicked ways,"* the Lord has promised, *"then will I hear from Heaven, and will forgive their sin, and will heal their land"* (II Chron. 7:14).

(11) "FOR, BEHOLD, THE LORD COMMANDS, AND HE WILL SMITE THE GREAT HOUSE WITH BREACHES, AND THE LITTLE HOUSE WITH CLEFTS."

The exegesis is:

1. The phrase, *"For, behold, the LORD commands,"* refers to Him executing what He commands.

2. The *"great house"* pertains to the Ten Tribes of the northern kingdom.

3. The *"little house"* refers to the Two

Tribes of the southern kingdom.

BOTH NATIONS

In this Eleventh Verse, the Lord predicts Judgment on both the northern kingdom of Israel and the southern kingdom of Judah. He does this even though the southern kingdom will not experience Judgment as quickly as the northern kingdom. In fact, it would be over 130 years after the destruction of the northern kingdom before the southern kingdom would experience destruction.

The northern kingdom did not have one godly king, while the southern kingdom was blessed with a few, namely Hezekiah, Jehoshaphat, and Josiah. Under these men, Judah experienced Revival to some degree. Unfortunately, after Josiah, there were no godly kings, and despite the prophesying of Jeremiah, Judah ultimately went to her doom.

WHY THE ACUTE UNBELIEF?

That's a good question.

While unbelief affects the entirety of society, most of the time, when it is addressed in the Word of God, it is speaking of those who claim to be Believers.

The way is very clear, very obvious, and open. Paul said:

"Take heed, brethren *(proclaims Paul warning Believers by the examples of Israel's failures in the wilderness)***, lest there be in any of you an evil heart of unbelief** *(the Greek order of words is, 'a heart evil with reference to unbelief')***, in departing from the Living God.** *(As stated, the problem is unbelief, and in modern terminology it refers to unbelief in Christ and the Cross)***"** (Heb. 3:12).

UNBELIEF AND THE CROSS

When the Holy Spirit through Paul gave us the warning about unbelief, as stated in the notes, he was speaking of a departure from the Cross of Christ to other things. How do we know that's what he was addressing? He continues, **"For we are made partakers of Christ** *(refers to Rom. 6:3-5)***, if we hold the beginning of our confidence stedfast unto the end** *(if our confidence remains steadfast in Christ and the Cross)***"** (Heb. 3:14).

The only way that one can be a *"partaker of Christ"* is by exhibiting Faith in Him and what He did for us at the Cross (Jn. 6:53). Please note the following very carefully:

• The only thing standing between mankind and eternal Hell is the Cross of Christ.

• The only thing standing between the Judgment of God and sinful man is the Cross of Christ.

• There is only one place that a thrice-Holy God can meet with sinful man, and that is the Cross of Christ.

Now, if the above is true, and if you know anything about your Bible, you know that it is true, then we must understand that the very center and circumference of Redemption is all wrapped up in Christ and what Christ did for us at the Cross.

Whenever the church begins to lose the Message of the Cross, that's when it begins to lose its way. This is where unbelief comes in, thereby, breeding deceitfulness, etc. Please understand that there is only one answer for sin, and that is the Cross of Christ. Mankind tries to address the problem of sin in many and various ways, all having failed, as all must fail. As stated, there is only one answer for this dread malady, one solution to this problem, and that is the Cross of Christ.

(12) "SHALL HORSES RUN UPON THE ROCK? WILL ONE PLOW THERE WITH OXEN? FOR YOU HAVE TURNED JUDGMENT INTO GALL, AND THE FRUIT OF RIGHTEOUSNESS INTO HEMLOCK."

The exegesis is:

1. *"For we have turned Judgment into gall, and the fruit of Righteousness into hemlock,"* refers to Israel turning the Word of God, and all that it promised, against themselves instead of for themselves.

2. Obedience brings blessing, while disobedience brings the opposite!

3. By the Holy Spirit addressing Israel with the questions, *"Shall horses run upon the rock? Will one plow there with oxen?"* it is meant to proclaim the fact that such cannot be done. So, the direction that Israel was heading could not contain Righteousness.

A CHURCH WITHOUT THE CROSS

Without the Message of the Cross, which is *"The Message,"* the church has no purpose.

The reason is simple:

The Cross of Christ is the only answer for mankind, so, if the church doesn't preach the Cross, then whatever it is that it is preaching is of no consequence.

Let's use as an example a thousand people who have a terminal disease. In other words, they are dying. The Church has the solution for that disease, which is the Cross of Christ, but instead, the church is giving them popsicles.

What good does it do to give a drowning man a new suit of clothes when he needs a life raft?

That's where humanity is. It needs the answer, which the Lord Alone can give, which is the Message of the Cross. Instead, it is getting everything but!

(13) "YOU WHO REJOICE IN A THING OF NOUGHT, WHO SAY, HAVE WE NOT TAKEN TO US HORNS BY OUR OWN STRENGTH?"

The exegesis is:

1. *"You who rejoice in a thing of naught,"* pertains to Israel trusting idols.

2. The question, *"Have we not taken to us horns by our own strength?"* refers to military strength and Israel's belief that they were impregnable.

3. Their boast was a consequence of the successful wars with the Syrians (II Ki. 14:25-28). The Prophet proceeds to demolish their proud vaunt.

(14) "BUT, BEHOLD, I WILL RAISE UP AGAINST YOU A NATION, O HOUSE OF ISRAEL, SAYS THE LORD THE GOD OF HOSTS; AND THEY SHALL AFFLICT YOU FROM THE ENTERING IN OF HEMATH UNTO THE RIVER OF THE WILDERNESS."

The overview is:

1. The first phrase of Verse 14 refers to the Assyrians.

2. The last phrase of the Verse predicts the entirety of Israel being wrecked by the Assyrians.

3. We find from these Passages that the Lord is able to raise up or bring down.

4. For those who walk in pride, God knows how to destroy.

"The Love of Christ constrains;

"Oh, let the watchword ring,
"Till all the word adoring,
"To Jesus' Feet it bring.
"Till north and south the kingdoms,
"Shall own His glorious Sway,
"And east and west the nations,
"Rejoice to see His Day."

"The Love of Christ constrains;
"At home, abroad, wherever,
"By sea or shore abiding,
"His Name and Sign we bear.
"We ask not that our service,
"Or great or small may be,
"If only You will own it,
"Dear Lord, as unto Thee."

"The Love of Christ constrains;
"And we who trust His Word.
"Who know and feel its Power,
"To gladder service stirred,
"Shall neither faint nor falter,
"Though dark the night and long,
"And weak our hands that labor,
"His Strength shall make us strong."

"The Love of Christ constrains,
"Then let us work and pray,
"And watch the glad appearing,
"Of that triumphant day,
"When Father, Son, and Spirit,
"By every tongue confessed,
"All Earth His broad Dominion,
"In His dear Love shall rest."

CHAPTER 7

(1) "THUS HAS THE LORD GOD SHOWED UNTO ME; AND, BEHOLD, HE FORMED GRASSHOPPERS IN THE BEGINNING OF THE SHOOTING UP OF THE LATTER GROWTH; AND, LO, IT WAS THE LATTER GROWTH AFTER THE KING'S MOWINGS."

The diagram is:

1. The revelation of the first nine Verses of this Chapter is: persistence in evil, after repeated forgiveness, will ultimately meet with eternal Judgment.

2. The first phrase of the Verse refers to locusts coming upon the harvest.

3. The latter phrase refers to the king taking the first crop of hay and the locusts taking the second, with nothing remaining for the unhappy people.

4. The entirety of this Verse points to the moral Government of God, Who uses Nature to work His Purposes.

THE REVELATION OF THE LORD

The Lord showed Amos how that the king would take his part of the crops as taxes, which was about half, with the Lord then using grasshoppers to take the other half. As would be obvious, there was nothing left for the people. Why would the Lord desire to do this?

He doesn't desire to do it! In fact, He does many things before it comes to such Judgment, hopefully, to turn His People around. However, when He does such, it is only as a matter of last resort, using stern measures in order to turn the people back to God. Regrettably, it seldom works!

WILL GOD SEND JUDGMENT UPON AMERICA?

He is already doing so!

I refer to inclement weather, such as hurricanes, tornadoes, etc. As well, I refer to the ruptured oil pipe off the coast of Louisiana that has spewed hundreds of millions of barrels of oil into the Gulf. In fact, the list could go on and on.

No matter how consecrated and godly the Church might be, still, there is enough sin being committed in any state and in any country in the world that it demands Judgment. However, such Judgment can either be little or large, all according to the spiritual condition of the Church. Regrettably, the church, and I speak of the church all over the world, is in worse spiritual condition presently than at any time since the Reformation half a millennia ago. Now, of course, there are some few Churches on fire for God, which means the Pastors are on fire for God, and are doing their very best to reach this world for Christ. However, that number is smaller than ever and getting smaller almost by the day.

If one pulls aside the churches which are immersed in the *"Purpose Driven Life"*

NOTES

scheme, the *"Seeker Sensitive"* scheme, or the *"Word of Faith,"* which is no faith at all, at least, that God will recognize, plus other weird doctrines, not much is left.

To be sure, precious few people enjoy reading words of this nature, much less hearing it preached and taught. Nevertheless, what we are saying is the truth. Concerning these last days, Paul stated:

ITCHING EARS

"For the time will come when they will not endure sound Doctrine (*'sound Doctrine' pertains to overriding principles: the Salvation of the sinner and the Sanctification of the Saint; the Cross is the answer for both, and is the only answer for both*); **but after their own lusts shall they heap to themselves teachers, having itching ears** (*refers to the people who have ears that 'itch' for the smooth and comfortable word, and are willing to reward handsomely the man who is sufficiently compromising to speak it; hearers of this type have rejected the Truth and prefer to hear the lie*);

"And they shall turn away *their* ears from the Truth (*those who follow false teachers not only turn away their ears from the Truth, but see to it that the ears are always in a position such that they will never come in contact with the Truth*), **and shall be turned unto fables.** (*If it's not the 'Message of the Cross,' then it is 'fables' [I Cor. 1:18]*)" **(II Tim. 4:3-4).**

THE ONLY CORRECT DOCTRINE IS THE CROSS OF CHRIST

If the preacher is not preaching the Cross, then whatever it is he is preaching, while it may be very clever and very educated, still, it's not the Gospel. Paul said:

"For Christ sent me not to baptize (*presents to us a Cardinal Truth*), **but to preach the Gospel** (*the manner in which one may be Saved from sin*): **not with wisdom of words** (*intellectualism is not the Gospel*), **lest the Cross of Christ should be made of none effect.** (*This tells us in no uncertain terms that the Cross of Christ must always be the emphasis of the Message*)" **(I Cor. 1:17).**

The Apostle went on to say, **"For the preaching** (*Word*) **of the Cross is to them who perish foolishness** (*Spiritual things cannot be discerned by unredeemed people, but that doesn't matter; the Cross must be preached just the same, even as we shall see*); **but unto us who are Saved it is the Power of God.** (*The Cross is the Power of God simply because it was there that the total sin debt was paid, giving the Holy Spirit, in Whom the Power resides, latitude to work mightily within our lives*)" **(I Cor. 1:18).**

Then the Apostle said, **"But we preach Christ Crucified** (*this is the Foundation of the Word of God and, thereby, of Salvation*), **unto the Jews a stumblingblock** (*the Cross was the stumblingblock*), **and unto the Greeks foolishness** (*both found it difficult to accept as God a dead Man hanging on a Cross, for such Christ was to them*)" **(I Cor. 1:23).**

Many preachers today refuse to preach the Cross, the Blood, etc., because they say it *"might offend people."* This Twenty-third Verse is Paul's answer to such stupidity. It wasn't primary to the Apostle that the Cross of Christ was a stumblingblock to the Jews, or foolishness to the Greeks (Gentiles), still, he preached *"Christ Crucified,"* simply because that was the answer and, in fact, the only answer.

And finally the Apostle said, **"For I determined not to know anything among you** (*with purpose and design, Paul did not resort to the knowledge or philosophy of the world regarding the preaching of the Gospel*), **save Jesus Christ, and Him Crucified** (*that and that alone is the Message, which will save the sinner, set the captive free, and give the Believer perpetual victory*)" **(I Cor. 2:2).**

I believe we unmistakably learn from all of this as to what the Gospel of Jesus Christ really is. Let's say it again:

• Jesus Christ is the Source of all things we receive from God (Jn. 1:1-2, 14, 29; Col. 2:10-15).

• The Cross of Christ is the Means by which these things are given to us (Rom. 6:3-5; I Cor. 1:17-18; 2:2; Gal. 6:14).

• The Cross of Christ must ever be the Object of our Faith (Rom. 6:1-14; Gal., Chpt. 5).

• The Holy Spirit superintends all of this (Rom. 8:1-2, 10-11; Eph. 2:13-18).

(2) "AND IT CAME TO PASS, THAT WHEN THEY HAD MADE AN END OF EATING THE GRASS OF THE LAND, THEN I SAID, O LORD GOD, FORGIVE, I BESEECH YOU: BY WHOM SHALL JACOB ARISE? FOR HE IS SMALL."

The exposition is:

1. When praying for personal pardon, sin should be magnified. When pleading for the pardon of a neighbor, sin should be minimized.

2. The first phrase of Verse 2 refers to the exhaustion of all sustenance, with no one to help them but the Lord. And sadly, they had no right to ask Him for anything because they had sinned greatly against Him.

3. The last phrase records Amos acting as an Intercessor on behalf of this hapless people, which the Lord graciously answered because He is a God of Mercy.

AMOS, THE INTERCESSOR

Having heard the tremendous pronouncements regarding coming Judgment and that almost all would be killed, he could not see how the people could survive at all. Therefore, in his mind, it seemed that the Lord, because of the great sins of the people and their refusal to repent, would totally annihilate them, not only as a Nation but as a people. In other words, *"Jacob"* will be no more!

His prayer is somewhat like the prayer of Moses of old, who cried to God when the Lord threatened Judgment upon the entirety of the people He had delivered from Egypt.

Moses said to the Lord that day, *". . . Oh, this people have sinned a great sin, and have made them gods of gold."*

"Yet now, if You will forgive their sin; and if not, blot me, I pray You, out of Your Book which You have written" (Ex. 32:31-32).

Amos, not carrying it as far as Moses, still, entered into great Intercession for a people who would not live for God and, in fact, hated Amos as well!

He pleads that *"Jacob"* will be totally exterminated if the Lord carries through these predictions.

WHY DID THE PEOPLE OF THAT DAY HATE AMOS SO MUCH?

If the person doesn't like the message,

they will find fault with the messenger, and there is always fault to be found in some way.

As we stated in the Introduction to this Book, Amos is said to have been relatively uneducated. In fact, his main occupation was a herdsman and a gatherer of sycamore fruit, which meant that he most definitely was not of the aristocracy of Israel. He was a man who worked with his hands. So, no doubt, the aristocracy of Israel looked at him, instantly found fault with him, and determined not to heed the things he said. *"How could this country bumpkin tell them anything?"* they must have mused!

However, as we now know, every Word that Amos uttered at that time, concerning the coming Judgment of the northern kingdom of Israel, was, in fact, the Word of God, and would come to pass exactly as stated in all of its horror. It is almost positive that Amos did not live to see this happen, but happen it did!

The truth is, everything any Preacher proclaims must be judged according to the Word of God. Is it Scriptural? If it is Scriptural, we had best pay heed, irrespective as to who the individual might be.

(3) "THE LORD REPENTED FOR THIS: IT SHALL NOT BE, SAYS THE LORD."

The construction is:

1. The first phrase of Verse 3 literally means that God changed His Direction.

2. The use of the word *"repent,"* at least as it refers to the Lord, infers no wrongdoing whatsoever on His Part. It merely means that He wills a change without changing His Will; for that He cannot do.

3. *"It shall not be, says the LORD,"* concerns this particular destruction, in this particular way, but not the overall thrust of the Judgment, barring the people's Repentance.

THE REPENTANCE OF THE LORD

As we have stated, the word *"repented,"* as it refers to the Lord, in no way means that the Lord has done anything wrong, for that cannot be. It merely means, as stated, that He has changed His Direction.

God has ordained Laws to the degree that He governs Himself. His Way is that most

NOTES

of the time, whatever it is that He does is according to what people do. He willed it in the very beginning, and I speak of the Creation of man. If man obeys God's Word, the Lord will do certain things concerning Blessing. If man disobeys God's Word, the Lord will do certain things based on that, such as sending Judgment, etc.

As it regards God and the Laws that He has devised, by which He governs everything, even Himself, that will never change. In fact, the Lord said through the great Prophet Malachi, *"For I am the LORD, I change not; therefore you sons of Jacob are not consumed"* (Mal. 3:6).

IT SHALL NOT BE, SAYS THE LORD

The phrase, *"It shall not be, says the LORD,"* did not mean that Judgment was not going to come upon the northern kingdom of Israel, barring Repentance. It just meant that the Lord would lessen that Judgment somewhat. It would still be awful, to say the least!

Even though the people had no regard for Amos and, no doubt, treated him very shabbily, still, he was crying to God on their behalf. He was definitely able to effect some good as it regarded the Nation as a whole and what would happen in the future. Regrettably and sadly, none of this made any difference to Israel, for they would not repent!

INTERCESSION

Intercession speaks of Believers who cry to God on behalf of particular individuals, circumstances, or even an entire nation. The Lord, weighing heavily the petition of His Saints, oftentimes will stop the course of events in answer to such prayer.

Tragically, there is presently very little of such Intercession in the modern church. Most have little knowledge as to what prayer is all about. The modern church has been so psychologized, which, of necessity, pulls men away from the Bible, that it little believes in the great Truths here expounded.

As well, another great segment of the church, which claims great Faith, does not even believe in seeking the Lord thusly, claiming that one only has to confess certain situations into reality.

Such teaching takes the leadership out of the Hands of God and places it into the faltering hands of mere mortals, which the Lord will never accept. Jesus said to His prospective Disciples, *"Follow Me!"* There is no place in the Bible where it even hints of Him following the Disciples or anyone else, for that matter!

When petition is made, such as Amos, Abraham (Gen., Chpt. 18), Moses (Ex., Chpt. 32), and Paul (Phil. 4:6) made, the Lord will do all He can do, outside of negating His Will. This is because of the *"Authority of the Believer,"* which is freely given by Christ. Therefore, circumstances and situations are often changed by individuals interceding before God.

Consequently, any village, city, or country, having godly people within its boundaries, is tremendously blessed, as here Israel was blessed by Amos. Tragically, the people seldom recognize the Children of God as such, and often try to hinder them.

(4) "THUS HAS THE LORD GOD SHOWED UNTO ME: AND, BEHOLD, THE LORD GOD CALLED TO CONTEND BY FIRE, AND IT DEVOURED THE GREAT DEEP, AND DID EAT UP A PART."

The structure is:

1. *"Thus has the Lord GOD showed unto me,"* refers to a further Judgment that had been decided in the high Counsels of Heaven against Israel.

2. It was a *"Judgment by fire,"* and was to be so great that it would *"devour the great deep,"* which means to drink up the very ocean itself.

3. As bad as this seems, due to the prayer of Amos, it appears that this Judgment was lessened in its intensity dramatically so. Therefore, the people were given more time to repent, which, sadly, they did not.

GOD CONTROLS ALL . . .

Probably the particular calamity alluded to is the second invasion of Tiglath-Pileser II, when he conquered Gilead and the northern part of the kingdom and carried some of the people captive to Assyria (II Ki. 15:29).

Due to the prayer of Amos, it seems that this invasion, which was originally intended to be much more severe, was lessened in its intensity, and dramatically so. Perhaps it was not only lessened in intensity but delayed, as well, giving Israel more time. Of course, the Lord knew that none of this would effect any positive results, but He did it just the same.

(5) "THEN SAID I, O LORD GOD, CEASE, I BESEECH YOU: BY WHOM SHALL JACOB ARISE? FOR HE IS SMALL."

The composition is:

1. The petition of Verse 5 is the same as Verse 2, except Jacob says here, "cease," instead of "forgive."

2. Actually, the word "cease" fits perfectly in that the second invasion of Tiglath-Pileser II was cut short, no doubt, in answer to this prayer.

3. Amos looked beyond the aristocracy of Israel who hated him and, instead, saw the Nation as a whole. Thus, he interceded!

(6) "THE LORD REPENTED FOR THIS: THIS ALSO SHALL NOT BE, SAYS THE LORD GOD."

The synopsis is:

1. Once again, Amos importunes, and once again, the Lord answers.

2. All of this is similar to that which Abraham asked of the Lord concerning Sodom and Gomorrah (Gen., Chpt. 18).

3. In all of this, we see the Mercy of God, with the Lord, it seems, looking for any excuse to show His Mercy. What a wonderful Lord we serve!

(7) "THUS HE SHOWED ME: AND, BEHOLD, THE LORD STOOD UPON A WALL MADE BY A PLUMBLINE, WITH A PLUMBLINE IN HIS HAND."

The composition is:

1. Every evidence is that Amos actually saw the Lord in a Vision.

2. "And, behold, the LORD stood upon a wall made by a plumbline," actually speaks of the "wall" as the kingdom of Israel, once carefully built up, solidly constructed, and accurately arranged.

3. In effect, the Lord is saying that Israel, from henceforth, will have to measure up to the "plumbline," and that all the Mercy that could be shown to Israel, due to the petitions of Amos, had been shown, and could not be extended.

NOTES

THE PLUMBLINE

The "plumbline" is the Word of God. And it should be quickly added, there is no other plumbline.

The "plumbline" is a builder's tool used to ascertain that the work is even and perpendicular, meaning "exactly upright."

The phrase, "With a plumbline in His Hand," actually pertains to symbolism!

Ultimately, the "plumbline" of the Word of God must be applied to every single individual, situation, or circumstance. The Lord will show Mercy as long as is possible, particularly, according to the petition of His People. But, still, the Word of God is the ultimate authority and, sooner or later, must be applied.

If it wasn't, chaos would ultimately prevail, with the whole of humanity ultimately being destroyed. Therefore, the "plumbline," i.e., Word of God, is, within itself, an act of Mercy, as should be obvious.

THE PLUMBLINE IS ALSO THE MESSAGE OF THE CROSS

In effect, the "Word of God" and the "Message of the Cross" are one and the same. The great Atoning Work at Calvary is the story of the entirety of the Word of God. It is where our Lord gave Himself as a Sacrifice, shedding His Life's Blood, which atoned for every sin. Everything bends toward the great Redemption Plan of God. In fact, that great Plan was formulated by the Godhead from before the foundation of the world, which also means that it was long before man was ever created (I Pet. 1:18-20).

While the Lord gave to Moses the great Law, it was to Paul that He gave the meaning of the New Covenant, which, in effect, is the meaning of the Cross. It is that to which every Sage, every Prophet, and every Patriarch pointed. Of the millions of lambs offered in sacrifice, which began on the first page of human history (Gen., Chpt. 4), all were a symbol of the Cross of Christ. So, the Word of God is saturated with blood, the blood of innocent victims, all symbolizing the Blood of the most innocent One, which would be shed for you and me. We speak, of course, of the Lord Jesus Christ.

The truth is, the following must be noted as it regards the Cross:

• The Believer never matures beyond the Cross! In other words, according to one's knowledge of the Cross is their maturity (I Cor., Chpt. 2).

• It cost God's Son everything to redeem humanity, but it cost us nothing (Jn. 3:16).

• The only alternative to the Cross is to fall back once again upon one's own resources, which guarantees defeat (Rom. 8:10).

• It is very obvious as to how Paul looked at the Message of the Cross by the way he introduced his Epistle to the Galatians (Gal., Chpt. 1).

• Turning from the Cross of Christ means to turn from the only way of coming to God and the only way of having fellowship with God (Rom. 6:3-5, 11).

• When we look at all the wonderful things the Lord has done for us in this Christian life, we must realize that they haven't come to us because of our efforts. They were all made possible by the Cross of Christ (Col. 2:10-15).

• Paul accused the Galatians who had turned from the Cross, which means to turn from Grace and, thereby, to Law, as being *"bewitched"* (Gal. 3:1).

• The Cross of Christ tells us that God is for us and not against us (Rom. 8:2).

• Why Christ Crucified? It is because a perfect substitute was needed in order to reconcile man to God. The Cross alone could do that (Jn. 1:1-2, 14, 29)!

• Fear is dispelled in no other way but by the Cross of Christ.

• The Cross of Christ is the only thing that stands between man and eternal Hell (Jn. 3:16).

• A thrice-Holy God can meet sinful man only in one place, and that is the Cross of Christ (I Cor. 2:2).

• The infinite Son of God became Man, hung upon a Cross, and was made a curse by God, so that you and I might not be cursed, but rather be free from the curse (Gal. 3:13).

• The Gospel of Jesus Christ is not something that is based upon our changing moods, but is rather anchored in the Cross of Christ, which will never change. It

NOTES

is called by Paul, *"The Everlasting Gospel"* (Heb. 13:20).

• The Gospel of Jesus Christ is not based upon our moral condition; it is based on His Moral Condition (Heb. 7:26).

• It is not my worth but the Worth of Christ that saves us, and did so by the Cross (Heb. 1:3).

• Irrespective of all the claims, there are, in fact, only two religions in the world, the religion of the Law and the Gospel of Grace (Rom. 6:14).

• There is freedom in the Cross of Christ, and there is freedom only in the Cross of Christ (Rom. 8:1-2).

• The Good News of the Gospel declares you must get rid of the idea that you can do anything to be accepted by God! It is one hundred percent Christ and what He did for us at the Cross, and our Faith in that Finished Work (Eph. 2:8-9).

• The only thing that stands between sinful man and the Judgment of God is the Cross of Christ (I Cor. 1:17).

• Understanding that the Cross of Christ is the sinew, which holds the fabric of the Gospel together, should it not be understandable that we *"preach the Cross"* (I Cor. 1:23)?!

(8) "AND THE LORD SAID UNTO ME, AMOS, WHAT DO YOU SEE? AND I SAID, A PLUMBLINE. THEN SAID THE LORD, BEHOLD, I WILL SET A PLUMBLINE IN THE MIDST OF MY PEOPLE ISRAEL: I WILL NOT AGAIN PASS BY THEM ANY MORE."

The exegesis is:

1. The first phrase of Verse 8 portrays the intimacy of the fellowship between Immanuel and the Prophet, and appears with peculiar sweetness in the Prophet being addressed as *"Amos"* (Jn. 10:3).

2. *"I will not again pass by them anymore,"* means He would not spare or forgive anymore, and the Prophet is, thereby, instructed to intercede no more.

3. The Judgment is irremediable, with the final conquest by Shalmaneser typified here.

EVERYTHING JUDGED BY THE PLUMBLINE

This means, as previously stated, that everything is judged by the Word of God.

If I remember correctly, the year was 1992. In 1991, in the month of October, the Lord instructed me to begin two prayer meetings a day, morning and night. This we instituted immediately, with the exception of Wednesday and Sunday nights, which were Service times. We did this with a small group from Family Worship Center, meeting at 10 a.m. each morning and 6:30 p.m. each evening. Even though the times have changed somewhat, I continue this regimen on a personal basis even unto this hour.

At that time, the Lord only told me one thing. He said to me, *"Do not seek Me so much for what I can do, but rather for Who I am."* So, these prayer meetings were begun on that basis, which, as is obvious, was an establishment of greater relationship.

About a year passed, and even though I was greatly blessed in these prayer meetings, still, I could not honestly say that the Lord had done anything great in my life. In fact, I did not even really know that for which I was praying. I was just going before the Lord each morning and each night and, as stated, was greatly blessed, but I could see nothing tangible.

DISCOURAGED

At a point in time, I began to ask the Lord as to why it was taking so long. Little did I know or realize at that time that it would be another five years before the Lord would perform a great Work in my life and Ministry by giving me a Revelation of the Cross, which, in effect, was that which had already been given to the Apostle Paul.

At any rate, at that particular time in 1992, I asked the Lord as to why it was taking so long? And yet, and, as stated, I didn't even really know that for which I was seeking.

I sought the Lord, I suppose, for several weeks about this thing, but no answer came. I went on day after day and night after night, seeking the Lord as I had been doing, and finally forgetting the petition I had made to Him about the delay. Then, one particular night at prayer meeting, the Lord gave me an answer.

He brought it all back to me as to exactly what I had asked and then answered me.

NOTES

PRECEPT MUST BE UPON PRECEPT, LINE UPON LINE

The Lord said to me, *"You have asked as to why it is taking so long? This is My Answer to you:"*

He said, *"For precept must be upon precept, precept upon precept; line upon line, line upon line; here a little, and there a little"* (Isa. 28:10).

As the Presence of the Lord covered me, I knew that what I had received was from the Lord, but I didn't understand it. To me, at that time, this was a most strange Verse attempting to explain something. And yet, as I continued to pray about it, I came to the place that I felt I knew what the Lord was telling me. It was:

• The phrase, *"For precept must be upon precept, precept upon precept; line upon line, line upon line,"* proclaimed the fact that everything in my life and Ministry must line up perfectly with the Word of God. When the Lord says something once, it is of extreme significance; however, when He says it four times, then its significance cannot be measured.

• The phrase, *"Here a little, and there a little,"* ultimately let me know that what the Lord would do would be *a little here and a little there,"* until the Work was completed.

This is the *"Plumbline"* demanded by the Lord, not only of me, but of all who proclaim His Name.

THE WORD OF THE LORD

The attention of Amos is drawn to the *"Plumbline,"* specifying that Israel must measure up to this line, which, in fact, she could not!

The phrase, *"And I said, A plumbline,"* refers to the lesson taught to the Prophet by symbolism, which means that all must measure up to the Word of God or else be destroyed. Everything built on the Word, which is the Rock, will stand; everything built on anything other than the Word, i.e., *"the Rock,"* will fall. As well, the *"plumbline"* is used not only for building but also for pulling down.

This is actually what the seven churches of Asia were measured by, and with the verdict given by Christ Himself (Rev., Chpts. 2-3).

MY PEOPLE

The phrase, *"Then said the LORD, Behold, I will set a plumbline in the midst of My People Israel,"* refers to the Lord, at least, for the first time in this Book, referring to Israel as *"My People."*

"The midst" referred to the city of Samaria, portraying that the Judgment would reach even to this fortified city. The first destruction fell on Gilead (Vs. 4) which was the frontier; the final Judgment upon Samaria, the capital.

Concerning all of this, in effect, the people had not sought forgiveness, having engaged in no repentance to speak of, with the Lord showing Mercy only according to the Intercession of the Prophet. Therefore, what is said is chilling, to say the least!

(9) "AND THE HIGH PLACES OF ISAAC SHALL BE DESOLATE, AND THE SANCTUARIES OF ISRAEL SHALL BE LAID WASTE; AND I WILL RISE AGAINST THE HOUSE OF JEROBOAM WITH THE SWORD."

The construction is:

1. The first phrase of Verse 9 refers to the entirety of Israel and ultimately was fulfilled to the letter.

2. The latter phrase was fulfilled, as well, as recorded in II Kings 15:10.

3. Although the Lord will bear long with His People, if, ultimately, Repentance is not forthcoming, Judgment will come.

THE JUDGMENT

As stated, all of this was fulfilled to the letter.

The northern kingdom of Israel was destroyed approximately 60 years from the time of the Prophecies of Amos. The kingdom of Judah was destroyed nearly 200 years from that particular time. So, in all of this, we can see the Mercy of God, especially, in giving warning many, many years before the Judgment would fall. But, regrettably, the warnings were little heeded, if at all.

At the present time, the Word of God plainly tells us that Judgment is coming upon this world in the form of tribulation

such as it has never known before. Jesus said it would be worse than ever had been (Mat. 24:21). But yet, most Christians do not believe this, choosing rather to believe a lie.

For instance, a great segment of the modern church teaches that no Judgment is coming, but rather the world is getting better and better, with Christianity becoming more and more dominant. However, the Bible doesn't teach anything of this nature. Rather, Paul said, **"This know also, that in the last days** (*the days in which we now live*) **perilous times shall come.** (*This speaks of difficult dangerous times, which Christians living just before the Rapture will encounter*)" **(II Tim. 3:1).** Paul said these particular times, as it regards the Church, would **". . . have a form of godliness** (*refers to all the trappings of Christianity but without the power*), **but denying the power thereof** (*the modern church, for all practical purposes, has denied the Cross; in doing this, they have denied that through which the Holy Spirit works, and in Whom the power resides [Rom. 8:1-2, 11; I Cor. 1:18]*): **from such turn away.** (*No half measures are to be adopted here. The command is clear! It means to turn away from churches that deny or ignore the Cross*)" **(II Tim. 3:5).**

He also said, **"For the time will come when they will not endure sound Doctrine** (*'sound Doctrine' pertains to overriding principles: the Salvation of the sinner and the Sanctification of the Saint; the Cross is the answer for both, and is the only answer for both*); **but after their own lusts shall they heap to themselves teachers, having itching ears** (*refers to the people who have ears that 'itch' for the smooth and comfortable word, and are willing to reward handsomely the man who is sufficiently compromising to speak it; hearers of this type have rejected the Truth and prefer to hear the lie*);

"And they shall turn away *their* **ears from the Truth** (*those who follow false teachers not only turn away their ears from the Truth, but see to it that the ears are always in a position such that they will never come in contact with the Truth*), **and shall be turned unto fables.** (*If it's not the*

'Message of the Cross,' then it is 'fables' [I Cor. 1:18])" **(II Tim. 4:3-4).**

THE CHURCH AT LAODICEA

In Chapters 2 and 3 of Revelation, our Lord proclaims seven Messages to the seven churches of Asia. Actually, this pertained to the entirety of the Church Age. The church at Laodicea epitomizes the modern church. Read carefully as to what Jesus said about this church. It parallels the modern church completely.

"And unto the Angel (Pastor) **of the church of the Laodiceans write** (this is the 'apostate church'; we do not know when it began, but we do know it has begun; it is the last church addressed by Christ, so that means the Rapture will take place very shortly)**; These things says the Amen, the faithful and true witness** (by contrast to His Church, which is not faithful and true)**, the beginning of the Creation of God** (Jesus is the Creator of all things)**."**

LUKEWARM

"I know your works, that you are neither cold nor hot (characterizes that which is prevalent at this present time)**: I would you were cold or hot** (half measures won't do).

"So then because you are lukewarm, and neither cold nor hot (if a person is lukewarm towards something, it means he hasn't rejected it, but at the same time, he has by no means accepted it; in the Mind of God, a tepid response is equal to a negative response)**, I will spue you out of My Mouth.** (There is no prospect of Repentance here on the part of this church, or Restoration. In fact, there is Divine rejection.)**"**

HAVE NEED OF NOTHING

"Because you say, I am rich, and increased with goods, and have need of nothing (they equated the increase in material goods with Spiritual Blessings, which they were not)**; and know not that you are wretched, and miserable, and poor, and blind, and naked** (the tragedy lay in the fact that while this church gloated over material wealth, she was unconscious of her spiritual poverty; again indicative of the modern church!)**."**

GOLD TRIED IN THE FIRE

"I counsel you to buy of Me gold tried in the fire, that you may be rich (what they needed to 'buy' could not be purchased with money, but only with the precious Blood of Christ, which price has already been paid; but the modern church is not interested!)**; and white raiment, that you may be clothed, and that the shame of your nakedness do not appear** (refers to Righteousness which is exclusively of Christ, and is gained only by Faith in Christ and the Cross; this tells us that the Laodicean church is extremely self-righteous; not having the Righteousness of Christ, they are 'naked' to the Judgment of God)**; and anoint your eyes with eyesalve, that you may see.** (The modern church is also spiritually blind.)**"**

CHASTISEMENT

"As many as I love, I rebuke and chasten (implies a remnant)**: be zealous therefore, and repent.** (The modern church desperately needs to repent for its rebellion against God's Divine Order [Christ and the Cross] and for following cunningly devised fables [II Pet. 1:16].)**"**

THE APPEAL OF OUR LORD

"Behold, I stand at the door, and knock (presents Christ outside the church)**: if any man hear My Voice** (so much religious racket is going on that it is difficult to 'hear His Voice')**, and open the door** (Christ is the True Door, which means the church has erected another door)**, I will come in to him, and will sup with him, and he with Me.** (Having been rejected by the church, our Lord now appeals to individuals, and He is still doing so presently.)**"**

HEAR WHAT THE SPIRIT IS SAYING

"To him who overcomes will I grant to sit with Me in My Throne (the overcomer will gain the prize of the Throne, which can only be done by one ever making the Cross the Object of his Faith)**, even as I also overcame, and am set down with My Father in His Throne.** (This presents Christ as our Substitute, going before us, and doing for us what we could not do for ourselves.)

"He who has an ear, let him hear what the

Spirit says unto the churches. *(In plain language, the Holy Spirit is saying, 'Come back to Christ and the Cross!')"* **(Rev. 3:14-22).**

(10) "THEN AMAZIAH THE PRIEST OF BETH-EL SENT TO JEROBOAM KING OF ISRAEL, SAYING, AMOS HAS CONSPIRED AGAINST YOU IN THE MIDST OF THE HOUSE OF ISRAEL: THE LAND IS NOT ABLE TO BEAR ALL HIS WORDS."

The overview is:

1. The first phrase of Verse 10 portrays the fact that the type of preaching done by Amos was out of place in the royal chapel. A state religion negates any civil and religious liberty. If it is of human origination, it cannot endure the testimony of Truth.

2. Not to be a member of the state church is to be, in a degree, a rebel. The king, being the head of the church, said that no religious teaching could be permitted that was displeasing to him and to the priests whom he appointed (I Ki. 12:31; 13:1-4).

3. Amaziah was one of these man-made priests. He was not of the House of Aaron. His charge that Amos predicted the death of the king was a falsehood. Amos predicted the doom of the *"house of Jeroboam."*

4. Verse 10 also means that at least some few of the Israelites had been convinced by the Prophet's words and had joined ranks with him. Hence, Amaziah speaks of a *"conspiracy"* against the king.

5. The phrase, *"The land is not able to bear all his words,"* reveals the effect the Ministry of Amos had on Israel. God give us more today as Amos!

AMAZIAH THE PRIEST

As we've already stated, Amaziah was no true Priest. His office had been devised by the king of Israel, which means it had no scriptural validity whatsoever.

Millions today follow in the train of Amaziah. They aren't called to preach and, in fact, look at the Ministry as a profession. Please understand the following:

The Call to preach the Gospel presents itself as the highest Calling on the face of the Earth because that Calling comes straight from the Throne of God. Any man or woman who is truly Called of God for one of the fivefold Ministry Offices (Eph. 4:11) would

have to step down to a much lower level to be the President of the United States. But far too many modern preachers, who have been truly Called of God, have abdicated, in other words, compromised their Calling. We live in an age when people have *"itching ears,"* meaning they really don't want to hear the Gospel of Jesus Christ, but rather a message that will make them feel good despite their sins (II Tim. 4:3-4). Unfortunately, there are plenty of preachers who are ready and willing to serve this purpose. In other words, they trim their message to where it is no longer the Word of God but only a religious overtone of their own making. Please read the following carefully:

If the world applauds our message, then something is badly wrong with our message. As someone has rightly said:

"The world loves its own, and its own loves the world."

A CONSPIRACY?

Amaziah the priest went to king Jeroboam, claiming that Amos was conspiring against him and the State of Israel, etc.

There was no conspiracy here whatsoever, only the delivery by Amos of the Word of God to Israel. Amos was telling Israel that they were going in the wrong direction, and if they continued in that direction, destruction would ultimately come, which would completely lay waste the Nation in every capacity. Admittedly, it wasn't a pleasant message to hear, but it just happened to be the truth.

Presently, when we state that homosexuality is a sin, we aren't conspiring against homosexuals. Homosexuals, as human beings, should be treated with the same respect that any other human being is treated. When we preach against alcoholism, that doesn't mean we are conspiring against alcoholics, or when we preach against drug addiction, it doesn't mean we are conspiring against addicts. We are merely saying that these things are wrong. We must always remember, Jesus loved the sinner while, at the same time, hating the sin (Jn. 3:16). But yet, the state is claiming that when we say that homosexuality is a sin against God and, as well, against mankind in general, we are engaging in *"hate speech."* Actually, there are powerful people in places of leadership in this nation, who would stop any Preacher of the Gospel from saying that anything is a sin. As stated, they want words that make them feel comfortable in their sin and, regrettably, they can find plenty of preachers who will function in that capacity. These elements aren't satisfied to merely oppose what true Preachers are saying, but they want to stop the voice of the Preacher as well.

CAIN AND ABEL

This spirit did not begin yesterday. Actually, it began on the first page of human history. Cain wasn't satisfied to say to Abel, whose sacrifice that God had accepted, that Abel could preach his message, and Cain could preach his. He had to stop the mouth of Abel, so he murdered his brother.

If the law of the land allowed such, there are untold thousands of preachers in this nation, who would stop every voice except their own and those who preach their message, whatever it might be. The only reason they don't do such is because they cannot do such.

One only has to go back to the Dark Ages and observe the Catholic church, who murdered all, or sought to do so, who would not acquiesce to the Pope. Please understand that the hearts of evil men have not changed, only the law that forbids them.

THE WORD OF THE LORD

The phrase, *"The land is not able to bear all his words,"* reveals the powerful effect the Prophecies of Amos had on Israel and the people at large.

In 1988, one of the religious leaders of the largest Pentecostal denomination in America stated to two of my associates, speaking of me personally, *"We will get him off of television, and we will use any method we have to use to do it!"*

They meant exactly what they said and, in fact, no effort was spared in order to carry out this task, despite the fact that hundreds of thousands of people were being brought to a Saving Knowledge of Jesus Christ.

Now, several decades later, and sadly so,

that religious denomination is all but bereft of the Moving and Operation of the Holy Spirit. It has embraced totally and completely the Purpose Driven Life scheme as well as other such like particulars.

While many things might be said and other so-called reasons supposedly given, the real reason they didn't like me was because of the message I preached. For instance, that particular denomination had embraced humanistic psychology in totality. We were standing on the largest television platform in the world pertaining to Gospel and saying that Jesus Christ Alone was and is the answer. They didn't want to hear that. So, that's the reason they wanted to stop our voice. Thank God, even though they were a tool in the hand of Satan and did everything they could do to carry out their threat, they were not able to do so. We give the Lord the praise and the glory for that.

No, Israel did not like the Message given by Amos simply because it was not what they wanted to hear. Man doesn't desire to be told he is wrong! He doesn't like to hear that he is going in the wrong direction. Most of the time, he wants to hear a message that will make him feel good about himself and, at the same time, allow him to remain in his sins. And, one more thing, I might quickly add:

When the church begins to preach the Cross, it's going to find opposition coming from both the world and religion.

WHY IS THE CROSS OF CHRIST AN OFFENSE?

Paul said, **"And I, brethren, if I yet preach Circumcision, why do I yet suffer persecution?** *(Any message other than the Cross draws little opposition.)* **then is the offense of the Cross ceased.** *(The Cross offends the world and most of the church. So, if the preacher ceases to preach the Cross as the only way of Salvation and Victory, then opposition and persecution will cease, but so will Salvation!)"* **(Gal. 5:11).**

The Cross of Christ is an offense to the world and to most of the church for particular reasons. Some of those reasons are:

• The Cross of Christ shows us how sinful and wicked that man actually is.

- The Cross of Christ shows us how loving that God is, considering that He would give His Only Begotten Son to die on a Cross in order that man might be Saved.
- The Cross of Christ is an offense because it exposes man's self-righteousness.
- The Cross of Christ is an offense because it shoots down all of man's ways to bring about Righteousness.
- The Cross of Christ is an offense because it tells man that it is the only way.
- When the Cross of Christ is accepted, allegiance to everything else falls by the wayside.
- The Cross of Christ proclaims the fact that, pure and simple, the flesh is incapable.
- The Cross of Christ draws attention solely to Christ, which, at the same time, exposes self.
- The Cross of Christ is altogether God's Way, which sets aside all of man's ways.

(11) "FOR THUS AMOS SAID, JEROBOAM SHALL DIE BY THE SWORD, AND ISRAEL SHALL SURELY BE LED AWAY CAPTIVE OUT OF THEIR OWN LAND."

The diagram is:

1. The first phrase of Verse 11 pertained to the false accusation of Amaziah that Amos had predicted the death of the king. He had only predicted the destruction of the *"house of Jeroboam with a sword"* (Vs. 9).

2. The latter phrase of Verse 11 was correct in that it predicted the captivity of Israel.

3. Such is the most hurtful lie of all, in that it contains some truth!

TWIST THE MESSAGE

Amaziah carefully omits the fact that Amos had merely been the mouthpiece of God in all his announcements. As well, when he stated that Amos had foretold the captivity of Israel, he said nothing of the sins which led to this doom, of the hope held out to Repentance, or of the Prophet's Intercession on behalf of Israel.

Amaziah saw his place and position of authority and wealth greatly threatened if, in fact, Israel heeded the words of Amos, and did repent. Therefore, to protect this place and position, he would go to any lengths.

RELIGIOUS MEN

Religious men have absolutely no regard for the Will of God, only for their religious position. In their self-made position they cannot abide any God-called Prophet because such cannot be controlled, and control is the essence of religion.

To protect their positions, they must control the minds of the people, and they do this by controlling what is said.

Inasmuch as the true Prophet gets his Word from the Lord and brooks no go-between, such individuals must be silenced at all cost. That's the reason that the greatest of Satan's evil is not sins of passion, etc., as bad as they are, but instead, religion.

The definition of religion, at least, in this case, is that which is man-originated and not God-given. In fact, Bible Christianity is not a religion at all but a relationship with a Person, the Man, Christ Jesus.

In Christ's day, the Pharisees of that time had impeccable reputations. In fact, they were the religious leaders of Israel, controlling most all religious activity in that country. They claimed to be sticklers for the Word of God and, in fact, would have been called the *"fundamentalists"* of this present day.

And yet, Jesus said of them, *". . . beware of the leaven of the Pharisees . . ."* (Mk. 8:15).

LEAVEN

The *"leaven"* was their own man-instituted rules and regulations, which did not coincide with the Word of God. As such, it was labeled by Christ as false.

Had anyone asked about the reputation of the Pharisees, they, no doubt, would have been given the highest recommendation. And yet, they were evil beyond words, showing that it is not *"he that commends himself is approved, but whom the Lord commends"* (II Cor. 10:18). To be sure, God's Rule of Commendation has absolutely nothing to do with man's rule.

These same Pharisees hated Christ because they could not control Him, and, consequently, they crucified Him.

Therefore, the modern Believer must be very careful that he not merely follows the denominational line but that he follows the

Word of God.

Please remember, reputation is what men think you are, character is what God knows you are.

(12) "ALSO AMAZIAH SAID UNTO AMOS, O YOU SEER, GO, FLEE YOU AWAY INTO THE LAND OF JUDAH, AND THERE EAT BREAD, AND PROPHESY THERE."

The construction is:

1. In other words, Amaziah the Priest said to Amos, *"You are not wanted here!"*

2. There is no record that Jeroboam took any steps in consequence of this accusation, either deeming the words of Amos to be unworthy of serious consideration or, like Herod (Mat. 14:5), fearing the people, who had been impressed by the Prophet's words and bold bearing.

3. Amaziah seeks by his own authority to make Amos leave the country. He evidently thought that Amos, like himself, preached for money.

(13) "BUT PROPHESY NOT AGAIN ANY MORE AT BETH-EL: FOR IT IS THE KING'S CHAPEL, AND IT IS THE KING'S COURT."

The exegesis is:

1. This heathen priest, as he speaks of the *"king's chapel"* and the *"king's court,"* acts as if human authority is everything, and that the Lord, of Himself, has no claims on the land or the place.

2. In effect, this heathen priest is saying that there will be no coming Judgment.

3. The Cross of Christ is the only thing on this Earth that can stop Judgment; however, this heathen priest did not at all believe in such.

THE STATE CHURCH

Preaching of the character that was given out by Amos was out of place in the chapel royal. A state religion robs of civil and spiritual liberty. If it is of human origination, it cannot endure the testimony of truth, which, of course, characterized totally the northern kingdom. Not to be a member of the state church is to be, in a degree, a rebel. The king, being the head of the church, said that no spiritual teaching could be permitted, which was displeasing to him and to the priest that he appointed (I Ki. 12:31;

13:1-4). Amaziah was one of these man-made priests.

(14) "THEN ANSWERED AMOS, AND SAID TO AMAZIAH, I WAS NO PROPHET, NEITHER WAS I A PROPHET'S SON; BUT I WAS AN HERDMAN, AND A GATHERER OF SYCAMORE FRUIT."

The exegesis is:

1. The first phrase of Verse 14 proclaims the fact that Amos was not a Preacher of his own will or of the will of others. He was not meaning that he was not a *"Prophet,"* but that his Calling was not of human origin but of God.

2. The northern kingdom of Israel didn't like the message, so they attacked the messenger. That has always been the motif.

3. Anytime the Cross of Christ is preached, there will be opposition, both from the world and the church.

THE PROPHET

The statement, as given by Amos, was not only in verification of his own Spiritual position, but, as well, it was in opposition to Amaziah as a hireling.

Amaziah knew that he had no right to be a priest, and that the entirety of the worship of Israel was a fabrication of man and was, thereby, blasphemy. In fact, the exercise of the Prophetical Office, as ordained by God, was restricted neither to gender nor rank. There were many Prophetesses in Israel (Judg. 4; II Ki. 22:14; Neh. 6:14).

The phrase, *"Neither was I a Prophet's son,"* means that Amos was neither self-commissioned nor trained in any human institution.

The phrase, *"But I was an herdman, and a gatherer of sycamore fruit,"* portrays his humble position, of which he was not ashamed.

His terminology shows that he had no desire to elevate self, nor did he concern himself with what Amaziah thought of him. He was simply there to deliver a message, a Message ordained by God.

(15) "AND THE LORD TOOK ME AS I FOLLOWED THE FLOCK, AND THE LORD SAID UNTO ME, GO, PROPHESY UNTO MY PEOPLE ISRAEL."

The synopsis is:

1. The first phrase of Verse 15 proclaims the fact that Prophets are not born such, nor are they self-made, nor made by others. The Calling comes strictly from the Lord (Eph. 4:11).

2. *"Go, prophesy unto My People Israel,"* specifies that the Lord gave Amos a direct Message for Israel, which was not to be added to or taken from.

3. Amos, as a true Prophet, met with opposition, while all true Prophet's presently also meet with opposition.

THE OFFICE OF THE PROPHET

Before the Cross, the Lord guided His People by the Ministry and Message of the Prophet. Some, if not most all of the Prophets engaged in foretelling, that is, what was going to come upon this Earth in the future. However, most of all, they were Preachers of Righteousness. In other words, God used them to whip the Nation back into shape.

There are still Prophets in the Church presently, with their Ministry being the same as Old Testament Prophets, but with one exception. Now, the Lord uses Apostles to serve as the de-facto leaders of the Church. The mark of the Apostle is the Message he brings. We learn this from Paul as well as others in the New Testament.

The Holy Spirit knows what the Church needs and, thereby, lays it on the heart of the Apostle to deliver the Message, whatever it might be.

The phrase, *"Go, prophesy unto My People Israel,"* specifies that the Lord gave Amos a direct Message for Israel, which was not to be added to or taken from!

(16) "NOW THEREFORE HEAR YOU THE WORD OF THE LORD: YOU SAY, PROPHESY NOT AGAINST ISRAEL, AND DROP NOT YOUR WORD AGAINST THE HOUSE OF ISAAC."

The construction is:

1. God had not renounced His Rights as the God of Israel.

2. He called them *"My People Israel,"* and, therefore, pronounced a Judgment upon Amaziah.

3. *"Now therefore hear you the Word of the LORD,"* refers to a Prophecy being

directed to this heathen priest personally. The pronoun *"you"* emphasizes this.

THE MINISTRY OF THE PROPHET

There were not many true Prophets in the Israel of the day of Amos. In fact, there may have been no other Prophets other than this one man.

As well, at the present time, there are precious few true Prophets. Most of the time, the Ministry of the Prophet does not come to the fore until there is something negative that needs to be said. As a result, the opposition is fierce. That's at least one of the reasons there aren't too many true Prophets. And yet, at the same time, there are many false prophets, who are ready and willing to tell the people what the people want to hear. These individuals are quick to satisfy the *"itching ears."*

As it regards true Prophets, Jesus said:

"O Jerusalem, Jerusalem *(presents Jesus standing in the Temple when He gave this sorrowing account)*, **you who kill the Prophets, and stone them which are sent unto you** *(presents the terrible animosity tendered toward these Messengers of God)*, **how often would I have gathered your children together, even as a hen gathers her chickens under** *her* **wings, and you would not!** *(Proclaims every effort made by the Lord, and made 'often,' to bring Israel back to her senses.)*

"Behold, your house *(the Temple or Jerusalem is no longer God's habitation)* **is left unto you desolate** *(without God, which means they were at the mercy of Satan)*" **(Mat. 23:37-38).**

FALSE PROPHETS

Jesus also said:

"Beware of false prophets, which come to you in sheep's clothing, but inwardly they are ravening wolves *('beware of false prophets' is said in the sternest of measures! there will be and are false prophets and are some of Satan's greatest weapons)."*

CHECK THE FRUIT

"You shall know them by their fruits *(this is the test as given by Christ as it regards identification of false prophets and* *false apostles).* **Do men gather grapes of thorns, or figs of thistles?** *(It is impossible for false doctrine, generated by false prophets, to bring forth good fruit.)*

"Even so every good tree brings forth good fruit; but a corrupt tree brings forth evil fruit *(the good fruit is Christlikeness, while the evil fruit is self-likeness).*

"A good tree cannot bring forth evil fruit, neither *can* a corrupt tree bring forth good fruit *(the 'good tree' is the Cross, while the 'corrupt tree' pertains to all of that which is other than the Cross).*

"Every tree that brings not forth good fruit is hewn down, and cast into the fire *(Judgment will ultimately come on all so-called gospel, other than the Cross [Rom. 1:18]).*

"Wherefore by their fruits you shall know them *(the acid test)*" **(Mat. 7:15-20).**

(17) "THEREFORE THUS SAYS THE LORD; YOUR WIFE SHALL BE AN HARLOT IN THE CITY, AND YOUR SONS AND YOUR DAUGHTERS SHALL FALL BY THE SWORD, AND YOUR LAND SHALL BE DIVIDED BY LINE; AND YOU SHALL DIE IN A POLLUTED LAND: AND ISRAEL SHALL SURELY GO INTO CAPTIVITY FORTH OF HIS LAND."

The pattern is:

1. If, in Amos, we have an example of a faithful Prophet, in Amaziah, we have an example of an unfaithful priest.

2. The fate predicted for Amaziah was indeed terrible; but we discern in its appointment, not the malice of a human foe, but the justice of a Divine Ruler.

3. Concerning the demand of Amaziah, *"You shall not prophesy,"* Amos' keen retort was, *"Thus says the LORD."* Such will always be the case with the true Prophet of God.

THE TERRIBLE JUDGMENT PRONOUNCED

This Prophecy, as Amos gave it to Amaziah and to Israel, contained five principles. They are:

1. His wife should be dishonored in the streets of the city by heathen soldiers.

2. His children would be slaughtered.

3. His property portioned off to others.

4. He himself should die as a slave in a foreign land.

5. His Nation would be carried away into helpless captivity.

One can well imagine the response of Amaziah at this prediction. There is no record whatsoever that he heeded the Divine Call and repented, but instead, he continued to rebel, and in the face of a sure announcement.

Among the circumstances, which enhanced the horror of this fate, is mentioned the pollution of the heathen land in which the wicked priest will close his life. By so doing, the Holy Spirit was saying that inasmuch as Amaziah did not want the True Word of God and desired idol-worship, he would be banished to a land where there was nothing but idol-worship.

Some have supposed that because certain nations were appointed by Divine Providence to be the ministers of retribution upon Israel, these nations must have been morally admirable or even superior to that upon which their power was exercised for purposes of chastisement.

A PERMITTED JUDGMENT OF GOD

However, that is definitely not the case! The records of the Old Testament Scriptures are decisive upon this point. Idolatrous people were permitted to scourge Israel for idolatry. A polluted land was to be the means of cleansing those polluted by sin. Consequently, when Amaziah said, *"You shall not prophesy,"* Amos' keen retort was, *"Thus says Jehovah."*

Such will always be the case of the true Prophet of God.

In closing this Chapter, and as an Evangelist, the question must be asked of any and all Preachers of the Gospel as to what class you belong.

Is it that represented by Amaziah, who, though recognized by his king and country as the true teacher, was, nevertheless, destitute of loyalty to the One True God? Or, is it that represented by Amos, who altogether a poor laborer, unrecognized by his country as a true teacher, yet, was Called of God and manfully fulfilled his Divine Mission?

*"Christian, seek not yet repose,
"Hear your gracious Saviour say;*

"You are in the midst of foes:
"Watch and pray."

"Principalities and powers,
"Mustering their unseen array,
"Wait for your unguarded hours:
"Watch and pray."

"Gird your Heavenly armor on,
"Wear it ever night and day;
"Ambushed lies the Evil One:
"Watch and pray."

"Hear the victors who overcame,
"Still they mark each warrior's way;
"All with one sweet voice exclaim,
"Watch and pray."

"Hear, above all, hear your Lord.
"Him you love to obey;
"Hide within your heart His Word:
"Watch and pray."

"Watch, as if on that alone,
"Hung the issue of the day;
"Pray, that help may be sent down:
"Watch and pray."

CHAPTER 8

(1) "THUS HAS THE LORD GOD SHOWED UNTO ME: AND BEHOLD A BASKET OF SUMMER FRUIT."

The synopsis is:

1. The gathering of fruit was the last harvest of the year and was done in October.

2. As it was the last harvest of the year, it also fitly typified the final warning to Israel.

3. Why did the Lord bother when He knew what the outcome would be?

SUMMER FRUIT

With Amaziah's interruption disposed of, the fourth symbol follows those of the locusts, the drought, and the plumbline.

There were three major harvests in Israel. They were:

1. The barley harvest: this took place in April. It was the time also of the Passover Feast, the Feast of Unleavened Bread, and the Feast of Firstfruits. All typified Christ with the Passover a picture of His Crucifixion on Calvary's Cross. Unleavened Bread

pictured His Perfect Life and Perfect Body. Firstfruits pictured His Resurrection.

2. The wheat harvest: this came about the first of June. This was the time, as well, of the Feast of Pentecost, which typified Christ as the Baptizer with the Holy Spirit.

3. The fruit harvest: this took place, as stated, in October and typified the harvest of souls that would be brought about as a result of what Jesus did at the Cross. The Feast of Trumpets, the Atonement, and the Feast of Tabernacles took place at this time. The Feast of Trumpets portrayed Christ coming back to this Earth as it regards the Second Coming. Atonement proclaims Israel accepting Him as Saviour and as Lord. Tabernacles represent the coming Kingdom Age when Christ will rule and reign for a thousand years.

(2) "AND HE SAID, AMOS, WHAT DO YOU SEE? AND I SAID, A BASKET OF SUMMER FRUIT. THEN SAID THE LORD UNTO ME, THE END IS COME UPON MY PEOPLE OF ISRAEL; I WILL NOT AGAIN PASS BY THEM ANY MORE."

The construction is:

1. The last phrase of Verse 2 means that the Lord will not forgive Israel anymore or show any more Mercy because of their refusal to repent.

2. God's Mercy is predicated on the individual meeting God's Terms. Those terms, to be brief, are an admittance that we are wrong and that He is Right.

3. While God is overly patient, still, there always comes a time that His Patience wears out.

4. As great as will be His Mercy if one will repent, as great will be His Judgment for those who will not repent.

WHAT DO YOU SEE?

The question, *"And He said, Amos, what do you see?"* once more, proclaims the affecting intimacy of the Divine Fellowship with the Prophet.

The phrase, *"And I said, a basket of summer fruit,"* declares, as stated, the approaching end of summer; the fruit was ripe and had already been plucked from the trees.

The phrase, *"Then said the LORD unto me, The end is come upon My People of*

Israel," symbolizes the announced end of the kingdoms, its ripeness for Judgment, and that its citizens would be plucked out of the land.

"I will not again pass by them anymore," means, *"I will not forgive them anymore or show any more Mercy."*

To be sure, this is not an arbitrary decision but a decision based upon Israel's refusal to repent, despite the Pleadings of the Holy Spirit through the Prophet.

(3) "AND THE SONGS OF THE TEMPLE SHALL BE HOWLINGS IN THAT DAY, SAYS THE LORD GOD: THERE SHALL BE MANY DEAD BODIES IN EVERY PLACE; THEY SHALL CAST THEM FORTH WITH SILENCE."

The exposition is:

1. *"Howlings"* portray the coming disposition of Israel changed from its present occupation of revelry, luxury, and entertainment to one of Judgment, desolation, destitution, and stark terror.

2. The Lord is represented here as casting dead bodies to the ground so that death is everywhere, with the interjection, *"Hush!"* as an admonition to bend beneath the Hand of an avenging God.

3. Judgment was much more pronounced then because the Cross was yet in the future. The Cross alone assuages Judgment.

HOWLINGS

The phrase, *"There shall be many dead bodies in every place,"* is more forcible in the original Hebrew: *"Many the corpses; in every place He has cast them forth. Hush!"*

The phrase, *"They shall cast them forth with silence,"* also means that the dead bodies of the revelers should not be laid in stately tombs but cast forth as carrion, in other words, for the buzzards. In addition, the silence of terror shall replace the accustomed funeral pomp and eloquence.

RAW UNBELIEF

It is an amazing thing at the ability of mankind to resist the Holy Spirit. Hearing Prophecies of the nature given here by Amos, which spoke of unprecedented horror, seemingly had no effect at all upon the Israel of his day. It was business as usual!

NOTES

If warning is given, and Repentance is rejected, God has no alternative but to send Judgment. Israel's refusal to repent could only be chalked up to raw unbelief. They simply did not believe what the Prophet was saying. Or, if they did give some credence to his words, their thinking was that it would take place only in the distant future, so it would not involve them. In fact, it would be approximately 60 years in the future before this terrible thing came to pass, but, ultimately, it did come to pass exactly as the Lord had spoken through the Prophet.

JUDGMENT ON THIS PRESENT WORLD

The Book of Revelation vividly proclaims the fact that Judgment is soon to come upon the entirety of this world, which will be the worst it has ever known, and so bad that it will never see such again. This is what Jesus said (Mat. 24:21).

But yet, as clearly as it is presented in that great Book, the last Book, incidentally, in the Bible, still, the world believes it not at all. In fact, most of the modern church gives little credence to that which is given to us. Irrespective, what our Lord said will happen, to be sure, will most definitely happen.

Some in the church have claimed that the Book of Revelation has already been fulfilled. Well, of course, that is hard to believe when one considers that the Nineteenth Chapter of Revelation, proclaims the fact of the Second Coming of our Lord. That has not yet happened, so that means that the Great Tribulation has not taken place yet, either. The following is that which the Bible portrays as soon to come to pass:

• The Rapture of the Church: the words *"Rapture"* and *"Resurrection"* actually are just two different words for the same event. While we may argue the timing of this event, we cannot argue the fact of this event, that is, if we want to be true to the Word of God. The Apostle Paul gave us a preview of what this will be like, found in I Thessalonians 4:13 through 18. This Passage tells us what will take place at that time, with I Corinthians, Chapter 15, telling us how it will happen.

• The Rise of the Antichrist: the Prophet Daniel tells us of the rise of the man of sin, found in Chapters 7, 8 and 11 of the great Book which bears his name. Paul also gave us a preview of the rise of the man of sin in II Thessalonians, Chapter 2.

• The Great Tribulation Period: Daniel also told us of this coming time and how long it would last in his Book (Dan. 9:27). John the Beloved gave us an account of this coming time in Chapters 6 through 18 of the Book of Revelation.

• Battle of Armageddon: Ezekiel tells us of this coming event, which, without a doubt, will be the most cataclysmic conflict ever engaged. It is found in Chapters 38 and 39 of the Book that bears his name.

• The Second Coming of the Lord: in Chapters 38 and 39 of Ezekiel, the great Prophet portrays the Second Coming. John the Beloved also gave us another account in Chapter 19 of the Book of Revelation.

• The Kingdom Age: this will begin immediately after the Second Coming and will last a thousand years. Isaiah gave us the greatest account of this coming grand time (Isa., Chpt. 2, 11, etc.).

• The Perfect Age to come: this will last forever and forever and is outlined in Chapters 21 and 22 of the Book of Revelation. At that time, the Lord will transfer His Headquarters from Planet Heaven to Planet Earth. Then the world will be, and forever, that which the Lord originally intended.

(4) "HEAR THIS, O YOU WHO SWALLOW UP THE NEEDY, EVEN TO MAKE THE POOR OF THE LAND TO FAIL."

The composition is:

1. God's Love for the poor and His burning Anger against their oppressors once more appears.

2. We must ever remember that the Lord sees all and knows all.

3. All of this means that He notes every transaction, every direction, in fact, everything that is done.

THE POOR AND THE NEEDY

The idea of Verse 4 presents the planning schemes of the upper class, who look for every opportunity to take from the poor what little they have. They closed all credit to them, or if they did give credit, charged an exorbitant rate of interest, which, within

itself, presented every likelihood of failure.

As well, the judges were corrupt and seldom gave the poor a fair hearing in court, using their legal position to make it all but impossible for the poor to succeed, hence, *"even to make the poor of the land to fail."*

(5) "SAYING, WHEN WILL THE NEW MOON BE GONE, THAT WE MAY SELL CORN? AND THE SABBATH, THAT WE MAY SET FORTH WHEAT, MAKING THE EPHAH SMALL, AND THE SHEKEL GREAT, AND FALSIFYING THE BALANCES BY DECEIT?"

The overview is:

1. By reducing the size of the ephah, by overcharging, and by falsifying the scales, they robbed the defenseless. Plunging them into debt, they sold them into slavery for a trifle in defiance of Leviticus 25:39.

2. *"Saying, When will the new moon be gone, that we may sell corn?"* refers to the first day of the month on which all trade was supposed to be suspended (Num. 28:18).

3. These greedy individuals kept the festivals, but they grudged the time given to them and considered them as wasted. In other words, they had no time for the Lord.

DISHONESTY

Those who have no regard for the Ways of God soon put aside equity and practice dishonesty.

The phrase, *"And falsifying the balances by deceit,"* portrays the increase of their gains by falsifying their scales and using fraudulent weights. Thus, they cheated the poor probably in three ways—by small measure, exorbitant prices, and light weight.

By now, it should be readily observable as to what the Lord thinks of dishonest measures, and that refers to dishonesty in any capacity.

One of the hallmarks of the Christian Faith is, *". . . Provide things honest in the sight of all men"* (Rom. 12:17).

THE SHEKEL

The word, *"shekel,"* as used here, does not denote coins, but rather the meaning of a certain weight, as is obvious from the Text.

It doesn't seem that Israel began using coins made out of certain metals, such as copper, silver, or gold, until after the Babylonian captivity.

Thus, in ordinary transactions, at least before that particular time, the term *"silver"* is often omitted, but yet, understood. Solomon purchased chariots at 600 shekels weight of silver and horses at 150 shekels weight of silver (I Ki. 10:29).

So, at that time, *"shekels"* denoted weight instead of a particular exchange of money.

(6) "THAT WE MAY BUY THE POOR FOR SILVER, AND THE NEEDY FOR A PAIR OF SHOES; YES, AND SELL THE REFUSE OF THE WHEAT?"

The synopsis is:

1. The idea of this Verse is that the poor, because of the dishonesty of much of the upper class, kept getting poorer, and they were compelled to pay their debt by selling themselves into slavery.

2. *"And the needy for a pair of shoes,"* means that they dealt harshly even for the smallest debt.

3. *"Yes, and sell the refuse of the wheat,"* referred to a type of scale, which, when the grain was poured into it for weighing, had openings in the bottom, not visible to the seller, which caused as much as ten to twenty percent of the grain to sift into an unseen container, giving a short weight. They would then sell that which was called *"refuse,"* which had actually been stolen, adding more dishonest gain to their already dishonest gain.

(7) "THE LORD HAS SWORN BY THE EXCELLENCY OF JACOB, SURELY I WILL NEVER FORGET ANY OF THEIR WORKS."

The exposition is:

1. *"The excellency of Jacob,"* speaks of God Himself.

2. In Verse 2, He says, *"I will not forgive."* Now He says, *"I will never forget,"* expressing His Pity for the oppressed and His eternal Anger against the oppressors.

3. There are books in Heaven (Rev. 20), which note every action, good and bad, by every person. The bad can be erased but only in one way, and that's by the Precious Blood of the Lord Jesus Christ. When the believing sinner accepts Christ and makes Him his Lord, the record of evil is then wiped clean.

I WILL NEVER FORGET

Actually, the phrase, *"I will never forget,"* refers to the guarantee that God will not leave such action unpunished.

Therefore, be it known that God sees all, and that all, whether it be honest or dishonest, will *". . . receive a just recompence of reward"* (Heb. 2:2).

(8) "SHALL NOT THE LAND TREMBLE FOR THIS, AND EVERY ONE MOURN WHO DWELLS THEREIN? AND IT SHALL RISE UP WHOLLY AS A FLOOD; AND IT SHALL BE CAST OUT AND DROWNED, AS BY THE FLOOD OF EGYPT."

The overview is:

1. The idea of Verse 8 is that coming Judgment shall flood the land.

2. As a flood covers everything, likewise, the Judgment of God against Israel will cover everything.

3. The Mills of God grind slowly, but they grind exceedingly fine, meaning they miss nothing.

TO TREMBLE

The question, *"Shall not the land tremble for this?"* speaks of the oppression and robbery. There is a suggestion that the earthquake of Amos 1:1 was at least a part of the Divine Judgment upon this evil.

However, the balance of the phrase, *"And everyone mourn who dwells therein,"* speaks of the coming invasion of Assyria, which would affect the entirety of the land, and not a part only!

The phrase, *"And it shall rise up wholly as a flood,"* and the accompanying clause, speak of the Nile River in Egypt, which overflowed its banks at certain times of the year, inundating the countryside.

The idea is, as stated, that coming Judgment shall flood the land.

(9) "AND IT SHALL COME TO PASS IN THAT DAY, SAYS THE LORD GOD, THAT I WILL CAUSE THE SUN TO GO DOWN AT NOON, AND I WILL DARKEN THE EARTH IN THE CLEAR DAY."

The overview is:

1. Verse 9 speaks of an eclipse of the sun.

2. At exactly what time the Holy Spirit is speaking of in this particular Passage is

not known.

3. If the Lord says that something will *"come to pass,"* one can rest assured that ever how long it takes, it will *"come to pass."*

TOTAL CONTROL

It should be understood that the Lord, Who created the elements, has total and complete control over the elements. Everything is at His Command. In fact, in the coming Great Tribulation, which Jesus said would be the worst the world has ever known (Mat. 24:21), the elements will then be affected to a greater degree in the negative sense than history has ever known before. In fact, during that coming seven-year period of time (Dan. 9:27), quite possibly, half the population of Planet Earth could die. These Judgments at that time will not be happenchance but will originate with the Lord.

IS GOD FAIR IN DOING SUCH A THING?

Along with the Judgments that will come upon this Earth in those days, resulting in the deaths of untold hundreds of millions, every effort will be made to get people to repent. In fact, during that time, the Scripture says emphatically they, *". . . repented not of the works of their hands"* (Rev. 9:20), *"Neither repented they of their murders . . ."* (Rev. 9:21), *". . . they repented not to give Him glory"* (Rev. 16:9), *". . . and repented not of their deeds"* (Rev. 16:11).

God is a God of Love and a God of great Mercy and Compassion.

Even though hundreds of thousands of people, if not millions, will be Saved at that particular time, still, due to the fact that the true Church has been raptured out of this world, evil will then be predominant in a way that cannot even now begin to be imagined.

It is amazing as to the ability of man to resist his Maker despite all the evidence to the contrary.

(10) "AND I WILL TURN YOUR FEASTS INTO MOURNING, AND ALL YOUR SONGS INTO LAMENTATION; AND I WILL BRING UP SACKCLOTH UPON ALL LOINS, AND BALDNESS UPON EVERY HEAD; AND I WILL MAKE IT AS THE MOURNING OF AN ONLY SON, AND THE END THEREOF AS A BITTER DAY."

The exposition is:

1. The last phrase, *"And the end thereof as a bitter day,"* sums up the entirety of this Passage.

2. It speaks of the attack by the Assyrians and the shock of its brutal force finally registering upon Israel.

3. Out of the entirety of the Universe, God has the Power to back up every single thing that He says.

THE BITTER DAY

The idea of Verse 10 pertains to the coming Judgment and that it would not conclude until all was destroyed. In other words, there would be no respite!

The *"baldness"* spoke of the shaving of the head in *"mourning and lamentation."*

As Amos delivered this message, how many people took the time to stop and listen?

Especially considering the opposition of Amaziah, quite possibly, even those who were interested were afraid to listen for fear of reprisal by the priestly order or even the government.

As a result of the religious leadership demeaning the message, and especially considering that the secular leadership was uninterested, it was not popular at all to side with Amos, which meant that most, if not all, ridiculed him.

Most individuals, even Christians, cannot swim against the tide of public opinion, therefore, it is easier to ridicule or, at the least, remain silent!

The ridicule was, no doubt, heavy especially considering the present prosperity and strength of the Nation. That these things would come to pass was preposterous, to say the least, at least, in their thinking.

However, the ridicule, sarcasm, and unbelief, in no way negated the actual fulfillment of these events. They came to pass exactly as the Word of God predicted.

THE WORD OF GOD

Likewise, every single prediction in the Bible, even, Jesus said, down to the *"jot and tittle,"* shall be completely fulfilled. Men can ignore it, disbelieve it, or ridicule it; however, such response in no way affects the outcome.

When one considers that the Bible is the only Book on Earth, which tells what the outcome shall be, it would seem that men would actively peruse its contents. However, the Bible, as with Israel of old, is, by and large, an unread Book even among many Christians.

(11) "BEHOLD, THE DAYS COME, SAYS THE LORD GOD, THAT I WILL SEND A FAMINE IN THE LAND, NOT A FAMINE OF BREAD, NOR A THIRST FOR WATER, BUT OF HEARING THE WORDS OF THE LORD."

The exposition is:

1. What the leaders of Israel had demanded of Amos, that he cease preaching the Word of God, they will now get!

2. They will be carted away to captivity, at least those who were left, with the results being that there would be no more *"hearing the Words of the LORD."*

3. What Israel wanted, Israel got. However, what she got did not turn out to be what she thought she wanted!

A SCARCITY OF THE WORD OF GOD

The phrase, *"Behold, the days come,"* referring to a scarcity of the Word of God, happened exactly as predicted! Israel, at least those who remained, was carted off to captivity in a heathen land, which knew nothing of the Word of God, and which opposed any such type of worship.

The *"famine"* here spoken of was far worse than a *"famine of bread, or thirst for water."* It was a *"famine"* of *"hearing the Words of the LORD."*

To be sure, there is a *"famine"* of hearing the True Word of the Lord in America presently, as well as many other countries of the world. While the Bible is still the best seller, still, it is mostly an unread Book and, therefore, an unpreached Book in most churches.

If one will take the time to peruse the book offerings of most Christian bookstores, one will find that a large percent actually pertains to psychology and not the Word of God. In reality, most of the degrees offered in modern so-called Bible colleges and seminaries are psychology courses of one type or the other, with most not even offering a degree in Bible.

NOTES

(What would you think of a law school that did not offer a degree in law?)

It is even suggested in some Pentecostal and Fundamentalist circles that modern man is facing problems that are not addressed in the Bible, and, therefore, psychology must be wedded to the Bible in order to bring about the desired results.

For one to say such shows a blatant ignorance of the Word of God at least, or blasphemy at worst!

ALL THINGS THAT PERTAIN UNTO LIFE AND GODLINESS

Peter said:

"According as His Divine Power has given unto us all things (the Lord with large-handed generosity has given us all things) **that *pertain* unto life and godliness** (pertains to the fact that the Lord Jesus has given us everything we need regarding life and living)**, through the knowledge of Him Who has called us to Glory and Virtue** (the 'knowledge' addressed here speaks of what Christ did at the Cross, which alone can provide 'Glory and Virtue')**:"**

PRECIOUS PROMISES

"Whereby are given unto us exceeding great and Precious Promises (pertains to the Word of God, which alone holds the answer to every life problem)**: that by these** (Promises) **you might be partakers of the Divine Nature** (the Divine Nature implanted in the inner being of the believing sinner becomes the source of our new life and actions; it comes to everyone at the moment of being 'Born-Again')**, having escaped the corruption that is in the world through lust.** (This presents the Salvation experience of the sinner and the Sanctification experience of the Saint)**" (II Pet. 1:3-4).**

In effect, the church, as a whole, does not even believe the Bible anymore. This would include Pentecostals, Charismatics, and Fundamentalists. Of course, there are exceptions, but those exceptions are few and given little or no credence whatsoever in the religious community.

SOUND DOCTRINE

Most preaching and teaching presently

NOTES

consists of man's ideas, heresy, and outright fabrications. Paul said, *"For the time will come when they will not endure sound doctrine; but after their own lusts shall they heap to themselves teachers, having itching ears;*

"And they shall turn away their ears from the Truth, and shall be turned unto fables" (II Tim. 4:3-4).

Inasmuch as most false doctrine is slickly produced much of the time and, as well, contains some truth, because of an ignorance of the True Word of God, it is readily accepted.

(12) "AND THEY SHALL WANDER FROM SEA TO SEA, AND FROM THE NORTH EVEN TO THE EAST, THEY SHALL RUN TO AND FRO TO SEEK THE WORD OF THE LORD, AND SHALL NOT FIND IT."

The construction is:

1. Then the Word of the Lord would be eagerly desired, but not realized; sought, but not found; called for, but not answered!

2. And it must be quickly added, nothing could be worse! On all counts, the prosperity of a people and a nation is *"the Word of the LORD."* Deprived of that, the people are left aimless and without direction.

3. There is nothing more precious than the *"Word of the LORD."*

A FAMINE OF THE WORD

When men are in prosperity, they ridicule or neglect the Word of God, but when in adversity, they desire it, or, at least, some do; but a just Judgment declares they *"shall not find it."*

It is the idea that if men will to know the Word of God, the Lord wills that such be brought about. As well, if they will the opposite, He wills a famine of the *"Word of the LORD."*

The idea of the Passage speaks of the coming desolation when Israel would be destroyed, and approximately 130 years later, Judah would, as well, suffer the same fate. At that time, Nebuchadnezzar would completely destroy the Temple, with all of its priestly functions brought to a halt, etc. Consequently, and exactly as predicted, there would be no *"Word of the LORD,"* because the voice of the Prophets would be silenced, with all spiritual activity brought to a halt.

SEEKING A DIVINE MESSAGE

As well, the Hebrew word structure in this Passage has the sense of vainly seeking a Divine Message from idolatry in any part of the world.

When it speaks of *"sea to sea,"* it means from the Mediterranean to the Dead Sea, that is, from the west to the south, i.e., from the gods of the Philistines to the gods of the Egyptians.

"From the north even to the east," refers to the gods of the Assyrians on the north to the gods of the Chaldeans on the east.

As the *"Word of the LORD"* could not be found in idols, neither can it be found in the Book of Mormon, the Koran, the teachings of the Catholic church, Christian Science, Jehovah's Witnesses, modern thought, neo-orthodoxy, psychology, or all such like fabrication.

(13) "IN THAT DAY SHALL THE FAIR VIRGINS AND YOUNG MEN FAINT FOR THIRST."

The overview is:

1. The *"thirst"* spoken of here concerns Spiritual Thirst, which can only be satisfied by the *"Word of the LORD."*

2. Nothing could be worse in any land than to have the Word of God taken away.

3. The only hope for mankind is found in the Word of the Lord.

THIRST AGAIN

Jesus said, *". . . Whosoever drinks of this water shall thirst again:*

"But whosoever drinks of the water that I shall give him shall never thirst; but the water that I shall give him shall be in him a well of water springing up into Everlasting Life" (Jn. 4:13-14).

(14) "THEY WHO SWEAR BY THE SIN OF SAMARIA, AND SAY, YOUR GOD, O DAN, LIVES; AND, THE MANNER OF BEER-SHEBA LIVES; EVEN THEY SHALL FALL, AND NEVER RISE UP AGAIN."

The synopsis is:

1. Samaria, Dan, Beth-el, Gilgal, and Beer-sheba were centers of idolatry in Israel (Hos. 4:15; 9:15; 12:11; I Ki. 12:27-30).

2. This truth is demonstrated by the fate

of the Jews who will not receive Christ as the Promised Messiah and, consequently, have fallen to *"never rise up again."*

3. And so shall it be for all who reject Christ as their Eternal Saviour!

"O Holy, Holy, Holy Lord!
"Thou God of Hosts by all adored;
"The Earth and heavens are full of Thee,
"Your Light, Your Power, Your Majesty."

"Loud hallelujahs to Your Name,
"Angels and Seraphim proclaim:
"By all the powers and thrones in Heaven,
"Eternal praise to You be given."

"Apostles join the glorious throng,
"And swell the loud, triumphant song;
"Prophets and martyrs hear the sound,
"And spread the hallelujahs round."

"Glory to You, O God Most High!
"Father, we praised Your Majesty;
"The Son, the Spirit we adore,
"One Godhead, blest forevermore."

CHAPTER 9

(1) "I SAW THE LORD STANDING UPON THE ALTAR: AND HE SAID, SMITE THE LINTEL OF THE DOOR, THAT THE POSTS MAY SHAKE: AND CUT THEM IN THE HEAD, ALL OF THEM; AND I WILL KILL THE LAST OF THEM WITH THE SWORD: HE WHO FLEES OF THEM SHALL NOT FLEE AWAY, AND HE WHO ESCAPES OF THEM SHALL NOT BE DELIVERED."

The overview is:

1. The first phrase of Verse 1 refers to Amos actually and literally seeing the Lord as He stood upon the *"Brazen Altar"* in front of the Temple in Jerusalem.

2. Even though the pronouncement of Judgment is more pointedly against the northern kingdom, still, the whole of both kingdoms is meant because the Restoration of both kingdoms is referred to in Verses 11 through 15.

3. The phrase, *"And He said, Smite the lintel of the door, that the posts may shake,"* refers to the destruction of the Temple, which would take place nearly 200 years from Amos' time. The implication is: total destruction from summit to base.

THE AWFUL PRONOUNCEMENT

Judgment begins at the House of God. From that Judgment, there will be no escape; for the Judge is Omniscient (all-knowing) and Irresistible.

The phrase, *"And cut them in the head, all of them,"* refers to the falling building covering the post with ruins. The overthrown Temple presents a forcible picture of the destruction of the theocracy.

The phrase, *"Shall not be delivered,"* refers to those who may try to escape but would be cut off. The only One Who can truly deliver is the Lord, and He, due to their failure to repent, was not there to deliver but, instead, to destroy.

SALT THAT HAS LOST ITS SAVOR

Jesus said, **"You are the salt** (preservative) **of the Earth: but if the salt have lost his savour, wherewith shall it be salted? it is thenceforth good for nothing, but to be cast out, and to be trodden underfoot of men.** *('Salt' is a type of the Word of God; the professing Believer who no longer holds to the Word is of no use to God or man)"* **(Mat. 5:13).**

Believers, who are consecrated to the Lord, present the greatest blessing that any community, city, or country could ever have. However, Believers who no longer believe, and who have lost their way with the Lord and refuse to repent, irrespective of the warnings, are not only good for nothing but are actually a curse, bringing harm to their locality and even the entirety of the nation.

I'm afraid to say that most of the modern church, sadly and regrettably, falls into the latter category. Some of you have heard me say it any number of times that the problem in this nation is not really emanating from the White House or the State House, but the blame can rather be laid at the doorstep of the church.

THE CHURCH AND
THE CROSS

When the church ceases to preach the Cross, seeing the Cross of Christ alone stands between mankind and the Judgment of God, the church has then lost its savor and is good for nothing.

THE CURSE

Considering this, this means that the Lord is doing the world a favor by destroying the northern kingdom of Israel, and this powerful truth holds true unto this present hour as well. Paul said:

"For as many as are of the works of the Law are under the curse: for it is written, Cursed is everyone who continues not in all things which are written in the Book of the Law to do them" (Gal. 3:10; Deut. 27:26).

(2) "THOUGH THEY DIG INTO HELL, THENCE SHALL MY HAND TAKE THEM; THOUGH THEY CLIMB UP TO HEAVEN, THENCE WILL I BRING THEM DOWN."

The diagram is:

1. The Holy Spirit, upon reading the minds of the people as they heard the words of Amos, proclaims to them the folly of their thoughts of escape.

2. Men presently, and for all time, have *"dug into Hell,"* i.e., delved into witchcraft, but found that demon spirits could not protect them from the Hand of God.

3. As well, they have *"climbed up to heaven,"* the exploration of near space. But, despite the Russian Cosmonauts declaring that they nowhere saw God, still, *"He brought them down,"* i.e., destroyed the Soviet Union.

THE ENTIRETY OF MANKIND, AND FOR
ALL TIME, WILL ULTIMATELY FACE
THE LORD JESUS CHRIST

Man can face Christ at the Cross of Calvary, which means to accept Him as the Saviour of one's soul and, thereby, make Him the Lord of one's life. That is the reason for the great price paid by our Lord at Calvary's Cross. The door is wide open, and all may come who desire to come, whomever they might be, and whatever it is that

NOTES

they have done. If they will exercise Faith in Christ, all will be forgiven, and Eternal Life bestowed. As someone has well said, *"It is the greatest story ever told."*

But if men refuse to meet Christ at the Cross of Calvary, they will ultimately meet Him at the Great White Throne Judgment. But meet Him they shall! In describing this event, John the Beloved said:

"And I saw a Great White Throne (proclaims the final Judgment of the unredeemed, which will take place at the end of the Kingdom Age)**, and Him Who sat on it** (proclaims none other than God; however, we must understand that it is the Person of the Godhead, the Lord Jesus Christ [Mat. 25:31]; He is the Saviour today; He will be the Judge tomorrow)**, from Whose Face the Earth and the Heaven fled away; and there was found no place for them.** (This means a New Heaven and New Earth are in the offing.)"

THE BOOKS

"And I saw the dead, small and great, stand before God (pertains to the second Resurrection, the Resurrection of Damnation [I Cor., Chpt. 15; I Thess. 4:13-18; Jn. 5:29])**; and the Books were opened: and another Book was opened, which is *the Book* of Life: and the dead were judged out of those things which were written in the Books, according to their works** (proclaims the manner of Judgment)."

ACCORDING TO THEIR WORKS

"And the sea gave up the dead which were in it; and death and Hell delivered up the dead which were in them (points to the fact that every unredeemed person who has ever lived will face the Great White Throne Judgment; none will be exempted)**: and they were judged every man according to their works** (records the fact that this Judgment is not arbitrary but is based on absolute Justice)."

THE SECOND DEATH

"And death and Hell were cast into the Lake of Fire (combined, includes the wicked of all ages). **This is the second death** (Eternal separation from God and the Lake of Fire).

"And whosoever was not found written in the Book of Life *(refers to the record of all the Redeemed)* was cast into the Lake of Fire. *(This includes every single individual who isn't redeemed, beginning with Adam and Eve. That is, if they didn't come back to God)*" (Rev. 20:11-15).

SOME PARTICULARS ABOUT THE GREAT WHITE THRONE JUDGMENT

• Where will it be conducted? Every evidence is it will be conducted on Earth (Rev. 20:11).

• Who will be the Judge? The Lord Jesus Christ (Rev. 20:11).

• Who will be judged? Every person who has ever lived, who did not make Jesus Christ his Saviour and Lord (Rev. 20:12).

• What will be the basis of Judgment? *"The Books,"* which will contain every action of every person. In other words, proverbially speaking, it's all in black and white (Rev. 20:12).

• What will be the Judgment? It will be the Lake of Fire, which will last forever and forever (Rev. 20:15).

MAN

Man is created spirit, soul, and body. The spirit and the soul are eternal, meaning they will never die. The physical body as it is now will die, awaiting the Judgment (Heb. 9:27).

There are two Resurrections in the future. The first is the *"Resurrection of Life"* (Jn. 5:29). This Resurrection could actually take place at any time. It is sometimes referred to as the *"Rapture"* of the Church. While one may argue the timing of this Resurrection, one cannot argue the fact of this Resurrection.

The second Resurrection, which is referred to as the *"Resurrection of Damnation,"* will take place approximately 1,000 years after the first Resurrection. As only the Redeemed will be in the Resurrection of Life, only the unredeemed will be in the *"Resurrection of Damnation."* All will be given an indestructible body, the former to spend eternity with God, which will be forever and forever, with the latter being in the Lake of Fire, which will also be forever and forever.

Considering the implications of all of

this, don't you think it would be prudent to serve the Lord and to do so with all of our strength?

Eternity is a long, long time, in fact, something that will never end. It would be bad enough to have to spend one hour in Hell, worse yet to spend a month, worse still to spend a year, but to think of forever is beyond comprehension. But that's exactly what it is, forever and forever (Rev. 20:10).

(3) "AND THOUGH THEY HIDE THEMSELVES IN THE TOP OF CARMEL, I WILL SEARCH AND TAKE THEM OUT THENCE: AND THOUGH THEY BE HID FROM MY SIGHT IN THE BOTTOM OF THE SEA, THENCE WILL I COMMAND THE SERPENT, AND HE SHALL BITE THEM."

The overview is:

1. The idea is: there will be no escaping this coming Judgment!

2. Over and over again, the Holy Spirit makes it clear that whatever it is that God has spoken, it will most definitely come to pass.

3. Men have ever tried to hide from God, but such effort is futile, to say the least.

(4) "AND THOUGH THEY GO INTO CAPTIVITY BEFORE THEIR ENEMIES, THENCE WILL I COMMAND THE SWORD, AND IT SHALL SLAY THEM: AND I WILL SET MY EYES UPON THEM FOR EVIL, AND NOT FOR GOOD."

The construction is:

1. For the Lord to do such a thing means that countless opportunities for Repentance have been spurned, with every plea by the Holy Spirit rejected.

2. All of this could be avoided if Israel would only repent.

3. At the same time, Hell, where most will go, could be totally and completely avoided if men would only accept the Lord Jesus Christ as their Saviour. However, sadly and regrettably, most won't. Jesus said, *". . . broad is the way, that leads to destruction, and many there be that go in thereat"* (Mat. 7:13).

FOR EVIL AND NOT FOR GOOD

The last clause of Verse 4 is fearful indeed, *"And I will set My Eyes upon them for evil, and not for good."*

For the Lord to do such a thing means

that countless opportunities for Repentance have been spurned, with every plea by the Holy Spirit rejected. One can basically see the fate of Israel from that day forward. Even though they enjoyed a short time of revival after the dispersion, still, they soon resorted to their old ways and murdered the Prophet Zechariah.

After the Prophet Malachi, there was no Prophet in Israel for a little over 400 years until John the Baptist. Of course, it is obvious what they did to Christ, which caused their total destruction.

Now, for nearly 2,000 years, they have wandered as outcasts among the nations of the world. For the tens of millions who lived and died during this time, almost all lost their souls due to their rejection of Christ. As such, they will *"never rise up again,"* at least, as far as the Resurrection of Life is concerned, but will be in the Resurrection of Damnation.

However, as Amos will soon tell us, and other Prophets saw, as well, there will be a Restoration for those who are alive at the time of the Second Coming. But it will be only after they accept Christ as their Saviour and make Him the Lord of their lives. Then and only then will the Blessings of God rest upon Israel, with them enjoying what, in effect, they could have had all along.

(5) "AND THE LORD GOD OF HOSTS IS HE WHO TOUCHES THE LAND, AND IT SHALL MELT, AND ALL WHO DWELL THEREIN SHALL MOURN: AND IT SHALL RISE UP WHOLLY LIKE A FLOOD; AND SHALL BE DROWNED, AS BY THE FLOOD OF EGYPT."

The synopsis is:

1. The title, *"Lord GOD of Hosts,"* in the Hebrew is *"Jehovah Elohim Zebaoth,"* and represents God not only as Ruler of the heavenly bodies, but as the Monarch of a multitude of Heavenly Spirits, who execute His Will, worship Him in His Abiding-place, and are attendants and witnesses of His Glory.

2. As the Nile River in Egypt then at times flooded the land, likewise, the Judgment of God would cover Israel.

3. The problem with Israel then, as it is with untold millions now, is unbelief.

LIKE A FLOOD

The phrase, *"And the Lord GOD of Hosts is He Who touches the land,"* refers to touching it in wrath.

Men are fond of portraying God as a God of Love, and rightly so; however, He, as is here obvious, is also a God of Wrath. The Scripture plainly says of Him:

"For the Wrath of God (*God's Personal Emotion with regard to sin*) **is revealed from Heaven** (*this anger originates with God*) **against all ungodliness and unrighteousness of men** (*God must unalterably be opposed to sin*)**, who hold the truth in unrighteousness** (*who refuse to recognize Who God is, and what God is*)**" (Rom. 1:18).**

Some people think that because this is the Dispensation of Grace, and it definitely is, such forgoes the Wrath of God. In other words, they think that, due to the fact of this particular time, God's Wrath is held in check.

Not so!

To be frank, in this Dispensation of Grace, because greater light is given, God's Wrath is exhibited more presently than ever before. Once again, the Scripture says, and concerning this very thing:

"And the times of this ignorance God winked at (*does not reflect that such ignorance was Salvation, for it was not! before the Cross, there was very little Light in the world, so God withheld Judgment*)**; but now commands all men everywhere to repent** (*but since the Cross, the 'Way' is open to all; it's up to us Believers to make that 'Way' known to all men*)**:**

"Because He has appointed a day (*refers to the coming of the Great White Throne Judgment [Rev. 20:11-15]*)**, in the which He will judge the world in Righteousness by *that* Man Whom He has ordained** (*this Righteousness is exclusively in Christ Jesus and what He has done for us at the Cross, and can be gained only by Faith in Him [Eph. 2:8-9; Rom. 10:9-10, 13; Rev. 22:17]*)**; *whereof* He has given assurance unto all *men*, in that He has raised Him from the dead** (*refers to the Resurrection ratifying that which was done at Calvary, and is applicable to all men, at least to all who will believe!*)**" (Acts 17:30-31).**

THE PRINCE OF THE POWERS
OF THE AIR

While Satan is the Prince of the powers of the air, meaning that he is the indirect cause of all inclement weather conditions, still, he can only do what God allows him to do. Satan is not running wild, so to speak, rather he answers to God for everything (Job, Chpts. 1-2).

In the original Creation of the Earth and mankind, God never intended for there to be war, inclement weather of any nature, hunger, crime, etc. Of course, sin brought all of this in. Jesus has addressed sin at the Cross of Calvary, and now it remains for Satan and his demon spirits and fallen Angels to be locked away, which they will be very shortly. Then the Lord is going to completely redo this Planet, cleansing it from all past situations, with it becoming what He originally intended. Then the Evil One, plus all demon spirits and fallen Angels, and every unbeliever who has followed Satan, will be cast into the Lake of Fire, where they will remain forever and forever (Rev. 20:10). As previously stated, the last two Chapters of Revelation give us a preview of what that new world and that new time is going to be like. In fact, it is so overwhelmingly wonderful as to defy all description. What a privilege it is to live for God, to enjoy His bountiful Blessings, and then to have the privilege of living with Him forever and forever in the New Jerusalem.

(6) "IT IS HE WHO BUILDS HIS STORIES IN THE HEAVEN, AND HAS FOUNDED HIS TROOP IN THE EARTH; HE WHO CALLS FOR THE WATERS OF THE SEA, AND POURS THEM OUT UPON THE FACE OF THE EARTH: THE LORD IS HIS NAME."

The synopsis is:

1. The phrase, *"It is He Who builds His Stories in the Heaven,"* refers to God's Headquarters on Planet Heaven.

2. *"And has founded His Troop in the Earth,"* seems, in the original language, to have the idea of making the arch of the heavens above the Earth, that is, the immediate heaven surrounding the Earth, i.e., the expanse, clouds, atmosphere, etc.

3. The phrase, *"The LORD is His Name,"* refers to God as Creator of all things and not mindless evolution.

PLANET HEAVEN

Some may blanch at the term, *"Planet Heaven;"* however, there is no Scripture in the Bible that would contradict such, and, as well, there are many Scriptures which lend credence to the term.

We know that there is a city in Heaven called the *"New Jerusalem,"* and in this city, there are mansions, streets, rivers, trees, etc. As well, there are horses and probably many other different types of animals.

There are many other things, which could be named, as well, and speak of great similarity to Earth, although on a higher plane. Therefore, the term *"Planet Heaven"* does violence to no Passage of Scripture.

THE RAIN

The phrase, *"He Who calls for the waters of the sea, and pours them out upon the face of the Earth,"* refers to the manner in which rain is brought about, therefore, watering the earth.

The phrase, *"The LORD is His Name,"* refers to God as Creator of all things and not mindless evolution.

Actually, it takes far more Faith to believe in the drivel of evolution than it does to believe that behind Creation is a Creator.

(7) "ARE YOU NOT AS CHILDREN OF THE ETHIOPIANS UNTO ME, O CHILDREN OF ISRAEL? SAYS THE LORD. HAVE NOT I BROUGHT UP ISRAEL OUT OF THE LAND OF EGYPT? AND THE PHILISTINES FROM CAPHTOR, AND THE SYRIANS FROM KIR?"

The exegesis is:

1. The proud boast of the Israelites, namely, that they were God's peculiar People and that their Redemption from Egypt demonstrated that they were His Favorites, was a fleshly boast and is combatted by this Verse.

2. Spiritually, the Israelites were *"as Ethiopians"* (Jer. 13:23). Historically, they could only rank as the Philistines and the Syrians, whom God, in His Providence, had also delivered from captivity and probably had also brought out of Egypt originally.

3. As Israel of old, election by God cannot and, in fact, does not guarantee Salvation when the conduct does not correspond with God's Word.

THE CHOSEN PEOPLE?

Israel's election to be God's People could not save them unless their conduct corresponded with God's Word. If they obeyed not, they were no better in His Eyes than the heathen, and their delivery from Egypt had no more significance than the migration of pagan nations.

Consequently, as Israel of old, election by God cannot and, in fact, does not guarantee Salvation when the conduct does not correspond with God's Word. Therefore, the unscriptural doctrine of *"Unconditional Eternal Security"* is shot down in this Passage, as well as countless others.

During the Ministry of John the Baptist, he referred to this when he said, **"And think not to say within yourselves, We have Abraham to *our* father** *(pride)*: **for I say unto you, that God is able of these stones to raise up children unto Abraham** *(the Lord has raised up the Gentiles as children unto Abraham [Gal. 3:7, 14]).*

"And now also the axe is laid unto the root of the trees: therefore every tree which brings not forth good fruit is hewn down, and cast into the fire *(Israel was cut down because of unbelief [Rom. 11:20])*" **(Mat. 3:9-10).**

(8) "BEHOLD, THE EYES OF THE LORD GOD ARE UPON THE SINFUL KINGDOM, AND I WILL DESTROY IT FROM OFF THE FACE OF THE EARTH; SAVING THAT I WILL NOT UTTERLY DESTROY THE HOUSE OF JACOB, SAYS THE LORD."

The exposition is:

1. *"And I will destroy it from off the face of the Earth,"* refers to both Israel and ultimately Judah ceasing as independent nations.

2. The Ten-Tribe kingdom was destroyed by the Assyrians a few years after the time of Amos, never to rise again. About 130 years after their destruction, Judah also fell!

3. After the dispersion, elements of all the Tribes came back to the Promised Land,

although as a vassal state to a foreign power until their destruction in A.D. 70.

4. For nearly 2,000 years, they ceased to be a Nation but did remain as a people. Only since 1948 have they enjoyed statehood, but they are to see some very difficult days not too far into the future.

PREDESTINATION?

Some would call Verse 8 *"Predestination."* Actually, that is correct! However, it is the Plan of God that is predestined and not who will be in that Plan.

In other words, God has predestined that a *"Remnant"* out of Israel will be Saved, but as to who will be in that *"Remnant"* is not predestined. That is according to *"Whosoever will"* (Rev. 22:17).

I WILL NOT UTTERLY DESTROY

The phrase, *"Behold, the Eyes of the Lord GOD are upon the sinful kingdom,"* refers to both Israel and Judah, as the Lord *"Standing upon the Altar"* in Jerusalem implies!

The phrase, *"And I will destroy it from off the face of the Earth,"* refers to both Israel and ultimately Judah ceasing as nations.

At the conclusion of the Great Tribulation, called *"the time of Jacob's Trouble"* (Jer. 30:7), that particular period, including the Battle of Armageddon, will once again push Israel to the brink of extinction. However, the Second Coming of the Lord at that particular time will save Israel, with the *"Remnant"* fulfilling this phrase, *"Saving that I will not utterly destroy the House of Jacob, says the LORD."*

Despite the destruction of the wicked, God's Promises hold true, and there is still a *"Remnant"* who shall be Saved (Jer. 30:11).

(9) "FOR, LO, I WILL COMMAND, AND I WILL SIFT THE HOUSE OF ISRAEL AMONG ALL NATIONS, LIKE AS CORN IS SIFTED IN A SIEVE, YET SHALL NOT THE LEAST GRAIN FALL UPON THE EARTH."

The synopsis is:

1. In Verses 8 and 9, the Lord says, *"I will destroy," "I will command," "I will sift."*

2. God Himself promises to be the Principal. Even though it sounds extremely negative, still, this is all lovely and consoling to Faith. It secures the absolute Salvation

of the Remnant.

3. The smallest grain is as sure of eternal safety as the largest, hence, the phrase, *"Yet shall not the least grain fall upon the earth."*

I WILL SIFT

The word, *"sift,"* implies, *"to shake violently to and fro."* This shaking shall show who are the true Israelites and who are the false, who retain their Faith and cleave to the Lord under all difficulties, and who lose their hold of true Salvation and assimilate themselves to the heathen among whom they dwell.

To be sure, there would not be many who would do this, reckoning the small number who returned from the captivity, and the small number who followed Christ in His earthly Ministry.

As well, the *"sifting"* continued in the Early Church, with only a few Israelites following Paul, along with the Lord's Apostles.

This *"sifting"* will continue, extensively so, in the coming Great Tribulation and will conclude only with the Remnant accepting Christ as Saviour and Messiah at the Second Coming (Zech. 12:10).

(10) "ALL THE SINNERS OF MY PEOPLE SHALL DIE BY THE SWORD, WHO SAY, THE EVIL SHALL NOT OVERTAKE NOR PREVENT US."

The pattern is:

1. Even though the Lord calls Israel *"My People,"* still, He also calls them *"sinners."*

2. Barring Repentance, these *"sinners"* will *"die by the sword."*

3. As well, they will lose their eternal souls! And there could be nothing worse than that.

SALVATION

The phrase, *"All the sinners of My People,"* presents a contrast that should be heeded carefully.

There has always been only one type of Salvation for any and all. In other words, people were Saved before Christ exactly as they are Saved presently. It is the Cross of Calvary that has effected Salvation, and only the Cross of Calvary that has effected Salvation.

People were Saved before the Cross by

NOTES

looking forward to that Prophetic event, while people are Saved now by looking backward to that historical event. In any case, it was and always will be the Cross of Christ which makes Salvation possible.

As a result, the Lord has always dealt identically with all, whether under the Old Covenant or under the New Covenant. As only a few Israelites were truly Saved, as well, only a few in the modern church are truly Saved!

Even though the entirety of the *"House of Israel"* was called *"My People,"* still, only those who truly served the Lord were truly His People.

Also, their serving Him faithfully for awhile did not at all guarantee their Salvation, that is, if they ultimately turned their backs on Him (Ezek. 3:20).

The same is true in the modern church. Being truly Born-Again does not guarantee Salvation, unless one abides faithful to the end (Mat. 7:21).

Claiming that one continues to be Saved, no matter what they do or how they act, even ceasing to believe, is the same as the *"sinners"* of Amos' day saying, *"The evil shall not overtake nor prevent us."*

HOW IS SALVATION EFFECTED?

As stated, it is the Cross of Christ, which makes Salvation possible. We speak of what Jesus there did, which was to give Himself as a Perfect Sacrifice, which God the Father accepted, thereby, opening the door to all who will come in (Heb. 1:3; 9:28; Rev. 22:17).

Salvation is effected by the means of Faith (Eph. 2:8-10; Rom. 5:1-2).

It must be understood, however, one's Faith must have the correct Object, and that correct Object is, *"Jesus Christ and Him Crucified"* (I Cor. 1:23). In other words, one's Faith must be in Christ and the Cross. While the believing sinner will have very little understanding of Christ and what He did at the Cross, still, it is the Cross alone, meaning what Jesus there did, that makes Salvation possible.

The Lord expects very little out of the believing sinner who is coming to Christ, but He does expect that we understand these things once we are Saved.

VICTORY OVER THE WORLD, THE FLESH, AND THE DEVIL

Fortunately, most Believers understand the Cross of Christ as it refers to Salvation, but, unfortunately, most have no understanding of the Cross at all as it regards our every day living for God. The truth is, the Cross of Christ plays as great a part in our life and living as it does our initial Salvation. In fact, one could say that it plays even a bigger part.

Salvation is a once for all Work that is accomplished instantly upon Faith. Our living for God on a daily basis is something that goes on day-by-day, even every day and year of our lives in our living for God. In fact, unless the Believer understands the Cross of Christ as it regards our every day living, even as Paul gave this information to us, such a Believer can be Saved, but they cannot live a victorious life. That's why Jesus said the following as it regards the Cross:

TAKE UP THE CROSS DAILY

"And He said to *them* **all, If any** *man* **will come after Me** (the criteria for Discipleship), **let him deny himself** (not asceticism as many think, but rather that one denies one's own willpower, self-will, strength, and ability, depending totally on Christ), **and take up his cross** (the benefits of the Cross, looking exclusively to what Jesus did there to meet our every need) **daily** (this is so important, our looking to the Cross; that we must renew our Faith in what Christ has done for us, even on a daily basis, for Satan will ever try to move us away from the Cross as the Object of our Faith, which always spells disaster), **and follow Me** (Christ can be followed only by the Believer looking to the Cross, understanding what it accomplished, and by that means alone [Rom. 6:3-5, 11, 14; 8:1-2, 11; I Cor. 1:17-18, 21, 23; 2:2])" **(Lk. 9:23).**

Jesus then said:

"And whosoever does not bear his Cross, and come after Me, cannot be My Disciple" (Lk. 14:27).

(11) "IN THAT DAY WILL I RAISE UP THE TABERNACLE OF DAVID THAT IS FALLEN, AND CLOSE UP THE

BREACHES THEREOF; AND I WILL RAISE UP HIS RUINS, AND I WILL BUILD IT AS IN THE DAYS OF OLD."

The synopsis is:

1. *"In that day,"* refers to the future day of the Restoration of Israel, which will take place at the Second Coming and, of course, will follow the present night of desolation.

2. As well, it is the *"Tabernacle of David,"* which is to be raised up, and not of Jeroboam, nor of Jehu, etc.

3. *"And I will build it as in the days of old,"* is also quoted in Acts 15:14-18. It refers to the fact that this will be fulfilled only after the Church Age, actually in the Kingdom Age.

THE RESTORATION OF ISRAEL

The phrase, *"Will I raise up,"* along with *"I will close up," "I will build," "I will perform," "I will bring,"* and *"I will plant,"* proclaims the *"I wills"* of God in Grace and contrast with His *"I wills"* of wrath found in Verses 8 and 9.

WHEN WILL THIS RESTORATION TAKE PLACE?

As stated, it will take place, or rather will have its beginning immediately after the Second Coming. Before the Restoration can take place, however, Israel must accept Jesus Christ as their Saviour and, thereby, make Him the Lord of their very beings. There is every indication in the Word of God that every Jew in the world will at that time accept Christ (Isa. 54:13; Zech. 9:1, 16).

The great Prophet Zechariah also said:

"And I will pour upon the House of David and upon the inhabitants of Jerusalem, the Spirit of Grace and of Supplications: and they shall look upon Me Whom they have pierced, and they shall mourn for Him, as one mourns for his only son, and shall be in bitterness for Him, as one that is in bitterness for his firstborn" (Zech. 12:10).

I quote the following word for word from THE EXPOSITOR'S STUDY BIBLE.

I WILL POUR . . .

"'And I will pour . . . ,' refers to the Lord pouring out fire upon Zion's adversaries, but the Holy Spirit upon her inhabitants

(II Thess., Chpt. 1). If one is to notice, the Messiah Himself is speaking in the entirety of the Twelfth Chapter of Zechariah as far as the word 'pierced'; then the Holy Spirit points to the moral effect produced by the revelation. 'Upon the House of David,' proclaims the Promise originally given to David concerning his seed upon the Throne of Israel (II Sam. 7:12-16)."

THE SPIRIT OF GRACE

"The phrase, 'I will pour upon them the Spirit of Grace,' concerns the Goodness of God and means that Israel is no longer trusting in their Law, but instead the 'Grace of God,' which is found only in the Lord Jesus Christ. 'And I will pour upon them the Spirit of Supplications,' speaks of Israel supplicating the Lord and the Lord supplicating the Father on their behalf. The word means 'to ask humbly and earnestly.'"

THE ONE WHOM THEY HAVE PIERCED

"'And they shall look upon Me Whom they have pierced,' identifies who and what they are and Who He is. 'And they shall mourn for Him, as one mourns for his only son,' now proclaims the moral effect produced by this Revelation, as given by the Holy Spirit. They will then make their supplications to Him for Mercy and Forgiveness. 'And they shall be in bitterness for Him,' means 'a sense of intense shame.' It speaks of true Repentance."

THE FIRSTBORN

"The last phrase, 'As one who is in bitterness for his firstborn,' refers to the loss of an only son, the firstborn. In effect, they killed their own son, and the firstborn at that, which meant that the family line could not continue; it was, in fact, destroyed, at least as far as the Covenant was concerned; however, this 'Son,' or 'Firstborn,' rose from the dead. Even though they would not accept it then, they will accept it now – and because He lives, they shall live also!"

ISRAEL, THE LEADING NATION IN THE WORLD

This small country in the Middle East known as *"Israel,"* which is about the size

of the State of New Jersey, will be the leading Nation on the face of the Earth in the coming Kingdom Age. One might say that it will be the priestly Nation. Ezekiel proclaims that in the last nine Chapters of his great Book.

Then the borders of Israel will be that which was originally promised to Abraham (Gen. 15:18).

This means that in the Kingdom Age the borders of Israel in the east will go to the River Euphrates, which will take in about half of Iraq and also Jordan. It will also take in Syria and Lebanon to the north. On the south, it will take in the Arabian Peninsula, which will border the Persian Gulf and will include all of the Arabian countries in that vicinity. On the west, of course, the border will be the Mediterranean Sea. On the south, Israel, in that day, will also extend to the present Gulf of Suez, which also incorporates the Suez Canal. In fact, the size of Israel in the coming Kingdom Age will probably be about a fourth of the size of the United States, and possibly a little larger than that.

(12) "THAT THEY MAY POSSESS THE REMNANT OF EDOM, AND OF ALL THE HEATHEN, WHICH ARE CALLED BY MY NAME, SAYS THE LORD WHO DOES THIS."

The overview is:

1. The phrase, *"That they may possess the remnant of Edom, and of all the heathen,"* actually refers to *"Adam,"* that is, all of mankind.

2. The new-born Israel, after the Second Coming of the Lord, will take possession of all nations and bring them to Immanuel, thus, totally fulfilling the Commission of Matthew 28:19.

3. As well, these nations will come willingly and gladly, realizing that Israel is the source of all blessings.

THE POSSESSION

Thus, the Holy Spirit in Amos sets out the Ways of God with His People; reviews their moral condition from the time of the golden calf of Sinai to that of Beth-el; declares the consequent Judgment; and predicts the Spiritual Birth of the Twelve

Tribes and the physical transformation of their ancient home.

THE MUSLIMS

The resurgence of Islam at this particular time is not without Spiritual weight. It is Satan's attempt to keep Israel from fulfilling what God has intended for her, and what is glaringly promised in the Word of God. Of course, we know from the Word of God that Satan will not succeed, but it will not be from lack of trying.

In fact, the darkest days that Israel has ever known are just ahead, and please understand, Israel has already seen some dark days in the past. But what is coming, Jesus said would be worse than anything the world had previously seen. His exact Words were:

"For then shall be great tribulation (the last three and one half years)**, such as was not since the beginning of the world to this time, no, nor ever shall be** (the worst the world has ever known, and will be so bad that it will never be repeated)**.**

"And except those days should be shortened, there should no flesh be saved (refers to Israel coming close to extinction)**: but for the elect's** (Israel's) **sake those days shall be shortened** (by the Second Coming)**" (Mat. 24:21-22).**

Of all the tasks given by God to America at this present time, the protection of Israel is probably the most important. However, under the present Administration (2010), the situation doesn't look good at all. In fact, the Administration is much more sympathetic to the Muslims than they are to Israel. I personally think there is no sympathy for Israel whatsoever. This poses an extreme danger for this nation, perhaps the greatest danger it has ever known.

To be sure, the Promise the Lord gave to Abraham some 4,000 years ago still holds true to this present hour. He said to the Patriarch:

"I will bless them who bless you, and curse him who curses you: and in you shall all families of the Earth be blessed" (Gen. 12:3).

When the Lord said that He would curse the person, or the nation, who cursed Israel, He meant exactly what He said. We must

NOTES

ever understand, the Curse of God is just as bad in the negative sense as the Blessings of God are good in the positive sense.

THE DEMANDS OF THE MUSLIMS

Much of the world thinks that the problem in the Middle East is because Israel is denying the Palestinians a homeland. Let us address ourselves to that.

There is no such thing as Palestinians. Actually, the name, *"Palestinian,"* comes from the ancient name of *"Philistines,"* and there are no more Philistines and have not been for several thousands of years. In fact, the Arabs in Israel are Egyptians, Syrians, and mostly Jordanians, etc. Not a single Muslim country will allow any of these people to immigrate to their respective countries, even though they have plenty of room. To be frank, they will give precious little help to the Palestinians, with the exception of weapons, desiring that they live in abject poverty, so they can point it out to the entirety of the world. The United States has given about a billion dollars a year in tax dollars to the Palestinians, the majority of which finds a resting place in Swiss bank accounts. But Uncle Sam (Uncle Sap) keeps pouring it out. For instance, when Arafat died, he was found to have nearly a half billion dollars in French bank accounts.

The truth is, the Palestinians have no interest whatsoever in a part of Israel for their so-called homeland. They rather want the entirety of the State of Israel and every Israeli dead. That's their goal, and that is the cause of the bone of contention.

WHAT IS GOING TO HAPPEN IN THE NEAR FUTURE?

President after president in this country have claimed that before they left office, they would have a peace treaty between Israel and the Palestinians. Actually, there have been all kinds of treaties signed but with the Palestinians breaking them almost before the ink was dry.

But there is coming one to whom the Bible refers as the *"Antichrist,"* who is going to manage to do what no one else has been able to do, namely, formulate a seven-year peace treaty between Israel and the

Palestinians, guaranteeing the safety and protection of Israel, etc. This man will be a Jew but will be greatly respected by the Muslims, and I'll tell you why in a moment.

The whole world will acclaim the wisdom of the *"man of sin,"* when he is able to broker this treaty, in fact, something no one else has been able to do. Israel will declare him as their long hoped for Messiah, and the whole world will rejoice. In fact, during this time, Israel will be able to build her Temple, no doubt, on the same site where Solomon built his Temple.

Now, the great question arises as to how the Antichrist can get the Muslims to agree to having their Dome of the Rock torn down, which is claimed to be the third most holy site of Islam, and in its place the Jews build their Temple (Dan. 7:8; 8:9-11, 23-25; II Thess. 2:4).

While the Bible doesn't say how the Antichrist will convince the Muslims to give up their Dome of the Rock, the following is quite possibly at least a way that it could happen.

THE GREAT DECEIVER

We do know that for Israel and the Muslims to sign a seven-year, nonaggression pact, guaranteeing the borders and protection of Israel for some seven years, is going to take great persuasive power. How will the Antichrist pull that off?

He could very well call a meeting of all the Muslim leaders and explain to them how he is drawing Israel into his trap. When he is strong enough, he will turn on Israel and defeat them. Then the Muslims can have the entirety of the land of Israel and rename it to their satisfaction. Now, whether he will carry it out in this way, the Bible doesn't say, but it could very well be close to the truth. But, the actual truth is, even though he is a Jew, for Israel would not accept anyone as their Messiah who was not Jewish, still, he hates Israel with a passion, more so than anyone else. However, he will not have any love for the Muslims, either, and, in fact, will hate all religions, thereby, setting himself up as god.

True to his promise, he will turn on Israel about midpoint of the Great Tribulation

NOTES

(after some three and a half years), with Israel suffering her first military defeat since becoming a Nation in 1948. In fact, he would totally destroy them then, but Daniel said that he will hear tidings out of the north and out of the east, which will trouble him, which means that he has to leave Israel for another time (Dan. 11:44).

It will take him about three and a half years to clean up that situation, which will probably be with Russia and China, etc. Then he will come down on the land of Israel, which the Bible calls the *"Battle of Armageddon."* That's when he will meet the King of kings and Lord of lords, and it will be a meeting that he will long regret— actually, for all of eternity. I speak of the Second Coming.

THE SECOND COMING

Please understand, when Jesus Christ comes back the second time, He will not come back to be beaten, spit upon, lampooned, and crucified, but He will rather come back with a Power such as the world has never known before. The Antichrist and his mighty army will be decimated, in fact, with five-sixths of all his soldiers being killed (Ezek., Chpts. 38-39). Then Israel, which has come close to extinction, with some two-thirds dying in the Great Tribulation Period, will then accept the Lord Jesus as their Saviour and their Lord. This will be the beginning of their Restoration, which will culminate with this tiny Nation then being the greatest in the world, but all under Christ.

(13) "BEHOLD, THE DAYS COME, SAYS THE LORD, THAT THE PLOWMAN SHALL OVERTAKE THE REAPER, AND THE TREADER OF GRAPES HIM WHO SOWS SEED; AND THE MOUNTAINS SHALL DROP SWEET WINE, AND ALL THE HILLS SHALL MELT."

The overview is:

1. *"Behold, the days come, says the LORD,"* pertains to the certitude of this action.

2. As the Day of Judgment was sure to come, likewise, the Day of Blessing is sure to come, as well, that is, if one finally lines up with the Word of God.

3. Verse 13 speaks of the coming

Kingdom Age, when Israel will truly be a land flowing with *"milk and honey,"* which will bless the entirety of the Earth.

THE BLESSINGS

The phrase, *"Behold, the days come, says the LORD,"* refers to the certitude of this action.

The idea is, irrespective of world conditions, these Passages shall be fulfilled to the letter.

The phrase, *"That the plowman shall overtake the reaper, and the treader of grapes him who sows seed,"* refers to the planting and the harvest, which shall be continuous, without interval as presently. Then the curse will be lifted from the Earth, and it will produce as God originally intended. Paul said, *"For we know that the whole Creation groans and travails in pain together until now,"* signifying this coming day (Rom. 8:22).

Hunger will then be a thing of the past, as the Earth will produce so abundantly as to defy description!

The phrase, *"And the mountains shall drop sweet wine, and all the hills shall melt,"* is similar to Joel 3:18.

It is thought that Amos possibly prophesied some time after Joel, and, if so, the Holy Spirit gave him similar words as He had given Joel.

All of this will be during the coming Kingdom Age when Christ will Personally rule the entirety of the world with His Capital being Jerusalem. Actually, the great Prophet Ezekiel, in the last nine Chapters of the Book that bears his name, tells us what the spiritual condition of Israel will then be.

THE PROPHET ISAIAH

The great Prophet Isaiah also stated the following concerning world conditions at that time:

"And many people shall go and say, Come you, and let us go up to the mountain of the LORD, to the House of the God of Jacob; and He will teach us of His Ways, and we will walk in His Paths: for out of Zion shall go forth the Law, and the Word of the LORD from Jerusalem. *(The 'Law,' as referred to here, has no reference to the*

Law of Moses, but rather to instruction, direction, and teaching. Again, this is the coming Kingdom Age when the Messiah, 'The Greater than Solomon,' will rule the world by Wisdom, Grace, and Love.)"

NO MORE WAR

"And He shall judge among the nations, and shall rebuke many people: and they shall beat their swords into plowshares, and their spears into pruninghooks: nation shall not lift up sword against nation, neither shall they learn war anymore. *(The words, 'judge among,' should read 'arbitrate between,' and 'rebuke' would have been better translated 'decide the disputes of.' Man's courts of arbitration are doomed to failure, but, to Messiah's Court, success is promised here)"* **(Isa. 2:3-4).**

CONDITIONS DURING THE MILLENNIUM

The great Prophet, by the Power of the Holy Spirit, tells us here something so spectacular as to defy description. It speaks of the entirety of the complexion of Planet Earth totally changing. The Scripture says:

"The wolf also shall dwell with the lamb, and the leopard shall lie down with the kid; and the calf and the young lion and the fatling together; and a little child shall lead them. *(The character and nature of the Planet, including its occupants and even the animal creation, will revert to their posture as before the Fall.)*

"And the cow and the bear shall feed *(feed together)***; their young ones shall lie down together: and the lion shall eat straw like the ox.** *(This Passage plainly tells us that the carnivorous nature of the animal kingdom will be totally and eternally changed.)*

"And the sucking child shall play on the hole of the asp, and the weaned child shall put his hand on the cockatrice' den. *(Even though some of the curse will remain on the serpent in the Millennium, in that he continues to writhe in the dust, still, the deadly part will be removed [Gen. 3:14])"* **(Isa. 11:6-8).**

The world will then know a time of prosperity and peace such as it has never known before in all of its history. To think of a world without war, without crime, without man's inhumanity to his fellowman, presents something that we have never seen before, but, most assuredly, all who are redeemed by the Blood of the Lamb will see that coming glad day. And it's not too long in coming!

(14) "AND I WILL BRING AGAIN THE CAPTIVITY OF MY PEOPLE OF ISRAEL, AND THEY SHALL BUILD THE WASTE CITIES, AND INHABIT THEM; AND THEY SHALL PLANT VINEYARDS, AND DRINK THE WINE THEREOF; THEY SHALL ALSO MAKE GARDENS, AND EAT THE FRUIT OF THEM."

The synopsis is:

1. Verses 13 through 15 concerns the coming Restoration of Israel, which will take place immediately following the Second Coming.

2. *"And I will bring again the captivity of My People of Israel,"* concerns a length of time that has now lasted for nearly 2,000 years. If we count the time they were a vassal state, it is some 2,500 years.

3. The tone and intent of Verse 14 also claim that the contesting of the land of Israel will be forever ended. This signifies that Satan's day is done!

MY PEOPLE ISRAEL

Satan hates Israel for many and varied reasons.

He hates them because they have produced, even though they do not now believe it, the Son of the Living God, the Lord Jesus Christ, Who has defeated the Evil One at Calvary's Cross.

As well, Satan hates Israel simply because the Word of God, despite their present difficulties, promises their Restoration to a place of glory and a position of Righteousness that literally defies description.

As we have previously stated, the rise of Islam in these last days is not without purpose and design. Of course, the design is of Satan. But he will not succeed!

The ancient land of Israel does not belong to the Muslims, or anyone else, for that matter. In fact, it belongs to God, and His Tenant, so to speak, is Israel.

AN INTERVIEW

I had the privilege to hear over television

NOTES

one of the last interviews given by Clark Clifford, who had been an advisor to every democratic president, beginning with Harry Truman and, last of all, Jimmy Carter. He died soon after this interview was given. The interview lasted for over an hour, and I had the privilege of hearing almost all of it. If I remember correctly, Mr. Clifford was then in his late 80's.

At any rate, almost the entirety of the interview dealt with Israel.

Mr. Clifford spoke of those days with Harry Truman, stating that he (Clifford) was the youngest advisor there. Even though he attended all the meetings, his advice was seldom asked about anything. Israel, who had lost some six million dead to the Nazi butchers, was demanding their ancient homeland. They were also demanding that it be named *"Israel,"* exactly as it is in the Bible.

Powerful forces were demanding of President Truman that he not allow this to be. In fact, his closest friend, George Marshall, was advising that America purchase a small country in Central America and give that to the Jews.

During this time, when the president was searching his soul, Clifford wrote a letter to the president concerning Israel. He stated in the letter that the ancient homeland of the Bible must be given to Israel as their state, and it must be named the same as it always had been—Israel.

THE WAYS OF THE LORD

He didn't have enough place and position to get a personal audience with the president, so he had to write this letter. He gave it to someone to give to the president and was assured that it would be delivered.

He was asked the question by the interviewer as to why he felt so strongly about Israel, considering that he was not Jewish himself.

As he contemplated the question, he finally spoke up and said, *"I don't know why I felt the way I did, but this I do know, my feelings were strong in this regard."*

He forgot about the letter, when several days later, the president sent for him. He had no idea it was about the letter.

He was ushered into the Oval Office and

stood there before the president. He saw his letter open on the president's desk.

He went on to relate that day as to how the president sat there for a few moments and said nothing. And then, finally, he looked up and said to Mr. Clifford, *"Clark, why do you feel that the ancient homeland of the Jews be given to them, and that it must be named Israel, exactly as it is in the Bible?"*

He wasn't anticipating the question and did not really know how to answer. Finally, he blurted out, *"Mr. President, I feel strongly about this because it is the right thing to do."*

The president stared at him for a few moments and said nothing. He finally said, *"That is all, you may leave."*

When asked if he thought his letter had anything to do with the favorable position ultimately given by Mr. Truman concerning the Jews and the State of Israel, he affirmed that he did not know. But one thing was certain, just a few days later, President Truman announced to America and the world that America would stand behind the Jews in their reclaiming of their ancient homeland, that given in the Bible. In addition, it would be named according to their request, the land of *"Israel."*

Not long before his death, President Truman was asked by a reporter as to what He (the president) thought was his greatest achievement while in office.

The reporter was thinking of the ending of World War II and the president's decision to drop the atomic bombs, which ended that war. He was thinking of the Marshall Plan, which saved Western Europe from the Communist. But the president left the reporter somewhat nonplussed when he stated, *"You have asked me what I think was my greatest contribution in being the president. My answer is this,"* he exclaimed! *"Putting the power, prestige, and strength of America behind Israel becoming a Nation was, I think, my greatest contribution."*

The president could not have been more right. That was his greatest contribution. Nearing his death, quite possibly, the president was thinking more on Spiritual lines than ever before.

(15) "AND I WILL PLANT THEM UPON THEIR LAND, AND THEY SHALL NO

MORE BE PULLED UP OUT OF THEIR LAND WHICH I HAVE GIVEN THEM, SAYS THE LORD YOUR GOD."

The diagram is:

1. Thus, Amos closes his great Book with the words, *"says the LORD your God,"* which seal the Predictions and Promises.

2. The Lord said, *"I will . . ."* and, to be sure, He most definitely shall.

3. The land He gave them, which was actually first promised to Abraham even before there was an Israel, shall then be theirs forever and forever. To be sure, this is the way it will be and, again, because of what the Holy Spirit said through the Prophet, *"says the LORD your God."*

GIVEN TO ISRAEL

Plainly and simply, in this great Passage, which closes out the Book of Amos, the Holy Spirit through the great Prophet has stated what the future for Israel will be. And to be certain, that's exactly the way it will be. He said:

• *"And I will plant them upon their land"*: The Muslims should read this Verse, and everyone else, for that matter. While the land of Israel actually belongs to the Lord, here the Lord proclaims the fact that He will then give it to Israel.

• *"And they shall no more be pulled up out of their land which I have given them"*: From the time the Lord promised this land to Abraham and, therefore, his seed, which is the Jews, Satan has contested it. In fact, the greatest contest is just ahead. But the Evil One will lose that battle, and the land of Israel will be contested no more.

• *"Says the LORD your God"*: What a way to end this Promise, and, to be sure, it will come to pass exactly as the Lord has said.

CONCLUSION

It is July 19, 2010, twenty minutes after 4 p.m., as I finish our efforts with this Commentary, which includes the Books of Hosea, Joel, and Amos. If you, the reader, enjoy our efforts half as much as I have enjoyed the research in the writing of this Volume, then we will both be blessed.

When we handle the Word of God, we are handling the greatest Work this side of

Heaven. The Word of God is the road map for life and the blueprint for eternity. There is no other because there need be no other.

BIBLIOGRAPHY

CHAPTER 1

Edward Gibbon, *The history of the decline and fall of the Roman Empire,* Philadelphia, B.F. French, 1830, pg. 263.

CHAPTER 2

C.H. Mackintosh, *Notes on the Pentateuch: Notes on Leviticus,* Neptune, New Jersey, Loizeaux Brothers, 1972, pgs. 388-389.
George Williams, *The Student's Commentary on the Holy Scriptures,* Grand Rapids, Kregel Publications, 1949, pg. 648.

CHAPTER 3

George Williams, *The Student's Commentary on the Holy Scriptures,* Grand Rapids, Kregel Publications, 1949, pg. 648.

CHAPTER 5

C.H. Mackintosh, *Notes on the Pentateuch: Notes on Leviticus,* Neptune, New Jersey, Loizeaux Brothers, 1972, pgs. 389.

REFERENCE BOOKS

Atlas Of The Bible — Rogerson
Expository Dictionary of Bible Words — L.O. Richards
Matthew Henry Commentary On The Holy Bible — Matthew Henry
New Bible Dictionary — Tyndale
Strong's Exhaustive Concordance Of The Bible
The Complete Word Study Dictionary
The Essential Writings — Josephus
The Interlinear Greek — English New Testament — George Ricker Berry
The International Standard Bible Encyclopedia
The Pulpit Commentary — H.D.M. Spence
The Student's Commentary On The Holy Scriptures — George Williams
The Zondervan Pictorial Encyclopedia Of The Bible
Vine's Expository Dictionary Of New Testament Words
Webster's New Collegiate Dictionary
Word Studies In The Greek New Testament, Volume I — Kenneth S. Wuest
Young's Literal Translation Of The Holy Bible

NOTES

INDEX

The index is listed according to subjects. The treatment may include a complete dissertation or no more than a paragraph. But hopefully it will provide some help.

As well, even though extended treatment of a subject may not be carried in this Commentary, one of the other Commentaries may well include the desired material.

For all information concerning the
Jimmy Swaggart Bible Commentary,
please request a Gift Catalog.

You may inquire by using Books of the Bible.

- Genesis (639 pages) (11-201)
- Exodus (639 pages) (11-202)
- Leviticus (435 pages) (11-203)
- Numbers
  Deuteronomy (493 pages) (11-204)
- Joshua
  Judges
  Ruth (329 pages) (11-205)
- I Samuel
  II Samuel (528 pages) (11-206)
- I Kings
  II Kings (560 pages) (11-207)
- I Chronicles
  II Chronicles (528 pages) (11-226)
- Ezra
  Nehemiah
  Esther (288 pages) (11-208)
- Job (320 pages) (11-225)
- Psalms (688 pages) (11-216)
- Proverbs (320 pages) (11-227)
- Ecclesiastes
  Song Of Solomon (11-228)
- Isaiah (688 pages) (11-220)
- Jeremiah
  Lamentations (688 pages) (11-070)
- Ezekiel (508 pages) (11-223)
- Daniel (403 pages) (11-224)
- Hosea
  Joel
  Amos (496 pages) (11-229)
- Obadiah
  Jonah
  Micah
  Nahum
  Habakkuk
  Zephaniah *(will be ready Spring 2013)* (11-230)

- Matthew (625 pages) (11-073)
- Mark (606 pages) (11-074)
- Luke (626 pages) (11-075)
- John (532 pages) (11-076)
- Acts (697 pages) (11-077)
- Romans (536 pages) (11-078)
- I Corinthians (632 pages) (11-079)
- II Corinthians (589 pages) (11-080)
- Galatians (478 pages) (11-081)
- Ephesians (550 pages) (11-082)
- Philippians (476 pages) (11-083)
- Colossians (374 pages) (11-084)
- I Thessalonians
  II Thessalonians (498 pages) (11-085)
- I Timothy
  II Timothy
  Titus
  Philemon (687 pages) (11-086)
- Hebrews (831 pages) (11-087)
- James
  I Peter
  II Peter (730 pages) (11-088)
- I John
  II John
  III John
  Jude (377 pages) (11-089)
- Revelation (602 pages) (11-090)

For telephone orders you may call 1-800-288-8350 with bankcard information. All Baton Rouge residents please use (225) 768-7000. For mail orders send to:

Jimmy Swaggart Ministries
P.O. Box 262550
Baton Rouge, LA 70826-2550

Visit our website: www.jsm.org

NOTES

NOTES

NOTES

NOTES

NOTES

NOTES